LOBBYING
IN THE
EUROPEAN UNION

LOBBYING IN THE EUROPEAN UNION

4th edition

Routledge
Taylor & Francis Group

LONDON AND NEW YORK

First published 1998
Fourth edition 2005

© **Routledge 2005**
Haines House, 21 John Street,
London, WC1N 2BP, United Kingdom
(a member of the Taylor & Francis Group)

ISBN 1 85743 336 X
ISSN 1373-3397

Typeset in 9 on 10 pt Times New Roman

Typeset by AJS Solutions, Huddersfield ● Dundee
Printed and bound in Great Britain by MPG Books,
Bodmin, Cornwall

FOREWORD

Over the years, public affairs have become increasingly complex and it is now standard practice to turn to professionals in the field of lobbying. The fourth edition of Lobbying in the European Union is an essential reference source providing contact details of key personnel and institutions focused on the European Union

Part One of the publication provides an overview of the principal European Union institutions, together with the names and contact details of key personnel at the European Commission, the European Parliament and the Council of the European Union, and other useful contact information.

Part Two covers the fields of trade and professional associations, interest groups and non-governmental organizations, trade unions, employers' organizations, chambers of commerce and industry, agricultural organizations, regional representations, national associations, diplomatic corps accredited to the European Union, consultants specializing in EU questions and law firms specializing in the law of the European Union.

Indexes of acronyms, full names and keywords have been extracted to facilitate access to organizations and institutions listed in the book's main sections, while the sections on consultants and lawyers are each accompanied by an index of specialities.

October 2005

CONTENTS

CONTENTS

THE PROFESSION OF LOBBYIST

Introduction

Wherever decisions are made in an open society which directly affect people's lives or livelihoods, lobbyists will be seeking to shape those decisions in their own or in their own clients' best interests. This is a necessary and healthy feature of democratic decision-making: necessary because it is essential that all those involved as bureaucrats or legislators in the making of laws should know as precisely as possible what the impact of those laws is going to be; and healthy because in the long run nothing would more rapidly undermine the validity of representative democracy than law-makers who were evidently ignorant of and uninterested in the quality of legislation. No conscientious law-maker would ever wish to be anything other than well-informed; to have a grasp of both sides of the case; and to be satisfied that a particular measure will be not merely effective but cost-effective too. It is these three functions – information on the matter which the measure seeks to address, presentation of a case, and analysis of the likely impact of the measure – which lie at the heart of the lobbyist's role. And once the confidence of the law-maker has been gained, the lobbyist can preceed to the final and most important stage: suggesting ways in which the measure, while still in draft form and in a fashion consistent with its basic purpose, could be modified.

Of course lobbying, like much else in the democratic process, is open to abuse, and some of these abuses are touched on in more detail below. The best general safeguard against abuse is openness: and this in turn strengthens the case for lobbying to be accepted as a healthy and necessary part of democratic decision-making. Openness allows for the facts and arguments marshalled by the lobbyist to be open to scrutiny and so to debate. It allows law-makers freely to accept or reject the lobbyist's case, and be seen to do so. And it gives the measure as finally enacted the additional moral weight which flows from its having been based on the widest possible consultation.

Origin of Lobbying

The word 'lobby' in its original architectural sense of "in the House of Commons, and other houses of legislature, a large entrance-hall or apartment open to the public, and chiefly serving for interviews between members and persons not belonging to the house" dates from 1640. Two centuries later, initially in the United States, it had acquired as a verb the sense with which we are here concerned: "to influence members of a house of legislature in the exercise of their legislative function by frequenting the lobby. Also to procure the passing of a measure ... by means of such influence". The expressions lobbying and lobbyist were both in use by the 1860s. Although *The Times* of 6 January 1862 remarked rather dismissively that "lobbying, as it is termed, is a well known institution at Washington", the suggestion that the original lobby was that of Washington Willard Hotel can be discounted.

Washington continues to host the world's largest concentration of lobbyists. Lobbying is regulated by law under the Foreign Agents Registration Act (1938) and the Federal Regulation of Lobbying Act (1946). In addition to the several thousand lobbyists active upon Capitol Hill itself, the big corporations have very large government affairs departments on the lookout for any legislation which might, however remotely, affect their interests. Trade and professional assocations lobby very vigorously on behalf of their members' interests, whether their members be farmers, steelmakers, small shopkeepers, college professors, or whatever. Labour unions large and small are similarly engaged. Separate from these are the pressure groups, the single-issue lobbies active in such fields as animal rights, abortion law, the environment, development aid, consumer interests, and so on, or active on behalf of particular sectors of society, such as old people, Veterans of Foreign Wars, the National Association for the Advancement of Colored People, and many others.

Think-tanks of every possible orientation are also seeking to bring influence to bear both on the overall character and on the detail of government legislation. Finally – although they might not think of themselves as lobbyists in the conventional sense – there are innumerable foreign governments and international organizations which, through their embassies or representative offices, are monitoring the legislative process. When we bear all this in mind and remember that, with the exception of the last two categories, much of this lobbying is replicated at the State level, we can gain some idea of the extent and complexity of lobbying in the United States.

Lobbying in the European Union

Lobbying in the European Union has developed very rapidly in recent years. One recent estimate puts the number of lobbyists in Brussels – if large corporations are included – at 10,000 people. Although still at the formative stage, it is well beyond the embryonic. Certain features already distinguish it very markedly from lobbying in the United States. Some of these features spring from the fundamental character of the Union itself, while others are bound up with the unique nature of the Union's institutions and their mode of operation.

First, the fact of the Union's much greater heterogeneity by comparison with the United States – in the case of living standards, prosperity, culture, patterns of consumption, attitudes, and much else – means that on any given issue the range of interests and points of view to be accommodated is correspondingly wider. Second, there are very real problems bound up with the use of the many languages of the various Member States. Ultimately all law must find its final expression in language, and part of the Union's current drive towards 'better law-making' is the requirement that this language be both unambiguous and accessible to the ordinary person. To produce legal texts which mean exactly the same from Athens to Aberdeen, and from Jerez to Helsinki, requires expertise of a very high order. The scope for linguistic nuance, extensive in any language, becomes near-infinite in the many languages of the European Union. And upon such nuances may depend not only questions of interpretation but also substantial costs for those involved in the application of the law in question. The good lobbyist will be aware of this.

A detailed account of the European Union's law-making process is given below, together with a description of the main institutions involved in it. Here we shall note a few general features which affect the work of the lobbyist. First, it is a relatively open process, thanks primarily to a more active, full-time, directly elected European Parliament more conscious of its responsibilities to the electorate than its pre-1979 predecessor, which had been appointed by national parliaments. This culture of greater openness has spread both to the Commission, which now makes more use of consultative papers (green and white) before drafting legislation, and to the Council of the European Union and the European Council, although not without a good deal of hesitation on the part of some Member States. At the legal level this greater openness has been powerfully endorsed by the Court of Justice and at the technical level revolutionized by the development of the Internet and other forms of access to documents.

Second, although the European Union's law-making process is comparatively open, it remains ill-understood, not only by the electorate but even on the part of many bodies with a direct interest in the legislation which emerges from it. This is hardly surprising. Few people have a clear and detailed understanding of the law-making process, at any level, in their own country and of the powers and procedures of the institutions involved in it. How much less likely is it, therefore, that they will know much about the way the European Union's institutions work and the scope for influencing legislative outcomes? It follows from this that much of the lobbyist's preparatory work often takes the form of the most basic explanations of the interaction, for example, between the Council of the European Union, the European Parliament, and the Commission.

Third, account must be taken of the role of the media. Although the situation, at least as far as the serious newspapers and broadcasters are concerned, has improved in recent years, and coverage of European Union affairs is now wider and more accurate than ever before, it remains the case that much reporting is intentionally sensational, biased and concerned far more with confirming readers' and viewers' prejudices than with the facts. Obviously, this kind of reporting can give rise to real alarm. A manufacturer may suddenly learn via a newspaper that his principal product line is under some vague 'threat from Brussels', or a voter may be assured that some precious aspect of national life is about to disappear as a consequence of a decision 'taken by Europe'. Such stories, even when subsequently shown to be untrue or at least wildly overstated, leave a residue of distaste for the European Union, thereby acting as a further barrier to an active engagement in its processes, and heighten the sense that relations with the Union are at heart based on an adversarial 'us and them' model very much at variance with the way decisions are actually made. Although there must be many occasions when inaccurate reporting, intentional or otherwise, has prompted someone to turn, perhaps for the first time, to a lobbyist, the responsible lobbyist will know that the first essential is to disentangle the story with a view to identifying what really is the point at issue and how it might be resolved.

The fourth and final general point is bound up with one of the most fundamental features of the way European Union law is drawn up and applied. To take the commonest form of legislative instrument, the Directive, we can identify three quite distinct stages. First comes enactment, which is wholly the responsibility of the European Union's own institutions. Second comes implementation, i.e. introduction into the domestic law of Member States. Although this is under the active supervision of the European Commission, in its role as the guardian of the Treaties, the details of implementation are worked out largely by national authorities, including most obviously national parliaments and governments. Finally comes enforcement. This is wholly a matter for national, regional, or local authorities, depending on the subject dealt with by the Directive. Redress in the case, for example, of unfair or discriminatory enforcement must normally be sought at the national level, since only in a limited number of areas – of which perhaps the most important is competition policy – does the Commission have a direct responsibility for enforcement under the Treaty of Rome. Much of the alarm prompted by real or imaginary legislative action on the part of the European Union springs from a failure to understand the course which a piece of legislation follows from its first appearance in an internal working document of the Commission to enforcement at the local level. Such a failure also makes more difficult the task of identifying exactly what (if anything) has gone wrong, exactly who is responsible, where and how that person or agency can best be reached, and what can be done to put the matter right as expeditiously as possible.

The Various Types of Lobby

Although there are many people and agencies with an interest in bringing influence to bear upon the legislative process in Brussels, only a minority among them are normally classified as lobbyists. Three main types may be distinguished:

- Single-issue lobbies, many of them well-established pressure groups in fields such as animal rights, the environment, food safety, development policy and so on.

- Trade associations and trade unions with particular interest in specific sectors of economic activity as well as in more general economic questions such as employment law, the overall direction of economic policy, the impact of Economic and Monetary Union, and the Union's relations with the global trading system.

- Commercial lobbyists, who will take up any case on behalf of a client in any way the client wishes. Sometimes the service is limited solely to keeping the client supplied with information, but in many cases the full range of the lobbyist's experience, contacts, expertise, and presentational skills are deployed on behalf of the client's case.

Across these broad categories other distinctions may be applied. First, some lobbyists are concerned not with a specific issue but with a specific geographical area (Catalonia, Flanders, maritime regions, etc.) or with a particular sector of society. There are now large numbers of offices in Brussels representing regions, metropolitan areas, counties, and cities, and these are an increasingly important and influential adjunct to the more conventional form of State representation embodied in the Council of the European Union and Member States' Permanent Representations.

Second, lobbying may be reactive or pro-active. Some lobbying is designed to prevent legislation from being drawn up, but more commonly lobbying is brought into play when a legislative proposal, the desirability or necessity of which is already generally accepted, can be shaped in conformity with the client's interest.

Codes of Conduct

Most abuses of the lobbying system fall into one of two categories. The first is obtaining information dishonestly, which is an abuse of the privileged access that accredited lobbyists enjoy with respect to the Brussels institutions and which might well entail a breach of trust on the part of an official. The second is bribing or otherwise suborning officials or politicians. As far as officials are concerned, this compromises the impartiality and objectivity which are essential qualifications for their work. Politicians also have a duty to exercise independent judgement. Rule 2 of the European Parliament Rules of Procedure specifies that members shall not be bound by any instructions and shall not receive a binding mandate. To agree to vote a particular way in exchange for whatever blandishments a lobbyist may be prepared to offer is clearly tantamount to accepting a 'binding mandate'. The only legitimate instrument a lobbyist can deploy is reasoned argument.

The growth of lobbying and the greater sensitivity of the institutions of the European Union to their public image have led to lobbying now being more closely regulated than was formerly the case. Lobbyists themselves (or 'public affairs practitioners') have drawn up their own code of conduct, which requires them always to "identify themselves by name and company" and to specify the client that they represent. The code outlaws anything which might be constructed as bribing officials or politicians. The European Parliament has its own 10-point code of conduct on lobbying, set out in Annex IX of the Parliament Rules of Procedure. This too requires lobbyists to "refrain from any action designed to obtain information dishonestly" and moreover "not to claim any formal relationship with Parliament in any dealings with third parties". Lobbyists, defined as "persons who wish to enter Parliament's premises frequently with a view to supplying information to Members ... in their own interests or those of third parties", are required to sign a register, and are issued with special orange-coloured passes which distinguish them from any other visitors. Both the Council of the European Union and the European Commission also maintain registers of lobbyists. Accredited lobbyists are allowed fairly open access to both institutions, with one significant exception: they are not allowed in the Commission's press centre, to forestall the possibility of their using the Commission's press conference to raise matters in their own or in their client's interests.

The basic purpose of these codes of conduct is to bring lobbying into the open. Although there is still pressure in some quarters in favour of making the codes legally binding, others argue that this is not necessary as long as the codes are vigorously and consistently enforced. In any case, lobbyists all recognize that it is not in their interests to be suspected of underhand practices and that the maintenance of good relations with all the Brussels institutions is essential.

The Different Kinds of Law in the European Union

Strictly speaking, the expression 'European Union law' is incorrect. What is drawn up under the Treaty of Rome (the European Community Treaty), adopted by the Council of the European Union and/or the European Parliament, and interpreted when necessary by the Court of Justice or the Court of First Instance, is European Community law. However, the use of European Union to mean European Community is so widespread that even some authoritative legal textbooks use 'EU law' to denote the whole body of law which underpins the Union, including both the *acquis communautaire* (i.e. laws already adopted) and law in the process of gestation.

Basically, there are three categories of law in the European Union: primary legislation, i.e. the Treaties and other agreements possessing similar status; secondary legislation, i.e. Directives, Regulations, etc. (see below), which draw their legal authority from the Treaties; and case-law of the Court of Justice and the Court of First Instance. A fourth category of law is the international treaties (bilateral or multilateral) to which the European Community is a party. Such treaties, especially if they contain provisions with a bearing on trade, can be of real significance to lobbyists and their clients, but they are not dealt with by the institutions in the same way as other legislation and the procedures are described separately below.

The lobbyist is rarely concerned with primary legislation. Most lobbying is directed towards secondary legislation. The case-law of the Court of Justice and the Court of First Instance is a matter for lawyers rather than lobbyists, although there are many lobbying firms active in Brussels which command substantial legal expertise.

The original impulse which may lead in the end to European Union legislation can come from a number of different sources. It may emanate from a decision of the European Council; it may be the result of pressure from business and industry; it may arise directly from public concern, whether or not articulated through the European Parliament; it may result from external factors (from some change, for example, in the rules of international commerce); or it may arise in response to a serious crisis, such as BSE, in an area in which the European Union has a broad measure of responsibility and the power to take direct action. But whatever the source of the idea, it is the European Commission which has the **right of initiative** – that is, the right to decide what action should be taken. It exercises its right by forming a draft proposal for legislation. However, it is essential to bear in mind that the Commission must find a **legal base** in the Treaties for what is proposed. Often there will be a choice of possible bases, and the choice is important (and may be challenged in the Court of Justice). Not only will it affect the chance of getting the legislation through the system, it will decide what course the draft follows through the institutions as they scrutinize and possibly amend the Commission's proposal, and what majorities are necessary at different stages in the process to uphold or overturn, as the case may be, the Commission's draft or the amendments put forward by other institutions.

The choice of legal instrument is important too. There are several types:

- A **Regulation**, once adopted by the Council of the European Union and/or the European Parliament (in certain areas the Commission can also adopt Regulations), is "binding in its entirety and directly applicable in all Member States". It does not need to be embodied in national law.

- A **Directive** also has binding effect with respect to the end result, but leaves to national authorities a choice as to the legislative means by which the result is to be achieved. The entry of Directives into national law is closely monitored by the Commission and must normally take place to a strict deadline. The expression **Framework Directive** is used to denote a Directive which identifies policy objectives over a broad field, thereby preparing the way for legislative action on specific points.

- A **Decision** is "binding in its entirety upon those to whom it is addressed". The power to take Decisions is limited to the Council of the European Union and the Commission.

- **Opinions** and **Recommendations** have no binding force and some authorities do not recognize them as legal instruments.

A temporary waiver from a Regulation or a Directive is known as a **Derogation**. Normally Derogations, which are strictly time-limited, can only be granted by the unanimous consent of the Council of the European Union and are seldom renewed.

The Legislative Process

Contrary to what is generally supposed, the legislative process in the European Union is remarkably open, and no more complicated than the process used in the Member States. Since the entry into force in May 1999 of the Treaty of Amsterdam (the result of the 1996–1997 Intergovernmental Conference convened to review and revise the Treaties upon which the Union is founded), the great majority of laws are drawn up under a procedure known as **co-decision**. As the name implies, the procedure is one in which the Council of the European Union and the European Parliament have equal weight.

The procedure is set out in Article 251 of the Treaty of Rome (the European Community Treaty), supplemented by a joint Council–Commission–Parliament declaration of 4 May 1999 on the practical arrangements necessary to make the procedure work. As is the case with all European Union legislation, the procedure is set in train by the Commission forwarding a draft proposal to the Council and to the Parliament. The proposal is then considered by one of the Council's working-parties and by one or more of the Parliament's specialized committees. At this stage the Council may, and in some cases must, seek the opinions of the European Economic and Social Committee and the Committee of the Regions. Once Parliament's examination of the proposal in committee has been completed and embodied in a report, the Parliament proceeds to its **first reading** in plenary session, at which it normally adopts, by simple majority, amendments to the Commission's proposal. These are forwarded to the Council, which, if it agrees with the Parliament's views or if the Parliament has no amendments to suggest, may then proceed formally to adopt the legislation.

If the Council does not agree with the Parliament's amendments, it adopts a **common position**. The proposal then goes back onto the Parliament's agenda for a **second reading**. At this point there are four possibilities. The Parliament may *accept* the Council's common position or it may *fail to reach a decision*: in either case the Council may adopt the legislation. The Parliament may, by an absolute majority of its total membership, decide to *reject* the common position, in which case the legislation cannot be adopted. Or the Parliament may, by an absolute majority, *amend* the common position, thereby presenting the Council with two possibilities. It may approve the Parliament's amendments (by unanimity in the case of amendments with which the Commission disagrees) and proceed to adopt the legislation; or it may convene the joint Council–Parliament *Conciliation Committee* to resolve the differences between the views of the two institutions. If the Committees can reach an agreement (which must be endorsed by a qualified majority in the Council and by a simple majority in the Parliament), the legislation can be adopted, duly modified in accordance with the agreement. If the Committee cannot reach an agreement, the proposal is deemed to have been rejected.

The **co-operation procedure**, now used only in a very small number of areas, differs from the co-decision procedure in that it does not allow the Parliament a *de facto* right of veto and does not provide for a Conciliation Committee. There is also a one-stage procedure, known as the **consultation procedure**, under which the Parliament can give its opinion. The main areas in which this procedure is used are the Common Foreign and Security Policy (CFSP) and Economic and Monetary Union (EMU).

The procedure for the adoption of the European Union's **budget** is similar to the co-decision procedure in that it also allows the European Parliament's two readings and provides for a conciliation committee. The Commission draws up the preliminary draft budget (PDB), which is examined and amended by the Council and forwarded to the Parliament as the draft budget (DB). The Parliament's amendments are sent back to the Council and, wherever possible, differences are resolved in a joint Council–Parliament Conciliation Committee. Within a maximum rate of increase, the Parliament has the last word on so-called 'non-compulsory expenditure', i.e. expenditure other than that undertaken by virtue of a legal obligation such as a Treaty commitment (including, most significantly, price support under the Common Agricultural Policy). About 55 per cent of the budget is non-compulsory expenditure. As a last resort, the Parliament may reject the budget as a whole. The budget can be important to lobbyists anxious to secure on their own or their clients' account support from the budget for particular projects: for a research programme, for example, or for regional development.

Finally, there is the procedure which governs the negotiation and conclusion of the international treaties and agreements, bilateral or unilateral, to which the European Union is a party. The Commission acts as the negotiator on behalf of the Member States, but must first submit a draft negotiation mandate to the Council of the European Union. Once this has been approved, the negotiations can begin, and they are monitored by the European Parliament. Most international treaties and agreements have to be approved by the Parliament under the **assent procedure** set out in Article 300 of the Treaty of Rome.

When, Whom, and How to Lobby

Effective lobbying depends not only on understanding the process by which laws are made but also on knowing what goes on behind the scenes. With this in mind, there are several conclusions to be drawn from the summary description of the various procedures given above.

The first is the cardinal importance of the Commission. The best time to influence the substance of a proposal is while it is still under discussion within the Commission, before it is the subject of a green or white paper, before it is featured in the Commission's annual work programme, and certainly before it is published as a formal proposal and printed in the *Official Journal*. To this end the lobbyist needs to keep in touch with the A (administrative) grade officials in the Commission responsible for the actual drafting. At this and every stage in the procedure, a general observation on the proposal is of little value unless it is backed up by a specific form of words which meets the point. This is especially true of technical proposals, which often include highly detailed annexes in which the real substance of the measure, with all its compliance cost implications, may well be found.

Once the proposal has been published, the lobbyist's attention needs to be directed towards the Council of the European Union and the European Parliament (and in many areas of policy to the European Economic and Social Committee and the Committee of the Regions). The preparatory work on all legislative proposals is done by Council working parties composed of national officials from Member States' Permanent Representations to the European Union. At a later stage, the proposals are filtered through Coreper, the Permanent Representatives Committee, before reaching the agenda of the full Council. It is important that any points with a bearing upon a particular national interest are brought to the attention of officials and that the relevant national bodies are alerted and mobilized. Lobbyists should be aware that, by the time a matter is on the Council agenda, compromises will have been reached on key points, making them more difficult to amend in any way. And under the post-Amsterdam co-decision procedure described above, there may be only one opportunity to influence the Council's thinking since, if the Council and the Parliament are in agreement, the proposal can be adopted after the first reading.

At the same time as the various bodies attached to the Council are considering the it, the proposal will be examined by one or more of the specialist committees of the European Parliament. One committee (known as the committee *au fond*) is principally responsible for drawing up a report complete with amendments. To this end one of the members of the committee will be appointed Rapporteur, and the report will be prepared in that Member's name. The Parliament can be lobbied in three ways: directly to the Members or their assistants; by approaching the officials of the Parliament attached to the relevant committee; and via the political groups. It is of prime importance to establish good contacts with the Rapporteur. Again, as with the Council, it is important too for lobbying to be done as early as possible before too many compromises and trade-offs have been reached within the responsible committee. It goes without saying that the more a case can be given a cross-national, cross-party dimension, the better its chance of acceptance. The same broad general rules apply to lobbying directed at the European Economic and Social Committee and the Committee of the Regions. Lobbyists should be aware that although many proposals are subject to a second reading in the Parliament, Rule 80 of the Parliament's Rules of Procedure severely limits the scope for bringing forward new amendments at the second reading stage and virtually prohibits the retabling of amendments which were not adopted at the first reading.

Contacts with the European Parliament can be valuable in other ways. Lobbyists can make use of the Members' right to put questions, oral or written, to the Commission and the Council, to raise matters both with Commissioners or with representatives of the Council in committee, to initiate debates and, exceptionally, to set up Committees of Inquiry under Article 193 of the Treaty of Rome. Also of great interest to lobbyists are the public hearings which are now an established feature of committee work.

PART I

THE EUROPEAN COMMISSION

The European Commission forms what might be called the 'government' of the Member States. The Commissioners are responsible for the Directorates-General as well as for various services.

The procedure for selecting and approving the Commission is as follows. First, a candidate for President is nominated by the European Council. The choice requires endorsement by a majority of the Members of the European Parliament. If the proposed candidate does not receive a majority of votes, the European Council must, within one month, nominate another candidate. The Commission's President-elect chooses the Commissioners from lists of three nominees per Member State. The College is then collectively submitted to a vote of approval by the European Parliament.

The first part of this section provides the names, responsibilities and telephone numbers of the Commissioners, and similar details for the Directors-General and other key posts in the Commission's main operational services.

All written correspondence should be addressed to the individual concerned, giving the name of the Directorate-General, Directorate and Unit to which the person belongs (e.g. Enterprise DG/A/3), and should be sent to The European Commission, 1049 Brussels, Belgium.

Letters to the President of the Commission should be addressed as follows: Mr José Manuel Barroso, President of the Commission, European Commission, 1049 Brussels, Belgium.

The number of the Commission's central switchboard in Brussels is: (+32) 2-2991111 and the main fax numbers are (+32) 2-2950138 and (+32) 2-2950139. Officials can also be contacted by e-mail using the standard pattern firstname.surname@cec.eu.int. The Commission have their website at http://europa.eu.int/comm.

General contact details for units based in Luxembourg are: The European Commission, Rue Alcide de Gasperi, 2920 Luxembourg, Luxembourg; tel. (+352) 43011 (switchboard); fax (+352) 430135049.

THE COMMISSIONERS

The Commission is the executive of the European Union. It currently has 25 members and is appointed for a five-year period.

BARROSO José Manuel
President
Tel. (+32) 2-2991559
Tel. (+32) 2-2967246

WALLSTRÖM Margot
Vice-President (Institutional Relations and
  Communication Strategy)
Tel. (+32) 2-2981800
Tel. (+32) 2-2994917

VERHEUGEN Günther
Vice-President (Enterprise and Industry)
Tel. (+32) 2-2981100
Tel. (+32) 2-2993869

BARROT Jacques
Vice-President (Transport)
Tel. (+32) 2-2981500
Tel. (+32) 2-2981506

KALLAS Siim
Vice-President (Administrative Affairs, Audit
  and Anti-Fraud)
Tel. (+32) 2-2988762

FRATTINI Franco
Vice-President (Justice, Freedom and Security)
Tel. (+32) 2-2987500

REDING Viviane
Member of the Commission (Information
  Society and Media)
Tel. (+32) 2-2981600
Tel. (+32) 2-2958992

DIMAS Stavros
Member of the Commission (Environment)
Tel. (+32) 2-2982000
Tel. (+32) 2-2982001

ALMUNIA Joaquín
Member of the Commission (Economic and
   Monetary Affairs)
Tel. (+32) 2-2980900

HÜBNER Danuta
Member of the Commission (Regional Policy)
Tel. (+32) 2-2988625

BORG Joe
Member of the Commission (Fisheries and
   Maritime Affairs)
Tel. (+32) 2-2988685

GRYBAUSKAITĖ Dalia
Member of the Commission (Financial
   Programming and Budget)
Tel. (+32) 2-2988731

POTOČNIK Janez
Member of the Commission (Science and
   Research)
Tel. (+32) 2-2988670

FIGEL' Ján
Member of the Commission (Education,
   Training, Culture and Multilingualism)
Tel. (+32) 2-2988716

KYPRIANOU Markos
Member of the Commission (Health and
   Consumer Protection)
Tel. (+32) 2-2988700

REHN Olli
Member of the Commission (Enlargement)
Tel. (+32) 2-2957957

MICHEL Louis
Member of the Commission (Development and
   Humanitarian Aid)
Tel. (+32) 2-2959600

KOVÁCS László
Member of the Commission (Taxation and
   Customs Union)
Tel. (+32) 2-2988400

KROES Neelie
Member of the Commission (Competition)

FISCHER BOEL Mariann
Member of the Commission (Agriculture and
   Rural Development)
Tel. (+32) 2-2993400

FERRERO-WALDNER Benita
Member of the Commission (External
   Relations and Neighbourhood Policy)
Tel. (+32) 2-2994900

MCCREEVY Charlie
Member of the Commission (Internal Market
   and Services)
Tel. (+32) 2-2988040

ŠPIDLA Vladimir
Member of the Commission (Employment,
   Social Affairs and Equal Opportunities)
Tel. (+32) 2-2988530

MANDELSON Peter
Member of the Commission (Trade)
Tel. (+32) 2-2988590

PIEBALGS Andris
Member of the Commission (Energy)
Tel. (+32) 2-2988747

SECRETARIAT-GENERAL OF THE COMMISSION

Rue de la Loi 200, 1049 Brussels, Belgium
Tel: (+32) 2-2991111
E-mail: to pattern firstname.surname@
   cec.eu.int
URL: http://europa.eu.int/comm/dgs/
   secretariat_general/index_en.htm

O'SULLIVAN David
Secretary-General
Tel. (+32) 2-2950948
Tel. (+32) 2-2950098

MOAVERO MILANESI Enzo
Deputy Secretary-General (with special
   responsibility for Directorates A, B, C, D
   and E)
Tel. (+32) 2-2953427
Tel. (+32) 2-2969481

GUTH Eckart
Deputy Secretary-General (with special
   responsibility for Directorates F, G and H)
Tel. (+32) 2-2981702
Tel. (+32) 2-2981703

ONESTINI Cesare
Assistant to the Secretary-General
Tel. (+32) 2-2957571

DE OLIVEIRA E SOUSA Jorge
Chief Adviser
Tel. (+32) 2-2960393

Directorate A – Registry and Commission Decision-Making Process

BUGNOT Patricia
Director
Tel. (+32) 2-2950731
Tel. (+32) 2-2950033

Directorate B – Relations with Civil Society

NYMAND CHRISTENSEN Jens
Director
Tel. (+32) 2-2993317
Tel. (+32) 2-2966432

Directorate C – Programming and Administrative Co-ordination

[post vacant]
Director

Directorate D – Policy Co-ordination

BISARRE Sylvain
Director
Tel. (+32) 2-2954695
Tel. (+32) 2-2952449

Directorate E – Resources and General Matters

HARFORD Marleen
Director
Tel. (+32) 2-2953518

Directorate F – Relations with the Council

BORCHARDT Gustaaf
Director
Tel. (+32) 2-2966583
Tel. (+32) 2-2966670

Directorate G – Relations with the European Parliament, the European Ombudsman, the European Economic and Social Committee, the Committee of the Regions and National Parliaments

MASSANGIOLI Guiseppe
Director
Tel. (+32) 2-2950746
Tel. (+32) 2-2963297

Directorate H – Institutional Matters

PONZANO Paolo
Director
Tel. (+32) 2-2951934

LEGAL SERVICE

E-mail: to pattern firstname.surname@ cec.eu.int
URL: http://europa.eu.int/comm/dgs/legal_ service/index_en.htm

PETITE Michel
Director-General
Tel. (+32) 2-2965052
Tel. (+32) 2-2952521

SANTAOLALLA GADEA Francisco
Deputy Director-General (acting)

O'LEARY William
Assistant to the Director-General
Tel. (+32) 2-2966221
Tel. (+32) 2-2952934

VAN RIJN Thomas
Principal Legal Adviser – Agriculture and fisheries
Tel. (+32) 2-2951818
Tel. (+32) 2-2959864

JONCZY-MONTASTRUC Marie-José
Principal Legal Adviser – Employment and social affairs
Tel. (+32) 2-2952974
Tel. (+32) 2-2998387

DURAND Claire-Françoise
Principal Legal Adviser – Internal market
Tel. (+32) 2-2951192
Tel. (+32) 2-2959168

BENYON Frank
Principal Legal Adviser – Business law
Tel. (+32) 2-2058241
Tel. (+32) 2-2965788

KUIJPER Pieter Jan
Principal Legal Adviser – External relations
Tel. (+32) 2-2961273

SANTAOLALLA GADEA Francisco
Principal Legal Adviser – State aids and
　dumping
Tel. (+32) 2-2962776
Tel. (+32) 2-2955257

GRÜNWALD Juergen
Principal Legal Adviser – Budget, personnel
　and administration
Tel. (+32) 2-2958263
Tel. (+32) 2-2965817

HARTVIG Hans Peter
Principal Legal Adviser – Institutions
Tel. (+32) 2-2951192

DE MARCH Eugenio
Principal Legal Adviser (acting) – Justice,
　Freedom and Security, Private Law and
　Criminal Law
Tel. (+32) 2-2957281

CHRISTOFOROU Theofanis
Principal Legal Adviser (acting) – Competition
　and Mergers
Tel. (+32) 2-2950168
Tel. (+32) 2-2951904

CROSSLAND Hans
Legal Adviser
Tel. (+32) 2-2955746
Tel. (+32) 2-2965804

WOELKER Ulrich
Legal Adviser
Tel. (+32) 2-2966268
Tel. (+32) 2-2952831

CURRALL Julian
Legal Adviser
Tel. (+32) 2-2957900
Tel. (+32) 2-2953864

WHITE Eric
Legal Adviser
Tel. (+32) 2-2954856
Tel. (+32) 2-2993352

TRAVERSA Enrico
Legal Adviser
Tel. (+32) 2-2955921
Tel. (+32) 2-2965297

DÍAZ-LLANOS LA ROCHE Miguel
Legal Adviser
Tel. (+32) 2-2962715
Tel. (+32) 2-2965297

MAIDANI Dominique
Legal Adviser
Tel. (+32) 2-2994913
Tel. (+32) 2-2962132

TUFVESSON Christina
Legal Adviser
Tel. (+32) 2-2959203
Tel. (+32) 2-2993352

DOCKSEY Christopher
Legal Adviser
Tel. (+32) 2-2955717
Tel. (+32) 2-2950066

VAN NUFFEL Pieter
Legal Adviser
Tel. (+32) 2-2950029
Tel. (+32) 2-2966361

SACK Jörn
Legal Adviser
Tel. (+32) 2-2957317
Tel. (+32) 2-2950956

ROZET Gérard
Legal Adviser
Tel. (+32) 2-2957218
Tel. (+32) 2-2967842

HETSCH Patrick
Legal Adviser
Tel. (+32) 2-2951151
Tel. (+32) 2-2965788

BANKS Karen
Legal Adviser
Tel. (+32) 2-2952824
Tel. (+32) 2-2965788

FORMAN John
Legal Adviser
Tel. (+32) 2-2952829
Tel. (+32) 2-2958209

VAN SOLINGE Alain
Legal Adviser
Tel. (+32) 2-2955854
Tel. (+32) 2-2960068

BOUFLET Jean-Jacques
Legal Adviser
Tel. (+32) 2-2990152
Tel. (+32) 2-2991753

CLARKE-SMITH Bevis
Head of Legal Revisers Group
Tel. (+32) 2-2952828
Tel. (+32) 2-2953462

PRESS AND COMMUNICATION DIRECTORATE-GENERAL

E-mail: to pattern firstname.surname@ cec.eu.int
URL: http://europa.eu.int/comm/dgs/press_ communication/index_en.htm

CARVOUNIS Panayotis
Director-General (acting)

ROUDIÉ François
Assistant to the Director-General
Tel. (+32) 2-2966898

LE BAIL Françoise
Deputy Director-General, and Commission Spokesperson (acting)
Tel. (+32) 2-2992243

LE BAIL Françoise
Chief Adviser
Tel. (+32) 2-2992243

CROONEN Edwin
1. Audit

CHAMLA Jean-Jacques
2. Inspection
Tel. (+32) 2-2957823

BOUYGUES Sixtine
3. Planning, Programming and Evaluation

RIBEIRO DA SILVA Leonor
Deputy Spokesperson
Tel. (+32) 2-2088155

AHRENKILDE HANSEN Pia
Deputy Spokesperson
Tel. (+32) 2-2953070

KREUZHUBER Gregor
Spokesperson (enterprise and industry)
Tel. (+32) 2-2966565

TODD Jonathan
Spokesperson (competition)
Tel. (+32) 2-2994107

DREWES Oliver
Spokesperson (internal market and services)
Tel. (+32) 2-2992421

TORRES Amélia
Spokesperson (economic and monetary affairs)
Tel. (+32) 2-2954629

DOWGIELEWICZ Mikolay
Spokesperson (communication and institutional relations)
Tel. (+32) 2-2950051

SELMAYR Martin
Spokesperson (information society and media)
Tel. (+32) 2-2981230

VINCENT Frederic
Spokesperson (education, training and culture)
Tel. (+32) 2-2987166

RAMPI Valérie
Spokesperson (administration, audit and the fight against fraud)
Tel. (+32) 2-2966367

ASSIMAKOPOULOU Maria
Spokesperson (taxation and customs union)
Tel. (+32) 2-2959842

HEDLUND Ewa
Spokesperson (financial programming and budget)
Tel. (+32) 2-2991223

DE RYNCK Stefaan
Spokesperson (transport)
Tel. (+32) 2-2999279

KRIETEMEYER Rupert
Spokesperson (energy)
Tel. (+32) 2-2990784

MOCHAN Antonia
Spokesperson (science and research)
Tel. (+32) 2-2969921

UDWIN Emma
Spokesperson (external relations)
Tel. (+32) 2-2959577

VERON-REVILLE Claude
Spokesperson (trade)
Tel. (+32) 2-2961159

ALTAFAJ TARDIO Amadeu
Spokesperson (development and humanitarian
   aid)
Tel. (+32) 2-2952658

NAGY Krisztina
Spokesperson (enlargement)
Tel. (+32) 2-2988663

VON SCHNURBEIN Katharina
Spokesperson (employment and social affairs)
Tel. (+32) 2-2981408

LAISSY Ana-Paula
Spokesperson (regional policy)
Tel. (+32) 2-2953258

ROSCAM ABBING Friso
Spokesperson (justice, liberty and security)
Tel. (+32) 2-2966746

MANN Michael
Spokesperson (agriculture and rural
   development)
Tel. (+32) 2-2999780

THOM Mireille
Spokesperson (fishing and maritime affairs)
Tel. (+32) 2-2991630

TOD Philip
Spokesperson (health and consumer protection)
Tel. (+32) 2-2965911

HELFFERICH Barbara
Spokesperson (environment)
Tel. (+32) 2-2982010

Directorate A – Information and Communication Strategies and Policies

CARVOUNIS Panayotis
Director
Tel. (+32) 2-2952173

Directorate B – Communication, Media and Services

DUMORT Alain
Director (acting)

Directorate C – Resources

VANDERSTEEN Jean-Pierre
Director
Tel. (+32) 2-2986170

BUREAU OF EUROPEAN POLICY ADVISERS (BEPA)

E-mail: group-advisers@cec.eu.int
*URL: http://europa.eu.int/comm/dgs/policy_*
   advisers/team/index_en.htm

TAVARES Carlos
Director
Tel. (+32) 2-2920891
Tel. (+32) 2-2985296

CANOY Marcel
Adviser

MARTIN SMITH Peter
Adviser
Tel. (+32) 2-2953994

BELESSIOTIS Tassos
Adviser

OLIGBO Una
Adviser

LEVIN Mattias
Adviser

CLAIRET Paul
Adviser
Tel. (+32) 2-2966789
Tel. (+32) 2-2968474

MELICH Anna
Adviser
Tel. (+32) 2-2999172

WENINGER Michael
Adviser

SOCHACKI Myriam
Adviser

GOZI Sandro
Adviser

ROGERS Michael
Adviser
Tel. (+32) 2-2950641
Tel. (+32) 2-2968474

CARVALHO Maria da Graca
Adviser

FIELDING Andrew
Adviser

HUBERT Agnès
Adviser
Tel. (+32) 2-2958889
Tel. (+32) 2-2963624

COLOMBO Paola
Adviser

MOMMENS Patricia
Adviser

ECONOMIC AND FINANCIAL AFFAIRS DIRECTORATE-GENERAL

E-mail: to pattern firstname.surname@ cec.eu.int
URL: http://europa.eu.int/comm/dgs/economy_ finance/index_en.htm

REGLING Klaus
Director-General
Tel. (+32) 2-2994366
Tel. (+32) 2-2994360

PFLÜGER Stefan
Assistant to the Director-General
Tel. (+32) 2-2993413

SIMONETTI Sylvain
Internal audit
Tel. (+32) 2-2936343
Tel. (+32) 2-2935110

LELAKIS Vassili
Director responsible for relations with the EBRD (acting)

STEMITSIOTIS Loukas
Secretary of the Economic and Financial Committee and the Economic Policy Committee (acting)

Directorate A – Economic Studies and Research

KRÖGER Jürgen
Director
Tel. (+32) 2-2993488
Tel. (+32) 2-2994399

Directorate B – National Economies

BUTI Marco
Director
Tel. (+32) 2-2962246
Tel. (+32) 2-2996261

Directorate C – Economy of the Euro Zone and the Union

DEROOSE Servaas
Director
Tel. (+32) 2-2994375
Tel. (+32) 2-2994424

Directorate D – International Economic and Financial Affairs

DE LECEA FLORES DE LEMUS Antonio
Director

Directorate E – Economic Evaluation Service

SCHMIDT Jan Host
Director
Tel. (+32) 2-2957904
Tel. (+32) 2-2994385

Directorate L – Financial Operations, Programmes Management and Liaison with the EIB Group

MCGLUE David
Director
Tel. (+32) 2-2934067
Tel. (+32) 2-2936206

Directorate R – Resources

CAS GRANJE Alexandra
Director
Tel. (+32) 2-2956269
Tel. (+32) 2-2954785

9

ENTERPRISE AND INDUSTRY DIRECTORATE-GENERAL

E-mail: to pattern firstname.surname@ cec.eu.int
URL: http://europa.eu.int/comm/dgs/enterprise/ index_en.htm

REICHENBACH Horst
Director-General
Tel. (+32) 2-2994396
Tel. (+32) 2-2951258

ZOUREK Heinz
Deputy Director-General (Directorates C, D, E and H)
Tel. (+32) 2-2991604
Tel. (+32) 2-2962176

THERY Nicolas
Adviser
Tel. (+32) 2-2982240

SALMI Heikki
Adviser
Tel. (+32) 2-2951497

LUCHNER Johannes
Assistant to the Director-General
Tel. (+32) 2-2968811

Directorate R – Management and Resources

PYKE Belinda
Director
Tel. (+32) 2-2961673

Directorate A – Co-ordination for Competitiveness

MATTHIAS Ruete
Director
Tel. (+32) 2-2950734

Directorate B – Industrial Policy and Economic Reforms

KOOPMAN Gert-Jan
Director
Tel. (+32) 2-2993381

Directorate C – Regulatory Policy

AYRAL Michel
Director
Tel. (+32) 2-2955643

Directorate D – Innovation Policy

WHITE David
Director
Tel. (+32) 2-2955724

Directorate E – Promotion of SMEs' Competitiveness

RUTE Maive
Director
Tel. (+32) 2-2959159

Directorate F – Consumer Goods

LALIS Georgette
Director
Tel. (+32) 2-2987930

Directorate G – Chemicals and Construction

HENNESSY Patrick
Director
Tel. (+32) 2-2963355

Directorate H – Aerospace, Security, Defence and Equipment

WEISSENBERG Paul
Director
Tel. (+32) 2-29633358

Directorate I — Basics and Design Industries, Tourism, IDABC

ORTUN Pedro
Director
Tel. (+32) 2-2952084

COMPETITION DIRECTORATE-GENERAL

E-mail: to pattern firstname.surname@ cec.eu.int
URL: http://europa.eu.int/comm/dgs/ competition/index_en.htm

LOWE Philip
Director-General
Tel. (+32) 2-2965040
Tel. (+32) 2-2954562

DRAUZ Götz-Heinrich
Deputy Director-General (with special responsibility for mergers)
Tel. (+32) 2-2958681
Tel. (+32) 2-2996728

ROCCA Gianfranco
Deputy Director-General (with special responsibility for antitrust activities)
Tel. (+32) 2-2951152
Tel. (+32) 2-2951139

[post vacant]
Deputy Director-General (with special responsibility for state aid)

PESARESI Nicola
Assistant to the Director-General
Tel. (+32) 2-2992906
Tel. (+32) 2-2992132

DEISENHOFER Thomas
Assistant to the Director-General

Directorate R – Strategic Planning and Resources

NORBERG Sven
Director
Tel. (+32) 2-2952178
Tel. (+32) 2-2963603

Directorate A – Policy and Strategic Support

PAULIS Emil
Director
Tel. (+32) 2-2965033
Tel. (+32) 2-2952871

Directorate B – Energy, Basic Industries, Chemicals and Pharmaceuticals

[post vacant]
Director

Directorate C – Information, Communication and Media

TRADACETE COCERA Angel
Director
Tel. (+32) 2-2952462
Tel. (+32) 2-2950900

Directorate D – Services

EVANS Lowri
Director
Tel. (+32) 2-2965029
Tel. (+32) 2-2965036

Directorate E – Industries, Consumer Goods and Manufacturing

MEHTA Kirtikumar
Director

Directorate F – Cartels

[post vacant]
Director

Directorate G – State Aid I: Cohesion and Competitiveness

DRABBE Humbert
Director
Tel. (+32) 2-2950060
Tel. (+32) 2-2952701

11

Directorate H – State Aid II: Network Industries, Liberalized Sectors and Services

DORMAL-MARINO Loretta
Director
Tel. (+32) 2-2958603
Tel. (+32) 2-2953731

Directorate I – State Aid Policy and Strategic Co-ordination

VAN HOOF Marc
Director

EMPLOYMENT, SOCIAL AFFAIRS AND EQUAL OPPORTUNITIES DIRECTORATE-GENERAL

E-mail: to pattern firstname.surname@ cec.eu.int
URL: http://europa.eu.int/comm/dgs/ employment_social/index_en.htm

QUINTIN Odile
Director-General
Tel. (+32) 2-2992277

SAMUEL Lenla
Deputy Director-General

OLSSON Erick Stefan
Assistant to the Director-General
Tel. (+32) 2-2953569

Directorate A – Employment & ESF Policy Co-ordination

KASTRISSIANAKIS Antonis
Director
Tel. (+32) 2-2957380

Directorate B – National Employment and Social Inclusion Monitoring & ESF Operations I

JØRGENSEN Peter Stub
Director
Tel. (+32) 2-2986000

Directorate C – National Employment and Social Inclusion Monitoring & ESF Operations II

KJELLSTRÖM Sven
Director
Tel. (+32) 2-2954010

Directorate D – Adaptability, Social Dialogue and Social Rights

JANSEN Bernhard
Director
Tel. (+32) 2-2957604

Directorate E – Social Protection and Social Integration

VIGNON Jérôme
Director
Tel. (+32) 2-2954602

Directorate F – Resources

PRADO Raoul
Director
Tel. (+32) 2-2969646

Directorate G – Horizontal and International Issues

PAVAN-WOOLFE Luisella
Director
Tel. (+32) 2-2956638

Directorate H – National Employment and Social Inclusion, Monitoring and ESF Operations III

PRATS MONNE Xavier
Director
Tel. (+32) 2-2961230

AGRICULTURE AND RURAL DEVELOPMENT DIRECTORATE-GENERAL

E-mail: to pattern firstname.surname@ cec.eu.int
URL: http://europa.eu.int/comm/dgs/ agriculture/index_en.htm

SILVA RODRÍGUEZ José Manuel
Director-General
Tel. (+32) 2-2951910
Tel. (+32) 2-2953274

HOELGAARD Lars Christian
Deputy Director-General (Directorates B, C and D)
Tel. (+32) 2-2963314
Tel. (+32) 2-2962615

AHNER Dirk
Deputy Director-General (Directorates E, F and G)
Tel. (+32) 2-2957555
Tel. (+32) 2-2965215

DEMARTY Jean-Luc
Deputy Director-General (Directorates H, I and J)
Tel. (+32) 2-2956126
Tel. (+32) 2-2953290

[post vacant]
Adviser hors classe (analyses concerning different aspects of the Common Agricultural Policy)

LORIZ-HOFFMANN Josefine
Assistant to the Director-General
Tel. (+32 2) 295 79 77

VERLET Nicolas
Assistant to the Director-General
Tel. (+32) 2-2961508
Tel. (+32) 2-2959392

[post vacant]
Principal Adviser

Directorate AI – International Affairs I, in particular WTO Negotiations

MINCH Mary
Director
Tel. (+32) 2-2961651

Directorate AII – International Affairs II, in particular Enlargement

PACHECO João José
Director

Directorate B – Relations with other Institutions; Communication and Documentation

LEGUEN DE LACROIX Eugène
Director (acting)

Directorate C – Economics of Agricultural Markets (and CMO)

MILDON Russell
Director
Tel. (+32) 2-2953224
Tel. (+32) 2-2968890

Directorate D – Direct Support, Market Measures, Promotion

JAFFRELOT Jean-Jacques
Director (acting)
Tel. (+32) 2-2952836

Directorate EI – Rural Development Programmes I

SOUSA UVA José Manuel
Director
Tel. (+32) 2-2959318
Tel. (+32) 2-2950653

Directorate EII – Rural Development Programmes II

CONSTANTINOU Antonis
Director
Tel. (+32) 2-2952638

Directorate F – Horizontal Aspects of Rural Development

SIVENAS Nikiforos
Director
Tel. (+32) 2-2959662
Tel. (+32) 2-2994338

Directorate G – Economic Analyses and Evaluation

BENSTED-SMITH John
Director
Tel. (+32) 2-2957443
Tel. (+32) 2-2961261

Directorate H – Agricultural Legislation

GENCARELLI Fabio
Director (acting)
Tel. (+32) 2-2956276

Directorate I – Internal Resource Management

DE WINNE Prosper
Director
Tel. (+32) 2-2956394

Directorate J – Audit of Agricultural Expenditure

HEBETTE Chantal
Director
Tel. (+32) 2-2961814
Tel. (+32) 2-2993243

ENERGY AND TRANSPORT DIRECTORATE-GENERAL

E-mail: to pattern firstname.surname@ cec.eu.int
URL: http://europa.eu.int/comm/dgs/energy_ transport/index_en.html

LAMOUREUX François
Director-General
Tel. (+32) 2-2951992
Tel. (+32) 2-2965002

KAZATSAY Zoltán
Deputy Director-General (co-ordination of transport activities, supervision of Directorates E, F and G)

DE ESTEBAN ALONSO Fernando
Deputy Director-General (co-ordination of nuclear activities, supervision of Directorates H and I)
Tel. (+352) 430132420

HENNINGSEN Jörgen
Chief Adviser to the Director-General
Tel. (+32) 2-2992965
Tel. (+32) 2-2969504

LANDRESSE Gaston
Adviser (to the Deputy Director-General in charge of the analysis of the technical aspects of the files)
Tel. (+352) 430137165
Tel. (+352) 430132247

GANTELET Gilles
Assistant to the Director-General
Tel. (+32) 2-2994896

MAYET Remi
Assistant to the Director-General
Tel. (+32) 2-2964677

Directorate A – General Affairs and Resources

RISTORI Dominique
Director
Tel. (+32) 2-2992460
Tel. (+32) 2-2992461

Directorate B – Trans-European Networks – Energy and Transport

HILBRECHT Heinz
Director
Tel. (+32) 2-2968174
Tel. (+32) 2-2992006

Directorate C – Conventional Sources of Energy

SCHMIDT VON SYDOW Helmut
Director
Tel. (+32) 2-2954256
Tel. (+32) 2-2961491

Directorate D – New Sources of Energy, Demand Management and Sustainable Development

GONZÁLEZ FINAT Alfonso
Director
Tel. (+32) 2-2968287
Tel. (+32) 2-2968441

Directorate E – Inland Transport

GRILLO PASQUARELLI Enrico
Director
Tel. (+32) 2-2956203
Tel. (+32) 2-2957213

Directorate F – Air Transport

CALLEJA CRESPO Daniel
Director

Directorate G – Maritime and River Transport and Intermodality

KARAMITSOS Fotis
Director
Tel. (+32) 2-2963461
Tel. (+32) 2-2968305

Directorate H – Nuclear Energy

WAETERLOOS Christian
Director
Tel. (+352) 430134342

Directorate I – Nuclear Guarantees

CLEUTINX Christian
Director
Tel. (+352) 430136236
Tel. (+352) 430135540

Directorate J – Security: Protection of Persons, Assets and Facilities

TRESTOUR Jean
Director (acting)

Euratom Supply Agency (ESA)

WAETERLOOS Christian
Director-General (acting)
Tel. (+352) 430134342

ENVIRONMENT DIRECTORATE-GENERAL

E-mail: to pattern firstname.surname@ cec.eu.int
URL: http://europa.eu.int/comm/dgs/ environment/index_en.htm

DAY Catherine
Director-General
Tel. (+32) 2-2958312
Tel. (+32) 2-2952303

HARGADON Malachy
Assistant to the Director-General
Tel. (+32) 2-2968450

Directorate A – Governance, Communication and Civil Protection

LAWRENCE David
Director (acting)
Tel. (+32) 2-2953537

Directorate B – Protecting the Natural Environment

DAY Catherine
Director (acting)
Tel. (+32) 2-2958312
Tel. (+32) 2-2952303

Directorate C – Air and Chemicals

DELBEKE Jos
Director
Tel. (+32) 2-2968804
Tel. (+32) 2-2967380

Directorate D – Water and Environmental Programmes

LAWRENCE David
Director
Tel. (+32) 2-2953537

Directorate E – International Affairs

BLANCO Soledad
Director
Tel. (+32) 2-2995182

Directorate F – Resources

GROEBNER Viola
Director
Tel. (+32) 2-2990078
Tel. (+32) 2-2960752

Directorate G – Sustainable Development and Economic Analysis

MÄKELÄ Timo
Director
Tel. (+32) 2-2962634

RESEARCH DIRECTORATE-GENERAL

E-mail: to pattern firstname.surname@ cec.eu.int
URL: http://europa.eu.int/comm/dgs/research/ index_en.htm

MITSOS Achilleas
Director-General
Tel. (+32) 2-2958560
Tel. (+32) 2-2962785

STANCIC Zoran
Deputy Director-General
Tel. (+32) 2-2962475

[post vacant]
Deputy Director-General

ANDRÉ Michel
Adviser (responsible for research policy matters)
Tel. (+32) 2-2960781

CHATZIPANAGIOTOU Stavros
Assistant to the Director-General
Tel. (+32) 2-2993915

Directorate A – Co-ordination of Community Activities

ESCRITT Richard
Director
Tel. (+32) 2-2950725
Tel. (+32) 2-2960790

Directorate B – Structuring the European Research Area

SMITS Robert-Jan
Director (acting)

Directorate C – Science and Society

GEROLD Rainer
Director
Tel. (+32) 2-2952716
Tel. (+32) 2-2951946

Directorate D – Human Factor, Mobility and Marie Curie Actions

LIBERALI Raffaele
Director
Tel. (+32) 2-2958673
Tel. (+32) 2-2958879

Directorate E – Biotechnology, Agriculture and Food

PATERMANN Mark
Director
Tel. (+32) 2-2951815
Tel. (+32) 2-2954070

Directorate F – Health

QUINTANA TRIAS Octavio
Director
Tel. (+32) 2-2989330

Directorate G – Industrial Technologies

ANDRETA Ezio
Director
Tel. (+32) 2-2951660

Directorate H – Space and Transport

METTHEY Jack
Director
Tel. (+32) 2-2968870

Directorate I – Environment

VALETTE Pierre
Director (acting)
Tel. (+32) 2-2956356
Tel. (+32) 2-2957412

Directorate J – Energy

FERNÁNDEZ RUIZ Pablo
Director
Tel. (+32) 2-2953461
Tel. (+32) 2-2990031

Directorate K – Social Sciences and Humanities; Foresight

LENNON Theodius
Director
Tel. (+32) 2-2959986
Tel. (+32) 2-2955404

Directorate M – Investment in Research and Links with other Policies

SARAGOSSI Isi
Director (acting)
Tel. (+32) 2-2955517
Tel. (+32) 2-2991165

Directorate N – International Scientific Co-operation

SIEGLER Andras
Director
Tel. (+32) 2-2980182

Directorate R – Resources

SOARES Maria Manuela
Director
Tel. (+32) 2-2962148
Tel. (+32) 2-2962092

JOINT RESEARCH CENTRE

E-mail: to pattern firstname.surname@ cec.eu.int
URL: http://www.jrc.cec.eu.int

Brussels: *Rue de la Loi 200, 1049 Brussels, Belgium*
Tel: (+32) 2-291111
Fax: (+32) 2-2950146

Ispra: *21020 Ispra (Varese), Italy*
Tel: (+39) 0332-786750
Fax: (+39) 0332-789157

Geel: *Steenweg op Retie, 2240 Geel, Belgium*
Tel: (+32) 14-571272
Fax: (+32) 14-584273

Karlsruhe: *Postfach 2340, 76125 Karlsruhe, Germany*
Tel: (+49 7247) 951156
Fax: (+49 7247) 951591

Petten: *Westerduinweg 3, Postbus Nr 2, 1755 ZG Petten, Netherlands*
Tel: (+31 224) 565278
Fax: (+31 224) 565630

Seville: *Edificio Expo, Garcilaso s/n, 41092 Seville, Spain*
Tel: (+34) 954-488348
Fax: (+34) 954-488339

SCHENKEL Roland
Director-General (acting)
Tel. (+32) 2-2999840
Tel. (+32) 2-2961490

SCHENKEL Roland
Deputy Director-General (with special responsibility for nuclear activities, the comprehensive decommissioning programme)
Tel. (+32) 2-2999840
Tel. (+32) 2-2961490

VAN LEEUWEN Cornelis
Principal adviser (reporting to the Director-General)
Tel. (+32) 2-2980936

Directorate A – Institutional and Scientific Relations (Brussels)

FAHY Michael
Director (acting)
Tel. (+32) 2-2967216
Tel. (+32) 2-2953701

Directorate B – Programme and Resource Management (Brussels, Ispra)

DEZEURE Freddy
Director (acting)
Tel. (+32) 2-2959805
Tel. (+32) 2-2957223

Directorate C – Ispra Site Directorate

WILKINSON David
Director
Tel. (+39) 0332-786750

Directorate D – Institute for Reference Materials and Measurements (Geel)

HERRERO MOLINA Alejandro
Director

Directorate E – Institute for Transuranium Elements (Karlsruhe)

LANDER Gerard
Director

Directorate F – Institute for Energy (Petten)

TÖRRÖNEN Kari
Director
Tel. (+31 224) 565401

Directorate G – Institute for the Protection and the Security of the Citizen (Ispra)

CADIOU Jean-Marie
Director
Tel. (+39) 0332-789947

Directorate H – Institute for Environment and Sustainability (Ispra)

GRASSERBAUER Manfred
Director
Tel. (+39) 0332-786680

Directorate I – Institute for Health and Consumer Protection (Ispra)

KOTZIAS Dimitrios
Director (acting)

Directorate J – Institute for Prospective Technological Studies (Seville)

KIND Peter
Director
Tel. (+34) 954-488273

INFORMATION SOCIETY AND MEDIA DIRECTORATE-GENERAL

E-mail: to pattern firstname.surname@ cec.eu.int
URL: http://europa.eu.int/comm/dgs/ information_society/index_en.htm

COLASANTI Fabio
Director-General
Tel. (+32) 2-2994374

ZANGL Peter
Deputy Director-General
Tel. (+32) 2-2954147

[post vacant]
Principal Adviser

WILKINSON Christopher
Adviser
Tel. (+32) 2-2969538

OTRUBA Heinrich
Adviser (ERG Secretariat)
Tel. (+32) 2-2968879

HEALY Jean-Claude
Adviser (seconded to WHO)
Tel. (+32) 2-2963506
Tel. (+32) 2-2961200

STREITENBERGER Wolfgang
Adviser
Tel. (+32) 2-2984426

PELHATE Pierrette
Adviser
Tel. (+32) 2-2969633

VERHOEF Paul
Adviser (seconded to ICANN)

WATSON John
Assistant to Director-General
Tel. (+32) 2-2964166

ALVAREZ HIDALGO Paloma
Assistant to Director-General
Tel. (+32) 2-2955079

Directorate R – Resources

LIBERTALIS Bernard
Director
Tel. (+32) 2-2968952

Directorate S – General Affairs

BINNS Susan
Director

Directorate A – Audiovisual, Media, Internet

PAULGER Gregory
Director
Tel. (+32) 2-2999434

Directorate B – Electronic Communications Policy

LANGEHEINE Bernd
Director
Tel. (+32) 2-2991855

Directorate C – Lisbon Strategy and Policies for the Information Society

DE BRUÏNE Reinier
Director
Tel. (+32) 2-2968538

Directorate D – Network and Communication Technologies

DA SILVA João Augusto
Director
Tel. (+32) 2-2992005

Directorate E – Content

FORSTER Horst
Director
Tel. (+352) 430132133

Directorate F – Emerging Technologies and Infrastructures

DAHLSTEN Ulf
Director
Tel. (+32) 2-2994931

Directorate G – Components and Systems

ZOBEL Rosalie
Director
Tel. (+32) 2-2968168

Directorate H – ICT for Citizens and Businesses

[post vacant]
Director

FISHERIES AND MARITIME AFFAIRS DIRECTORATE-GENERAL

E-mail: to pattern firstname.surname@ cec.eu.int
URL: http://europa.eu.int/comm/dgs/fisheries/ index_en.htm

HOLMQUIST Jörgen
Director-General
Tel. (+32) 2-2955192
Tel. (+32) 2-2965192

PAPAIOANNOU Emmanouil-Georgios
Assistant to the Director-General
Tel. (+32) 2-2969988

Directorate A – Conservation Policy

FARNELL John
Director
Tel. (+32) 2-2956397

Directorate B – External Policy and Markets

DEBEN ALFONSO César
Director
Tel. (+32) 2-2993224

Directorate C – Structural Policy

VERSTRAETE Lea
Director
Tel. (+32) 2-2954561
Tel. (+32) 2-2995925

Directorate D – Control and Enforcement

LAUREC Alain
Director
Tel. (+32) 2-2986652
Tel. (+32) 2-2950288

Directorate E – Resources and Relations with Stakeholders

MASTRACCHIO Emilio
Director
Tel. (+32) 2-2955568
Tel. (+32) 2-2954387

INTERNAL MARKET AND SERVICES DIRECTORATE-GENERAL

E-mail: to pattern firstname.surname@ cec.eu.int
URL: http://europa.eu.int/comm/dgs/internal_ market/index_en.htm

SCHAUB Alexander
Director-General
Tel. (+32) 2-2952387
Tel. (+32) 2-2958819

STOLL Thierry
Deputy Director-General
Tel. (+32) 2-2952438
Tel. (+32) 2-2994970

THÉBAULT Jean-Claude
Adviser (detached to the President's Cabinet)

KLAUS Henning
Assistant to the Director-General
Tel. (+32) 2-2994310

MUYLLE Jean-Yves
Assistant to the Director-General
Tel. (+32) 2-2967537

Directorate A – Planning, Administrative Support and Communication

POST Henrik
Director
Tel. (+32) 2-2966606

Directorate B – Horizontal Policy Development

HOUTMAN Anne
Director
Tel. (+32) 2-2959628

Directorate C – Public Procurement Policy

CARSIN Bertrand
Director
Tel. (+32) 2-2955795

Directorate D – Knowledge-Based Economy

MINOR Jacqueline
Director
Tel. (+32) 2-2957226
Tel. (+32) 2-2969069

Directorate E – Services

BERARDIS Guido
Director
Tel. (+32) 2-2994012

Directorate F – Free Movement of Capital, Company Law and Corporate Governance

DELSAUX Pierre
Director

Directorate G – Financial Services Policy and Financial Markets

WRIGHT David
Director
Tel. (+32) 2-2958626
Tel. (+32) 2-2960921

Directorate H – Financial Institutions

SCHWIMANN Irmfried
Director

REGIONAL POLICY DIRECTORATE-GENERAL

E-mail: to pattern firstname.surname@ cec.eu.int
URL: http://europa.eu.int/comm/dgs/regional_ policy/index_en.htm

MEADOWS Graham
Director-General
Tel. (+32) 2-2956181
Tel. (+32) 2-2960299

PASCA-RAYMONDO Michele
Deputy Director-General
Tel. (+32) 2-2956447
Tel. (+32) 2-2994829

LEYGUES Jean-Charles
Deputy Director-General
Tel. (+32) 2-2991257

GOULET Raphael
Assistant to the Director General
Tel. (+32) 2-2992470
Tel. (+32) 2-2996883

Directorate A – Resources

SEYLER Jean-Marie
Director
Tel. (+32) 2-2954681
Tel. (+32) 2-2953589

Directorate B – Conception and Reform of Cohesion Policy, Co-ordination, Legal Matters, Solidarity Fund

HALL Ronald
Director (acting)

Directorate C – Thematic Development, Impact, Evaluation and Innovative Actions

KAZLAUSKIENE Natalia
Director

Directorate D – Territorial Co-operation, Urban Actions and Outermost Regions

HELANDER Ester Elisabeth
Director
Tel. (+32) 2-2950354
Tel. (+32) 2-2961116

Directorate E – Programmes and Projects in Austria, Denmark, Germany, Latvia, Lithuania, Slovakia, Sweden and the United Kingdom

PALMA ANDRÉS José
Director
Tel. (+32) 2-2951531
Tel. (+32) 2-2959578

Directorate F – Programmes and Projects in Belgium, the Czech Republic, Estonia, Finland, Ireland, Luxembourg and Spain

MATHERNOVÁ Katarína
Director

Directorate G – Programmes and Projects in Cyprus, Greece, Hungary, Italy, Malta and the Netherlands

SHOTTON Robert
Director
Tel. (+32) 2-2956838
Tel. (+32) 2-2984544

Directorate H – Programmes and Projects in France, Poland, Portugal and Slovenia; ISPA

RIERA FIGUERAS Luis
Director
Tel. (+32) 2-2965068
Tel. (+32) 2-2951183

Directorate I – Audit

MARTYN Nicholas
Director (acting)
Tel. (+32) 2-2962941
Tel. (+32) 2-2958089

TAXATION AND CUSTOMS UNION DIRECTORATE-GENERAL

E-mail: to pattern firstname.surname@ cec.eu.int
URL: http://europa.eu.int/comm/dgs/taxation_ customs/index_en.htm

VERRUE Robert
Director-General
Tel. (+32) 2-2954376

BERTIN Lilian
Assistant to the Director-General
Tel. (+32) 2-2968929

[post vacant]
Principal Adviser

Directorate A – Co-ordination and Programmes

DE GRAAFF Marinus
Director
Tel. (+32) 2-2952025

Directorate B – International Affairs and Tariff Matters

ARNAL MONREAL Manuel
Director
Tel. (+32) 2-2963328

Directorate C – Customs Policy

ZIELINSKI Miroslaw
Director
Tel. (+32) 2-2958183

Directorate D – Indirect Taxation and Tax Administration

WIEDOW Alexander
Director
Tel. (+32) 2-2953605

EDUCATION AND CULTURE DIRECTORATE-GENERAL

E-mail: to pattern firstname.surname@ cec.eu.int
URL: http://europa.eu.int/comm/dgs/ education_culture/index_en.htm

VAN DER PAS Nikolaus
Director-General
Tel. (+32) 2-2968308
Tel. (+32) 2-2996670

[post vacant]
Principal Adviser

TSOLAKIS Alexandros
Adviser (ad personam)
Tel. (+32) 2-2959981

GIBERT-MORIN Nicolas
Assistant to the Director-General
Tel. (+32) 2-2991120

Directorate A – Education

COYNE David
Director
Tel. (+32) 2-2955741
Tel. (+32) 2-2993677

Directorate B – Lifelong Learning: Education and Training, Programmes and Actions

RICHONNIER Michel
Director
Tel. (+32) 2-2950973
Tel. (+32) 2-2969545

Directorate C – Culture and Communication

BOON-FALLEUR Christine
Director (acting)
Tel. (+32) 2-2957596

Directorate D – Youth, Sport and Relations with the Citizen

MAIRESSE Pierre
Director (acting)
Tel. (+32) 2-2962009

Directorate E – Resources

GASCARD Gilbert
Director
Tel. (+32) 2-2950017
Tel. (+32) 2-2950048

HEALTH AND CONSUMER PROTECTION DIRECTORATE-GENERAL

E-mail: to pattern firstname.surname@ cec.eu.int
URL: http://europa.eu.int/comm/dgs/health_ consumer/index_en.htm

MADELIN Robert
Director-General
Tel. (+32) 2-2963338
Tel. (+32) 2-2999090

HUSU-KALLIO Jaana
Deputy Director-General (Directorates D, E and F)
Tel. (+32) 2-2996887
Tel. (+32) 2-2995819

THEVENARD Eric
Assistant to the Director General
Tel. (+32) 2-2969966

MOYNAGH James
Assistant to the Deputy Director-General
Tel. (+32) 2-2958086

JIMENEZ BELTRAN Domingo
Adviser

PAUL Jan-Peter
Adviser (reporting to the Deputy Director-General)
Tel. (+32) 2-2995064

Directorate A – General Affairs

JANSSENS Daniel
Director (acting)

Directorate B – Consumer Affairs

PANTELOURI Agne
Director
Tel. (+32) 2-2990131
Tel. (+32) 2-2958306

Directorate C – Public Health and Risk Assessment

SAUER Fernand
Director
Tel. (+32) 2-2932719
Tel. (+32) 2-2935640

Directorate D – Food Safety, Production and Distribution Chain

TESTORI Paola
Director
Tel. (+32) 2-2953430

Directorate E – Food Safety; Plant Health, Animal Health and Welfare, International Questions

VAN GOETHEM Bernard
Director (acting)

Directorate F – Food and Veterinary Office

GAYNOR Michael
Director
Tel. (+353 1) 2070858

JUSTICE, FREEDOM AND SECURITY DIRECTORATE-GENERAL

E-mail: to pattern firstname.surname@ cec.eu.int
URL: http://europa.eu.int/comm/dgs/justice_ home/index_en.htm

FAULL Jonathan
Director-General
Tel. (+32) 2-2958658
Tel. (+32) 2-2986269

SUTTON Michelle
Assistant to the Director-General
Tel. (+32) 2-2960239
Tel. (+32) 2-2987085

Directorate A – General Affairs

MARGUE Tung-Lai
Director
Tel. (+32) 2-2954437

Directorate B – Immigration, Asylum and Borders

DE BROUWER Jean-Louis
Director

Directorate C – Civil Justice, Fundamental Rights and Citizenship

FONSECA MORILLO Francisco
Director

EXTERNAL RELATIONS DIRECTORATE-GENERAL

E-mail: to pattern firstname.surname@ cec.eu.int
URL: http://europa.eu.int/comm/dgs/external_ relations/index_en.htm

LANDÁBURU ILLARRAMENDI Eneko
Director-General
Tel. (+32) 2-2951968
Tel. (+32) 2-2962211

KOVANDA Karel
Deputy Director-General (CFSP, Multilateral relations, North America, East Asia, Australia, New Zealand, EEA and EFTA – Directorates A, B and C)
Tel. (+32) 2-2980765

LEIGH
Deputy Director-General (European Neighbourhood Policy, relations with Eastern Europe, Southern Caucasus and Central Asia, Middle East and Southern Mediterranean – Directorates D, E and F)

JOUANJEAN Hervé
Deputy Director-General (Asia and Latin America – Directorates G and H
Tel. (+32) 2-2992210

SANNINO Stefano
Principal Adviser (representative of the Commission to the Political and Security Committee)
Tel. (+32) 2-2956352

MAVROMICHALIS Petros
Assistant to the Director-General
Tel. (+32) 2-2994443

Directorate A – CFSP and ESDP: Commission Co-ordination and Contribution

BRIET Lodewyk
Director
Tel. (+32) 2-2966665
Tel. (+32) 2-2990794

Directorate B – Multilateral Relations and Human Rights

SMADJA Danièle
Director
Tel. (+32) 2-2998976

Directorate C – North America, East Asia, Australia, New Zealand, EEA, EFTA, San Marino, Andorra, Monaco

WRIGHT Richard
Director
Tel. (+32) 2-2988598

Directorate D – Co-ordination of the European Neighbourhood Policy (ENP)

WISSELS Rutger
Director
Tel. (+32) 2-2993482

Directorate E – Eastern Europe, the Southern Caucasus, Central Asian Republics

MINGARELLI Hugues
Director
Tel. (+32) 2-2999180

Directorate F – Middle East, Southern Mediterranean

LEFFLER Christian
Director
Tel. (+32) 2-2950502

Directorate G – Latin America

DUPLA DELL MORAL Tomás
Director
Tel. (+32) 2-2992313
Tel. (+32) 2-2990184

Directorate H – Asia (except Japan and Korea)

FOTIADIS Fokion
Director
Tel. (+32) 2-2992302
Tel. (+32) 2-2990610

Directorate I – Headquarters Resources, Information, Interinstitutional Relations

LIPMAN David
Director
Tel. (+32) 2-2990755
Tel. (+32) 2-2990655

Directorate K – External Service

SAINT MAURICE Thierry
Director

Directorate L – Strategy, Co-ordination and Analysis

AVERY Graham
Director
Tel. (+32) 2-2992202
Tel. (+32) 2-2999225

TRADE DIRECTORATE-GENERAL

*E-mail: to pattern firstname.surname@
cec.eu.int*
*URL: http://europa.eu.int/comm/dgs/trade/
index_en.htm*

CARL Mogens Peter
Director-General
Tel. (+32) 2-2992205
Tel. (+32) 2-2994006

FALKENBERG Karl-Friedrich
Deputy Director-General

DEVIGNE Luc
Assistant to the Director-General
Tel. (+32) 2-2991873

Directorate A – General Affairs; Resources, Bilateral Trade Relations I

DEPYPERE Stefaan
Director
Tel. (+32) 2-2990713

Directorate B – Trade Defence Instruments

WENIG Fritz Harald
Director
Tel. (+32) 2-2958684
Tel. (+32) 2-2995657

Directorate C – Development and Management of Free Trade and Economic Partnership Agreements with ACP Countries, Latin America, GCC and Iran. GSP.

[post vacant]
Director

Directorate D – Development and Management of Trade Relations with Neighbourhood Countries and with South-East Asia

GARCÍA BERCERO Ignacio
Director
Tel. (+32) 2-2995661
Tel. (+32) 2-2958718

Directorate E – Industrial Trade Issues. Bilateral Trade Relations II. Market Access. Export-Related Trade Policy

WILKINSON Ian
Director
Tel. (+32) 2-2984274

Directorate F – Co-ordination of WTO and OECD Matters; Dispute Settlement; Trade Barriers Regulation

PETRICCIONE Mauro Raffaele
Director
Tel. (+32) 2-2961666
Tel. (+32) 2-2990051

Directorate G – Services. Agricultural Trade Questions. Sustainable Development

AGUIAR MACHADO João
Director
Tel. (+32) 2-2996310

Directorate H – Textiles, New Technologies, Intellectual Property, Public Procurement. Trade Analysis

VANDOREN Paul
Director (acting)
Tel. (+32) 2-2992436
Tel. (+32) 2-2992010

DEVELOPMENT DIRECTORATE-GENERAL

E-mail: to pattern firstname.surname@ cec.eu.int
URL: http://europa.eu.int/comm/dgs/ development/index_en.htm

MANSERVISI Stefano
Director-General
Tel. (+32) 2-2957169

THEODORAKIS Athanassios
Deputy Director-General
Tel. (+32) 2-2993238
Tel. (+32) 2-2993237

LUYCKX Olivier
Assistant to the Director General

Directorate A – General Matters and Operational Support

BARREIROS Maria
Director
Tel. (+32) 2-2993268

Directorate B – Development Policy and Sectoral Questions

PETIT Bernard
Director
Tel. (+32) 2-2993255
Tel. (+32) 2-2955409

Directorate C – Horn of Africa, East and Southern Africa, Indian Ocean, Pacific

HENRIKSSON Anders
Director
Tel. (+32) 2-2969228
Tel. (+32) 2-2996337

Directorate D – West and Central Africa, the Caribbean and the OCTs

BROUWER Sipke
Director
Tel. (+32) 2-2951364
Tel. (+32) 2-2992233

Directorate D – Financial Instruments

MEGANCK Dirk
Director
Tel. (+32) 2-2961380
Tel. (+32) 2-2995100

Directorate E – General Matters and Resources

BONUCCI Augusto
Director
Tel. (+32) 2-2993197
Tel. (+32) 2-2953985

ENLARGEMENT DIRECTORATE-GENERAL

E-mail: to pattern firstname.surname@ cec.eu.int
URL: http://europa.eu.int/comm/dgs/ enlargement/index_en.htm

BARBASO Fabrizio
Director-General (acting)
Tel. (+32) 2-2956739
Tel. (+32) 2-2954354

VERGER Myriam
Assistant to the Director-General
Tel. (+32) 2-2969119

Directorate A – Acceding countries

[post vacant]
Director

Directorate B – Candidate Countries

MIREL Pierre
Director
Tel. (+32) 2-2956172

Directorate C – Other Western Balkans

PRIEBE Reinhard
Director
Tel. (+32) 2-2950161
Tel. (+32) 2-2954989

EUROPEAID CO-OPERATION OFFICE

E-mail: to pattern firstname.surname@ cec.eu.int
URL: http://europa.eu.int/comm/dgs/europeaid/ index_en.htm

RICHELLE Koos
Director-General
Tel. (+32) 2-2963638

RICHARDSON Hugh
Deputy Director-General
Tel. (+32) 2-2959096
Tel. (+32) 2-2965924

DELLA MONICA Sabato
Adviser
Tel. (+32) 2-2992542

TOLEDANO LAREDO Emma
Assistant to the Director-General
Tel. (+32) 2-2966204
Tel. (+32) 2-2966492

STAUSBOLL Hans
Assistant to the Director-General
Tel. (+32) 2-2991681
Tel. (+32) 2-2965433

Directorate A – Europe, Southern Mediterranean, Middle East and Neighbourhood Policy

WEBER Richard
Director
Tel. (+32) 2-2953055
Tel. (+32) 2-2960293

Directorate B – Latin America

CARDESA GARCÍA Fernando
Director
Tel. (+32) 2-2992329
Tel. (+32) 2-2995282

Directorate C – Sub-Saharan Africa, Caribbean, Pacific

QUINCE Gary
Director
Tel. (+32) 2-2954859

Directorate D – Asia and Central Asia

MULLER Erich
Director
Tel. (+32) 2-2990775
Tel. (+32) 2-2992856

Directorate E – Operations Quality Support

[post vacant]
Director

Directorate F – General Operations Support

DE ANGELIS Francesco
Director
Tel. (+32) 2-2958400
Tel. (+32) 2-2961292

Directorate G – Resources

STATHOPOULOS Constantin
Director
Tel. (+32) 2-2952463

HUMANITARIAN AID DIRECTORATE-GENERAL (ECHO)

E-mail: to pattern firstname.surname@ cec.eu.int
URL: http://europa.eu.int/comm/dgs/ humanitarian_aid/index_en.htm

CAVACO António
Director-General
Tel. (+32) 2-2959428
Tel. (+32) 2-2956993

TRAUTMANN Henrike
Assistant to the Director-General

EUROSTAT

Bâtiment Jean Monnet, 2920 Luxembourg, Luxembourg
Tel: (+352) 43011
E-mail: to pattern firstname.surname@ cec.eu.int
URL: http://europa.eu.int/comm/dgs/eurostat/ index_en.htm

HANREICH Günther
Director-General

BOHATA Marie
Deputy Director-General
Tel. (+352) 430137630

NÄSLUND Annika
Assistant to the Director-General
Tel. (+352) 430133055

CALÒ Guiseppe
Chief Adviser
Tel. (+352) 430137210
Tel. (+352) 430137209

REEH Klaus
Adviser
Tel. (+352) 430133523

Directorate A – Resources

KAISER Stephen
Director
Tel. (+352) 430133073
Tel. (+352) 430134484

Directorate B – Principal Indicators and Statistical Tools

DIAZ MUÑOZ Pedro
Director
Tel. (+352) 430135474
Tel. (+352) 430133448

Directorate C – Economic and Monetary Statistics

MEGANCK Bart
Director
Tel. (+352) 430133533
Tel. (+352) 430133988

Directorate D – Internal Market, Employment and Social Statistics

GLAUDE Michel
Director
Tel. (+352) 4301336848

Directorate E – Agriculture, Fisheries, Structural Funds and Environmental Statistics

NØRLUND Laurs
Director
Tel. (+352) 430136850

Directorate F – External Relations Statistics

EVERAERS Pieter
Director
Tel. (+352) 430136847

PERSONNEL AND ADMINISTRATION DIRECTORATE-GENERAL

E-mail: to pattern firstname.surname@ cec.eu.int
URL: http://europa.eu.int/comm/dgs/ personnel_administration/index_en.htm

CHENE Claude
Director-General
Tel. (+32) 2-2952437
Tel. (+32) 2-2955615

LINDER Christian
Assistant to the Director-General
Tel. (+32) 2-2986917

LEVASSEUR Christian
Assistant to the Director-General
Tel. (+352) 4301365580

GÓMEZ REINO Santiago
Adviser hors classe
Tel. (+32) 2-2996312

KITZMANTEL Edith
Adviser hors classe

TANZILLI Rocco
Chief Adviser
Tel. (+32) 2-2961011

NANOPOULOS Photius
Chief Adviser
Tel. (+32) 2-2932443

BRANDT Eberhard
Adviser (with responsibility for organization and control. Financial Irregularities Panel)
Tel. (+32) 2-2959969

DENUIT Renaud
Adviser
Tel. (+32) 2-2956607
Tel. (+32) 2-2950464

DALY Emer
Permanent Rapporteur to the CCA
Tel. (+32) 2-2960503
Tel. (+32) 2-2953231

Directorate A – Staff and Careers

SOUKA Irène
Director
Tel. (+32) 2-2957206
Tel. (+32) 2-2995313

Directorate B – Staff Regulations: Policy, Management and Advisory Services

JACOB Daniel
Director
Tel. (+32) 2-2959870
Tel. (+32) 2-2986402

Directorate C – Social Welfare Policy, Luxembourg Staff, Health, Safety

DE SOLA DOMINGO Mercedes
Director
Tel. (+32) 2-2956272
Tel. (+32) 2-2992292

Directorate D – Resources

VANTILBORGH Hendrik
Director (acting)

Directorate DS – Security

HUTCHINS Stephen
Director (acting)
Tel. (+32) 2-2956168
Tel. (+32) 2-2964277

Directorate IDOC – Investigation and Disciplinary Office

VAN LIER Hendrik
Director
Tel. (+32) 2-2957595

INFORMATICS DIRECTORATE-GENERAL (DIGIT)

E-mail: to pattern firstname.surname@ cec.eu.int
URL: http://europa.eu.int/comm/dgs/ informatics/index_en.htm

GARCÍA MORÁN Francisco
Director-General (acting)
Tel. (+32) 2-2934561
Tel. (+32) 2-2935747

GARCÍA MORÁN Francisco
Deputy Director-General
Tel. (+32) 2-2934561
Tel. (+32) 2-2935747

Directorate A – Infrastructure

JORTAY Marcel
Director (acting)

Directorate B – Information Systems

DEASY Declan
Director
Tel. (+32) 2-2932060
Tel. (+32) 2-2934322

Directorate R – Resources and Logistics

CABALLERO BASSEDAS Arturo
Director
Tel. (+32) 2-2953974

BUDGET DIRECTORATE-GENERAL

E-mail: to pattern firstname.surname@ cec.eu.int
URL: http://europa.eu.int/comm/dgs/budget/ index_en.htm

ROMERO REQUENA Luis
Director-General
Tel. (+32) 2-2995150
Tel. (+32) 2-2953771

GRAY Brian
Deputy Director-General (Commission accounting officer)
Tel. (+32) 2-2954627
Tel. (+32) 2-2965510

MAMER Eric
Assistant to the Director-General
Tel. (+32) 2-2994073

SPENCE James
Adviser (budgetary procedure and reporting)
Tel. (+32) 2-2981704

VANHEUKELEN Marc
Adviser
Tel. (+32) 2-2993405

Directorate R – Resources

DALPOZZO Luca
Director (acting)
Tel. (+32) 2-2951771

Directorate A – Expenditure

BRÜCHERT Fritz
Director
Tel. (+32) 2-2956688

Directorate B – Own Resources, Evaluation and Financial Programming

BACHE Jean-Pierre
Director
Tel. (+32) 2-2951679

Directorate C – Budget Execution

GRAY Brian
Director (acting)
Tel. (+32) 2-2954627

Directorate D – Central Financial Service

TAVERNE Philippe
Director
Tel. (+32) 2-2953590

INTERNAL AUDIT SERVICE

E-mail: to pattern firstname.surname@ cec.eu.int
URL: http://europa.eu.int/comm/dgs/internal_ audit/index_en.htm

DEFFAA Walter
Director-General (internal auditor of the Commission)
Tel. (+32) 2-2957752

MAGENHANN Bernard
Assistant to the Director-General
Tel. (+32) 2-2999482

Directorate A – Horizontal Affairs

HÜNKE Horst
Director and Deputy Head of Service
Tel. (+32) 2-2968572

Directorate B – Audit Process

MERCHÁN CANTOS Francisco
Director and Head of the Audit Staff Pool
Tel. (+32) 2-2996730

EUROPEAN ANTI-FRAUD OFFICE (OLAF)

E-mail: to pattern firstname.surname@ cec.eu.int
URL: http://europa.eu.int/comm/dgs/anti_ fraud/index_en.htm

BRÜNER Franz-Hermann
Director-General
Tel. (+32) 2-2969063
Tel. (+32) 2-2950327

SPITZER Harald
Assistant to the Director-General (policy)
Tel. (+32) 2-2991633
Tel. (+32) 2-2962976

HEINKELMANN Bärbel
Assistant to the Director-General (operations)
Tel. (+32) 2-2998730

Directorate A – Policy, Legislation and Legal Affairs

LECOU Claude
Director
Tel. (+32) 2-2957736
Tel. (+32) 2-2994419

Directorate B – Investigations and Operations

PERDUCA Alberto
Director
Tel. (+32) 2-2958508
Tel. (+32) 2-2990427

Directorate C – Intelligence, Operational Strategy and Information Services

ILETT Nicholas
Director
Tel. (+32) 2-2984986
Tel. (+32) 2-2994036

OLAF – Supervisory Committee

DARRAS Jean
Director (Secretary of the Supervisory Committee)
Tel. (+352) 430130010
Tel. (+352) 430130013

INTERPRETATION DIRECTORATE-GENERAL

E-mail: to pattern firstname.surname@ cec.eu.int
URL: http://europa.eu.int/comm/scic/index_ en.htm

BENEDETTI Marco
Director-General
Tel. (+32) 2-2957058
Tel. (+32) 2-2960947

BAKER David
Assistant to the Director-General
Tel. (+32) 2-2985078
Tel. (+32) 2-2955631

BODDIN Johan
Adviser

DELAVA Jean-Pierre
Adviser

Directorate A – Interpreting

FOX Brian
Director
Tel. (+32) 2-2955416

Directorate B – Administration and Resources

ALEGRIA Carlos
Director

Directorate C – Provision of Interpreting

D'HAEN BERTIER Ann
Director
Tel. (+32) 2-2950993

Directorate D – Conferences

HAMACHER Jupp
Director

TRANSLATION DIRECTORATE-GENERAL

E-mail: to pattern firstname.surname@ cec.eu.int
URL: http://europa.eu.int/comm/dgs/ translation/index_en.htm

LÖNNROTH Karl-Johan
Director-General
Tel. (+32) 2-2937825

ORY Carole
Assistant to the Director-General
Tel. (+32) 2-2951930
Tel. (+32) 2-2956366

Directorate A – Translation (Luxembourg)

O'LEARY Marian
Director
Tel. (+32) 2-2934229
Tel. (+32) 2-2932236

VAN DER HORST Cornelis
Adviser
Tel. (+32) 2-2932397

Directorate B – Translation (Brussels)

VLACHOPOULOS George
Director
Tel. (+32) 2-2958618

Directorate C – Resources

[post vacant]
Director

Directorate D – Translation Strategy

DE VICENTE Francisco
Director
Tel. (+32) 2-2960094

PUBLICATIONS OFFICE

E-mail: to pattern firstname.surname@
  cec.eu.int
URL: http://publications.eu.int/index_en.html

CRANFIELD Thomas L.
Director-General
Tel. (+352) 292942222

BERGER Albrecht
Adviser (responsible for the Secretariat of
  interinstitutional committees)
Tel. (+32) 2-2957552
Tel. (+32) 2-2956260

BOCK Veronica
Assistant to the Director-General
Tel. (+352) 292942438

Directorate Resources
REYNOLDS Bernard
Director
Tel. (+352) 292942090

**Directorate Official Journal and Access
to Law**

RAYBAUT Jacques
Director
Tel. (+352) 292942408

**Directorate Publications and
Dissemination**

RAYBAUT Jacques
Director (acting)
Tel. (+352) 292942408

OFFICE FOR INFRASTRUCTURE AND LOGISTICS – BRUSSELS (OIB)

E-mail: to pattern firstname.surname@
  cec.eu.int
*URL: http://europa.eu.int/comm/oib/index_*
  en.htm

VERLEYSEN Piet
Director
Tel. (+32) 2-2957349
Tel. (+32) 2-2968192

[post vacant]
1. Principal adviser (with responsibility for the
   co-ordination of logistical units)

MIGOYA GARNICA Alvaro
Adviser (with responsibility for co-ordination
  with other departments on health and safety
  matters)
Tel. (+32) 2-2963169

GERMAIN Daniel
Adviser (with responsibility for new policies
  and interinstitutional co-operation)

MAMBOURG André
Assistant to the Director
Tel. (+32) 2-2969222

PELEMAN Marc
Assistant to the Director
Tel. (+32) 2-2952717
Tel. (+32) 2-2968192

OFFICE FOR INFRASTRUCTURE AND LOGISTICS – LUXEMBOURG (OIL)

REICHERTS Martine
Director
Tel. (+352) 292932620

33

WILLEME Claude
Adviser
Tel. (+352) 292934898
Tel. (+352) 292934537

OFFICE FOR ADMINISTRATION AND PAYMENT OF INDIVIDUAL ENTITLEMENTS (PMO)

DESHAYES Dominique
Director
Tel. (+32) 2-2956156

RIGON Francis
Adviser with responsibility for the NAP
Tel. (+32) 2-2998198

EUROPEAN PERSONNEL SELECTION OFFICE (EPSO)

HALSKOV Erik
Director
Tel. (+32) 2-2962451
Tel. (+32) 2-2994959

JENSEN Hans
Adviser
Tel. (+32) 2-2955020

LEVY Carlos
Assistant to the Director

WALKER David
European School of Administration
Tel. (+32) 2-2999300

EUROPEAN COMMISSION OFFICES IN MEMBER STATES

AUSTRIA

Kärntner-Ring 5–7, 1010 Vienna, Austria
Tel. (+43 1) 51618-0
Fax (+43 1) 5134225
E-mail burvie@cec.eu.int
URL http://europa.eu.int/austria
Head Karl Doutlik

BELGIUM

Rue Archimède 73, 1000 Brussels, Belgium
Tel. (+32) 2-2953844
Fax (+32) 2-2950166
E-mail represent-bel@cec.eu.int
URL http://europa.eu.int/comm/represent/be
Head Willy Hélin

CYPRUS

PO Box 23480, 1683 Nicosia, Cyprus
Premises at: Iris Tower (8th Floor), 2 Agapinor
  Street, 1076 Nicosia, Cyprus
Tel. (+357) 22817770
Fax (+357) 22768926
E-mail press-rep-cyprus@cec.eu.int
URL http://www.delcyp.cec.eu.int
Head Themis Themistocleous

CZECH REPUBLIC

PO Box 811, 111 21 Prague 1, Czech Republic
Premises at: Jungmannova 24, 110 00 Prague 1,
  Czech Republic
Tel. (+420) 224312835
Fax (+420) 224312850
E-mail press-rep-czech@cec.eu.int
URL www.evropska-unie.cz
Head (acting) Katerina Thompson

DENMARK

Hojbrohus, Østergade 61, Postboks 144, 1004
  Copenhagen K, Denmark
Tel. (+45) 33-14-41-40
Fax (+45) 33-11-12-03
E-mail eu@europa-kommissionen.dk
URL www.europa-kommissionen.dk
Head Fritz von Nordheim

ESTONIA

Kohtu 10, 10130 Tallinn, Estonia
Tel. (+372) 6264400
Fax (+372) 6264439
E-mail press-rep-estonia@cec.eu.int
URL http://eng.euroopaliit.ee

FINLAND

Pohjoisesplanadi 31, PO Box 1250, 00101
  Helsinki, Finland
Tel. (+358 9) 6226544
Fax (+358 9) 656728
E-mail burhel@cec.eu.int
URL http://europa.eu.int/finland
Head (acting) Paavo Mäkinen

FRANCE

288 Boulevard Saint-Germain, 75007 Paris,
  France
Tel. (+33) 1-40-63-38-00
Fax (+33) 1-45-51-52-53
E-mail burpar@cec.eu.int
URL http://europa.eu.fr/france
Head Yves Gazzo

2 rue Henri Barbusse, 13241 Marseille
  Cedex 01, France
Tel. (+33) 4-91-91-46-00
Fax (+33) 4-91-90-98-07
E-mail antmar@cec.eu.int
URL http://europa.eu.int/france/marseille

GERMANY

Unter den Linden 78, 10117 Berlin, Germany
Tel. (+49 30) 2280-2000
Fax (+49 30) 2280-2222
E-mail eu-de-kommission@cec.eu.int
URL http://www.eu-kommission.de
Head Gerhard Sabathil

Bertha-von-Suttner-Platz 2–4, 53111 Bonn,
  Germany
Tel. (+49 228) 53009-0
Fax (+49 228) 53009-50
E-mail eu-de-bonn@cec.eu.int
Head Barbara Gessler

Erhardtstr. 27, 80331 Munich, Germany
Tel. (+49 89) 242448-0
Fax (+49 89) 242448-15
E-mail eu-de-muenchen@cec.eu.int
Head Jochen Kubosch

GREECE

Vassilissis Sofias 2, 106 74 Athens, Greece
Tel. (+30) 210-7272100
Fax (+30) 210-7244620
E-mail burath@cec.eu.int
URL http://europa.eu.int/hellas
Head [post vacant]

HUNGARY

Bérc u. 23, 1016 Budapest, Hungary
Tel. (+36 1) 2099700
Fax (+36 1) 4664221
E-mail press-rep-hungary@cec.eu.int
URL www.eudelegation.hu
Head Gábor György

IRELAND

European Union House, 18 Dawson Street,
  Dublin 2, Ireland
Tel. (+353 1) 6341111
Fax (+353 1) 6341112
E-mail eu-ie-info-request@cec.eu.int
URL www.euireland.ie
Head Martin Territt

ITALY

Via IV Novembre 149, 00187 Rome, Italy
Tel. (+39) 06-699991
Fax (+32) 06-6791658
E-mail eu-it-info@cec.eu.int
URL http://europa.eu.int/italia
Head Pier Virgilio Dastoli

Corso Magenta 59, 20123 Milan, Italy
Tel. (+39) 02-4675141
Fax (+32) 02-4818543
E-mail antmil@cec.eu.int
URL http://europa.eu.int/italia/milano
Head Roberto Santaniello

LATVIA

Aspazijas bulvāris 28, 1050 Riga, Latvia
Tel. (+371) 7985400
Fax (+371) 7085448
E-mail press-rep-latvia@cec.eu.int
URL www.eiropainfo.lv

LITHUANIA

Naugarduko 10, 01141 Vilnius, Lithuania
Tel. (+370 523) 13191
Fax (+370 523) 13192
E-mail press-rep-lithuania@cec.eu.int
URL www.eudel.lt
Head Laimute Pilukaite

LUXEMBOURG

Bâtiment Jean Monnet, Rue Alcide de Gasperi,
  2920 Luxembourg, Luxembourg
Tel. (+352) 430132925
Fax (+352) 430134433

E-mail burlux@cec.eu.int
URL http://europa.eu.int/luxembourg

MALTA

'The Vines', 51 Ta'Xbiex Sea Front, Ta'Xbiex
MSD 11, Malta
Tel. (+356) 21345111
Fax (+356) 21344897
E-mail press-rep-malta@cec.eu.int
URL www.delmlt.cec.eu.int
Head (acting) Axel R. Bunz

NETHERLANDS

Postbus 30465, 2500 GL The Hague,
Netherlands
Premises at: Korte Vijverberg 5, 2513 AB The
Hague, Netherlands
Tel. (+31 70) 3135300
Fax (+31 70) 3646619
E-mail burhay@cec.eu.int
URL http://europa.eu.int/netherlands
Head (acting) Klasja van de Ridder

POLAND

Warsaw Financial Centre, ul. Emilii Plater 53,
00-113 Warsaw, Poland
Tel. (+48 22) 520-82-00
Fax (+48 22) 520-82-82
E-mail delegation-poland@cec.eu.int
URL www.europa.delpol.pl
Head Róża Thun

PORTUGAL

Largo Jean Monnet 1 – 10°, 1069-068 Lisbon,
Portugal
Tel. (+351) 213509800
Fax (+351) 213509801
E-mail burlis@cec.eu.int
URL http://europa.eu.int/portugal

SLOVAKIA

Palisády 29, 811 06 Bratislava, Slovakia
Tel. (+421 2) 54431718
Fax (+421 2) 54432980
E-mail press-rep-slovakia@cec.eu.int
URL www.europa.sk
Head Andrea Elschekova-Matisova

SLOVENIA

Breg 14, 1000 Ljubljana, Slovenia
Tel. (+386 1) 2528800
Fax (+386 1) 4252085

E-mail press-rep-slovenia@cec.eu.int
URL www.evropska-unija.si

SPAIN

Paseo de la Castellana 46, 28046 Madrid, Spain
Tel. (+34) 91-4238000
Fax (+34) 91-5760387
E-mail eu-es-docu@cec.eu.int
URL http://europa.eu.int/spain
Head José Luis González Vallvé

Passeig de Gràcia 90, 08008 Barcelona, Spain
Tel. (+34) 93-4677380
Fax (+34) 93-4677381
URL http://europa.eu.int/spain
Head Josep Coll i Carbó

SWEDEN

Nybrogatan 11, Box 7323, 103 90 Stockholm,
Sweden
Tel. (+46 8) 56-24-44-11
Fax (+46 8) 56-24-44-12
E-mail bursto@cec.eu.int
URL www.eukomm.se

UNITED KINGDOM

8 Storey's Gate, London SW1P 3AT,
United Kingdom
Tel. (+44 20) 7973-1992
Fax (+44 20) 7973-1900
URL www.cec.org.uk
Head Reijo Kemppinen

9 Alva Street, Edinburgh EH2 4PH,
United Kingdom
Tel. (+44 131) 225-2058
Fax (+44 131) 226-4105
URL www.cec.org.uk/scotland
Head Elizabeth Holt

2 Caspian Point, Caspian Way, Cardiff
CF10 4QQ, United Kingdom
Tel. (+44 29) 2089-5020
Fax (+44 29) 2089-5035
Head Andy Klom

9–15 Bedford Street, Belfast BT2 7EG,
United Kingdom
Tel. (+44 28) 9024-0708
Fax (+44 28) 9024-8241
E-mail eddie.mcveigh@cec.eu.int
URL www.cec.org.uk/ni
Head Eddie McVeigh

THE EUROPEAN PARLIAMENT

Composed of 732 members elected for five years (the next elections will be in 2009), the European Parliament represents the interests of some 457 million EU citizens and exercises an increasingly important influence on the EU legislative procedure (especially since the Single Act and the Maastricht, Amsterdam and Nice Treaties). It adopts the budget, supervises the activities of the Commission and the Council, adopts or repeals international agreements and enjoys powers of legislative co-decision. The following ratio of MEPs is attributed to the different Member States: Germany: 99; France, Italy and the United Kingdom: 78; Poland and Spain: 54; Netherlands: 27; Belgium, Czech Republic, Greece, Hungary and Portugal: 24; Sweden: 19; Austria: 18; Denmark, Finland and Slovakia: 14; Ireland and Lithuania: 13; Latvia: 9; Slovenia: 7; Cyprus, Estonia and Luxembourg: 6; Malta: 5.

The Political Groups

MEPs are not grouped in national delegations but according to the political group to which they belong. The groups are of central importance in both the political and organizational work of the Parliament. Eight groups are currently represented:

PPE–DE – Group of the European People's Party and European Democrats comprising Christian Democrat and Centre Right parties (266 MEPs)

PSE – Group of the Party of European Socialists (201 MEPs)

ALDE – Alliance of Liberals and Democrats for Europe (89 MEPs)

Verts/ALE – Greens/European Free Alliance. This comprises MEPs, from Green parties, who have formed an alliance with MEPs from home rule parties in several Member States (42 MEPs)

GUE/NGL – Confederal Group of the European United Left/Nordic Green Left (41 MEPs)

UEN – Union for a Europe of Nations Group is pledged to defend the nation state and is opposed to further integration (27 MEPs)

IND/DEM – Independence and Democracy Group comprises Eurosceptic MEPs (36 MEPs)

NI – Group of Non-attached Members (29 MEPs).

The different political groups are serviced by their own secretariats, based in Brussels, and the level of resources available to each secretariat depends on the number of members belonging to that group.

The Committees

The Parliament's work is prepared in 22 specialist Committees and sub-committees. In addition to standing committees, the EP may also set up temporary committees or committees of inquiry to examine specific problems. The Committees draw up responses to legislative proposals from the Commission, and may formulate reports on their own initiative, though these do not form part of the legislative process. Committees may also organize public hearings at which experts give advice on the technical aspects of particular problems. Joint parliamentary committees maintain relations with the parliaments of states linked to the European Union by association agreements, while interparliamentary delegations maintain relations with the parliaments of many other countries and with international organizations. The Parliament's work is organized by a secretariat headed by a

Secretary-General with a permanent staff of about 3,500, in addition to which there are political group staff and Members' assistants.

The European Parliament's Secretariat

The secretariat is divided into eight Directorates-General (DGs). DG 4 (Information) co-ordinates a network of external offices in the Member States. These offices are the first point of contact between EU citizens and the European Parliament. They are well equipped to respond to requests for both information and documentation and are responsible for passing on the centralized information provided by Brussels and Strasbourg, but tailored to each Member State's specific requirements.

The Plenary Session

For ease of contact with the other institutions, the parliamentary committees generally meet in Brussels for two weeks a month. The third week is set aside for political group meetings and the fourth for the plenary session, which is held in Strasbourg.

Day-to-day operations of the Parliament and its bodies are the responsibility of the Bureau, though the Plenary session remains the final authority. The Bureau consists of the President of the Parliament and the 14 Vice-Presidents. There are five Quaestors who are responsible for internal administrative and financial matters.

When the Bureau and the Chairpersons of the political groups meet, they form the Enlarged Bureau. One of their main tasks is to draw up the draft agendas for Parliament's plenary sessions, which are then approved or amended by the Plenary session.

COMMITTEES AND DELEGATIONS

COMMITTEES

BUDG: Committee on Budgets

Chairman

LEWANDOWSKI Janusz

Vice-Chairs

LUNDGREN Nils

MULDER Jan

WALTER Ralf

Members

ANDRIKIENĖ Laima Liucija

ASHWORTH Richard James

BÖGE Reimer

BÖSCH Herbert

BONSIGNORE Vito

BUSUTTIL Simon

CASACA Paulol

DEPREZ Gérard

DOMBROVSKIS Valdis

DOUAY Brigitte

DÜHRKOP DÜHRKOP Bárbara

ELLES James

FAJMON Hynek

FAZAKAS Szabolcs

FERBER Markus

GARRIGA POLLEDO Salvador

GILL Neena

GROBOWSKI Dariusz Maciej

GRÄSSLE Ingeborg

GRECH Louis

GRIESBECK Nathalie

GUIDONI Umberto

GUY-QUINT Catherine

HAUG Jutta D.

ITÄLÄ Ville

JENSEN Anne E.

JØRGENSEN Dan

JUKNEVIČIENÉ Ona

KOCH-MEHRIN Silvana

KOZLÍK Sergej

KRARUP Ole

KUC Wiesław Stefan

KUŽMIUK Zbigniew Krzysztof

LAMASSOURE Alain

MAŇKA Vladimír

MAURO Mario

ONESTA Gérard

PAHOR Borut

PITTELLA Giovanni

ROSZKOWSKI Wojciech

SAMARAS Antonis

SAMUELSEN Anders

SEPPÄNEN Esko

ŠCOTTOVÁ Nina

STAES Bart

STUBB Alexander

SURJÁN László

TRÜPEL Helga

VAUGRENARD Yannick

VIRRANKOSKI Kyösti Tapio

XENOGIANNAKOPOULOU Marilisa

CONT: Committee on Budgetary Control

Chairman

FAZAKAS Szabolcs

Vice-Chairs

BÖSCH Herbert

DUCHOŇ Petr

Members

AYALA SENDER Inés

BONSIGNORE Vito

VAN BUITENEN Paul

BUSUTTIL Simon

CAMRE Mogens N. J.

CASACA Paulol

CESA Lorenzo

ELLES James

FERBER Markus

FJELLNER Christofer

GRÄSSLE Ingeborg

KRATSA-TSAGAROPOULOU Rodi

MARTIN Hans-Peter

MASTENBROEK Edith

MATHIEU Véronique

MULDER Jan

PÁLFI István

PÓMES RUIZ José Javier

STARKEVIČIŪTÉ Margarita

TITFORD Jeffrey

VIRRANKOSKI Kyösti Tapio

WYNN Terence

XENOGIANNAKOPOULOU Marilisa

ECON: Committee on Economic and Monetary Affairs

Chairwoman

BERÈS Pervenche

Vice-Chairs

GARCÍA-MARGALLO Y MARFIL José Manuel

KRASTS Guntars

PURVIS John

Members

BECSEY Zsolt László

BERSANI Pier Luigi

BERTINOTTI Fausto

BULLMANN Udo

VAN DEN BURG Ieke

CASA David

CIRINO POMICINO Paolo

COHN-BENDIT Daniel Marc

EHLER Jan Christian

EVANS Jonathan

GAUZÈS Jean-Paul

GOEBBELS Robert

GOLLNISCH Bruno

HAMON Benoît

HÖKMARK Gunnar

HOPPENSTEDT Karsten Friedrich

HUDGHTON Ian

IN 'T VELD Sophia

KARAS Othmar

KAUPPI Piia-Noora

KLINZ Wolf

KONRAD Christoph

LAUK Kurt Joachim

LETTA Enrico

LULLING Astrid

MARTIN Hans-Peter

MITCHELL Gay

MONTORO ROMERO Cristobal

MUSCAT Joseph

RADWAN Alexander

RAPKAY Bernhard

RIIS-JØRGENSEN Karin

ROSATI Dariusz

RYAN Eoin

SÁNCHEZ PRESEDO Antolín

DOS SANTOS Manuel António

SKINNER Peter

STARKEVIČIŪTĖ Margarita

STREJČEK Ivo

WAGENKNECHT Sahra

WATSON Graham

WHITTAKER John

WOHLIN Lars

EMPL: Committee on Employment and Social Affairs

Chairman

ANDERSSON Jan

Vice-Chairs

MANN Thomas

PANZERI Pier Antonio

FIGUEIREDO Ilda

Members

BACHELOT-NARQUIN Roselyne

BENNAHMIAS Jean-Luc

BOZKURT Emine

BUSHILL-MATTHEWS Philip

CABRNOCH Milan

CAMRE Mogens N. J.

CERCAS Alejandro

CHRISTENSEN Ole

CLARK Derek Roland

COCILOVO Luigi

COTTIGNY Jean-Louis

DE POLI Antonio

DE ROSSA Proinsias

DÉSIR Harlem

ETTL Harald

FALBR Richard

FATUZZO Carlo

HASSE FERREIRA Joel

HELMER Roger

HUGHES Stephen

JÖNS Karin

JUKNEVIČIENÉ Ona

KUŁAKOWSKI Jan Jerzy

KUSSTATSCHER Sepp

LAMBERT Jean

LANG Carl

LANGENDRIES Raymond

LEHIDEUX Bernard

LYNNE Elizabeth

MCDONALD Mary Lou

MANTOVANI Mario

MASIEL Jan Tadeusz

MAŠTÁLKA Jiří

MATO ADROVER Ana

MATSOUKA Maria

OOMEN-RUIJTEN Ria

ŐRY Csaba

OVIIR Siiri

PANAYOTOPOULOS-CASSIOTOU Marie

PROTASIEWICZ Jacek

SILVA PENEDA José Albino

SINNOTT Kathy

SPAUTZ Jean

STEVENSON Struan

VAN LANCKER Anne

ZIMMER Gabriele

ENVI: Committee on the Environment, Public Health and Food Safety

Chairman

FLORENZ Karl-Heinz

Vice-Chairs

ANDREJEVS Georgs

BLOKLAND Johannes

HASSI Satu

Members

ADAMOU Adamos

AYLWARD Liam

BOWIS John

BREPOELS Frederika

BREYER Hiltrud

CALLANAN Martin

CORBEY Dorette

DAVIES Chris

DOYLE Avri

DRČAR MURKO Mojca

ESTRELA Edite

EVANS Jillian

FERREIRA Anne

FOGLIETTA Alessandro

GLANTE Norbert

GROSSETÊTE Françoise

GUTIÉRREZ-CORTINES Cristina

HEGYI Gyula

HONEYBALL Mary

ISLER BÉGUIN Marie Anne

JACKSON Caroline

JØRGENSEN Dan

KLASS Christa

KORHOLA Eija-Riitta

KRAHMER Holger

KRUPA Urszula

KUŠĶIS Aldis

LIENEMANN Marie-Noëlle

LIESE Peter

MAATEN Jules

MCAVAN Linda

MATSAKIS Marios

MUSACCHIO Roberto

MYLLER Riitta

OLAJOS Péter

OUZKÝ Miroslav

PAPADIMOULIS Dimitrios

POLI BORTONE Adriana

PRODI Vittorio

RIES Frédérique

ROTH-BEHRENDT Dagmar

SACCONI Guido

SCHEELE Karin

SCHLYTER Carl

SCHNELLHARDT Horst

SEEBER Richard

SINNOTT Kathy

SJÖSTEDT Jonas

SONIK Bogusław

SORNOSA MARTÍNEZ María

TRAKATELLIS Antonios

TZAMPAZI Evangelia

ULMER Thomas

VERNOLA Marcello

DE VILLIERS Philippe

WEISGERBER Anja

WESTLUND Åsa

WIJKMAN Anders

ITRE: Committee on Industry, Research and Energy

Chairman

CHICHESTER Giles

Vice-Chairs

BRUNETTA Renato

RANSDORF Miloslav

THOMSEN Britta

Members

ATTARD-MONTALTO John

BELET Ivo

BIRUTIS Šarūnas

BŘEZINA Jan

BUSQUIN Philippe

BUZEK Jerzy

CALABUIG RULL Joan

DEL CASTILLO VERO Pilar

CESA Lorenzo

CHATZIMARKAKIS Jorgo

DE MICHELIS Gianni

DOVER Den

DUIN Garrelt

EK Lena

FONTAINE Nicole

GIEREK Adam

GUIDONI Umberto

GYÜRK András

HALL Fiona

HAMMERSTEIN MINTZ David

HARMS Rebecca

HUDACKÝ Ján

JORDAN CIZELJ Romana

LANGEN Werner

LAPERROUZE Anne

LOCATELLI Pia Elda

LUNDGREN Nils

MORGAN Eluned

MUSUMECI Sebastiano (Nello)

NIEBLER Angelika

PAASILINNA Reino

PANZERI Pier Antonio

PEILLON Vincent

PIRILLI Umberto

REMEK Vladimír

REUL Herbert

RIERA MADURELL Teresa

ROTHE Mechtild

RÜBIG Paul

SCHENARDI Lydia

TARAND Andres

TOIA Patrizia

TRAUTMANN Catherine

TURMES Claude

VAKALIS Nikolaos

VIDAL-QUADRAS ROCA Alejo

VLASTO Dominique

IMCO: Committee on the Internal Market and Consumer Protection

Chairman

WHITEHEAD Phillip

Vice-Chairs

RIZZO Marco

ROITHOVÁ Zuzana

Members

BLOOM Godfrey

DE VITS Mia

DOORN Bert

FOURTOU Janelly

GEBHARDT Evelyne

HANDZLIK Malgorzata

HARBOUR Malcolm

HEATON-HARRIS Christopher

HEDH Anna

HERCZOG Edit

JÄÄTTEENMÄKI Anneli

JONCKHEER Pierre

KAMIŃSKI Michał Tomasz

KRISTENSEN Henrik Dam

LAMBSDORFF Alexander

LECHNER Kurt

LEHTINEN Lasse

MCCARTHY Arlene

MANDERS Toine

MEDINA ORTEGA Manuel

NEWTON DUNN Bill

PATRIE Béatrice

PLEŠTINSKÁ Zita

PODESTÀ Guido

RUDI UBEDA Luisa Fernanda

43

RÜHLE Heide

RUTOWICZ Leopold Józef

SCHWAB Andreas

SVENSSON Eva-Britt

SZÁJER József

THYSSEN Marianne

TOUBON Jacques

VERGNAUD Bernadette

WEILER Barbara

WUERMELING Joachim

TRAN: Committee on Transport and Tourism

Chairman

COSTA Paolo

Vice-Chairs

CHRUSZCZ Sylwester

QUEIRÓ Luís

SAVARY Gilles

Members

ALBERTINI Gabriele

ATKINS Robert

AUKEN Margrete

AYALA SENDER Inés

BARSI-PATAKY Etelka

BRADBOURN Philip

CRAMER Michael

DEGUTIS Arūnas

DE VEYRAC Christine

DIONISI Armando

DUCHOŇ Petr

EL KHADRAOUI Saïd

EVANS Robert

FERNANDES Emanuel Jardim

DE GRANDES PASCUAL Luis

GROSCH Mathieu

HEDKVIST PETERSEN Ewa

HENNIS-PLASSCHAERT Jeanine

JAŁOWIECKI Stanisław

JARZEMBOWSKI Georg

KOCH Dieter-Lebrecht

KOHLÍČEK Jaromir

KRATSA-TSAGAROPOULOU Rodi

LEICHTFRIED Jörg

LE RACHINEL Fernand

LIBERADZKI Boqusław

LICHTENBERGER Eva

LOUIS Patrick

MEIJER Erik

MOTE Ashley

NATTRASS Michael Henry

NAVARRO Robert

Ó NEACHTAIN Seán

ONYSZKIEWICZ Janusz

ORTUONDO LARREA Josu

PIECYK Willi

RACK Reinhard

ROMAGNOLI Luca

SCHMITT Ingo

SOMMER Renate

STERCKX Dirk

STOCKMANN Ulrich

TITLEY Gary

TOUSSAS Georgios

VINCENZI Marta

WORTMANN-KOOL Corien

ZĪLE Roberts

REGI: Committee on Regional Development

Chairman

GALEOTE QUECEDO Gerardo

Vice-Chairs

ATTWOOLL Elspeth

FAVA Giovanni Claudio

OLBRYCHT Jan

Members

ANDRIA Alfonso

ARNAOUTAKIS Stavros

BEAUPUY Jean-Marie

BEREND Rolf

BIELAN Adam Jerzy

BOBOŠÍKOVÁ Paní Jana

BOOTH Graham

BOSSI Umberto

BOURZAI Bernadette

DE BRÚN Bairbre

GARCÍA PÉREZ Iratxe

GENTVILAS Eugenijus

GERINGER DE OEDENBERG Lidia Joanna

GUELLEC Ambroise

GUERREIRO Pedro

GURMAI Zita

HARANGOZÓ Gábor

HARKIN Marian

HATZIDAKIS Konstantinos

HIGGINS Jim

HUTCHINSON Alain

ITURGAIZ ANGULO Carlos José

JANOWSKI Mieczysław Edmund

KALLENBACH Gisela

KELAM Tunne

KOTEREC Miloš

KREHL Constanze Angela

MADEIRA Jamila

MARQUES Sérgio

MATSIS Yiannakis

MIKOLÁŠIK Miroslav

MUSOTTO Francesco

NICHOLSON James

VAN NISTELROOIJ Lambert

PÁLFI István

PIEPER Markus

PLEGUEZUELOS AGUILAR Francisca

POIGNANT Bernard

SCHROEDTER Elisabeth

SMITH Alyn

STANISZEWSKA Grażyna

STIHLER Catherine

SUDRE Margie

TATARELLA Salvatore

TRIANTAPHYLLIDES Kyriacos

VLASÁK Oldřich

ŽELEZNÝ Vladimír

AGRI: Committee on Agriculture and Rural Development

Chairman

DAUL Joseph

Vice-Chairs

FRUTEAU Jean-Claude

GRAEFE ZU BARINGDORF Friedrich-Wilhelm

WOJCIECHOWSKI Janusz

Members

ADWENT Filip

AUBERT Marie-Hélène

BACO Peter

BATZELI Katerina

BERLATO Sergio

BERMAN Thijs

BUSK Niels

CAPOULAS SANTOS Luis Manuel

CASTIGLIONE Giuseppe

DESS Albert

DIDŽIOKAS Gintaras

EBNER Michl

FRAGA ESTÉVEZ Carmen

FREITAS Duarte

GKLAVAKIS Ioannis

GOEPEL Lutz

GOLIK Bogdan

HERRANZ GARCÍA María Esther

JEGGLE Elisabeth

KINDERMANN Heinz

LE FOLL Stéphane

LIOTARD Kartika Tamara

MAAT Albert Jan

MCGUINNESS Mairead

MANOLAKOU Diamanto

MARTINEZ Jean-Claude

MIGUÉLEZ RAMOS Rosa

PARISH Neil

SALINAS GARCÍA María Isabel

SCHIERHUBER Agnes

SCHUTH Willem

SIEKIERSKI Czesław Adam

TABAJDI Csaba Sándor

TARABELLA Marc

TITFORD Jeffrey

TOMCZAK Witold

VIRRANKOSKI Kyösti Tapio

PECH: Committee on Fisheries

Chairman

MORILLON Philippe

Vice-Chairs

DE POLI Antonio

DE VILLIERS Philippe

MIGUÉLEZ RAMOS Rosa

Members

ALLISTER James Hugh

ARNAOUTAKIS Stavros

ATTWOOLL Elspeth

AUBERT Marie-Hélène

BUSK Niels

CAPOULAS SANTOS Luis Manuel

CAROLLO Giorgio

CASA David

CASACA Paulol

CHMIELEWSKI Zdzisław Kazimierz

D'ALEMA Massimo

FRAGA ESTÉVEZ Carmen

GKLAVAKIS Ioannis

GOMOLKA Alfred

GUERREIRO Pedro

HUDGHTON Ian

JARZEMBOWSKI Georg

KINDERMANN Heinz

KRISTENSEN Henrik Dam

MAAT Albert Jan

MEYER PLEITE Willy

MUSUMECI Sebastiano (Nello)

Ó NEACHTAIN Seán

PARISH Neil

PIECYK Willi

POIGNANT Bernard

STERCKX Dirk

STEVENSON Struan

STIHLER Catherine

SUDRE Margie

VARELA SUANZES-CARPEGNA Daniel

CULT: Committee on Culture and Education

Chairman

SIFUNAKIS Nikolaos

Vice-Chairs

MAVROMMATIS Manolis

SCHMITT Pál

TRÜPEL Helga

Members

BADÍA I CUTCHET María

BEAZLEY Christopher

BERLINGUER Giovanni

BONO Guy

DE SARNEZ Marielle

DESCAMPS Marie-Hélène

DIČKUTÉ Jolanta

FLASAROVÁ Věra

GAL'A Milan

GIBAULT Claire

GRAÇA MOURA Vasco

GRÖNER Lissy

HENNICOT-SCHOEPGES Erna

HERRERO-TEJEDOR Luis

HIERONYMI Ruth

JOAN I MARÍ Bernat

LAIGNEL André

LE PEN Marine

MIKKO Marianne

NOVAK Ljudmila

PACK Doris

PAVILIONIS Ronaldas

PODKAŃSKI Zdzisław Zbigniew

PORTAS Miguel

PRETS Christa

RESETARITS Karin

ROSZKOWSKI Wojciech

SALVINI Matteo

TAKKULA Hannu

WEBER Henri

WISE Thomas

ZATLOUKAL Tomáš

JURI: Committee on Legal Affairs

Chairman

GARGANI Giuseppe

Vice-Chairs

LÉVAI Katalin

SZEJNA Andrzej Jan

WIELAND Rainer

Members

BERGER Maria

CZARNECKI Marek Aleksander

DI PIETRO Antonio

DOORN Bert

FRASSONI Monica

KAUPPI Piia-Noora

LECHNER Kurt

LEHNE Klaus-Heiner

LICICKI Marcin

LIPIETZ Alain

LÓPEZ-ISTÚRIZ WHITE Antonio

MASIP HIDALGO Antonio

MAYER Hans-Peter

MOHÁCSI Viktória

SAKALAS Aloyzas

STROŽ Daniel

WALLIS Diana

ZINGARETTI Nicola

ZVĚŘINA Jaroslav

ZWIEFKA Tadeusz

LIBE: Committee on Civil Liberties, Justice and Home Affairs

Chairman

CAVADA Jean-Marie

Vice-Chairs

GAUBERT Patrick

LAMBRINIDIS Stavros

ZAPPALA' Stefano

Members

ALVARO Alexander Nuno

ANGELILLI Roberta

ANTONIOZZI Alfredo

BAUER Edit

BLOKLAND Johannes

BORGHEZIO Mario

BREJC Mihael

CASHMAN Michael

CATANIA Giusto

CEDERSCHIÖLD Charlotte

COELHO Carlos

CORREIA Fausto

DÍAZ DE MERA GARCÍA CONSUEGRA Agustín

DÍEZ GONZÁLEZ Rosa

DUQUESNE Antoine

GÁL Kinga

DE GROEN-KOUWENHOVEN Elly

GRUBER Lilli

HAZAN Adeline

JÁRÓKA Lívia

KIRKHOPE Timothy

KLAMT Ewa

KÓSÁNÉ KOVÁCS Magda

KRARUP Ole

KREISSL-DÖRFLER Wolfgang

KUDRYCKA Barbara

LA RUSSA Romano Maria

LAX Henrik

LOMBARDO Raffaele

LUDFORD Sarah

MASTENBROEK Edith

MAYOR OREJA Jaime

MORAES Claude

MUSSOLINI Alessandra

NASSAUER Hartmut

PAFILIS Athanasios

PĘK Bogdan

PISTELLI Lapo

ROURE Martine

SANTORO Michele

SBARBATI Luciana

SEGELSTRÖM Inger

VANHECKE Frank

VARVITSIOTIS Ioannis

WEBER Manfred

ŽDANOKA Tatjana

STUBB Alexander

WIERZEJSKI Wojciech

AFCO: Committee on Constitutional Affairs

Chairman

LEINEN Jo

Vice-Chairs

GUARDANS CAMBÓ Ignasi

VENTRE Riccardo

VOGGENHUBER Johannes

Members

ALLISTER James Hugh

BONDE Jens-Peter

CARNERO GONZÁLEZ Carlos

COHN-BENDIT Daniel Marc

CORBETT Richard

CROWLEY Brian

DEHAENE Jean-Luc

DEMETRIOU Panayiotis

DUFF Andrew

ESTEVES Maria da Assunção

FRIEDRICH Ingo

GEREMEK Bronisław

GRABOWSKA Genowefa

HANNAN Daniel

KAUFMANN Sylvia-Yvonne

MÉNDEZ DE VIGO Íñigo

MÖLZER Andreas

PAHOR Borut

PĪKS Rihards

POETTERING Hans-Gert

REYNAUD Marie-Line

SOUSA PINTO Sérgio

FEMM: Committee on Women's Rights and Gender Equality

Chairwoman

ZÁBORSKÁ Anne

Vice-Chairs

ESTRELA Edite

GURMAI Zita

SVENSSON Eva-Britt

Members

BAUER Edit

BOZKURT Emine

BREYER Hiltrud

CARLSHAMRE Maria

FIGUEIREDO Ilda

FLASAROVÁ Věra

FONTAINE Nicole

GIBAULT Claire

GRÖNER Lissy

HERRANZ GARCÍA María Esther

JÄÄTTEENMÄKI Anneli

JÁRÓKA Lívia

KAUPPI Piia-Noora

KRATSA-TSAGAROPOULOU Rodi

KRUPA Urszula

LOCATELLI Pia Elda

LULLING Astrid

NIEBLER Angelika

OVIIR Siiri

PACK Doris

PANAYOTOPOULOS-CASSIOTOU Marie

PRETS Christa

REYNAUD Marie-Line

RIERA MADURELL Teresa

ROEVA I RUEDA Raül

SARTORI Amalia

SCHENARDI Lydia

SZYMAŃSKI Konrad

THOMSEN Britta

VAN LANCKER Anne

WORTMANN-KOOL Corien

PETI: Committee on Petitions

Chairman

LICICKI Marcin

Vice-Chairs

CASHMAN Michael

MATSOUKA Maria

Members

ATKINS Robert

AYALA SENDER Inés

BATTILOCCHIO Alessandro

BORGHEZIO Mario

DE ROSSA Proinsias

DOBOLYI Alexandra

FOURTOU Janelly

DE GROEN-KOUWENHOVEN Elly

HAMMERSTEIN MINTZ David

HELMER Roger

ITURGAIZ ANGULO Carlos José

MCGUINNESS Mairead

MARTIN David

MARTÍNEZ MARTÍNEZ Miguel Angel

MAVROMMATIS Manolis

MEYER PLEITE Willy

PANAYOTOPOULOS-CASSIOTOU Marie

SBARBATI Luciana

SCHWAB Andreas

SEEBER Richard

WALLIS Diana

WIELAND Rainer

AFET: Committee on Foreign Affairs

Chairman

BROK Elmar

Vice-Chairs

ILVES Toomas Hendrik

NICHOLSON OF WINTERBOURNE

VAN ORDEN Geoffrey

Members

AGNOLETTO Vittorio

BEER Angelika

BEGLITIS Panagiotis

BELDER Bastiaan

BEŇOVÁ Monika

BONINO Emma

BRIE André

CLAEYS Philip

COÛTEAUX Paul Marie

COVENEY Simon

CZARNECKI Ryszard

D'ALEMA Massimo

DE KEYSER Véronique

DIMITRAKOPOULOS Giorgos

EURLINGS Camiel

FOTYGA Elzbieta

GAWRONSKI Jas

GIERTYCH Maciej Marian

GOMES Ana Maria

GOMOLKA Alfred

HÄNSCH Klaus

HOWITT Richard

IBRISAGIC Anna

KACIN Jelko

KARATZAFERIS Georgios

KASOULIDES Ioannis

KLICH Bogdan

KUHNE Helmut

LAGENDKJK Joost

LANDSBERGIS Vytautas

LASCHET Armin

MCMILLAN-SCOTT Edward

MALMSTRÖM Cecilia

MENÉNDEZ DEL VALLE Emilio

MEYER PLEITE Willy

MILLÁN MON Francisco José

MORILLON Philippe

MOSCOVICI Pierre

NAPOLETANO Pasqualina

NEYTS-UYTTEBROECK Annemie

OBIOLS I GERMÀ Raimon

ÖGER Vural

ÖZDEMIR Cem

PALECKIS Justas Vincas

PETERLE Alojz

PFLÜGER Tobias

PINHEIRO João de Deus

PIOTROWSKI Mirosław Mariusz

PISKORSKI Paweł Bartłomiej

POLFER Lydie

POSSELT Bernd

RASMUSSEN Poul Nyrup

ROCARD Michel

ROEVA I RUEDA Raül

SALAFRANCA SÁNCHEZ-NEYRA José Ignacio

SARYUSZ-WOLSKI Jacek Emil

SCHÖPFLIN György

SEEBERG Gitte

SIWIEC Marek Maciej

STENZEL Ursula

SUMBERG David

SWOBODA Hannes

SZENT-IVÁNYI István

SZYMAŃSKI Konrad

TAJANI Antonio

TANNOCK Charles

VÄYRYNEN Paavo

VAIDERE Inese

VATANEN Ari

WIERSMA Jan Marinus

VON WOGAU Karl

WURTZ Francis

YAÑEZ-BARNUEVO GARCÍA Luis

ZIELENIEC Josef

DROI: Sub-Committee on Human Rights

Chairwoman

FLAUTRE Hélène

Vice-Chairs

HOWITT Richard

TANNOCK Charles

VAN HECKE Johan

Members

AGNOLETTO Vittorio

ANDRIKIENĖ Laima Liucija

BELOHORSKÁ Irena

DE KEYSER Véronique

DIMITRAKOPOULOS Giorgos

DUKA-ZÓLYOMI Árpád

ESTEVES Maria da Assunção

GAHLER Michael

GÁL Kinga

HORÁČEK Milan

KARIM Sajjad

KORHOLA Eija-Riitta

MORGANTINI Luisa

NAPOLETANO Pasqualina

NICHOLSON OF WINTERBOURNE

OBIOLS I GERMÀ Raimon

PETERLE Alojz

PINIOR Józef

RIBEIRO E CASTRO José

RIES Frédérique

ROEVA I RUEDA Raül

SCHÖPFLIN György

SCHULZ Martin

SPERONI Francesco Enrico

TABAJDI Csaba Sándor

VALENCIANO MARTÍNEZ-OROZCO María Elena

VERGES Paul

SEDE: Sub-Committee on Security and Defence

Chairman

VON WOGAU Karl

Vice-Chairs

BREJC Mihael

GOMES Ana Maria

KRISTOVSKIS G irts Valdis

Members

BATTEN Gerard

BEER Angelika

BEGLITIS Panagiotis

CHIESA Giulietto

CLAEYS Philip

D'ALEMA Massimo

IBRISAGIC Anna

KELAM Tunne

KUHNE Helmut

LAGENDKJK Joost

LANDSBERGIS Vytautas

MALMSTRÖM Cecilia

MORILLON Philippe

ONYSZKIEWICZ Janusz

PAFILIS Athanasios

PFLÜGER Tobias

QUEIRÓ Luís

ROCARD Michel

SEEBERG Gitte

STENZEL Ursula

SWOBODA Hannes

TAJANI Antonio

VAN ORDEN Geoffrey

VERNOLA Marcello

WIERSMA Jan Marinus

YAÑEZ-BARNUEVO GARCÍA Luis

DEVE: Committee on Development

Chairwoman

MORGANTINI Luisa

Vice-Chairs

BUDREIKAITÉ Danuté

GAHLER Michael

VAN DEN BERG Margrietus

Members

AUKEN Margrete

BATTILOCCHIO Alessandro

CARLOTTI Marie-Arlette

CORNILLET Thierry

DEVA Nirj

DILLEN Koenraad

DOBOLYI Alexandra

FERNÁNDEZ MARTÍN Fernando

GOUDIN Hélène

HYBÁŠKOVÁ Jana

KACZMAREK Filip Andrzej

KINNOCK Glenys

KREISSL-DÖRFLER Wolfgang

KRISTOVSKIS G¸irts Valdis

MARTENS Maria

MARTÍNEZ MARTÍNEZ Miguel Angel

MITCHELL Gay

PINIOR Józef

PÓMES RUIZ José Javier

RIBEIRO E CASTRO José

SAVI Toomas

SCHAPIRA Pierre

SCHMIDT Frithjof

SCHRÖDER Jürgen

UCA Feleknas

VALENCIANO MARTÍNEZ-OROZCO
  María Elena

VERGES Paul

ZÁBORSKÁ Anne

ZAHRADIL Jan

ZANI Mauro

INTA: Committee on International Trade

Chairman

BARÓN CRESPO Enrique

Vice-Chairs

CHIESA Giulietto

ŠŤASTNÝ Peter

VARELA SUANZES-CARPEGNA Daniel

Members

ARIF Kader

ASSIS Francisco

BOURLANGES Jean-Louis

CASPARY Daniel

CASTEX Françoise

FARAGE Nigel

FJELLNER Christofer

FORD Glyn

GLATTFELDER Béla

HENIN Jacky

KARIM Sajjad

LE PEN Jean-Marie

LIPIETZ Alain

LUCAS Caroline

MANN Erika

MARKOV Helmuth

MARTIN David

MORENO SÁNCHEZ Javier

MUSCARDINI Cristiana

PAPASTAMKOS Georgios

QUISTHOUDT-ROWOHL Godelieve

ROGALSKI Bogusław

SAÏFI Tokia

STURDY Robert

VAN HECKE Johan

ZALESKI Zbigniew

INTERPARLIAMENTARY DELEGATIONS

Delegation for Relations with the Countries of South-East Europe

Chairwoman

PACK Doris

Vice-Chairs

POLI BORTONE Adriana

SWOBODA Hannes

Members

BECSEY Zsolt László

BŘEZINA Jan

CZARNECKI Ryszard

GUARDANS CAMBÓ Ignasi

KALLENBACH Gisela

KRISTENSEN Henrik Dam

LUDFORD Sarah

MUSACCHIO Roberto

PROTASIEWICZ Jacek

ROTHE Mechtild

TRAKATELLIS Antonios

XENOGIANNAKOPOULOU Marilisa

Delegation for Relations with Belarus

Chairman

KLICH Bogdan

Vice-Chairs

KUŠĶIS Aldis

MUSCAT Joseph

Members

FJELLNER Christofer

FLASAROVÁ Věra

GENTVILAS Eugenijus

GOMOLKA Alfred

KUDRYCKA Barbara

LANG Carl

ONYSZKIEWICZ Janusz

SAKALAS Aloyzas

SCHROEDTER Elisabeth

SZEJNA Andrzej Jan

SZYMAŃSKI Konrad

WIERZEJSKI Wojciech

Delegation for Relations with Israel

Chairwoman

HYBÁŠKOVÁ Jana

Vice-Chairs

BELDER Bastiaan

BEŇOVÁ Monika

Members

CERCAS Alejandro

CZARNECKI Marek Aleksander

FERBER Markus

GAUBERT Patrick

GUTIÉRREZ-CORTINES Cristina

HAMMERSTEIN MINTZ David

LE PEN Marine

MASTENBROEK Edith

PANNELLA Marco

RIES Frédérique

SCHAPIRA Pierre

ŠŤASTNÝ Peter

STOCKMANN Ulrich

SVENSSON Eva-Britt

TAJANI Antonio

VOGGENHUBER Johannes

ZALESKI Zbigniew

Delegation for Relations with the Palestinian Legislative Council

Chairman

ADAMOU Adamos

Vice-Chairs

DE ROSSA Proinsias

KASOULIDES Ioannis

Members

ALVARO Alexander Nuno

AUKEN Margrete

BACHELOT-NARQUIN Roselyne

BOWIS John

CASPARY Daniel

CASTEX Françoise

DAVIES Chris

DE VEYRAC Christine

EVANS Jillian

HEDH Anna

LE FOLL Stéphane

LUCAS Caroline

MASIP HIDALGO Antonio

MORGANTINI Luisa

ZAPPALA' Stefano

Delegation for Relations with the Maghreb Countries and the Arab Maghreb Union (including Libya)

Chairwoman

RUDI UBEDA Luisa Fernanda

Vice-Chairs

BUSUTTIL Simon

HUTCHINSON Alain

Members

COÛTEAUX Paul Marie

FLAUTRE Hélène

FRAGA ESTÉVEZ Carmen

KOCH-MEHRIN Silvana

KRISTOVSKIS G,irts Valdis

LAIGNEL André

LETTA Enrico

LIOTARD Kartika Tamara

LOMBARDO Raffaele

NAPOLETANO Pasqualina

PIEPER Markus

DOS SANTOS Manuel António

SCHENARDI Lydia

SILVA PENEDA José Albino

SONIK Bogusław

YAÑEZ-BARNUEVO GARCÍA Luis

Delegation for Relations with the Mashreq Countries

Chairwoman

PATRIE Béatrice

Vice-Chairs

BONINO Emma

RADWAN Alexander

Members

CARNERO GONZÁLEZ Carlos

DE KEYSER Véronique

DIMITRAKOPOULOS Giorgos

DIONISI Armando

HAZAN Adeline

IN 'T VELD Sophia

KÓSÁNÉ KOVÁCS Magda

MADEIRA Jamila

MUSOTTO Francesco

MUSSOLINI Alessandra

MUSUMECI Sebastiano (Nello)

PORTAS Miguel

PURVIS John

VENTRE Riccardo

VINCENZI Marta

ZAHRADIL Jan

Delegation for Relations with the Gulf States (including Yemen)

Chairwoman

GRUBER Lilli

Vice-Chairs

DOYLE Avri

PFLÜGER Tobias

Members

ANGELILLI Roberta

ATTARD-MONTALTO John

BOURLANGES Jean-Louis

CAPOULAS SANTOS Luis Manuel

FONTAINE Nicole

GAL'A Milan

GROSSETÊTE Françoise

KARIM Sajjad

LAGENDKJK Joost

LOUIS Patrick

MYLLER Riitta

NIEBLER Angelika

REYNAUD Marie-Line

SAÏFI Tokia

Delegation for Relations with Iran

Chairwoman

BEER Angelika

Vice-Chairs

LA RUSSA Romano Maria

PRETS Christa

Members

BUSHILL-MATTHEWS Philip

CASACA Paulol

CASTIGLIONE Giuseppe

CATANIA Giusto

DÍAZ DE MERA GARCÍA CONSUEGRA Agustín

FRIEDRICH Ingo

GAUZÈS Jean-Paul

LOCATELLI Pia Elda

MARTIN Hans-Peter

NICHOLSON OF WINTERBOURNE

PURVIS John

ROUČEK Libor

SAMUELSEN Anders

SAVARY Gilles

Delegation for Relations with the United States

Chairman

EVANS Jonathan

Vice-Chairs

BONSIGNORE Vito

HAMON Benoît

Members

ANDRIA Alfonso

BARÓN CRESPO Enrique

BRADBOURN Philip

BROK Elmar

COVENEY Simon

CROWLEY Brian

DE BRÚN Bairbre

DESCAMPS Marie-Hélène

DUCHOŇ Petr

FATUZZO Carlo

GALEOTE QUECEDO Gerardo

GIERTYCH Maciej Marian

GRAÇA MOURA Vasco

GUIDONI Umberto

ILVES Toomas Hendrik

JÄÄTTEENMÄKI Anneli

JORDAN CIZELJ Romana

KUHNE Helmut

LAMBRINIDIS Stavros

LAMBSDORFF Alexander

LAUK Kurt Joachim

MCCARTHY Arlene

MOSCOVICI Pierre

NEYTS-UYTTEBROECK Annemie

PANZERI Pier Antonio

PINIOR Józef

RESETARITS Karin

SINNOTT Kathy

SKINNER Peter

SUMBERG David

Delegation for Relations with Canada

Chairman

Ó NEACHTAIN Seán

Vice-Chairs

LEHTINEN Lasse

SAVI Toomas

Members

ATTWOOLL Elspeth

CHRUSZCZ Sylwester

DOVER Den

DÜHRKOP DÜHRKOP Bárbara

FREITAS Duarte

GURMAI Zita

HARKIN Marian

HIERONYMI Ruth

HIGGINS Jim

HUDGHTON Ian

SCHIERHUBER Agnes

TRAUTMANN Catherine

Delegation for Relations with the Countries of Central America

Chairman

OBIOLS I GERMÀ Raimon

Vice-Chairs

GARCÍA-MARGALLO Y MARFIL José Manuel

RIZZO Marco

ROEVA I RUEDA Raül

Members

ANTONIOZZI Alfredo

AYALA SENDER Inés

BELOHORSKÁ Irena

COTTIGNY Jean-Louis

ESTRELA Edite

FALBR Richard

GARGANI Giuseppe

HEATON-HARRIS Christopher

HERRERO-TEJEDOR Luis

HUGHES Stephen

KRAHMER Holger

LIESE Peter

MEYER PLEITE Willy

ORTUONDO LARREA Josu

PAVILIONIS Ronaldas

PISTELLI Lapo

QUEIRÓ Luís

SONIK Bogusław

Delegation for Relations with the Countries of the Andean Community

Chairman

LIPIETZ Alain

Vice-Chairs

VAN DEN BERG Margrietus

Members

BUDREIKAITÉ Danuté

DEGUTIS Arūnas

FAVA Giovanni Claudio

FERNÁNDEZ MARTÍN Fernando

FLORENZ Karl-Heinz

GRÄSSLE Ingeborg

LEICHTFRIED Jörg

MEDINA ORTEGA Manuel

MENÉNDEZ DEL VALLE Emilio

MONTORO ROMERO Cristobal

VAN NISTELROOIJ Lambert

ROGALSKI Bogusław

VERNOLA Marcello

VLASÁK Oldřich

WAGENKNECHT Sahra

Delegation for Relations with Mercosur

Chairman

D'ALEMA Massimo

Vice-Chairs

DUQUESNE Antoine

Members

AYUSO GONZÁLEZ María del Pilar

BIELAN Adam Jerzy

CEDERSCHIÖLD Charlotte

COCILOVO Luigi

DESS Albert

FIGUEIREDO Ilda

FRASSONI Monica

GLATTFELDER Béla

GRIESBECK Nathalie

HANDZLIK Malgorzata

HANNAN Daniel

HENNICOT-SCHOEPGES Erna

HUDACKÝ Ján

KARATZAFERIS Georgios

KREISSL-DÖRFLER Wolfgang

MORENO SÁNCHEZ Javier

NAVARRO Robert

PINHEIRO João de Deus

RASMUSSEN Poul Nyrup

ROMAGNOLI Luca

SALAFRANCA SÁNCHEZ-NEYRA José Ignacio

SALINAS GARCÍA María Isabel

SOUSA PINTO Sérgio

Delegation for Relations with Japan

Chairman

JARZEMBOWSKI Georg

<table>
<tr><td>

Vice-Chairs

VIRRANKOSKI Kyösti Tapio

ZVĚŘINA Jaroslav

Members

ANDERSSON Jan

BADÍA I CUTCHET María

BREYER Hiltrud

CORBETT Richard

DOUAY Brigitte

DUIN Garrelt

GOLLNISCH Bruno

HARBOUR Malcolm

ITÄLÄ Ville

ITURGAIZ ANGULO Carlos José

KARAS Othmar

KAUFMANN Sylvia-Yvonne

LEWANDOWSKI Janusz

NEWTON DUNN Bill

ROSZKOWSKI Wojciech

SALVINI Matteo

SÁNCHEZ PRESEDO Antolín

STARKEVIČIŪTĖ Margarita

SZÁJER József

WALTER Ralf

WORTMANN-KOOL Corien

Delegation for Relations with the People's Republic of China

Chairman

STERCKX Dirk

Vice-Chairs

DEHAENE Jean-Luc

ROURE Martine

</td><td>

Members

ATKINS Robert

BATZELI Katerina

BRUNETTA Renato

CALABUIG RULL Joan

DEL CASTILLO VERO Pilar

CORBEY Dorette

DE MICHELIS Gianni

FAJMON Hynek

GEBHARDT Evelyne

HOPPENSTEDT Karsten Friedrich

JØRGENSEN Dan

KAUPPI Piia-Noora

KIRKHOPE Timothy

LAPERROUZE Anne

LICICKI Marcin

MANDERS Toine

MAVROMMATIS Manolis

OLBRYCHT Jan

OOMEN-RUIJTEN Ria

PAPADIMOULIS Dimitrios

PĘK Bogdan

PĪKS Rihards

REUL Herbert

RIIS-JØRGENSEN Karin

ROUČEK Libor

SACCONI Guido

TRÜPEL Helga

TURMES Claude

ZIMMER Gabriele

</td></tr>
</table>

Delegation for Relations with the Countries of South Asia and the South Asia Association for Regional Co-operation (SAARC)

Chairman

GILL Neena

Vice-Chairs

KOHLÍČEK Jaromir

MULDER Jan

Members

BELET Ivo

BERGER Maria

BUSHILL-MATTHEWS Philip

COSTA Paolo

DEVA Nirj

EHLER Jan Christian

ESTEVES Maria da Assunção

EVANS Robert

GERINGER DE OEDENBERG Lidia Joanna

GOEBBELS Robert

GOLIK Bogdan

JÁRÓKA Lívia

LAMASSOURE Alain

LAMBERT Jean

LEINEN Jo

LYNNE Elizabeth

MANN Thomas

PIOTROWSKI Mirosław Mariusz

RYAN Eoin

Delegation for Relations with the Countries of Southeast Asia and the Association of South East Asian Nations (ASEAN)

Chairman

NASSAUER Hartmut

Vice-Chairs

MATHIEU Véronique

TARABELLA Marc

Members

DIDŽIOKAS Gintaras

DOORN Bert

GAWRONSKI Jas

GROBOWSKI Dariusz Maciej

LAVARRA Vincenzo

MAATEN Jules

ŐRY Csaba

PAFILIS Athanasios

PETERLE Alojz

POIGNANT Bernard

PÓMES RUIZ José Javier

RIERA MADURELL Teresa

SCHMIDT Frithjof

WEILER Barbara

WOHLIN Lars

Delegation for Relations with the Korean Peninsula

Chairwoman

STENZEL Ursula

Vice-Chairs

GRECH Louis

SZENT-IVÁNYI István

Members

FORD Glyn

HELMER Roger

JARZEMBOWSKI Georg

LE RACHINEL Fernand

ONESTA Gérard

QUISTHOUDT-ROWOHL Godelieve

SPERONI Francesco Enrico

TARAND Andres

ULMER Thomas

WATSON Graham

ZINGARETTI Nicola

Delegation for Relations with Australia and New Zealand

Chairman

PARISH Neil

Vice-Chairs

PIOTROWSKI Mirosław Mariusz

WYNN Terence

Members

BEAUPUY Jean-Marie

BERLATO Sergio

BÖGE Reimer

VAN DEN BURG Ieke

CHICHESTER Giles

CLAEYS Philip

CRAMER Michael

HÄNSCH Klaus

KLAMT Ewa

KOTEREC Miloš

MARTIN David

NICHOLSON James

RACK Reinhard

RUTOWICZ Leopold Józef

TAKKULA Hannu

TRIANTAPHYLLIDES Kyriacos

VARELA SUANZES-CARPEGNA Daniel

Delegation for Relations with South Africa

Chairman

DI PIETRO Antonio

Vice-Chairs

MARQUES Sérgio

THOMSEN Britta

Members

BARSI-PATAKY Etelka

BENNAHMIAS Jean-Luc

BRADBOURN Philip

BREJC Mihael

DE SARNEZ Marielle

FERREIRA Anne

KRARUP Ole

KRUPA Urszula

MORAES Claude

SCHMITT Ingo

VAIDERE Inese

Delegations for Relations with the NATO Parliamentary Assembly

Chairman

CASACA Paulo

Vice-Chairs

ALBERTINI Gabriele

PISKORSKI Paweł Bartłomiej

Members

BEER Angelika

KOTEREC Miloš

KRAHMER Holger

PFLÜGER Tobias

VAN ORDEN Geoffrey

VON WOGAU Karl

ZINGARETTI Nicola

DELEGATIONS TO PARLIAMENTARY CO-OPERATION COMMITTEES

Delegation to the EU-Armenia, EU-Azerbaijan and EU-Georgia Parliamentary Co-operation Committees

Chairwoman

ISLER BÉGUIN Marie Anne

Vice-Chairs

DUKA-ZÓLYOMI Árpád

LANDSBERGIS Vytautas

Members

ANDREJEVS Georgs

BATTILOCCHIO Alessandro

BLOKLAND Johannes

BREPOELS Frederika

DEMETRIOU Panayiotis

EL KHADRAOUI Saïd

LASCHET Armin

MANOLAKOU Diamanto

OVIIR Siiri

SIFUNAKIS Nikolaos

SPAUTZ Jean

SWOBODA Hannes

ZWIEFKA Tadeusz

Delegation to the EU-Moldova Parliamentary Co-operation Committee

Chairwoman

MIKKO Marianne

Vice-Chairs

KACIN Jelko

PODKAŃSKI Zdzisław Zbigniew

Members

ANDRIKIENĖ Laima Liucija

CARLSHAMRE Maria

GOMOLKA Alfred

MAŠTÁLKA Jiří

PITTELLA Giovanni

SCHROEDTER Elisabeth

WIERSMA Jan Marinus

Delegation to the EU-Russia Parliamentary Co-operation Committee

Chairman

EURLINGS Camiel

Vice-Chairs

PAASILINNA Reino

SEPPÄNEN Esko

Members

BUSQUIN Philippe

CABRNOCH Milan

CHIESA Giulietto

ESTEVES Maria da Assunção

FOTYGA Elzbieta

GARRIGA POLLEDO Salvador

GEREMEK Bronisław

GLATTFELDER Béla

JENSEN Anne E.

KELAM Tunne

KREHL Constanze Angela

LAX Henrik

LEHNE Klaus-Heiner

LE PEN Jean-Marie

LIBERADZKI Bogusław

PALECKIS Justas Vincas

REMEK Vladimír

ROGALSKI Bogusław

SAMARAS Antonis

SANTORO Michele

SARYUSZ-WOLSKI Jacek Emil

SEEBER Richard

STAES Bart

SUDRE Margie

TABAJDI Csaba Sándor

WEBER Henri

ŽDANOKA Tatjana

ŽELEZNÝ Vladimír

Delegation to the EU-Ukraine Parliamentary Co-operation Committee

Chairman

SIWIEC Marek Maciej

Vice-Chairs

ADWENT Filip

TANNOCK Charles

Members

BERMAN Thijs

BIRUTIS Šarūnas

BOBOŠÍKOVÁ Paní Jana

BUZEK Jerzy

HARMS Rebecca

HERCZOG Edit

KRASTS Guntars

MARKOV Helmuth

PÁLFI István

PLEŠTINSKÁ Zita

RAPKAY Bernhard

STANISZEWSKA Grażyna

THYSSEN Marianne

Delegation to the EU-Kazakhstan, EU-Kyrgyzstan and EU-Uzbekistan Parliamentary Co-operation Committees, and Delegation for Relations with Tajikistan, Turkmenistan and Mongolia

Chairwoman

JUKNEVIČIENĖ Ona

Vice-Chairs

BOURZAI Bernadette

MAAT Albert Jan

Members

BERSANI Pier Luigi

BLOKLAND Johannes

CIRINO POMICINO Paolo

CORREIA Fausto

GIEREK Adam

HASSI Satu

JEGGLE Elisabeth

JÖNS Karin

MOHÁCSI Viktória

MUSCARDINI Cristiana

OLAJOS Péter

RANSDORF Miloslav

WOJCIECHOWSKI Janusz

ZATLOUKAL Tomáš

DELEGATIONS TO JOINT PARLIAMENTARY COMMITTEES

Delegation to the European Economic Area (EEA) Joint Parliamentary Committee, and Delegation for Relations with Switzerland, Iceland and Norway (SIN)

Chairwoman

WALLIS Diana

Vice-Chairs

BONDE Jens-Peter

Members

BARSI-PATAKY Etelka

DIČKUTĖ Jolanta

GOEPEL Lutz

HEDKVIST PETERSEN Ewa

JANOWSKI Mieczysław Edmund

LÉVAI Katalin

MCDONALD Mary Lou

PANAYOTOPOULOS-CASSIOTOU Marie

ROTH-BEHRENDT Dagmar

RÜBIG Paul

SCHUTH Willem

ŠCOTTOVÁ Nina

SMITH Alyn

STIHLER Catherine

VANHECKE Frank

Delegation to the EU-Bulgaria Joint Parliamentary Committee

Chairwoman

GUY-QUINT Catherine

Vice-Chairs

TOUSSAS Georgios

VÄYRYNEN Paavo

Members

BELDER Bastiaan

CASA David

CHATZIMARKAKIS Jorgo

DE VITS Mia

ETTL Harald

GARCÍA PÉREZ Iratxe

GIBAULT Claire

DE GROEN-KOUWENHOVEN Elly

IBRISAGIC Anna

KARATZAFERIS Georgios

KUC Wiesław Stefan

KUŽMIUK Zbigniew Krzysztof

LECHNER Kurt

MÉNDEZ DE VIGO Íñigo

MORGAN Eluned

PIRILLI Umberto

STUBB Alexander

TZAMPAZI Evangelia

VARVITSIOTIS Ioannis

WEBER Manfred

WUERMELING Joachim

Delegation to the EU-Croatia Joint Parliamentary Committee

Chairman

SCHMITT Pál

Vice-Chairs

MALMSTRÖM Cecilia

PAHOR Borut

Members

BACO Peter

EBNER Michl

FAZAKAS Szabolcs

HORÁČEK Milan

KINDERMANN Heinz

MEIJER Erik

POSSELT Bernd

PRODI Vittorio

SIEKIERSKI Czesław Adam

STREJČEK Ivo

TITLEY Gary

TOMCZAK Witold

Delegation to the EU-Former Yugoslav Republic of Macedonia (FYROM) Joint Parliamentary Committee

Chairman

PAPASTAMKOS Georgios

Vice-Chairs

HEGYI Gyula

KARATZAFERIS Georgios

Members

BERTINOTTI Fausto

DRČAR MURKO Mojca

GARCÍA PÉREZ Iratxe

GYÜRK András

HONEYBALL Mary

KOCH Dieter-Lebrecht

KUSSTATSCHER Sepp

MATSOUKA Maria

ŐRY Csaba

PIECYK Willi

Delegation to the EU-Romania Joint Parliamentary Committee

Chairman

PODESTÀ Guido

Vice-Chairs

GÁL Kinga

LIENEMANN Marie-Noëlle

Members

ARNAOUTAKIS Stavros

BATTILOCCHIO Alessandro

BAUER Edit

BEAZLEY Christopher

BORGHEZIO Mario

CASHMAN Michael

CAVADA Jean-Marie

CHRISTENSEN Ole

GAUZÈS Jean-Paul

HARANGOZÓ Gábor

HENNIS-PLASSCHAERT Jeanine

KONRAD Christoph

MCGUINNESS Mairead

MASIEL Jan Tadeusz

RÜHLE Heide

SBARBATI Luciana

STROŽ Daniel

TATARELLA Salvatore

VAKALIS Nikolaos

VAUGRENARD Yannick

WIERSMA Jan Marinus

Delegation to the EU-Turkey Joint Parliamentary Committee

Chairman

LAGENDKJK Joost

Vice-Chairs

BEGLITIS Panagiotis

DUFF Andrew

SOMMER Renate

TOUBON Jacques

Members

ARIF Kader

BOZKURT Emine

CAMRE Mogens N. J.

DEPREZ Gérard

HASSE FERREIRA Joel

HATZIDAKIS Konstantinos

HÖKMARK Gunnar

HOWITT Richard

JAŁOWIECKI Stanisław

LANGEN Werner

LUNDGREN Nils

MATSAKIS Marios

MATSIS Yiannakis

MÖLZER Andreas

ÖGER Vural

ÖZDEMIR Cem

SCHÖPFLIN György

UCA Feleknas

VAN ORDEN Geoffrey

VIDAL-QUADRAS ROCA Alejo

Delegation to the EU-Chile Joint Parliamentary Committee

Chairman

BRIE André

Vice-Chairs

KLASS Christa

SURJÁN László

Members

ASSIS Francisco

BÖSCH Herbert

FOGLIETTA Alessandro

FOURTOU Janelly

GLANTE Norbert

GRAEFE ZU BARINGDORF Friedrich-Wilhelm

DE GRANDES PASCUAL Luis

MIGUÉLEZ RAMOS Rosa

SALVINI Matteo

STEVENSON Struan

TOIA Patrizia

Delegation to the EU-Mexico Joint Parliamentary Committee

Chairwoman

MANN Erika

Vice-Chairs

SCHRÖDER Jürgen

Members

ASHWORTH Richard James

BERLINGUER Giovanni

BONO Guy

DÍEZ GONZÁLEZ Rosa

GKLAVAKIS Ioannis

GROSCH Mathieu

GUELLEC Ambroise

GUERREIRO Pedro

KLINZ Wolf

LICHTENBERGER Eva

MATO ADROVER Ana

SPERONI Francesco Enrico

POLITICAL GROUPS' SECRETARIATS

Group of the European People's Party (Christian Democrats) and European Democrats (PPE–DE)

Brussels office
Tel: (+32) 2-2842111
Fax: (+32) 2-2306208 (Parliamentary work)
Fax: (+32) 2-2309793 (Press service)

Strasbourg office
Tel: (+33) 3-88-17-40-01
Fax: (+33) 3-88-17-15-21 (Parliamentary work)
Fax: (+33) 3-88-35-39-25 (Press)

POETTERING Hans-Gert
Chairman
Tel. Brussels (+32) 2-2845769
Tel. Strasbourg (+33) 3-88-17-57-69
E-mail: hpoettering@europarl.eu.int

RUHRMANN Katrin
Spokesperson
Tel. Brussels (+32) 2-2842573
Tel. Strasbourg (+33) 3-88-17-48-30
E-mail: kruhrmann@europarl.eu.int

PEDERSEN Niels
Secretary-General
Tel. Brussels (+32) 2-2843022
Tel. Strasbourg (+33) 3-88-17-48-79
E-mail: npedersen@europarl.eu.int

BIESMANS John
Internal Organization – Deputy Secretary-General
Tel. Brussels (+32) 2-2843026
Tel. Strasbourg (+33) 3-88-17-48-52
E-mail: jbiesmans@europarl.eu.int

LICANDRO Paolo
Central Secretariat – Deputy Secretary-General
Tel. Brussels (+32) 2-2842596
Tel. Strasbourg (+33) 3-88-17-45-01
E-mail: plicandro@europarl.eu.int

FONTAINE Pascal
Documentation, Publication, Research – Deputy Secretary-General
Tel. Brussels (+32) 2-2842445
Tel. Strasbourg (+33) 3-88-17-48-57
E-mail: pfontaine@europarl.eu.int

PAPI BOUCHER Miguel
Finance – Deputy Secretary-General
Tel. Brussels (+32) 2-2844620
Tel. Strasbourg (+33) 3-88-17-48-62
E-mail: mpapi@europarl.eu.int

KAMP Martin
Parliamentary Business – Official Responsible
Tel. Brussels (+32) 2-2843265
Tel. Strasbourg (+33) 3-88-17-44-19
E-mail: mkamp@europarl.eu.int

KORDHOUDT Guy
Deputy Secretary-General
Tel. Brussels (+32) 2-2831209
Tel. Strasbourg (+33) 3-88-17-48-90
E-mail: korthoudt@europarl.eu.int

Group of the Party of European Socialists (PSE)

Brussels office
Tel: (+32) 2-2842111
Fax: (+32) 2-2306664 (Secretariat)
Fax: (+32) 2-2849026 (Press)

Luxembourg office
Tel: (+352) 430022731
Fax: (+352) 437256

Strasbourg office
Tel: (+33) 3-88-17-40-01
Fax: (+33) 3-88-35-48-65 (Secretariat)
Fax: (+33) 3-88-25-55-13 (Press)

SCHULZ Martin
Chairman
Tel. Brussels (+32) 2-2845503
Tel. Strasbourg (+33) 3-88-17-55-03
E-mail: mschultz@europarl.eu.int

MCAVAN Linda
Treasurer
Tel. Brussels (+32) 2-2845438
Tel. Strasbourg (+33) 3-88-17-49-33
E-mail: lmcavan@europarl.eu.int

HARLEY David
Secretary-General
Tel. Brussels (+32) 2-2843909
Tel. Strasbourg (+33) 3-88-17-45-07
E-mail: dharley@europarl.eu.int

ROBINSON Tony
Press and Communications Co-ordinator
Tel. Brussels (+32) 2-2843061
E-mail: trobinson@europarl.eu.int

COLOMBO Anna
Deputy Secretary-General
Tel. Brussels (+32) 2-2842270
Tel. Strasbourg (+33) 3-88-17-43-86
E-mail: acolombo@europarl.eu.int

SCHUNCK Jesper
Administrative Affairs – Deputy Secretary-
 General
Tel. Brussels (+32) 2-2843084
Tel. Strasbourg (+33) 3-88-17-43-73
E-mail: jschunck@europarl.eu.int

The Greens/European Free Alliance (Verts/ALE)

Brussels office
Tel: (+32) 2-2843045
Fax: (+32) 2-2307837

Strasbourg office
Tel: (+33) 3-88-17-58-80
Fax: (+33) 3-88-24-11-96

TSETSI Vula
Secretary-General
Tel. Brussels (+32) 2-2842117
Tel. Strasbourg (+33) 3-88-17-58-79
E-mail: vtsetsi@europarl.eu.int

DENKINGER Joachim
Deputy Secretary-General
Tel. Brussels (+32) 2-2843095
Tel. Strasbourg (+33) 3-88-17-48-65
E-mail: jdenkinger@europarl.eu.int

FERGUSSON Neil
Deputy Secretary-General
Tel. Brussels (+32) 2-2842250
Tel. Strasbourg (+33) 3-88-17-50-24
E-mail: nfergusson@europarl.eu.int

LINAZASORO José Luis
EFA Co-ordinator
Tel. Brussels (+32) 2-2843040
Tel. Strasbourg (+33) 3-88-17-40-33
E-mail: jlinazasoro@europarl.eu.int

WEIXLER Helmut
Press Attaché
Tel. Brussels (+32) 2-2844683

Tel. Strasbourg (+33) 3-88-17-47-60
E-mail: hweixler@europarl.eu.int

Confederal Group of the European United Left/Nordic Green Left (GUE/NGL)

Brussels office
Tel: (+32) 2-2842683
Fax: (+32) 2-2841780

Strasbourg office
Tel: (+33) 3-88-17-43-97
Fax: (+33) 3-88-17-42-44

D'ALIMONTE Maria
Secretary-General
Tel. Brussels (+32) 2-2842682
Tel. Strasbourg (+33) 3-88-17-43-96
E-mail: mdalimonte@europarl.eu.int

HERMANSSON Stellan
Deputy Secretary-General
Tel. Brussels (+32) 2-2844571
Tel. Strasbourg (+33) 3-88-17-44-63
E-mail: shermansson@europarl.eu.int

RAECK Thomas
Deputy Secretary-General
Tel. Brussels (+32) 2-2846282
Tel. Strasbourg (+33) 3-88-17-29-40
E-mail: traeck@europarl.eu.int

HERMANSSON Stellan
Co-ordinator for the Nordic Green Left (NGL)
Tel. Brussels (+32) 2-2844571
Tel. Strasbourg (+33) 3-88-17-44-63
E-mail: shermansson@europarl.eu.int

Union for Europe of the Nations Group (UEN)

Brussels office
Tel: (+32) 2-2842111
Fax: (+32) 2-2846972

Strasbourg office
Tel: (+33) 3-88-17-40-01
Fax: (+33) 3-88-25-16-01

BARRETT Frank
Secretary-General
Tel. Brussels (+32) 2-2842971
Tel. Strasbourg (+33) 3-88-17-42-24
E-mail: fbarrett@europarl.eu.int

PRETA Eugenio
Deputy Secretary-General
Tel. Brussels (+32) 2-2844359
Tel. Strasbourg (+33) 3-88-17-46-59
E-mail: epreta@europarl.eu.int

CIUFFREDA Pasquale
Head of Press Office and Internet Site Editor
Tel. Brussels (+32) 2-2841418
Tel. Strasbourg (+33) 3-88-17-35-16
E-mail: pciuffreda@europarl.eu.int

Group of Non-attached Members (NI)

BUGALHO Eduardo
Secretary-General Co-ordinator
Tel. Brussels (+32) 2-2842466
Tel. Strasbourg (+33) 3-88-17-22-97
E-mail: ebugalho@europarl.eu.int

Independence/Democracy Group (IND/DEM)

Brussels office
Tel: (+32) 2-2842111
Fax: (+32) 2-2849144

Strasbourg office
Tel: (+33) 3-88-17-40-91
Fax: (+33) 3-88-17-90-41

VANGRUNDERBEECK Claudine
Co-Secretary-General
Tel. Brussels (+32) 2-2843043
Tel. Strasbourg (+33) 3-88-17-40-69
E-mail: cvangrunderbeeck@europarl.eu.int

VERHEIRSTRAETEN Herman
Co-Secretary-General
Tel. Brussels (+32) 2-2840926
Tel. Strasbourg (+33) 3-88-17-22-62
E-mail: hverheirstraeten@europarl.cu.int

TOWLER Gwain
Press Attaché
Tel. Brussels (+32) 2-2846384
Tel. Strasbourg (+33) 3-88-17-35-49
E-mail: gtowler@europarl.eu.int

Alliance of Liberals and Democrats for Europe (ALDE)

Brussels office
Tel: (+32) 2-2842111
Fax: (+32) 2-2302485

Strasbourg office
Tel: (+33) 3-88-17-40-01
Fax: (+33) 3-88-17-90-44

BEELS Alexander
Secretary-General
Tel. Brussels (+32) 2-2842561
Tel. Strasbourg (+33) 3-88-17-42-16
E-mail: abeels@europarl.eu.int

RINALDI Niccolò
Deputy Secretary-General
Tel. Brussels (+32) 2-2842073
Tel. Strasbourg (+33) 3-88-17-41-70
E-mail: nrinaldi@europarl.eu.int

PAULI François
Deputy Secretary-General
Tel. Brussels (+32) 2-2841415
Tel. Strasbourg (+33) 3-88-17-66-50
E-mail: fpauli@europarl.eu.int

CORLETT Neil
Spokesperson and Head of the Press Office
Tel. Brussels (+32) 2-2842077
Tel. Strasbourg (+33) 3-88-17-41-67
E-mail: ncorlett@europarl.eu.int

EUROPEAN PARLIAMENT: ADMINISTRATION

Rue Wiertz 60, 1047 Brussels, Belgium
Tel: (+32) 2-2842111

Plateau du Kirchberg, 2929 Luxembourg,
Luxembourg

Allée du Printemps, 67070 Strasbourg, France

Tel: (+33) 3-88-17-40-01
URL: www.europarl.eu.int

President's Office

BORRELL FONTELLES Josep
President

VERGER Christine
Director-General
Tel. Brussels (+32) 2-2844661
Tel. Strasbourg (+33) 3-88174323
E-mail: cverger@europarl.eu.int

AGUIRIANO NALDA Luis Marco
Director
Tel. Brussels (+32) 2-2843036
Tel. Strasbourg (+33) 3-88172433
E-mail: maguiriano@europarl.eu.int

TORRELL Ricard
Head of Cabinet
Tel. Brussels (+32) 2-2841129
Tel. Strasbourg (+33) 3-88173127
E-mail: rtorrell@europarl.eu.int

NANCY Jacques
Spokesman for the President
Tel. Brussels (+32) 2-2842485
Tel. Strasbourg (+33) 3-88174082
E-mail: jnancy@europarl.eu.int

KEARNS Helen
Press Attaché
Tel. Brussels (+32) 2-2841650
Tel. Strasbourg (+33) 3-88173125
E-mail: hkearns@europarl.eu.int

SAMPER Ignacio
Adviser
Tel. Brussels (+32) 2-2844895
Tel. Strasbourg (+33) 3-88172427
E-mail: isamper@europarl.eu.int

OBERHAUSER Susanne
Adviser
Tel. Brussels (+32) 2-2843048
Tel. Strasbourg (+33) 3-88173871
E-mail: soberhauser@europarl.eu.int

DRAGONI Doriano
Adviser
Tel. Brussels (+32) 2-2843518
Tel. Strasbourg (+33) 3-88173763
E-mail: ddragoni@europarl.eu.int

COSTELLO Patrick
Adviser
Tel. Brussels (+32) 2-2841137
Tel. Strasbourg (+33) 3-88173999
E-mail: pcostello@europarl.eu.int

SENK Daniela
Adviser
Tel. Brussels (+32) 2-2841033
Tel. Strasbourg (+33) 3-88173124
E-mail: dsenk@europarl.eu.int

MIGO Monika
Adviser
Tel. Brussels (+32) 2-2843035
Tel. Strasbourg (+33) 3-88174412
E-mail: mmigo@europarl.eu.int

FAY Ester
Adviser
Tel. Brussels (+32) 2-2841052
Tel. Strasbourg (+33) 3-88174353
E-mail: efay@europarl.eu.int

Secretariat

PRIESTLEY Julian
Secretary-General
Tel. Brussels (+32) 2-2842613
Tel. Luxembourg (+352) 430022483
Tel. Strasbourg (+33) 3-88174531
E-mail: jpriestley@europarl.eu.int

Directorate-General 1 – Presidency

RØMER Harald
Deputy Secretary-General
Tel. Brussels (+32) 2-2843028
Tel. Luxembourg (+352) 430022553
Tel. Strasbourg (+33) 3-88174884
E-mail: hromer@europarl.eu.int

Directorate-General 2 – Internal Policies of the Union

WELLE Klaus
Director-General
Tel. Brussels (+32) 2-2846242
Tel. Strasbourg (+33) 3-88174831
E-mail: kwelle@europarl.eu.int

Directorate-General 3 – External Policies

NICKEL Dietmar
Director-General
Tel. Brussels (+32) 2-2842759
Tel. Strasbourg (+33) 3-88174079
E-mail: dnickel@europarl.eu.int

Directorate-General 4 – Information

RATTI Francesca
Director-General

Tel. Brussels (+32) 2-2843921
Tel. Luxembourg (+352) 430022188
Tel. Strasbourg (+33) 3-88173913
E-mail: fratti@europarl.eu.int

Directorate-General 5 – Personnel

WILSON Barry
Director-General
Tel. Brussels (+32) 2-2842068
Tel. Luxembourg (+352) 430022068
Tel. Strasbourg (+33) 3-88174307
E-mail: bwilson@europarl.eu.int

Directorate-General 6 – Infrastructure and Interpretation

RIEFFEL Nicolas-Pierre
Director-General
Tel. Brussels (+32) 2-2843493

Tel. Luxembourg (+352) 430022734
Tel. Strasbourg (+33) 3-88174591

Directorate-General 7 – Translation and Publishing

BOKANOWSKI Gérard
Director-General
Tel. Brussels (+32) 2-2842350
Tel. Luxembourg (+352) 430027799
Tel. Strasbourg (+33) 3-88174731
E-mail: gbokanowski@europarl.eu.int

Directorate-General 8 – Finance

VANHAEREN Roger
Director-General
Tel. Brussels (+32) 2-2845100
Tel. Luxembourg (+352) 430025100
Tel. Strasbourg (+33) 3-88175100
E-mail: rvanhaeren@europarl.eu.int

EUROPEAN PARLIAMENT INFORMATION OFFICES

Austria

Kärntner-Ring 5–7, 1010 Vienna, Austria
Tel (+43 1) 51617-0
Fax (+43 1) 5132515
E-mail epwien@europarl.eu.int
URL www.europarl.at

Belgium

Rue Wiertz 60, 1047 Brussels, Belgium
Tel (+32) 2-2842005
Fax (+32) 2-2307555
E-mail epbrussels@europarl.eu.int
URL www.europarl.eu.int/brussels

Cyprus

5A Demophontas Street, PO Box 23440,
    1683 Nicosia, Cyprus
Tel (+357) 22460694
Fax (+357) 22767733
E-mail epnicosia@europarl.eu.int
URL www.europarl.eu.int/nicosia

Czech Republic

Jungmannova 24, 110 00 Prague 1, Czech
    Republic
Tel (+420) 255708208
Fax (+420) 255708200
E-mail eppraha@europarl.eu.int
URL www.evropsky-parlament.cz

Denmark

Christian IX's Gade 2,2, 1111 Copenhagen K,
    Denmark
Tel (+45) 33-14-33-77
Fax (+45) 33-15-08-05
E-mail epkobenhavn@europarl.eu.int
URL www.europarl.dk

Estonia

Swiss House, Roosikrantsi 11, 10119 Tallinn,
    Estonia
Tel (+372) 6676320
Fax (+372) 6676322
E-mail eptallinn@europarl.eu.int

Finland

Pohjoisesplanadi 31, PL 26, 00131 Helsinki,
    Finland
Tel (+358 9) 6220450
Fax (+358 9) 6222610
E-mail ephelsinki@europarl.eu.int
URL www.europarl.fi/ep/index.jsp

France

288 Blvd Saint-Germain, 75341 Paris Cedex
    07, France
Tel (+33) 1-40-63-40-00
Fax (+33) 1-45-51-52-53
E-mail epparis@europarl.eu.int
URL www.europarl.eu.int/paris

2 rue Henri Barbusse, 13241 Marseille, France
Tel (+33) 4-91-91-46-00
Fax (+33) 4-91-90-95-03
E-mail epmarseille@europarl.eu.int
URL www.europarl.eu.int/marseille

Allée du Printemps, Bâtiment Louis Weiss, BP
    1024 / F, 67070 Strasbourg, France
Tel (+33) 3-88-17-40-01
Fax (+33) 3-88-17-51-84
E-mail epstrasbourg@europarl.eu.int

Germany

Unter den Linden 78, 10117 Berlin, Germany
Tel (+49 30) 2280-1000
Fax (+49 30) 2280-1111
E-mail epberlin@europarl.eu.int
URL www.europarl.de

Erhardtstr. 27, 80331 Munich, Germany
Tel (+49 89) 202 0879-0
Fax (+49 89) 202 0879-73
E-mail epmuenchen@europarl.eu.int
URL www.europarl.de

Greece

Leof. Amalias 8, 105 57 Athens, Greece
Tel (+30) 210-3278900
Fax (+30) 210-3311540
E-mail epathinai@europarl.eu.int
URL www.europarl.gr

Hungary

Országház, Kossuth Lajos tér 1–3,
    1357 Budapest, Hungary
Tel (+36 1) 4416602
Fax (+36 1) 4416603
E-mail epbudapest@europarl.eu.int
URL www.euparl.hu

Ireland

European Union House, 43 Molesworth Street,
    Dublin 2, Ireland
Tel (+353 1) 6057900
Fax (+353 1) 6057999
E-mail epdublin@europarl.eu.int
URL www.europarl.ie

Italy

Corso Magenta 59, 20123 Milan, Italy
Tel (+39) 02-4344171
Fax (+39) 02-434417500
E-mail epmilano@europarl.eu.int

Via IV Novembre 149, 00187 Rome, Italy
Tel (+39) 06-699501
Fax (+39) 06-69950200
E-mail eproma@europarl.eu.int
URL www.europarl.it

Latvia

Aspazijas Blvd 28, 1050 Riga, Latvia
Tel (+371) 7085460
Fax (+371) 7085470
E-mail epriga@europarl.eu.int
URL www.europarl.lv

Lithuania

Naugarduko 10, 01141 Vilnius, Lithuania
Tel (+370 521) 20766
Fax (+370 526) 19828
E-mail epvilnius@europarl.eu.int

Luxembourg

Bâtiment Robert Schuman, Place de l'Europe,
    2929 Luxembourg, Luxembourg
Tel (+352) 430022597
Fax (+352) 430022457
E-mail epluxembourg@europarl.eu.int

Malta

280 Republic Street, Valletta VLT 04, Malta
Tel (+356) 21235075
Fax (+356) 21227580
E-mail epvalletta@europarl.eu.int
URL www.europarl.eu.int/valletta

Netherlands

Korte Vijverberg 6, 2513 AB The Hague,
    Netherlands
Tel (+31 70) 3624941
Fax (+31 70) 3647001
E-mail epdenhaag@europarl.eu.int
URL www.europeesparlement.nl

Poland

Biuro informacyjne Parlamentu Europejskiego,
    Warszawskie Centrum Finansowe, ul. Emilii
    Plater 53, 19 pitro, 00-113 Warsaw, Poland
Tel (+48 22) 5206655
Fax (+48 22) 5206659
E-mail epwarszawa@europarl.eu.int
URL www.europarl.eu.int/warszawa

Portugal

Centro Europeu Jean Monnet, Largo Jean
    Monnet 1–6, 1269-070 Lisbon, Portugal
Tel (+351) 213504900
Fax (+351) 213540004
E-mail eplisboa@europarl.eu.int
URL www.parleurop.pt

Slovakia

Informacná kancelária Európskeho parlamentu,
    Palisády 29, 811 06 Bratislava, Slovakia
Tel (+421 2) 59203297
Fax (+421 2) 54648013
E-mail epbratislava@europarl.eu.int

Slovenia

Trg Republike 3, 1000 Ljubljana, Slovenia
Tel (+386 1) 4269887
Fax (+386 1) 4269906
E-mail epljubljana@europarl.eu.int
URL www.europarl.si

Spain

Paseo de la Castellana 46, 28046 Madrid, Spain
Tel (+34) 91-4364747
Fax (+34) 91-5771365
E-mail epmadrid@europarl.eu.int
URL www.europarl.es

Passeig de Gràcia 90 (1a planta),
    08008 Barcelona, Spain
Tel (+34) 93-2722044
Fax (+34) 93-2722045
E-mail epbarcelona@europarl.eu.int

Sweden

Nybrogatan 11, 3 tr., 114 39 Stockholm,
    Sweden
Tel (+46 8) 56-24-44-55
E-mail info@europarl.se
URL www.europarl.se

United Kingdom

2 Queen Anne's Gate, London SW1H 9AA,
    United Kingdom
Tel (+44 20) 7227-4300
E-mail eplondon@europarl.eu.int
URL www.europarl.org.uk

The Tun, 4 Jackson's Entry, Holyrood Road,
    Edinburgh EH8 8PJ, United Kingdom
Tel (+44 131) 557-7866
Fax (+44 131) 557-4977
E-mail epedinburgh@europarl.eu.int
URL www.europarl.org.uk/office/
    ScotlandOfficeMain.htm

THE COUNCIL OF THE EUROPEAN UNION

Rue de la Loi 175, 1048 Brussels, Belgium
Tel. (+32) 2-2856111
Fax (+32) 2-2857397
E-mail public.info@consilium.eu.int
URL ue.eu.int

The Council of the European Union is the main decision-making body of the European Union. Its functions include: passing laws, often legislating jointly with the European Parliament, and in principle on the basis of proposals formulated by the European Commission; co-ordinating the broad economic policies of the member states; defining and implementing the EU's common foreign and security policy, based on guidelines set by the European Council; concluding, on behalf of the Community and the Union, international agreements between the EU and one or more states or international organizations; and co-ordinating the actions of member states and adopting measures in the area of police and judicial co-operation in criminal matters. The Council and the European Parliament together constitute the budgetary authority that adopts the Community's budget.

The Council's acts can take the form of regulations, directives, decisions, common actions or common positions, recommendations or opinions. The Council can also adopt conclusions, declarations or resolutions.

The presidency of the Council is held for six months by each Member State in rotation, and voting takes place, on the basis of a simple majority, a qualified majority or unanimity, depending on the type of case, as defined by the Treaties. The distribution of votes among the Member States is as follows: France, Germany, Italy and the United Kingdom have 29 votes each; Poland and Spain have 27 votes each; the Netherlands has 13 votes; Belgium, the Czech Republic, Greece, Hungary and Portugal have 12 votes each; Austria and Sweden have 10 votes each; Denmark, Finland, Ireland, Lithuania and Slovakia have 7 votes each; Cyprus, Estonia, Latvia, Luxembourg and Slovenia have 4 votes each; and Malta has 3 votes.

Meetings in the Council of the European Union are attended by the appropriate ministers from the governments of the Member States, depending on the subject under consideration.

The Member States' Permanent Representatives usually meet each week in a committee known as the Permanent Representatives' Committee (Coreper). That Committee is divided into two parts, one being composed of the Permanent Representatives and the other of their Deputies. Coreper is responsible for preparing the Council's proceedings.

COUNCIL OF THE EUROPEAN UNION: ADMINISTRATION

Rue de la Loi 175, 1048 Brussels, Belgium
Tel: (+32) 2-2856111
Fax: (+32) 2-2857397
E-mail: public.info@consilium.eu.int
URL: http://ue.eu.int

Secretariat-General

SOLANA Javier
Secretary-General and High Representative
Tel. (+32) 2-2855660

DE BOISSEAU Javier
Deputy Secretary-General
Tel. (+32) 2-2856215

Secretary-General's Private Office

SCHIAVO Leonardo
Head of Cabinet of the Secretary-General /
  High Representative / Director
Tel. (+32) 2-2855575

SERRANO DE HARO Pedro Antonio
Deputy Head of Cabinet of the Secretary-
  General / High Representative (CFSP, liaison
  with the PPEWU)
Tel. (+32) 2-2855572

DE VRIES Gijs
Co-ordinator for the fight against terrorism
Tel. (+32) 2-2859998

GIANNELLA Annalisa
Personal Representative of the Secretary-
  General / High Representative / Director
Tel. (+32) 2-2858044

GALLOWAY David
Head of Cabinet of the Deputy Secretary-
  General / Director
Tel. (+32) 2-2856194

REIDERMANN Paul
Adviser
Tel. (+32) 2-2858704

KAESSNER Ralph
Adviser
Tel. (+32) 2-2859422

Departments Attached to the Secretary-General / High Representative

PPEWU – Policy Planning and Early Warning Unit

HEUSGEN Christoph
Director
Tel. (+32) 2-2855430

TASK FORCE: EUROPEAN SECURITY AND
DEFENCE POLICY (ESDP)

WEISSERTH Hans Bernard
Tel. (+32) 2-2855848

TASK FORCE: MEDITERRANEAN / BARCELONA –
MIDDLE EAST

CHARLAT Pascal
Head of Unit
Tel. (+32) 2-2855324

TASK FORCE 'AFRICA'

VERVAEKE Koen
Tel. (+32) 2-2859734

TASK FORCE 'EUROPE (NEW NEIGHBOURS),
CENTRAL ASIA, TRANSATLANTIC RELATIONS'

VAN RIJ Cornelis
Head of Unit
Tel. (+32) 2-2855328

TASK FORCE: ASIA

KOZLOWSKI Tomasz
Tel. (+32) 2-2353680

TASK FORCE: WESTERN BALKANS

LEHNE Stefan
Director
Tel. (+32) 2-2855327

TASK FORCE 'UNITED NATIONS, LATIN AMERICA'

PASCUAL DE LA PARTE Nicolás
Tel. (+32) 2-2855322

TASK FORCE 'HORIZONTAL SECURITY MATTERS'

PAPACONSTANTINOU Andreas
Tel. (+32) 2-2855840

Military Staff

PERRUCHE Jean-Paul
Army Corps General / Director-General of the
  European Union Military Staff
Tel. (+32) 2-2855990

Joint Situation Centre of the European Union

SHAPCOTT William
Director
Tel. (+32) 2-2855824

Communications Centre (COMCEN), Consular Affairs

PORZIO Giorgio
Head of Unit
Tel. (+32) 2-2856102

Departments Attached to the Secretary-General / High Representative and to the Deputy Secretary-General

Directorate for General Political Questions

KELLER-NOËLLET Jacques
Deputy Director-General
Tel. (+32) 2-2857417

GENERAL POLITICAL QUESTIONS/MEETINGS

ZBYSZEWSKI Georges
Head of Unit
Tel. (+32) 2-2857659

Security Office

LEGEIN Alexandro
Head of Unit
Tel. (+32) 2-2858519

Internal Audit

VAN HÖVELL François
Head of Unit
Tel. (+32) 2-2857268

Data Protection

VERNHES Pierre
Tel. (+32) 2-2859009

Infosec (Information Systems Security)

MANENTI Bartolomeo
Head of Unit
Tel. (+32) 2-2857645

Prevention

DHAEYER Guy
Tel. (+32) 2-2855456

Department for General Administrative Affairs

LEPOIVRE Marc
Director-General
Tel. (+32) 2-2858267

Legal Service

PIRIS Jean-Claude
Director-General, Legal Adviser to the Council
Tel. (+32) 2-2856227

BLANCHET Thérèse
Assistant to the Director-General
Tel. (+32) 2-2858775

Team I – Internal Market, Industry, Telecommunications, Tourism, Energy, Civil Protection, Research, Trans-European Networks, Transport, Social Affairs, Culture, Education, Youth, Regional Policy, Environment, Harmonization of Food Legislation, Consumer Protection, Health, Competition Rules/Public Procurement

JACQUÉ Jean-Paul
Director
Tel. (+32) 2-2856226

Team II – Agriculture, Fisheries, Economic and Monetary Union (EMU), Taxation, Free Movement of Capital, Structural Funds and Generally All Matters for the Ecofin Council Prepared by Coreper II

MIDDLETON Timothy
Director
Tel. (+32) 2-2857919

Team III – External Relations (including CFSP, Development Co-operation, ACP, All Questions Relating to International Agreements and Relations with International Organizations) and Enlargement

GOSALBO BONO Ricardo
Director
Tel. (+32) 2-2856259

Team IV – Institutional/Budgetary Questions

MAGANZA Giorgio
Director
Tel. (+32) 2-2857950

Team V – Justice and Home Affairs

SCHUTTE Julian
Director
Tel. (+32) 2-2856229

Interinstitutional Relations

LOPES-SABINO Amadeu
Director
Tel. (+32) 2-2857109

Research and Documentation Unit

MAVRAKOS Christos
Head of Unit
Tel. (+32) 2-2857190

Legal/Linguistic Experts

GALLAS Tito
Head of Lawyer-Linguists Group / Head of Unit
Tel. (+32) 2-2857474

Directorate-General A – Personnel and Administration

GRIFFO Vittorio
Director-General
Tel. (+32) 2-2856540

GROSJEAN Gérard
Special Adviser to the Director-General / Head of Unit
Tel. (+32) 2-2857576

HELLWIG Dirk
Assistant to the Director-General
Tel. (+32) 2-2856958

Unit for Implementation of New Staff Regulations, and Communication Policy

KRAVCENKO Evija
Tel. (+32) 2-2859769

Directorate 1A – Human Resources

SCHILDERS Dirk
Director
Tel. (+32) 2-2859989

Directorate 1B – Personnel and Administration

RADAUER Leopold
Director
Tel. (+32) 2-2858915

Directorate 2 – Conferences, Organization, Infrastructures, Information Technology

ELLIS Stephen
Director
Tel. (+32) 2-2857624

Directorate 3 – Translation and Document Production

LACERDA Margarida
Director (together with her duties in Central Co-ordination)
Tel. (+32) 2-2857205

Directorate 4 – Finances

MARIGUESA José Antonio
Tel. (+32) 2-2856058

Directorate-General B – Agriculture, Fisheries

BOIXAREU CARRERA Ángel
Director-General
Tel. (+32) 2-2856234

Directorate I – Market Organizations, Veterinary and Zootechnical Questions, including International Aspects

MAZZASCHI Luigi
Director
Tel. (+32) 2-2857571

Directorate 2 – Agricultural Structures, Agrimonetary and Agrofinancial Questions, Phytosanitary, Organic Products

MATUT ARCHANCO Francisco Javier
Director
Tel. (+32) 2-2856626

Directorate 3 – Fisheries, including External Relations

WALL Frank
Director
Tel. (+32) 2-2858055

Directorate-General C – Internal Market, Competitiveness, Industry, Research, Energy, Transport, Information Society

GRETSCHMANN Klaus
Director-General
Tel. (+32) 2-2855550

Directorate 1 – Internal Market, Competition, Customs Union

OLANDER Anders
Director
Tel. (+32) 2-2856392

Directorate 2 – Industry, Research, Energy, Atomic Questions

HUMPHREYS ZWART Barbara
Director
Tel. (+32) 2-2857215

Directorate 3 – Transport and Information Society

ALTEKÖSTER Elisabeth
Director
Tel. (+32) 2-2859770

Directorate-General E – External Economic Relations, Common Foreign and Security Policy

COOPER Robert
Director-General
Tel. (+32) 2-2858522

VIKAS Anastassios
Deputy Director-General (Common Foreign and Security Policy; Regional Affairs)
Tel. (+32) 2-2856825

FEITH Pieter Cornelis
Deputy Director-General (European Security and Defence Policy)
Tel. (+32) 2-2855220

STIFANI Elda
Deputy Director-General (United Nations Liaison Office in New York)
Tel. (+1) (212) 2928608

Co-ordination Unit

D'ANIELLO Cesira
Head of Unit
Tel. (+32) 2-2858253

Directorate 1 – Enlargement

KATHARIOS Christos
Head of Unit
Tel. (+32) 2-2857567

Directorate 2 – Development and ACP; Multilateral Economic Affairs and non-EU Western Europe

CULLEY Paul
Tel. (+32) 2-2856197

Directorate 4 – Transatlantic Relations, United Nations and Human Rights

CLOOS Jim
Director
Tel. (+32) 2-2859330

Directorate 5 – Mediterranean Basin, Middle East, Africa, Asia

Director: (vacant).

Directorate 6 – Western Balkans Region, Eastern Europe and Central Asia

LEHNE Stefan
Director
Tel. (+32) 2-2855327

Directorate 8 – Defence Aspects

ARNOULD Claude-France
Director
Tel. (+32) 2-2856185

Directorate 9 – Civilian Crisis Management and Co-ordination

MATTHIESSEN Michael
Director
Tel. (+32) 2-2855321

Office of the Personal Representative of the High Representative for Matters of Non-Proliferation

GIANNELLA Annalisa
Personal Representative of the Secretary-
General / High Representative
Tel. (+32) 2-2858044

Geneva – Office for Liaison with the European Office of the United Nations

BRODIN Jacques
Director / Head of the Liaison Office
Tel. (+41) 22-9197408

New York – United Nations Liaison Office

STIFANI Elda
Deputy Director-General / Head of the Liaison
Office
Tel. (+1 212) 292-8608

Directorate-General F – Press, Communication, Protocol

BRUNMAYR Hans
Director-General / Head of Protocol
Tel. (+32) 2-2859197

Unit 1 – Press

MARRO Dominique-George
Head of Unit
Tel. (+32) 2-2856423

Spokesperson to the Secretary-General / High Representative for Common Foreign and Security Policy

GALLACH Cristina
Head of Unit (attached to the Secretary-
General / High Representative)
Tel. (+32) 2-2856467
Fax: (+32) 2-2855694

Unit 2 – Communication

BIELEK Peter
Head of Unit
Tel. (+32) 2-2858783
Fax: (+32) 2-2855333

Unit 3 – Registry, Archives, Libraries

JIMÉNEZ FRAILE Ramón
Head of Unit
Tel. (+32) 2-2856176
Fax: (+32) 2-2855333

Budget

DAIDONE Gerda
Tel. (+32) 2-2857168

Protocol

BERTACCA Maria Cristina
Tel. (+32) 2-2856438

Directorate-General G – Economic and Social Affairs

KORKMAN Sixten
Director
Tel. (+32) 2-2856213

Co-ordination, Horizontal Questions and Management

ALMEIDA Alexandra
Tel. (+32) 2-2856313

Directorate 1 – Economic Affairs

BLIZKOVSKY Petr
Director
Tel. (+32) 2-2855130

Directorate 2 – Social and Regional Affairs

Director: (vacant).

Directorate 3 – Budget and Financial Regulations

BRYAN-KINNS Merrick
Director
Tel. (+32) 2-2856583

Directorate-General H – Justice and Home Affairs

BIZJAK Ivan
Director-General
Tel. (+32) 2-2858505

Directorate 1 – Asylum and Immigration

GONZÁLEZ SÁNCHEZ Enrique
Director
Tel. (+32) 2-2856546

Directorate 2 – Police, Customs and Judicial Co-operation

DE KERCHOVE D'OUSSELGHEM Gilles
Director
Tel. (+32) 2-2857933

Directorate-General I — Protection of the Environment and Consumers, Civil Protection, Health, Foodstuffs, Education, Youth, Culture, Audiovisual

NIBLAEUS Kerstin
Tel. (+32) 2-2857421

Directorate 1 – Protection of the Environment, Civil Protection

EHMKE GENDRON Sabine
Tel. (+32) 2-2858569

Directorate 2 – Education and Youth, Culture, Audiovisual, Health, Consumer Protection, Food Products

SZABÓ Sandor
Director
Tel. (+32) 2-2858841

THE COUNCIL'S COMMITTEES AND WORKING PARTIES

The Council is assisted in its work by a series of committees and working parties, the most important being the Permanent Representatives Committee (COREPER) which prepares the Council's work and carries out any instructions given to it by the Council. The Committee meets in two parts – Deputy Permanent Representatives (Part I) and Ambassadors (Part II).

Permanent Representatives Committee – Part 1 (COREPER I)

TUTS Geneviève
Deputy Permanent Representative of Belgium

Rond-Point Schuman 6, 1040 Brussels, Belgium
Tel. (+32) 2-2332111
Fax: (+32) 2-2311075
E-mail: belrep@belgoeurop.diplobel.fed.be

STAVINOHA Luděk
Minister Counsellor
Deputy Permanent Representative of the Czech Republic
Rue Caroly 15, 1050 Brussels, Belgium
Tel. (+32) 2-2130110
Fax: (+32) 2-5137154
E-mail: eu.brussels@embassy.mzv.cz

TRANHOLM-MIKKELSEN Jeppe
Ambassador

Deputy Permanent Representative of Denmark
Rue d'Arlon 73, 1040 Brussels, Belgium
Tel. (+32) 2-2330811
Fax: (+32) 2-2309384
E-mail: brurep@um.dk

WITT Peter
Ambassador
Deputy Permanent Representative of Germany
Rue Jacques de Lalaing 19–21, 1040 Brussels,
    Belgium
Tel. (+32) 2-2381811
Fax: (+32) 2-2381978
E-mail: eurogerma@brueeur.auswaertiges
    -amt.de

RAHUOJA Margus
Minister
Deputy Permanent Representative of Estonia
Rue Guimard 11/13, 1040 Brussels, Belgium
Tel. (+32) 2-2273910
Fax: (+32) 2-2273925
E-mail: mission@estemb.be

RALLIS Dimitrios
Ambassador Extraordinary and
    Plenipotentiary
Deputy Permanent Representative of Greece
Rue Montoyer 25, 1000 Brussels, Belgium
Tel. (+32) 2-5515601
Fax: (+32) 2-5515602
E-mail: mea.bruxelles@rp-grece.be

GONZÁLEZ-ALLER JURADO Cristóbal
Ambassador
Deputy Permanent Representative of Spain
Boulevard du Régent 52–54, 1000 Brussels,
    Belgium
Tel. (+32) 2-5098611
Fax: (+32) 2-5111023
E-mail: reper.reper@mae.es

MASSET Christian
Minister Plenipotentiary
Deputy Permanent Representative of France
Place de Louvain 14, 1000 Brussels, Belgium
Tel. (+32) 2-2298211
Fax: (+32) 2-2298282
E-mail: bruxelles-dfra@diplomatie.gouv.fr

GUNNING Peter
Minister Plenipotentiary
Deputy Permanent Representative of Ireland
Rue Froissart 89–93, 1040 Brussels, Belgium
Tel. (+32) 2-2308580
Fax: (+32) 2-2303203
E-mail: irlprb@iveagh.gov.ie

PIGNATTI MORANO DI CUSTOZA
    Alessandro
Minister Plenipotentiary
Deputy Permanent Representative of Italy
Rue du Marteau 9, 1000 Brussels, Belgium
Tel. (+32) 2-2200411
Fax: (+32) 2-2193449
E-mail: rp@rpue.it

KORNELIOU Kornelios
First Counsellor
Deputy Permanent Representative of Cyprus
Square Ambiorix 2, 1000 Brussels, Belgium
Tel. (+32) 2-7353510
Fax: (+32) 2-7354552
E-mail: be.cydelegation.eu@mfa.gov.cy

LICE-LICITE Lelde
Ambassador
Deputy Permanent Representative of Latvia
Rue d'Arlon 30–41, 1000 Brussels, Belgium
Tel. (+32) 2-2820360
Fax: (+32) 2-2820369
E-mail: missioneu@mfa.gov.lv

ŠVEDAS Romas
Minister Plenipotentiary
Deputy Permanent Representative of Lithuania
Rue Belliard 41–43, 1040 Brussels, Belgium
Tel. (+32) 2-7710140
Fax: (+32) 2-7714597
E-mail: office@lt-mission-eu.be

BRAUN Christian
Deputy Permanent Representative of
    Luxembourg
President of the Permanent Representatives
    Committee (Part I)
Avenue de Cortenbergh 75, 1000 Brussels,
    Belgium
Tel. (+32) 2-7352060
Fax: (+32) 2-7361429
E-mail: secretariat@rpue.etat.lu

DIENES-OEHM Egon
Ambassador
Deputy Permanent Representative of Hungary
Rue de Trèves 92–98, 1040 Brussels, Belgium
Tel. (+32) 2-2341200
Fax: (+32) 2-2340784
E-mail: sec@hunrep.be

CUTAJAR Theresa
Deputy Permanent Representative of Malta

Rue Belliard 65–67, 1040 Brussels, Belgium
Tel. (+32) 2-3430195
Fax: (+32) 2-3430106
E-mail: maltarep@gov.mt

SCHUWER H. J. J.
Minister Plenipotentiary
Deputy Permanent Representative of the
  Netherlands
Avenue Hermann Debroux 48, 1160 Brussels,
  Belgium
Tel. (+32) 2-6791511
Fax: (+32) 2-6791775
E-mail: bre@minbuza.nl

GRAHAMMER Walter
Minister
Deputy Permanent Representative of Austria
Avenue de Cortenbergh 30, 1040 Brussels,
  Belgium
Tel. (+32) 2-2345122
Fax: (+32) 2-2356122
E-mail: bruessel-ov@bmaa.gv.at

SYNOWIEC Ewa
Minister Counsellor
Deputy Permanent Representative of Poland
Avenue de Tervuren 282–284, 1150 Brussels,
  Belgium
Tel. (+32) 2-7777220
Fax: (+32) 2-7777297
E-mail: mail@pol-mission-eu.be

FEZAS VITAL Domingos
Minister Plenipotentiary
Deputy Permanent Representative of Portugal
Avenue de Cortenbergh 12–22, 1040 Brussels,
  Belgium
Tel. (+32) 2-2864211
Fax: (+32) 2-2310026
E-mail: reper@reper-portugal.be

JAGER Marjeta
Deputy Permanent Representative of Slovenia
Avenue Marnix 30, 1000 Brussels, Belgium
Tel. (+32) 2-5124466
Fax: (+32) 2-5120997
E-mail: missionbruxelles@gov.si

NOCIAR Juraj
Counsellor
Deputy Permanent Representative of Slovakia
Avenue de Cortenbergh 79, 1000 Brussels,
  Belgium
Tel. (+32) 2-7436811
Fax: (+32) 2-7436888
E-mail: slovakmission@pmsreu.be

VASKUNLAHTI Nina
Minister
Deputy Permanent Representative of Finland
Rue de Trèves 100, 1040 Brussels, Belgium
Tel. (+32) 2-2878411
Fax: (+32) 2-2878400
E-mail: to pattern firstname.lastname@formin.fi

HJELT AF TROLLE Ingrid
Minister Plenipotentiary
Deputy Permanent Representative of Sweden
Square de Meeûs 30, 1000 Brussels, Belgium
Tel. (+32) 2-2895611
Fax: (+32) 2-2895600
E-mail: representationen.bryssel@
  foreign.ministry.se

LAMBERT Anne
Deputy Permanent Representative of the United
  Kingdom
Avenue d'Auderghem 10, 1040 Brussels,
  Belgium
Tel. (+32) 2-2878211
Fax: (+32) 2-2878398
E-mail: ukrep@fco.gov.uk

Permanent Representatives Committee
– Part 2
(COREPER II)

DE BOCK Jan
Ambassador Extraordinary and
  Plenipotentiary
Permanent Representative of Belgium
Rond-Point Schuman 6, 1040 Brussels,
  Belgium
Tel. (+32) 2-2332111
Fax: (+32) 2-2311075
E-mail: belrep@belgoeurop.diplobel.fed.be

KOHOUT Jan
Ambassador Extraordinary and
  Plenipotentiary
Permanent Representative of the Czech
  Republic
Rue Caroly 15, 1050 Brussels, Belgium
Tel. (+32) 2-2130110
Fax: (+32) 2-5137154
E-mail: eu.brussels@embassy.mzv.cz

GRUBE Klaus
Ambassador Extraordinary and
  Plenipotentiary
Permanent Representative of Denmark

Rue d'Arlon 73, 1040 Brussels, Belgium
Tel. (+32) 2-2330811
Fax: (+32) 2-2309384
E-mail: brurep@um.dk

SCHÖNFELDER Wilhelm
Ambassador Extraordinary and
  Plenipotentiary
Permanent Representative of Germany
Rue Jacques de Lalaing 21–21, 1040 Brussels,
  Belgium
Tel. (+32) 2-2381811
Fax: (+32) 2-2381978
E-mail: eurogerma@
  brueeur.auswaertiges-amt.de

REINART Väinto
Ambassador Extraordinary and
  Plenipotentiary
Permanent Representative of Estonia
Rue Guimard 11/13, 1040 Brussels, Belgium
Tel. (+32) 2-2273910
Fax: (+32) 2-2273925
E-mail: mission@estemb.be

KASKARELIS Vassilis
Ambassador Extraordinary and
  Plenipotentiary
Permanent Representative of Greece
Rue Montoyer 25, 1000 Brussels, Belgium
Tel. (+32) 2-5515637
Fax: (+32) 2-5126950
E-mail: mea.bruxelles@rp-grece.be

BASTARRECHE SAGÜES Carlos
Ambassador Extraordinary and
  Plenipotentiary
Permanent Representative of Spain
Boulevard du Régent 52–54, 1000 Brussels,
  Belgium
Tel. (+32) 2-5098611
Fax: (+32) 2-5111023
E-mail: reper.reper@mae.es

SELLAL Pierre
Ambassador Extraordinary and
  Plenipotentiary
Permanent Representative of France
Place de Louvain 14, 1000 Brussels, Belgium
Tel. (+32) 2-2298211
Fax: (+32) 2-2298282
E-mail: bruxelles-dfra@diplomatie.gov.fr
URL: http://rpfrance-ue.org

ANDERSON Anne
Ambassador Extraordinary and
  Plenipotentiary

Permanent Representative of Ireland
Rue Froissart 89–93, 1040 Brussels, Belgium
Tel. (+32) 2-2308580
Fax: (+32) 2-2303203
E-mail: irlprb@iveagh.gov.ie

CANGELOSI Rocco Antonio
Ambassador Extraordinary and
  Plenipotentiary
Permanent Representative of Italy
Rue du Marteau 9, 1000 Brussels, Belgium
Tel. (+32) 2-2200411
Fax: (+32) 2-2193449
E-mail: rp@rpue.it

EMILIOU Nicholas
Ambassador Extraordinary and
  Plenipotentiary
Permanent Representative of Cyprus
Square Ambiorix 2, 1000 Brussels, Belgium
Tel. (+32) 2-7353510
Fax: (+32) 2-7354552
E-mail: be.cydelegation.eu@mfa.gov.cy

STIPRAIS Eduards
Ambassador Extraordinary and
  Plenipotentiary
Permanent Representative of Latvia
Rue d'Arlon 39–41, Brussels, Belgium
Tel. (+32) 2-2820360
Fax: (+32) 2-2820369
E-mail: missioneu@mfa.gov.lv

JUSYS Oskaras
Ambassador Extraordinary and
  Plenipotentiary
Permanent Representative of Lithuania
Rue Belliard 41–43, 1040 Brussels, Belgium
Tel. (+32) 2-7710140
Fax: (+32) 2-7714597
E-mail: office@lt-mission-eu.be

SCHOMMER Martine
Ambassador Extraordinary and
  Plenipotentiary
Permanent Representative of Luxembourg
President of the Permanent Representatives
  Committee (Part 2)
Avenue de Cortenbergh 75, 1000 Brussels,
  Belgium
Tel. (+32) 2-7352060
Fax: (+32) 2-7361429
E-mail: secretariat@rpue.etat.lu

KISS Tibor
Ambassador Extraordinary and
  Plenipotentiary

Permanent Representative of Hungary
Rue de Trèves 92–98, 1040 Brussels, Belgium
Tel. (+32) 2-2341200
Fax: (+32) 2-2340784
E-mail: sec@hunrep.be

CACHIA CARUANA Richard
Ambassador Extraordinary and
Plenipotentiary
Permanent Representative of Malta
Rue Belliard 65–67, 1040 Brussels, Belgium
Tel. (+32) 2-3430195
Fax: (+32) 2-3430106
E-mail: maltarep@gov.mt

DE BRUIJN T. J. A. M.
Ambassador Extraordinary and
Plenipotentiary
Permanent Representative of the Netherlands
Avenue Hermann Debroux 48, 1160 Brussels,
Belgium
Tel. (+32) 2-6791511
Fax: (+32) 2-6791775
E-mail: bre@minbuza.nl

WOSCHNAGG Gregor
Ambassador Extraordinary and
Plenipotentiary
Permanent Representative of Austria
Avenue de Cortenbergh 30, 1040 Brussels,
Belgium
Tel. (+32) 2-2345100
Fax: (+32) 2-2345300
E-mail: bruessel-ov@bmaa.gv.at

GRELA Marek
Ambassador Extraordinary and
Plenipotentiary
Permanent Representative of Poland
Avenue de Tervuren 282–284, 1150 Brussels,
Belgium
Tel. (+32) 2-7777220
Fax: (+32) 2-7777297
E-mail: mail@pol-mission-eu.be

MENDONÇA E MOURA Álvaro
Ambassador Extraordinary and
Plenipotentiary
Permanent Representative of Portugal
Avenue de Cortenbergh 12/22, 1040 Brussels,
Belgium
Tel. (+32) 2-2864211
Fax: (+32) 2-2310026
E-mail: reper@reper-portugal.be

ŠTOKELJ Ciril
Ambassador Extraordinary and
Plenipotentiary
Permanent Representative of Slovenia
Avenue Marnix 30, 1000 Brussels, Belgium
Tel. (+32) 2-5124466
Fax: (+32) 2-5120997
E-mail: missionbruxelles@gov.si

ŠEFČOVIČ Maroš
Ambassador Extraordinary and
Plenipotentiary
Permanent Representative of Slovakia
Avenue de Cortenbergh 79, 1000 Brussels,
Belgium
Tel. (+32) 2-7436811
Fax: (+32) 2-7436888
E-mail: slovakmission@pmsreu.be

KOSONEN Eikka
Ambassador Extraordinary and
Plenipotentiary
Permanent Representative of Finland
Rue de Trèves 100, 1040 Brussels, Belgium
Tel. (+32) 2-2878411
Fax: (+32) 2-2878400
E-mail: to pattern firstname.lastname@
formin.fi

PETERSSON Sven-Olof
Ambassador Extraordinary and
Plenipotentiary
Permanent Representative of Sweden
Square de Meeûs 30, 1000 Brussels, Belgium
Tel. (+32) 2-2895611
Fax: (+32) 2-2895600
E-mail: representationen.bryssel@
foreign.ministry.se

GRANT CMG John
Ambassador Extraordinary and
Plenipotentiary
Permanent Representative of the United
Kingdom
Avenue d'Auderghem 10, 1040 Brussels,
Belgium
Tel. (+32) 2-2878211
Fax: (+32) 2-2878398
E-mail: ukrep@fco.gov.uk

THE COURT OF JUSTICE AND THE COURT OF FIRST INSTANCE

Court of Justice of the European Communities, 2925 Luxembourg, Luxembourg
Tel (+352) 4303-1
Fax (+352) 4303-2600
Fax – Press and Information Team (+352) 4303-2500
URL http://curia.eu.int

Cases brought by Member States, the EU institutions, private individuals or companies may be referred to the Court of Justice. The Court of Justice operated alone until 1989. The Court of First Instance was then added so as to improve the legal protection of the EU's citizens and to enable the Court of Justice to concentrate its efforts on its primary task of ensuring that Community law is interpreted uniformly, working closely with national judges through the preliminary ruling procedure.

The Court of First Instance is empowered to deal with all actions brought by individuals and companies against EU institutions and bodies. The judgments of the Court of First Instance may go to further appeal to the Court of Justice, but the appeal is limited to points of law.

Having no political message to convey, the Court of Justice's basic information role is to bring to the public's knowledge the caselaw created via its judgments. It also informs EU citizens about its organization, powers and procedures. The Court is made up of 25 judges and is assisted by 8 advocates-general. The members of these bodies are appointed for a renewable six-year term of office by common agreement of the Member States' governments. The judges select one of their number to be President of the Court for a renewable term of three years. The President directs the work of the Court and presides at hearings and deliberations. The advocates-general assist the Court in its task. They deliver, in open court and with complete impartiality and independence, opinions on the cases brought before the Court.

The Court of First Instance is composed of 25 judges appointed by the governments of the Member States to hold office for a renewable term of six years. The Members of the Court of First Instance select one of their number as President. There are no permanent advocates-general in the Court of First Instance. The duties of advocate-general are performed, in a limited number of cases, by one of the judges.

The Court of Justice may sit in plenary session or in chambers of three or five judges. It sits in plenary session when a Member State or a Community institution that is a party to the proceedings so requests, or in particularly complex or important cases. Other cases are heard by a chamber. The Court of First Instance sits in chambers of three or five judges. It too may sit in plenary session in certain particularly important cases.

The Court of Justice does not have any external information offices and its business takes place at the Court's seat in Luxembourg. Information about the Court can be obtained via Commission offices in the Member States. Some documents may also be ordered from the Office for Official Publications of the European Communities or its sales offices.

THE EUROPEAN ECONOMIC AND SOCIAL COMMITTEE

Rue Belliard 99, 1040 Brussels, Belgium
Tel. (+32) 2-5469011
Fax (+32) 2-5134893
URL www.esc.eu.int

Made up of 317 representatives drawn from economic and social interest groups in Europe, the European Economic and Social Committee (EESC) acts in an advisory capacity in the EU decision-making process. The representatives are divided into three groups – Employers (I), Employees (II) and Various Interests (III) – and membership is distributed as follows among the respective Member States: France, Germany, Italy and the United Kingdom have 24 members each; Poland and Spain have 21 members; Austria, Belgium, the Czech Republic, Greece, Hungary, the Netherlands, Portugal and Sweden have 12 members; Denmark, Finland, Ireland, Lithuania and Slovakia have 9 members; Estonia, Latvia and Slovenia have 7 members; Cyprus and Luxembourg have 6 members; and Malta has 5 members. Members are nominated by national governments and appointed by the Council of the European Union for a renewable four-year term.

Employers' Group (Group I). The Employers' Group (Group I) has members from private and public sectors of industry, chambers of commerce, wholesale and retail trade, banking and insurance, transport and agriculture.

Group I policy in general reflects the opinion of European industrial federations in supporting the development of a European Union of free market economies with freedom of trade and movement within the internal market, in the belief that this is the best road to growth, competitiveness and employment.

Employees' Group (Group II). The vast majority of the workers' group at the European Economic and Social Committee belong to the European Trade Union Confederation. Others are members of the Organization of Managerial and Executive Staff. The group has its own secretariat.

The objectives of the group are the battle against unemployment; the improvement of living and working conditions (worker information and consultation, inter alia); the protection of fundamental freedoms; relations with third countries and world peace; tackling the repercussions of economic globalization and defending the EU's social achievements.

Various Interests Group (Group III). The unique feature which forges Group III's identity is the wide range of categories represented therein. Its members are drawn from farmers' organizations, small businesses, the crafts sector, the professions, co-operatives and non-profit associations, consumer organizations, environmental organizations, associations representing the family, women, persons with disabilities, and the scientific and academic community.

The EESC elects from amongst its number, for a two-year period, a bureau of 37 members and a President and two Vice-Presidents chosen in rotation from each of the three groups. The president represents the EESC in relations with outside bodies. Joint briefs (relations with EFTA, CEEC, AMU, ACP countries, Latin American and other third countries, and Citizens' Europe) fall within the remit of the EESC bureau and the EESC president. The basic function of the bureau is to organize the Committee's work.

The EESC is divided into six sections and the Consultative Committee on Industrial Change (CCIC). The sections are:

ECO   Economic and Monetary Union and Economic and Social Cohesion
INT   Single Market, Production and Consumption

TEN   Transport, Energy, Infrastructure and the Information Society
SOC   Employment, Social Affairs and Citizenship
NAT   Agriculture, Rural Development and the Environment
REX   External Relations

The sections' opinions are prepared by study groups, which usually comprise 12 members, including a *rapporteur*, and which are assisted by experts.

The EESC's plenary assembly adopts opinions by simple majority on the basis of the sections' opinions. These opinions are then forwarded to the institutions and published in the *Official Journal of the European Communities*.

THE COMMITTEE OF THE REGIONS

Rue Belliard 101, 1040 Brussels, Belgium
Tel. (+32) 2-2822211
Fax (+32) 2-2822325
URL www.cor.eu.int

Established by the Treaty on European Union, the Committee of the Regions (CoR) provides a voice for the regional and local authorities of the European Union, enabling them to take part, in an advisory capacity, in the Community decision making process.

Under the terms of the Treaties, the CoR must be consulted in the following areas of Union policy: economic and social cohesion; trans-European infrastructure networks; health; education; culture; employment; social issues; environment; training; transport.

The Council or the Commission may also consult the CoR on other matters where they consider it appropriate to do so, especially in the field of cross-border co-operation. The European Parliament may also consult the CoR on matters of mutual interest. The CoR is informed when the European Economic and Social Committee is consulted, and may issue an opinion on the matter if it considers specific regional interests are concerned. Finally, the CoR may issue an opinion on its own initiative if it judges such action appropriate.

There are 317 members of the Committee of the Regions and an equal number of alternate members. There are 24 members each for France, Germany, Italy and the United Kingdom, 21 for Poland and Spain, 12 for Austria, Belgium, the Czech Republic, Greece, Hungary, the Netherlands, Portugal, and Sweden, 9 for Denmark, Finland, Ireland, Lithuania and Slovakia, 7 for Estonia, Latvia and Slovenia, 6 for Cyprus and Luxembourg, and 5 for Malta. Members and alternate members are appointed for four years, the term of office being renewable. The CoR elects a President and Bureau from among its members for a two-year term.

The CoR maintains the following six Commissions, each of which comprises members of the CoR:

COTER Commission for Territorial Cohesion Policy
ECOS   Commission for Economic and Social Policy
DEVE   Commission for Sustainable Development
EDUC   Commission for Culture and Education
CONST Commission for Constitutional Affairs and European Governance
RELEX Commission for External Relations

THE EUROPEAN INVESTMENT BANK

Blvd Konrad Adenauer 100, 2950 Luxembourg, Luxembourg.
Tel. (+352) 43791
Fax (+352) 43793122
URL www.eib.org

The European Investment Bank (EIB) was established in 1958 as part of the decision to create a European Economic Community. Its aims are to contribute to the steady and balanced development of the European Union by providing loans for capital investment projects furthering Union policy objectives, in particular: the economic development of the Union's less developed regions; the improvement of European transport and telecommunications infrastructure; the protection of the environment and the quality of life; the attainment of the Union's energy policy objectives, strengthening the international competitiveness of industry and promoting its integration at Union level; and supporting the activities of small and medium-sized enterprises.

Outside the European Union, the EIB participates in the implementation of the Union's development policy in countries in the Mediterranean region, in African, Caribbean and Pacific countries which are signatories to the Cotonou Agreement, in South Africa, in the countries of Central and Eastern Europe and in many countries in Latin America and Asia.

EIB Information Structures

The Communication and Information Department is responsible for external information and press contacts. Enquiries may be addressed to: Communication and Information Department, Blvd Konrad Adenauer 100, 2950 Luxembourg, Luxembourg; tel. (+352) 43793122; fax (+352) 43793191; e-mail info@eib.org.

Contacts for information related to EIB activities within the European Union:

Austria: Dusan Ondrejicka; tel. (+352) 43792142; e-mail d.ondrejicka@eib.org
Belgium, France, Luxembourg: Sabine Parisse; tel. (+352) 43792146; e-mail s.parisse@eib.org
Denmark, Finland, Sweden: Pé Verhoeven; tel. (+352) 43793118; e-mail p.verhoeven@cib.org
Germany: Paul Gerd Löser; tel. (+352) 43792159; e-mail p.loeser@eib.org
Greece: Helen Kavvadia; tel. (+352) 43793134; e-mail h.kavvadia@eib.org
Ireland, United Kingdom: Adam McDonaugh; tel. (+352) 43791; e-mail a.mcdonaugh@eib.org
Italy: Daniela Sacchi; tel. (+352) 43793138; e-mail d.sacchi@eib.org
Portugal, Spain: Juan Manuel Sterlin Balenciaga; tel. (+352) 43791; e-mail j.sterlin@eib.org
The Netherlands: Yvonne Berghorst; tel. (+352) 43793154; e-mail y.berghorst@eib.org

Contacts for information related to EIB activities outside the European Union:

Accession countries (AC): Dusan Ondrejicka; tel. (+352) 43792142; e-mail d.ondrejicka@eib.org
Mediterranean countries (MED) and Balkan countries (BLK): Helen Kavvadia; tel. (+352) 43793134; e-mail h.kavvadia@eib.org

African, Caribbean and Pacific countries (ACP) and South Africa (SA): Bram Schim van der Loeff; tel. (+352) 43793130; e-mail a.schimvanderloeff@eib.org

Asian and Latin American countries (ALA) and non EU-OECD countries: Orlando Arango; tel. (+32) 2-2350084; e-mail o.arango@eib.org

EFTA countries: Pé Verhoeven; tel. (+352) 43793118; e-mail p.verhoeven@eib.org

Contact for information related to EIB's electronic media:

Electronic media: Marc Bello; tel. (+352) 43793119; e-mail m.bello@eib.org

THE EUROPEAN COURT OF AUDITORS

Rue Alcide De Gasperi 12, 1615 Luxembourg, Luxembourg
Tel. (+352) 43981
Fax (+352) 439846430
E-mail euraud@eca.eu.int
URL www.eca.eu.int

The European Court of Auditors examines the accounts of all the revenue and expenditure of the Community. The Court of Auditors audits not only the general budget of the European Union but also Community loans and borrowings as well as the operations of the European Development Fund, which are financed outside the budget by contributions from the Member States. It also provides a Statement of Assurance as to the reliability of the accounts and the legality and regularity of the underlying transactions.

The Court of Auditors comprises 25 members – one from each EU Member State – appointed unanimously by the Council, after consultation with the Parliament, for a renewable term of six years, having been nominated for the position by their Member State. The members sit as a College, which is the main decision-making body of the Court, and elect a President from among their number for a renewable term of three years. The Court examines the accounts of revenue and expenditure of all bodies set up by the Community in so far as the relevant constituent instrument does not preclude such examination. In addition, the Court has a consultative role. It is involved in the Community's legislative process in the fields of finance and budgeting. As far as financial regulations are concerned, the Court of Auditors is required to deliver an opinion which is published in the *Official Journal*. Furthermore, it may also, at any time, submit observations on specific questions and deliver opinions at the request of one of the Institutions of the Community.

The Court's External Relations Department is responsible for handling any request for information concerning documents adopted by the Court. The department's direct telephone number is (+352) 439845410.

THE EUROPEAN CENTRAL BANK

Postfach 16 03 19, 60066 Frankfurt am Main, Germany
Located at: Kaiserstr. 29, 60311 Frankfurt am Main, Germany
Tel. (+49 69) 1344-0
Fax (+49 69) 1344-6000
E-mail info@ecb.int
URL www.ecb.int

On 25 May 1998, the governments of the eleven Member States participating in the third stage of Economic and Monetary Union appointed the President, the Vice-President and four other members of the Executive Board of the European Central Bank (ECB), the successor to the European Monetary Institute. Their appointment took effect on 1 June 1998 and marked the establishment of the European Central Bank. The ECB and the national central banks form the European System of Central Banks (ESCB), which formulates and defines the single monetary policy in the third stage of EMU.

The basic tasks of the ESCB are: to define and implement the monetary policy of the Community; to conduct foreign exchange operations; to hold and manage the official foreign reserves of the participating Member States; to promote the smooth operation of payment systems; to contribute to the smooth conduct of policies pursued by the competent authorities relating to the prudential supervision of credit institutions and the stability of the financial system.

The ESCB is governed by the decision-making bodies of the European Central Bank – the Governing Council, the Executive Board and the General Council.

The Governing Council of the European Central Bank (ECB) comprises the members of the Executive Board of the ECB and the governors of the National Central Banks which have adopted the Euro.

The Executive Board comprises the President, the Vice-President and four other members, all chosen from among persons with professional experience in monetary or banking matters, and appointed by common accord of the governments of the Member States.

The General Council is composed of the President and the Vice-President and the governors of all 25 National Central Banks, and performs the tasks which the ECB took over from the European Monetary Institute (EMI).

THE EUROPEAN OMBUDSMAN

1 ave du Président Robert Schuman, BP 403, 67001 Strasbourg Cedex, France
Tel. (+3) 3-88-17-23-13
Fax (+33) 3-88-17-90-62
E-mail euro-ombudsman@europarl.eu.int
URL www.euro-ombudsman.eu.int

The idea of an ombudsman for the European Union was launched by the European Parliament as of 1979. The right of appeal to the European Ombudsman was finally included in the chapter of the Maastricht Treaty introducing EU citizenship. In 1995, the European Parliament elected Jacob Soderman as the EU's first ombudsman. The present incumbent is Nikiforos Diamandouros.

The Ombudsman's basic task is to check and report on poor administration within the EU's institutions and agencies. Only the Court of Justice and the Court of First Instance – in the exercise of their legal functions – fall outside the Ombudsman's remit. The Ombudsman usually conducts his enquiries on the basis of a complaint, assisted by a team of lawyers and administrators. Any EU citizen or any legal or natural person residing in or having their registered office in an EU Member State may contact the Ombudsman. The Ombudsman also has the right to conduct checks on his own initiative.

INDEX OF KEYWORDS IN PART I

PART II

TRADE AND PROFESSIONAL ASSOCIATIONS IN THE EUROPEAN UNION

AAC

Association of the European Starch Industries of the EU

Association des Amidonneries de Céréales de l'UE

Avenue des Arts 43, 1040 Brussels, Belgium
Tel. (+32) 2-2896760
Fax (+32) 2-5135592
E-mail aac@aac-eu.org
URL www.aac-eu.org
Pres. Bram Klaeijsen
Contact Lorenza Squarci (Man. Dir)

ACE

Alliance for Beverage Cartons and the Environment

Av. Louise 250, Box 106, 1050 Brussels, Belgium
Tel. (+32) 2-5040710
Fax (+32) 2-5040719
E-mail information@ace.be
URL www.ace.be
Pres. Erika Mink
Contact Dr Kevin Bradley (Dir-Gen.)

ACE / CAE

Architects' Council of Europe

Conseil des Architectes d'Europe

Rat der Architekten Europa's

Rue Paul Emile Janson 29, 1050 Brussels, Belgium
Tel. (+32) 2-5431140
Fax (+32) 2-5431141
E-mail info@ace-cae.org
URL www.ace-cae.org
Pres. Marie-Hélène Lucas
Sec.-Gen. Alain Sagne
Contact Adrian Joyce (Senior Adviser)

ACEA

Association of European Automobile Manufacturers

Association des Constructeurs Européens d'Automobiles

Rue du Noyer 211, 1000 Brussels, Belgium
Tel. (+32) 2-7325550
Fax (+32) 2-7387310
E-mail af@acea.be
Sec.-Gen. Ivan Hodac
Contact Alfredo Filippone (Communication Officer)

ACEM

Association des Constructeurs Européens de Motocycles

Avenue de la Joyeuse Entrée 1, 1040 Brussels, Belgium
Tel. (+32) 2-2309732
Fax (+32) 2-2301683
E-mail acembike@acembike.org
URL www.acembike.org
Pres. Herbert Diess
Sec.-Gen. Jacques Compagne
Contact Filippo Belcari (Vice-Pres.)

ACI EUROPE

Airports Council International – European Region

Conseil International des Aéroports – Region Europe

Internationaler Flughafenrat – Region Europa

Square de Meeûs 6, 1000 Brussels, Belgium
Tel. (+32) 2-5520982
Fax (+32) 2-5025637
E-mail info@aci-europe.org
URL www.aci-europe.org
Pres. Prof. Dr Manfred Schölch
Contact Prof. Ir. Pierre Klees (Member of the Exec. Communication)

ACME

Association of European Cooperative and Mutual Insurers

Association des Assureurs Coopératifs et Mutualistes Européens

Europäischer Genosserschaftlicher und Wechselseitiger Versicherungsverband

Rue d'Arlon 50, 1000 Brussels, Belgium
Tel. (+32) 2-2310828
Fax (+32) 2-2800399
E-mail acme@skynet.be
URL www.acme.eu.org
Contact Catherine Hock

ACT

Association of Commercial Television in Europe

Association des Télévisions Commerciales Européennes

Rue Joseph II 9/13, 1000 Brussels, Belgium
Tel. (+32) 2-7360052
Fax (+32) 2-7354172
E-mail info@acte.be
URL www.acte.be

Pres. Nicolas De Tavernost
Sec.-Gen. Ross Biggam
Contact Ross Biggam (Dir-Gen.)

ACTIP

Animal Cell Technology Industrial Platform

POB 9143, 3007 AC Rotterdam, Netherlands
Tel. (+31 10) 4828306
Fax (+31 10) 4827750
E-mail actip@actip.org
URL www.actip.org

Pres. Dr H. van den Berg
Contact Dr Helma Hermans (Exec. Sec.)

ACTUARIES

European Actuarial Consultative Group

Groupe Consultatif Actuariel Européen

Napier House, 4 Worcester Street, Oxford OX1 2AW, United Kingdom
Tel. (+44 18) 6526-8218
Fax (+44 18) 6526-8244
E-mail mlucas@gcactuaries.org
URL www.gcactuaries.org

Pres. Tom Ross
Contact Paul Grace (Chair.)

ADDE

Association of Dental Dealers in Europe

Association des Dépôts Dentaires en Europe

Moosstrasse 2, 3073 Gumligen-Berne, Switzerland
Tel. (+41) 31-952-78-92
Fax (+41) 31-952-76-83
E-mail uwanner@swissonline.ch
URL www.adde.info

Pres. Frank Bruggeman
Sec.-Gen. Dr Ulrich Wanner
Contact Alex Engelberger (Vice-Pres.)

AEA

Association of European Airlines

Avenue Louise 350, 1050 Brussels, Belgium
Tel. (+32) 2-6398989
Fax (+32) 2-6398999
E-mail aea.secretariat@aea.be
URL www.aea.be

Pres. Jean-Cyril Spinetta
Sec.-Gen. Ulrich Schulte-Strathaus
Contact Fernando Pinto (Chair.)

AECMA

European Association of Aerospace Industries

Europäischer Verband der Luft- und Raumfahrt Industrie

Gulledelle 94–B5, 1200 Brussels, Belgium
Tel. (+32) 2-7758110
Fax (+32) 2-7758111
E-mail info@aecma.org
URL www.aecma.org

Pres. Dr Bengt Halse
Sec.-Gen. Roger W. Hawksworth
Contact Marc J. Haese (Public Relations and Press Officer)

AEDE

European Association of Teachers

Association Européenne des Enseignants

Europäische Erzieherbund

68 Rue du Faubourg National, 67000 Strasbourg, France
Tel. (+33) 3-88-32-63-67
Fax (+33) 3-88-22-48-34
E-mail aede.sgeurope@wanadoo.fr
URL www.aede.org

Pres. Rick Matser
Sec.-Gen. Jean-Claude Gonon

AEDT

European Association of National Organizations of Textiles Retailers

Association Européenne des Organisations Nationales de Détaillants en Textiles

Europäische Vereinigung der Spitzenverbande des Textileinzelhandels

1040 Brussels, Belgium
Tel. (+32) 2-2305296
Fax (+32) 2-2302569
E-mail info@aedt.org
URL www.aedt.org
Pres. Betty van Arenthals – Kramer Freher
Sec.-Gen. Alessandro Bedeschi
Contact Carlo Massoletti (Vice-Pres.)

AEEBC

Association of European Building Surveyors

Association d'Experts Européens du Bâtiment et de la Construction

C/o Mr. M. Russell-Croucher, 12 Great George Street, London SW1P 3AD, United Kingdom
Tel. (+44 20) 7334-3734
Fax (+44 20) 7695-1526
E-mail aeebc@rics.org.uk
URL www.aeebc.org
Pres. Prof. Trevor Mole
Sec.-Gen. Francis Wargnies
Contact Paul Caillon (Vice-Pres.)

AEGPL

European LPG Association

Association Européenne des Gaz de Pétrole Liquéfiés

Europäischer Flüssiggasverband

6 Rue Galilée, 75782 Paris Cedex 16, France
Tel. (+33) 1-47-23-52-74
Fax (+33) 1-47-23-52-79
E-mail aegpl@aol.com
URL www.aegpl.com
Pres. Lindenhovius
Sec.-Gen. Patrick Segarra
Contact Chapotot (Dir-Gen.)

AEGRAFLEX

European Association of Engravers and Flexographers

Association Européenne des Graveurs et des Flexographes

Europäische Vereinigung der Graveure und Flexografen

Postfach 1869, 65008 Wiesbaden, Germany
Tel. (+49 611) 803-115
Fax (+49 611) 803-117
E-mail so@bvdm-online.de
URL www.aegraflex.org
Pres. Waage Leif
Sec.-Gen. Dipl.-Ing. Torben Thorn

AEJ / AJE

Association of European Journalists

Association des Journalistes Européens

Vereinigung Europäischer Journalisten

Calle Cedaceros 11, 3° F, 28014 Madrid, Spain
Tel. (+34) 91-4296869
Fax (+34) 91-4292754
E-mail info@apeuropeos.org
URL www.apeuropeos.org
Pres. Carlos-Louis Alvarez
Sec.-Gen. Miguel Angel Aguilar

AEMUM

Association of European Municipal Equipment Manufacturers

Lyonerstrasse 18, 60528 Frankfurt am Main, Germany
Tel. (+49 69) 66031301
Fax (+49 69) 66032301
E-mail carmen.simon@vdma.org
URL www.vdma.org
Contact Dr Bernd Scherer

AEPOC

European Association for the Protection of Encrypted Works and Services

Association Européenne pour la Protection des Oeuvres et Services Cryptés

Avenue Louise 165, 1050 Brussels, Belgium
Tel. (+39) 2-89011980
Fax (+39) 2-86996069
E-mail contact@aepoc.org
URL www.aepoc.org
Pres. Jean Grenier
Sec.-Gen. Davide Rossi
Contact Jean Grenier (Chair.)

AER

Association of European Radios

Association Européenne des Radios

Av. d'Auderghem 76, 1040 Brussels, Belgium
Tel. (+32) 2-7369131
Fax (+32) 2-7328990

E-mail aer@aereurope.org
URL www.aereurope.org
Pres. Christer Jungeryd
Sec.-Gen. Frederik Stucki
Contact Christina Sleszynska (Man.)

AEROBAL

European Association of Aluminium Aerosol Container Manufacturers

Association Européenne des Fabricants de Boîtes en Aluminium pour Aérosol

Europäische Vereinigung der Hersteller von Aluminium-Aerosoldosen

Haus der Metalle, 2nd floor, Am Bonneshof. 5, 40474 Düsseldorf, Germany
Tel. (+49 211) 4796144
Fax (+49 211) 4796408
E-mail aerobal@aluinfo.de
URL www.aerobal.org
Pres. Emmanuel Perret
Sec.-Gen. Perret Spengler

Aertel

European Ribbon, Braid and Elastic Fabrics Association

Association Européenne Rubans, Tresses, Tissus Elastiques

Europäische Vereinigung der Bandweber- und Flechterindustrie

Poortakkerstraat 98, 9051 Gent (Sint-Denijs-Westrem), Belgium
Tel. (+32) 9-2429820
Fax (+32) 9-2429829
E-mail pvm@gent.febeltex.be
Pres. P. Gleich
Contact P. van Mol (Gen. Man.)

AESAD

European Association of Care and Help at Home

Association Européenne de Soins et d'Aides à Domicile

Avenue Ad. Lacomblé 69, 1030 Brussels, Belgium
Tel. (+32) 2-7367972
Fax (+32) 2-7367498
E-mail EACHH@skynet.be
URL www.aeosad.org
Contact Roland Seutin (Dir-Gen.)

AESGP

Association of the European Self-Medication Industry

Association Européenne des Spécialités Pharmaceutiques Grand Public

Europäischer Fachverband der Arzneimittel-Hersteller

Avenue de Tervuren 7, 1040 Brussels, Belgium
Tel. (+32) 2-7355130
Fax (+32) 2-7355222
E-mail info@aesgp.be
URL www.aesgp.be
Pres. Albert Esteve
Contact Dr Hubertus Cranz (Dir-Gen.)

AEXEA

Association of European Registered Experts

Association des Experts Européens Agréés

Arbeitsgemeinschaft der Europäischen Anerkannten Savchverständigen

49 rue Lamartine, 78000 Versailles, France
Tel. (+33) 1-39-51-48-71
Fax (+33) 1-39-51-48-71
E-mail alinea.sa@wanadoo.fr
URL www.aexea.org
Pres. Bernard Robert
Sec.-Gen. Lygia Négrier-Dormont
Contact Michel Binard (Vice-Pres.)

AFCASOLE

Association of Soluble Coffee Manufacturers of the European Community

Association des Fabricants de Café Soluble des Pays de la Communauté Européenne

Vereinigung der Hersteller von Löslichem Kaffee der Europäischen Gemeinschaft

Tourniairestraat 3, 1065 KK Amsterdam, Netherlands
Tel. (+31 20) 5113870
Fax (+31 20) 5113810
E-mail vnkt@koffiethee.nl
URL www.vnkt.nl
Pres. G. Lemorehedec
Sec.-Gen. Roland Vaessen

AFECOR

European Control Manufacturers' Association

Association des Fabricants Européens d'Appareils de Contrôle et de Régulation

Verband Europäischer Kontrollgerätehersteller

C/o Honeywell, Phileas Foggstraat 7, 7821 AJ Emmen, Netherlands
Tel. (+31 591) 695323
Fax (+31 591) 695203
E-mail gerhard.vedder@honeywell.com
Sec.-Gen. T. Khai Tu
Contact G. J. Vedder (Representative)

AFEMS

Association of European Manufacturers of Sporting Ammunition

Association des Fabricants Européens de Munitions de Sport

Vereinigung der Europäischen Sportmunitionshersteller

Rue Th. de Cuyper 100, 1200 Brussels, Belgium
Tel. (+32) 2-6767211
Fax (+32) 2-6767303
E-mail afems@afems.org
Contact B. Jensen

AFERA

European Adhesive Tapes Manufacturers Association

Association des Fabricants Européens de Rubans Auto-Adhésifs

Verband des Europäischen Klebebandhersteller

Laan Copes van Cattenburch 79, POB 85612, 2508 CH The Hague, Netherlands
Tel. (+31 70) 3123916
Fax (+31 70) 3636348
E-mail mail@afera.com
URL www.afera.com
Pres. Peter Rambusch
Sec.-Gen. Astrid Lejeune
Contact Lutz Jacob (Technical Committee Chair.)

AFG

Association of the Glucose Producers in the EU

Association des Fabricants de Glucose de l'UE

Av. de la Joyeuse Entrée 1 bte 10, 1040 Brussels, Belgium
Tel. (+32) 2-2302031

Fax (+32) 2-2300245
E-mail aac@aac-eu.org
Contact Sqarce

AFTA

Association for Fair Trade in Alcohol

J.B. Denayerstraat 25, 1560 Hoeilaart, Belgium
Tel. (+32) 2-6576679
Fax (+32) 2-6573569
E-mail afta@pandora.be
URL www.afta.be
Contact Vierhout

AGE

Automotive Glazing Europe UEMV

POB 416, 1800 AK Alkmaar, Netherlands
Tel. (+31 72) 5114161
Fax (+31 72) 5113783
E-mail info@uemv.com
Pres. Berresford Dutton
Contact Pim de Ridder (Chair.)

AICV

Association of the Cider and Fruit Wine Industry of the EU

Association des Industries des Cidres et Vins de Fruits de l'UE

Vereinigung der Obst- und Fruchtweinindustrie der EG

Rue de la Loi 221, PO Box 5, 1040 Brussels, Belgium
Tel. (+32) 2-2350620
Fax (+32) 2-2829420
E-mail aicv@aicv.org
URL www.aicv.org
Pres. Anders Gronquist
Sec.-Gen. Jan Hermans
Contact Denis Hayes (Vice-Pres.)

AIDA

International Association for the Distributive Trade

Association Internationale de la Distribution

Internationale Vereinigung des Handels

Rue Marianne 34, 1180 Brussels, Belgium
Tel. (+32) 2-3459923
Fax (+32) 2-3460204
E-mail info@cbd_bcd.be
URL www.infocbd.bcd
Pres. Campbell
Contact Leon Wegnez

AIE

European Association of Electrical Contractors

Association Européenne de l'Installation Electrique

Europäische Vereinigung der Unternehmungen für Elektrische Anlagen

J. Chantraineplantsoen 1, 3070 Kortenberg, Belgium
Tel. (+32) 2-2534222
Fax (+32) 2-2536763
E-mail info@aie-elec.org
URL www.aie-elec.org
Pres. Karl-Heinz Bertram
Sec.-Gen. Evelyne Schellekens
Contact Guy Geffroy (Vice-Pres.)

AIECE

Association of European Conjuncture Institutes

Association d'Instituts Européens de Conjoncture Economique

Vereinigung der Europäischen Wirtschaftsprognoseinstitute

Place Montesquieu 3, 1348 Louvain-la-Neuve, Belgium
Tel. (+32) 10-474143
Fax (+32) 1-0473945
E-mail olbrechts@aiece.org
URL www.aiece.org
Pres. P Vartia
Sec.-Gen. Paul Olbrechts

AIJN

Association of the Industry of Juices and Nectars from Fruits and Vegetables of the EU

Association de l'Industrie des Jus et Nectars de Fruits et de Légumes de l'UE

Vereinigung der Fruchtsaftindustrie der EG

Rue de la Loi 221, PO Box 5, 1040 Brussels, Belgium
Tel. (+32) 2-2350620
Fax (+32) 2-2829420
E-mail aijn@ajin.org
URL www.aijn.org
Pres. Andrew Biles
Sec.-Gen. Jan Hermans
Contact Thiel Peter (Vice-Pres.)

AIM

European Brands Association

Association des Industries de Marque

Europäischer Markenverband

Avenue des Gaulois 9, 1040 Brussels, Belgium
Tel. (+32) 2-7360305
Fax (+32) 2-7346702
E-mail brand@aim.be
URL www.aim.be
Pres. Lars Olofsson
Contact Alain Galaski (Dir-Gen.)

AIMA

Alternative Investment Management Association Limited

Meadows House, 20–22 Queen Street, London W1J 5PR, United Kingdom
Tel. (+44 20) 7659-9920
Fax (+44 20) 7659-9921
E-mail info@aima.org
URL www.aima.org
Pres. Christopher Fawcett
Contact Alison Pernek (Administrator)

AIPCE

EU Fish Processors Association

Association des Industries du Poisson de l'UE

Avenue de Roodebeek 30, 1030 Brussels, Belgium
Tel. (+32) 2-7438730
Fax (+32) 2-7368175
E-mail aipcee@sia-dvi.be
Pres. Hyldtoft Peter
Sec.-Gen. Coenen Michel
Contact Commere Pierre (Vice-Pres.)

AISE

International Association of the Soap, Detergent and Maintenance Products

Association Internationale de la Savonnerie, de la Détergence et des Produits d'Entretien

Internationaler Verband der Seifen-, Wasch-, Putz- und Pflegemittelindustrie

Square Marie-Louise 49, 1000 Brussels, Belgium
Tel. (+32) 2-2308371
Fax (+32) 2-2308288
E-mail aise.main@aise-net.org
URL www.aise-net.org

Pres. Charles Laroche
Sec.-Gen. Dr Hans Verbeek
Contact Maarten G. Labberton (Dir-Gen.)

AIUFFASS

International Association of Users of Artificial and Synthetic Filament Yarns and of Natural Silk

Association Internationale des Utilisateurs de Fils de Filaments Artificiels et Synthétiques et de Soie Naturelle

Internationaler Verband der Verarbeiter von Chemiefaser Filament- und Naturseidengamen

Poortakkerstraat 98, 9051 Gent (Sint-Denijs-Westrem), Belgium
Tel. (+32) 9-2429820
Fax (+32) 9-2429829
E-mail pvm@gent.febeltex.be
Sec.-Gen. P. Vanmol

AMAFE

Association of Manufacturers of Animal-derived Food Enzymes

Association des Fabricants d'Enzymes Alimentaires Dérivés d'Animaux

Vereinigung der Tierischen Nahrungsenzymhersteller

CSK Food Enrichment, POB 225, 8901 BA Leeuwarden, Netherlands
Tel. (+31 58) 2885255
Fax (+31 58) 2880673
E-mail vanboven@cskfood.nl
Pres. P. Visschelijk
Contact A. van Boven

AMFEP

Association of Manufacturers and Formulators of Enzyme Products

Roodebeeklaan, Avenue de Roodebeek 30, 1030 Brussels, Belgium
Tel. (+32) 2-7438730
Fax (+32) 2-7368175
E-mail amfep@sia-dvi.be
URL www.amfep.org
Pres. Hubb Scheres
Sec.-Gen. Michel Coenen
Contact Karolien de Never

ANEC

European Association for the Co-ordination of Consumer Representation in Standardisation

Porte-parole des Consommateurs Européens dans la Normalisation

Avenue de Tervuren 32, PO Box 27, 1040 Brussels, Belgium
Tel. (+32) 2-7432470
Fax (+32) 2-7065430
E-mail anec@anec.org
URL www.anec.org
Pres. Benedicte Federspiel
Sec.-Gen. Dr Gottlobe Fabisch
Contact Florence Nicolas (Vice-Pres.)

AOCFI-Europe

Association of Career Management Consulting Firms International-Europe

Jansweg 40, 2011 KN Haarlem, Netherlands
Tel. (+31 23) 5535985
Fax (+31 23) 5535988
E-mail secretariat@aocfi-europe.com
URL www.aocfi-europe.com
Pres. Herbert Mühlenhoff
Sec.-Gen. A. Lefevre
Contact Bob Hueglin (Sec.)

APAG

European Oleochemicals & Allied Products Group

Groupement Européen des Produits Oléochimiques & Associés

Avenue E. van Nieuwenhuyse 4, PO Box 1, 1160 Brussels, Belgium
Tel. (+32) 2-6767255
Fax (+32) 2-6767301
E-mail cdc@cefic.be
URL www.apag.org
Pres. Graham Beesley
Sec.-Gen. Chantal de Cooman
Contact Andersson Börje (Deputy Chair.)

APEAL

Association of European Producers of Steel for Packaging

Association Professionnelle des Producteurs Européens d'Acier pour Emballage

Vereinigung der Europäischen Hersteller von Stahl für Verpackung

Avenue Louise 89, 1050 Brussels, Belgium

Tel. (+32) 2-5379151
Fax (+32) 2-5378649
E-mail info@apeal.be
URL www.apeal.org
Contact Philippe Wolper (Gen. Man.)

APFE

European Glass Fibre Producers Association
Association des Producteurs de Fibres de Verre Européens
Europäischer Verband der Glasfaserhersteller

Avenue Louise 89 Box 2, 1050 Brussels, Belgium
Tel. (+32) 2-5384446
Fax (+32) 2-5378469
E-mail v.favry@cpivglass.be
Pres. Gaarenstroom
Sec.-Gen. Gilbert Maeyaert

API / AAC

Association of the Producers of Isoglucose of the EU
Association des Producteurs d'Isoglucose de l'UE

Avenue des Arts 43, 1000 Brussels, Belgium
Tel. (+32) 2-2896760
Fax (+32) 2-5135592
E-mail aac@aac-eu.org
URL www.aac-eu.org/
Contact Illiana Axiotiades

APME

Association of Plastics Manufacturers in Europe (Plastics Europe)
Association des Producteurs de Matieres Plastiques en Europe
Verband der Kunststoffhersteller in Europa

Avenue van Nieuwenhuyse 4, Box 3, 1160 Brussels, Belgium
Tel. (+32) 2-6753297
Fax (+32) 2-6753935
E-mail info@plasticseurope.org
URL www.plasticseurope.org
Pres. Dr Werner Prätorius
Contact Nancy Russotto (Exec. Dir)

APPE

Association of Petrochemical Producers in Europe

Association des Producteurs de Produits Pétroléochimiques en Europe
Verband der Hersteller von Petrochemikalien in Europa

Avenue E. van Nieuwenhuyse 4, 1160 Brussels, Belgium
Tel. (+32) 2-6767211
Fax (+32) 2-6767300
E-mail pfe@cefic.be
URL www.petrochemistry.net
Pres. Theo Walthie
Contact Jacques Autin (Dir)

AQUA EUROPA

European Water Conditioning Association
Fédération Européenne du Traitement de l'Eau
Europäische Vereinigung für Wasseraufbereitung

Rue de Louvrandes 58, 1325 Dion-Valmont, Belgium
Tel. (+32) 10-245236
Fax (+32) 10- 225659
E-mail henderyckx.aqua@skynet.be
Pres. Frank Torfs
Sec.-Gen. Y. Henderyckx

AQUA

European Association of Water Meters Manufacturers
Association Européenne des Fabricants de Compteurs d'Eau
Europäische Vereinigung der Hersteller von Wasserzählern

Rue Louis Blanc 39–41, 92038 Paris La Défense, France
Tel. (+33) 1-43-34-76-80
Fax (+33) 1-43-34-76-82
E-mail aqua@syndicat-mesure.fr
URL www.syndicat-mesure.fr
Pres. Bonnard
Sec.-Gen. Valitchek
Contact J.M. Loeser (Vice-Pres.)

AREA

Air Conditioning & Refrigeration European Association

Beau Site Première Avenue 88, 1330 Rixensart, Belgium
Tel. (+32) 2-6538835
Fax (+32) 2-6523872

E-mail info@area-eur.be
URL www.area-eur.be
Pres. Jean Jacquin
Sec.-Gen. R. Berckmans
Contact J. Hoogkamer

ARGE

European Federation of Associations of Lock and Builders Hardware Manufacturers

Fédération Européenne des Associations de Fabricants de Serrures et de Ferrures

Arbeitsgemeinschaft der Verbände der Europäischen Schloss- und Beschlagindustrie

4502 Solothurn, Switzerland
Tel. (+41) 32-621-91-76
Fax (+41) 32-621-91-77
E-mail arge.europe@bluewin.ch
URL www.arge.nu
Pres. Henri Morel
Sec.-Gen. Alfred Scheurer
Contact Juan Miguel (Vice-Pres.)

ARTGLACE

Confederation of Associations of Ice Manufacturers of the EC

Confédération des Associations des Artisans Glaciers de la CE

Konföderation der Eishersteller der EG

Via del Parco 3, 32013 Longarone (Belluno), Italy
Tel. (+39) 04-37577577
Fax (+39) 04-37770340
E-mail info@artglace.org
URL www.artglace.org
Pres. Italo De Lorenzo
Sec.-Gen. Jose Luis Gisbert Valls

ASERCOM

Association of European Refrigeration Compressor and Controls Manufacturers

Motzstrasse 91, 10779 Berlin, Germany
Tel. (+49 30) 21479872
Fax (+49 30) 21479871
E-mail asercomjaw@t-online.de
URL www.asercom.org
Pres. Jochen A. Winkler
Contact Hans P. Meurer (Chair.)

ASPEC

Association of Sorbitol Producers within the EEC

Avenue des Gaulois 9, 1040 Brussels, Belgium
Tel. (+32) 2-7365354
Fax (+32) 2-7323427
E-mail wirkler@asercom.com
Contact Michael Bellingham

ASSIFONTE

Association de l'Industrie de la Fonte de Fromage de l'UE

Adenauerallee 148, 53113 Bonn, Germany
Tel. (+49 228) 959-690
Fax (+49 228) 371-535
E-mail info@milchindestrie.de
URL www.milchindustrie.de
Pres. J Ruys
Sec.-Gen. D.E Hetzner

ASSUC

Association of Professional Organizations of the Sugar Trade in the EU

Association des Organisations Professionnelles du Commerce des Sucres pour les Pays de l'UE

Verband der Fachorganisationen des Zuckerhandels in den Ländern der EU

Suare Ambiorix F4/Boite 24 32, 1000 Brussels, Belgium
Tel. (+32) 2-7367997
Fax (+32) 2-7326766
E-mail assuc@pro.tiscali.be
URL www.sugartraders.co.uk
Pres. Loomans Peter
Sec.-Gen. Rouhier Pascale
Contact John Ireland (Chair.)

ASSURRE

Association for the Sustainable Use and Recovery of Resources in Europe

Rue du Luxembourg 19–21, 1000 Brussels, Belgium
Tel. (+32) 2-7725252
Fax (+32) 2-7725419
E-mail management@assurre.org
URL www.assurre.org
Pres. Kay Twitchen
Contact William R Duncan (Man. Dir)

AVEC

Association of Poultry Processors and Poultry Import and Export Trade in the EU countries

Association des Centres d'Abattage de Volailles et du Commerce d'Importation et d'Exportation de Volailles des Pays de l'UE

Trommesalen 5, 1614 Copenhagen, Denmark
Tel. (+45) 33-25-41-00
Fax (+45) 33-25-35-52
E-mail avec@poultry.dk
URL www.avec.dk
Pres. Jacques Risse
Sec.-Gen. Tage Lysgaard
Contact Peter Bradnock (Chief Exec.)

BCME

Beverage Can Makers Europe

Fabricants de Boîtes pour Boissons en Europe

Hersteller von Getränkdosen in Europa

Rue Theodore Decuyper 284, 1200 Brussels, Belgium
Tel. (+32) 2-7612371
Fax (+32) 2-7612373
E-mail bobschmitz@compuserve.com
URL www.bcme.org
Pres. L. Emilson
Contact L. Emilson (Chair.)

BEDA

Bureau of European Designers' Associations

Bureau des Associations de Designers Européens

Büro der Europäischen Designer-Verbanden

Diagonal 452, 5°, 08006 Barcelona, Spain
Tel. (+34) 934-153655
Fax (+34) 934-155419
E-mail office@beda.org
URL www.beda.org
Pres. Francisco Carrera

BIBM

International Bureau for Precast Concrete

Bureau International du Béton Manufacturé

Internationale Büro der Beton- und Fertigteilindustrie

Rue Voltastraat 12, 1050 Brussels, Belgium
Tel. (+32) 2-7356069

Fax (+32) 2-7347795
E-mail mail@febe.be
URL www.bibm.org
Pres. Zanbergen
Contact Dano (Chief Exec. Officer)

BIPAR

International Federation of Insurance Intermediaries

Bureau International des Producteurs d'Assurances et de Réassurances

Internationaler Dachverband der Versicherungs- und Ruckversicherungsvermittler

Av. Albert-Elisabeth 40, 1200 Brussels, Belgium
Tel. (+32) 2-7356048
Fax (+32) 2-7321418
E-mail bipar@skynet.be
URL www.biparweb.org
Pres. K. Sedler
Contact H. Krauss (Dir)

BLIC

European Association of the Rubber Industry

Bureau de Liaison des Industries du Caoutchouc de l'UE

Avenue des Arts 2, PO Box 12, 1210 Brussels, Belgium
Tel. (+32) 2-2184940
Fax (+32) 2-2186 62
E-mail info@blic.be
URL www.blic.be
Pres. Richard Fraussen
Sec.-Gen. Fazilet Cinaralp
Contact Bruno Philippe (Dir)

CAEF

Committee of Associations of European Foundries

Sohnstrasse 70, 40237 Düsseldorf, Germany
Tel. (+49 21) 16871215
Fax (+49 21) 16871205
E-mail info@caef-eurofoundry.org
URL www.caef-eurofoundry.org
Pres. Theo Lammers
Sec.-Gen. Dr Klaus Urbat

CAFIM

Confederation of European Music Industries

Confédération des Associations des Facteurs d'Instruments de Musique de la CEE

Vereinigung der Musikinstrumenten-Herstellerverbande in der EG

Tennelbachstrasse 25, 65193 Wiesbaden, Germany
Tel. (+49 61) 19545886
Fax (+49 61) 19545885
E-mail info@cafim.org
URL www.cafim.org
Pres. Gerhard A. Meinl
Sec.-Gen. Winfried Baumbach
Contact Patrick Selmer (Vice-Pres.)

CAMME

Committee of Apparel Machinery Manufacturers in Europe

C/o VDMA, Richard Strauss Strasse 56/III, 81677 Munich, Germany
Tel. (+49 89) 27828750
Fax (+49 89) 27828722
E-mail bul@vdma.org
Pres. Diether Klingelnberg
Contact Elgar Straub (Man. Dir)

CANDLES

Association of European Candle Manufacturers

Association Européenne des Syndicats de Fabricants de Bougies et de Cierges

Europäische Vereinigung der Verbände der Kerzenhersteller

118 Avenue Achille Peretti, 92200 Neuilly-sur-Seine, France
Tel. (+33) 1-46-37-22-06
Fax (+33) 1-46-37-22-06
E-mail bougies@fncg.fr
Pres. Beaumont
Sec.-Gen. Jean-Claude Barsacq
Contact Herbert Hofer (Chair.)

CAOBISCO

Association of the Chocolate-, Biscuit- and Confectionery Industries of the UE

Association des Industries de la Chocolaterie, Biscuiterie-Biscotterie et Confiserie de l'UE

Rue Defacqz 1, 1000 Brussels, Belgium
Tel. (+32) 2-5391800
Fax (+32) 2-5391575
E-mail david.zimmer@caobisco.be
URL www.caobisco.com
Pres. Jacques Ruh
Sec.-Gen. David Zimmer
Contact Micheline Boeykens (Exec. Sec.)

CAPIEL

Coordinating Committee for the Associations of Manufacturers of Industrial Electrical Switchgear and Controlgear in the European Union

Comité de Coordination des Associations de Constructeurs d'Appareillage Industriel Electrique de l'Union Européenne

Koordinierendes Komitee der Fachverbände der Schaltgerätehersteller in der Europäischen Union

Sercobe, Principe de Vergara 74, 28006 Madrid, Spain
Tel. (+34) 91-4115115
Fax (+34) 91-5621922
E-mail g_eisenberg@terra.es
Pres. Michel Duret
Sec.-Gen. Nadi Assaf

CARTOON

European Association of Animation Film

Association Européenne du Film d'Animation

Europäische Vereinigung des Zeichentrickfilms

Bd Lambermont 314, 1030 Brussels, Belgium
Tel. (+32) 2-2451200
Fax (+32) 2-2454689
E-mail info@cartoon.skynet.be
URL www.cartoon-media.be
Pres. Bob Balser
Contact Iain Harvey (Vice-Pres.)

CBMC

Brewers of Europe

Brasseurs Européens

Europäischen Brauer

Rue Caroly 23-25, 1050 Brussels, Belgium
Tel. (+32) 2-6722392
Fax (+32) 2-6609402
E-mail info@brewersofeurope.org
URL www.brewersofeurope.org
Pres. Piero Perron

Sec.-Gen. Rodolphe de Looz-Corswarem
Contact Pierre-Olivier Bergeron (Dir)

CCACE

Coordination Committee of European Cooperative Associations
Comité de Coordination des Associations Coopératives Européennes
Koordinierung der Europäischen Genossenschaftsverbande

Rue Guillaume Tell 59, 1060 Brussels, Belgium
Tel. (+32) 2-5431033
Fax (+32) 2-5431037
E-mail info@point-be.be
URL www.ccace.org
Pres. Etienne Pflimlin
General Delegate Rainer Schlüter
Contact Giuliano Poletti (Vice-Pres.)

CCA-EUROPE

Calcium Carbonate Association – Europe

Bd.Sylvain Dupuis 233, PO Box 124, 1070 Brussels, Belgium
Tel. (+32) 2-5245500
Fax (+32) 2-5244575
E-mail secretariat@ima-eu.org
URL www.ima-eu.org/cca.html
Sec.-Gen. M. Wyart Remy

CCBE

Council of the Bars and Law Societies of the European Union
Conseil des Barreaux de l'Union Européenne
Rat der Anwaltschaften der Europäischen Union

Avenue de la Joyeuse entree 1-5, 1040 Brussels, Belgium
Tel. (+32) 2-2346510
Fax (+32) 2-2346511
E-mail ccbe@ccbe.org
URL www.ccbe.org
Pres. Bernard Vatier
Contact Manuel Cavaleiro Brandao (Vice-Pres.)

CEA

European Federation of National Insurance Associations
Comité Européen des Assurances

3 bis rue de la Chaussee d'Antin, 75009 Paris, France
Tel. (+33) 1-44-83-11-83
Fax (+33) 1-47-70-03-75
E-mail caudet@cea.assur.org
URL www.cea.assur.org
Pres. Gerard de la Martiniere
Contact Daniel Schante (Dir-Gen.)

CEAB / CEI

European Confederation of Property Managers
Confédération Européenne des Administrateurs de Biens
Europäische Konföderation der Immobilienmakler

Avenue de Tervuren 36, Bte 2, 1040 Brussels, Belgium
Tel. (+32) 2-7354990
Fax (+32) 2-7359988
E-mail cepi@cepi.be
URL www.cepi.be
Pres. Winand van Coillie
Sec.-Gen. Joachim Schmidt
Contact Martin van Adorp

CEBP

European Confederation of National Bakery and Confectionery Organizations
Confédération Européenne des Organisations Nationales de la Boulangerie et de la Pâtisserie

Bd Louis Mettewie 83, Bte 42, 1080 Brussels, Belgium
Tel. (+32) 2-4692000
Fax (+32) 2-4692140
E-mail admin@cebp.be
URL www.bakeruib.org
Pres. Jacques van de Vall
Sec.-Gen. Dr Eberhard Groebel
Contact Claes

CEC

European Confederation of Managerial Staff
Confédération Européenne des Cadres

Rue de la Loi 81A, 1040 Brussels, Belgium
Tel. (+32) 2-4201051
Fax (+32) 2-4201292
E-mail info@cec-managers.org
URL www.cec-managers.org

Pres. Maurizio Angelo
Sec.-Gen. Claude Cambus
Contact Alexe von Wurmb

CEC

European Confederation of the Footwear Industry
Confédération Européenne de l'Industrie de la Chaussure
Europäische Konföderation der Schuhindustrie
Rue François Bossaerts 53, 1030 Brussels, Belgium
Tel. (+32) 2-7365810
Fax (+32) 2-7361276
E-mail cec@vidac.be
URL www.cecshoe.be
Pres. Antonio Brotini
Contact Roeland Smets (Man. Dir)

CECA

Committee of European Coffee Associations
Tourniairestraat 3, 1065 BK Amsterdam, Netherlands
Tel. (+31 20) 5113858
Fax (+31 20) 5113810
E-mail ceca@coffee-associations.org
Pres. P. Installe
Sec.-Gen. C. Krietemeijer

CECAPI

European Committee of Electrical Installation Equipment Manufacturers
Comité Européen des Constructeurs d'Appareillage Electrique d'Installation
Avenue de la Joyeuse Entrée 1, 1040 Brussels, Belgium
Tel. (+32) 2-2861234
Fax (+32) 2-2306908
E-mail cecapi@skynet.be
URL www.cecapi.org
Pres. Jozef de Backer
Sec.-Gen. Rainer Schilling

CECCM

Confederation of European Community Cigarette Manufacturers
Confédération des Fabricants de Cigarettes de la Communauté Européenne
Avenue Louise 125, 1050 Brussels, Belgium
Tel. (+32) 2-5410031
Fax (+32) 2-5410045
E-mail ceccm@ceccm.be

CECE

Committee for European Construction Equipment
Comité Européen des Matériels de Génie Civil
Europäisches Baumaschinen Komitee
Blvd Reyers 80, 1030 Brussels, Belgium
Tel. (+32) 2-7068225
Fax (+32) 2-7068229
E-mail info@cece-eu.org
URL www.cece-eu.org
Pres. Massimo Arghinenti
Sec.-Gen. Ralf Wezel

CECED

Federation of European Manufacturers of Domestic Appliances
Conseil Européen des Constructeurs d'Appareils Ménagers
Blvd Auguste Reyers 80, 1030 Brussels, Belgium
Tel. (+32) 2-7068290
Fax (+32) 2-7068289
E-mail secretariat@ceced.be
URL www.ceced.org
Pres. Kurt-Ludwig Gutberlet
Contact Luigi Meli (Dir-Gen.)

CECIMO

European Committee for Co-operation of the Machine Tools Industries
Europäisches Komitee für die Zusammenarbeit der Werkzeugmaschinenindustrien
Avenue Louise 66, 1050 Brusscls, Bclgium
Tel. (+32) 2-5027090
Fax (+32) 2-5026082
E-mail info@cecimo.be
URL www.cecimo.be
Pres. Keith Bailey
Sec.-Gen. René Groothedde
Contact Elisabeth Vilain (Exec. Asst)

CECIP

European Committee of Scale and Weighing Machines Manufacturers
Comité Européen des Constructeurs d'Instruments de Pesage

Europäisches Komitee der Hersteller von Waagenapparaturen

4 Domaine d'Armainvilliers, Impasse François Coli, 77330 Ozoir-la-Ferrière, France
Tel. (+33) 1-60-02-89-58
Fax (+33) 1-60-02-89-58
E-mail turpain.cecip@wanadoo.fr
URL www.cecip.de
Pres. David Castle
Contact Caroline Obrecht (Vice-Pres.)

CECOD

Committee of European Manufacturers of Petroleum Measuring and Distributing Equipment

Comité des Fabricants Européens d'Installation et de Distribution de Pétrole

Komitee der Europäischen Hersteller von Einrichtungen zur Messung und Verteilung von Flüssigen Brennstoffen

C/o Syndicat de la Mesure, 92038 Paris La Défense Cedex, France
Tel. (+33) 1-43-34-76-81
Fax (+33) 1-43-34-76-82
E-mail cecod@syndicat-mesure.fr
URL www.syndicat-mesure.fr
Pres. Dell Omo
Sec.-Gen. Patrick Antoine

CECODE

European Retail Trade Centre

Centre Européen du Commerce de Détail

Zentrum des Europäischen Einzelhandels

Gothaer Allée 2, 50969 Cologne, Germany
Tel. (+49 221) 93655-770
Fax (+49 221) 93655-779
E-mail nzilat.hde@einzelhandel.de
URL www.bbeberatung.com
www.einzelhandel.de
Pres. J. Demesmacre

CECOF

European Committee of Industrial Furnace and Heating Equipment Manufacturers

Comité Européen des Constructeurs de Fours et d'Equipements Thermiques Industriels

Europäisches Komitee der Hersteller von Industrieöfen und Industrie-Wärmeanlagen

Lyoner Strasse 18, 60528 Frankfurt, Germany

Tel. (+49 69) 66031413
Fax (+49 69) 66032278
E-mail cecof@vdma.org
URL www.cecof.org
Pres. Mike Debier
Sec.-Gen. Dr Gutmann Habig
Contact Susanne Flenner

CECOMAF

European Committee of Manufacturers of Refrigeration Equipment

Comité Européen des Constructeurs de Matériel Frigorifique

Boulevard Reyers 80, 1030 Brussels, Belgium
Tel. (+32) 2-7067985
Fax (+32) 2-7067966
E-mail info@eurovent-cecomaf.org
URL www.eurovent-cecomaf.org
Pres. Georg Mager
Sec.-Gen. Michel van der Horst
Contact Sule Becirspahic (Dir)

CECOP

European Confederation of Workers' Co-operatives, Social Co-operatives and Participative Enterprises

Confédération Européenne des Coopératives de Production et de Travail Associé, des Coopératives Sociales et des Entreprises Participatives

Rue Guillaume Tell 59 B, 1060 Brussels, Belgium
Tel. (+32) 2-5431033
Fax (+32) 2-5431037
E-mail cecop@cecop.org
URL www.cecop.coop
Pres. Felice Scalvini
Sec.-Gen. Rainer Schluter
Contact Jan Wiesner (Vice-Pres.)

CECRA

European Council for Motor Trades and Repairs

Conseil Européen du Commerce et de la Réparation Automobiles

Europäischer Verband des Kraftfahrzeuggewerbes

Boulevard de la Woluwe 46, Bte 17, 1200 Brussels, Belgium
Tel. (+32) 2-7719656
Fax (+32) 2-7726567

E-mail mail@cecra.org
URL www.cecra.org
Pres. Jürgen Creutzig
Sec.-Gen. Rita Soetaert
Contact Massimo Campilli (Vice-Pres.)

CECT

European Committee of Boiler, Vessel and Pipework Manufacturers
Comité Européen de la Chaudronnerie et de la Tuyauterie
Europäisches Komitee für den Dampfkessel, Behälter- und Rohrleitungsbau

C/o SNCT, 39–41 Rue Louis Blanc, 92038 Courbevoie, France
Tel. (+33) 1-47-17-62-71
Fax (+33) 1-47-17-62-77

Contact M.Y. Marez

CED

European Hardware Trade Confederation
Confédération Européenne de la Droguerie
Konföderation der Europäischen Drogistenverbänd

Vogelsanger Strasse. 165, 50823 Cologne, Germany
Tel. (+49 22) 1952917
Fax (+49 22) 1952917
E-mail bfv-vdd@einzelhandel.de
URL www.drogistenverband.de

CEDEC

European Federation of Local Public Energy Distribution Companies
Confédération Européenne des Distributeurs d'Energie Publics Communaux
Europäischer Dachverband der Öffentlichen Kommunalen Energieversorgungsunternehmen

Rue Royale 55, 1000 Brussels, Belgium
Tel. (+32) 2-2178117
Fax (+32) 2-2192056
E-mail melanie.zylverberg@cedec.com
URL www.cedec.com
Pres. Achille Diegenant
Sec.-Gen. Gert de Block
Contact Jacques Glorieux (Representative)

CEDI

European Confederation of Independents
Confédération Européenne des Indépendants
Europaverband der Selbständigen-CEDI

Hüttenbergstrasse. 38–40, 66538 Neunkirchen, Germany
Tel. (+49 68) 21306240
Fax (+49 68) 21306241
E-mail info@bvd-cedi.de
URL www.bvd-cedi.de

CEDIP

European Committee of Professional Diving Instructors
Comite Européen des Moniteurs de Plongée Professionnels
Europäischer Verband der Berufstauchlehrer

62 Avenue des Pins du Cap, 06160 Antibes – Juan les Pins, France
Tel. (+33) 4-93-61-45-45
Fax (+33) 4-93-67-34-93
E-mail cedip.antibes@wanadoo.fr
URL www.cedip.org
Pres. Daniel Mercier
Sec.-Gen. Valérie Houchard

CEDT

European Confederation of Cigarette Dealers
Confédération Européenne des Détaillants en Tabac

Avenue de Broqueville 158, 1200 Brussels, Belgium
Tel. (+32) 2-7721305
Fax (+32) 2-7724401
E-mail cedt@skynet.be
Pres. M. J. Fernandez Vicario
Sec.-Gen. G. Risso
Contact M. Speranza

CEEC

European Committee of Construction Economists
Comité Européen des Economistes de la Construction
Europäischer Ausschuss der Bauwirtschaftler

8 Avenue Percier, 75008 Paris, France

Tel. (+44) 2-07-33-43-87-7
Fax (+44) 2-07-33-43-84-4
E-mail john.frewen-lord@pgcn.net
Pres. M. Webb
Sec.-Gen. C. Deprez
Contact Laurence Marcouly (Sec.)

CEEP

European Centre for Enterprises with Public Participation and of Enterprises of General Economic Interest
Centre Européen des Entreprises à Participation Publique et des Entreprises d'Intérêt Economique Général
Rue de la Charité 15, Bte 12, 1210 Brussels, Belgium
Tel. (+32) 2-2192798
Fax (+32) 2-2181213
E-mail ceep@ceep.org
URL www.ceep.org
Pres. João Cravinho
Sec.-Gen. Rainer Plassmann
Contact Inge Reichert (Dir-Gen.)

CEEREAL

European Breakfast Cereal Association
Rond Point Schumann 9, Bte 11, 1040 Brussels, Belgium
Tel. (+32) 2-2304354
Fax (+32) 2-2309493
E-mail w.hees@verbaende-hees.de
Contact W. Hees

CEETB

European Technical Contractors Committee for the Construction Industry
Comité Européen des Equipements Techniques du Bâtiment
Europäischer Verband der Technischen Gebaüdeausrüstung
Rue Jacques de Lalaing 4, 1040 Brussels, Belgium
Tel. (+32) 2-2850727
Fax (+32) 2-2307861
E-mail contact@ceetb.org
URL www.ceetb.org
Pres. Jan Heeres
Sec.-Gen. Oliver Loebel

CEETTAR

European Confederation of Technical Agricultural and Rural Contractors
Confédération Européenne des Entrepreneurs de Travaux Techniques Agricoles et Ruraux
Europäische Konföderation der Technischen, Landwirtschaftlichen und Ländlichen Unternehmen
Rue d'Alost 7, 1000 Brussels, Belgium
Tel. (+32) 2-2133874
Fax (+32) 2-2133637
E-mail ceettar.europe@skynet.be
Pres. Robert Sabathie
Sec.-Gen. J. Maris

CEEV

European Committee of Wine Companies
Comité Européen des Entreprises Vins
Avenue des Arts 43 5e, 1040 Brussels, Belgium
Tel. (+32) 2-2309970
Fax (+32) 2-5130218
E-mail ceev@ceev.be
URL www.ceev.be
Pres. George Sandeman
Sec.-Gen. Marion Wolfers

CEFACD

European Committee of Manufacturers of Domestic Heating and Cooking Appliances
Comité Européen des Fabricants d'Appareils de Chauffage et de Cuisine Domestique
Europäischer Auschuss der Heiz- und Kochgeräte Industrie
Agoria, Diamant Building, Blvd Auguste Reyers 80, 1030 Brussels, Belgium
Tel. (+32) 2-7067961
Fax (+32) 2-7067966
E-mail françois-xavier.belpaire@agoria.be
URL www.agoria.be
Pres. C. Berlaimont
Contact F.X. Belpaire

CEFIC

European Chemical Industry Council
Conseil Européen de l'Industrie Chimique
Europäischer Rat der Chemischen Industrie

Avenue E. van Nieuwenhuyse 4, PO Box 1,
1160 Brussels, Belgium
Tel. (+32) 2-6767211
Fax (+32) 2-6767300
E-mail mail@cefic.be
URL www.cefic.org
Pres. Peter Elverding
Contact Alain Perroy (Dir-Gen.)

CEFS

European Committee for Sugar Manufacturers

Comité Européen des Fabricants de Sucre

Avenue de Tervueren 182, 1150 Brussels,
Belgium
Tel. (+32) 2-7620760
Fax (+32) 2-7710026
E-mail info@cefs.org
URL www.cefs.org
Pres. Johann Marihart
Sec.-Gen. Jean-Louis Barjol

CEHP/UEHP

European Committee of Private Hospitals and European Union of Independent Hospitals

Comité Européen de l'Hospitalisation Privée et Union Européenne de l'Hospitalisation Privée

Avenue A. Solvay 5, 1170 Brussels, Belgium
Tel. (+32) 2-6603550
Fax (+32) 2-6729062
E-mail genevieve.robin@skynet.be
URL www.uehp.org
Pres. Max Pomseille
Sec.-Gen. Paolo Giordano
Contact H. Anrys

CEI

European Confederation of Estate Agents
Confédération Européenne de l'Immobilier

Sainctelettesquare 11–12, 1000 Brussels,
Belgium
Tel. (+32) 2-2194008
Fax (+32) 2-2178841
E-mail asgroot@yahoo.com
URL www.web-cei.com
Pres. André Groot
Sec.-Gen. I. Tonge
Contact Ph. Ruelens

CEI-BOIS

European Confederation of Woodworking Industries

Confédération Européenne des Industries du Bois

Zentralverband der Europäischen Holzindustrie

Allee Hof-Ter-Vleest 5/4, 1070 Brussels,
Belgium
Tel. (+32) 2-5562585
Fax (+32) 2-5562595
E-mail info@cei-bois.org
URL www.cei-bois.org
Pres. Bo Borgstrom
Sec.-Gen. Filip de Jaeger
Contact Dr Guy van Steertegem (Advisor)

CEIR

European Committee for the Valve Industry
Comité Européen de l'Industrie de la Robinetterie
Europäisches Komitee der Armaturenindustrie

C/o Orgalime, Boulevard Reyers 80, 1030
Brussels, Belgium
Tel. (+32) 2-7068237
Fax (+32) 27068253
E-mail l.platteur@marketseurope.eu.com
URL www.ceir-online.org
Pres. Fransisco Lafuente
Sec.-Gen. Guy van Doorslaer
Contact Janet Almond (Asst)

CEJA

European Council of Young Farmers
Conseil Européen des Jeunes Agriculteurs
Europäischer Rat der Junglandwirte

Rue Belliard 23/A, Bte 8, 1040 Brussels,
Belgium
Tel. (+32) 2-2304210
Fax (+32) 2-2801805
E-mail ceja@ceja.be
URL www.ceja.org
Pres. Giacomo Ballari
Sec.-Gen. Henriette Christensen
Contact Albert Falip Gasull (Vice-Pres.)

CEJH

European Community of Young Horticulturists

Communautée Européenne des Jeunes de l'Horticulture

Europäische Gemeinschaft der Jungen Gartenbauer

Giessener Strasse 47, 35305 Grünberg, Germany
Tel. (+49 64) 01910150
Fax (+49 64) 01910176
E-mail info@cejh.org
URL www.cejh.org
Pres. Klaus Schnaidt
Sec.-Gen. Jörg Disselborg
Contact N. Becker

CELCAA

European Liaison Committee for the Agri-Food Trade

Comité Européen de Liaison des Commerces Agricoles et Agro-Alimentaires

Europäischer Verbindungsausschuss für den Handel mit Landwirtschaftlichen Produkten und Lebensmitteln

Rue du Trône 98, 1050 Brussels, Belgium
Tel. (+32) 2-2300370
Fax (+32) 2-2304323
E-mail celcaa@Schuman9.com
URL www.schuman9.com
Pres. Christian de Cannière
Sec.-Gen. Bernd Gruner
Contact Kathrin Renner (Policy Adviser)

CEMA

European Committee of Associations of Manufacturers of Agricultural Machinery

Comité Européen des Groupements de Constructeurs du Machinisme Agricole

Europäisches Komitee der Verbände der Landmaschinenhersteller

19 Rue Jacques Bingen, 75017 Paris, France
Tel. (+33) 1-42-12-85-90
Fax (+33) 1-40-54-95-60
E-mail cema@sygma.org
URL www.cema-agri.org
Pres. M. Siebert
Sec.-Gen. J. Dehollain

CEMAFON

European Committee for Materials and Products for Foundries

Comité Européen des Matériels et Produits pour la Fonderie

Europäisches Komitee der Hersteller von Giessereimaschinen und Giessereiausrüstungen

Lyoner Strasse 18, 60528 Frankfurt, Germany
Tel. (+49 69) 66031278
Fax (+49 69) 66032278
E-mail cemafon@vdma.org
URL www.cemafon.org
Pres. Gabriel Galante
Sec.-Gen. Dr jur. Arnold Lahrem
Contact Dr Gutmann Habig (Man. Dir)

CEMATEX

European Committee of Textile Machinery Manufacturers

Comité Européen des Constructeurs de Machines Textiles

Europäisches Komitee der Textilmaschinenhersteller

C/o UCMTF, 92038 Paris La Défense Cedex, France
Tel. (+33) 1-47-17-63-45
Fax (+33) 1-47-17-63-48
E-mail ucmt@worlnet.fr
URL www.cematex.org
Pres. Edward Roberts
Sec.-Gen. Evelyne Cholet

CEMBUREAU

European Cement Association

Association Européenne du Ciment

Rue d'Arlon 55, 1040 Brussels, Belgium
Tel. (+32) 2-2341011
Fax (+32) 2-2304720
E-mail general.secretariat@cembureau.be
URL www.cembureau.be
Pres. Dr Jurgen Lose
Sec.-Gen. Alain van der Vaet
Contact Jean-Marie Chandelle (Chief Exec.)

CEMEP

European Committee of Manufacturers of Electrical Machines and Power Electronics

Comité Européen de Constructeurs de Machines Electriques et d'Electronique de Puissance

Europäisches Komitee der Hersteller von Elektrischen und Kraftelektronischen Maschinen

Rue Evariste Galois, Site de Chalembert BP 31,
  86130 Jaunay Clan, France
Tel. (+33) 5-49-62-86-16
Fax (+33) 5-49-62-86-19
E-mail jmolina@gimelec.fr
URL www.cemep.org

CEN

European Committee for Standardization
Comité Européen de Normalisation
Europäisches Komitee für Normung

Rue de Stassart 36, 1050 Brussels, Belgium
Tel. (+32) 2-5500811
Fax (+32) 2-5500819
E-mail infodesk@cenorm.be
URL www.cenorm.be
Pres. Dkfm. Hans-Joachim Bäurle
Sec.-Gen. Hermann Wilhelm Ahls
Contact Karsten Meinhold (Chair.)

CENELEC

European Committee for Electrotechnical
Standardization
Comité Européen de Normalisation
Electrotechnique
Europäisches Komitee für Elektrotechnische
Normung

Rue de Stassartstraat 35, 1050 Brussels,
  Belgium
Tel. (+32) 2-5196871
Fax (+32) 2-5196919
E-mail info@cenelec.org
URL www.cenelec.org
Pres. Dr Ulrich Spindler
Contact David Start (Vice-Pres.)

CEOAH

European Committee for Agricultural and
Horticultural Tools and Implements
Comité Européen de l'Outillage Agricole et
Horticole
Europäisches Komitee der Gerätehersteller
für Landwirtschaft und Garten

Light Trades House, Melbourne Avenue 3,
  Sheffield S10 2QJ, United Kingdom
Tel. (+44 114) 266-3084
Fax (+44 114) 267-0910
E-mail light.trades@virgin.net
URL www.britishtools.co.uk

Pres. D. Macdomhnaill
Contact J.G. Till

CEOC

European Confederation of Organisations
for Testing, Inspection, Certification and
Prevention
Confédération Européenne des Organismes
de Contrôle Technique, d'Inspection, de
Certification et de Prévention
Europäische Vereinigung der
Organisationen für Prüfung,
Überwachung, Zertifizierung und
Prävention

Rue du Commerce 20–22, 1000 Brussels,
  Belgium
Tel. (+32) 2-5115065
Fax (+32) 2-5025047
E-mail voelzow@ceoc.com
URL www.ceoc.com

Pres. Hugo Eberhardt
Sec.-Gen. Michael Volzow
Contact Jean-Rémi Gouze (Vice-Pres.)

CEP

Federation of National Organisations of
Importers and Exporters of Fish
Comité des Organisations Nationales des
Importateurs et Exportateurs de Poisson

Avenue de Roodebeek 30, 1030 Brussels,
  Belgium
Tel. (+32) 2-7438730
Fax (+32) 2-7368175
E-mail aipcee@sia-dvi.be
Pres. Pastoor Guus
Sec.-Gen. Michel Coenen
Contact Mozos Juan (Vice-Pres.)

CEPA

Confederation of European Pest Control
Associations
Confédération Européenne des Associations
de Pesticides Appliqués

Rue de l'Association 27, 1000 Brussels,
  Belgium
Tel. (+32) 2-2258330
Fax (+32) 2-2258339
E-mail info@cepa-europe.org
URL www.cepa-europe.org
Pres. Robert Stuyt
Contact Marc Esculier (Vice-Pres.)

CEPE

European Council of Paint, Printing Ink and Artists' Colours Industry

Conseil Européen de l'Industrie des Peintures, des Encres d'Imprimerie et des Couleurs d'Art

Europäische Vereinigung der Lack-, Druckfarben und Künstlerfarbenindustrie

Avenue van Nieuwenhuyse 4, 1160 Brussels, Belgium
Tel. (+32) 2-6767480
Fax (+32) 2-6767490
E-mail secretariat@cepe.org
URL www.cepe.org
Pres. Neville Petersen
Sec.-Gen. Jean Schoder
Contact Paul Keymolen (Asst Sec.-Gen.)

CEPEC

Confédération Européenne des Professionnels de l'Esthétique Cosmétique

64 rue de la Briquetterie, 17000 La Rochelle, France
Tel. (+33) 5-46-41-69-79
Fax (+33) 5-46-42-25-96
E-mail info@fngae.fr
URL www.fngae.fr
Pres. Michelle Lamoureux-Stern
Sec.-Gen. E. Forte

CEPI

Confederation of European Paper Industries

Confédération des Industries Papetières Européennes

Europäische Konföderation der Papierindustrien

Avenue Louise 250, Bte 80, 1050 Brussels, Belgium
Tel. (+32) 2-6274911
Fax (+32) 2-6468137
E-mail c.carlisle@cepi.org
URL www.cepi.org
Contact Carl Bjornberg (Chair.)

CEPI

European Council for Real Estate Professions

Conseil Européen des Professions Immobilières

Europäischer Immobilien Rat

Avenue de Tervueren 36, Bte 2, 1040 Brussels, Belgium
Tel. (+32) 2-7354990
Fax (+32) 2-7359988
E-mail cepi@cepi.be
URL www.cepi.be
Pres. Andrea Merello
Sec.-Gen. Alexander Benedetti
Contact Martine van Adorp (Office Man.)

CEPIS

Council of European Professional Informatics Societies

C/o VDE-Haus, Stresemannallee 15, 60596 Frankfurt am Main, Germany
Tel. (+49 696) 308-392
Fax (+49 69) 96315233
URL www.cepis.org
Pres. J. Ruissafo

CEPLIS

European Council of the Liberal Professions

Conseil Europeen des Professions Liberales

Rue Jacques de Lalaing 4, 1040 Brussels, Belgium
Tel. (+32) 2-5114439
Fax (+32) 2-5110124
E-mail ceplis@pi.be
URL www.ceplis.org
Pres. Adrien Bedossa
Sec.-Gen. Estelle Mangold
Contact John Ferguson (Vice-Pres.)

CEPM

Confédération Européenne des Producteurs de Maïs

21 Siège Social, Chemin de Pau, 64121 Montardon, France
Tel. (+33) 5-59-12-67-00
Fax (+33) 5-59-12-67-10
Pres. Christophe Terrain

CEPMC

Council of European Producers of Materials for Construction

Conseil Européen des Producteurs de Matériaux de Construction

Vereinigung Europäischer Baustoffhersteller

Gulledelle 98, PO Box 7, 1200 Brussels, Belgium
Tel. (+32) 2-7758491

Fax (+32) 2-7713056
E-mail info@cepmc.org
URL www.cepmc.org
Pres. Jim O'Brien
Sec.-Gen. Philip Bennett
Contact Han de Groot (Chair.)

CEPS

European Spirits Organisation
Confédération Européenne des Producteurs de Spiritueux
Avenue de Tervueren 192, Bte 3, 1150 Brussels, Belgium
Tel. (+32) 2-7792423
Fax (+32) 2-7729820
E-mail ceps1@skynet.be
URL www.europeanspirits.org
Pres. Jean-Paul Bouyat
Sec.-Gen. Robby Schreiber
Contact Anthony Arke (Dir-Gen.)

CEPT

European Conference of Postal and Telecommunications Administrations
Conférence Européenne des Administrations des Postes et des Télécommunications
Europäische Konferenz der Verwaltungen für Post und Telekommunikation
Avenue de l'astronomie 14, Bte 21, 1210 Brussels, Belgium
Tel. (+32) 2-2268896
Fax (+32) 2-2268877
E-mail cerp.secretariat@ibpt.be
URL www.cept.org
Pres. Marc Furrer
Contact Chris van Diepenbeek (Chair.)

CER

Community of European Railways
Communauté des Chemins de Fer Européens
Gemeinschaft der Europäischen Bahnen
Avenue des Arts 53, 1000 Brussels, Belgium
Tel. (+32) 2-2130870
Fax (+32) 2-5125231
E-mail contact@cer.be
URL www.cer.be
Pres. Giancarlo Cimoli
Contact Dr Johannes Ludewig (Exec. Dir)

CERP

European Public Relations Confederation
Confédération Européenne des Relations Publiques
Europäische Konföderation der Public Relations Gesellschaften
Chaussée de Gand 443, Bte 4, 1080 Brussels, Belgium
Tel. (+32) 2-4140432
Fax (+32) 2-4149605
E-mail secretariat@bprc.be
URL www.cerp.org
Pres. Jean-Jaques Strijp
Sec.-Gen. Daniel de Marto
Contact Thierry Habotte (Vice-Pres.)

CERAME-UNIE

Liaison Office of the European Ceramic Industries
Bureau de Liaison des Industries Céramiques Européennes
Verbindungsbüro der europäischen Keramikindustrie
Rue des Colonies 18–24, Bte 17, 1000 Brussels, Belgium
Tel. (+32) 2-5113012
Fax (+32) 2-5115174
E-mail sec@cerameunie.net
URL www.cerameunie.net
Pres. Luitwin Gisbert von Boch
Sec.-Gen. Rogier Chorus

CESA

Committee of European Union Shipbuilders Associations
Rue Marie de Bourgogne 52–54, 3rd floor, 1000 Brussels, Belgium
Tel. (+32) 2-2302791
Fax (+32) 2-2304332
E-mail info@cesa-shipbuilding.org
URL www.cesa-shipbuilding.org
Pres. Dr Luken
Sec.-Gen. Dr Reinhard Lüken
Contact Arkadiusz Aszyk (Policy Adviser)

CESCE

European Committee for Business Support Services
Comité Européen des Services de Soutien aux Entreprises
Kanselarijstraat 19, 1000 Brugge, Belgium

Tel. (+32) 2-2274940
Fax (+32) 2-2276391
E-mail fabienne.sorba@ffcgea.fr
URL www.cesce.org
Pres. Jean Claude Bachelot
Contact Jean Claude Bachelot (Gen. Man.)

CESI

**European Confederation of Independent
Trade Unions**

**Confédération Européenne des Syndicats
Indépendants**

**Europäische Union der Unabhängigen
Gewerkschaften**

Avenue de la Joyeuse Entrée 1–5, 1040
Brussels, Belgium
Tel. (+32) 2-2821870
Fax (+32) 2-2821871
E-mail info@cesi.org
URL www.cesi.org
Pres. Valerio Salvatore
Sec.-Gen. Helmut Müllers
Contact Claudia Buley (Sec.)

CET

**European Ceramic Tile Manufacturers'
Federation**

**Fédération Européenne des Producteurs de
Carreaux**

**Europäischer Industrieverband der
Keramikfliesen**

Rue des Colonies 18–24, 1000 Brussels,
Belgium
Tel. (+32) 2-5113012
Fax (+32) 2-5115174
E-mail sec@cerameunie.net
URL www.cerameunie.net
Pres. Luitwin Gisbert von Boch
Sec.-Gen. Roiger Chorus

CET

Taxi Radio Bruxellois S.A.

Confédération Européenne des Taxis

Europäische Konföderation der Taxis

Rue des Carburants 54–56, 1190 Brussels,
Belgium
Tel. (+32) 2-3494143
Fax (+32) 2-3494142
E-mail m.petre@taxis.be
URL www.taxis.be

Pres. Petre
Contact Van Lauwe (Sec.)

CETOP

**European Oil Hydraulic and Pneumatic
Committee**

**Comité Européen des Transmissions
Oléohydrauliques et Pneumatiques**

**Europäisches Komitee Ölhydraulik und
Pneumatik**

Lyoner Strasse 18, 60528 Frankfurt am Main,
Germany
Tel. (+49 69) 66031319
Fax (+49 69) 66031459
E-mail info@cetop.org
URL www.cetop.org
Pres. Dr Ing. Amadio Bolzani
Sec.-Gen. Sylvia Grohmann Mundschenk
Contact Peter Abplanalp (Vice-Pres.)

CFE

Confédération Fiscale Européenne

Neue Promenade 4, 10178 Berlin-Mitte,
Germany
Tel. (+49 30) 2400870
Fax (+49 30) 24008799
E-mail generalsecretary@cfe-eutax.org
URL www.cfe-eutax.org
Pres. François Lambrechts
Sec.-Gen. Weiler
Contact Prof. Mario Boidi (Vice-Pres.)

CIAA

**Confederation of the Food and Drink
Industries of the EU**

**Confédération des Industries Agro-
Alimentaires de l'UE**

Avenue des Arts 43, 1040 Brussels, Belgium
Tel. (+32) 2-5141111
Fax (+32) 2-5112905
E-mail ciaa@ciaa.be
URL www.ciaa.be
Pres. Jean Martin
Contact Israelachwilli (Dir-Gen.)

CIBE

**International Confederation of European
Beet Growers**

**Confédération Internationale des
Betteraviers Européens**

Internationale Vereinigung Europaeischer Rübenanbauer

29 Rue du Général Foy, 75008 Paris, France
Tel. (+33) 1-44-69-39-00
Fax (+33) 1-42-93-28-93
E-mail lodiers@textielnet.nl
Pres. Von Arnold
Sec.-Gen. Hubert Chavanes

CIDE / CIDE

European Dehydrators Association

Commission Intersyndicale des Déshydrateurs Européens

Arbeitsgemeinschaft Europäischer Trockungsbetriebe

Rue Froissart 57, 1040 Brussels, Belgium
Tel. (+33) 1-42617294
Fax (+33) 1-49270273
E-mail contact@dehy.net
URL www.luzerne.org
Pres. Naglia
Sec.-Gen. Guillemot

CIELFFA

International Research Committee for Cold-Rolled Strips

Comité International d'Etude du Laminage à Froid du Feuillard d'Acier

Kaiserswerther Strasse 137, Postfach 300333, 40474 Düsseldorf, Germany
Tel. (+49 211) 478060
Fax (+49 211) 4780622
E-mail info@cielffa.org
URL www.cielffa.org
Pres. Gerhard Tichler
Contact Dr Friedrich Neuhaus (Sec.)

CIMO

European Fresh Produce Importers Association

Av. de Broqueville 272, 1200 Brussels, Belgium
Tel. (+32) 2-7713635
Fax (+32) 2-2629425
E-mail info@freshfel.org
URL www.cimo.be
Contact Philipe Binard

CIPF

International Committee for Cold-Rolled Sections

Comité International du Profilage à Froid

C/o Confederation of British Metal Forming, National Metal Forming Centre, Birmingham Road 47, West Bromwich B70 6TW, United Kingdom
Pres. M. Bertrams
Contact J. Field

CIPF

International Confederation for Trade in Straw, Fodders and Derivatives

Confédération Internationale du Commerce et de l'Industrie des Pailles, Fourrages, Tourbes et Dérivés

2 Rue de Viarmes, Paris Cedex 01, 75040 Paris, France
Tel. (+33) 1-42-36-84-35
Fax (+33) 1-42-36-44-93
E-mail ucipf@mageos.com
Pres. Bernard Creuwels
Contact Guy Coudert

CIRCCE

International Confederation of the Commercial Representation of the European Community

Confédération Internationale de la Représentation Commerciale de la Communauté Européenne

Internationale Vereinigung der Handelsvertretung der Europäischen Gemeinschaft

2 Rue d'Hauteville, 75010 Paris, France
Tel. (+33) 1-48-24-97-59
Fax (+33) 1-45-23-19-48
E-mail csm.secretariat@libertysurf.fr
URL www.csm.fr
Pres. J. P. Broggi
Sec.-Gen. S. James

CIRFS

International Rayon and Synthetic Fibres Committee

Comité International de la Rayonne et des Fibres Synthétiques

Internationale Chemiefaservereinigung

Avenue E. van Nieuwenhuyse 4, 1160 Brussels,
Belgium
Tel. (+32) 2-6767455
Fax (+32) 2-6767454
E-mail info@cirfs.org
URL www.cirfs.org
Sec.-Gen. Monique Gerritsma
Contact Colin Purvis (Dir-Gen.)

CITPA

**International Confederation of Paper and
Board Converters in Europe**

Avenue Louise 250, Box 108, 1050 Brussels,
Belgium
Tel. (+32) 2-6269838
Fax (+32) 2-6466460
E-mail info@citpa-europe.org
URL www.citpa-europe.org
Pres. Sanguinazzi
Sec.-Gen. Pfeiffer

CLCCR

**Liaison Committee of the Body and Trailer
Building Industry**

**Comité de Liaison de la Construction de
Carrosseries et de Remorques**

**Verbindungsausschuss der Aufbauen- und
Anhängerindustrie**

C/o Verband der Automobilindustrie e.V.
(VDA), Westendstrasse 61, 60325 Frankfurt
am Main, Germany
Tel. (+49 69) 97507308
Fax (+49 69) 97507261
E-mail heibach@vda.de
URL www.vda.be
Pres. H.J. Nooteboom
Sec.-Gen. Dr M. Heibach
Contact D. Reed (Vice-Pres.)

CLECAT

**European Association for Forwarding,
Transport, Logistic and Customs Services**

Rue du Commerce 77, 1040 Brussels, Belgium
Tel. (+32) 2-5034705
Fax (+32) 2-5034752
E-mail info@clecat.org
URL www.clecat.org
Pres. Manfred Boes
Sec.-Gen. Han van Os
Contact Marco Sorgetti (Dir-Gen.)

CLEDIPA

**European Liaison Committee of the
Independent Distribution of Spare Parts
and Equipment for Motor Cars**

**Comité de Liaison Européen de la
Distribution Indépendante de Pièces de
Rechange et Equipement pour
Automobiles**

**Europäischer Verbindungsausschuss der
Selbsständigen Verteilung von
Ersatzteilen & Ausrüstungen für
Kraftwagen**

Blvd de la Woluwe 46, Bte 12, 1200 Brussels,
Belgium
Tel. (+32) 2-7786200
Fax (+32) 2-7621255
E-mail figiefa@federauto.be
URL www.figiefa.org
Pres. F. van Heck
Sec.-Gen. S. Gotzen

CLEO

European Liaison Committee of Osteopaths

**Comité de Liaison Européen des
Ostéopathes**

**Europäisches Verbindungskomitee der
Osteopathen**

116 Avenue des Champs Elysées, 75008 Paris,
France
Tel. (+33) 1-44-21-80-75
Fax (+33) 1-44-21-82-99
Pres. J. Barkworth
Sec.-Gen. F.P. Berthenet

CLEPA

**European Association of Automotive
Suppliers**

**Association Européenne des Equipementiers
Automobiles**

Verband der Europäischen Autozulieferer

Blvd Brand Whitlock 87, Bte 1, 1200 Brussels,
Belgium
Tel. (+32) 2-7439130
Fax (+32) 2-7320055
E-mail info@clepa.be
URL www.clepa.be
Pres. Jürgen Harnisch
Contact Maggy Creplet (Head of
Administration)

CLGE

Council of European Geodetic Surveyors

Comité de Liaison des Géomètres Européens

Bürgerstrasse 34, 6010 Innsbruck, Austria
Tel. (+43 512) 58841160
Fax (+43 512) 58841161
E-mail gerda.schennach@bev.gv.at
URL www.clge.org
Pres. Klaus Rurup
Sec.-Gen. Gerda Schennach
Contact Henning Elmstroem (Vice-Pres.)

CLITRAVI

Liaison Centre for the Meat Processing Industries in the EU

Centre de Liaison des Industries Transformatrices de Viandes de l'UE

Blvd Baudouin 18, Bte 4, 1000 Brussels, Belgium
Tel. (+32) 2-2035141
Fax (+32) 2-2033244
E-mail devries@skypro.be
Sec.-Gen. Dirk Dobbelaere

CLPUE

Liaison Committee of Podiatrists of the EU

Comité de Liaison des Podologues de l'UE

Verbindungskomitee für Podologen der EU

St. Bernardse Steenweg 1000, 2620 Hemiksen, Belgium
Tel. (+32) 3-8773938
Fax (+32) 3-8775902
E-mail fip.roofthooft.jose@pi.be
Pres. Christophe Jacobs

CNUE

Conférence des Notariats de l'Union Européenne

Avenue de Cortenbergh, 52, 1000 Brussels, Belgium
Tel. (+32) 2-5139529
Fax (+32) 2-5139382
E-mail info@cnue.be
URL www.cnue.be
Pres. Paolo Piccoli

COCERAL

Committee of Cereals, Oilseeds, Animal Feed, Olive Oil, Oils and Fats and Agrosupply Trade in the EU

Comité du Commerce des Céréales, Aliments du Bétail, Oléagineux, Huile d'Olive, Huiles et Graisses et Agrofournitures

Komitee des Getreide-, Futtermittel-, Ölsaaten, Olivenöl, Ölen und Fetten und landwirtschaftliche Betriebsmittelhandels in der EG

Rue du Trône 98, 4ème étage, 1050 Brussels, Belgium
Tel. (+32) 2-5020808
Fax (+32) 2-5026030
E-mail secretariat@coceral.com
URL www.coceral.com
Pres. Andrew Barnard
Sec.-Gen. Chantal Fauth

COCIR

European Coordination Committee of the Radiological and Electromedical Industries

Comité Européen de Coordination des Industries Radiologiques et Electromédicales

C/o ZVEI Fachverband, Electromedizinische Technik, Stresemannallee 19, 60596 Frankfurt am Main, Germany
Tel. (+49 69) 6302207
Fax (+49 69) 6302390
E-mail office@cocir.org
URL www.cocir.org
Pres. Tom Egelund
Sec.-Gen. Hans-Peter Bursig

COFAG

Glutamic Acid Manufacturers Association of the EU

Comité des Fabricants d'Acide Glutamique de l'UE

Glutaminsaüre Herstellers Komitee bei der EG

C/o Ajinomoto Eurolysine, 153 rue de Courcelles, 75817 Paris, France
Tel. (+33) 1-44-40-12-29
Fax (+33) 1-44-40-12-15
E-mail Guion_Philippe@eli.ajinomoto.com
URL www.glutamat.com
Contact Philippe Guion (Sec.Exec.)

COFALEC

Committee of Bakers Yeast Manufacturers of the EU

Comité des Fabricants de Levure Panification de l'UE

Komitee der Hefeindustrie in der EG

14 Rue de Turbigo, 75001 Paris, France
Tel. (+33) 1-45-08-54-82
Fax (+33) 1-42-21-02-14
E-mail info@cofalec.com
URL www.cofalec.com
Pres. André de Schepper
Sec.-Gen. Hubert Bocquelet

COGECA

General Committee for Agricultural Cooperation in the EU

Comité Général de la Coopération Agricole de l'UE

Allgemeiner Ausschuss des Ländlichen Genossenschaftswesens der Europäischen Union

Rue de Trèves, 61, 1040 Brussels, Belgium
Tel. (+32) 2-2872711
Fax (+32) 2-2872700
E-mail mail@copa-cogeca.be
URL www.copa-cogeca.be
Pres. Eduardo Baamonde
Sec.-Gen. Franz-Josef Feiter
Contact Joël Castany (Vice-Pres.)

COGEN EUROPE

European Association for the Promotion of Cogeneration

Association Européenne pour la Promotion de la Cogénération

Gulledelle 98, 1200 Brussels, Belgium
Tel. (+32) 2-7728290
Fax (+32) 2-7725044
E-mail info@cogen.org
URL www.cogen.org
Pres. G. van Ingen
Contact Dr Simon Minett (Man. Dir)

COLIBI

Liaison Committee of European Bicycle Manufacturers

Comité de Liaison des Fabricants de Bicyclettes de la Communauté Européenne

Verbindungskomitee der Fahrradhersteller in der Europäischen Gemeinschaft

Blvd de la Woluwe 46, B 16, 1200 Brussels, Belgium

Tel. (+32) 2-7786458
Fax (+32) 2-7628171
E-mail contact@colibi.com
URL www.colibi.com
Pres. René Takens
Sec.-Gen. Greet Engelen
Contact Davide Brambilla (Vice-Pres.)

COLIPA

European Cosmetic, Toiletry and Perfumery Association

Avenue Hermann Debroux 15A, 1160 Brussels, Belgium
Tel. (+32) 2-2276610
Fax (+32) 2-2276627
E-mail colipa@colipa.be
URL www.colipa.com
Pres. Puig
Sec.-Gen. Bertil Heerink
Contact Sebastian Marx (Communication Man.)

COLIPED

Association of the European Two-Wheeler Parts' and Accessories' Industry

Blvd de la Woluwe 46, B 16, 1200 Brussels, Belgium
Tel. (+32) 2-7786458
Fax (+32) 2-7628171
E-mail greet.engelen@coliped.com
URL www.coliped.com
Pres. Willo Blome
Contact Pascal Marchand (Vice-Pres.)

CONCAWE

Oil Companies' European Organization for Environment, Health and Safety

Organisation Européenne des Compagnies Pétrolières pour l'Environnement, la Santé et Sécurité

Europäische Organisation der Ölgesellschaften für Umwelt, Gesundheit und Sicherheit

Blvd du Souverain 165, 1160 Brussels, Belgium
Tel. (+32) 2-5669160
Fax (+32) 2-5669181
E-mail info@concawe.org
URL www.concawe.org
Pres. Wilhelm Bonse Geuking
Sec.-Gen. Jean Castelein
Contact Herman Meyer (Dir)

COPA

Committee of Agricultural Organizations in the EU

Comité des Organisations Professionnelles Agricoles de l'UE

Rue de Trèves, 61, 1040 Brussels, Belgium
Tel. (+32) 2-2872711
Fax (+32) 2-2872700
E-mail mail@copa-cogeca.be
URL www.copa-cogeca.be
Pres. Peter Gaemelke
Sec.-Gen. Franz-Josef Feiter
Contact Joël Castany (Vice-Pres.)

COTANCE

Confederation of National Associations of Tanners and Dressers of the EC

Confédération des Associations Nationales de Tanneurs et Mégissiers de la CE

Vereinigung der Nationalen Verbanden der Lederindustrie

Rue Belliard 3, 1040 Brussels, Belgium
Tel. (+32) 2-5127703
Fax (+32) 2-5129157
E-mail info@euroleather.com
URL www.euroleather.com
Pres. Josep Costa
Sec.-Gen. Gustavo Gonzalez-Quijano

COTREL

Committee of Associations of European Transformers Manufacturers

Comité des Associations de Constructeurs de Transformateurs dans la Communauté Européenne

EG-Zusammenarbeit der Fachverbände der Transformatorenhersteller

Agoria, Boulevard Reyers 80, 1030 Brussels, Belgium
Tel. (+32) 2-7068000
Fax (+32) 2-7068009
E-mail herman.looghe@agoria.be
URL www.cotrel.com

CPE

European Farmers Coordination

Coordination Paysanne Européenne

Europäische Bauern Koordination

Rue de la Sablonnière, 18, 1000 Brussels, Belgium
Tel. (+32) 2-2173112
Fax (+32) 2-2184509
E-mail cpe@cpefarmers.org
URL www.cpefarmers.org
Contact Gérard Choplin (Co-ordinator)

CPIV

Permanent International Vinegar Committee

Comité Permanent International du Vinaigre

Ständiger Internationaler Ausschuss der Essighersteller – Gemeinsamer Markt

Reuterstrasse 151, 53113 Bonn, Germany
Tel. (+49 228) 212-017
Fax (+49 228) 229-460
E-mail info@verbaendeburo.de
Pres. Dothley
Sec.-Gen. Dr Murau

CPIV

Standing Committee of the European Glass Industries

Comité Permanent des Industries du Verre Européennes

Ständiger Ausschuss der europäischen Glasindustrien

Avenue Louise 89, 1050 Brussels, Belgium
Tel. (+32) 2-5384446
Fax (+32) 2-5378469
E-mail info@cpivglass.be
URL www.cpivglass.be
Pres. David Workman
Sec.-Gen. Frédéric van Houte
Contact Véronique Favry Dupuis (Asst)

CPLOL

Standing Liaison Committee of EU Speech Therapists and Logopedists

Comité Permanent de Liaison des Orthophonistes-Logopèdes de l'UE

145 Blvd Magenta, 75010 Paris, France
Tel. (+33) 1-40-35-63-75
Fax (+33) 1-40-37-41-42
E-mail info@cplol.org
URL www.cplol.org
Pres. Birgitta Rosén Gustafsson
Sec.-Gen. Bent Kjaer
Contact Aileen Patterson (Vice-Pres.)

CPME
Standing Committee of European Doctors
Comité Permanent des Médecins Européens
Rue de la Science 41, 1040 Brussels, Belgium
Tel. (+32) 2-7327202
Fax (+32) 2-7327344
E-mail secretariat@cpme.be
URL www.cpme.be
Pres. Dr Bernhard Grevin
Sec.-Gen. Lisette Tiddens Engwirda
Contact Dr Poulsen (Vice-Pres.)

CRIET
European Textile Finishers' Organisation
Comités Réunis de l'Industrie de l'Ennoblissement Textile dans les Communautés Européennes
POB 518, 3900 AM Veenendaal, Netherlands
Tel. (+31 318) 564488
Fax (+31 318) 564487
E-mail criet@criet.org
URL www.criet.org
Sec.-Gen. Cees Lodiers
Contact Koen Buyse (Vice-Pres.)

DHAEMAE-SIS
Disposable Hypodermic and Allied Equipment Manufacturers' Association of Europe
Association des Fabricants d'Aiguilles Hypodermiques et Produits Connexes en Europe
Vereinigung der Hersteller von Wegwerfbaren Subkutanspritzen und Verwandten Produkten in Europa
Place Saint Lambert 14, 1200 Brussels, Belgium
Tel. (+32) 2-7722212
Fax (+32) 2-7713909
E-mail richard.moore@eucomed.be
URL www.eucomed.be
Pres. Aerts

DLC / CLD / ZAV
Dental Liaison Committee in the EU
Comité de Liaison des Praticiens de l'Art Dentaire des Pays de l'UE
Zahnärztlicher Verbindungsausschuss zur EU
Avenue de la Renaissance 1, 1000 Brussels, Belgium

Tel. (+32) 2-7363429
Fax (+32) 2-7355407
E-mail ct@bzak.be
Pres. Dr W. Doneus
Contact Claudia Ritter (Office Man.)

EAA
European Aluminium Association
Association Européenne d'Aluminium
Avenue de Broqueville 12, 1150 Brussels, Belgium
Tel. (+32) 2-7756363
Fax (+32) 2-7790531
E-mail eaa@eaa.be
URL www.aluminium.org
Pres. Bark Jones
Sec.-Gen. Patrick de Schrynmaker
Contact Jan te Bos (Dir Public Affairs)

EAAP / FEZ / EVT
European Association for Animal Production
Fédération Européenne de Zootechnie
Europäische Vereinigung für Tierproduktion
Via Nomentana 134, 00162 Rome, Italy
Tel. (+39) 06-86329141
Fax (+39) 06-86329263
E-mail eaap@eaap.org
URL www.eaap.org
Pres. J. Flanagan
Sec.-Gen. Andrea Rosati
Contact L. Fésüs (Vice-Pres.)

EACA
European Association of Communications Agencies
Blvd Brand Whitlock 152, 1200 Brussels, Belgium
Tel. (+32) 2-7400710
Fax (+32) 2-7400717
E-mail info@eaca.be
URL www.eaca.be
Pres. James Best
Contact Dominic Lyle (Dir-Gen.)

EACB / GEBC
European Association of Cooperative Banks
Groupement Européen des Banques Coopératives

Europäische Vereinigung der Genossenschaftsbanken

Rue de l'industrie 26–38, 1040 Brussels, Belgium
Tel. (+32) 2-2301124
Fax (+32) 2-2300649
E-mail secretariat@eurocoopbanks.coop
URL www.eurocoopbanks.coop
Pres. Etienne Pflimlin
Sec.-Gen. Hervé Guider
Contact Kumar Dasgupta (Project Man.)

EADP

European Association of Directory and Database Publishers

Association Européenne des Editeurs d'Annuaires et de Bases de Données

Europäischer Verband der Adressbuch- und Datenbankverlegger

Avenue Franklin Roosevelt 127, 1050 Brussels, Belgium
Tel. (+32) 2-6463060
Fax (+32) 2-6463637
E-mail mailbox@eadp.org
URL www.eadp.org
Pres. Dr Christoph Dumrath
Sec.-Gen. Anne Lerat
Contact Richard Duggleby (Vice-Pres.)

EADTU

European Association of Distance Teaching Universities

Association Européenne des Universités d'Enseignement à Distance

Europäischer Verband der Universitaten für Fernstudien

POB 2960, 6401 DL Heerlen, Netherlands
Tel. (+31 45) 5672214
Fax (+31 45) 5741473
E-mail secretariat@eadtu.nl
URL www.eadtu.nl
Pres. Prof. Jorgen Bang
Sec.-Gen. Piet Henderikx

EAEVE / AEEEV

European Association of Establishments for Veterinary Education

Association Européenne des Etablissements d'Enseignement Vétérinaire

Europäischer Verband der Veterinarmedizinischen Ausbildungsstatten

Rue Leys 34, 1000 Brussels, Belgium
Tel. (+32) 2-7368029
Fax (+32) 2-7337862
E-mail eaeve@yahoo.co.uk
URL www.eaeve.org
Pres. Dr Tito Horacio Fernandes
Contact B. Jones (Sec.)

EAFE

European Association of Fisheries Economists

FOI, Rolighedsvej 25, 1958 Frederiksberg, Denmark
Tel. (+45) 35-28-68-93
Fax (+45) 35-28-68-00
E-mail elsebeth@foi.dk
URL www.eafe-fish.org
Pres. Rodgers
Sec.-Gen. Sabatena

EAHP / AEPH

European Association of Hospital Pharmacists

Association Européenne des Pharmaciens des Hôpitaux

Europäische Vereinigung der Krankenhaus Apotheker

Walzegem 6, 9860 Oosterzele, Belgium
Tel. (+32) 9-3603789
Fax (+32) 9-3613010
E-mail info@eahponline.org
URL www.eahponline.org
Pres. Jacqueline Surugue
Sec.-Gen. Prof. Fanny Chabirand
Contact Elfriede Dolinar (Vice-Pres.)

EALM / AEMB

European Association of Livestock Markets

Association Européenne des Marchés aux Bestiaux

Europäischer Viehmärkteverband

Rue de la Loi 81A Bte 9, 1040 Brussels, Belgium
Tel. (+32) 2-2304603
Fax (+32) 2-2309400
E-mail uecbv@scarlet.be
URL www.uecbv.eunet.be
Pres. Harrison Boyd

Sec.-Gen. Jesus Lanchas
Contact Tom Doyle (Vice-Pres.)

EANPC / AECNP

**European Association of National
    Productivity Centres**

**Association Européenne des Centres
    Nationaux de Productivité**

Rue de la Concorde 60, 1050 Brussels,
    Belgium
Tel. (+32) 2-5117100
Fax (+32) 2-5112401
E-mail eanpc@skynet.be
URL www.eanpc.org
Pres. Peter Rehnstrom
Sec.-Gen. Dr Sim Moors
Contact Antoine Hengen (Vice-Pres.)

EAPA

European Animal Protein Association

**Association Européenne de Protéine
    Animale**

Europäische Vereinigung für Tierprotein

Blvd Baudouin 18–4th floor, 1000 Brussels,
    Belgium
Tel. (+32) 2-2035141
Fax (+32) 2-2033244
E-mail devries@skypro.be
Pres. Chris Penning
Sec.-Gen. Dirk Dobbelaere

EAPA

European Asphalt Pavement Association

**Association Européenne des Producteurs des
    Enrobés**

Europäische Asphalt Verband

Rue du Commerce 77, 1040 Brussels, Belgium
Tel. (+32) 2-5025888
Fax (+32) 2-5022358
E-mail info@EAPA.org
URL www.eapa.org
Pres. Dariusz Slotwinski
Sec.-Gen. Jürgen Sturm

EAPO / AEOP

**European Association of Fish Producers
    Organisations**

**Association Européenne des Organisations
    de Producteurs dans le Secteur de la Pêche**

H. Baelskaai 25, 8400 Oostende, Belgium
Tel. (+32) 5-9321876

Fax (+32) 5-9322840
E-mail info@eapo.be
URL www.eapo.com
Pres. John Goodland
Sec.-Gen. Luc Corbisier
Contact Jose Suarez Llaros (Sec.)

EARTO

**European Association of Research and
    Technology Organisations**

Rue du Luxembourg 3, 1000 Brussels, Belgium
Tel. (+32) 2-5028698
Fax (+32) 2-5028693
E-mail info@earto.org
URL www.earto.org
Pres. Jan Dekker
Sec.-Gen. Dr Hendrik Schlesing
Contact Theo Gumpelmayer (Vice-Pres.)

EAS

European Aquaculture Society

Société Européenne d'Aquaculture

**Europäische Gesellschaft für
    Wasserlandwirtschaft**

Slijkensesteenweg 4, 8400 Oostende, Belgium
Tel. (+32) 5-9323859
Fax (+32) 5-9321005
E-mail eas-AT-aquaculture.cc
URL www.easonline.org
Pres. Johan Verreth
Contact Els Vanderperren (Project Asst)

EASA

European Advertising Standards Alliance

Rue de la Pépinière 10, 1000 Brussels,
    Belgium
Tel. (+32) 2-5137806
Fax (+32) 2-5132861
E-mail library@easa-alliance.org
URL www.easa-alliance.org
Contact Jean Pierre Teyssier (Chair.)

EATP

European Association for Textile Polyolefins

**Association Européenne des Textiles
    Polyolefines**

**Europäischer Verband der
    Polyolefintextilien**

Avenue E. van Nieuwenhuyse 4, 1160 Brussels,
    Belgium
Tel. (+32) 2-6767455

Fax (+32) 2-6767454
E-mail info@cirfs.org
URL www.eatp.org
Contact Allan Thompson (Chair.)

EAZA

European Association of Zoos and Aquaria
Association Européenne des Zoos et des
Aquariums
POB 20164, 1000 HD Amsterdam, Netherlands
Tel. (+31 20) 5200753
Fax (+31 20) 5200754
E-mail info@eaza.net
URL www.eaza.net
Contact Dr Koen Brouwer (Exec. Dir)

EBA

European Borates Association
Bd S. Dupuis 233, 1070 Brussels, Belgium
Tel. (+32) 2-5245500
Fax (+32) 2-5244575
E-mail secretariat@ima-eu.org
URL www.ima-eu.org/eba.html
Pres. Kieran Quill
Sec.-Gen. Wyart-Remy Michelle

EBC

European Brewery Convention
Convention Européenne de la Brasserie
Europäische Brauereikonvention
POB 510, 2380 BB Zoeterwoude, Netherlands
Tel. (+31 71) 5456047
Fax (+31 71) 5410013
E-mail secretariat@ebc-nl.com
URL www.ebc-nl.com
Pres. Jan Vesely
Sec.-Gen. Marjolein Wijngaarden
Contact Stéphane Dupire (Vice-Pres.)

EBC

European Builders Confederation
Confédération Européenne de l'Artisanat,
des Petites et Moyennes Entreprises du
Bâtiment
Europäische Konföderation des Handwerks
und der Kleinen und Mittleren
Bauunternehmen
Rue Jacques de Lalaing 4, 1040 Brussels,
Belgium
Tel. (+32) 2-5142323
Fax (+32) 2-5140015

E-mail secretariat@eubuilders.org
URL www.eubuilders.org
Pres. Jean Lardin
Sec.-Gen. Agnes Thibault
Contact Antonio Delgado (Vice-Pres.)

EBF / FEL

European Booksellers Federation
Fédération Européenne des Libraires
Chaussée de Charleroi 51b, Boite 1, 1060
Brussels, Belgium
Tel. (+32) 2-2234940
Fax (+32) 2-2234938
E-mail frandubruille.eurobooks@skynet.be
URL www.ebf-eu.org
Pres. John McNamee
Contact Françoise Dubruille (Dir)

EBU / UER

European Broadcasting Union
Union Européenne de Radio-Télévision
Ancienne Route 17A, 1218 Grand-Saconnex,
Switzerland
Tel. (+41) 22-717-21-11
Fax (+41) 22-747-40-00
E-mail ebu@ebu.ch
URL www.ebu.ch/en/index.php
Pres. Arne Wessberg
Sec.-Gen. Jean Réveillon
Contact Boris Bergant (Vice-Pres.)

ECA

European Carpet Association
Association Européenne du Tapis
Europäischer Teppichverband
Rue Montoyer 24, 1000 Brussels, Belgium
Tel. (+32) 2-2801813
Fax (+32) 2-2801809
E-mail paulette.de.wilde@euratex.org
Pres. Mike Mills
Sec.-Gen. S. van de Vrande

ECA

European Cockpit Association
Association Européenne du Cockpit
Europäischer Cockpitverband
Rue du Commerce 41, 1000 Brussels, Belgium
Tel. (+32) 2-7053293
Fax (+32) 2-7050877
E-mail eca@eca.skynet.be

URL www.eurocockpit.be
Pres. Martin Chalk
Sec.-Gen. Philip Schöppenthau
Contact Henk Vries (Vice-Pres.)

ECA / USC

European Chimney Association

Union Syndicale des Cheminées

39–41 Rue Louis Blanc, 92038 Paris La
　Défense Cedex, France
Tel. (+33) 1-47-17-62-92
Fax (+33) 1-47-17-64-27
E-mail eca@dial.oleane.com
Pres. Goddek Heinrich
Sec.-Gen. Pascal Folempin

ECA-PME

**European Confederation of Associations of
Small and Medium-Sized Enterprises**

**Confédération Européenne des Associations
de Petites et Moyennes Entreprises**

Avenue de la Renaissance 1, 1000 Brussels,
　Belgium
Tel. (+32) 2-7396359
Fax (+32) 2-7360571
E-mail info@cea-pme.org
URL www.cea-pme.org
Pres. Mario Ohoven
Sec.-Gen. Walter Grupp

ECATRA

European Car and Truck Rental Association

**Association Européenne des Entreprises de
Location de Véhicules**

Avenue de Tervuren 402, 1150 Brussels,
　Belgium
Tel. (+32) 2-7616614
Fax (+32) 2-7770505
E-mail ecatra@ecatra.org
URL www.ecatra.org
Pres. Bernard Pollak
Sec.-Gen. Jacques Mollet
Contact Peter Verkuyl (Vice-Pres.)

ECBP

European Council for Building Professionals

**Conseil Européen des Professionnels de la
Construction**

Europäischer Rat für Baufachleute

Ny Vesergade 13, 3rd floor, 1471 Copenhagen,
　Denmark

Tel. (+45) 33-36-41-50
Fax (+45) 33-36-41-60
E-mail ecbp@ecbp.org
URL www.ecbp.org
Pres. Kevin Sheridan
Sec.-Gen. Doug Goodsir

ECBTA

**European Community Banana Trade
Association**

**Association du Commerce de la Banane de la
Communauté Européenne**

**Verband der Bananenhandler der
Europäischen Gemeinschaft**

Avenue de Broqueville, Bte 17, 272, 1200
　Brussels, Belgium
Tel. (+32) 2-7771585
Fax (+32) 2-7771586
E-mail secretariat@ecbta.com
Sec.-Gen. Binard Philippe

ECCA

**European Cable Communications
Association**

Avenue des Arts 36, Kunstlaan 36, 6th floor,
　1040 Brussels, Belgium
Tel. (+32) 2-5211763
Fax (+32) 2-5217976
E-mail ecca@ecca.be
URL www.ecca.be
Pres. Bernard Cottin
Sec.-Gen. Peter Kokken
Contact Dirk Jaeger (Technical Dir)

ECCA

European Coil Coating Association

Rue du Luxembourg 19–21, 1000 Brussels,
　Belgium
Tel. (+32) 2-5136052
Fax (+32) 2-5114361
E-mail ecca@eccacoil.com
URL www.eccacoil.com
Pres. Frans Eschauzier
Sec.-Gen. P.J. Franck

ECCO

**European Confederation of Conservators /
Restorers Organizations**

**Confédération Européenne des
Organisations de Conservateurs**

Michael van Gompen, Rue Archimède 46,
 1000 Brussels, Belgium
Tel. (+32) 2-2307291
Fax (+32) 2-2801797
E-mail horlogerie.vangompen@proximedia.be
URL www.ecco-eu.org
Pres. Y. Player-Dahnsjo
Sec.-Gen. Y. van Reebum
Contact G. van Gompen

ECCS / CECM / EKS

**European Convention for Constructional
 Steelwork**

**Convention Européenne de la Construction
 Métallique**

Europäische Konvention für Stahlbau

Av. des Ombrages 32, 1200 Brussels, Belgium
Tel. (+32) 2-7620429
Fax (+32) 2-7620935
E-mail eccs@steelconstruct.com
URL www.steelconstruct.com
Pres. Jacques Huillard
Sec.-Gen. Georges Gendebien
Contact Allan Collins (Chair.)

ECED

**European confederation of Equipment
 Distributors**

**Confédération Européenne des Distributeurs
 d'Equipement AISBL**

Blvd de la Woluwe 46 b 14, 1200 Brussels,
 Belgium
Tel. (+32) 2-7786200
Fax (+32) 2-7786222
E-mail sigma@federauto.be
URL www.eced-association.org
Pres. Leo Lubbers
Sec.-Gen. Philippe Decrock
Contact Peter Tüttenberg (Vice-Pres.)

ECETOC

**European Centre for Ecotoxicology and
 Toxicology of Chemicals**

**Centre Européen d'Ecotoxicologie et de
 Toxicologie de Produits Chimiques**

**Europäisches Zentrum für Ökotoxikologie
 und Chemietoxikologie**

Avenue Edmond van Nieuwenhuyse 4 Bte 6,
 1160 Brussels, Belgium
Tel. (+32) 2-6753600
Fax (+32) 2-6753625

E-mail info@ecetoc.org
URL www.ecetoc.org
Pres. Peter Peschak
Sec.-Gen. Dr M. Gribble
Contact G. Gérits (Office Man.)

ECF

European Coffee Federation

Fédération Européenne du Café

Tourniairestraat 3, POB 90445, 1006 BK
 Amsterdam, Netherlands
Tel. (+31 20) 5113815
Fax (+31 20) 5113892
E-mail ecf@coffee-associations.org
URL www.ecf-coffee.org
Pres. Mario Cerutti
Sec.-Gen. Roel Vaessen
Contact Mirjam Jonker Stegeman (Account
 Asst)

ECMA INTERNATIONAL

**International Europe-based Industry
 Association for Standardizing Information
 and Communication Systems**

Rue du Rhône 114, 1204 Geneva, Switzerland
Tel. (+41) 22-849-60-00
Fax (+41) 22-849-60-01
E-mail helpdesk@ecma-international.org
URL www.ecma-international.org
Pres. Theis
Sec.-Gen. Van den Beld
Contact Statt (Vice-Pres.)

ECMA

European Carton Makers Association

POB 85612, 2508 CH The Hague, Netherlands
Tel. (+31 70) 3123911
Fax (+31 70) 3636348
E-mail mail@ecma.org
URL www.ecma.org
Pres. Dr Georg Wall
Sec.-Gen. Jules Lejeune

ECNAIS

**European Council of National Associations
 of Independent Schools**

**Conseil Européen d'Associations Nationales
 d'Ecoles Indépendantes**

**Europäischer Rat Nationaler Verbande von
 Freien Schulen**

Ny Kongensgade 10, 1472 Copenhagen,
　Denmark
Tel. (+45) 70-20-26-42
Fax (+45) 70-20-26-43
E-mail ecnais@ecnais.org
URL www.ecnais.org
Sec.-Gen. Per Kristensen
Contact Carlos Diaz Muniz (Chair.)

ECOO

European Council of Optometry and Optics
**Conseil Européen de l'Optométrie et de
　l'Optique**
Europäischer Rat für Optometrie und Optik

61 Southwark St, London SE1 0HL,
　United Kingdom
Tel. (+44 20) 7207-2193
Fax (+44 20) 7620-1140
E-mail postbox@aop.org.uk
Pres. Robert Chappell
Sec.-Gen. Richard Carswell

ECPA

European Crop Protection Association
**Association Européenne pour la Protection
　des Cultures**
Europäischer Pflanzenschutzverband

Avenue E. van Nieuwenhuyse 6, 1160 Brussels,
　Belgium
Tel. (+32) 2-6631550
Fax (+32) 2-6631560
E-mail ecpa@ecpa.be
URL www.ecpa.be
Pres. Roger Doig
Contact Friedhelm Schmider (Dir-Gen.)

ECPCI

**Association of the European Cigarette Paper
　Converting Industry**
**Association Européenne de l'Industrie de
　Transformation du Papier à Cigarettes**
**Verband der Europäischen Zigaretten
　Papier Verarbeitenden Industrie**

Rheinallee 25 B, 53173 Bonn, Germany
Tel. (+49 228) 934-460
Fax (+49 228) 934-4620
E-mail info@verband-rauchtabak.de
Pres. W. Hinz
Contact F.P. Marx (Man. Dir)

ECSA

**European Community Shipowners'
　Associations**

Rue Ducale 45, 1000 Brussels, Belgium
Tel. (+32) 2-5113940
Fax (+32) 2-5118092
E-mail mail@ecsa.be
URL www.ecsa.be
Pres. Lennart Simonsson
Sec.-Gen. Alfons Guinier
Contact Philippe Louis Dreyfus (Vice-Pres.)

ECSA / ANAC

**European Community Seamen's
　Associations**
**Association des Navigants de la
　Communauté Européenne**

Rue Ducale 45, 1000 Brussels, Belgium
Tel. (+32) 2-5113940
E-mail mail@ecsa.be
URL www.ecsa.be
Pres. Lennart Simonsson
Sec.-Gen. Alfons Guinier
Contact Philippe Louis-Dreyfus (Vice-Pres.)

ECSLA

**European Cold Storage and Logistics
　Association**

Avenue de Broqueville 272, bte 8, 1200
　Brussels, Belgium
Tel. (+32) 2-7627780
Fax (+32) 2-7627782
E-mail info@ecsla.be
URL www.ecsla.be
Pres. Wim van Bon
Sec.-Gen. Carole Prier
Contact Jean Eudes Tesson (Vice-Pres.)

ECTA

**European Communities Trade Mark
　Association**
**Association Communautaire du Droit des
　Marques**
**Vereinigung für Warenzeichen der
　Europäischen Gemeinschaften**

Bisschoppenhoflaan 286, PO Box 5, 2100
　Deurne Antwerpen, Belgium
Tel. (+32) 3-3264723
Fax (+32) 3-3267613
E-mail ecta@ecta.org
URL www.ecta.org
Pres. Max Oker Blom

Sec.-Gen. Keith Havelock
Contact Mireia Curell (Vice-Pres.)

ECTA

European Cutting Tools Association

**Association Européenne d'Outillage
Mécanique**

**Europäischer Verband der Hersteller für
Ausrüstungen von Schneidewerkzeugen**

Light Trades House, Sheffield S10 2QJ,
United Kingdom
Tel. (+44 114) 266-3084
E-mail light.trades@virgin.net
URL www.britishtools.com

Pres. W. Sengerbusch

ECTAA

**Group of National Travel Agents' and Tour
Operators' Associations within the EU**

**Groupement des Unions Nationales des
Agences et Organisateurs de Voyages de
l'UE**

Rue Dautzenberg 36, 1050 Brussels, Belgium
Tel. (+32) 2-6443450
Fax (+32) 2-6442421
E-mail secretariat@ectaa.org
URL www.ectaa.org

Pres. Norbert Draskovits
Sec.-Gen. Michel de Blust
Contact Romana Engeman (Vice-Pres.)

ECTP / CEU

European Council of Town Planners

Conseil Européen des Urbanistes

**Europäischer Rat der Stadt- Regional- und
Landesplaner**

chaussée de La Hulpe 177 bte 5, 1170 Brussels,
Belgium
Tel. (+32) 2-6396300
Fax (+32) 2-6401990
E-mail cub@urbanistes.be
URL www.urbanistes.be

Pres. B. Clerbaus
Sec.-Gen. F. Hennequin
Contact P. Cox (Vice-Pres.)

ECYC

**European Confederation of Youth Clubs
Organisations**

**Confédération Européenne des
Organisations des Centres de Jeunes**

Ornevej 45, 2400 Copenhagen, Denmark
Tel. (+45) 38-10-80-38
Fax (+45) 38-10-46-55
E-mail ecycdk@centrum.dk
URL www.ecyc.org

Pres. Oskar Dyrmundur Olafsson
Sec.-Gen. Andrew Cummings
Contact Annina Hirvonen (Vice-Pres.)

ECYF4HC

**European Committee for Young Farmers'
and 4H Clubs**

**Comité Européen des Clubs de Jeunes
Agriculteurs et Clubs 4H**

**Europäisches Komitee für Jungbauern und
4H Klubs**

Schauflergasse 6, 1014 Wien, Austria
Tel. (+45 1) 53441-8600
Fax (+45 1) 53441-8609
E-mail ecyf4hc@pklwk.at
URL www.ecyf4hc.org

Pres. Linda Steele
Sec.-Gen. Sabine Klocker

EDA

European Dairy Association

Association Laitière Européenne

Europäischer Milchindustrieverband

Rue Montoyer 14, 1000 Brussels, Belgium
Tel. (+32) 2-5495040
Fax (+32) 2-5495049
E-mail eda@euromilk.org
URL www.euromilk.org

Pres. Veijo Merilainen
Sec.-Gen. Dr Joop Kleibeuker
Contact Agnès Vaillier (Asst Sec.-Gen.)

EDA

European Decaffeinators Association

Association Européenne des Décaféineurs

Europäischer Verband der Entcoffeinierer

18 Rue de la Pépinière, 75008 Paris, France
Tel. (+33) 1-53-42-13-38
Fax (+33) 1-53-42-13-39
E-mail b-dufrene@wanadoo.fr

Pres. Dr Bernhard Bichsel

EDA

European Demolition Association

Association Européenne de Démolition

Europäischer Abbruchverband

POB 12, 3740 AA Baarn, Netherlands
Tel. (+31 35) 5427505
Fax (+31 35) 5427605
E-mail eda@eda-demolition.com
URL www.eda-demolition.com
Pres. Brandis

EDANA

European Disposables and Nonwovens Association

Avenue Eugène Plasky 157, 1030 Brussels, Belgium
Tel. (+32) 2-7349310
Fax (+32) 2-7333518
E-mail info@edana.org
URL www.edana.org
Contact Knud Hansen (Chair.)

EDIG

European Defence Industries Group

Gulledelle 94–B5, 1200 Brussels, Belgium
Tel. (+32) 2-7758135
Fax (+32) 2-7758131
E-mail edig@skynet.be
URL www.edig.org
Pres. Corrado Antonini
Sec.-Gen. Jean Wesner

EDiMA

European Digital Media Association
Association Européenne des Médias Numériques

Friars House, Office 118, 157–168 Blackfriars Road, London SE1 8EZ, United Kingdom
Tel. (+32) 2-6261990
Fax (+32) 2-6269501
E-mail info@edima.org
URL www.europeandigitalmediaassociation.org
Contact Lucy Cronin (Exec. Dir)

EDMA

European Diagnostic Manufacturers Association

Place Saint Lambert 14, 1200 Brussels, Belgium
Tel. (+32) 2-7722225
Fax (+32) 2-7722329
E-mail edma@edma-ivd.be
URL www.edma-ivd.be

Pres. Chris Tobin
Contact Christine Tarrajat (Dir-Gen.)

EDTNA/ERCA

European Dialysis and Transplant Nurses' Association / European Renal Care Association

Association Européenne du Personnel Soignant en Dialyse et Greffes / Association Européenne des Soins Rénaux

Verband des Europäischen Dialyse- und Transplantationspflegepersonals / Verband des Europäischen Nierenpflegepersonals

Pilatusstrasse 35, Postfach 3052, 6002 Luzern, Switzerland
Tel. (+41) 41-766-05-80
Fax (+41) 41-766-05-85
E-mail info@edtna-erca.org
URL www.edtna-erca.org
Pres. Althea Mahon
Sec.-Gen. Josefa Fenselau
Contact Lorna Engblom (Treasurer)

EEA

European Elevator Association

Avenue Louis Gribaumont 1/5, 1150 Brussels, Belgium
Tel. (+32) 2-7721093
Fax (+32) 2-7718661
E-mail info@eea-geie.org
URL www.eea-eeig.org
Pres. William Orchard
Sec.-Gen. Luc Rivet
Contact Yasmine Quintin (Office Man.)

EEA

European Express Association

Avenue de Cortenbergh 118, PO Box 8, 1000 Brussels, Belgium
Tel. (+32) 2-7379576
Fax (+32) 2-7379501
E-mail ghodgson@hillandknowlton.com
URL www.euroexpress.org
Pres. Jaap Mulders
Sec.-Gen. Russell Patten
Contact Harald Schönfelder (Chair.)

EECA

European Electronic Component Manufacturers' Association

Association Européenne des Fabricants de Composants Electroniques

Europäische Vereinigung der Elektronischen Komponentenhersteller

Diamant Building, Blvd Auguste Reyers 80, 1030 Brussels, Belgium
Tel. (+32) 2-7068600
Fax (+32) 2-7068605
E-mail secretariat.gen@eeca.be
URL www.eeca.org
Pres. Enrico Villa
Sec.-Gen. Martin Spät
Contact Merten Koolen (Chair.)

EEPA

European Egg Processors Association

Association des Producteurs Européens d'Ovoproduits

Euro Eiprodukten Fabrikanten Verband

Bilkske 93, 8000 Brugge, Belgium
Tel. (+32) 5-0440070
Fax (+32) 5-0440077
E-mail filiepsr@eepa.org
URL www.eepa.org
Pres. J.Y. Justeau
Sec.-Gen. F. van Bosstraeten

EFA

European Driving Schools Association

Fédération Européenne des Auto-Ecoles

Europäische Fahrlehrer-Assoziation eV

Hofbrunnstrasse 13, PO Box 710969, 81479 Munich, Germany
Tel. (+49 89) 74914940
Fax (+49 89) 74914944
E-mail info@efa-eu.com
URL www.efa-eu.com
Pres. Gerhard von Bressensdorf
Contact Lars Gunnarson (Vice-Pres.)

EFAA

European Federation of Accountants and Auditors for SMEs

Rue Jaques de Lalaing, 4, 1040 Brussels, Belgium
Tel. (+32) 2-7368886
Fax (+32) 2-7362964
E-mail info@efaa.com
URL www.efaa.com
Pres. Klas Erik Hjorth

Sec.-Gen. Peter Poulsen
Contact Fritz Vogt (Vice-Pres.)

EFAH / FEDESA

European Federation of Animal Health

Fédération Européenne de la Santé Animale

Europäische Föderation für Tiergesundheit

Rue Defacqz 1, Bte 8, 1000 Brussels, Belgium
Tel. (+32) 2-5437560
Fax (+32) 2-5370049
E-mail info@fedesa.be
URL www.fedesa.be
Pres. P. James
Contact B. Williams

EFAMA / FEFSI

European Fund and Asset Management Association

Fédération Européenne des Fonds et Sociétés d'Investissement

Square de Meeûs 18, 1050 Brussels, Belgium
Tel. (+32) 2-5133969
Fax (+32) 2-5132643
E-mail info@fefsi.be
URL www.fefsi.org
Pres. Dr Wolfgang Mansfeld
Sec.-Gen. Steffen Matthias
Contact Bernard Delbecque (Senior Economic Adviser)

EFAMRO

European Federation of Associations of Market Research Organisations

Fédération Européenne des Associations d'Instituts de Marketing

Europäische Föderation der Marktforschungsinstitutsverbande

26 Chester Close North, Regent's Park, London NW1 4JE, United Kingdom
Tel. (+44 20) 7224-3873
Fax (+44 20) 7224-3873
E-mail efamro@aol.com
URL www.efamro.org
Pres. Vincent Ravet
Contact Bryan Bates (Dir-Gen.)

EFAPIT

Royal Dutch Grain and Feed Trade Association

Fédération Européenne des Importateurs et Négociants en Protéine Animale

Europäische Föderation der Tierproteinimporteure und -Händler

Heer Bokelweg 157B, 3000 Rotterdam, Netherlands

Tel. (+31 10) 4673188

Fax (+31 10) 4678761

E-mail cvg@graan.com

URL www.graan.com

Pres. O. Derome

Sec.-Gen. Marselle Stegehuis

Contact G.J. van Noortwijk (Chair.)

EFB

European Federation of Biotechnology

Fédération Européenne de Biotechnologie

Europäische Föderation Biotechnologie

Pg. Lluis Companys 23, 08010 Barcelona, Spain

Tel. (+34) 932-687703

Fax (+34) 932-683768

E-mail info@efbweb.org

URL www.efbweb.org

Pres. Pierre Crooy

Sec.-Gen. Christian Suojanen

Contact Børge Diderichsen (Vice-Pres.)

EFBS / FEECL / EuBV

European Federation of Building Societies

Fédération Européenne d'Epargne et de Crédit pour le Logement

Europäische Bausparkassenvereinigung

Klingerhöfer Strasse 4, 10785 Berlin, Germany

Tel. (+49 30) 590091913

Fax (+49 30) 590091917

E-mail info@efbs.org

URL www.efbs.org

Pres. Miquel Capellà

Contact Andreas Zehnder (Man. Dir)

EFBWW / FETBB / EFBH

European Federation of Building and Woodworkers

Fédération Européenne des Travailleurs du Bâtiment et du Bois

Europäische Föderation der Bau- und Holzarbeiter

Rue Royale 45, Bte 3, 1000 Brussels, Belgium

Tel. (+32) 2-2271040

Fax (+32) 2-2198228

E-mail info@efbh.be

URL www.efbww.org

Pres. Arne Johansen

Sec.-Gen. Harrie Bijen

Contact Marina Saegerman (Office Man.)

EFCA

European Federation of Engineering Consultancy Associations

Fédération Européenne des Associations d'Ingénieurs-Conseils et Bureaux d'Ingenierie

EuropäischeVereinigung der Verbände Beratender Ingenieure

Avenue des Arts 3, 4 & 5, 1210 Brussels, Belgium

Tel. (+32) 2-2090770

Fax (+32) 2-2090771

E-mail efca@efca.be

URL www.efcanet.org

Pres. Yann Leblais

Sec.-Gen. Jan van der Putten

Contact Pablo Bueno Tomás (Vice-Pres.)

EFCE

European Federation of Chemical Engineering

Fédération Européenne du Génie Chimique

Europäische Föderation für Chemie-Ingenieurwesen

C/o Dechema eV, Theodor-Heuss-Allee 25, 60486 Frankfurt am Main, Germany

Tel. (+49 69) 7564143

Fax (+49 69) 7564201

E-mail efce@decherma.de

Pres. Prof. Charpentier

Sec.-Gen. Prof. Kreysa

Contact Prof. Nomen (Exec.Vice-Pres.)

EFCEM

European Federation of Catering Equipment Manufacturers

Fédération Européenne des Constructeurs d'Equipement de Grandes Cuisines

Europäischer Verband der Hersteller von Grosskochanlagen

C/o Syng, 39/41 rue Louis Blanc, 92400 Courbevoie, France

Tel. (+33) 1-47-17-63-62

Fax (+33) 1-47-17-68-69

E-mail efcem@syneg.org

URL www.efcem.org

Pres. Thierry Brener

Sec.-Gen. Thierry Allix
Contact Guerrini

EFCF

European Federation of City Farms

Schapenstraat 14, 1750 Sint-Martens-Lennik,
   Belgium
Tel. (+32) 2-5320190
Fax (+32) 2-5322322
E-mail efcf@vgc.be
URL www.cityfarms.org
Pres. Marc de Staercke

EFCI / FENI

European Federation of Cleaning Industries

**Fédération Européenne du Nettoyage
   Industriel**

**Europäischer Dachverband der
   Gebäudereinigung**

Rue de l'Association 27, 1000 Brussels,
   Belgium
Tel. (+32) 2-2258330
Fax (+32) 2-2258339
E-mail office@feni.be
URL www.feni.be
Pres. John Oliver
Sec.-Gen. Martyn Vesey
Contact Guy Auffret (Vice-Pres.)

EFCLIN

**European Federation of the Contact Lens
   Industry**

**Fédération Européenne des Industries de
   Lentilles de Contact**

Waterwilg 1, 4761 WN Zeren Bergen,
   Netherlands
Tel. (+31 16) 8329308
Fax (+31 16) 8327069
E-mail info@efclin.com
URL www.efclin.com
Pres. Graham Avery
Sec.-Gen. Etten-Leur
Contact Henk van Bruggen (Vice-Pres.)

EFEMA

**European Food Emulsifiers Manufacturers'
   Association**

**Association des Fabricants Européens
   d'Emulsifiants Alimentaires**

**Verband Europäischer Hersteller von
   Nahrungsmittelemulgatoren**

Avenue des Gaulois 9, 1040 Brussels, Belgium
Tel. (+32) 2-6767396
Fax (+32) 2-6767332
E-mail efema@ecco-eu.com
URL www.emulsifiers.org
Pres. Vanoverstraten

EFER

**European Federation of Electronics
   Retailers**

**Fédération Européenne des Commerçants en
   Electronique Domestique et
   Electroménager**

**Europäische Föderation der Einzelhändler
   für Elektronischen Hausgeräte**

Regentlaan 58, 1000 Brussels, Belgium
Tel. (+32) 2-5501714
Fax (+32) 2-5501729
E-mail dirk.rutten@nelectra.be
Pres. van Hove
Sec.-Gen. Rutten

EFF

European Franchise Federation

Fédération Européenne de la Franchise

Europäische Franchiseföderation

Avenue Louise 179, 1050 Brussels, Belgium
Tel. (+32) 2-5201607
Fax (+32) 2-5201735
E-mail info@eff.franchise.com
URL www.eff-franchise.com
Pres. Pierre Jeanmart
Contact Carol Chopra (Exec. Dir)

EFFA

European Flavour & Fragrance Association

**Association des Industries d'Arômes et de
   Parfums**

Square Marie Louise, 49, 1000 Brussels,
   Belgium
Tel. (+32) 2-2389905
Fax (+32) 2-2300265
E-mail secretariat@effaorg.org
URL www.effa.be
Pres. Bodife
Sec.-Gen. Dils

EFFAT

**European Federation of Trade Unions in the
   Food, Agriculture and Tourism sectors
   and allied branches**

Fédération Européenne des Syndicats des Secteurs de l'Alimentation, de l'Agriculture et du Tourisme et des Branches Connexes

Europäische Föderation der Gewerkschaften des Lebens-, Genussmittel-, Landwirtschafts- und Tourismussektors und verwandter Branchen

Rue Fossé-aux-Loups 38 Boîte 3, 1000 Brussels, Belgium
Tel. (+32) 2-2187730
Fax (+32) 2-2183018
E-mail effat@effat.org
URL www.effat.org
Sec.-Gen. Harald Wiedenhofer
Contact Wendy van Haver (Project Administration)

EFFC

European Federation of Foundation Contractors

Fédération Européenne des Entreprises de Fondations

Europäischer Verband der Spezialtiefbauer

Forum Court, 83 Copers Cope Road, Beckenham BR3 1NR, United Kingdom
Tel. (+44 20) 8663-0948
Fax (+44 20) 8663-0949
E-mail effc@effc.org
URL www.effc.org
Pres. Patrice Runacher
Contact Dianne Jennings

EFFCA

European Food and Feed Cultures Association

Association Européenne des Fabricants de Ferments à Usage Agro-alimentaire

Europäische Vereinigung der Fermenthersteller für Nahrungsmittelindustriegebrauch

85 Blvd Haussmann, 75008 Paris, France
Tel. (+33) 1-42-65-41-58
Fax (+33) 1-42-65-02-05
E-mail effca@effca.com
URL www.effca.com
Pres. Lars Frederiksen
Sec.-Gen. Bernard Billon
Contact Fabienne Saadane-Oaks (Vice-Pres.)

EFFCM / FEPFC

European Federation of Fibre Cement Manufacturers

Fédération Européenne des Producteurs de Fibres-Ciment

Europäische Vereinigung der Faserzement-Hersteller

Avenue de Tervuren 361, 1150 Brussels, Belgium
Tel. (+32) 2-7781211
Fax (+32) 2-7781212
E-mail communication@etexgroup.com
URL www.etexgroup.com
Pres. M Vandenbosh
Sec.-Gen. Nous
Contact Philippe Coens (Man. Dir)

EFFOST

European Federation of Food Science and Technology

Fédération Européenne de la Science et de la Technologie Alimentaire

Europäische Föderation der Nahrungsmittelwissenschaft und -Technologie

PO Box 17, 6700 AA Wageningen, Netherlands
Tel. (+31 317) 476457
Fax (+31 317) 475347
E-mail info@effost.org
URL www.effost.org
Pres. Prof. Lars Thomas Ohlsson
Sec.-Gen. Dr Christina Goodacre
Contact N.M. Sander

EFFS

European Federation of Funeral Services

Fédération Européenne de Services Funéraires

Europäischer Vereinigung für Bestattungsdienste

Obere Donaustrasse 53, 1020 Wien, Austria
Tel. (+43 1) 71737-6235
Fax (+43 1) 71737-6262
E-mail office@effs.at
URL www.effs.org
Pres. Wolfgang Zocher
Sec.-Gen. Peter Skyba

EFIA

European Fertilizer Import Association

Association Européenne des Importateurs d'Engrais

Europäischer Verband der Düngemittelimporteure

Rue de la Loi 62, 1040 Brussels, Belgium
Tel. (+32) 2-2191620
Fax (+32) 2-2191626
E-mail fvermeeren@whitecase.com
Pres. Oscar Geyer
Contact Fabienne Vermeeren

EFIP / FEPI

European Federation of Inland Ports

Fédération Européenne des Ports Intérieurs

Europäischer Verband der Binnenhafen

Place des Armateurs 6, 1000 Brussels, Belgium
Tel. (+32) 2-4207037
Fax (+32) 2-4200371
E-mail efip@skynet.be
URL www.inlandports.be
Pres. Charles Huygens
Sec.-Gen. Jurgen Sturm
Contact Ph. Binard

EFJ/IFJ / FEJ/FIJ / EJF/IJF

European Federation of Journalists

Fédération Européenne des Journalistes

Europaische Journalisten-Föderation

Résidence Palace (Bloc C), Rue de la Loi 155, 1040 Brussels, Belgium
Tel. (+32) 2-2352200
Fax (+32) 2-2352219
E-mail efj@ifj.org
URL www.ifj.org
Pres. Gust Glattfelder
Sec.-Gen. Aiden White
Contact Renate Schroeder (Dir)

EFLA / AEDA

European Food Law Association

Association Européenne pour le Droit de l'Alimentation

Europäische Vereinigung für Lebensmittelrecht

Rue de la Loi, 235, 1040 Brussels, Belgium
Tel. (+32) 2-2304845
Fax (+32) 2-2308206
E-mail secretariat@efla-aeda.org

URL www.efla-aeda.org
Pres. Charles Cockbill
Sec.-Gen. Nicole Coutrelis
Contact Alain Gérard (Vice-Pres.)

EFLA / FEAP

European Foundation for Landscape Architecture

Fondation Européenne pour l'Architecture du Paysage

Rue Washington 38–40, 1150 Brussels, Belgium
Tel. (+32) 2-3463862
Fax (+32) 2-3469876
E-mail efla.feap@skynet.be
URL www.efla.org
Pres. Teresa Andresen
Sec.-Gen. Robert Holden
Contact Karen Foley (Vice-Pres.)

EFMA

European Fertilizer Manufacturers Association

Association Européenne des Producteurs d'Engrais

Europäischer Verband der Düngemittelhersteller

Avenue E. van Nieuwenhuyse 4, 1160 Brussels, Belgium
Tel. (+32) 2-6753550
Fax (+32) 2-6753961
E-mail main@efma.be
URL www.efma.org
Pres. Clauw
Sec.-Gen. Aldinger
Contact Helmuth Aldinger (Dir-Gen.)

EFMD

European Foundation for Management Development

Fondation Européenne pour le Développement de la Gestion

Europäische Management-Entwicklungsstiftung

Rue Gachard 88, PO Box 3, 1050 Brussels, Belgium
Tel. (+32) 2-6290810
Fax (+32) 2-6290811
E-mail info@efmd.be
URL www.efmd.be

Pres. Gerard van Schaik
Contact Martine Plompen (Dir)

EFOMP

European Federation of Organisations in Medical Physics

Centre G.-F. Leclerc, Service de
  Radiophysique, 1 rue Pr Marion, BP 77980,
  21034 Dijon Cedex, France
Tel. (+33) 3-80-73-75-00
Fax (+33) 3-80-67-19-15
E-mail snaudy@dijon.fnclcc.fr
URL www.efomp.org
Pres. Alberto del Guerra
Sec.-Gen. Dr Suzanne Naudy
Contact Noel

EFPA

European Food Service and Packaging Association

Association Européenne d'Emballages Alimentaires à Usage Unique

Europäischer Verband für Lebensmittelverpackungen und Einweggeschirr

Avenue Livingstone 13–15, 1000 Brussels,
  Belgium
Tel. (+32) 2-2869496
Fax (+32) 2-2869495
E-mail efpa@eamonnbates.com
URL www.efpa.com
Pres. Jorge Mallo Esteban
Sec.-Gen. Eamonn Bates
Contact David Schisler (Vice-Pres.)

EFPIA

European Federation of Pharmaceutical Industries and Associations

Fédération Européenne d'Associations et d'Industries Pharmaceutiques

Rue du Trône 108, 1050 Brussels, Belgium
Tel. (+32) 2-6262555
Fax (+32) 2-6262566
E-mail info@efpia.org
URL www.efpia.org
Pres. Franz Humer
Contact Brian Ager (Dir-Gen.)

EFPRA

European Fat Processors and Renderers Association

Blvd Baudouin 18, Bte 4, 1000 Brussels,
  Belgium
Tel. (+32) 2-2035141
Fax (+32) 2-2033244
E-mail devries@skypro.be
Sec.-Gen. Dirk Dobbelaere

EFQM

European Foundation for Quality Management

Fondation Européenne du Contrôle de la Qualité

Avenue des Pléiades 15, 1200 Brussels,
  Belgium
Tel. (+32) 2-7753511
Fax (+32) 2-7753535
E-mail info@efqm.org
URL www.efqm.org
Contact A. De Dommartin (Chief Exec.)

EFR

European Ferrous Recovery and Recycling Federation

Fédération Européenne de la Récupération et du Recyclage des Ferrailles

Europäischer Recycling-Verband für Eisen und Stahl

C/o BIR, Avenue Franklin Roosevelt 24, 1050
  Brussels, Belgium
Tel. (+32) 2-6275770
Fax (+32) 2-6275773
E-mail bir.sec@skynet.be
URL www.efr2.org
Pres. Christian Rubach
Contact Francis Veys (Dir-Gen.)

EFTC / EVH

European Federation of Timber Construction

Fédération Européenne de la Construction Bois

Europäische Vereinigung des Holzbaus

Circuit de la Foire Internationale 2, 1016
  Luxembourg-Kirchberg, Luxembourg
Tel. (+352) 4245111
Fax (+352) 424525
E-mail info@fda.lu
URL www.fda.lu
Pres. Georg König
Sec.-Gen. Jeannot Franck

EFWSID

European Federation of Wine and Spirit Importers and Distributors

Fédération Européenne des Importateurs et Distributeurs des Vins et Boissons Alcoolisées

Europäische Föderation der Wein- und Spirituosenimporteure und Grosshändler

5 King House, 1 Queen Street Place, London EC4R 1XX, United Kingdom
Tel. (+44 20) 7248-5377
Fax (+44 20) 7489-0322
E-mail EFWSID@wsa.org.uk
Pres. Francis Clottu
Contact Quentin Rappoport (Dir)

EGA

European Generic Medicines Association

Association Européenne des Médicaments Génériques

Europäischer Verband der Generikaindustrie

Rue d'Arlon 15, 1050 Brussels, Belgium
Tel. (+32) 2-7368411
Fax (+32) 2-7367438
E-mail info@egagenerics.com
URL www.egagenerics.com
Pres. Emile G.W.H. Loof
Sec.-Gen. Greg Perry
Contact Nadene McClay (Dir)

EGGA

European General Galvanizers Association

Association Européenne des Industries de Galvanisation d'Articles Divers

Europäische Vereinigung der Industrien für die Galvanisierung

Maybrook House, Godstone Road, Caterham, Surrey CR3 6RE, United Kingdom
Tel. (+44 1883) 331277
Fax (+44 1883) 331287
E-mail mail@egga.com
URL www.egga.com
Pres. Jo Verstappen
Contact Michael Burcher (Dir)

EGOLF

European Group of Organisations for Fire Testing, Inspection and Certification

Holmesfield Road, Warrington, Cheshire WA1 2DS, United Kingdom
Tel. (+44 1925) 646665
Fax (+44 1925) 646630
E-mail ruth.boughey@egolf.org.uk
URL www.egolf.org.uk
Pres. Twilt
Sec.-Gen. Ruth Boughey

EGTA

European Group of Television Advertising

Groupe Européen de la Publicité Télévisée

Europäische Gruppe für Fernsehwerbung

Rue Wiertz 50, 1150 Brussels, Belgium
Tel. (+32) 2-2903131
Fax (+32) 2-2903139
E-mail info@egta.com
URL www.egta.com
Pres. Walter Neuhauser
Sec.-Gen. Grégoire Michel
Contact Vanessa Marschner (Office Man.)

EHA / GEH

European Helicopter Association

Groupement Européen de l'Hélicoptère

Europäischer Hubschrauberverband

P.C. Hooftstraat 83–1, 1071 BP Amsterdam, Netherlands
Tel. (+31 20) 4707020
Fax (+31 20) 4707021
E-mail stuurman@eha.nl
URL www.eha.nl
Pres. Lord Glenarthur
Contact Jan Willem Stuurman (Chief Exec.)

EHI

Association of the European Heating Industry

Blvd A. Reyers 80, 1030 Brussels, Belgium
Tel. (+32) 2-7067962
Fax (+32) 2-7067966
E-mail info@ehi.coma
URL www.aehi.be
Sec.-Gen. Udo Wasser
Contact Giorgio Crivelli (Chair.)

EHIA

European Herbal Infusions Association

Association Européenne des Infusions d'Herbe

Europäische Vereinigung der nationalen Verbände für Kräuter- und Früchtetee

Gotenstrasse 21, 20097 Hamburg, Germany
Tel. (+49 40) 23601614
Fax (+49 40) 23601610
E-mail ehia@wga-hh.de
URL www.ehia-online.org
Pres. Nick Revett
Sec.-Gen. Dr Monika Beutgen
Contact Christoph Strohmeyer (Vice-Pres.)

EHIMA

European Hearing Instrument Manufacturers Association

Association Européenne des Fabricants d'Audioprothèses

Europäische Vereinigung der Hörgerätehersteller

Bosch 135, 1780 Wemmel, Belgium
Tel. (+32) 2-4613752
Fax (+32) 2-4613647
E-mail ehima@skynet.be
URL www.ehima.com
Pres. Jesper Mailand
Sec.-Gen. Anne Marie Wolters
Contact Tom Westermann (Chair.)

EHMA

European Health Management Association

Association Européenne de Gestion des Systèmes de Santé

Europäische Vereinigung für Management im Gesundheitswesen

Vergemount Hall, Clonskeagh, Dublin 6, Ireland
Tel. (+353 1) 2839299
Fax (+353 1) 2838653
E-mail info@ehma.org
URL www.ehma.org
Pres. Laraine Joyce
Contact Philip Berman (Dir)

EHPM

European Federation of Associations of Health Product Manufacturers

Groupement Européen des Associations des Fabricants de Produits de Réforme

Europäische Vereinigung der Verbände der Reformwaren-Hersteller

Rue de l'Association 50, 1000 Brussels, Belgium
Tel. (+32) 2-2091145
Fax (+32) 2-2233064
E-mail lorenecourrege@ehpm.be
URL www.ehpm.org
Contact David Richardson (Prof.)

EICTA / AEIIT

European Information, Communications and Consumer Electronics Technology Industry Association

Association Européenne des Industries de l'Informatique et des Télécommunications et des Industries de Produits Electroniques Grand Public

Blvd. A Reyers 80, 1030 Brussels, Belgium
Tel. (+32) 2-7068470
Fax (+32) 2-7068479
E-mail info@eicta.org
URL www.eicta.org
Pres. Andy Mattes
Contact Mark MacGann (Dir-Gen.)

EIGA

European Industrial Gases Association

Association Européenne des Gaz Industriels

Europäischer Verband für Technische Gase

Avenue des Arts 3–5, 1210 Brussels, Belgium
Tel. (+32) 2-2177098
Fax (+32) 2-2198514
E-mail info@eiga.org
URL www.eiga.org
Sec.-Gen. Frank H. Finger
Contact Klaus Krinninger (Chair.)

EIHSA / IEACS / EIJS

European Institute for Hunting and Sporting Arms

Institut Européen des Armes de Chasse et de Sport

Europäisches Institut für Jagd- und Sportwaffen

6 Cap de Bos, 33430 Gajac, France
Tel. (+33) 5-56-25-24-46
Fax (+33) 5-56-25-24-49
E-mail eldwynn@aol.com
Pres. Carlo Peroni
Sec.-Gen. Henri Heidebroek

EIPG / GPIE

European Industrial Pharmacy Group

Groupe des Pharmaciens de l'Industrie en Europe

Délégation aux Affaires Extérieures, Rue du Zéphir 58B, 1200 Brussels, Belgium
Tel. (+32) 3-8902778
Fax (+32) 3-8902935
E-mail paul.nelis@alconlabs.com
Pres. Jane Nicholson
Contact P. Neils

EIRMA

European Industrial Research Management Association

Association Européenne pour l'Administration de la Recherche Industrielle

Asociación Europea para la Administración de la Investigación Industrial

46 Rue Lauriston, 75116 Paris, France
Tel. (+33) 1-53-23-83-10
Fax (+33) 1-47-20-05-30
E-mail info@eirma.asso.fr
URL www.eirma.asso.fr
Pres. Walter Steinlin
Sec.-Gen. Dr Andrew Dearing
Contact Léopold Demiddeleer (Vice-Pres.)

EKA

European Kaolin Association

Boulevard S. Dupuis 233, PO Box 124, 1070 Brussels, Belgium
Tel. (+32) 2-5245500
Fax (+32) 2-5244575
E-mail secretariat@ima-eu.org
URL www.ima-eu.org
Pres. Ron Shuttleworth
Sec.-Gen. Christophe Sykes
Contact Olivier Vandermarcq (Vice-Pres.)

ELA

European Lift Association

Avenue Louis Gribaumont 1, Bte 6, 1150 Brussels, Belgium
Tel. (+32) 2-7795082
Fax (+32) 2-7721685
E-mail info@ela-aisbl.org
URL www.ela-aisbl.org
Sec.-Gen. S. Lutrivet

ELA

European Logistics Association

Association Européenne de Logistiques

Europäische Logistikvereinigung

Avenue des Arts 19, Kunstlaan, 1210 Brussels, Belgium
Tel. (+32) 2-2300211
Fax (+32) 2-2308123
E-mail ela@elalog.org
URL www.elalog.org
Pres. Graham Ewer
Sec.-Gen. Marc Fourny
Contact Nicole Geerkens (Exec. Officer)

ELC

European Lamp Companies Federation

Fédération Européenne des Entreprises d'Eclairage

Europäische Föderation der Beleuchtungsunternehmen

Boulevard Reyers 80, 1030 Brussels, Belgium
Tel. (+32) 2-7068608
Fax (+32) 2-7068609
E-mail info@eicfed.org
URL www.elcfed.org
Pres. Jan Denneman
Sec.-Gen. Gerald Strickland
Contact E.C. Guest (Vice-Pres.)

ELC

Federation of European Food Additives, Food Enzymes and Food Cultures Industries

Fédération des Industries Européennes d'Additifs et d'Enzymes Alimentaires

Föderation der Europäischen Industrien für Nahrungszusätze und -Enzyme

Avenue des Gaulois 9, 1040 Brussels, Belgium
Tel. (+32) 2-7365354
Fax (+32) 2-7323427
E-mail elc@ecco-eu.com
URL www.elc-eu.org
Pres. C. Guittard
Sec.-Gen. Dionne Heijnen

ELCA

European Landscape Contractors Association

Association des Entrepreneurs Paysagistes Européens

Gemeinschaft des Europäischen Garten-, Landschafts- und Sportplatzbaues

Alexander-von-Humboldt-Strasse 4, 53604 Bad Honnef, Germany

Tel. (+49 22) 24770720

Fax (+49 22) 24770777

E-mail contact@elca.info

URL www.elca.info

Pres. Toni Berger

Sec.-Gen. Dr H. J. Kurth

Contact Dr Hermann J. Kurth (Sec.)

ELCDHyg

European Liaison Committee for Dental Hygiene

C/o School of Dental Hygiene, Glasgow Dental Hospital & School, 378 Sauchiehall Street, Glasgow G2 3JZ, United Kingdom

Tel. (+44 141) 211-9774

Fax (+44 129) 4476-2653

E-mail eagray.dief@virgin.net

Contact E A Gray

ELF

European Locksmith Federation

C/o Safetyset Oy, Makelankatu 2, 00500 Helsinki, Finland

Tel. (+358 9) 27091880

Fax (+358 9) 739736850

E-mail secretary@eurolockfed.com

URL www.eurolockfed.com

Pres. Dave O'Toole

Sec.-Gen. T. Kajan

Contact Ona Luomala (Sec.)

ELMA

European Association for Length Measuring Instruments and Machines

Forge House, 3 Summerleys Road, Princes Risborough, Bucks HP27 9DT, United Kingdom

Tel. (+44 1844) 274222

Fax (+44 1844) 274227

E-mail gtma@gtma.co.uk

ELVHIS

European Association of High Intensity Gas Infrared Heater Manufacturers

Association Européenne Principale des Fabricants de Panneaux Infrarouges Lumineux à Gaz

Europäischer Leitverband der Hersteller von Gaz-Infrarot-Hellstrahlern e.V.

Marienburgerstrasse 15, 50968 Cologne, Germany

Tel. (+49 22) 13764830

Fax (+49 22) 13764861

E-mail figawa@t-online.de

URL www.elvhis.com

Pres. B.H. Schwank

Sec.-Gen. Dr Burger

EMA

European Medical Association

Place de Jamblinne de Meux 12, 1030 Brussels, Belgium

Tel. (+32) 2-7342980

Fax (+32) 2-7342023

E-mail contact@EMAnet.org

URL www.EMAnet.org

Pres. Dr Vincenzo Costigliola

Sec.-Gen. P. Kettelaer

EMA

European Metallizers Association

Association Européenne de la Métallisation

Europäischer Metallisierungsverband

POB 85612, 2508 CH The Hague, Netherlands

Tel. (+31 70) 3123917

Fax (+31 70) 3636348

E-mail mail@eurometallizers.org

URL www.eurometallizers.org

Pres. Mark Gooseman

Sec.-Gen. Manon Kienjet

Contact Eduardo Beasley (Exec. Dir)

EMA / ASFE

European Midwives Association

Association des Sages-Femmes Européennes

POB 18, 3720 AA Bilthoven, Netherlands

Tel. (+31 30) 2294299

Fax (+31 30) 2294162

E-mail ema@knov.nl

URL www.europeanmidwives.org

Pres. Dorthe Taxbøl

Contact Gloria Seguranyes (Vice-Pres.)

EMAA

European Management Accountants Association

Association Européenne de Comptables Agréés

Europäischer Verband der Bilanbuchhalter

Am Propsthof 15–17, 53121 Bonn, Germany
Tel. (+49 228) 639-318
Fax (+49 228) 639-314
E-mail kontakt@emaa.de
URL www.emaa.de
Pres. Udo Binias
Sec.-Gen. Peter Poulsen
Contact Herbert Mattle (Vice-Pres.)

EMBO

European Molecular Biology Organization

Meyerhofstrasse 1, 69117 Heidelberg, Germany
Tel. (+49 62) 2188910
Fax (+49 62) 218891200
E-mail embo@embo.org
URL www.embo.org
Sec.-Gen. Christiane Nüsslein-Volhard
Contact Frank Gannon (Exec. Dir)

EMC

European Marketing Confederation

Place des Chasseurs Ardennais 20, 1030 Brussels, Belgium
Tel. (+32) 2-7421780
Fax (+32) 2-7421785
E-mail infodesk@emc.be
URL www.emc.be
Pres. Nikos Pannossopoulos
Sec.-Gen. J. Ridsdale-Jaw
Contact Daniel Viane (Vice-Chair.)

EMCEF

European Mine, Chemical and Energy Workers' Federation

Fédération Européenne des Syndicats des Mines, de la Chimie et de l'Energie

Europäische Föderation der Bergbare-, Chemie- und Energiegewerkschaften

Avenue Emile de Béco 109, 1050 Brussels, Belgium
Tel. (+32) 2-6262180
Fax (+32) 2-6460685
E-mail info@emcef.org
URL www.emcef.org

Pres. Hubertus Schmoldt
Sec.-Gen. Reinhard Reibsch
Contact Paul Lootens (Vice-Pres.)

EMF / FEM / EMB

European Metalworkers' Federation

Fédération Européenne des Métallurgistes

Europäischer Metallgewerkschaftsbund

Rue Royale 45, Bte 2, 1000 Brussels, Belgium
Tel. (+32) 2-2271010
Fax (+32) 2-2175963
E-mail emf@emf-fem.org
URL www.emf-fem.org
Pres. Tony Janssen
Sec.-Gen. Peter Scherrer

EMF / FHE / EHV

European Mortgage Federation

Fédération Hypothécaire Européenne

Europäischer Hypothekenverband

Avenue de la Joyeuse Entrée 14/2, 1040 Brussels, Belgium
Tel. (+32) 2-2854030
Fax (+32) 2-2854031
E-mail emfinfo@hypo.org
URL www.hypo.org
Pres. Philip Williamson
Sec.-Gen. Judith Hardt

EMO

European Mortar Industry Organization

Association de l'Industrie Européenne des Mortiers

Verband der Europäischen Mortelindustrie

Düsseldorfer Strasse 50, 47051 Duisburg, Germany
Tel. (+49 20) 3992390
Fax (+49 20) 39923997
E-mail hans-peter.braus@baustoffverbaende.de
URL www.euromortar.com
Pres. Louis Moynard
Sec.-Gen. Hans-Peter Braus
Contact Rainer Algars (Vice-Pres.)

EMOTA / AEVPC

European Mail Order Traders' Association

Association Européenne de Vente par Correspondance

Europäische Vereinigung des Versandverkaufs

Rue Wiertz 50/28, 1050 Brussels, Belgium
Tel. (+32) 2-4016195
Fax (+32) 2-4016868
E-mail info@emota.org
URL www.emota-aevpc.org
Pres. Gerard Marsman
Sec.-Gen. Aad Weening
Contact Maitane Olabarria Uzquiano (Dir)

EMU

European Metal Union
Union Européenne du Métal
Europäische Metall-Union

Postbus 2600, Einsteinbaan 1, 3430
    Nieuwegein, Netherlands
Tel. (+31 30) 6053344
Fax (+31 30) 6063115
E-mail emu@metaalunie.nl
URL www.emu-pass.com
Pres. W. van Gaardingen
Contact Harm Jan Keijer (Dir)

ENERO

European Network of Environmental Research Organisations

URL www.enero.dk
Pres. Bert Don
Sec.-Gen. Jean-Claude Maquinay
Contact Philippe Janti (Vice-Pres.)

ENGAGE

European Network of Engineering for Agriculture and Environment

MTT/vakola, Vakolantie 55, 03400 Vihti,
    Finland
Tel. (+358 9) 224251
Fax (+358 9) 2246210
E-mail hannu.haapala@mtt.fi
URL www.fal.de/engage/index.htm
Sec.-Gen. Kim Kaustell
Contact Prof. Dr Hannu Happala (Vice-Pres.)

ENGVA

European Natural Gas Vehicle Association

Kruisweg 813 A, 2132 NG Hoofdorp,
    Netherlands
Tel. (+31 23) 5543050
Fax (+31 23) 5579065

E-mail info@engva.nl
URL www.engva.org
Pres. Jeffrey Seisler
Contact Jeffrey M. Seisler (Exec. Dir)

ENPA

European Newspaper Publishers' Association
Association Europeenne des Editeurs de Journaux
Verband Europäischer Zeitungsverleger

Rue des Pierres 29, Bte 8, 1000 Brussels,
    Belgium
Tel. (+32) 2-5510190
Fax (+32) 2-5510199
E-mail enpa@enpa.be
URL www.enpa.be
Pres. Per Lyngby
Contact Alan Crosbie (Vice-Pres.)

ENS / SEEN

European Nuclear Society
Société Européenne de l'Energie Nucléaire
Europäische Kernenergie Gesellschaft

Rue de la Loi 57, 1040 Brussels, Belgium
Tel. (+32) 2-5053050
Fax (+32) 2-5023902
E-mail ens@euronuclear.org
URL www.euronuclear.org
Pres. Bertrand Barré
Sec.-Gen. Dr Peter Haug
Contact Andrew Teller (Man.)

ENSCA

European Natural Sausage Casing Association
Association Européenne des Industries et Commerces de Boyauderie
Europejskie Stowarzyszenie Naturalnych Osłonek do Wędlin

Gotenstrasse 21, 20097 Hamburg, Germany
Tel. (+49 40) 23601622
Fax (+49 40) 23601610
E-mail ensca@wga-hh.de
URL www.ensca.be
Pres. Lindy Munkholm
Sec.-Gen. Dr Monika Beutgen
Contact M. Beutgen

EOQ

European Organization for Quality
Organisation Européenne pour la Qualité
Europäische Organisation für Qualität

Rue du Luxembourg 3, 1000 Brussels, Belgium
Tel. (+32) 2-5010735
Fax (+32) 2-5010736
E-mail bjouslin@compuserve.com
URL www.eoq.org
Pres. Wolfgang Kaerkes
Sec.-Gen. Bertrand Jouslin de Noray
Contact Hendric Niyazy (Vice-Pres.)

EOS

European Organisation of the Sawmill
Industry
Organisation Européenne des Scieries
Europäische Organisation der Sägewerke

Allée Hof-ter-Vleest 5, PO Box 4, 1070
Brussels, Belgium
Tel. (+32) 2-5562597
Fax (+32) 2-5562595
E-mail eos@cei-bois.org
Pres. Hans Michael Offner
Sec.-Gen. Filip de Jaeger
Contact Paula Serranao

EOTA

European Organisation for Technical
Approvals
Organisation Européenne pour l'Agrément
Technique
Europäische Organisation für Technische
Zulassungen

Kunstaan, Avenue des Arts 40, 1040 Brussels,
Belgium
Tel. (+32) 2-5026900
Fax (+32) 2-5023814
E-mail info@eota.be
URL www.eota.be
Pres. R. Mikulits
Sec.-Gen. P. Caluwaerts
Contact C. De Pauw (Chair.)

EPA

European Association of Polyol Producers
Association Européenne des Producteurs de
Polyols
Europäischer Verband der Polyol Hersteller

Avenue des Gaulois 9, 1040 Brussels, Belgium
Tel. (+32) 2-7365354
Fax (+32) 2-7323427
E-mail epa@ecco-eu.com
URL www.polyols-eu.org
Sec.-Gen. Heijnen

EPAG

European Property Agents Group

Avenue de Tervuren 36, Bte 2, 1040 Brussels,
Belgium
Tel. (+32) 2-7354990
Fax (+32) 2-7359988
E-mail cepi@cepi.be
URL www.cepi.be
Pres. Gerhard Steller
Sec.-Gen. Joachim Schmidt
Contact Winand van Coillie (Vice-Pres.)

EPBA

European Portable Battery Association
Association Européenne des Piles Portables
Europäische Vereinigung der Tragbaren
Batterien

Avenue Marcel Thiry 204, 1200 Brussels,
Belgium
Tel. (+32) 2-7749602
Fax (+32) 2-7749690
E-mail epba@eyam.be
URL www.epbaeurope.net
Pres. Rémy Burel
Sec.-Gen. Rachel Barlow

EPC

European Publishers' Council
Conseil Européen des Editeurs
Europäischer Verlegerrat

49 Park Town, Oxford OX2 6SL,
United Kingdom
Tel. (+44 18) 65310732
Fax (+44 18) 65310739
E-mail angelamills@epceurope.org
URL www.epceurope.org
Pres. Sir Frank Rogers
Sec.-Gen. Michel Viaud
Contact Angela Mills Wade (Exec. Dir)

EPDCC

European Pressure Die Casting Committee
Comité Européen des Fondeurs
Europäisches Komitee der Metallgiessereien

Am Bonneshof 5, 40474 Düsseldorf, Germany
Tel. (+49 211) 4796154
Fax (+49 211) 4796409
E-mail Gerhard.Kluegge@gdm-metallguss.de
URL www.gdm-metallguss.de
Sec.-Gen. Gerhard Klügge

EPF

European Panel Federation

Fédération Européenne des Panneaux à Base de Bois

Europäischer Holswerkstoffverband

Allée Hof-ter-Vleest 5, PO Box 5, 1070
    Brussels, Belgium
Tel. (+32) 2-5562589
Fax (+32) 2-5562594
E-mail info@europales.org
URL www.europanels.org
Pres. Ladislaus Döry
Sec.-Gen. Kris Wijnendaele
Contact Frans de Cock

EPHA

European Public Health Alliance

Alliance Européenne de la Santé Publique

Europäische Allianz für öffentliche Gesundheit

Rue d'Arlon 39–41, 1000 Brussels, Belgium
Tel. (+32) 2-2303056
Fax (+32) 2-2333880
E-mail epha@epha.org
URL www.epha.org
Pres. Andrew Hayes
Sec.-Gen. Tamsin Rose
Contact Prof. Ulf Magnusson

EPIA

European Photovoltaïc Industry Association

Avenue Charles Quint 124, 1083 Brussels,
    Belgium
Tel. (+32) 2-4653884
Fax (+32) 2-4682430
E-mail epia@epia.org
URL www.epia.org
Pres. Murray Cameron
Sec.-Gen. Michel Viaud
Contact Ernesto Macias (Vice-Pres.)

EPMA

European Powder Metallurgy Association

Association Européenne de Poudre Métallurgique

Europäische Vereinigung des Metallpuders

2nd Floor, Talbot House, Market Street,
    Shrewsbury SY1 1LG, United Kingdom
Tel. (+44 1743) 248899
Fax (+44 1743) 362968
E-mail info@epma.com
URL www.epma.com
Pres. Dr Cesar Molins
Contact Jonathan Wroe (Exec. Dir)

EPPF / SNPPA

European Profiles and Panels Producers Federation

Syndicat National du Profilage des Produits Plats en Acier

6/14 rue La Pérouse, 75784 Paris, France
Tel. (+33) 1-40-69-58-90
Fax (+49) 2-11-67-20-34
E-mail b.fulton@snppa.fr
URL www.eppf.com
Pres. Annie-Claude Bourcier
Sec.-Gen. R. Podleschny
Contact Dr Torsten Schlüter (Vice-Pres.)

EPSU / FSESP / EGÖD

European Federation of Public Service Unions

Fédération Syndicale Européenne des Services Publics

Europäischer Gewerkschaftsverband für den Öffentlichen Dienst

Rue Royale 45, PO Box 1, 1000 Brussels,
    Belgium
Tel. (+32) 2-2501080
Fax (+32) 2-2501099
E-mail epsu@epsu.org
URL www.epsu.org
Pres. Anna Salfi
Sec.-Gen. Fischbach Pyttel

EPTA

European Power Tool Association

Elektrowerkzeuge

Postfach 701261, 60591 Frankfurt am Main,
    Germany

Tel. (+49 69) 6302298
Fax (+49 69) 6302386
E-mail werkzeuge@zvei.org
Pres. U.E. Ruepp
Contact Klaus Greefe (Man. Dir)

ERA

European Regions Airline Association
Association des Compagnies d'Aviation des Régions d'Europe
Verband der Fluglinien Europäischer Regionen

The Baker Suite, Fairoaks Airport, Chobham GU24 8HX, United Kingdom
Tel. (+44 1276) 856495
Fax (+44 1276) 857038
E-mail info@eraa.org
URL www.eraa.org
Pres. Antonis Simigdalas
Contact Mike Ambrose (Dir-Gen.)

ERA

European Rotogravure Association
Association Européenne de Héliogravure
Verband des Europäischen Tiefdruchindustrie

Swakopmunder Strasse 3, 81827 Munich, Germany
Tel. (+49 89) 4395051
Fax (+49 89) 4394107
E-mail info@era.eu.org
URL www.era.eu.org
Pres. Nikolaus Broschek
Sec.-Gen. James Siever
Contact Alberto de Matthaeis (Vice-Pres.)

EREC / CEI

European Real Estate Confederation
Confédération Européenne de l'Immobilier
Europäische Makleronföderation

Sainctelette Square 11/12, 1000 Brussels, Belgium
Tel. (+32) 2-2194008
Fax (+32) 2-2178841
E-mail cei@web-cei.com
URL www.web-cei.com
Pres. André Groot

ERF

European Union Road Federation

Avenue Louise 113, 1050 Brussels, Belgium
Tel. (+32) 2-6445877
Fax (+32) 2-6475934
E-mail info@erf.be
URL www.erf.be
Pres. Aniceto Zaragoza
Sec.-Gen. José Papí
Contact Brendan Halleman (Dir)

ERMCO

European Ready Mixed Concrete Organisation
Association Européenne du Béton Prêt à l'Emploi
Europäischer Transportbetonverband

Rue Volta 8, 1050 Brussels, Belgium
Tel. (+32) 2-6455212
Fax (+32) 2-7351467
E-mail secretariat@ermco.org
URL www.ermco.org
Pres. Didier Levy
Sec.-Gen. Francesco Biasioli

ERPA

European Recovered Paper Association

Avenue Franklin Roosevelt 24, 1050 Brussels, Belgium
Tel. (+32) 2-6275770
Fax (+32) 2-6275773
E-mail bir.sec@skynet.be
URL www.erpa.info
Pres. Marteen Kleiweg de Zwaan
Contact Francis Veys (Exec. Dir)

ESA

European Sealing Association e.V.

Tegfryn, Tregarth, Gwynedd LL57 4PL, United Kingdom
Tel. (+44 1248) 600250
Fax (+44 1248) 600250
E-mail bse@europeansealing.com
URL www.europeansealing.com
Pres. M. Werner
Sec.-Gen. Dr Brian S Ellis
Contact Dr Jürgen Koch

ESA

European Snacks Association

6 Catherine St, London WC2B 5JJ,
United Kingdom
Tel. (+44 20) 7420-7220
Fax (+44 20) 7420-7221
E-mail esa@esa.org.uk
URL www.esa.org.uk
Pres. Andreas F. Schubert
Sec.-Gen. Steve Chandler
Contact Dr Robert Foot (Regulatory Affairs)

ESA

European Spice Association
Association Européenne de l'Epice
Europäische Vereinigung des Gewürzes

Reuterstrasse 151, 53113 Bonn, Germany
Tel. (+49 228) 216-162
Fax (+49 228) 229-460
E-mail weber@verbaendebuero.de
Pres. M. Rendlen
Sec.-Gen. Dr Hans-Joachim Murau
Contact S. Ludtke

ESBG / GECE / ESV

European Savings Banks Group
**Groupement Européen des Caisses
d'Epargne**
Europäische Sparkassenvereinigung

Rue Marie-Thérèse 11, 1000 Brussels, Belgium
Tel. (+32) 2-2111111
Fax (+32) 2-2111199
E-mail info@savings-banks.com
URL www.savings-banks.com
Pres. Charles Milhaud
Contact Dr Sandro Molinari (Vice-Pres.)

ESBO

European Solid Board Organisation

Laan Copes van Cattenburch 79, PO Box
85612, 2508 CH The Hague, Netherlands
Tel. (+31 70) 3123918
Fax (+31 70) 3636348
E-mail mail@esbo.nl
URL www.esbo.nl
Pres. Dirk Schut
Sec.-Gen. Herman Voskamp
Contact Ad Smit (Vice-Pres.)

ESDREMA

**European Surgical Dressings
Manufacturers' Association**

C/o Dr Massima Poretti, Via San Giovanni
s/Muro 1, 20121 Milan, Italy
Pres. Dr Massima Poretti

ESF

European Safety Federation

Rue Gachardstraat 88 (b 4), 1050 Brussels,
Belgium
Tel. (+32) 3-4600231
Fax (+32) 3-4600213
E-mail Info@european-safety-federation.org
URL www.european-safety-federation.org/
Pres. Dr David Harris
Sec.-Gen. Henk Vanhoutte
Contact Rita Boel (Sec.)

ESF

European Spring Federation

Goldene Pforte 1, 58093 Hagen, Germany
Tel. (+49 23) 31958851
Fax (+49 23) 31587484
E-mail contact@esf-springs.com
URL www.esf-springs.com
Pres. Dr Hans Jochem Steim
Sec.-Gen. Horst Dieter Dannert

ESGG / FNAMS

European Seed Growers Group
**Fédération Nationale des Agriculteurs
Multiplicateurs de Semences**

74/76 Rue Jean-Jacques Rousseau, 75001
Paris, France
Tel. (+33) 1-44-82-73-33
Fax (+33) 1-44-82-73-40
E-mail esgg@wanadoo.fr
Pres. G. Matteucci
Contact S. Prin

ESHA

European School Heads' Association
**Association des Chefs d'Etablissements
d'Enseignement**
**Europäische Schulleiter Vereinigung im
Sekundarbereich II**

C/o Ria van Peperstraten, Kromme
  Nieuwegracht 50, 3512 HK Utrecht,
  Netherlands
Tel. (+31 30) 2349090
Fax (+31 30) 2349099
E-mail r.vpeperstraten@vvo.nl
URL www.esha.org
Pres. Antonino Petrolino
Sec.-Gen. Jorma Lempinen
Contact Kees den Ouden (Dir)

ESHP / SEG / EGS

**European Society of Handwriting
  Psychology**

Société Européenne de Graphologie

**Europäische Gesellschaft für
  Schriftpsychologie und Schriftexpertise**

PO Box 2077, 8041 Zurich, Switzerland
Tel. (+41) 44-481-62-18
Fax (+41) 44-481-62-88
E-mail egs-secretariat@web.de
URL www.egs-graphologie.ch
Pres. Rudolf Kanzig-Muller
Contact Herbert Scholpp (Chair.)

ESOMAR

World Association of Research Professionals

**Association Européenne pour les Etudes
  d'Opinion et de Marketing**

**Europäische Gesellschaft für Meinungs- und
  Marketing-Forschung**

Vondelstraat 172, 1054 GV Amsterdam,
  Netherlands
Tel. (+31 20) 6642141
Fax (+31 20) 6642922
E-mail email@esomar.org
URL www.esomar.org
Pres. José Ortega
Contact Ted Vonk (Dir-Gen.)

ESPA

European Salt Producers' Association

**Association Européenne des Producteurs de
  Sel**

Europäische Vereinigung der Salzhersteller

Avenue de l'Yser 4, 1040 Brussels, Belgium
Tel. (+32) 2-7371090
Fax (+32) 2-7371099
E-mail info@eusalt.com
URL www.eu-salt.com

Pres. David Goadby
Contact Robert Speiser (Man. Dir)

ESPO

European Sea Ports Organisation

**Organisation des Ports Maritimes
  Européens**

Treurenberg 6, 1000 Brussels, Belgium
Tel. (+32) 2-7363463
Fax (+32) 2-7366325
E-mail mail@espo.be
URL www.espo.be
Sec.-Gen. Patrick Verhoeven
Contact D. Whitehead

ESRA

European Synthetic Rubber Association

Association des Caoutchoucs Synthétiques

Europäischer Synthesekeutschukverband

The Green 8, Richmond upon Thames
  TW9 1PL, United Kingdom
Tel. (+44 20) 8332-1113
Fax (+44 20) 8332-9292
E-mail sue@iisrpes.stech.co.uk
URL www.cefic.org
Sec.-Gen. Sue Cain

ESTA

European Security Transport Association

**Association Européenne du Transport et
  Convoyage de Valeurs**

**Europäische Vereinigung für Geldtransport
  und -Begleitung**

Rue D. Lefevre 252, 1020 Brussels, Belgium
Tel. (+32) 2-4670283
Fax (+32) 2-4670728
E-mail francis.ravez@esta.biz
URL www.esta.biz
Pres. N Buckles
Sec.-Gen. Francis Ravez
Contact Bernard Dumoulin (Exec. Vice-Pres.)

ESTA

European Smoking Tobacco Association

Association Europeenne de Tabac a Fumer

Rond Point Schumanplein 9, PO Box 1, 1040
  Brussels, Belgium
Tel. (+32) 2-2308092
Fax (+32) 2-2308214
E-mail info@esta.be
URL www.esta.be

Pres. Sluiter
Contact Peter van den Driest (Dir)

ESTA
European Steel Tube Association
Association Européenne du Tube d'Acier
130 rue de Silly, 92100 Boulogne-Billancourt,
    France
Tel. (+33) 1-49-09-35-91
Fax (+33) 1-49-09-35-91
E-mail esta.cl@wanadoo.fr
Sec.-Gen. Raymond Barbier

ESTA
European Surgical Trade Association
Buchenstrasse 76, 28211 Bremen, Germany
Tel. (+49 42) 13478608
Fax (+49 42) 13491866
E-mail esta@esta-office.com
URL www.esta-office.com
Pres. Oscar Rizzi

ESTOC
European Smokeless Tobacco Council
Conseil Européen du Tabac sans Fumée
Europäischer Rat für Rauchlosen Tabak
Streekbaan 100, 1800 Vilvoorde, Belgium
Tel. (+32) 2-7322204
Fax (+32) 2-7321926
E-mail 101553.3357@compuserve.com
URL www.estoc.org
Pres. Sture Lindmark
Contact Monique Verhulst (Representative)

ETA
European Tube Association
**Association Européenne des Fabricants de
    Tubes Souples**
Europäische Tuben Vereinigung
Am Bonneshof 5, 40474 Düsseldorf, Germany
Tel. (+49 211) 4796144
Fax (+49 211) 4796408
E-mail eta@aluinfo.de
Sec.-Gen. Gregor Spengler

ETAD
**Ecological and Toxicological Association of
    Dyes and Organic Pigments
    Manufacturers**
PO Box, 4005 Basel, Switzerland

Tel. (+41) 61-690-99-66
Fax (+41) 61-691-42-78
E-mail info@etad.com
URL www.etad.com
Pres. Dr Frank-Michael Stöhr
Contact Dr Herbert Motschi (Exec. Dir)

ETC / CET
European Tea Committee
Comité Européen du Thé
Europäisches Komitee des Tees
3 rue de Copenhague, 75008 Paris, France
Tel. (+33) 1-53-42-13-38
Fax (+33) 1-53-42-13-39
E-mail b-dufrene@wanadoo.fr
Pres. Thijs Kramer
Sec.-Gen. Dr Monika Beutgen
Contact Dr Barbara Dufrene

ETC / CET
European Travel Commission
Commission Européenne du Tourisme
Comisión Europea del Turismo
Avenue Marnix 19a, PO Box 25, 1000
    Brussels, Belgium
Tel. (+32) 2-5489000
Fax (+32) 2-5141843
E-mail info@etc-corporate.org
URL www.etc-corporate.org
Pres. Arthur Oberascher
Contact Jaime-Axel Ruiz Baudrihaye

ETF
European Transport Workers' Federation
**Fédération Européenne des Travailleurs des
    Transports**
Europäische Transportarbeiter-Föderation
Rue du Midi 165, 1000 Brussels, Belgium
Tel. (+32) 2-2854660
Fax (+32) 2-2800817
E-mail etf@etf-europe.org
URL www.itf.org.uk/etf
Pres. Wilhelm Haberzettl
Sec.-Gen. Eduardo Chagas
Contact Graham Stevenson (Vice-Pres.)

ETNO
**European Telecommunications Network
    Operators' Association**
Avenue Louise 54, 1050 Brussels, Belgium

Tel. (+32) 2-2193242
Fax (+32) 2-2196412
E-mail etno@etno.be
URL www.etno.be
Contact Michael Bartholomew (Dir)

ETRTO

European Tyre and Rim Technical Organisation

Organisation Technique Européenne du Pneumatique et de la Jante

Technische Organisation der Europäischen Reifen- und Felgenhersteller

Avenue Brugmann 32, Bte 2, 1060 Brussels, Belgium
Tel. (+32) 2-3444059
Fax (+32) 2-3441234
E-mail info@etrto.org
URL www.etrto.org
Pres. J. Musy
Sec.-Gen. JC. Noirhomme
Contact T. Neddenriep (Vice-Pres.)

ETSA

European Telecommunication Services Association

Association Européenne des Entreprises de Service en Télécommunication

Rue de Spa 18, 1000 Brussels, Belgium
Tel. (+32) 2-2302388
Fax (+32) 2-2801755
E-mail dcm@etsa.org
URL www.etsa.org
Pres. Maurizio Esitini
Sec.-Gen. Baronne de Coninck de Merckem Dominique
Contact Jaime Soto Somano (Vice-Pres.)

ETSA

European Textile Services Association

Rue Montoyer 24, PO Box 7, 1000 Brussels, Belgium
Tel. (+32) 2-2820990
Fax (+32) 2-2820999
E-mail etsa@etsa-europe.org
URL www.etsa-europe.org
Sec.-Gen. Robert Long
Contact Thomas Krautschneider (Vice-Pres.)

ETTFA

European Tourism Trade Fairs Association

Association des Foires Touristiques Européennes

Europäischer Fremdenverkehrsmessenverband

PO Box 585, Richmond upon Thames TW9 1YQ, United Kingdom
Tel. (+44 20) 8948-6656
Fax (+44 20) 8948-8097
E-mail secretariat@ettfa.org
URL www.ettfa.org
Pres. Tom Nutley
Sec.-Gen. M. Lapter

ETUC / CES / EGB

European Trade Union Confederation

Confédération Européenne des Syndicats

Europäischer Gewerkschaftsbund

Blvd du Roi Albert II 5, 1210 Brussels, Belgium
Tel. (+32) 2-2240411
Fax (+32) 2-2240454
E-mail etuc@etuc.org
URL www.etuc.org
Pres. Candido Mendez
Sec.-Gen. John Monks
Contact Patricia Grillo (Head of Press and Communication)

ETUCE / CSEE / EGBW

European Trade Union Committee for Education

Comité Syndical Européen de l'Education

Europäisches Gewerkschaftskomitee für Bildung und Wissenschaft

Blvd du Roi Albert II 5, 9th floor, 1210 Brussels, Belgium
Tel. (+32) 2-2240691
Fax (+32) 2-2240694
E-mail secretariat@csee-etuce.org
URL www.csee-etuce.org
Pres. Doug McAvoy
Sec.-Gen. Martin Romer
Contact D. Verschueren

ETUCO / ASE / EGA

European Trade Union College

Académie Syndicale Européenne

Europäische Gewerkschaftsakademie

Boulevard du Roi Albert II 5, PO Box 7, 1210
  Brussels, Belgium
Tel. (+32) 2-2240530
Fax (+32) 2-2240520
E-mail etuco@etuc.org
URL www.etuc.org/etuco
Pres. Cándido Méndez Rodríguez
Sec.-Gen. John Monks
Contact Eva Berger (Sec.)

ETUF : TCL / FSE : THC / EGV : TBL

**European Trade Union Federation : Textiles,
Clothing and Leather**

**Fédération Syndicale Européenne du Textile,
de l'Habillement et du Cuir**

**Europäischer Gewerkschaftsverband Textil,
Bekleidung und Leder**

Rue J. Stevens 8, 1000 Brussels, Belgium
Tel. (+32) 2-5115477
Fax (+32) 2-5118154
E-mail fse.ths@skynet.be
Pres. Valeria Fedeli
Sec.-Gen. Patrick Itschert
Contact Jean Lapeyre (Deputy Sec.-Gen.)

ETV

European Tobacco Wholesalers Association

**Association Européenne des Grossistes en
Produits du Tabac**

**Europäischer Tabakwaren-Grosshandels-
Verband E.V.**

Stadtwaldgürtel 44, 50931 Cologne, Germany
Tel. (+49 221) 400700
Fax (+49 221) 4007020
E-mail info@bdta.de
URL www.bdta.de
Pres. Erich Spengler
Contact Peter Lind (Man. Dir)

EUAC

European Union of Aquarium Curators

**Union Européenne des Conservateurs
d'Aquarium**

Eugeen Fahylaan 34, 2100 Antwerp, Belgium
Tel. (+32) 3-3241008
Fax (+32) 3-2756913
E-mail paul.van.den.sande@euac.org
URL www.euac.org
Pres. Jürgen Lange
Sec.-Gen. Nadia Ounais
Contact Paul van den Sande (Exec. Dir)

EUBA

European Bentonite Producers' Association

Boulevard S. Dupuis 233, PO Box 124, 1070
  Brussels, Belgium
Tel. (+32) 2-5245500
Fax (+32) 2-5244575
E-mail secretariat@ima-eu.org
URL www.ima-eu.org
Pres. Kriton Anavlavis
Sec.-Gen. Roger Doome
Contact Ulrich Werneck (Vice-Pres.)

EUCA

**European Federation of Associations of
Coffee Roasters**

**Fédération Européenne des Associations de
Torréfacteurs de Café**

**Europäische Vereinigung der
Rösterverbände**

Tourniairestraat 3, PO Box 90445, 1006 BK
  Amsterdam, Netherlands
Tel. (+31 20) 5113814
Fax (+31 20) 5113892
E-mail euca@coffee-associations.org
Pres. Dr Mario Cerutti
Sec.-Gen. J.A.J.R. Vaessen
Contact Mirjam Jonker-Stegeman
  (Accountant Asst)

EUCAR

**European Council for Automotive Research
and Development**

**Conseil Européen pour la Recherche et
Développement dans le Secteur
Automobile**

Rue du Noyer 211, 1000 Brussels, Belgium
Tel. (+32) 2-7387352
Fax (+32) 2-7387312
E-mail eucar@acea.be
URL www.eucar.be
Pres. M. Reitz
Contact Dr Arnold Vanzyl (Dir)

EUCARPIA

**European Association for Research on Plant
Breeding**

**Association Européenne pour l'Amélioration
des Plantes**

**Europäische Gesellschaft für
Züchtungsforschung**

Gregor Mendel Str. 33, 1180 Vienna, Austria

Tel. (+43 1) 47654-3309
Fax (+43 1) 47654-3342
E-mail hans.vollmann@iname.com
URL www.eucarpia.org
Pres. Prof. Dr Jaime Prohens-Tomás
Sec.-Gen. Dr Maria Luisa Badenes
Contact Dr Zoltán Bedö (Vice-Pres.)

EUCEPA
European Liaison Committee for Pulp and Paper
Comité Européen de Liaison pour la Cellulose et le Papier
Europäische Technische Vereinigung der Zellstoff- und Papierindustrie
154 Blvd Haussmann, 75008 Paris, France
Tel. (+33) 1-45-62-11-91
Fax (+33) 1-45-63-53-09
E-mail eucepa@yahoo.fr
URL www.eucepa.com
Pres. Angelo Loureiro
Sec.-Gen. Virginie Batais

EuCIA / GPRMC
European Composites Industry Association
Groupement Européen des Plastiques Renforcés / Matériaux Composites
Diamant Building, Blvd A. Reyers 80, 1030 Brussels, Belgium
Tel. (+32) 2-7067960
Fax (+32) 2-7067966
E-mail gustaaf.bos@agoria.be
URL www.gprmc.be
Pres. Volker Fritz
Sec.-Gen. Gustaaf Bos
Contact Jan Verhaeghe (Vice-Pres.)

EUCOLAIT
European Union of Dairy Trade
Union Européenne du Commerce des Produits Laitiers et Dérivés
Europäische Union des Handels mit Milcherzeugnissen
Avenue Livingstone 26, 1000 Brussels, Belgium
Tel. (+32) 2-2304448
Fax (+32) 2-2304044
E-mail dairy.trade@eucolait.be
URL www.eucolait-dairytrade.org
Pres. Ivan Hayes

Sec.-Gen. Anne Randles
Contact Patricia Portetelle (Office Man.)

EUCOMED
European Medical Technology Industry Association
Place St Lambert 14, Woluwe St Lambert, 1200 Brussels, Belgium
Tel. (+32) 2-7722212
Fax (+32) 2-7713909
E-mail eucomed@eucomed.be
URL www.eucomed.be
Pres. Wilson
Contact Maurice Wagner (Dir-Gen.)

EUDA
European Dredging Association
Association européenne de Dragage
Rue de Praetere 2–4, 1000 Brussels, Belgium
Tel. (+32) 2-6468183
Fax (+32) 2-6466063
E-mail info@euda.be
URL www.european-dredging.info
Pres. Marc Stordiau
Sec.-Gen. Fredrik J Mink
Contact F.A. Verhoeven (Treasurer)

EUF
Federation of European Tile Fixers Associations
Union Européenne des Fédérations des Entreprises de Carrelage
Europäische Union der Fliesen Fachverbände
Kolbenholz 4–6, 66121 Saarbrücken, Germany
Tel. (+49 681) 9356520
Fax (+49 681) 9356519
E-mail info@eufgs.com
URL www.eufgs.com
Pres. George Pardon
Sec.-Gen. Werner Altmayer
Contact Hans-Josef Aretz (Vice-Pres.)

EUFED
European Union Federation of Youth Hostel Associations
Fédération des Auberges de Jeunesse de l'Union Européenne
Rue Haute 25, 1000 Brussels, Belgium
Tel. (+32) 2-5028066

Fax (+32) 2-5025578
E-mail info@eufed.org
URL www.eufed.org
Pres. Peter Kaiser
Sec.-Gen. Sue Cassell
Contact Patrick Bernard (Vice-Pres.)

EuLA

European Lime Association

Association Européenne de la Chaux

Europäischer Kalkverband

Rue du Trône 61, 1050 Brussels, Belgium
Tel. (+32) 2-5113128
Fax (+32) 2-5140923
E-mail secretariat@eula.be
URL www.eula.be
Pres. M.R. Goffin
Sec.-Gen. Y. de Lespinay
Contact Dr G. Schaefer (Vice-Pres.)

EUMABOIS

**European Federation of Woodworking
Machinery Manufacturers**

Centro Direzionale Milanofiori, 1a Strada
Palazzo F3, 20090 Assago (Milano), Italy
Tel. (+39) 28-9210200
Fax (+39) 28-259009
E-mail info@eumabois.com
URL www.eumabois.com
Pres. Gianni Ghizzoni
Sec.-Gen. Zanibon

EUMAPRINT

**European Committee of Printing and Paper
Converting Machinery Manufacturers**

**Comité Européen des Constructeurs de
Machines pour les Industries Graphiques
et Papetières**

**Europäisches Komitee der Hersteller von
Druck- und Papiermaschinen**

Kirchenweg 4, Postfach, 8032 Zurich,
Switzerland
Tel. (+41 1) 384-41-11
Fax (+41 1) 384-48-46
E-mail eumaprint@npes.org
URL www.eumaprint.com
Pres. Philippe de Preux
Sec.-Gen. Dr Regis J. Delmontagne

EUMC

**European Union for Small and Medium-
Sized Enterprises**

**Union Européenne des Entreprises de Taille
Moyenne**

**Europäischen Union Mittelständischer
Unternehmen**

Rue Posschier 2, 1040 Brussels, Belgium
Tel. (+32) 2-6461187
Fax (+32) 2-6498762
E-mail eumc@skynet.be
Pres. J. Kiers
Sec.-Gen. Gerhard Hammerschimied

EUMETSAT

**European Organisation for the Exploitation
of Meteorological Satellites**

**Organisation européenne pour l'exploitation
des satellites météorologiques**

**Europäische Organisation zur Nutzung
Meteorologischer Satelliten**

Am Kavalleriesand 31, PO Box 100555, 64295
Darmstadt, Germany
Tel. (+49 61) 51807345
Fax (+49 61) 51807555
URL www.eumetsat.de
Pres. Dr Lars Prahvn
Contact Dr Livia Briese (Communication
Man.)

EuPC

European Plastics Converters

Confédération Européenne de la Plasturgie

Avenue de Cortenbergh 66, PO Box 4, 1000
Brussels, Belgium
Tel. (+32) 2-7324124
Fax (+32) 2-7324218
E-mail info@eupc.org
URL www.eupc.org
Pres. David Williams
Contact Alexandre Dangis (Man. Dir)

EUPG / UEVG / EUWEP

**European Union of Poultry, Egg and Game
Association**

Union Europeenne de la Volaille et du Gibier

**Europäische Vereinigung des Eier, Wild-
und Geflügelgross- und Aussenhandels eV
Ausschuss Geflugel und Wild**

Hochkreuzallee 72, 53175 Bonn, Germany

Tel. (+49 228) 959-600
Fax (+49 228) 959-6050
E-mail info@epega.org
URL www.epega.org
Pres. Biegi
Sec.-Gen. Dipl.-Ing Caspar von der Crone

EURACOAL

European Association for Coal and Lignite
Association Européenne du Charbon et du
Lignite

Av. de Tervueren 168, PO Box 11, 1150
Brussels, Belgium
Tel. (+32) 2-7719974
Fax (+32) 2-7714104
E-mail eurocoal@eurocoal.org
URL www.eurocoal.org
Pres. Nigel Yaxley
Sec.-Gen. Léopold Janssens
Contact Dr Constantinos Kavouridis
(Vice-Pres.)

EURADA

European Association of Development
Agencies
Association Européenne des Agences de
Développement
Europäischer Verband der
Wirtschaftsförderungsagenturen

Avenue des Arts 12, PO Box 7, 1210 Brussels,
Belgium
Tel. (+32) 2-2184313
Fax (+32) 2-2184583
E-mail info@eurada.org
URL www.eurada.org
Pres. Goran Ekstrom
Contact Christian Saublens (Dir)

EURATEX

European Apparel and Textile Organisation
Organisation Européenne de l'Habillement
et du Textile

Rue Montoyer 24, Bte 10, 1000 Brussels,
Belgium
Tel. (+32) 2-2854880
Fax (+32) 2-2306054
E-mail info@euratex.org
URL www.euratex.org
Pres. Filiep Libeert
Contact William Lakin (Dir-Gen.)

EUREAU

European Union of National Associations of
Water Suppliers and Waste Water
Services
Union Européenne des Associations
Nationales de Distributeurs d'Eau et de
Services d'Assainissement

Rue Colonel Bourg 127, 1140 Brussels,
Belgium
Tel. (+32) 2-7064080
Fax (+32) 2-7064081
E-mail eureau@skynet.be
URL www.eureau.org
Pres. Phillips
Sec.-Gen. F. Rillaerts

EUREL

Convention of National Societies of
Electrical Engineers of Europe

Avenue Roger Vandendriessche 18, 1150
Brussels, Belgium
Tel. (+32) 2-6467600
Fax (+32) 2-6463032
E-mail eurel@eurel.org
URL www.eurel.org
Pres. Prof. Vilim Simanek
Sec.-Gen. Dr F Rillaerts
Contact Dr Pavel Drasar (Exec. Dir)

EURELECTRIC

Union of the Electricity Industry
Groupement Européen des Entreprises
d'Electricité
Europäische Vereinigung der
Elektrizitätsversorgung

Boulevard de l'Impératrice 66, 1000 Brussels,
Belgium
Tel. (+32) 2-5151000
Fax (+32) 2-5151010
E-mail eurelectric@eurelectric.org
URL www.eurelectric.org
Pres. Rafael Robredo
Sec.-Gen. Paul Bulteel
Contact Lars Josefsson (Vice-Pres.)

EURIMA

European Insulation Manufacturers
Association
Association Européenne des Fabricants de
Matériaux d'Isolation

Europäische Vereinigung von Dämmstoff-Herstellern

Avenue Louise 375, PO Box 4, 1050 Brussels, Belgium
Tel. (+32) 2-6262090
Fax (+32) 2-6262099
E-mail info@eurima.org
URL www.eurima.org
Pres. Jan van Brummen
Contact Biedermann Horst (Dir-Gen.)

EURO CHLOR

Avenue E van Nieuwenhuyse 4, PO Box 2, 1160 Brussels, Belgium
Tel. (+32) 2-6767211
Fax (+32) 2-6767241
E-mail eurochlor@cefic.be
URL www.eurochlor.org
Contact Barrie S Gilliatt (Exec. Dir)

EURO COOP

European Community of Consumer Cooperatives

Communauté Européenne des Coopératives de Consommateurs

Europäische Gemeinschaft der Verbrauchergenossenschaften

Rue Archimède 17, 1000 Brussels, Belgium
Tel. (+32) 2-2850070
Fax (+32) 2-2310757
E-mail info@eurocoop.coop
URL www.eurocoop.coop
Pres. Giuseppe Fabretti
Sec.-Gen. Donal Walshe
Contact Louise Ousted Olsen (Senior Adviser)

EUROADSAFE

European Road Safety Equipment Federation

Fédération Européenne des Equipements Routiers de Sécurité

Europäische Föderation für Strassen Sicherheitsausrüstung

152 rue de Picpus, 95012 Paris Cedex, France
Tel. (+33) 1-43-42-26-36
Fax (+33) 1-43-42-47-71
Contact B.W. Wink (Vice-Pres.)

EURO-AIR

European Association of Air Heater Manufacturers

Marienbürger Strasse 15, 50968 Cologne, Germany
Tel. (+49 22) 13764830
Fax (+49 22) 13764861
E-mail figawa@t-online.de
URL www.euro-air.com
Pres. Joseph Boeckx
Sec.-Gen. N. Burger
Contact Dr Thomas Wittleder (Vice-Pres.)

EUROALLIAGES

Association of European Ferro-alloy Producers

Comité de Liaison des Industries de Ferro-Alliages

Avenue de Broqueville 12, 1150 Brussels, Belgium
Tel. (+32) 2-7756301
Fax (+32) 2-7756303
E-mail euroalliages@skynet.be
URL www.euroalliages.com
Pres. Bernard Epron
Sec.-Gen. Inès van Lierde

EUROBAT

Association of European Storage Battery Manufacturers

Association de Fabricants Européens d'Accumulateurs

Vereinigung Europäischer Akkumulatoren-Hersteller

Avenue Marcel Thiry 204, 1200 Brussels, Belgium
Tel. (+32) 2-7749653
Fax (+32) 2-7749690
E-mail eurobat@eyam.be
URL www.eurobat.org
Pres. W. Wever
Sec.-Gen. Alfons Westgeest
Contact Veerle Guns (Senior Asst)

EUROCADRES

Council of European Professional Managerial Staff

Conseil des Cadres Européens

Rat der Europäischen Fach- und Führungskrafte

Bd du Roi Albert II 5, 1210 Brussels, Belgium

Tel. (+32) 2-2240730
Fax (+32) 2-2240733
E-mail sat@eurocadres.org
URL www.eurocadres.org
Pres. Michel Rousselot
Contact Gina Ebner (Project Coordinator)

EUROCAE

European Organisation for Civil Aviation Equipment

Organisation Européenne pour l'Equipement de l'Aviation Civile

17 rue Hamelin, 75783 Paris Cedex 16, France
Tel. (+33) 1-45-05-72-35
Fax (+33) 1-45-05-72-30
E-mail eurocae@eurocae.com
URL www.eurocae.org
Pres. Prof. Terence Knibb
Sec.-Gen. Gilbert Amato
Contact Francis Grimal

EURO-CASE

European Council of Applied Sciences Technology and Engineering

28 Rue Saint Dominique, 75007 Paris, France
Tel. (+33) 1-53-59-53-40
Fax (+33) 1-53-59-53-41
E-mail mail@euro-case.org
URL www.euro-case.org
Sec.-Gen. Pierre Fillet
Contact Valentin van Den Balck (Chair.)

EUROCHAMBRES

Association of European Chambers of Commerce and Industry

Association des Chambres Européennes de Commerce et d'Industrie

Vereinigung der Europäischen Industrien- und Handelskammern

Avenue des Arts 19 A/D, 1000 Brussels, Belgium
Tel. (+32) 2-2820850
Fax (+32) 2-2300038
E-mail eurochambres@eurochambres.be
URL www.eurochambres.be
Pres. Christoph Leitl
Sec.-Gen. Arnaldo Abruzzini
Contact Paul Skehan (Deputy Sec.-Gen.)

EUROCINEMA

Association of Producers of Cinema and Television

Association de Producteurs de Cinéma et de Télévision

Rue Stévin 212, 1000 Brussels, Belgium
Tel. (+32) 2-7325830
Fax (+32) 2-7333657
E-mail eurocinema@eurocinema.be
URL www.eurocinema.com
Contact Yvon Thiec

EUROCOMMERCE

Association for retail, wholesale and international trade interests

Commerce de détail, de gros et international en Europe

Gegründet und Vertritt den Einzel-, Groß- und Außenhandel in Europa

Avenue des Nerviens 9–31, 1040 Brussels, Belgium
Tel. (+32) 2-7370598
Fax (+32) 2-2300078
E-mail bastings@eurocommerce.be
URL www.eurocommerce.be
Pres. Bernet
Sec.-Gen. Xavier R Durieu
Contact Fabienne Bastings (Gen. Admin.)

EUROCORD

Federation of European Rope, Twine and Netting Industries

Fédération Européenne des Industries de Corderie-Ficellerie et de Filets

EG-Verbindungsausschuss der Hartfaser- und Tauwerkindustrie

47 Rue de Monceau, 75008 Paris, France
Tel. (+33) 1-53-75-10-04
Fax (+33) 1-53-75-10-02
E-mail eurocord@eurocord.com
URL www.eurocord.com
Pres. Manuel Alberto Pereira
Sec.-Gen. Dr Anne Jourdain
Contact Edmond Blommaerts (Vice-Pres.)

EUROCOTON

Committee of the Cotton and Allied Textile Industries

Komitee der Baumwoll- und Verwandten Textilindustriën der EG

Rue Montoyer 24, Bte 13, 1000 Brussels,
  Belgium
Tel. (+32) 2-2303239
Fax (+32) 2-2303622
E-mail michele.anselme@eurocoton.org
Pres. Jean-Francois Gribomont
Sec.-Gen. Michèle Anselme
Contact Tito Burgi (Vice-Pres.)

EUROFEDOP

**European Federation of Public Service
Employees**

**Fédération Européenne du Personnel des
Services Publics**

**Europäische Föderation der
Öffentlichbediensteten**

Montoyerstraat 39, 1000 Brussels, Belgium
Tel. (+32) 2-2303865
Fax (+32) 2-2311472
E-mail info@infedop-eurofedop.com
URL www.eurofedop.org
Pres. Fritz Neugebauer
Sec.-Gen. Bert van Caelenberg
Contact Valentin Rasking (Translator)

EUROFEL

European Association of Feldspar Producers

Blvd. S. Dupuis, 233, PO Box 124, 1070
  Brussels, Belgium
Tel. (+32) 2-5245500
Fax (+32) 2-5244575
E-mail secretariat@ima-eu.org
URL www.ima-eu.org
Pres. Marc Lebrun
Sec.-Gen. Dr Michelle Wyart-Remy

EUROFER

**European Confederation of Iron and Steel
Industries**

Association Européenne de la Sidérurgie

**Europäische Wirtschaftsvereinigung der
Eisen- und Stahlindustrie**

Rue du Noyer, 211, 1000 Brussels, Belgium
Tel. (+32) 2-7387920
Fax (+32) 2-7363001
E-mail mail@eurofer.be
URL www.eurofer.org
Pres. Guy Dollé
Contact Dietrich von Hülsen (Dir-Gen.)

EUROFEU

**European Committee of the Manufacturers
of Fire Protection Equipment and Fire
Fighting Vehicles**

**Comité Européen des Constructeurs de
Matériels d'Incendie et de Secours**

**Europäisches Komitee der Hersteller von
Fahrzeugen, Geräten und Anlagen für den
Brandschutz**

Lyonerstrasse 18, 60528 Frankfurt am Main,
  Germany
Tel. (+49 69) 66031305
Fax (+49 69) 66031464
E-mail bernd.scherer@vdma.org
URL www.eurofeu.org
Pres. Pierre Schiffers
Sec.-Gen. Bernd Scherer

EUROFINAS

**European Federation of Finance House
Associations**

**Fédération Européenne des Instituts de
Crédit**

**Europäische Vereinigung der Verbände von
Finanzierungsbanken**

Avenue de Tervuren 267, 1150 Brussels,
  Belgium
Tel. (+32) 2-7780560
Fax (+32) 2-7780579
E-mail eurofinas@eurofinas.org
URL www.eurofinas.org
Sec.-Gen. Baert
Contact Menezes Rodrigues (Vice-Chair.)

EUROFORGE

European Forging Associations

**Comité de Liaison des Industries
Européennes de l'Estampage et de la
Forge**

Europaischer Schmiedeverband

Goldene Pforte 1, 58093 Hagen, Germany
Tel. (+49 23) 31958812
Fax (+49 23) 3151046
E-mail ltutmann@euroforge.org
URL www.euroforge.org
Pres. Peter Sundström
Sec.-Gen. Dr Theodor L. Tutmann
Contact Ingrid Schallnus (Asst)

EUROGAS

European Union of the Natural Gas Industry
Union Européenne de l'Industrie du Gaz Naturel
Europäische Vereinigung der Erdgaswirtschaft

Avenue Palmerston 4, 1000 Brussels, Belgium
Tel. (+32) 2-2371127
Fax (+32) 2-2306291
E-mail eurogas@eurogas.org
URL www.eurogas.org
Pres. Willy Bosmans
Sec.-Gen. Devos
Contact Burckhard Bergmann (Vice-Pres.)

EUROGIRO

Giro and Postbank Organisations in Europe

Carl Gustavs Gade 3, 1 th., 2630 Taastrup, Denmark
Tel. (+45) 43-71-27-72
Fax (+45) 43-71-26-62
E-mail eurogiro@eurogiro.com
URL www.eurogiro.com
Contact Henrik Parl (Man. Dir)

EUROGLACES

Association of the Ice Cream Industries of the EC
Association des Industries des Glaces Alimentaires de la CE
Vereinigung der Speiseeisindustrie der EG

3 rue de Copenhague, 75008 Paris, France
Tel. (+33) 1-53-42-13-38
E-mail b-dufrene@wanadoo.fr
Pres. Dimitrius Nicolau
Sec.-Gen. Barbara Dufrene

EUROGYPSUM

Association of European Gypsum Industries
Association des Industries Européennes du Plâtre
Verband der Europäischen Gipsindustrien

Gulledelle 98, PO Box 7, 1200 Brussels, Belgium
Tel. (+32) 2-7758490
Fax (+32) 2-7713056
E-mail info@eurogypsum.org
URL www.eurogypsum.org
Pres. Bruce Slatton
Sec.-Gen. Philip Bennett

EUROHEAT & POWER

International Association for District Heating, District Cooling and Combined Heat and Power

Avenue de Tervuren 300, 1150 Brussels, Belgium
Tel. (+32) 2-7402110
Fax (+32) 2-7402119
E-mail info@euroheat.org
URL www.euroheat.org
Pres. Tomas Bruce
Contact Sabine Froning (Man. Dir)

EUROKOBRA EEIG

EUROKOBRA European Economic Interest Grouping

Boulevard Poincaré 79, 1060 Brussels, Belgium
Tel. (+32) 2-6557711
Fax (+32) 2-6530729
E-mail eurokobra@bbri.be
URL www.eurokobra.org

EUROLAB

European Federation of National Associations of Measurement, Testing and Analytical Laboratories

Unter den Eichen 87, 12205 Berlin, Germany
Tel. (+49 30) 81043762
Fax (+49 30) 81044628
E-mail eurolab@bam.de
URL www.eurolab.org
Pres. Marc Mortureux
Sec.-Gen. Gloze
Contact Dr Bent Larsen (Vice-Pres.)

EUROLATEX

Koningsbaan, 1, 2560 Nijlen, Belgium
Tel. (+32) 3-4101300
Fax (+32) 3-4817932
E-mail info@artilat.be
Sec.-Gen. Rouchal Josef

EUROM II

Optics Laser & Laboratory Instrumentation Group within European Federation of Precision Mechanical & Optical Industries

39 rue L. Blanc, Courbevoie, 92038 Paris La Défense, France
Tel. (+33) 1-47-17-64-05

Fax (+33) 1-47-17-64-81
E-mail eurom2@blwa.co.uk
Pres. Michel Leclercq
Sec.-Gen. Francis Pithon

EUROM

European Federation of Precision Mechanical and Optical Industries

Fédération Européenne de l'Industrie de l'Optique et de la Mécanique de Précision

Europäische Industrie-Vereinigung Feinmechanik und Optik

C/o ANFAO, Via pettiti 16, 20149 Milan, Italy
Tel. (+39) 02-32673673
Fax (+39) 02-324233
E-mail pposso@worldcom.ch
Pres. Veller
Sec.-Gen. Lambert

EUROMAISIERS

EU Maize Millers Association

Groupement des Associations des Maïsiers des Pays de la EU

Arbeitsgemeinschaft der Maismühlenverbände der EG-Länder

21 Arlington Street, London SW1A 1RN,
United Kingdom
Tel. (+44 20) 7529-7707
Fax (+44 20) 7493-6785
E-mail nabim@dial.pipex.com
Pres. Valluis
Sec.-Gen. Pearson
Contact Alexander Waugh

EUROMALT

Working Committee of the EU Malting Industry

Comité de Travail des Malteries de l'UE

Arbeitskomitee der Malzereien in der EG

Avenue des Gaulois 9, 1040 Brussels, Belgium
Tel. (+32) 2-7365354
Fax (+32) 2-7323427
E-mail euromalt@graininindustry.com
Sec.-Gen. Antero Leino
Contact Harald Relander (Chair.)

EUROMAT

European Federation of Coin Machine Associations

Fédération Européenne des Associations de l'Automatique

Europaische Vereinigung der Automaten-Verbände

Chaussée de Wavre 214d, 1050 Brussels,
Belgium
Tel. (+32) 2-6261993
Fax (+32) 2-6269501
E-mail secretariat@euromat.org
URL www.euromat.org
Pres. Eduardo Antoja
Contact Hans Rosenzweig (Vice-Pres.)

EUROMETAL

European Federation of Associations of Steel, Tubes and Metal Merchants

Fédération Européenne des Associations de Négociants en Aciers, Tubes et Métaux

Europaischer Federation der Nationalen Verbande der Stahl-, Rohre und Metall-Handelsverband

Bd de la Woluwe 46, Bte 7, 1200 Brussels,
Belgium
Tel. (+32) 2-7715340
Fax (+32) 2-7721977
E-mail contact@eurometal.net
URL www.eurometal.net
Pres. Josef von Riederer
Sec.-Gen. F. Van Remoortere

EUROMETAUX

European Association of Metals

Association Européenne des Métaux

Avenue de Broqueville 12, 1150 Brussels,
Belgium
Tel. (+32) 2-7756311
Fax (+32) 2-7790523
E-mail eurometaux@eurometaux.be
URL www.eurometaux.org
Pres. Leysen Thomas
Sec.-Gen. Thiran Guy

EUROMETREC

European Metal Trade and Recycling Federation

EFR C/o BIR, Av Franklin Roosevelt 24, 1050
Brussels, Belgium
Tel. (+32) 2-6275770
Fax (+32) 2-6275773
E-mail eurometrec@bir.org
URL www.eurometrec.org

Pres. Bjorn Grufman
Sec.-Gen. Francis Veys
Contact Elisabeth Christ (Press and Media
Relations)

EUROMOL

**European Organisation for the Manufacture
of Leather Accessories, Travelware and
Related Products**
Calle Marques de la Ensainada 2, 4° planta,
28004 Madrid, Spain
Tel. (+34) 91-3196252
Fax (+34) 91-3104954
E-mail asesna@asesna.com
Pres. O. Montecci
Sec.-Gen. F. Gutierrez
Contact Gemma

EUROMOT

**European Association of Internal
Combustion Engine Manufacturers**
C/o VDMA e.V., Lyonerstrasse 18, 60528
Frankfurt am Main, Germany
Tel. (+49 69) 66031354
Fax (+49 69) 66032354
E-mail euromot@vdma.org
URL www.euromot.org
Pres. Manlio Mattei
Sec.-Gen. Dr Hartmut Mayer
Contact Pierre Bousseau (Deputy Pres.)

EUROPABIO

**European Association for Bioindustries
Association européenne des BioIndustries**
Avenue de l'Armée 6, 1040 Brussels, Belgium
Tel. (+32) 2-7350313
Fax (+32) 2-7354960
E-mail mail@curopabio.org
URL www.europabio.org
Sec.-Gen. Dr Johan Vanhemelrijck
Contact Dr Hans Kast (Chair.)

EUROPACABLE

**European Confederation of National
Associations of Manufacturers of
Insulated Wires and Cable**
**Confédération européenne des associations
de fabricants de fils et de câbles isolés**
**Europäische Konföderation der
Vereinigungen der Kabel- und
Isolierdrahthersteller**

C/o Cablebel, Diamant Building, Blvd A.
Reyers 80, 1030 Brussels, Belgium
Tel. (+32) 2-7068735
Fax (+32) 2-7068737
E-mail info@europacable.com
URL www.europacable.com
Pres. Dr V. Battista
Sec.-Gen. T. Neesen
Contact Michael Kelly (Deputy Sec.-Gen.)

EUROPARKS

European Federation of Leisure Parks
**Federation Européenne des Parcs
d'Attraction**
Europäische Föderation der Freizeitparks
Rue Wiertz 50, Bte 28, 1050 Brussels, Belgium
Tel. (+32) 2-4016162
Fax (+32) 2-4016868
E-mail j.bertus@wxs.nl
URL www.europarks.org
Pres. David Cam
Sec.-Gen. Jeff Bertus
Contact Taminiau (Vice-Pres.)

EUROPATAT

European Union of the Potato Trade
**Union Européenne du Commerce des
Pommes de Terre**
Europäische Union des Kartoffelhandels
Rue de Spa 8, 1000 Brussels, Belgium
Tel. (+32) 9-3391252
Fax (+32) 9-3391251
E-mail europatat@fvphouse.be
URL www.europatat.org
Pres. Joop Stet
Sec.-Gen. Romain Cools
Contact Liam Glennon (Vice-Pres.)

EUROPEAN REGION OF WCPT

**European Region of the World
Confederation for Physical Therapy**
Rue de Pascale 16, 1040 Brussels, Belgium
Tel. (+32) 2-2315063
Fax (+32) 2-2315064
E-mail physio.europe@tiscali.be
URL www.physio-europe.org
Pres. Antonio Lopes
Sec.-Gen. David Gorria

EUROPECHE

Association of the National Organisations of Fishery Enterprises in the European Union

Association des Organisations Nationales d'Entreprises de Pêche de l'UE

Vereinigung der Nationalen Verbände von Fischereiunternehmen in der Europäischen Union

Rue Montoyer 24, 1000 Brussels, Belgium
Tel. (+32) 2-2304848
Fax (+32) 2-2302680
E-mail europeche@skynet.be
URL www.europeche.org
Pres. Niels Wichmann
Sec.-Gen. Guy Vernaeve
Contact Javier Garat Perez (Vice-Pres.)

EUROPEN

European Organization for Packaging and the Environment

Organisation Européenne pour l'Emballage et l'Environnement

Europäische Vereinigung für Verpackung und Umwelt

Le Royal Tervuren, Avenue de l'Armée Leger 6, 1040 Brussels, Belgium
Tel. (+32) 2-7363600
Fax (+32) 2-7363521
E-mail packaging@europen.be
URL www.europen.be
Pres. Harry Jongeneelen
Contact Julian Carroll (Man. Dir)

EUROPGEN

European Generating Set Association

Comité de Coordination du Groupe Electrogène en Europe

Koordinierungskomitee der Kraftwerksfachverbände in Europa

C/o AMPS, Kirkby House, Andover SP11 6JW, United Kingdom
Tel. (+44 1264) 365367
Fax (+44 1264) 362304
E-mail technical@amps.org.uk
Pres. Robert Beebee
Sec.-Gen. Wheadon

EUROPIA

European Petroleum Industry Association

Association de l'Industrie Pétrolière Européenne

Blvd du Souverain 165, 1160 Brussels, Belgium
Tel. (+32) 2-5669100
Fax (+32) 2-5669111
E-mail info@europia.com
URL www.europia.com
Pres. Wilhelm Bonse Geuking
Sec.-Gen. Peter Tjan

EUROPLANT

European Plantmakers Committee

Comité Européen des Ensembliers Industriels

Europäisches Komitee der Grossanlangen Bauwer

C/o VDMA, Lyonerstrasse 18, 60528 Frankfurt am Main, Germany
Tel. (+49 69) 66031275
Fax (+49 69) 66032858
E-mail agab@vdma.org
URL www.grossanlagerbau.vdma.org

EUROPUMP

European Association of Pump Manufacturers

Association Européenne des Constructeurs de Pompes

Europäische Vereinigung der Pumpenhersteller

Diamant Building, Blvd. A. Reyers 80, 1030 Brussels, Belgium
Tel. (+32) 2-7068230
Fax (+32) 2-7068253
E-mail secretariat@europump.org
URL www.europump.org
Pres. Paolo Marinovich
Sec.-Gen. Guy Van Doorslaer
Contact Frank Ennenbach (Commission Chair.)

EUROPUR

European Association of Flexible Polyurethane Foam Blocks Manufacturers

Association Européenne des Fabricants de Blocs de Mousse Souple de Polyuréthane

Verband der Europäischen Hersteller von Polyurethan Weichblockschann

Square Marie-Louise 49, 1000 Brussels,
Belgium
Tel. (+32) 2-2389742
Fax (+32) 2-2301989
E-mail tspeeleveld@fedichem.br
URL www.europur.com
Pres. Edward Dupont
Sec.-Gen. Ir. Theo Speeleveld
Contact Raffaella Salerno (Asst)

EURORAD

European Association of Manufacturers of Radiators

Association Européenne des Constructeurs de Corps de Chauffe

Europäische Vereinigung der Hersteller von Heizkörpern

C/o GFCC, 92038 Paris La Défense, France
Tel. (+33) 1-47-17-61-64
Fax (+33) 1-47-17-60-03
Pres. D. Eitel
Sec.-Gen. P. Toledano

EUROSAFE

European Committee of Safe Manufacturers Associations

Comité Européen des Associations de Fabricants de Coffres-Forts

Boerhavelaan 40, PO Box 190, 2700 AD
Zoetermeer, Netherlands
Tel. (+31 79) 3531267
Fax (+31 79) 3531365
E-mail eurosafe@fme.nl
Pres. P. Laecrar
Sec.-Gen. J. Kat

EUROSEED

European Seed Association

Rue du Luxembourg 23/15, 1000 Brussels,
Belgium
Tel. (+32) 2-7432860
Fax (+32) 2-7432869
E-mail secretariat@euroseed.org
URL www.euroseeds.org
Pres. Sten Moberg
Sec.-Gen. Garlich von Essen
Contact Bert Scholte (Technical Dir)

EUROSIL

European Association of Silica Producers

Bd. S. Dupuis 233, Bte 124, 1070 Brussels,
Belgium
Tel. (+32) 2-5245500
Fax (+32) 2-5244575
E-mail secretariat@ima-eu.org
URL www.ima-eu.org
Pres. Peter Overdick
Sec.-Gen. Michelle Wyart-Remy
Contact Speeckaert (Vice-Pres.)

EUROSMART

European Smart Card Association

Rue du Luxembourg 19–21, 1000 Brussels,
Belgium
Tel. (+32) 2-5068838
Fax (+32) 2-5068825
E-mail info@eurosmart.com
URL www.eurosmart.com
Pres. Olivier Piou
Sec.-Gen. Bruno Dupont

EUROSPACE

Organisation of the European Space Industry

Association de l'Industrie Spatiale Européenne

15–17 avenue de Ségur, 75007 Paris, France
Tel. (+33) 1-44-42-00-70
Fax (+33) 1-44-42-00-79
E-mail letterbox@eurospace.org
URL www.eurospace.org
Pres. Pascale Sourisse
Sec.-Gen. Alain Gaubert
Contact Rosy Plet (Public Relations and
Conference Man.)

EUROTALC

Scientific Association of the European Talc Industry

Bd. S. Dupuis 233, Bte 124, 1070 Brussels,
Belgium
Tel. (+32) 2-5245500
Fax (+32) 2-5244575
E-mail secretariat@ima-eu.org
URL www.ima-eu.org
Pres. Claude Stenneler
Sec.-Gen. Michelle Wyart-Remy

EURO-TOQUES
European Community of Chefs
Avenue des Arts 43, 5ème Etage, 1040
  Brussels, Belgium
Tel. (+32) 2-5031295
Fax (+32) 2-5130218
E-mail secretary@euro-toques.org
URL www.euro-toques.org
Pres. Pedio Subijana
Sec.-Gen. M. Bernard Fournier

EUROTRANS
**European Committee of Associations of
Manufacturers of Gears and Transmission
Parts**
**Comité Européen des Associations de
Constructeurs d'Engrenages et
d'Eléments de Transmission**
**Europäisches Komitee der Fachverbände
der Hersteller von Getrieben und
Antriebselementen**
Lyonerstrasse 18, 60528 Frankfurt am Main,
  Germany
Tel. (+49 69) 66031526
Fax (+49 69) 66031459
E-mail klaus.wuestenberg@vdma.org
URL www.euro-trans.org
Pres. Dulaey
Sec.-Gen. K. Wustenberg

EUROVENT
**European Committee of Air Handling and
Air Conditioning Equipment
Manufacturers**
**Comité Européen des Constructeurs de
Matériel Aéraulique**
Diamant Building, Blvd A. Reyers 80, 1030
  Brussels, Belgium
Tel. (+32) 2-7067985
Fax (+32) 2-7067988
E-mail info@eurovent-cecomaf.org
URL www.agoria.be
Pres. Georg Mager
Sec.-Gen. Michel Van der Horst
Contact Francesco Basa (Vice-Pres.)

EUROWATT
Room 8.4, Gresham House, 53 Clarendon
  Road, Watford WD17 1FR,
  United Kingdom
Tel. (+44 1923) 334144

Fax (+44 1923) 244180
Contact Mordue (Sec.)

EUSIDIC
**European Association of Information
Services**
**Association Européenne des Services
d'Information**
**Europäische Vereinigung der
Informationsdienste**
WG Plein 475, 1054 SH Amsterdam,
  Netherlands
Tel. (+31 20) 5893232
Fax (+31 20) 5893230
E-mail eusidic@caos.nl
URL www.eusidic.org
Pres. Johan van Halm
Contact A. Brackel

EUSP / UEPS
European Union of the Social Pharmacies
Union Européenne des Pharmacies Sociales
Route de Lennik 900, 1070 Brussels, Belgium
Tel. (+32) 2-5299240
Fax (+32) 2-5299376
E-mail ueps@multipharma.be
URL www.eurosocialpharma.org
Pres. William Janssens
Sec.-Gen. Marc-Henry Cornely

EUTECA
**European Technical Caramel Colour
Association**
**Association Européenne de Caramels
Colorants**
**Europäischer Verband der Hersteller von
Farbstoffkaramel**
C/o ECCO, Avenue des Gaulois 9, 1040
  Brussels, Belgium
Tel. (+32) 2-7365354
Fax (+32) 2-7323427
E-mail euteca@ecco-eu.com
Pres. M. Knowles
Sec.-Gen. Dionne Heijnen

EUTECER
European Technical Ceramics Federation
Rue des Colonies 18–24, Bte 17, 1000
  Brussels, Belgium
Tel. (+32) 2-5113012
Fax (+32) 2-5115174

E-mail chorus@cerameunie.org
URL www.cerameunie. Net
Pres. J. Huber
Sec.-Gen. Rogier Chorus

EUTO
European Union of Tourist Officers
Union Européenne des Cadres du Tourisme
Europäischer Verband für Tourismusfachleute

22a Eglinton Street, Irvine KA12 8AS,
   United Kingdom
Tel. (+44 1294) 313006
Fax (+44 1294) 313016
E-mail liz.buchanan@tbt.visitscotland.com
URL www.euto.org
Pres. Erik van Dyck
Sec.-Gen. J.T. Owen
Contact Liz Buchanan (Vice-Pres.)

EUTS
European Union of Tapestries and Saddlers
Union Européenne des Tapissiers- Décorateurs et Selliers
Europäische Union der Tapeziere- Dekorateure und Sattler

Gurzelngasse 27, 4500 Solothurn, Switzerland
Tel. (+41) 32-623-86-70
Fax (+41) 32-623-46-09
E-mail info@interieursuisse.ch
URL www.interieursuisse.ch
Pres. U. Kern
Sec.-Gen. P. Platzer

EUVEPRO
European Vegetable Protein Federation
Fédération Européenne des Protéines Végétales
Europäische Vereinigung für Pflanzliches Eiweiss

Avenue de Roodebeek 30, 1030 Brussels,
   Belgium
Tel. (+32) 2-7438730
Fax (+32) 2-7368175
E-mail info@euvepro.be
URL www.euvepro.org
Pres. Yves Goemans
Sec.-Gen. Karolien de Neve

EUWEP
European Union of Wholesale with Eggs, Egg Products, Poultry and Game
Union Européenne du Commerce du Gros des Oeufs, Produits d'Oeufs, Volaille et Gibier
Europäische Union des Grosshandels mit Eiern, Eiprodukten, Geflügel und Wild

89 Charterhouse Street, 2nd floor, London
   EC1M 6HR, United Kingdom
Tel. (+44 20) 7608-3760
Fax (+44 20) 7608-3860
E-mail mwill10198@aol.com
Pres. Kemp
Sec.-Gen. Mark Williams

EVA
European Vending Association

Rue van Eyck 44, 1000 Brussels, Belgium
Tel. (+32) 2-5120075
Fax (+32) 2-5022342
E-mail vending@eva.be
URL www.eva.be
Pres. Augusto Garulli
Contact Catherine Piana (Dir-Gen.)

EVCA
European Private Equity & Venture Capital Association
Association Européenne des Investissements en Capital à Risque
Europäischer Venture Capital Verband

Minervastraat 4, Zaventem, 1930 Brussels,
   Belgium
Tel. (+32) 2-7150020
Fax (+32) 2-7250704
E-mail evca@evca.com
URL www.evca.com
Pres. Herman Daems
Sec.-Gen. Javier Echarri
Contact Martine Steenhouwer (Admn. Dir)

EVL
European Federation of Illuminated Signs
Fédération Européenne de la Publicité Lumineuse
Europäischer Verband der Lichtwerbung

5 Orton Enterprise Centre, Bakewell Road,
   Orton Southgate, Peterborough PE2 6XU,
   United Kingdom

Tel. (+44 1733) 230033
Fax (+44 1733) 230993
E-mail evl-signs@btconnect.com
URL www.evl-signs.com
Pres. Nicholas M J Pearce
Contact Peter W Tipton (Sec.)

EWA

European Water Association

Theodor-Heuss-Allee 17, 53773 Hennef,
    Germany
Tel. (+49 22) 42872189
Fax (+49 22) 42872135
E-mail EWA@dwa.de
URL www.ewaonline.de
Pres. Haakon Thaulow
Sec.-Gen. Dr Sigurd Van Riesen
Contact Kirsten Overmann (Tech. Asst)

EWA

European Welding Association

**Association Européenne des Fabricants de
    Matériel de Soudage**

**Europäischer Verband der Hersteller von
    Schweisselektrodenapparaten**

Westminster Tower, 3 Albert Embankment,
    London SE1 7SL, United Kingdom
Tel. (+44 20) 7793-3038
Fax (+44 20) 7793-3003
E-mail awillman@beama.org.uk
Pres. Mann
Sec.-Gen. Andrew Willman

EWEA

European Wind Energy Association

Rue du Trône 26, 1000 Brussels, Belgium
Tel. (+32) 2-5461940
Fax (+32) 2-5461944
E-mail ewea@ewea.org
URL www.ewea.org
Pres. Prof. Arthouros Zervos
Contact Corin Maillais (Chief Exec.)

EWPA

European Whey Products Association

**Association Européenne des Produits de
    Lactosérum**

Europäischer Whey-Produkte-Verband

Rue Montoyer 14, 1000 Brussels, Belgium
Tel. (+32) 2-5495040
Fax (+32) 2-5495049

E-mail ewpa@euromilk.org
URL ewpa.euromilk.org
Sec.-Gen. Dr Joop Kleibeuker

EWPM

**European Wood Preservative
    Manufacturers Group**

1 Gleneigles House, Vernon Gate, Derby
    DE1 1UP, United Kingdom
Tel. (+44 1332) 225104
Fax (+44 1332) 225101
E-mail info@bwpda.co.uk
URL www.bwpda.co.uk
Pres. Dr Finn Imsgard
Contact Dr Chris Coggins (Dir)

EWRIS

**European Federation of Wire Rope
    industries**

**Fédération Européenne des Industries de
    Câbles d'Acier**

**Europäische Informationsdienststelle für
    Drahtseil**

47 Rue de Monceau, 75008 Paris, France
Tel. (+33) 1-53-75-10-04
Fax (+33) 1-53-75-10-02
E-mail ewris@ewris.com
URL www.ewris.com
Pres. M.Steve Rutherford
Sec.-Gen. Dr Anne Jourdain
Contact Bernard Laupretre (Vice-Pres.)

FACE

**Federation of Associations for Hunting and
    Conservation of the EU**

**Fédération des Associations de Chasse et
    Conservation de la Faune Sauvage de
    l'UE**

Rue F. Pelletier 82, 1030 Brussels, Belgium
Tel. (+32) 2-7326900
Fax (+32) 2-7327072
E-mail info@face-europe.org
URL www.face-europe.org
Pres. Gilbert de Turckheim
Sec.-Gen. Dr Yves Lecocq
Contact Michel Ebner (Co-ordinator)

FACOGAZ

**Association of European Gas Meter
    Manufacturers**

Allée Broc à l'Aye 14, 1400 Nivelles, Belgium

Tel. (+32) 6-7214602
Fax (+32) 6-7443251
E-mail jsenave@skynet.be
Pres. Dr Hubert Dombrowski
Sec.-Gen. Jacques Senave

FAECF

Federation of European Window and Curtain Wall Manufacturers' Associations
Fédération des Associations Européennes des Constructeurs de Fenêtres et de Façades
Föderation der Europäischen Fenster- und Fassadenhersteller-Verbände
Via Chieti 8, 20154 Milan, Italy
Tel. (+39) 02-3192061
Fax (+39) 02-34537610
E-mail general.secretariat@faecf.org
URL www.faecf.org
Pres. Panos Kallias
Sec.-Gen. Pietro Gimelli
Contact Frank Koos (Tech. Asst)

FAEP

European Federation of Magazine Publishers
Fédération Européenne d'Editeurs de Périodiques
Europäischer Verband der Zeitschriftenverleger
Rue d'Arlon 15, 1050 Brussels, Belgium
Tel. (+32) 2-2868094
Fax (+32) 2-2868095
E-mail david.mahon@faep.org
URL www.faep.or
Pres. Pauli Leimio
Contact David Mahon (Exec. Dir)

FAFPAS

Federation of the Associations of the EU Frozen Food Producers
Fédération des Associations de Fabricants de Produits Alimentaires Surgelés de l'UE
Föderation der Tiefgefriernahrungsmittelhersteller-Verbände der EG
Avenue de Roodebeek 30, 1030 Brussels, Belgium
Tel. (+32) 2-7438730
Fax (+32) 2-7368175

E-mail fafpas@sia-dvi.be
Pres. Michel Coenen

FAREGAZ

Union of European Manufacturers of Gas Pressure Controllers
Union des Fabricants Européens de Régulateurs de Pression de Gaz
Marienburger Str. 15, 50968 Cologne, Germany
Tel. (+49 22) 13764830
Fax (+49 22) 13764861
E-mail info@faregaz.org
URL www.faregaz.org
Pres. Ulmer
Contact Prof. Burger

FBE

Banking Federation of the European Union
Fédération Bancaire de l'Union Européenne
Rue Montoyer 10, 1000 Brussels, Belgium
Tel. (+32) 2-5083711
Fax (+32) 2-5112328
E-mail fbe@fbe.be
URL www.fbe.be
Pres. Sella Maurizio
Sec.-Gen. Nikolaus Bomcke
Contact Hein Blocks (Chair.)

FCC

Federation of Cocoa Commerce Ltd
Federation du Commerce des Cacaos
Cannon Bridge House, London EC4R 3XX, United Kingdom
Tel. (+44 20) 7379-2884
Fax (+44 20) 7379-2389
E-mail fcc@liffe.com
URL www.cocoafederation.com
Pres. Alan B. Cook
Sec.-Gen. Silde Lauand

FEA

European Aerosol Federation
Fédération Européenne des Aérosols
Square Marie-Louise 49, 1000 Brussels, Belgium
Tel. (+32) 2-2389829
Fax (+32) 2-2800929
E-mail info@aerosol.org
URL www.aerosol.org

Pres. K Cool
Sec.-Gen. Alain d'Haese

FEACO

European Federation of Management Consulting Associations

Fédération Européenne des Associations de Conseil en Organisation

Europäische Föderation der Unternehmensberaterverbände

Avenue des Arts 3/4/5, 1210 Brussels, Belgium
Tel. (+32) 2-2500650
Fax (+32) 2-2500651
E-mail feaco@feaco.org
URL www.feaco.org
Sec.-Gen. Bruce Petter
Contact Else Groen (Man.)

FEAD

European Federation of Waste Management and Environmental Services

Fédération Européenne des Activités du Déchet et de l'Environnement

Europäische Föderation der Entsorgungswirtschaft

Avenue des Gaulois 19, 1040 Brussels, Belgium
Tel. (+32) 2-7323213
Fax (+32) 2-7349592
E-mail info@fead.be
URL www.fead.be
Pres. Peter J. Kneissl
Sec.-Gen. Vanya Veras
Contact Nadine de Greef (Deputy Sec.-Gen.)

FEANI

European Federation of National Engineering Associations

Fédération Européenne d'Associations Nationales d'Ingénieurs

Föderation Europäischer Nationaler Ingenieurverbände

Avenue Roger van den Driesche 18, 1150 Brussels, Belgium
Tel. (+32) 2-6390390
Fax (+32) 2-6390399
E-mail secretariat.general@feani.org
URL www.feani.org
Pres. Konstantinos Alexopoulos

Sec.-Gen. Philippe Wauters
Contact Isabelle Vandenberghe (Public Relations Sec.)

FEAP

Federation of European Aquaculture Producers

Fédération Européenne des Producteurs Aquacoles

Rue Nicolas Fossoul 54, 4100 Boncelles, Belgium
Tel. (+32) 4-3382995
Fax (+32) 4-3379846
E-mail secretariat@feap.info
URL www.feap.info
Pres. John Stephanis
Sec.-Gen. Courtney Hough
Contact Paul Birger Torgnes (Vice-Pres.)

FEB

Fellowship of European Broadcasters

The Service Road 23, Potters Bar, Herts. EN6 1QA, United Kingdom
Tel. (+44 17) 0764-9910
Fax (+44 17) 0766-2653
E-mail feb@feb.org
URL www.feb.org
Pres. Harvey Thomas

FEBO

European Timber Trade Association

Avenue des Volontaires 2, 1040 Brussels, Belgium
Tel. (+32) 2-2293260
Fax (+32) 2-2293264
E-mail febo@fnn.be
URL www.febo.org
Pres. Jörg Reimer
Sec.-Gen. Pierre Steenberghen
Contact Sabine Heyman (Deputy Sec.-Gen.)

FEC

Federation of the European Cutlery, Flatware, Holloware and Cookware Industries

Fédération de l'Industrie Européenne de la Coutellerie et des Couverts de Table, de l'Orfèvrerie et des Articles Culinaires

Föderation der Europäischen Schneidwaren-, Besteck-, Tafelgeräte-, Küchengeschirr und Haushaltgeräteindustrie

C/o Unitam, 39–41 Rue Louis Blanc, 92400
  Courbevoie, France
Tel. (+33) 1-47-17-64-60
Fax (+33) 1-47-17-64-61
E-mail unitam@mail.finema.com
URL www.fecinfo.org
Pres. Rémi Descosse
Sec.-Gen. Emmanuel Descheemaeker

FECC

**European Association of Chemical
Distributors**
**Fédération Européenne du Commerce
Chimique**
**Europäische Föderation des Chemischen
Handels**

Chaussée de Wavre 1519, 1160 Brussels,
  Belgium
Tel. (+32) 2-6790260
Fax (+32) 2-6727355
E-mail vle@fecc.org
URL www.fecc.org
Pres. Jim Norman
Sec.-Gen. Christopher Gillibrand
Contact Hendrik Abma (Dir-Gen.)

FECC

**European Federation of Managers in the
Construction Industry**
**Fédération Européenne des Cadres de la
Construction**

15 Rue de Londres, 75009 Paris, France
Tel. (+33) 1-55-31-76-76
Fax (+33) 1-55-31-76-33
E-mail contact@cgcbtp.com
Pres. Janert
Sec.-Gen. Martineau

FECIMA

**European Federation of International Trade
in Agricultural Machines and Related
Activities**
**Fédération Européenne du Commerce
International des Machines Agricoles et
Activités Connexes**

Bd de la Woluwe 46, Bte 14, 1200 Brussels,
  Belgium
Tel. (+32) 2-7786200
Fax (+32) 2-7786222
E-mail tom.antonissen@federauto.be
URL www.fecima.org

Pres. Philippe Lagache
Sec.-Gen. Poncelet
Contact T. Antonissen (Deputy Sec.-Gen.)

FECS

**European Association for Chemical and
Molecular Sciences**
**Fédération des Sociétés Chimiques
Européennes**
**Föderation Europäischer Chemiker
Gesellschaften**

Royal Society of Chemistry, Burlington House,
  Piccadilly, London W1J 0BA,
  United Kingdom
Tel. (+44 20) 7440-3303
Fax (+44 20) 7437-8883
E-mail mcewane@rsc.org
URL www.euchems.org
Sec.-Gen. Evelyn McEwan

FECS

**European Federation of Ceramic Sanitary
Ware Manufacturers**
**Fédération Européenne des Fabricants de
Céramiques Sanitaires**
**Europäische Föderation der Sanitär-
Keramik-Hersteller**

3 Rue La Boétie, 75008 Paris, France
Tel. (+33) 1-58-18-30-40
Fax (+33) 1-42-66-09-00
E-mail sanitaire@ceramique.org
URL www.fecs.web.at.it
Pres. Luis Sabanes
Sec.-Gen. François

FEDARENE

**European Federation of Regional Energy
and Environment Agencies**
**Fédération Européenne des Agences
Régionales de l'Energie et de
l'Environnement**
**Europäische Dachorganisation Regionale
Energie- und Umweltbehorden**

Rue du Beau-Site 11, 1000 Brussels, Belgium
Tel. (+32) 2-6468210
Fax (+32) 2-6468975
E-mail fedarene@fedarene.org
URL www.fedarene.org
Pres. Roger Léron
Sec.-Gen. Michael Geissler
Contact Gerhard Dell (Vice-Pres.)

FEDEMAC

European Organisation of National Removals Associations

Schulstrasse 53, 65795 Hattersheim am Main, Germany
Tel. (+49 61) 90989811
Fax (+49 61) 90989820
E-mail fedemac.troska@web.de
URL www.fedemac.com
Pres. Denis Caulfield
Sec.-Gen. Dr Troska
Contact Tony Richman (Liaison Officer)

FEDFA / FEDARENE

Federation of European Deer Farmers Associations

Kuytegemstraat 66/2, 2890 Synt Amands, Belgium
Tel. (+32) 5-2341788
Fax (+32) 5-0500667
E-mail marc.peelman@skynet.be
URL www.fedfa.com
Pres. Johan Trygve Solheym
Sec.-Gen. Marc Peelman

FEDIAF

European Pet Food Industry Federation

Fédération Européenne de l'Industrie des Aliments pour Animaux Familiers

Europaischer Verband der Heimtiernahrungsindustrie

Avenue Louise 89, 1050 Brussels, Belgium
Tel. (+32) 2-5360520
Fax (+32) 2-5378469
E-mail fediaf@fediaf.org
URL www.fediaf.org
Pres. Richard Fisher
Sec.-Gen. Thomas Meyer

FEDIMA

European Federation of the Intermediate Products Industries for the Bakery and Confectionery Trades

Nolet de Brauwerestraat 21A/12, 1800 Vilvoorde, Belgium
Tel. (+32) 2-3067934
Fax (+32) 2-3069418
E-mail fedima.vanhecke@pandora.be
URL www.fedima.org
Pres. John Gillespie

Sec.-Gen. van Hecke
Contact Van Der Klooster (Chair.)

FEDIOL

EC Seed Crushers' and Oil Processors' Federation

Fédération de l'Industrie de l'Huilerie de la CE

Vereinigung der Ölmühlenindustrie der EG

Avenue de Tervueren 168 PO Box 12, 1150 Brussels, Belgium
Tel. (+32) 2-7715330
Fax (+32) 2-7713817
E-mail fediol@fediol.be
URL www.fediol.be
Pres. R. Pont
Contact P. Cogels

FEDMA

Federation of European Direct Marketing

Fédération Européenne du Marketing Direct

Avenue de Tervuren 439, 1150 Brussels, Belgium
Tel. (+32) 2-7794268
Fax (+32) 2-7794269
E-mail info@fedma.org
URL www.fedma.org
Contact Ara Cinar (Chair.)

FEDOLIVE

Federation of the Olive Oil Industry of the EC

Fédération de l'Industrie de l'Huile d'Olive de la CE

Föderation der Olivenölindustrie in der EG

118 Avenue Achille Perreti, 92200 Neuilly-sur-Seine, France
Tel. (+33) 1-46-37-22-06
Fax (+33) 1-46-37-15-60
E-mail huiledolive@fncg.fr
Pres. C. Rousse La Cordère
Sec.-Gen. J. C. Barsacq

FEDSA

Federation of European Direct Selling Associations

Fédération Europeenne des Associations de Vente Directe

Europäische Föderation für Haustürverkauf und Dienstleistung

Avenue de Tervueren 14, 1040 Brussels,
Belgium
Tel. (+32) 2-7361014
Fax (+32) 2-7363497
E-mail fedsa@fedsa.be
URL www.fedsa.be
Pres. Dr H. Adelmann
Contact M. La Croix

FEE

Federation of European Accountants
Fédération des Experts Comptables
Européens
Föderation der Europäischen
Wirtschaftsprüfer

Avenue d'Auderghem, 22–28, 1040 Brussels,
Belgium
Tel. (+32) 2-2854085
Fax (+32) 2-2311112
E-mail secretariat@fee.be
URL www.fee.be
Pres. David Devlin
Sec.-Gen. Henri Olivier

FEEDM

European Federation of Honey Packers and
Distributors
Fédération Européenne des Emballeurs et
Distributeurs de Miel
Europäischer Verband der Honig-Verpacker
und -Händler

Grosse Baeckerstrasse 4, 20095 Hamburg,
Germany
Tel. (+49 40) 37471913
Fax (+49 40) 37471926
E-mail feedm@waren-verein.de
URL www.feedm.com
Pres. Vincent Michaud
Sec.-Gen. Katrin Langner
Contact Hanna Liebig

FEEM

Federation of European Explosives
Manufacturers

Avenue E. van Nieuwenhuyse 4, Bte 1, 1160
Brussels, Belgium
Tel. (+32) 2-6767202
Fax (+32) 2-6767301
E-mail mca@cefic.be
URL www.cefic.org
Contact Mara Caboara

FEFAC

European Feed Manufacturers' Federation
Fédération Européenne des Fabricants
d'Aliments Composés
Europäischer Verband der
Mischfutterindustrie

Rue de la Loi 223, Bte 3, 1040 Brussels,
Belgium
Tel. (+32) 2-2850050
Fax (+32) 2-2305722
E-mail fefac@fefac.org
URL www.fefac.org
Pres. Martin Tielen
Sec.-Gen. Alexander Doring

FEFANA

European Assocation of Feed Additive
Manufacturers – Asbl.
Fédération Européenne des Fabricants
d'Adjuvants pour la Nutrition Animale
Europäischer Verband für Wirkstoffe in der
Tierernährung

FEFANA Asbl, Avenue Louise 120, PO Box
13, 1050 Brussels, Belgium
Tel. (+32) 2-6396660
Fax (+32) 2-6404111
E-mail info@fefana.org
URL www.fefana.org
Pres. Jan Poul ten Hove
Sec.-Gen. Didier Jans

FEFCO

European Federation of Corrugated Board
Manufacturers
Fédération Européenne des Fabricants de
Carton Ondulé
Europäische Föderation der
Wellpappefabrikanten

Avenue Louise 250, 1050 Brussels, Belgium
Tel. (+32) 2-6464070
Fax (+32) 2-6466460
E-mail information@fefco.org
URL www.fefco.org
Pres. Dr Dermot F. Smurfit
Sec.-Gen. Wim Hoebert
Contact Berry Wiersum (Vice-Pres.)

FEFPEB

European Federation of Wooden Pallet and
Packaging Manufacturers

Fédération Européenne des Fabricants de Palettes et Emballages en Bois

Europäischer Verband der Holzpackmittel und Palettenhersteller

PO Box 90154, 5000 LG Tilburg, Netherlands
Tel. (+31 13) 5944802
Fax (+31 13) 5944749
E-mail fefpeb@wispa.nl
URL www.fefpeb.org
Pres. Gil Covey
Sec.-Gen. Fons J.M. Ceelaert
Contact Paulo Verdasca (Vice-Pres.)

FEIBP

European Brushware Federation

Fédération Européenne de l'Industrie de la Brosserie et de la Pinceauterie

Europäische Föderation der Pinsel- und Burstenindustrie

Kaiserswerther Strasse 137, 40474 Düsseldorf, Germany
Tel. (+49 21) 16025343-0
Fax (+49 21) 16025343-15
E-mail info@euro-brush.de
URL www.eurobrush.com
Pres. Olivia Gonzalez
Contact Andrea Acquaderni (Vice-Pres.)

FEIC

European Federation of the Plywood Industry

Fédération Européenne de l'Industrie du Contreplaqué

Europäische Föderation der Sperrholzindustrie

Allée Hof-ter-Vleestdreef 5/4, 1070 Brussels, Belgium
Tel. (+32) 2-5562584
Fax (+32) 2- 5562595
E-mail info@europlywood.org
URL www.europlywood.org
Pres. U. Bikis
Sec.-Gen. K. Wijenendaele

FEICA

Association of European Adhesives Manufacturers

Fédération Européenne des Industries de Colles et Adhésifs

Verband Europäischer Klebstoffindustrien

Ivo Beucker Strasse 43, 40237 Düsseldorf, Germany
Tel. (+49 21) 167931-30
Fax (+49 21) 167931-88
E-mail jochen.beleke@feica.com
URL www.feica.com
Pres. Lorenzo Busetti
Sec.-Gen. Ansgar van Halteren

FEITIS

European Federation of Audiovisual and Cinema Technical Industries

Fédération Européenne des Industries Techniques de l'Image et du Son

Europäische Föderation der Bild- und Tontechnischen Industrien

11–17 Rue Hamelin, 75783 Paris Cedex 16, France
Tel. (+33) 1-45-05-72-55
Fax (+33) 1-45-05-72-50
E-mail davidcarr@m2tv.com

FELASA

Federation of European Laboratory Animal Science Associations

Fédération des Associations Européennes Scientifiques d'Expérimentation Animale

Föderation der Europäischen Versuchstierkundeverbände

25 Shaftesbury Avenue, London W1D 7EG, United Kingdom
Tel. (+44 20) 7405-0463
Fax (+44 20) 7831-9489
E-mail jguillen@unav.es
URL www.felasa.org
Pres. Ritskes-Hoitinga Merel
Sec.-Gen. Javier Guillen

FEMB

Fédération Européenne du Mobilier de Bureau

Kaiserwerther Strasse 137, 40474 Düsseldorf, Germany
Tel. (+49 21) 16025343-03
Fax (+49 21) 16025343-15
E-mail info@femb.org
URL www.femb.org
Pres. E. Floore
Sec.-Gen. Jeroen de Roos
Contact Michele Perini (Vice-Pres.)

FEMFM

Federation of European Manufacturers of Friction Materials

Fédération Européenne des Fabricants de Matériaux de Friction

Europäischer Verband der Hersteller von Reibmaterialen

79 Jean-Jacques Rousseau, 92158 Suresnes, France

Tel. (+33) 1-46-25-02-30

Fax (+33) 1-46-97-00-80

E-mail vriverbd@netcologne.de

URL www.femfm.com

Sec.-Gen. Günther Vosskotter

FEMGED

European Federation of Middle-Size and Major Retailers

Fédération Européenne des Moyennes et Grandes Entreprises de Distribution

Europäische Vereinigung der Mittel- und Grossunternehmen des Einzelhandels

Avenue des Vaillants 5, Bte 7, 1200 Brussels, Belgium

Tel. (+32) 2-7343289

E-mail femged@pi.be

Pres. R. Pangels

Contact C. Droulans

FEMIB

Federation of the European Building Joinery Associations

Fédération Européenne des Syndicats de Menuiseries Industrielles du Bâtiment

Vereinigung der Europäischen Verbände der Holzindustrie im Baubereich

Walter-Kolb-Strasse 1–7, 60594 Frankfurt am Main, Germany

Tel. (+49 69) 9550540

Fax (+49 69) 95505411

E-mail femib@window.de

URL www.eurowindow.org

Pres. Jaime Ribas

FEMIN

European Federation of Manufacturers and Traders of Cleaning Machines, Material and Accessories

Square Gutenberg 13, 1000 Brussels, Belgium

Tel. (+32) 2-2309869

Fax (+32) 2-2311644

E-mail pcosta@gmx.be

FEP / FEE

Federation of European Publishers

Fédération des Editeurs Européens

Rue Montoyer 31 Bte 8, 1000 Brussels, Belgium

Tel. (+32) 2-7701110

Fax (+32) 2-7712071

E-mail malemann@fep-fee.be

URL www.fep-fee.be

Pres. Dr Arne Bach

Contact Mechthild von Alemann (Consultant)

FEPA

Federation of European Producers of Abrasive

Fédération Européenne des Fabricants de Produits Abrasifs

Vereinigung der Europäische Schleifmittel-Hersteller

20 Avenue Reille, 75014 Paris, France

Tel. (+33) 1-45-81-25-90

Fax (+33) 1-45-81-62-94

E-mail fepa@fepa-abrasives.org

URL www.fepa-abrasives.org

Pres. Gianni Scott

Contact F. Verguet

FEPD

European Federation of Perfume Retailers

Fédération Européenne des Parfumeurs Détaillants

Europäischer Parfümerie-Verband

An der Engelsburg 1, 45657 Recklinghausen, Germany

Tel. (+49 23) 619248-0

Fax (+49 23) 619248-88

E-mail info@ParfuemerieVerband.de

URL www.parfuemerieverband.de

Pres. Reinhard Dieter Wolf

Contact W. Hariegel

FEPE

European Envelope Manufacturers' Association

Fédération Européenne des Producteurs d'Enveloppes

Europäische Vereinigung der Briefumschlagfabrikanten

Bergstrasse 110 Postfach, 8032 Zurich,
  Switzerland
Tel. (+41 1) 266-99-22
Fax (+41 1) 266-99-49
E-mail info@fepe.org
URL www.fepe.org
Pres. J. Madsen-Mygdal
Sec.-Gen. M. Haberli
Contact Niklaus Freuler (Man. Dir)

FEPEDICA

**Fédération Européenne du Personnel
d'Encadrement des Productions, des
Industries, des Commerces et des
Organismes Agroalimentaires**
59–63 Rue du Rocher, 75008 Paris, France
Tel. (+33) 1-55-30-13-30
Fax (+33) 1-55-30-13-31
E-mail agro@cfecgc.fr
Pres. Broquet
Sec.-Gen. Weber

FEPF

European Ceramics Industries
**Fédération Européenne des Industries de
Porcelaine et de Faïence de Table et
d'Ornementation**
Rue des Colonies 18–24, Bte 17, 1000
  Brussels, Belgium
Tel. (+32) 2-5113012
Fax (+32) 2-5115174
E-mail sec@cerameunie.org
URL www.cerameunie.net
Pres. Von Boch
Sec.-Gen. Rogier Chorus

FEPORT

**Federation of European Private Port
Operators**
**Fédération Européenne des Opérateurs
Portuaires Privés**
**Vereinigung Europäischer Privater
Hafenumschlag Betriebe**
Treurenberg 6, 1000 Brussels, Belgium
Tel. (+32) 2-7367552
Fax (+32) 2-7323149
E-mail info@feport.be
URL www.feport.be
Pres. Cecilia Battistello

Sec.-Gen. Diego Teurelincx
Contact Milenka Backes (Asst)

FEPPD

**International and European Federation of
European Dental Laboratory Owners**
**Fédération Européenne des Patrons
Prothésistes Dentaires**
Rue Jacques de Lalaing 4, 1040 Brussels,
  Belgium
Tel. (+32) 2-2310573
Fax (+32) 2-2305027
E-mail feppd@kmonet.org
URL www.feppd.org
Pres. David Smith
Sec.-Gen. Michel Rey
Contact Nancy Paulussen (Admin. Sec.)

FERCO

**European Federation of Contract Catering
Organisations**
**Fédération Européenne de la Restauration
Collective**
Bastion Tower, Place du Champ de Mars 5,
  Boîte 14, 1050 Brussels, Belgium
Tel. (+32) 2-5503676
Fax (+32) 2-2301737
E-mail info@ferco-catering.org
URL www.ferco-catering.org
Pres. Hans Rijnierse
Sec.-Gen. Marie-Christine Lefebvre
Contact Damien Verdier (Vice-Pres.)

FEROPA

**European Federation of Fibre-Board
Manufacturers**
**Fédération Européenne des Fabricants de
Panneaux de Fibres**
**Europäische Föderation der
Holzfaserplatten-Fabrikanten**
724 Traverse des Rougons, 83510 Lorgues,
  France
Tel. (+33) 4-94-73-75-99
Fax (+33) 4-94-67-67-07
E-mail feropa@feropa.org
URL www.feropa.org
Pres. Saikovski

FESE
Federation of European Securities Exchanges

Rue du Lombard 41, 1000 Brussels, Belgium
Tel. (+32) 2-5510180
Fax (+32) 2-5124905
E-mail info@fese.org
URL www.fese.org
Pres. George Möller
Sec.-Gen. Paul Arlman
Contact Cathy Detry (Exec. Asst)

FESI
European Federation of Associations of Insulation Contractors

Fédération Européenne des Syndicats d'Entreprises d'Isolation

Europäische Vereinigung der Verbände der Isolierunternehmen

C/o Hauptverband der Deutschen Bauindustrie e.V., BFA Wärme-, Kälte-, Schall- und Brandschutz, Kurfurstenstrasse 129, 10785 Berlin, Germany
Tel. (+49 30) 21286163
Fax (+49 30) 21286160
E-mail bfa.wksb@bauindustrie.de
Pres. Versteegh
Sec.-Gen. Jurgen Schmoldt

FESI
Federation of the European Sporting Goods Industry

Avenue de Janvier 3, 1200 Brussels, Belgium
Tel. (+32) 2-7628648
Fax (+32) 2-7718746
E-mail info@fesi-sport.org
URL www.fesi-sport.org
Pres. Horst Widmann
Sec.-Gen. Alberto Bichi
Contact Joëlle Derulle (Administration Man.)

FETRATAB
European Federation of Tobacco Transformers

Fédération Européenne des Transformateurs de Tabac

23 rue de Frémicourt, 75015 Paris, France
Tel. (+33) 1-45-66-86-43
Fax (+33) 1-45-66-00-06
E-mail MaisonTabac.TobaccoHouse@ Hebel.net

Pres. Chidichimo
Sec.-Gen. Ferat

FETSA
Federation of European Tank Storage Associations

Chaussée de Wavre 1519, 1160 Brussels, Belgium
Tel. (+32) 2-6790264
Fax (+32) 2-6727355
E-mail info@fetsa.org
URL www.fetsa.com
Pres. W. Dornhof
Sec.-Gen. H. J. P. Standaar
Contact R. Kellaway

FEUGRES
European Federation for the Vitrified Clay Pipe Industry

Fédération Européenne des Fabricants de Tuyaux en Grès

Europäische Vereinigung der Steinzeugröhrenindustrie

Rue des Colonies 18–24 Bte 17, 1000 Brussels, Belgium
Tel. (+32) 2-5113012
Fax (+32) 2-5115174
E-mail cec@cerameunie.org
Pres. Rodolfo Spotti
Sec.-Gen. Rogier Chorus

FEUPF
European Federation of Professional Florists' Associations

Fédération Européenne des Unions Professionnelles de Fleuristes

Föderation der Europäischen Fachverbände der Floristen

Zandlaan 18, 6717 LP Ede, Netherlands
Tel. (+31 318) 527568
Fax (+31 318) 542266
E-mail info@vbw-groenplein.nl
Pres. Robert Shteinman
Sec.-Gen. A. Zwitserlood
Contact Friderman Haug (Vice-Pres.)

FEVE
European Container Glass Federation

Fédération Européenne du Verre d'Emballage

**Europäischer Behälterglasindustrie-
Verband**

Avenue Louise 89, Bte 4, 1050 Brussels,
Belgium
Tel. (+32) 2-5393434
Fax (+32) 2-5393752
E-mail info@feve.org
URL www.feve.org
Pres. C. Perales
Sec.-Gen. Andrew Somogyi
Contact G. Robyns (Asst Sec.-Gen.)

FFI

Freight Forward International

Avenue Marcel Thiry 204, 1200 Brussels,
Belgium
Tel. (+32) 2-7749639
Fax (+32) 2-7749690
E-mail ffi@eyam.be
URL www.freightforwardinternational.org
Pres. Klaus Herms
Contact Maria Teresa Scardigli (Exec. Dir)

FIC EUROPE

**Federation of the Condiment Sauce
Industries, Mustard and Fruit and
Vegetables prepared in Oil and Vinegar of
the European Union**

**Fédération des Industries des Sauces
Condimentaires, de la Moutarde et des
Fruits et Légumes préparés à l'Huile et au
Vinaigre de l'Union Européenne**

Avenue de Roodebeek 30, 1030 Brussels,
Belgium
Tel. (+32) 2-7438730
Fax (+32) 2-7368175
E-mail fic.europe@sia-dvi.be
Sec.-Gen. Michel Coenen

FIDE

Federation of the European Dental Industry

**Fédération de l'Industrie Dentaire en
Europe**

**Vereinigung der Europäischen Dental-
Industrie**

Kirchweg 2, 50858 Cologne, Germany
Tel. (+49 221) 50068712
Fax (+49 221) 500687212
E-mail info@fide-online.org
URL www.fide-online.org
Pres. Dr Jürgen Eberlein

Sec.-Gen. Harald Russegger
Contact Dr Alessandro Gamberini (Vice-Pres.)

FIDE

International Federation for European Law

**Fédération Internationale pour le Droit
Européen**

Internationale Föderation für Europarecht

C/o British Institute of International and
Comparative Law, Charles Clore House, 17
Russell Square, London WC1B 5JP,
United Kingdom
Tel. (+44 20) 7862-5151
Fax (+44 20) 7862-5152
E-mail info@biicl.org
URL www.biicl.org
Sec.-Gen. M. Andenas
Contact Stephen Walzer (Dir)

FIEC

European Construction Industry Federation

**Fédération de l'Industrie Européenne de la
Construction**

Verband der Europäischen Bauwirtschaft

Avenue Louise 66, 1050 Brussels, Belgium
Tel. (+32) 2-5145535
Fax (+32) 2-5110276
E-mail info@fiec.org
URL www.fiec.org
Pres. Wilhelm Küchler
Contact Ulrich Paetzold (Dir-Gen.)

FITCE

**Federation of the Telecommunications
Engineers of the European Community**

**Fédération des Ingénieurs des
Télécommunications de la Communauté
Européenne**

Boulevard Reyers 80, 1030 Brussels, Belgium
Tel. (+32) 2-7067805
Fax (+32) 2-7068009
E-mail filip.geerts@agoria.be
URL www.fitce.org
Pres. Carlos González Mateos
Sec.-Gen. Filip Geerts

FORATOM

European Atomic Forum

Forum Atomique Europeen

Europaisches Atomforum

Rue de la loi 57, 1040 Brussels, Belgium
Tel. (+32) 2-5024595
Fax (+32) 2-5023902
E-mail foratom@foratom.org
URL www.foratom.org
Pres. Eduardo González
Sec.-Gen. Dr Peter Haug

FRESHFEL

Freshfel Europe

Avenue de Boqueville 272, Bte 4, 1200
  Brussels, Belgium
Tel. (+32) 2-7771580
Fax (+32) 2-7771581
E-mail info@freshfel.org
URL www.freshfel.org
Pres. Kai Krasemann
Contact Philippe Binard

FRUCOM

**European Federation of the Trade in Dried
Fruit, Edible Nuts, Preserved Foods,
Spices, Honey and Similar Foodstuffs**

**Fédération Européenne du Commerce en
Fruits Secs, Conserves, Epices et Miel**

**Europäische Vereinigung des Handels mit
Trockenfrüchten, Konserven, Gewürzen
und Honig und verwandten Waren**

Große Bäckerstr 4, 20095 Hamburg, Germany
Tel. (+49 30) 3747190
Fax (+49 40) 37471919
E-mail info@frucom.org
URL www.frucom.org
Pres. Rome Martin
Sec.-Gen. Rouhier Pascale
Contact Mamias Sylvie (Senior Adviser)

FTA

Foreign Trade Association
Association de Commerce Extérieur

Avenue de Cortenbergh 168, 1000 Brussels,
  Belgium
Tel. (+32) 2-7620551
Fax (+32) 2-7627506
E-mail info@fta-eu.org
URL www.fta-eu.org
Pres. Ferry den Hoed
Sec.-Gen. Jan Eggert
Contact Dominique Barea (Project Asst)

FVE

Federation of Veterinarians of Europe
Fédération Vétérinaire Européenne
Europäische Föderation der Tierärtze

Rue Defacqz 1, 1000 Brussels, Belgium
Tel. (+32) 2-5337020
Fax (+32) 2-5372828
E-mail info@fve.org
URL www.fve.org
Pres. Tjeerd Jorna
Contact John Williams (Vice-Pres.)

GAFTA

Grain and Feed Trade Association

Gafta House, 6 Chapel Place, Rivington Street,
  London EC2A 3SH, United Kingdom
Tel. (+44 20) 7814-9666
Fax (+44 20) 7814-8383
E-mail post@gafta.com
URL www.gafta.com
Pres. B. Vallius
Contact Pamela Kirby Johnson (Dir-Gen.)

GAM

European Flour Milling Association

**Groupement des Associations Meunières des
Pays de l'UE**

**Arbeitsgemeinschaft der
Handelsmühlenverbände in den EG-
Ländern**

C/o ECCO, Avenue des Gaulois 9, 1040
  Brussels, Belgium
Tel. (+32) 2-7365354
Fax (+32) 2-7323427
E-mail info@ecco-eu.com
URL www.ecco.be
Pres. H. François
Sec.-Gen. Laurent Reverdy

GEPVP

**European Association of Flat Glass
Manufacturers**

**Groupement Européen des Producteurs de
Verre Plat**

**Europäische Vereinigung von
Flachglashersteller**

Avenue Louise 89, 1050 Brussels, Belgium
Tel. (+32) 2-5384377
Fax (+32) 2-5378469
E-mail info@gepvp.org

URL www.gepvp.org
Pres. Stuart Chambers
Sec.-Gen. Edwina Bullen

GERA-Europe

Global Entertainment Retail Association –
Europe

Chaussee de Wavre 214d, 1050 Brussels,
  Belgium
Tel. (+32) 2-6261991
Fax (+32) 2-6269501
E-mail info@gera-europe.org
URL www.gera-europe.org
Pres. Njara Zafimehy
Sec.-Gen. Elodie Mohen

GERG

European Gas Research Group
Groupe Européen de Recherches Gazières

Avenue Palmerston 4, 1000 Brussels, Belgium
Tel. (+32) 2-2308017
Fax (+32) 2-2306788
E-mail davepinchbeck@gerg.info
URL www.gerg.info
Pres. E. van Ingelghem
Sec.-Gen. Dave Pinchbeck
Contact M. Florette (Vice-Pres.)

GIRP

European Association of Pharmaceutical
Full-Line Wholesalers

Groupement International de la Répartition
Pharmaceutique

Internationaler Verband der Europäischen
Pharmazeutischen Grosshandelsverbände

Avenue de Tervuren 13 b, 1040 Brussels,
  Belgium
Tel. (+32) 2-7779977
Fax (+32) 2-7703601
E-mail girp@girp.org
URL www.girp.org
Pres. Jeffrey Harris
Sec.-Gen. Monika Derecque-Pois
Contact Lisa McGowan (Communication
  Man.)

GISEMES – UNESEM

Groupement International et Union
Européenne des Sources d'Eaux
Minérales Naturelles

10 Rue de la Trémoille, 75008 Paris, France

Tel. (+33) 1-47-20-31-10
Fax (+33) 1-47-20-27-62
E-mail csem@wanadoo.fr
Pres. Torben Friis
Sec.-Gen. Françoise de Buttet

HOPE

Standing Committee of the Hospitals of the
European Union

Comité Permanent des Hôpitaux de l'Union
Européenne

Ständiger Ausschuss der Krankenhäuser der
Europäischen Union

Blvd Auguste Reyers 207–209 b7, 1030
  Brussels, Belgium
Tel. (+32) 2-7421320
Fax (+32) 2-7421325
E-mail sg@hope.be
URL www.hope.be
Pres. Gérard Vincent
Sec.-Gen. Pascal Garel
Contact Brian Edwards (Vice-Pres.)

HOTREC

Hotels, Restaurants and Cafés in Europe

Blvd Anspach 111, PO Box 4, 1000 Brussels,
  Belgium
Tel. (+32) 2-5136323
Fax (+32) 2-5024173
E-mail main@hotrec.org
URL www.hotrec.org
Pres. Bernd Geyer
Sec.-Gen. Michel de Blust
Contact Marguerite Sequaris (Chief Exec.)

IATM

International Association of Tour Managers
Ltd

397 Walworth Road, London SE17 2AW,
  United Kingdom
Tel. (+44 20) 7703-9154
Fax (+44 20) 7703-0358
E-mail iatm@iatm.co.uk
URL www.iatm.co.uk
Pres. Pauline Grey
Contact Ron Julian (Gen. Man.)

IBC / CIBC / IMV

International Butchers' Confederation

Confédération Internationale de la
Boucherie et de la Charcuterie

Internationaler Metzgermeister Verband
Rue Jacques de Lalaing 4, PO Box 10, 1040
    Brussels, Belgium
Tel. (+32) 2-2303876
Fax (+32) 2-2303451
E-mail info@cibc.be
Pres. Eugen Nagel
Sec.-Gen. Ingolf Jakobi
Contact Kirsten Diessner (Dir)

IBFI
**International Business Forms Industries –
    European Operations**
**Industrie Internationale des Formulaires –
    Secrétariat Européen**
Mosstrasse 2, 3073 Gumligen-Berne,
    Switzerland
Tel. (+41) 31-952-61-12
Fax (+41) 31-952-76-83
E-mail uwannet@swissonline.ch
Sec.-Gen. Dr U. Wanner

IDACE
**Association of the Food Industries for
    Particular Nutritional Uses of the
    European Union**
**Association des Industries des Aliments
    Diététiques de l'UE**
**Verband der Diätetischen
    Lebensmittelindustrie der EG**
194 Rue de Rivoli, 75001 Paris, France
Tel. (+33) 1-53-45-87-87
Fax (+33) 1-53-45-87-80
E-mail info@idaco.org
URL www.idaco.org
Sec.-Gen. Andrée Bronner

IDF / FIL
International Dairy Federation
Fédération Internationale de Laiterie
Diamant Building, Blvd Auguste Reyers 80,
    1030 Brussels, Belgium
Tel. (+32) 2-7339888
Fax (+32) 2-7330413
E-mail info@fil-idf.org
URL www.fil-idf.org
Pres. Jim Begg
Contact Christian Robert (Dir-Gen.)

IFAP / FIPA
**International Federation of Agricultural
    Producers**
**Fédération Internationale des Producteurs
    Agricoles**
60 Rue Saint-Lazare, 75009 Paris, France
Tel. (+33) 1-45-26-05-53
Fax (+33) 1-48-74-72-12
E-mail ifap@ifap.org
URL www.ifap.org
Pres. Jack Wilkinson
Sec.-Gen. David King
Contact Dr Vallat (Dir-Gen.)

IFEAT
**International Federation of Essential Oils
    and Aroma Trades**
**Fédération Internationale des Huiles
    Essentielles et du Commerce des Arômes**
**Internationale Föderation der Ätherischen
    Öle und des Aromahandels**
Gafta House, 6 Chapel Place, Rivington Street,
    London EC2A 3SH, United Kingdom
Tel. (+44 20) 7729-5904
Fax (+44 20) 7814-8383
E-mail secretariat@ifeat.org
URL www.ifeat.org
Pres. Richard Pisano
Contact Katrina Neale (Chair.)

IFSW
**International Federation of Social Workers –
    European Region/EU Committee**
**Fédération Internationale des Assistants
    Sociaux-Réseau Européen**
PERSONAL, C/o Local Transport Group,
    Department for Education and Skills, Area
    2Q, Sanctuary Buildings, Great Smith Street,
    Westminster, London SW1P 3BT,
    United Kingdom
Tel. (+44 16) 0441-4345
Fax (+44 20) 7925-5086
E-mail vpeur@ifsw.org
URL www.ifsw.org
Pres. D. N. Jones
Contact Ana Radulescu

IMACE
**International Margarine Association of the
    Countries of Europe**

Association des Industries Margarinieres de la CE

Vereinigung der Margarine-Industrie der EG-Lander

Avenue de Tervuren 168, Bte 12, 1150 Brussels, Belgium
Tel. (+32) 2-7723353
Fax (+32) 2-7714753
E-mail imace.ifma@imace.org
URL www.imace.org
Pres. Didier Dallemagne
Sec.-Gen. Inneke Herreman

IMA-EUROPE

Industrial Minerals Association – Europe

Bd S. Dupuis 233, PO Box 124, 1070 Brussels, Belgium
Tel. (+32) 2-5245500
Fax (+32) 2-5244575
E-mail secretariat@ima-eu.org
URL www.ima-eu.org
Pres. Claude Stenneler
Sec.-Gen. Michelle Wyart-Remy

INEC

European Institute of the Carob Gum Industries

Institut Européen des Industries de la Gomme de Caroube

Europaische Vereinigung der Johannisbrotkrenmehl-Hersteller

Swiss Federal Inst. of Technology, ETH-Zentrum LFO F18, Schmelzbergstrasse, 8092 Zurich, Switzerland
Tel. (+41 1) 632-53-68
Fax (+41 1) 632-11-56
E-mail zdenko.puhan@ilw.argl.ethz.ch
Sec.-Gen. Puhan

INTERGRAF

International Confederation for Printing and Allied Industries a.i.s.b.l.

Place E. Flagey 7, bte 8, 1050 Brussels, Belgium
Tel. (+32) 2-2308646
Fax (+32) 2-2311464
E-mail intergraf@intergraf.org
URL www.intergraf.org
Pres. Lars Fredrikson
Sec.-Gen. Beatrice Klose

Contact Suzanne Verhoeven (Office Administration)

IPPA

International Pectin Producers Association

PO Box 151, Hereford HR4 8YZ, United Kingdom
Tel. (+44 1432) 830529
Fax (+44 1432) 830716
E-mail executive-secretary@ippa.info
URL www.ippa.info
Pres. Hans Hjorth
Sec.-Gen. Dr Hans-Ulrich Endress
Contact Dr Colin May (Exec.Sec.)

IPTIC / CICILS

International Pulse Trade and Industry Confederation

Comité Permanent CEE de la Confédération Internationale du Commerce et des Industries des Légumes Secs

Ständiger EG Ausschuss der Internationalen Könferation des Handels und der Trockengemüseindustrien

Bureau 273, Bourse de Commerce, 2 Rue de Viarmes, 75040 Paris Cedex 01, France
Tel. (+33) 1-42-36-84-35
Fax (+33) 1-42-36-44-93
E-mail guy.coudert@cicilsiptic.org
URL www.cicilsiptic.org
Contact Coudert

IRU

International Road Transport Union

Avenue de Tervuren 32–34, Boite 37, 4th floor, 1040 Brussels, Belgium
Tel. (+32) 2-7432580
Fax (+32) 2-7432599
E-mail brussels@iru.org
URL www.iru.org
Pres. Paul Laeremans
Sec.-Gen. Martin Marmy
Contact Janusz Lacny (Vice-Pres.)

ISA / AIE / ISV

International Sweeteners Association

Association Internationale pour les Edulcorants

Internationaler Süssstoff Verband

Avenue des Gaulois 9, 1040 Brussels, Belgium
Tel. (+32) 2-7365354

Fax (+32) 2-7323427
E-mail isa@ecc-eu.com
URL www.sweeteners.org
Pres. Dr Chris Groeneveld
Sec.-Gen. Margrethe Saxegaard

ISOPA

European Diisocyanates and Polyol Producers Association
Avenue E. van Nieuwenhuyse 4, Box 9, 1160 Brussels, Belgium
Tel. (+32) 2-6767475
Fax (+32) 2-6767479
E-mail main@isopa.org
URL www.isopa.org
Pres. Dr Reinhard Leppkes
Sec.-Gen. Dr Mike Jeffs
Contact Kristine Dewaele (Office Man.)

IUCAB

International Union of Commercial Agents and Brokers
Union Internationale des Agents Commerciaux et des Courtiers
De Lairessestraat 131–135, 1075 HJ Amsterdam, Netherlands
Tel. (+31 20) 4700177
Fax (+31 20) 6710974
E-mail info@iucab.nl
URL www.iucab.nl
Pres. Wolfgang Hinderer
Sec.-Gen. J.W.B. Baron van Till
Contact W. Krammer (Vice-Pres.)

IVTIP

In Vitro Testing Industrial Platform
POB 9143, 3007 AC Rotterdam, Netherlands
Tel. (+31 10) 4828306
Fax (+31 10) 4827750
E-mail ivtip@ivtip.org
URL www.ivtip.org
Pres. Dr D. Eigler
Contact Joan-Albert Vericat (Chair.)

IWTO

International Wool Textile Organisation
Rue de l'Industrie 4, 1000 Brussels, Belgium
Tel. (+32) 2-5054010
Fax (+32) 2-5034785
E-mail info@iwto.org
URL www.iwto.org

Pres. Michael Lempriere
Contact Henrik Kuffner (Dir-Gen.)

IZA

International Zinc Association
Avenue de Tervueren 168, PO Box 4, 1150 Brussels, Belgium
Tel. (+32) 2-7760070
Fax (+32) 2-7760089
E-mail info@iza.com
URL www.zincworld.org
Pres. Wilkinson
Contact Berit Wirths (Project Leader Communications)

LANDOWNERS / PROPRIETE RURALE

European Landowners' Organisation
Organisation Européeene de la Propriété Rurale
Europäische Grundbesitzerorganisation
Rue de Treves 67, 1040 Brussels, Belgium
Tel. (+32) 2-2343000
Fax (+32) 2-2343009
E-mail elo@elo.org
URL www.elo.org
Pres. Mark Thomasin-Foster
Sec.-Gen. Thierry de l'Escaille
Contact Dominique Collinet (Vice-Pres.)

LEASEUROPE

European Federation of Leasing Company Associations
Fédération Européenne des Associations des Etablissements de Crédit-Bail
Europäische Vereinigung der Verbände von Leasing-Gesellschaften
Avenue de Tervuren 267, 1150 Brussels, Belgium
Tel. (+32) 2-7780560
Fax (+32) 2-7780579
E-mail leaseurope@leaseurope.org
URL www.leaseurope.org
Pres. Vervaet
Sec.-Gen. Marc Baert
Contact Alain Vervaet (Chair.)

MAILLEUROP

Committee for the Knitting Industries in the EEC
Comité des Industries de la Maille de la CEE

Rue Montoyer 24, Bte 12, 1000 Brussels,
Belgium
Tel. (+32) 2-2854892
Fax (+32) 2-2306054
E-mail francesco.marchi@euratex.org
Sec.-Gen. Francesco Marchi
Contact V. Giulini

MARCOGAZ

**Technical Association of the European
Natural Gas Industry**

Avenue Palmerston 4, 1000 Brussels, Belgium
Tel. (+32) 2-2371111
Fax (+32) 2-2304480
E-mail marcogaz@marcogaz.org
URL www.marcogaz.org
Pres. Klaus Homann
Sec.-Gen. Daniel Hec
Contact Luigi Scopesi (Vice-Pres.)

MARINALG

Marinalg International

Rue Blanche 25, 1060 Brussels, Belgium
Tel. (+32) 2-5383825
Fax (+32) 2-5383826
E-mail marinalg@marinalg.org
URL www.marinalg.org

NATCOL

Natural Food Colours Association

**Association de Colorants Alimentaires
Naturels**

**Natürliche
Nahrungsmittelfarbstoffvereinigung**

PO Box 3255, Boycestown, Carrigaline,
Co. Cork, Ireland
Tel. (+353 21) 4919673
Fax (+353 21) 4919673
E-mail secretariat@natcol.org
URL www.natcol.org
Pres. B. S. Henry
Sec.-Gen. Dr Mary O'Callaghan

OCE

Orthoptistes de la CE

Bierbeekstraat 14, 3001 Heverlee, Belgium
Tel. (+32) 16-239524
Fax (+33) 16-291809
E-mail info@euro-orthoptics.com
URL www.euro-orthoptistes.com

Pres. M. van Lammeren
Contact Marie-Hélène Abadie (Sec. Treasurer)

OEA

**Organisation of European Aluminium
Refiners and Remelters**

Am Bonneshof 5, 40474 Düsseldorf, Germany
Tel. (+49 211) 451-933
Fax (+49 211) 431-009
E-mail office@oea-alurecycling.org
URL www.oea-alurecycling.org
Pres. Jim Morrison
Sec.-Gen. Günter Kirchner

OEB / ESO

**European Organization of Inland Waterway
Transportation**

Organisation Européenne des Bateliers

Europäische Schifferorganisation

Blvd Bischoffsheim 36, 1000 Brussels,
Belgium
Tel. (+32) 2-2172208
Fax (+32) 2-2195486
E-mail eso.oeb@skynet.be
Pres. Johannes Conings

OEICTO

**European Organisation of Tomato
Industries**

**Organisation Européenne des Industries de
la Conserve de Tomates**

**Europäische Organisation der
Tomatenkonservenindustrie**

Avenue de Roodebeek 30, 1030 Brussels,
Belgium
Tel. (+32) 2-7438738
Fax (+32) 2-7368175
E-mail oeit@sia.dvi.be
Pres. D. Nomikos
Sec.-Gen. P. Keppenne

OEITFL

**Organisation of European Industries
Transforming Fruit and Vegetables**

**Organisation Européenne des Industries
Transformatrices de Fruits et Légumes**

**Europäische Organisation der Obst- und
Gemüseverarbeitenden Industrie**

Avenue de Roodebeek 30, 1030 Brussels,
Belgium

Tel. (+32) 2-7438730
Fax (+32) 2-7368175
E-mail oeiftl@sia-dvi.be
URL www.oeitfl.org
Pres. J.L. Heymans
Sec.-Gen. Pascale Keppenne
Contact J. Garcia Gomez (Vice-Pres.)

ORGALIME
Liaison Group of the European Mechanical, Electrical, Electronic and Metalworking Industries
Organisme de Liaison des Industries Métalliques Européennes
Verbindungsstelle der Europäischen Maschinenbau-, Metall Verarbeitenden und Elektroindustrie

Diamant Building, Blvd Auguste Reyers 80, 1030 Brussels, Belgium
Tel. (+32) 2-7068235
Fax (+32) 2-7068250
E-mail secretariat@orgalime.org
URL www.orgalime.org
Pres. Martine Clement
Sec.-Gen. Adrian Harris
Contact Beatrice Schwering (Personal Asst)

PGEU / GPUE
Pharmaceutical Group of the European Union
Groupement Pharmaceutique de l'Union Européenne

Rue du Luxembourg 19–21, 1000 Brussels, Belgium
Tel. (+32) 2-2380818
Fax (+32) 2-2380819
E-mail pharmacy@pgeu.org
URL www.pgeu.org
Pres. Pedro Capilla
Sec.-Gen. Flora Giorgio-Gerlach

PLASTEUROPAC
European Association of Plastics Packing Manufacturers
Association Européenne des Fabricants d'Emballages Plastiques
Europäische Vereinigung der Plastik Verpackungshersteller

5 Rue de Chazelles, 75017 Paris, France
Tel. (+33) 1-46-22-33-66
Fax (+33) 1-46-22-02-35

URL www.packplast.org
Contact Françoise Gerardi (Gen. Man.)

PNEUROP
European Committee of Manufacturers of Compressors, Vacuum Pumps and Pneumatic Tools
Comité Européen des Constructeurs de Compresseurs, Pompes à Vide et Outils à Air Comprimé
Europäisches Komitee der Hersteller von Kompressoren, Vakuumpumpen und Druckluftwerkzeugen

Diamant Building, Blvd Reyers 80, 1030 Brussels, Belgium
Tel. (+32) 2-7068237
Fax (+32) 2-7068253
E-mail secretariat@pneurop.org
URL www.pneurop.org
Pres. Henri Ysewijn
Sec.-Gen. Guy van Doorslaer
Contact R.D. Wall (Dir)

POSTEUROP
Association of European Public Postal Operators
Association des Opérateurs Postaux Publics Européens
Vereinigung der Öffentlichen Europäischen Postdienstbetreiber

Avenue du Bourget 44, 1130 Brussels, Belgium
Tel. (+32) 2-7247280
Fax (+32) 2-7263008
E-mail posteurop@posteurop.org
URL www.posteurop.org
Pres. Paul-Bernard Damiens
Sec.-Gen. Marc Pouw
Contact Murray Buchanan (Vice-Chair.)

POULTRY AND GAME / VOLAILLE ET GIBIER
Confederation of Retail Trade for Poultry and Game in the EU
Confédération des Détaillants en Volaille et Gibier des Pays de la CE

Rue Melsens 28, 1000 Brussels, Belgium
Tel. (+32) 2-5120947
Fax (+32) 2-5120374
Pres. P. van Gaever
Sec.-Gen. Van Der Crone

PPTA

Plasma Protein Therapeutics Association Europe

Blvd Brand Whitlock 114/5, 1200 Brussels, Belgium
Tel. (+32) 2-7055811
Fax (+32) 2-7055820
E-mail pptaeu@pptaglobal.org
URL www.plasmatherapeutics.org
Pres. Nachruf von Jan M. Bult
Contact Rainer Pabst (Chair.)

PRE

European Refractories Producers' Federation

Fédération Européenne des Fabricants de Produits Réfractaires

Europäische Industrieverband der Feuerfestkeramik

Cerame-Unie, Rue des Colonies 18–24, Bte 17, 1000 Brussels, Belgium
Tel. (+32) 2-5113012
Fax (+32) 2-5115174
E-mail sec@cerameunie.net
Sec.-Gen. Rogier Chorus

REHVA

Federation of European Heating and Airconditioning Associations

Fédération des Associations Européennes de Chauffage et Conditionnement d'Air

PO Box 82, 1200 Brussels, Belgium
Tel. (+32) 2-5141171
Fax (+32) 2-5129062
E-mail info@rehva.com
URL www.rehva.com
Pres. Prof. Dušan Petráš
Sec.-Gen. Lara Egli
Contact P. Novak (Vice-Pres.)

RIAE

Recording Media Industry Association of Europe

Rue Notre Dame 42, 2951 Luxembourg, Belgium
Tel. (+32) 2-2854616
Fax (+32) 2-2803936
E-mail info@riae.org
URL www.riae.org
Pres. Dr J. Eicher
Sec.-Gen. I. Tondeur

RICS EUROPE / ESCS

European Society of Chartered Surveyors

Avenue de Cortenbergh 52, 1000 Brussels, Belgium
Tel. (+32) 2-7331019
Fax (+32) 2-7429748
E-mail ricseurope@rics.org
URL www.rics.org
Pres. Barry Gilbertson
Contact Philippe Winssinger Frics (Chair.)

SCEPEA

Standing Committee of European Port Employers' Associations

Comité Permanent des Entreprises de Manutention dans les Ports Européens

Zentralverband der deutschen Seehafenbetriebe

Am Sandtorkai 2, 20457 Hamburg, Germany
Tel. (+49 40) 366203
Fax (+49 40) 366377
E-mail info@zds-seehaefen.de
URL www.zds-seehaefen.de
Contact Dietrich Peter (Chair.)

SCOPE

Standing Committee of Police in Europe

Comité Permanent de la Police en Europe

Standiger Ausschuss der Polizei in Europa

Rue Leys 34, 1000 Brussels, Belgium
Tel. (+32) 2-7368029
Fax (+32) 2-7337862
E-mail scofpol@hotmail.com
Sec.-Gen. P. White

SEFA

European Association of Steel Drum Manufacturers

Syndicat Européen de l'Industrie des Fûts en Acier

Verband der Europäischen Stahlfassindustrie

C/o Agoria, Diamant Building, Blvd A. Reyers 80, 1030 Brussels, Belgium
Tel. (+32) 2-7067963
Fax (+32) 2-7067966
E-mail sefa@agoria.be
URL www.sefa.be
Pres. F. de Miguel
Sec.-Gen. H. Dejonghe

SEFEL

European Secretariat of Manufacturers of Light Metal Packaging

Secrétariat Européen des Fabricants d'Emballages Métalliques Légers

Europäisches Sekretariat der Hersteller von Leichten Metallverpackungen

Diamant Building, Blvd Reyers 80, 1030 Brussels, Belgium
Tel. (+32) 2-7067953
Fax (+32) 2-7067966
E-mail sefel@agoria.be
URL www.sefel.net
Sec.-Gen. Pierre Diederich

SITS

Surface Treatment Manufacturers and Suppliers Trade Association

Syndicat général des Industries de matériels et procédés pour les Traitements de Surfaces

39/41 Rue Louis Blanc, 92038 Paris La Défense Cedex, France
Tel. (+33) 1-47-17-63-73
Fax (+33) 1-47-17-63-74
E-mail info@sits.fr
URL www.sits.fr/
Pres. Jean Galaud
Sec.-Gen. Françoise Leclerc

TBE

European Federation of Brick and Tile Manufacturers

Fédération Européenne des Fabricants de Tuiles et de Briques

Europäischer Verband der Mauerziegel- und Dachziegelhersteller

Rue des Colonies 18–24, 1000 Brussels, Belgium
Tel. (+32) 2-5113012
Fax (+32) 2-5115174
E-mail sec@cerameunie.net
URL www.ceramieunie.net
Pres. Schenck
Sec.-Gen. Rogier Chorus

TEGOVA

European Group of Valuers' Associations

Place de la Vieille Halle aux Blés 28, 1000 Brussels, Belgium

Tel. (+32) 2-5033234
Fax (+32) 2-5033232
E-mail tegova@skynet.be
URL www.tegova.org
Pres. François
Sec.-Gen. Champness
Contact Rebekah Lowe (Exec.Dir)

TIE

Toy Industries of Europe

Rue des Deux Eglises 58, 1000 Brussels, Belgium
Tel. (+32) 2-2275301
Fax (+32) 2-2500019
E-mail tie@tietoy.org
URL www.tietoy.org
Pres. A. Munn
Sec.-Gen. Laura Currie
Contact Alan Munn (Chair.)

TII

European Association for the Transfer of Technologies, Innovation and Industrial Information

Association Européenne pour le Transfert des Technologies, de l'Innovation et de l'Information Industrielle

Europäische Vereinigung für den Transfer von Technologien, Innovation und Industrieller Information

Rue Aldringen 3, 1118 Luxembourg, Luxembourg
Tel. (+352) 463035
Fax (+352) 462185
E-mail tii@tii.org
URL www.tii.org
Pres. Gordon Ollivere
Sec.-Gen. Robinson

TRANSBEUROP

European Federation of Butter Processing Industries

Fédération Européenne des Entreprises de Transformation du Beurre et de ses Composants

Europäischer Verband der Butter und dessen Bestandteile Verarbeitenden Unternehmen

Avenue Livingstone 26, 1000 Brussels, Belgium

Tel. (+32) 2-2304448
Fax (+32) 2-2304044
E-mail dairy.trade@eucolait.be
URL www.transbeurop.org
Pres. Norman Oldmeadow
Sec.-Gen. Anne Randles

TUTB

European Trade Union Technical Bureau for Health and Safety

Blvd du Roi Albert II 5, Bte 5, 1210 Brussels, Belgium
Tel. (+32) 2-2240560
Fax (+32) 2-2240561
E-mail tutb@etuc.org
URL www.etuc.org/tutb
Contact M Sapir (Dir)

UAE

European Lawyers' Union

Union des Avocats Européens

Europäischer Anwaltsverein

Grand-Rue 31, BP 222, 2012 Luxembourg, Luxembourg
Tel. (+352) 467346
Fax (+352) 467348
E-mail jlemmer@pt.lu
URL www.uae.lu
Pres. Gérard Abitbol
Sec.-Gen. Joë Lemmer

UCBD

European Hardwood Federation

Union pour le Commerce des Bois Durs dans l'UE

Galerie du Centre (Bloc I, 5è étage), Rue des Fripiers 15/17, 1000 Brussels, Belgium
Tel. (+32) 2-2194373
Fax (+32) 2-2293267
E-mail info@boisimport.be
URL www.boisimport.be
Pres. Mats Baath
Sec.-Gen. Daelmans

UCTE

Union for the Coordination of Transmission of Electricity

Union pour la Coordination du Transport de l'Electricité

Union für die Koordinierung des Transportes elektrischer Energie

Boulevard Saint-Michel 15, 1040 Brussels, Belgium
Tel. (+32) 2-7416940
Fax (+32) 2-7416949
E-mail info@ucte.org
URL www.ucte.org
Pres. M. Fuchs
Sec.-Gen. Marcel Bial
Contact Serrani (Vice-Pres.)

UEA

European Furniture Manufacturers Federation

Union Européenne de l'Ameublement

Verband der Europäischen Möbelindustrie

Rue Royale 163, 1210 Brussels, Belgium
Tel. (+32) 2-2181889
Fax (+32) 2-2192701
E-mail secretariat@uea.be
URL www.ueanet.com
Pres. Calixto Valenti
Sec.-Gen. Bart de Turck

UEAPME

European Association of Craft, Small and Medium-Sized Enterprises

Union Européenne de l'Artisanat et des Petites et Moyennes Entreprises

Europäische Union des Handwerks und der Klein- und Mittelbetriebe

Rue Jacques de Lalaing 4, 1040 Brussels, Belgium
Tel. (+32) 2-2307599
Fax (+32) 2-2307861
E-mail info@ueapme.com
URL www.ueapme.com
Pres. Paul Reckinger
Sec.-Gen. Hans-Werner Muller
Contact Christine Faes (Vice-Pres.)

European Union of Agrément

Union Européenne pour l'Agrément Technique dans la Construction (UEAtc)

Europäische Union für das Agrement im Bauwesen

PO Box 195, Bucknalls Lane, Garston, Watford WD25 9BA, United Kingdom
Tel. (+44 1923) 665300
Fax (+44 1923) 665301
E-mail mail@ueatc.com

URL www.ueatc.com
Pres. Maugard Alain
Sec.-Gen. Blaisdale William

UEC

Union Européenne de la Carrosserie

Blvd de la Woluwe 46, Bte 9, 1200 Brussels,
Belgium
Tel. (+32) 2-7786200
Fax (+32) 2-7786222
E-mail mail@federauto.be
URL www.federauto.be
Pres. René Heinix
Contact Hilde Vander Stichele

UECBV

**European Livestock and Meat Trading
Union**

**Union Européenne du Commerce du Bétail
et de la Viande**

Europäische Vieh- und Fleischhandelsunion

Rue de la Loi 81A, PO Box 9, Floor 4, 1040
Brussels, Belgium
Tel. (+32) 2-2304603
Fax (+32) 2-2309400
E-mail uecbv@scarlet.be
URL www.uecbv.be
Pres. Laurent Spanghero
Sec.-Gen. Jean-Luc Meriaux
Contact Piet Thijsse (Vice-Pres.)

UEEIV

**Union of European Railway Engineer
Associations**

**Union des Associations Européennes des
Ingénieurs Ferroviaires**

**Union Europäischer Eisenbahn-Ingenieur-
Verbände**

Kaiserstrasse 61, 60329 Frankfurt am Main,
Germany
Tel. (+49 69) 259329
Fax (+49 69) 259220
E-mail ueeiv@t-online.de
URL www.ueeiv.com
Pres. Heinrich Salzmann
Contact Brinkmann

UEIL

**Independent Union of the European
Lubricant Industry**

**Union Indépendante de l'Industrie
Européenne des Lubrifiants**

Square Marie-Louise 49, 1000 Brussels,
Belgium
Tel. (+32) 2-2389785
Fax (+32) 2-2300389
E-mail ueil@fedichem.be
URL www.ueil.org
Pres. Hugh Dowding
Sec.-Gen. Dominique de Hemptinne
Contact Fabio Parodi (Vice-Pres.)

UEITP

**European Association of Potato Processing
Industry**

**Union Européenne des Industries de
Transformation de la Pomme de Terre**

**Europäische Vereinigung der Kartoffel
Verarbeitenden Industrie**

Von-der-Heydt Strasse 9, 53177 Bonn,
Germany
Tel. (+49 228) 932-9111
Fax (+49 228) 932-9120
E-mail erikdemarrez@compuserve.de
Pres. Richard Harris
Sec.-Gen. E. Demarriz

UEMO

European Union of General Practitioners

**Union Européenne des Médecins
Omnipraticiens**

**Europäische Vereinigung der
Omnipraktizierenden Ärzte**

PO Box 5610, Villagatan 5, 11486 Stockholm,
Sweden
Tel. (+46 8) 790-34-52
Fax (+46 8) 20-57-18
E-mail info@uemo.org
URL www.uemo.org
Pres. Dr Christina Fabian
Sec.-Gen. Dr Carl-Eric Thors
Contact Elisabeth Sundström (Exec. Sec.)

UEMS

European Union of Medical Specialists
Union Européenne des Médecins Spécialistes
Europäische Vereinigung der Fachärzte

Avenue de la Couronne 20, 1050 Brussels,
Belgium
Tel. (+32) 2-6495164
Fax (+32) 2-6403730

E-mail SG@uems.net
URL www.uems.net
Pres. Dr Hannu Halila
Sec.-Gen. Dr Bernard Maillet
Contact Dr Ciro Costa (Vice-Pres.)

UEMV

European Glaziers Association
Union Européenne des Miroitiers Vitriers
Europäischer Dachverband des
  Gläserhandwerks

POB 41, 1483 ZG De Rijp, Netherlands
Tel. (+31 29) 9682614
Fax (+31 29) 9682619
E-mail info@uemv.com
URL www.uemv.com
Pres. Trevor Coles
Sec.-Gen. Pim H. K. de Ridder

UEPA

European Union of Alcohol Producers
Union Europeenne des Producteurs d'Alcool
Europäische Union der Alkoholhersteller

Avenue des Nerviens 65, bte 24, 1040 Brussels,
  Belgium
Tel. (+32) 2-7729830
Fax (+32) 2-7729824
E-mail uepa@skynet.be
Pres. Dreuillet
Sec.-Gen. Valérie Corre
Contact Koffi N'Guessan (Vice-Pres.)

UEPC

European Union of Developers and House
  Builders
Union Européenne des Promoteurs-
  Constructeurs
Europäische Union der Freien
  Wohnungsunternehmen

Rue de la Violette 43, 1000 Brussels, Belgium
Tel. (+32) 2-5112526
Fax (+32) 2-2197199
E-mail info@uepc.org
URL www.uepc.org
Pres. Pavan
Contact Buelens (Dir)

UEPG

European Aggregates Association

Union Européenne des Producteurs de
  Granulats
Europäischer Verband der Kies-, Sand- und
  Schotterproduzenten

Travesia de Tellez, Entreplanta Izquierda 4,
  28007 Madrid, Spain
Tel. (+34) 91-5021417
Fax (+34) 91-4339155
E-mail anefa@aridos.org
URL www.uepg.org
Pres. Cipriano Gómez Carrión
Sec.-Gen. Rafael Fernández Aller

UFE

Union of Potato Starch Factories of the
  European Union
Union des Féculeries de Pommes de Terre de
  l'Union Européenne
Vereinigung der Kartoffelstärken Betriebe
  der Europäischen Union

Rue de Treves 59–61, 1040 Brussels, Belgium
Tel. (+32) 2-2824677
Fax (+32) 2-2824693
E-mail ufe.brussels@worldonline.be
Pres. Krijne Pieter
Sec.-Gen. Cornelis Visser

UFEMAT

European Association of National Builders
  Merchants' Associations
Union Européenne des Fédérations
  Nationales des Négociants en Matériaux
  de Construction
Europäische Vereinigung der Nationalen
  Baustoffhändler-Verbände

Alois de Deckerstraat 20, 1731 Zellik, Belgium
Tel. (+32) 2-4662483
Fax (+32) 2-4632646
E-mail fema@telenet.be
URL www.ufemat.com
Contact Christian Leus (Dir)

UGAL

Union of Groups of Independent Retailers of
  Europe
Union des Groupements de Détaillants
  Indépendants de l'Europe aisbl
Union der Verbundgruppen selbständiger
  Einzelhändler Europas

Avenue des Gaulois 3, Bte 3, 1040 Brussels,
  Belgium
Tel. (+32) 2-7324660
Fax (+32) 2-7358623
E-mail info@ugal.org
URL www.ugal.org
Pres. Dr Peter Hampl
Sec.-Gen. Denis Labatut
Contact Harri Sivula (Vice-Pres.)

UITP – EuroTeam

**International Association of Public
  Transport – EuroTeam**

Union Internationale des Transports Publics

**Internationaler Verband für Öffentliches
  Verkehrswesen**

Rue Sainte Marie 6, 1080 Brussels, Belgium
Tel. (+32) 2-6736100
Fax (+32) 2-6601072
E-mail euroteam@uitp.com
URL www.uitp.com
Pres. Roberto Cavalieri
Sec.-Gen. Hans Rat
Contact Alain Flausch (Vice-Pres.)

UNESDA – CISDA

**Union of EU Soft Drinks Associations –
  Confederation of International Soft
  Drinks Associations**

Bd Saint Michel 77–79, 1040 Brussels,
  Belgium
Tel. (+32) 2-7434050
Fax (+32) 2-7325102
E-mail mail@unesda-cisda.org
URL www.unesda-cisda.org
Sec.-Gen. Alain Beamount

UNI Europa

**Regional European Organisation of Union
  Network International**

**Organisation Régionale Européenne
  d'Union Network International**

**Europäische Regionalorganisation von
  Union Network International**

Rue de l'Hôpital 31, PO Box 9, 1000 Brussels,
  Belgium
Tel. (+32) 2-2345656
Fax (+32) 2-2350870
E-mail uni-europa@union-network.org
URL www.uni-europa.org
Pres. Frank Bsirske

Sec.-Gen. Philip J Jennings
Contact Bernadette Tesch-Segol (Regional
  Sec.)

UNICE

**Union of Industrial and Employers'
  Confederations of Europe**

**Union des Confédérations de l'Industrie et
  des Employeurs d'Europe**

Avenue de Cortenbergh 168, 1000 Brussels,
  Belgium
Tel. (+32) 2-2376511
Fax (+32) 2-2311445
E-mail main@unice.be
URL www.unice.org
Pres. Dr Strube Jürgen
Sec.-Gen. Baron Philippe de Buck
Contact Fau Maria Fernanda (Comm. Dir)

UNIFE

Union of European Railway Industries

**Union des Industries Ferroviaires
  Européennes**

**Verband der Europäischen
  Eisenbahnindustrien**

Avenue Louise 221, Bte 11, 1050 Brussels,
  Belgium
Tel. (+32) 2-6261260
Fax (+32) 2-6261261
E-mail corinne.dhainaut@unife.org
URL www.unife.org
Contact Drewin Nieuwenhuis (Gen. Man.)

UNISTOCK

**Union of Professional Agribulk Warehouse
  Keepers**

**Union des Stockeurs Professionnels de
  Céréales dans l'UE**

**Vereinigung der Getreidelagerbetriebe der
  EG**

Rue du Trône 98, 1050 Brussels, Belgium
Tel. (+32) 2-5020808
Fax (+32) 2-5026030
E-mail info@unistock.be
URL www.unistock.be
Pres. Alberto Bravo
Sec.-Gen. Chantal Fauth
Contact Marleen Logghe (Asst)

UPEI

Union of European Petroleum Independents
Union Pétrolière Européenne Indépendante
Grosse Theater Strasse 1, 20354 Hamburg,
  Germany
Tel. (+49 40) 340858
Fax (+49 40) 344200
E-mail info@upei.org
URL www.upei.org
Pres. Hellmuth Weisser
Sec.-Gen. Bernd Schnittler
Contact Cornelia Audran (Office Man.)

UPFE

Union of Providence of European Officials
Union de Prévoyance des Fonctionnaires
  Européens
Rue Stévin 202, 1000 Brussels, Belgium
Tel. (+32) 2-7369843
Fax (+32) 2-7367019
E-mail info@upfe.be
URL www.upfe.be
Pres. A. Pratley
Contact J. Kieffer

USSPE

Union Syndicale – European Public Service
Union Syndicale – Service Public Européen
Avenue des Gaulois 36, 1040 Brussels,
  Belgium
Tel. (+32) 2-7339800
Fax (+32) 2-7330533
E-mail web@unionsyndicale.org
URL www.unionsyndicale.org
Pres. Alan Hick
Sec.-Gen. Pierre Blanchard
Contact Fabrice Andreone (Vice-Pres.)

WEI / IEO

Western European Institute for Wood
  Preservation
Institut de l'Europe Occidentale pour
  l'Imprégnation du Bois
West-Europäisches Institut für
  Holzimprägnierung
Allée Hof-ter-Vleest 5, Bte 4, 1070 Brussels,
  Belgium

Tel. (+32) 2-5562586
Fax (+32) 2-5562595
E-mail info@wei-ieo.org
URL www.wei-ieo.org
Pres. Tommy Karlsson
Sec.-Gen. Filip Jaeger
Contact Frederik Lauwaert

WFA / FMA

World Federation of Advertisers
Fédération Mondiale des Annonceurs
Avenue Louise 120, Bte 6, 1050 Brussels,
  Belgium
Tel. (+32) 2-5025740
Fax (+32) 2-5025666
E-mail info@wfanet.org
URL www.wfanet.org
Pres. Rolf Kreiner
Contact Bernhard Adriaensens (Man. Dir)

WINDSCREEN / VITRIERS

European Car Windscreen Association
Association Européenne des Vitriers pour
  l'Automobile
Fahrzeugverglasung Europa
Van Santenlaan 20–7, 1700 AA
  Heerhugowaard, Netherlands
Tel. (+31 72) 5440953
Fax (+31 72) 714432
Pres. P. S. Bain
Sec.-Gen. P. H. K. de Ridder

YES

Confederation of Young Entrepreneurs for
  Europe
Confédération des Jeunes Entrepreneurs
  pour l'Europe
Junge Unternehmer für Europa
Avenue de la Joyeuse Entrée 1, 1040 Brussels,
  Belgium
Tel. (+32) 2-2803425
Fax (+32) 2-2803317
E-mail secretariat@yes.be
URL www.yes.be
Pres. Murat Sarayli
Sec.-Gen. Marco Pezzini
Contact Matteo Colaninno (Vice-Pres.)

INTEREST GROUPS AND NON-GOVERNMENTAL ORGANIZATIONS

ACA

Academic Co-operation Association
Rue d'Egmont 15, 1000 Brussels, Belgium
Tel. (+32) 2-5132241
Fax (+32) 2-5131776
E-mail info@aca-secretariat.be
URL www.aca-secretariat.be
Pres. Prof. Peter Scott
Dir Bernd Wächter

ACRR

Association of Cities and Regions for Recycling
Association des Cités et Régions pour le Recyclage
Gulledelle 100, 1200 Brussels, Belgium
Tel. (+32) 2-7757701
Fax (+32) 2-7757635
E-mail acrr@ibgebim.be
URL www.acrr.org
Pres. Todd Neville
Exec. Sec. Francis Radermaker
Sec. Sir Fabrice Lesceu

AEBR / ARFE / AGEG

Association of European Border Regions
Association des Régions Frontalières Européennes
Arbeitsgemeinschaft Europäischer Grenzregionen
Enscheder Strasse 362, 48599 Gronau, Germany
Tel. (+49 2562) 70219
Fax (+49 2562) 70259
E-mail info@aebr.net
URL www.aebr.net
Pres. Lambert van Nistelrooij
Sec.-Gen. Jens Gabbe
Contact Marie-Lou Perou

AECA

American European Community Association
Avenue de Messidor 208, PO Box 1, 1180 Brussels, Belgium
Tel. (+32) 2-3445949
Fax (+32) 2-3445343
E-mail aeca@aeca-europe.org
Pres. Georges de Veirman
Chair. John Largent

AECC

Association for Emissions Control by Catalyst
Diamant Building, Blvd Auguste Reyers 80, 1030 Brussels, Belgium
Tel. (+32) 2-7068160
Fax (+32) 2-7068169
E-mail info@aecc.be
URL www.aecc.be
Exec. Dir Dirk Bosteels

AEF

European Affairs
Europäische Angelegenheiten
Avenue Livingstone 33, 1040 Brussels, Belgium
Tel. (+32) 2-2300410
Fax (+32) 2-2305601
Pres. Mary Anne Thompson
Man. Partner M. van den Heuvel

AEH

European Action of the Disabled
Europäische Behindertenaktion
Wurzerstrasse 4a, 53175 Bonn, Germany
Tel. (+49 228) 820-9333
Fax (+49 228) 820-9346
E-mail aeh@vdk.de
URL www.vdk.de/aeh
Pres. Walter Hirrlinger
Dir Ulrich Laschet

AEI

Action in Europe for Education, Invention and Innovation

Europäische Aktionsgemeinschaft Bildung Erfindung Innovation

27 Rue du Champ de Mars, Espace Entreprise, 57200 Sarreguemines, France
Tel. (+33) 3-87-98-75-75
Fax (+33) 3-87-98-27-27
Pres. Herrmann Georges

AEIDL

European Association for Information on Local Development

Association Européenne pour l'Information sur le Développement Local

Chaussée Saint Pierre 260, 1040 Brussels, Belgium
Tel. (+32) 2-7364960
Fax (+32) 2-7360434
E-mail aeidl@aiedl.be
URL www.aeidl.be
Chair. Marie-Lise Semblat
Man. Dir William van Dingenen

AEM

Association Européenne des Elus de Montagne

European Association of Elected Representatives from Mountain Areas

Europäische Vereinigung der Gewählten von Bergregionen

Avenue des Arts 1 bte 9, 1210 Brussels, Belgium
Tel. (+32) 2-2210439
Fax (+32) 2-2176987
E-mail aem@promote-aem.org
URL www.promonte-aem.org
Pres. Luciano Caveri
Sec.-Gen. Sir Carlos Pinto

AER / ARE / VRE

Assembly of European Regions

Assemblée des Régions d'Europe

Versammlung der Regionen Europas

Bureaux Europe, 20 Place des Halles, 67000 Strasbourg, France
Tel. (+33) 3-88-22-07-07
Fax (+33) 3-88-75-67-19
E-mail secretariat@a-e-r.org
URL www.are-regions-europe.org

Pres. Riccardo Illy
Sec.-Gen. Klaus Klipp
Man. Barbara Thauront

AEUSCO

European Association of Universities, Schools and Colleges of Optometry

Europäischer Verband der Schulen und Kollegien für Optometrie

134 Route de Chartres, 91440 Bures-sur-Yvette, France
Tel. (+33) 1-64-86-12-13
Fax (+33) 1-69-28-49-99
E-mail ico.direction@wanadoo.fr
URL http://ubista.ubi.pt/~aeusco
Pres. Gloria Rico
Sec.-Gen. Jean-Paul Roosen

AGE

European Older People's Platform

Plateforme Européenne des Personnes Âgées

Rue Froissart 111, 1040 Brussels, Belgium
Tel. (+32) 2-2801470
Fax (+32) 2-2801522
E-mail info@age-platform.org
URL www.age-platform.org
Pres. Steen Langebaek
Information Officer Catherine Daurèle

ALZHEIMER EUROPA / ALZHEIMER EUROPE

145 Route de Thionville, 2611 Luxembourg, Luxembourg
Tel. (+352) 297970
Fax (+352) 297972
E-mail info@alzheimer-europe.org
URL www.alzheimer-europe.org
Chair. Maurice O'Connel
Sec.-Gen. Jean Georges

AMNESTY INTERNATIONAL

Amnesty International EU Office

Rue d'Arlon 39–41, 1000 Brussels, Belgium
Tel. (+32) 2-5021499
Fax (+32) 2-5025686
E-mail amnesty-eu@aieu.be
URL www.amnesty-eu.org
Dir Dick Oosting

AMRIE

Alliance of Maritime Regional Interests in Europe

Alliance des Intérêts Maritimes Régionaux en Europe

Rue du Commerce 20–22, 1000 Brussels, Belgium

Tel. (+32) 2-7361755

Fax (+32) 2-7352298

E-mail info@amrie.org

Dir Michael Lloyd

ANPED

Northern Alliance for Sustainability

POB 59030, 1040 KA Amsterdam, Netherlands

Tel. (+31 20) 4751742

Fax (+31 20) 4751743

E-mail h.jeune@anped.org

URL www.anped.org

Exec. Dir Jan Rademaker

Programmes Officer Kirsten Kossen

ARTIS GEIE

Groupement Européen des Sociétés de Gestion Collective des Droits des Artistes Interprètes ou Exécutants

European Performers' Collecting Societies Organisations

Rue d'Egmont 15, 1000 Brussels, Belgium

Tel. (+32) 2-5123017

Fax (+32) 2-5144322

E-mail artisgeie.be@skynet.be

Pres. Luis Cobos

Sec.-Gen. Jean Vincent

Dir Francesca Greco

ATD

International Movement ATD Fourth World

Mouvement international ATD Quart Monde

Internationale Bewegung ATD Vierte Welt

Avenue Victor Jacobs 12, 1040 Brussels, Belgium

Tel. (+32) 2-6479900

Fax (+32) 2-6407384

E-mail atd.europe@tiscali.be

URL www.atd-fourthworld.org

Pres. Anoman Oguié

Representative Sarah Kenningham

ATEE

Association for Teacher Education in Europe

Vereinigung für Lehrerbildung in Europa

Rue de la Concorde 60, 1050 Brussels, Belgium

Tel. (+32) 2-5127505

Fax (+32) 2-5128425

E-mail atee@euronet.be

URL www.atee.org

Pres. Maureen Killeavy

Acting Exec. Dir Dr Vijay Reddy

AUTISM-EUROPE / AUTISME-EUROPE

Autism Europe Aisbl

Rue Montoyer 39, 1000 Brussels, Belgium

Tel. (+32) 2-6757505

Fax (+32) 2-757270

E-mail secretariat@autismeurope.org

URL www.autismeurope.org

Pres. Donata Vivanti

BEUC

European Consumers Organisation

Bureau Européen des Unions de consommateurs

Europäisches Büro der Verbraucherverbände

Avenue de Tervueren 36 bte 4, 1040 Brussels, Belgium

Tel. (+32) 2-7431590

Fax (+32) 2-7402802

E-mail consumers@beuc.org

URL www.beuc.org

Pres. Rasmus Kjeldahl

Dir Jim Murray

CAN-EUROPE

Climate Action Network Europe asbl

Klima-Netzwerk Europa

Rue de la Charité 48, 1210 Brussels, Belgium

Tel. (+32) 2-2295220

Fax (+32) 2-2295229

E-mail info@climnet.org

URL www.climnet.org

Dir Karla Schoeters

CARE FOR EUROPE / CARE POUR L'EUROPE

Christian Action Research & Education for Europe

Action Recherche et Enseignement Chrétien
Rue Archimede 55–57, 1000 Brussels, Belgium
Tel. (+32) 2-7321147
Fax (+32) 2-7321228
E-mail info@careforeurope.org
URL www.careforeurope.org
Pres. C. Colchester
Sec.-Gen. L. Browning
Man. David Fieldsend

CARE INTERNATIONAL
Blvd du Régent 58, PO Box 10, 1000 Brussels,
    Belgium
Tel. (+32) 2-5024333
Fax (+32) 2-5028202
E-mail info@care-international.org
URL www.care-international.org
Chair. Lydia Marshall
Sec.-Gen. Denis Caillaux

CARITAS EUROPA
Rue de Pascale 4, 1040 Brussels, Belgium
Tel. (+32) 2-2350394
Fax (+32) 2-2301658
E-mail info@caritas-europa.org
URL www.caritas-europa.org
Pres. Denis Viénot
Sec.-Gen. Marius Wanders
Communication Officer Annalisa Mazzella

CECODHAS
**European Liaison Committee for Social
    Housing**
**Comité européen de Coordination de
    l'Habitat Social**
**Europäische Verbindungsausschuss zur
    Koordinierung**
Rue Guillaume Tell 59b, 1060 Brussels,
    Belgium
Tel. (+32) 2-5346043
Fax (+32) 2-5345852
E-mail ino@cecoshas.org
URL www.cecodhas.org
Pres. Angelo Grasso
Sec.-Gen. Claire Roumet
Events and Information Officer Sorcha
    Edwards

CEDAG
**European Council for Non-Profit
    Organisations**

**Comité européen des associations d'intérêt
    général**
**Europäischer Rat für gemeinnützige
    Organisationen**
Rue de Toulouse 22, 1040 Brussels, Belgium
Tel. (+32) 2-2300031
Fax (+32) 2-2300041
E-mail cedag@cedag-eu.org
URL www.cedag-eu.org
Pres. Anne David
Sec.-Gen. Christiana Weidel
Dir Marine Ranty

CEDR
European Council for Agricultural Law
Europäisches Komitee für Agrarrecht
Avenue de la Toison d'Or 72, 1060 Brussels,
    Belgium
Tel. (+32) 2-5437208
Fax (+32) 2-5437399
E-mail marc.heyerick@vlm.be
URL www.cedr.org
Pres. Prof. Joseph Hudault
Sec.-Gen. Dr Jur. Marc Heyerick

CEJI
European Jewish Information Centre
Centre Européen Juif d'Information
Avenue Brugman 319, 1180 Brussels, Belgium
Tel. (+32) 2-3443444
Fax (+32) 2-3446735
E-mail ceji@ceji.org
URL www.ceji.org
Pres. Jacques Graubart
Sec.-Gen. Daniel Kropf
Dir-Gen. Pascale Charhon

CELSIG
**European Liaison Committee on Services of
    General Interest**
**Comité européen de liaison des services
    d'intérêt général**
66 rue de Rome, 75008 Paris, France
Tel. (+33) 1-43-71-20-28
Fax (+33) 1-42-94-10-37
E-mail celsig@celsig.org
URL www.celsig.org
Pres. Pierre Bauby
Sec.-Gen. Jean-Claude Boual

CEMR / CCRE / RGRE

Council of European Municipalities and Regions

Conseil des Communes et Régions d'Europe

Rat der Gemeinden und Regionen Europas

Rue d'Arlon 22, 1050 Brussels, Belgium
Tel. (+32) 2-5117477
Fax (+32) 2-5110949
E-mail cemr@ccre.org
URL www.ccre.org

Pres. Dr Michael Häupl
Sec.-Gen. Jeremy Smith

CENPO

Centre for European Non-Profit Organisations

Rue de la Concorde 57, 1050 Brussels, Belgium
Tel. (+32) 2-7400000
Fax (+32) 2-7400009
E-mail info@cenpo.org
URL www.cenpo.org

Dir David Wedgwood
Contact Carling Sarah

CES

Confederation of European Scouts

Confédération Européenne de Scoutisme

Bund Europäischer Pfadfinder

Rue de la Margelle 5, 1341 Ottignies, Belgium
Tel. (+32) 10-614278
E-mail pierredessy@versateladsl.be
URL www.ces-scouts.com

Pres. Pierre Dessy

CESD

Centre for European Security and Disarmament

Centre de Sécurité Européenne et Désarmement

Rue Stévin 115, 1000 Brussels, Belgium
Tel. (+32) 2-2300732
Fax (+32) 2-2302467
E-mail cesd@cesd.org
URL www.cesd.org

Dir Sharon Riggle

CESE

Planning Congressi

Via S. Stefano 97, 40125 Bologna, Italy

Tel. (+39) 051-300100
Fax (+39) 051-309477
E-mail m.galantino@planning.it
URL www.planning.it

Administrator Michele Galantino

CIDSE

International Cooperation for Development and Solidarity

Coopération Internationale pour le Développement et la Solidarité

Internationale Arbeitsgemeinschaft für Entwicklungund Solidarität

Rue Stévin 16, 1000 Brussels, Belgium
Tel. (+32) 2-2307722
Fax (+32) 2-2307082
E-mail postmaster@cidse.org
URL www.cidse.org

Sec.-Gen. Christiane Overkamp
Policy and Advocacy Officer Guillaume Légaut

CIFCA

Copenhagen Initiative for Central America

Rue de la Linière 11, 1060 Brussels, Belgium
Tel. (+32) 2-5361912
Fax (+32) 2-561943
E-mail marta.ibero@cifca.ngonet.be

Pres. Janneke van Eijk
Sec.-Gen. René Rodríguez
Exec. Sec. Luis Guillermo Pérez Casas

CITIZENSHIP / CIVISME

Centre Européen du Civisme

European Centre of Good Citizenship

Avenue Franklin Roosevelt 17 (CP 108), 1050 Brussels, Belgium
Tel. (+32) 2-6489476
Fax (+32) 2-6409393
URL www.europarl.eu.int

Pres. G. Haarsher
Sec.-Gen. Monique Lambert

CLONG

Liaison Committee of Development NGOs to the European Union

Square Ambiorix 10, 1000 Brussels, Belgium
Tel. (+32) 2-7438760
Fax (+32) 2-7321934
E-mail info@clong.be
Sec.-Gen. G. Dumon

CLRAE / CPLRE / KGRE

Congress of Local and Regional Authorities of Europe

Kongress der Gemeinden und Regionen Europas

Conseil de l'Europe, 67075 Strasbourg Cedex, France
Tel. (+33) 3-88-41-20-00
Fax (+33) 3-88-41-27-51
E-mail rinaldo.locatelli@coe.int
URL www.coe.fr/cplre
Pres. Llibert Cuatrecasas
Contact A. Schneider

COFACE

Confederation of Family Organisations in the European Union

Confédération des Organisations Familiales de l'Union Européenne

Bund der Familienorganisationen der EU

Rue de Londres 17, 1050 Brussels, Belgium
Tel. (+32) 2-5114179
Fax (+32) 2-5144773
E-mail coface@brutele.be
URL www.coface-eu.org
Pres. Dr. Steen Mogens Lauge Lasson
Sec.-Gen. Esther Pinilla
Dir William Lay

COIMBRA GROUP

Rue de Stassart 119, 1050 Brussels, Belgium
Tel. (+32) 2-5138332
Fax (+32) 2-5029611
E-mail cguniv@coimbra-group.be
URL www.coimbra-group.be
Pres. Tosi
Office Dir Koen Delaere

CONFLICT (Prevention of) / CONFLIT (Prévention)

European Platform on Conflict Prevention and Transformation

European Centre for Conflict Prevention, POB 14069, 3508 SC Utrecht, Netherlands
Tel. (+31) 302427777
Fax (+31) 302369268
E-mail info@conflict-prevention.net
URL www.euconflict.org
Exec. Dir Paul van Tongeren
Office Management Cora Bastiaansen

CRED

Centre for Research on the Epidemiology of Disasters

Zentrum der Katastrophenepidemiologieforschung

Clos Chapelle-aux-Champs 30–94, 1200 Brussels, Belgium
Tel. (+32) 2-7643327
Fax (+32) 2-7643441
E-mail cred@epid.ucl.ac.be
URL www.cred.be
Pres. Ph. Laurent
Dir Prof. Debarati Guha-Sapir

CREW

Rue Capouillet 25, 1060 Brussels, Belgium
Tel. (+32) 2-5349085
Fax (+32) 2-5348134
E-mail mail@crew.be
Dir Rebecca Franciskides

CRPM / CPMR

Conférence des Régions Périphériques Maritimes

Conference of Peripheral Maritime Regions of Europe

6 Rue St Martin, 35000 Rennes, France
Tel. (+33) 2-99-35-40-50
Fax (+33) 2-99-35-09-19
E-mail secretariat@crpm.org
URL www.crpm.org
Pres. Claudio Martini
Sec.-Gen. Xavier Gizard
Head of Communications Fanny Harling

CSREMB

Coopération Subrégionale des Etats de la Mer Baltique

Avenue Palmerston 20, 1000 Brussels, Belgium
Tel. (+32) 2-2854640
Fax (+32) 2-2854657
E-mail guenther.schulz@hobru.landsh.de
Contact Guenther Schulz

CSW-EU

Christian Solidarity Worldwide EU Office

Rue Archimède 55–57, 1000 Brussels, Belgium
Tel. (+32) 2-7422082
Fax (+32) 2-7422082
E-mail csw-eu@village.uunet.be
URL www.csw.org.uk
Liaison Officer Anna-Lee Stangl

CTA

Technical Centre for Agricultural and Rural Cooperation ACP-EU

Centre technique pour la coopération agricole et rurale ACP-UE

Rue Montoyer 39, 1000 Brussels, Belgium
Tel. (+32) 2-5137436
Fax (+32) 2-580868
E-mail cta@cta.int
URL www.cta.nl
Pres. Frank Kruesi
Dir Carl B. Greenidge

DEMYC

Democrat Youth Community of Europe

Union des jeunes démocrates européens

Demokratischer Jugendverband Europas

Danasvej 4–6, 1910 Frederiksberg C, Denmark
Tel. (+45) 33-23-40-95
Fax (+45) 33-31-40-68
E-mail demyc@demyc.org
URL www.demyc.org
Pres. Meinhard Friedl
Sec.-Gen. Mikkel Loft

EAA

European Anglers Alliance

Rue du Parnasse 42, 1050 Brussels, Belgium
Tel. (+32) 2-7320309
Fax (+32) 2-7320309
E-mail email@eaa-europe.org
URL www.eaa-europe.org
Pres. Harm Minekus
Sec.-Gen. Jan Kappel

EAEA

European Association for the Education of Adults

Europäischer Verband für Erwachsenenbildung

Rue de la Concorde 60, 1050 Brussels, Belgium
Tel. (+32) 2-5135205
Fax (+32) 2-5135734
E-mail eaea-main@eaea.org
URL www.eaea.org
Pres. Janos Sz. Tóth
Sec.-Gen. Ellinor Haase
Senior Exec. Theo van Malderen

EAGLE

European Association for Grey Literature Exploitation

Europäische Vereinigung für die Ausnutzung der Grauen Literatur

C/o Fiz Karlsruhe, Hermann-von-Helmholtz-Platz 1, 76344 Eggenstein – Leopoldshafen, Germany
Tel. (+49 7247) 808313
Fax (+49 7247) 808114
E-mail eagle@fiz-karlsruhe.de
URL www.kb.nl/eagle
Pres. Andrew Smith
Contact E. Hellmann

EAHIL / AEIBS

European Association for Health Information and Libraries

Association européenne pour l'information et des bibliothèques de santé

C/o NVB Bureau, Nieuwegracht 15, 3512 LC Utrecht, Netherlands
Tel. (+31 30) 2619663
Fax (+31 30) 2311830
E-mail eahil-secr@nic.surfnet.nl
URL www.eahil.org
Pres. Arne Jakobsson
Supervisor Suzanne Bakker

EAL / AEA

European Association of Lawyers

Association Européenne des Avocats

Avenue Louise 137 Bte 1, 1050 Brussels, Belgium
Tel. (+32) 2-5430200
Fax (+32) 2-5381378
E-mail legal@vancutsem.be
Pres. Clemens van Nispen

EAMDA

European Alliance of Muscular Dystrophy Associations

C/o MDG, 4 Malta, Gzira Road, GZR O4 Gzira, Malta
Tel. (+356) 21346688
Fax (+356) 21318024
E-mail eamda@hotmail.com
URL www.eamda.com
Exec. Dir C. Cryna

EAPN

European Anti Poverty Network

Rue du Congrès 37–41 Bte 2, 1000 Brussels,
  Belgium
Tel. (+32) 2-2304455
Fax (+32) 2-2309733
E-mail team@eapn.skynet.be
URL www.eapn.org
Pres. Maria Marinakou
Dir Fintan Farrell

EASE

European Association for Special Education

**Association Européenne pour l'Education
  Spéciale**

C/o Keith BOVAIR, 268 Cherry Hinton Road,
  Cambridge CB1 7AU, United Kingdom
Tel. (+44 1223) 413348
E-mail kbovair@aol.com
Pres. Keith Bovair
EU-Co-ordinator Liliane DeCock

EASSW

**European Association of Schools of Social
  Work**

**Association Européenne des Ecoles de
  Formation de Travailleurs Sociaux et
  d'Educateurs**

Stenvej 4, 8270 Hoejberg, Denmark
Tel. (+45) 86-27-66-22
Fax (+45) 86-27-74-76
E-mail dsh@dsh-ea.dk
URL www.eassw.org
Pres. Dr. Christine Labonté-Roset
Sec. Dr. Nol Reverda

EBAA

European Business Aviation Association

**Europäische Vereinigung der
  Geschäftsluftfahrt**

Brusselsesteenweg 2, 3080 Tervuren, Belgium
Tel. (+32) 2-7660070
Fax (+32) 2-7681325
E-mail info@ebaa.org
URL www.ebaa.org
Chair. Rodolfo Baviera
Pres. Francois Chavatte
CEO Brian M. Humphries

EBCD

**European Bureau for Conservation and
  Development**

**Bureau européen pour la conservation et le
  développement**

**Europäisches Büro für Naturschutz und
  Entwicklung**

Rue de la Science 10, 1000 Brussels, Belgium
Tel. (+32) 2-2303070
Fax (+32) 2-2308272
E-mail ebcd.info@ebcd.org
URL www.ebcd.org/ebcd
Pres. Bertrand des Clers
Sec.-Gen. Bertrand des Clers
Dir Despina Symons Pirovolidoua

EBCO / BEOC

**European Bureau for Conscientious
  Objectors**

**Europäisches Büro für
  Kriegsdienstverweigerung**

Avenue Stobbaerts 81a, 1030 Brussels,
  Belgium
Tel. (+32) 2-2157908
Fax (+32) 2-2456297
E-mail ebco@ebco-beoc.org
URL www.ebco-beoc.org
Pres. Gerd Greune
Sec.-Gen. Hans Dijkman

EBCU

European Beer Consumers Union

C/o CAMRA, 230 Hatfield Road, St Albans,
  Herts AL1 4LW, United Kingdom
Tel. (+44 1727) 867201
Fax (+44 1727) 867670
E-mail camra@camra.org.uk
URL www.camra.org.uk
National Chair. Dave Goodwin
Contact Iain R Loe

EBEN

European Business Ethics Network

Norwegian School of Management, PO Box
  580, 1301 Sandvika, Norway
Tel. (+47) 67-55-70-00
Fax (+47) 67-55-72-50
E-mail Heidi.Hoivik@bi.no
URL www.eben.org
Pres. Dr Heidi von Weltzien Høivik
Contact H.G. Vlam

EBF

European Business Foundation

Europäische Geschaftsstiftung

39 Broughton Road, London W13 8QW,
United Kingdom
Tel. (+44 20) 8579-4688
Fax (+44 20) 8840-7345
E-mail euro.business@dial.pipex.com
Pres. A. Frodsham
Sec.-Gen. G. D'Angelo

EBIS

European Brain Injury Society

**Association européenne d'étude des
traumatisés crâniens et de leur réinsertion**

**Europäische Gesellschaft für
Hirnverletzungen**

Rue de Londres 17, 1050 Brussels, Belgium
Tel. (+32) 2-5222003
Fax (+32) 2-5233952
E-mail ebis@euronet.be
URL www.ebissociety.org
Pres. Prof. Anna Mazzucchi
Sec.-Gen. C Vrieze

EBLIDA

**European Bureau of Library, Information
and Documentation Associations**

**Europäisches Büro der Bibliotheks-,
Informations-und
Dokumentationsverbande**

POB 16359, 2500 The Hague, Netherlands
Tel. (+31 70) 3090550
Fax (+31 70) 3090558
E-mail eblida@debibliotheken.nl
URL www.eblida.org
Pres. Jan-Ewout an der Putten

EBLUL

**European Bureau for Lesser Used
Languages**

Sr. Chill Dara, 46 Kildare St, Baile Átha Cliath,
Dublin 2, Ireland
URL www.eblul.org
Pres. Neasa Ní Chinneide
Sec.-Gen. Markus Warazin

EBU / UEA

European Blind Union

Union Européenne des Aveugles

Europäischen Blindenunion

58 avenue Bosquet, 75007 Paris, France
Tel. (+33) 1-47-05-38-20
Fax (+33) 1-47-05-38-21
E-mail ebu_uea@compuserve.com
URL www.euroblind.org
Pres. Colin Low
Sec.-Gen. Vaclav Polasek

EC

Eurocities

Square de Meeûs 18, 1050 Brussels, Belgium
Tel. (+32) 2-5520888
Fax (+32) 2-5520889
E-mail info@eurocities.be
URL www.eurocities.org
Pres. Richard Leese
CEO Catherine Parmentier

ECAS

Euro Citizen Action Service

Rue du Prince Royal 83, 1050 Brussels,
Belgium
Tel. (+32) 2-5480490
Fax (+32) 2-5480491
E-mail info@ecas.org
URL www.ecas.org
Dir Tony Venables

ECCE

European Council of Civil Engineers

Europäischer Rat für Zivilingenieuren

3 Springfields, Amersham, Bucks. HP6 5JU,
United Kingdom
Tel. (+44 20) 7222-7722
Fax (+44 20) 7222-7500
E-mail eccesecretariat@hotmail.com
URL www.eccenet.org
Pres. Yrjoe Matikainen
Sec.-Gen. Diana Maxwell

ECCO

**European Council of Conscripts
Organisations**

Sehlstedtsgatan 7, 115 82 Stockholm, Sweden
Tel. (+46 8) 782-69-12
Fax (+46 8) 598-33-73
E-mail ecco@home.se
URL www.xs4all.nl/~ecco
Pres. A. Walmer

ECCP

**European Coordinating Committee for
NGOs on the Question of Palestine**
Quai du Commerce 9, 1000 Brussels, Belgium
Tel. (+32) 2-2230756
Fax (+32) 2-2501263
E-mail eccp@skynet.be
Chair. Pierre Galand

ECE

Eco-Counselling Europe
Umweltberatung Europa
Mariahilferstrasse 89 / 22, 1060 Wien, Austria
Tel. (+43 1) 5811328
Fax (+43 1) 581132818
E-mail ecocounselling.europe@nextra.at
URL www.ecocounselling-europe.org
Pres. Christian Schreffel
Sec. Krisztina Szabo

ECEAE

**European Coalition to End Animal
Experiments**
**Coalition Européenne pour mettre fin à
l'expérimentation animale**
Europäische Koalition gegen Tierversuche
C/o BUAV, 16a Crane Grove, London N7 8NN,
United Kingdom
Tel. (+44 2) 7700-4888
Fax (+44 20) 7700-0252
E-mail info@eceae.org
URL www.eceae.org
Pres. Michelle Thew
Sec.-Gen. Etienne Verhack

ECF

European Cyclists' Federation
Europäischer Radfahrer Verband
Grünenstrasse 120, 28199 Bremen, Germany
Tel. (+49 421) 3462939
Fax (+49 421) 3462950
E-mail office@ecf.com
URL www.ecf.com
Pres. Manfred Neun
Sec.-Gen. Marie Caroline Coppieters

ECL

Association of European Cancer Leagues
Chaussée de Louvain 479, 1030 Brussels,
Belgium

Tel. (+32) 2-2562000
Fax (+32) 2-2562003
E-mail info@europeancancerleagues.org
URL www.europeancancerleagues.org
Pres. Bruno Meili
Man. Dir Catherine Hartmann
EU Liaison Officer Andrew Hayes

ECOSA

European Consumer Safety Association
**Europäische Vereinigung für die
Verbraucher-Sicherheit**
Rijswijkstraat 2, 1059 GK Amsterdam,
Netherlands
Tel. (+31 20) 5114513
Fax (+31 20) 5114510
E-mail secretariat@ecosa.org
URL www.ecosa.org
Sec.-Gen. Dr. Wim Rogmans

ECPSA / CEREC

**European Committee for Promotion and
Sponsoring of the Arts**
**Europäischer Ausschuss für die Annaherung
von Wirtschaft und Kultur**
Cala Tuset 8 – 1° 2ª, 08006 Barcelona, Spain
Tel. (+34) 93-2372682
Fax (+34) 93-2372284
E-mail contact@cerec.org
URL www.cerec.org
Chair. Colin Tweedy
Sec.-Gen. Francesca Minguella

ECRE

European Council on Refugees & Exiles
**Europäischer Rat für Fluchtlinge und im
Exil Lebende**
103 Worship Street, London EC2A 2DF,
United Kingdom
Tel. (+44 20) 7377-7556
Fax (+44 20) 7377-7586
E-mail ecre@ecre.org
URL www.ecre.org
Sec.-Gen. Peer Baneke

ECTARC

**European Centre for Training and Regional
Co-operation**
**Europäisches Zentrum für Traditionelle und
Regionale Kultur**

Parade Street, Llanollen LL20 8RB,
United Kingdom
Tel. (+44 1978) 861514
Fax (+44 1978) 861804
E-mail contact@llangollen.org.uk
URL www.ectarc.com
Exec. Dir Sharon Thomas

ECTU
European Council of Transport Users
Europäischer Rat der
Verkehrsmittelbenutzer
Rue Ravenstein 4, 1000 Brussels, Belgium
Tel. (+32) 2-5022300
Fax (+32) 2-5023242
Pres. B. Nielsen
Sec.-Gen. H. Baasch

EDF / FEPH
European Disability Forum
Forum européen des personnes handicapées
Rue du Commerce 39–41, 1000 Brussels,
Belgium
Tel. (+32) 2-2824600
Fax (+32) 2-2824609
E-mail info@edf-feph.org
URL www.edf-feph.org
Pres. Yannis Vardakastanis
Dir Carlotta Besozzi

EDRC
Environment & Development Resource
Centre
Zentrum für Umwelt- und
Entwicklungsressourcen
Damrak 2830, 1012 LJ, Amsterdam,
Netherlands
Tel. (+31 20) 4225028
Fax (+31 20) 4225028
E-mail edrc@edrc.net
URL www.edrc.net
Pres. R. A. Kingham
Dir W. J. Veening

EDUCATION (Restructuring) /
ENSEIGNEMENT (Réorganisation)
International Restructuring Education
Network Europe
Stationstraat 39, 5038 EC Tilburg, Netherlands

Tel. (+31 13) 5351523
Fax (+31 13) 5442578
E-mail PeterPennartz@irene-network.nl
URL www.irene-network.nl
Sec. Peter Pennartz

EEB / BEE
European Environmental Bureau
Europäisches Umweltbüro
Bd de Waterloo 34, 1000 Brussels, Belgium
Tel. (+32) 2-2891090
Fax (+32) 2-2891099
E-mail eeb@eeb.org
URL www.eeb.org
Sec.-Gen. John Hontelez
Exec. Sec. Chantal de Meersman

EEE-YFU
European Educational Exchanges – Youth
for Understanding
Echanges Educatifs en Europe – Youth for
Understanding
Youth for Understanding – Europäischer
Bildungstausch
Fleminggatan 21, 4 tr, 112 26 Stockholm,
Sweden
Tel. (+46 8) 650-25-40
Fax (+46 8) 650-50-29
E-mail office@eee-yfu.org
URL www.eee-yfu.org
Pres. Susanne Himstedt
Dir Asa Nilsson-Söderström

EECOD
European Ecumenical Organization for
Development
Europäische Ökumenische
Entwicklungsorganisation
Rue Joseph II 174, 1040 Brussels, Belgium
Tel. (+32) 2-2306105
Fax (+32) 2-231141394
Sec.-Gen. M. Clark

EEIG EURODEVELOPPEMENT / GEIE
EURODEVELOPPEMENT
European Economic Interest Group of
Regional Financial Companies
Rue de Stassart 32, 1050 Brussels, Belgium

Tel. (+32) 2-5481132
Fax (+32) 2-5115909
E-mail d.caron@europemail.com
URL www.eurodev.be
Sec.-Gen. Danielle Caron
Sec. C. Smissaert

EFA

European Federation of Asthma and Allergy Associations
Europäische Föderation der Asthma- und Allergievereine
Avenue Louise 327, 1050 Brussels, Belgium
Tel. (+32) 2-6469945
Fax (+32) 2-6464116
E-mail efaoffice@skynet.be
URL www.efanet.org
Pres. Svein-Erik Myrseth
Sec. Arne Heimdal
Exec. Officer Susanna Palkonen

EFAD

European Federation of the Associations of Dietitians
Föderation der Diätassistenten-Verbände
Square Vergote 43, 1030 Brussels, Belgium
Tel. (+32) 4-78482048
Fax (+32) 2-3808360
E-mail Secretariat@efad.org
URL www.efad.org
Pres. Irene Mackay
Secretariat Judith Liddell

EFAH / FEAP

European Forum for the Arts and Heritage
Forum Europeen pour les Arts et le Patrimoine
Rue des Sciences 10, 1060 Brussels, Belgium
Tel. (+32) 2-5344002
Fax (+32) 2-5341150
E-mail efah@efah.org
URL www.efah.org
Pres. Y. Raj Isar
Sec.-Gen. Ilona Kish

EFC

European Foundation Centre
Europäisches Stiftungszentrum
Rue de la Concorde 51, 1050 Brussels, Belgium

Tel. (+32) 2-5128938
Fax (+32) 2-5123265
E-mail efc@efc.be
URL www.efc.be
Chief Exec. John Richardson

EFCT / FEVC

European Federation of Conference Towns
Europäische Föderation der Kongressstädte
Avenue Louise 287, 2nd Floor, 1040 Brussels, Belgium
Tel. (+32) 2-6432044
Fax (+32) 2-6452671
E-mail secretariate@efct.com
URL www.efct.com
Pres. Henri Céran

EFCW

Eurochild AISBL
Rue de la Concorde 53, 1050 Brussels, Belgium
Tel. (+32) 2-5117083
Fax (+32) 2-5117298
E-mail info@eurochild.org
URL www.eurochild.org
Pres. Catriona Williams
Sec.-Gen. Heidi De Pauw

EFECOT

European Federation for the Education of Children of Occupational Travellers
Rue de la Limite 6, 1210 Brussels, Belgium
Tel. (+32) 2-2274060
Fax (+32) 2-2274069
E-mail efecot@efecot.net
URL www.efecot.net
Pres. De Zutter
Dir Ludo Knaepkens

EFGP

European Federation of Green Parties
Europäische Föderation von Grüne Parteien
Rue Wiertz, PHS 2C85, 1047 Brussels, Belgium
Tel. (+32) 2-2845135
Fax (+32) 2-2849135
E-mail efgp@europarl.eu.int
URL www.europeangreens.org
Sec.-Gen. Arnold Cassola

EFIL

European Federation for Intercultural Learning

Avenue Emile Max 150, 1030 Brussels, Belgium
Tel. (+32) 2-5145250
Fax (+32) 2-5142929
E-mail info@efil.be
URL www.efil.afs.org
Pres. H. Garcea
Sec.-Gen. Elisabeth Hardt
Sec. Martha Eiriksdottir

EFRP

European Federation for Retirement Provision

Rue Royale 97, 1000 Brussels, Belgium
Tel. (+32) 2-2891414
Fax (+32) 2-2891415
E-mail efrp@efrp.org
URL www.efrp.org
Pres. Alan Pickering
Sec.-Gen. Chris Verhaegen

EFTA

European Family Therapy Association
Europäischer Familientherapieverband

Rue du Bailli 9, 1000 Brussels, Belgium
Tel. (+32) 2-6464367
Fax (+32) 2-6464367
E-mail melkaim@ulb.ac.be
URL www.efta-europeanfamilytherapy.com
Pres. Arlene Vetere
Gen.-Sec. Annette Kreuz-Smolinski

EFTA

European Fair Trade Association

Rue de la Charité 43, 1210 Brussels, Belgium
Tel. (+32) 2-2173617
Fax (+32) 2-2173798
E-mail osterhaus at fairtrade-advocacy.org
URL www.eftafairtrade.org
Advocacy Officer Mariano Iossa

EGLEI / GEILE

European Group for Local Employment Initiatives
Europäischer Zusammenschluss zur Förderung Lokalen Beschäftigungsinitiativen

Square Ambiorix 45, 1040 Brussels, Belgium

Tel. (+32) 2-2310687
Fax (+32) 2-2800284
E-mail eglei@eglei.be
Pres. H. Le Marois
Contact Catherine Niarchos-Lentz

EGMF

European Garden Machinery Industry Federation
Europäischen Verbandes der Motorgartengeräteindustrie

Boulevard A. Reyers 80, 1030 Brussels, Belgium
Tel. (+32) 2-7068253
Fax (+32) 2-7068230
E-mail guy.vandoorslaer@orgalime.org
Pres. Dr. Nikolas Stihl
Sec.-Gen. Guy Van Doorslaer

EHN

European Heart Network
Europäisches Netzwerk Herz

Rue Montoyer 31, 1000 Brussels, Belgium
Tel. (+32) 2-5129174
Fax (+32) 2-5033525
E-mail ehn@skynet.be
URL www.ehnheart.org
Pres. Susanne Volqvartz
Sec.-Gen. Staffan Josephson
Dir Susanne Logstrup

EIA

European Information Association

Central Library, St Peter's Square, Manchester M2 5PD, United Kingdom
Tel. (+44 161) 228-3691
Fax (+44 161) 236-6547
E-mail eia@libraries.manchester.gov.uk
URL www.eia.org.uk
Pres. Ian Thomson
Man. Catherine Webb

EIB

European Information Bureau

9 Bower Street, Stoke on Trent ST1 3BH, United Kingdom
Tel. (+44 1782) 266712
E-mail euro_bureau@hotmail.com
Contact John Huff
Contact Zenam Khan

EIRA / ARIE

European Industrial Regions Association
Vereinigung Europäischer Industrieregionen
Rue Joseph II 36–38, 1000 Brussels, Belgium
Tel. (+32) 2-2309107
Fax (+32) 2-2302712
E-mail secretariat@eira.org
URL www.eira.org
Pres. Cllr Roger Stone

EISA

European Initiative for Sustainable
Development in Agriculture
Europäische Initiative für Nachaltige
Entwicklung in der Landwirtschaft
C/o FNL e.V., Konstantinstrasse 90, 53179
Bonn, Germany
Tel. (+49 228) 979-930
Fax (+49 228) 979-9340
E-mail info@fnl.de
URL www.sustainable-agriculture.org
Chair. Heinrich Kemper
Sec.-Gen. Susanne Witsch
Man. Dir Dr Jürgen Fröhling

ELEC / LECE

European League for Economic
Co-operation
Ligue Européenne de Coopération
Economique
Place du Champ de Mars 2 # 8, 1050 Brussels,
Belgium
Tel. (+32) 2-2198250
Fax (+32) 2-2190663
E-mail elec@easynet.be
URL www.elec.easynet.be
Pres. Ferdinand Chaffart
Sec.-Gen. Jean-Claude Koeune

ELNI

Environmental Law Network International
C/o Öko-Institut e.V., Rheinstr. 95, 64295
Darmstadt, Germany
Tel. (+49 6151) 819131
Fax (+49 6151) 819133
E-mail h.unruh@oeko.de
URL www.oeko.de/elni
Co-ordinator Ralf Juelich

ELSA

European Law Students' Association
Boulevard Général Jacques 239, 1050 Brussel,
Belgium
Tel. (+32) 2-6462626
Fax (+32) 2-6462923
E-mail elsa@brutele.be
URL www.elsa.org
Pres. Ruta Zarnauskaite
Sec.-Gen. Li Axrup

EM

European Movement
Europäische Bewegung
7 Holyrood Street, London SE1 2EL,
United Kingdom
Tel. (+44 20) 7940-5252
Fax (+44 20) 7940-5253
E-mail info@euromove.org.uk
URL www.euromove.org.uk
Pres. Claude Moraes
Information Officer Isabel Obert

EMMAÜS International

183 bis Rue Vaillant Couturier, P.O. Box 91,
94143 Alfortville Cedex, France
Tel. (+33) 1-48-93-29-50
Fax (+33) 1-43-53-19-26
E-mail contact@emmaus-international.org
URL www.emmaus-international.org
Pres. Renzo Fior
Sec.-Gen. Jean-Marie Viennet
Exec. Dir Alain Fontaine

EMSP / SCLEROSE EN PLAQUES

European Multiple Sclerosis Platform
Plateforme européenne sur la sclérose en
plaques
Avenue Plasky 173 Bte 11, 1030 Brussels,
Belgium
Tel. (+32) 2-3058012
Fax (+32) 2-3058011
E-mail ms-in-europe@pandora.be
URL www.ms-in-europe.org
Pres. Peter Kauffeldt
Sec.-Gen. Christoph Thalheim

ENAE

European Network on Ageing and Ethnicity
Causewayside House, 160 Causewayside,
Edinburgh EH9 1PR, United Kingdom

Tel. (+44 845) 833-0200
Fax (+44 845) 833-0759
E-mail enquiries@acscott.org.uk
URL www.ageconcernscotland.org.uk
Dir Maureen O'Neill

ENAR

European Network Against Racism
Réseau Européen Contre le Racisme
Europäischen Netzgegen Rassismus
Rue de la Charité 43, 1210 Brussels, Belgium
Tel. (+32) 2-2293570
Fax (+32) 2-2293570
E-mail info@enar-eu.org
URL www.enar-eu.org
Chair. Bashy Quraishy
Sec.-Gen. Vera Egenberger
Information Officer Anoush der Boghossian

ENOPF

European Network of One-Parent Families
C/o Gingerbread NI, 169 University Street,
    Belfast BT7 1HR, United Kingdom
Tel. (+44 28) 9023-1417
Fax (+44 28) 9024-0740
E-mail enquiries@gingerbreadni.org
URL www.gingerbreadni.org
Dir Marie Cavanagh

ENSP

European Network for Smoking Prevention
Chaussée d'Ixelles 144, 1050 Brussels,
    Belgium
Tel. (+32) 2-2306515
Fax (+32) 2-2307507
E-mail info@ensp.org
URL www.ensp.org
Pres. Dr Prins Trudy
Events and Information Officer Sophie
    Vandamme

ENU

European Network of the Unemployed
Reseau Europeen des Sans Emploi
Araby House, 8 North Richmond Street, Dublin
    1, Ireland
Tel. (+353 1) 8560088
Fax (+353 1) 8560090
E-mail inou@iol.ie
URL www.multimania.com/enu/
Pres. Karl Kunnas

EOEF / FEED

European Offender Employment Forum
C/o Inclusion, Camelford House, 87–89 Albert
    Embankment, London SE1 7TP,
    United Kingdom
Tel. (+44 20) 7582-7221
Fax (+44 20) 7582-6391
E-mail mike.stewart@cesi.org.uk
URL www.eoef.org
Pres. C. Coppes
Sec.-Gen. De Jong
Dir Mike Stewart

EORTC

**European Organisation for Research and
    Treatment of Cancer**
Avenue Mounierlaan, 83/11, 1200 Brussels,
    Belgium
Tel. (+32) 2-7741611
Fax (+32) 2-7723545
E-mail eortc@eortc.be
URL www.eortc.be
Pres. Alexander M.M. Eggermont
Sec.-Gen. Pierre Fumoleau
Dir-Gen. Françoise Meunier

EPA

European Parents Association
**L'Association Européenne des Parents
    d'Elèves**
Europäischer Elternverband
Rue de Trèves 49 bte 8, 1040 Brussels,
    Belgium
Tel. (+32) 2-2806340
Fax (+32) 2-2806338
E-mail epa@medineurope.com
URL www.epa-parents.org
Pres. Karin Schutz
Sec.-Gen. Francis Borg

EPE

European Partners for the Environment
**Partenaires Européens pour
    l'Environnement**
Europäische Partner für die Umwelt
Avenue de la Toison d'Or 67 (4th floor), 1060
    Brussels, Belgium
Tel. (+32) 2-7711534
Fax (+32) 2-5394815
E-mail info@epe.be
URL www.epe.be

Pres. Bart-Jan Krouwel
Exec. Dir Raymond van Ermen

ERDI

Consortium of European Research & Development Institutes for Adult Education

Konsortium der Europäischen Forschungs- und Entwicklungsinstitute für Erwachsenenbildung

Kardinaal Mercierplein 1, 2800 Mechelen, Belgium
Tel. (+32) 15-446500
Fax (+32) 15-446501
E-mail annemie.decrick@vocb.be
URL www.erdi.info
Pres. Dr Vida Mohorcic-Spolar
Sec.-Gen. Susanne Lattke

ESAN

European Social Action Network

Réseau Européen d'Action Sociale

Europäisches Netzwerk für Soziales Handeln

60 Rue Sainte Catherine, 59000 Lille, France
Tel. (+33) 3-20-55-10-99
Fax (+33) 3-20-55-10-99
E-mail info@esan.org
URL www.esan.org
Pres. Léon Dujardin

ESCRS

European Society of Cataract and Refractive Surgeons

Europäische Gesellschaft von Katarakt- und Refraktionsarzten

Temple House, Temple Road, Blackrock, Co. Dublin, Ireland
Tel. (+353 1) 2091100
Fax (+353 1) 2091112
E-mail escrs@agenda-comm.ie
URL www.escrs.org
Pres. Marie Jose Tassignon
Sec. Josep Guell

ESED

European Society for Environment and Development

Europäische Gesellschaft für Umwelt und Entwicklung

Rue de Meuse 47, 5541 Hastières-par-delà, Belgium

Tel. (+32) 82-644580
Fax (+32) 82-644511
E-mail m.dubrulle@worldonline.be
Pres. Mark Dubrulle
Sec.-Gen. Dr Steven Halls

ESF

European Science Foundation

Europäische Wissenschaftsstiftung

1 Quai Lezay-Marnesia, PO Box 90015, 67080 Strasbourg Cedex, France
Tel. (+33) 3-88-76-71-00
Fax (+33) 3-88-37-05-32
E-mail esf@esf.org
URL www.esf.org
Pres. Reiner van Duinen
Sec.-Gen. Prof. Enric Banda
Communication and Information Unit Head Claus Nowotny

ESIB

National Unions of Students in Europe

Avenue de la Toison d'Or 17A (5ème Etage), Box 80, 1050 Brussels, Belgium
Tel. (+32) 2-5022362
Fax (+32) 2-5117806
E-mail secretariat@esib.org
URL www.esib.org
Chair. Vanja Ivosevic
Sec.-Gen. Thomas Nilsson

ESIP

European Social Insurance Partners

Maison Européenne de la Protection Sociale

Rue d'Arlon 50, 1000 Brussels, Belgium
Tel. (+32) 2-2820560
Fax (+32) 2-2307773
E-mail esip@esip.org
URL www.esip.org
Dir Dr Franz Terwey

ETS

European Tissue Symposium

Avenue des Arts 44, 1040 Brussels, Belgium
Tel. (+32) 2-5495230
Fax (+32) 2-5021598
E-mail info@europeantissue.com
URL www.europeantissue.com
Pres. P. Forlin
Legal Advisor Peter Bogaert

ETSC

European Transport Safety Council

Rue du Cornet 34, 1040 Brussels, Belgium
Tel. (+32) 2-2304106
Fax (+32) 2-2304215
E-mail information@etsc.be
URL www.etsc.be
Chair. Prof. Herman De Croo
Exec. Dir Jörg Beckmann
Information Officer Franziska Achterberg

ETWELFARE

European Round Table of Charitable Social Welfare Associations

Rue de Pascale 4–6, 1040 Brussels, Belgium
Tel. (+32) 2-2304500
Fax (+32) 2-2305704
E-mail euvertretung@bag-wohlfahrt.de
URL www.etwelfare.com
Pres. Bernd Otto Kuper
Sec.-Gen. Geroms

EUD

European Union of the Deaf

Coupure Rechts 314, 9000 Gent, Belgium
Tel. (+32) 9-2250833
Fax (+32) 9-2250834
E-mail info@eudnet.org
URL www.eudnet.org
Pres. Helga Stevens
Administrator Karin van Puyenbroek

EUFAMI

European Federation of Associations of Families of Mentally Ill People

Diestsevest 100, 3000 Leuven, Belgium
Tel. (+32) 16-745040
Fax (+32) 16-745049
E-mail info@eufami.org
URL www.eufami.org
Pres. Inger Nilsson
Sec. Reina van Mourik

EUFORES

European Forum for Renewable Energy Sources

Europäisches Forum für Erneuerbare Energiequellen

Rue du Trône 26, 1000 Brussels, Belgium
Tel. (+32) 2-5461948
Fax (+32) 2-5461947
E-mail eufores@eufores.org
URL www.eufores.org
Pres. Mechtild Rothe
Sec.-Gen. Juan Fraga
Dir Marc Timmer

EUFORIC

Europe's Forum on International Co-operation

Wycker Grach Straat 38, 6221 CX Maastricht, Netherlands
Tel. (+31) 433285180
Fax (+31) 433285185
E-mail info@euforic.org
URL www.euforic.org
Pres. Ramesh Jaura
Exec. Asst Yvette Petit

EUJS

European Union of Jewish Students

Europäische Union Judischer Studenten

Avenue Antoine Depage 3, 1000 Brussels, Belgium
Tel. (+32) 2-6477279
Fax (+32) 2-6482431
E-mail info@eujs.org
URL www.eujs.org
Chair. Lionel Schreiber
Exec. Dir Marta Mucznik

EURACOM

Action for Mining Communities

Fédération Européenne des Personnes Âgées

9 Regent Street, Barnsley S70 2EG, United Kingdom
Tel. (+44 12) 2620-0768
Fax (+44 12) 2629-6532
E-mail martincantor@ccc-alliance.demon.co.uk
Pres. Bill Flanagen
Contact Martin Cantor

EURAG

European Federation of Older Persons

Wielandgasse 9, 8010 Graz, Austria

Tel. (+43 316) 814608
Fax (+43 316) 814608
E-mail office@eurag-europe.org
URL www.eurag-europe.org
Pres. Edmée Mangers-Anen
Sec.-Gen Dr Ulla Herfort-Woerndle
International Cooperation Officer Gertraud
　Daye

EUROCASO

**European Council of Aids Services
Organisations**

Rue Pierre-Fatio 17, 1204 Genève, Switzerland
Tel. (+41) 22-700-15-00
Fax (+41) 22-700-15-47
E-mail info@groupesida.ch
URL www.groupesida.ch

Dir David Perrot
Regional Secretariat Florian Hubner

EURODAD

**European Network on Debt and
Development**

Avenue Louise 176, 8th Floor, 1050 Brussels,
　Belgium
Tel. (+32) 2-5439064
Fax (+32) 2-5440559
E-mail info@eurodad.org
URL www.eurodad.org

Chair. Ted van Hees
Policy and Communications Officer Gail
　Hurley

EUROGROUP FOR ANIMAL WELFARE

Eurogruppe für die Tiergesundheit

Rue des Patriotes 6, 1000 Brussels, Belgium
Tel. (+32) 2-7400820
Fax (+32) 2-7400829
E-mail info@eurogroupanimalwelfare.org
URL www.eurogroupanimalwelfare.org

Dir Sonja van Tichelen
Communication Officer Véronique Schmit

EURONATUR

European Nature Heritage Fund
Stiftung Europäisches Naturerbe

Konstanzer Strasse 22, 78315 Radolfzell,
　Germany
Tel. (+49 7732) 92720
Fax (+49 7732) 927222
E-mail info@euronatur.org
URL www.euronatur.org

Pres. Claus-Peter Hutter
Exec. Dir Gabriel Schwaderer

EURO-ORIENTATION

**European Association for Orientation,
Vocational Guidance and Educational and
Professional Information**

Kortrijkstraat 343, 8870 Izegem, Belgium
Tel. (+32) 51-301362
Fax (+32) 51-301362
E-mail gerard.wulleman@clb-net.be

Pres. Gerard Wulleman
Sec.-Gen. R. Stufkens

EUROSTEP

**European Solidarity Towards Equal
Participation of People**
**Europäische Solidarität für eine Gleiche
Beteiligung der Völker**

Rue Stévin 115, 1000 Brussels, Belgium
Tel. (+32) 2-2311659
Fax (+32) 2-2303780
E-mail admin@eurostep.org
URL www.eurostep.org

Dir Simon Stocker

EUROTEAM

**European Action Committee for Public
Transport**
**Europäischer Aktionsausschuss für den
Öffentlichen Verkehr**

Rue Ste Marie 6, 1080 Brussels, Belgium
Tel. (+32) 2-6636627
Fax (+32) 2-6601072
E-mail euroteam@uitp.com

Dir Brigitte Ollier

EVC / CEV

European Volunteer Centre
Centre Européen du Volontariat
Europäisches Freiwilligenzentrum

Rue de la Science 10, 1000 Brussels, Belgium
Tel. (+32) 2-5117501
Fax (+32) 2-5145989
E-mail cev@cev.be
URL www.cev.be

Pres. Christopher Spence

EWL / LEF / EFL
European Women's Lobby
Lobby européen des femmes
Europäische Frauen Lobby
Rue Hydraulique 18, 1210 Brussels, Belgium
Tel. (+32) 2-2179020
Fax (+32) 2-2198451
E-mail ewl@womenlobby.org
URL www.womenlobby.org
Pres. Lydia La Rivière-Zijdel
Sec.-Gen. Mary McPhail
Communication Co-ordinator Clarisse Delorme

EWMD
**European Women's Management
Development Network**
Avenue Louise 149, 1050 Brussels, Belgium
Tel. (+41) 76-3892124
Fax (+41) 41-7549955
E-mail international-office@ewmd.org
URL www.ewmd.org
Joint Pres. Martine De Witte
Joint Pres. Gabriele Hantschel

EYCE
Ecumenical Youth Council in Europe
Ökumenischer Jugdenrat in Europa
Rue du Champs de Mars 5, 1050 Brussels,
Belgium
Tel. (+32) 2-5106187
Fax (+32) 2-5106172
E-mail info@eyce.org
URL www.eyce.org
Chair. Dirk Thesenvitz
Sec.-Gen. Daniel Muller

EYE Network
European Youth Exchange Network
Czerningasse 9, 1020 Vienna, Austria
Tel. (+43 1) 9143671
Fax (+43 1) 9143671
E-mail eyenetwork@eyenetwork.org
URL www.eyenetwork.org
Pres. Damon Bock
Sec.-Gen. Jose De Brito

FEANTSA
**European Federation of National
Organisations Working with the Homeless**

**Europäischer Föderation Nationaler mit
Obdachlosen Arbeitenden Organisationen**
Chaussée de Louvain 194, 1210 Brussels,
Belgium
Tel. (+32) 2-5386669
Fax (+32) 2-5394174
E-mail office@feantsa.org
URL www.feantsa.org
Pres. Donal McManus
Communication Officer Dearbhal Murphy

FEM
**Female Europeans of Medium and Small
Enterprises**
**Femmes Européennes des Moyennes et
Petites Entreprises**
**Frauen Europäischer Mittel- und
Kleinbetriebe**
Rue Jacques de Lalaing 4, 1040 Brussels,
Belgium
Tel. (+32) 2-2850714
Fax (+32) 2-2307599
E-mail d.rabetge@ueapme.com
URL www.fem-pme.com
Pres. Miriam Arnau
Secretariat Doris Rabetge

FEMA
**Federation of European Motorcyclists
Associations**
Fédération Française des Motards en Colère
Rue de Champs 62, 1040 Brussels, Belgium
Tel. (+32) 2-7369047
Fax (+32) 2-7369401
E-mail fema@chello.be
URL www.fema.kaalium.com
Pres. Kees Meijer
Sec.-Gen. Antonio Perlot
Admin. Officer Christina Gesios

FEPEDA
**European Federation of Parents of Hearing
Impaired Children**
**Fédération Européenne des Parents
d'Enfants Déficients Auditifs**
**Europäischer Verband der Eltern
hörgeschädigter Kinder**
C/o DHB, Kungsgatan 10, 702 11 Örebro,
Sweden

Tel. (+46 19) 17-08-30
Fax (+46 10) 44-99
E-mail fepeda@dhb.se
URL www.fepeda.net
Pres. Lena Fernström
Secretariat Birgitta Rudin

FERN
EU Forest Programme of the World Rainforest Movement
Avenue des Celtes 20, 1040 Brussels, Belgium
Tel. (+32) 2-7422436
Fax (+32) 2-7368054
E-mail info@fern.org
URL www.fern.org
Trade Policy Officer Chantal Marijnissen

FERPA
European Federation of Retired and Older People
Fédération européenne des retraités et des personnes âgées
Europäische Verband der Rentnerinnen und Rentner und älteren Menschen
Boulevard du Roi Albert II 5, 1210 Brussels, Belgium
Tel. (+32) 2-2240442
Fax (+32) 2-2240567
E-mail jmontiel@etuc.org
URL www.ferpa.info
Pres. Josette Neunez
Sec.-Gen. Luigina De Santis

FOEE / CEAT
Friends of the Earth Europe
Rue Blanche 15, 1060 Brussels, Belgium
Tel. (+32) 2-5420180
Fax (+32) 2-5375596
E-mail info@foeeurope.org
URL www.foeeurope.org
Pres. Vojtech Kotecky
Dir Martin Rocholl

FOOD BANKS / BANQUES ALIMENTAIRES
European Federation of Food Banks
Fédération Européenne des Banques Alimentaries
53 Avenue du général Leclerc, 92340 Bourg-la-Reine, France

Tel. (+33) 1-45-36-05-45
Fax (+33) 1-45-36-05-52
E-mail feba@eurofoodbank.org
URL www.eurofoodbank.org
Sec.-Gen. C. Vian

FRERES DES HOMMES
Rue de Londres 18, 1050 Brussels, Belgium
Tel. (+32) 2-5129794
Fax (+32) 2-5114761
E-mail fdhbel@skynet.be
URL www.freresdeshommes.org
Contact Cecilia Diaz

FUEN / UFCE / FUEV
Federal Union of European Nationalities
Union Fédéraliste des Communautés Ethniques Européennes
Föderalistische Union Europäischer Volksgruppen
Schiffbrücke 41, 24939 Flensburg, Germany
Tel. (+49 461) 12855
Fax (+49 461) 180709
E-mail info@fuen.org
URL www.fuen.org
Pres. Romedi Arquint
Sec.-Gen. Frank Nickelsen

FYEG
Federation of Young European Greens
C/o European Parliament, ASP 08G138 Rue Wiertz, 1047 Brussels, Belgium
Tel. (+32) 2-2842440
Fax (+32) 2-2849273
E-mail fyeg@europarl.eu.int
URL www.fyeg.org
Pres. Claudia Sadean
Communication Officer Markus Drake

GAIN
Graphic Arts Intelligence Network
Via Augusta 317, 08017 Barcelona, Spain
Tel. (+34) 93-2046563
Fax (+34) 93-2805727
E-mail general@rccsa.org
URL www.gain-europe.com
Pres. Herr Janssen Roelof
Sec.-Gen. Ricard Casals

GLOBEEU

Global Legislators Organisation for a Balanced Environment, European Union

Globale Gesetzgeberorganisation für eine Ausgewogene Umwelt, Europäische Union

Rue Boduagnot 13, 1000 Brussels, Belgium
Tel. (+32) 2-2306589
Fax (+32) 2-2309530
E-mail e.globe@innet.be
Pres. A. Mep

GREENPEACE

Greenpeace European Unit

Rue Belliard 199, 1030 Brussels, Belgium
Tel. (+32) 2-2741900
Fax (+32) 2-2741910
E-mail european.unit@diala.greenpeace.org
URL http://eu.greenpeace.org
Dir Jorgo Riss

HANDICAP INTERNATIONAL

Handicap International Belgium

Rue de Spa 67, 1000 Brussels, Belgium
Tel. (+32) 2-2801601
Fax (+32) 2-2306030
E-mail info@handicap.be
URL www.handicapinternational.be
Dir-Gen. Angelo Simonazzi

HAR / RQH

Humanitarian Affairs Review

La Maison de l'Europe at the Bibliothèque Solvay, Parc Léopold, Rue Belliard 137, 1040 Brussels, Belgium
Tel. (+32) 2-7387592
Fax (+32) 2-7391592
E-mail info@humanitarian-review.org
URL www.humanitarian-review.org
Editorial Co-ordinator Julie Bolle

HE

Habitants d'Europe

Square Albert 1er 32, 1070 Brussels, Belgium
Tel. (+32) 2-5229869
Fax (+32) 2-5241816
E-mail syndicatdeslocataires@swing.be
Pres. J. Garcia

HRW

Human Rights Watch

Rue van Campenhout 15, 1000 Brussels, Belgium
Tel. (+32) 2-7322009
Fax (+32) 2-7320471
E-mail hrwatcheu@skynet.be
URL www.hrw.org
Exec. Dir Kenneth Roth
Office and Press Co-ordinator Vanessa Saenen

ICDA

International Coalition for Development Action

Rue Stévin 115, 1000 Brussels, Belgium
Tel. (+32) 2-2300430
Fax (+32) 2-2305237
E-mail icda@icda.be
URL www.icda.be
Chair. Janice Goodson Foerde
Secretariat Emmanuel K. Bensah

IEEP

Institute for European Environmental Policy

Institut für Europäische Umweltpolitik

Avenue des Gaulois 18, 1040 Brussels, Belgium
Tel. (+32) 2-7387482
Fax (+32) 2-7324004
E-mail central@ieeplondon.org.uk
URL www.ieep.org.uk
Dir David Baldock
Secretary Jonathan Taylor

IFAW

International Fund for Animal Welfare

Rue Boduognat 13, 1000 Brussels, Belgium
Tel. (+32) 2-2309717
Fax (+32) 2-2310402
E-mail generaleu@ifaw.org
URL www.ifaw.org
Pres. Fred O'Regan
Contact Bridget Jones

IFHOH-EUROPE

European Region of the International Federation of Hard of Hearing People

Drenikova 24, 1000 Ljubljana, Slovenia
Tel. (+47 611) 74880
E-mail info@ifhoh.org
URL www.ifhoh.org/members.htm

Pres. Marcel Bobeldijk
Sec.-Gen. Darja Holec

IFIAS

Institute for International Assistance and Solidarity

Avenue Jan Stobbaerts 81A, 1030 Brussels, Belgium
Tel. (+32) 2-2157908
Fax (+32) 2-2456297
E-mail ifias@ifias.net
URL www.ifias.net
Pres. Gerd Greune
Dir Susanne Drake

IFIEC EUROPE

International Federation of Industrial Energy Consumers – European Section

Internationale Föderation Industrieller Energiekonsumenten – Sektion Europa

Chaussée de Charleroi 119, 1060 Brussels, Belgium
Tel. (+32) 2-5420687
Fax (+32) 2-5420692
E-mail ifieceurope@ifieceurope.org
URL www.ifiec-europe.be
Pres. Peter Claes
Sec.-Gen. Roger Goffin

IPPF

European Network of the International Planned Parenthood Federation

Rue Royale 146, 1000 Brussels, Belgium
Tel. (+32) 2-2500950
Fax (+32) 2-2500969
E-mail info@ippfen.org
URL www.ippfen.org
Pres. Carine Vrancken

IRIS

European Network on Women's Training

Rue Capouillet 25, 1060 Brussels, Belgium
Tel. (+32) 2-5349085
Fax (+32) 2-5348134
E-mail mail@iris-asbl.org
Dir Rebecca Franceskides

ISCA-EU

International Save the Children Alliance – European Union

Montoyer 39, 1000 Brussels, Belgium

Tel. (+32) 2-5127851
Fax (+32) 2-5134903
E-mail savechildbru@skynet.be
Pres. Burkhard Gnärig

IYCS-IMCS / JECI-MIEC

International Young Catholic Students – European Co-ordination – International Movement of Catholic Students

Jeunesse Etudiante Catholique Internationale – Coordination Internationale – Mouvement Internationale d'Etudiants Catholiques

Rue du Marteau 19, 1000 Brussels, Belgium
Tel. (+32) 2-2185437
Fax (+32) 2-2185437
E-mail jecimiec@skynet.be
URL www.users.skynet.be/jecimiec/index.htm
Admin. Sec. Michel van Damme

JEF

Young European Federalists

Jeunes Européens Fédéralistes

Junge Europäische Föderalisten

Chaussée de Wavre 214D, 1050 Brussels, Belgium
Tel. (+32) 2-5120053
Fax (+32) 2-5126673
E-mail info@jef-europe.net
URL www.jef-europe.net
Pres. Jon Worth
Sec.-Gen. Joan Marc Simon

JME

Jeunesses Musicales Europe

Palais des Beaux Arts, Rue Royale 10, 1000 Brussels, Belgium
Tel. (+32) 2-5139774
Fax (+32) 2-5144755
E-mail mail@jmi.net
URL www.jmi.net
Pres. Pierre A. Goulet
Sec.-Gen. Dag Franzén
Communications Officer Sophie Putcuyps

JRS

Jesuit Refugee Service Europe

Jesuitischer Fluchtlingsdienst – Europa

Rue du Progrès 333, first floor, 1030 Brussels, Belgium

Tel. (+32) 2-2503220
Fax (+32) 2-2503229
E-mail europe@jrs.net
URL www.jrseurope.org
Regional Dir Jan Stuyt

LIBER
European Research Libraries Organization
Ligue des Bibliothèques Européennes de Recherche
Royal Library, PO Box 2149, 1016
  Copenhagen K, Denmark
Tel. (+45) 33-47-43-01
Fax (+45) 33-32-98-46
E-mail ekn@kb.dk
URL www.kb.dk/liber/
Pres. Erland Kolding Nielsen
Sec. Peter K. Fox

MHE-SME
European Regional Council of the World Federation for Mental Health
Santé Mentale Europe
Blvd Clovis 7, 1000 Brussels, Belgium
Tel. (+32) 2-2800468
Fax (+32) 2-2801604
E-mail info@mhe-sme.org
URL www.mhe-sme.org
Pres. Claude Deutsch
Sec. Pino Pini
Exec. Dir Pascale van den Heede

MI
Mobility International
Boulevard Baudouin 18, 1000 Brussels,
  Belgium
Tel. (+32) 2-2015608
Fax (+32) 2-2015763
E-mail mobint@arcadis.be
Pres. Wolfgang Tigges
Dir Josyane Pierre

NIHIL
European Sustainable Cities & Towns Campaign
Europäische Kampagne zukunftsbeständiger Städte und Gemeinden
Rue de Trèves 49–51 box 3, 1040 Brussels,
  Belgium

Tel. (+32) 2-2305351
Fax (+32) 2-2308850
E-mail campaign.office@skynet.be
URL www.sustainable-cities.org
Campaign Co-ordinator Anthony Payne

NORMAPME
European Office of Crafts, Trades and Small and Medium-Sized Enterprises for Standardisation
Bureau européen de l'artisanat, et des petites et moyennes entreprises pour la Normalisation
Europäisches Büro des Handwerks und der Klein- und Mittelbetriebe für die Normung
Rue Jacques de Lalaing 4, 1040 Brussels,
  Belgium
Tel. (+32) 2-2820530
Fax (+32) 2-2820535
E-mail info@normapme.com
URL www.normapme.com
Pres. Müller Hans Werner
Dir Loucas Gourtsoyannis

OBESSU
Organizing Bureau of European Schools Student Unions
Rue Borrens 32, 1050 Brussels, Belgium
Tel. (+32) 2-6472390
Fax (+32) 2-6472390
E-mail obessu@obessu.org
URL www.obessu.org
Sec.-Gen. Jovana Bazerkovska

OCFE
Common Office for European Training
Office Commun de Formation Européenne pour la Jeunesse
Gemeinsames Büro für Europäische Bildung
Rue Petite Aise 13, 6061 Charleroi, Belgium
Tel. (+32) 71-414839
Fax (+32) 71-414739
E-mail ocfej@gate71.be
URL www.ocfe.org
Sec.-Gen. Zonta Ivanka

OSI
Open Society Institute
Rue des Minimes 26, 1000 Brussels, Belgium

Tel. (+32) 2-5054646
Fax (+32) 2-5024646
E-mail osi@osi-brussels.be
URL www.osi-az.org/network.shtml
Dir Mabel Wisse Smit
Pres. Aryeh Neier

PAEAC

European Institute for Research on Mediterranean and Euro-Arab Cooperation
Institut Européen de Recherche sur la Coopération Méditerranéenne et Euro-Arabe
Avenue Louise 287, 1050 Brussels, Belgium
Tel. (+32) 2-2311300
Fax (+32) 2-2310646
E-mail info@medea.be
URL www.medea.be
Pres. Charles Ferdinand Nothomb
Sec.-Gen. J.P. Robert Vandenbegine
Dir Johan Gezels

PEACE / PAIX / FRIEDEN

Foundation for Peace
Stiftung für den Frieden
C/ Casp 31-2-1a A, 08010 Barcelona, Spain
Tel. (+34) 93-305129
Fax (+34) 93-017562
E-mail info@fundacioperlapau.org
URL www.fundacioperlapau.org
Pres. Alfons Banda
Dir Jordi Armadans

POETRY / POESIE

European Association for the Promotion of Poetry
Vrijdagmarkt 36, 9000 Gent, Belgium
Tel. (+32) 9-2252225
Fax (+32) 9-2259054
E-mail info@poeziecentrum
URL www.poeziecentrum.be
Chair. Willy Tibergien

QCEA

Quaker Council for European Affairs
Quakerrat für Europäische Angelegenheiten
Square Ambiorix 50, 1040 Brussels, Belgium

Tel. (+32) 2-2304935
Fax (+32) 2-2306370
E-mail info@qcea.org
URL www.quaker.org/qcea
Office Manager Xavier Verhaeghe

RC / EU OFFICE

Red Cross / EU Office
Bureau Croix-Rouge/UE
Rue Belliard 65, PO Box 7, 1000 Brussels, Belgium
Tel. (+32) 2-2350680
Fax (+32) 2-2305464
E-mail infoboard@redcross-eu.net
URL www.redcross-eu.net
Dir Luc Henskens

SEFI

European Society for Engineering Education
Société européenne pour la Formation des Ingénieurs
Europäische Gesellschaft für Ingenieurausbildung
Rue de Stassart 119, 1050 Brussels, Belgium
Tel. (+32) 2-5023609
Fax (+32) 2-5029611
E-mail info@sefi.be
E-mail francoise.come@sefi.be
URL www.sefi.be
Pres. Dr Alfredo Soeiro
Sec.-Gen. Françoise Côme

SOCIAL

Platform of European Social NGOs
Square de Meeûs 18, 1050 Brussels, Belgium
Tel. (+32) 2-5113714
Fax (+32) 2-511909
E-mail platform@socialplatform.org
URL www.socialplatform.org
Dir Simon Wilson
Administrator Pearly Raynal

SOLIDAR

Rue du Commerce 22, 1000 Brussels, Belgium
Tel. (+32) 2-5001020
Fax (+32) 2-5001030
E-mail solidar@skynet.be
URL www.solidar.org
Pres. Pierre Schori
Sec.-Gen. Giampiero Alhadeff

T & E

European Federation for Transport and Environment
Europäischer Verband für Verkehr und Umwelt
Rue de la Pépinière 1, 1000 Brussels, Belgium
Tel. (+32) 2-5029909
Fax (+32) 2-5029908
E-mail info@t-e.nu
URL www.t-e.nu
Pres. Sonja Klingberg
Dir Jos Dings

UCUE

Union des Capitales de l'Union Européenne
Union of Capitals of the European Union
Hôtel de Ville, Grand-Place, 1000 Brussels, Belgium
Tel. (+32) 2-2794952
Fax (+32) 2-2792391
E-mail cabinet.secretaire@brucity.be
URL www.ucue.org
Pres. Gábor Demzky
Contact Francis Deleau

UEF

Union of European Federalists
Union des Fédéralistes Européens
Union der Europäischen Federalisten
Chaussée de Wavre 214 D, 1050 Brussels, Belgium
Tel. (+32) 2-5083030
Fax (+32) 2-6269501
E-mail info@federaleurope.org
URL www.federaleurope.org
Pres. Mercedes Bresso
Sec.-Gen. Bruno Boissière
Organisation Man. Anja Härtwig

UEPMD

European Union of Dentists
Schlippenweg 2, 45470 Mülheim-Ruhr, Germany
Tel. (+49 20) 8763095
Fax (+49 20) 87672006
E-mail secgen@europeandentists.org
URL www.europeandentists.org
Pres. Dr Samiréh Nikolakakos
Sec.-Gen. Dr Derek Watson

UNITED

UNITED for Intercultural Action
Postbus 413, 1000 AK Amsterdam, Netherlands
Tel. (+31 20) 6834778
Fax (+31 20) 6834582
E-mail info@unitedagainstracism.org
URL www.unitedagainstracism.org
Sec.-Gen. Saskia Daru
Dir Geert Ates

UnitéE

Association pour l'Unité européennE
7 Rue du Dr Rocheford, 78400 Chatou, France
Tel. (+33) 1-30-53-55-49
Fax (+33) 1-53-43-11-09
E-mail unitee@unitee.com
URL www.unitee.com
Pres. Marc Regnard
Sec. Christophe Donizeau

WIDE

Women in Development Europe
Rue de la Science 10, 1000 Brussels, Belgium
Tel. (+32) 2-5459070
Fax (+32) 2-5127342
E-mail info@wide-network.org
URL www.eurosur.org/wide
Chair. Brigitte Holzner
Information Officer Barbara Specht

World Vision – EU Liaison Office
Rue de Toulouse 22, 1040 Brussels, Belgium
Tel. (+32) 2-2301621
Fax (+32) 2-2801621
E-mail jane_backhurst@wvi.org
URL www.wvi.org
Dir Jane Backhurst

WOSM

World Organisation of the Scout Movement – European Region
Avenue Porte de Hal 38, 1060 Brussels, Belgium
Tel. (+32) 2-5343315
Fax (+32) 2-5343315
E-mail relex@euro.scout.org
URL www.scout.org
Dir David Mckee
Admin. Asst Nathalie Labar

WSCF EUROPE

World Student Christian Federation (Europe Region)

Christlicher Weltstudentenbund (Europa Region)

Kálvin Tér 8, 1091 Budapest, Hungary
Tel. (+36 1) 2195166
Fax (+31 20) 6755736
E-mail RegionalOffice@wscf-europe.org
URL www.wscfeurope.org

Chair. Silke Lechner
Sec.-Gen. Hanna K. Tervanotko

WWF

World Wide Fund for Nature, European Policy Office

Fonds mondiaux pour la nature, bureau européen de politique

E. Jacqmainlaan 90, 1000 Brussels,
Belgium
Tel. (+32) 2-3400999
Fax (+32) 2-3400933
E-mail info.web@wwf.be
URL www.wwf.be

Dir Tony Long
Contact L. Devaux

YAP

Youth Action for Peace

Action de la jeunesse pour la paix

Avenue du Parc Royal 3, 1020 Brussels,
Belgium
Tel. (+32) 2-4789410
Fax (+32) 2-4789432
E-mail info@yap.org
URL www.yap.org

Pres. Andras F. Toth

YFJ

European Youth Forum

Forum européen de la Jeunesse

Rue Joseph II Straat 120, 1000 Brussels,
Belgium
Tel. (+32) 2-2306490
Fax (+32) 2-2302123
E-mail youthforum@youthforum.org
URL www.youthforum.org

Pres. Renaldas Vaisbrodas
Sec.-Gen. Tobias Flessenkemper

EUROPEAN CHURCH ASSOCIATIONS

APRODEV

Association of World Council of Churches related Development Organisations in Europe

Blvd Charlemagne 28, 1000 Brussels, Belgium
Tel. (+32) 2-2345660
Fax (+32) 2-2345669
E-mail admin@aprodev.net
URL www.aprodev.net

Sec.-Gen. Rob van Drimmelen
Policy and Information Officer Karine Sohet

CCME / CEME / KKME

Churches' Commission for Migrants in Europe

Commission des Eglises auprès des Migrants en Europe

Kommission für Migranten in Europa

Rue Joseph II 174, 1000 Brussels, Belgium
Tel. (+32) 2-2346800
Fax (+32) 2-2311413
E-mail csc.bru@cec-kek.be
URL www.cec-kek.org

Sec.-Gen. Doris Peschke
Project Sec. Torsten Moritz

CEC / KEK

Conference of European Churches
Conférence des Eglises européennes
Konferenz Europäischer Kirchen

Route de Ferney 150, PO Box 2100, 1211 Geneva 2, Switzerland
Tel. (+41) 22-791-61-11
Fax (+41) 22-791-62-27
E-mail cec@cec-kek.org
URL www.cec-kek.org

Pres. Jérémie Caligiorgis
Sec.-Gen. Colin Williams

CEEC

European Committee for Catholic Education
Comité Européen pour l'Enseignement Catholique
Europäisches Komitee für das Katholische Schulwesen

Avenue Marnix 19A bte 6, 1000 Brussels, Belgium

Tel. (+32) 2-5114774
Fax (+32) 2-5138694
E-mail ceec@skynet.be
URL http://ceec-edu.org

Pres. Chanoine Armand Beauduin
Sec.-Gen. Etienne Verhack
Admin. and Financial Dir Myriam Badart

COMECE

Commission of the Bishops' Conferences of the European Community

Commission des Episcopats de la CE

Kommission der Bischofskonferenzen der EG

Rue Stévin 42, 1000 Brussels, Belgium
Tel. (+32) 2-2350510
Fax (+32) 2-2303334
E-mail comece@comece.org
URL www.comece.org

Pres. Josef Homeyer
Sec.-Gen. Monsignor Noel Treanor

OCIPE

Catholic European Study and Information Centre

Office Catholique d'Information et d'Initiative pour l'Europe

Katholisches Sekretariat für Europäische Fragen

Rue du Cornet 51, 1040 Brussels, Belgium
Tel. (+32) 2-7379720
Fax (+32) 2-7379729
E-mail infos@ocipe.org
URL www.ocipe.org

Pres. Laurent Grégoire
Dir-Gen. Jan Kerkhofs

RCE

Rabbinical Center of Europe

Rond Point Schuman 6, 1040 Brussels, Belgium
Tel. (+32) 2-2347722
Fax (+32) 2-2347768
E-mail rabbinicalcenter@europe.com
URL www.rce.eu.com

Exec. Dir Moshe Garelik
Co-ordinator Levi Matusof

MISCELLANEOUS

AUDIOVISUAL / AUDIOVISUEL

European Audiovisual Observatory

Observatoire Européen de l'Audiovisuel

Europäische Audiovisuelle Informationsstelle

76 Allée de la Robertsau, 67000 Strasbourg, France
Tel. (+33) 3-88-14-44-00
Fax (+33) 3-88-14-44-19
E-mail obs@obs.coe.int
URL www.obs.coe.int
Exec. Dir Wolfgang Closs
Production Officer Markus Booms

EPO / OEB

European Patent Office

Office Européen des Brevets

Europäisches Patentamt

Erhardtstrasse 27, 80331 Münich, Germany
Tel. (+49 89) 2399-0
Fax (+49 89) 2399-4560
URL www.european-patent-office.org
Pres. Prof. Alain Pompidou
Council Secretariat Head Yves Grandjean

EPPO / OEPP

European and Mediterranean Plant Protection Organization

Organisation Européenne et Méditerranéenne pour la Protection des Plantes

Europäische und Mediterranee Organisation für Pflanzenschutz

1 Rue le Nôtre, 75016 Paris, France

Tel. (+33) 1-45-20-77-94
Fax (+33) 1-42-24-89-43
E-mail hq@eppo.fr
URL www.eppo.org
Chair. Olivier Felix
Dir-Gen. Dr Ian M Smith
Information Officer Anne-Sophie Roy

ETSI

European Telecommunications Standards Institute

Institut Européen des Normes de Télécommunication

Europäisches Institut für Telekommunikationsnormen

650 Route des Lucioles, 06921 Sophia Antipolis Cedex, France
Tel. (+33) 4-92-94-42-00
Fax (+33) 4-93-65-47-16
E-mail etsi@etsi.fr
URL www.etsi.org
Chair. Francisco da Silva
Dir-Gen. Karl-Heinz Rosenbrock

EUROCONTROL

European Organisation for the Safety of Air Navigation

Organisation Européenne pour la Sécurité de la Navigation Aérienne

Europäische Organisation für Flugsicherung

Rue de la Fusée 96, 1130 Brussels, Belgium
Tel. (+32) 2-7299011
Fax (+32) 2-7299044
URL www.eurocontrol.int
Dir-Gen. Victor M. Aguado
Secretariat Dir-Gen. Gerhard Stadler

EMPLOYER ORGANIZATIONS AND TRADE UNION ORGANIZATIONS

AUSTRIA

Bundesarbeitkammer

Federal Chamber of Labour

Chambre Fédérale du Travail

Avenue de Cortenbergh 30, 1040 Brussels, Belgium

Tel. (+32) 2-2306254

Fax (+32) 2-2302973

E-mail office@aken.at

URL www.aken.at

Pres. Herbert Tumpel

Sec.-Gen. Thomas Delapina

Counsellor Dr Elisabeth Aufheimer

Österreichischer Gewekschaftsbund

Austrian Federation of Trade Unions

Bureau Européen de la Confédération des Syndicats

Avenue de Cortenbergh 30, 1040 Brussels, Belgium

Tel. (+32) 2-2307463

Fax (+32) 2-2311710

E-mail europabuero@oigb-eu.at

URL www.oegb.at

Pres. Fritz Verzetnitsch

Head of Bureau Evelyne Regner

CZECH REPUBLIC

Svaz Průmyslu a Dopravy České Republiky

Square Vergote 39, 1030 Brussels, Belgium

Tel. (+32) 2-7370402

Fax (+32) 2-7370400

E-mail cez.lukas@skynet.be

Pres. Peter Karas

Permanent Delegate Karel Lukas

DENMARK

Danish Employers' Confederation (DA)

Avenue de Cortenbergh 168, 1000 Brussels, Belgium

Tel. (+32) 2-2850540

Fax (+32) 2-2850545

E-mail da-bxl@da.dk

URL www.da.dk

Dir Jørgen Rønnest

Pres. Jorgen Vorsholt

Danish Teacher Trade Unions

Syndicats d'Enseignants Danois

Boulevard du Roi Albert II 5, 1210 Brussels, Belgium

Tel. (+32) 2-2240670

Fax (+32) 2-2240671

E-mail dli@dlint.org

URL www.dlint.org

Head of Office Birgitte Birkvad

Landorganisationen

Danish Confederation of Trade Unions

Blvd du roi Albert II 5, PO Box 24, 1210 Brussels, Belgium

Tel. (+32) 2-2040690

Fax (+32) 2-2035657

E-mail lbo@lo.dk

URL www.lo.dk

Pres. Hans Jensen

Senior International Adviser and Journalist Peder Munch Hansen

FINLAND

Confederation of Finnish Industries

Confédération des Entreprises Finlandaises

Hauptverband der Finnischen Wirtschaft

Rue de la Charité 17, 1210 Brussels, Belgium

Tel. (+32) 2-2094311

Fax (+32) 2-2230805

E-mail jukka.ahtela@tt.fi

URL www.tt.fi

Head of Office, Permanent Delegate Ulla Sirkeinen

FRANCE

Chambre Syndicale des Constructeurs de Navires (CSCN)

C/o AMRIE, Rue du Commerce 20–22, 1000 Brussels, Belgium

Tel. (+32) 2-7361755

Fax (+32) 2-7352298

E-mail info@amrie.org
URL www.amrie.org
Dir Michael Lloyd

GERMANY

Arbeitsgemeinschaft Berufsstandischer Versorgungseinrichtungen eV (ABV)

Rue d'Arlon 50, 1000 Brussels, Belgium
Tel. (+32) 2-2820566
Fax (+32) 2-2820599
E-mail abv.ev@skynet.be
URL www.abv.de

Man. Dir Michael Proliner
Ansprechpartnerin Madeleine Schavoir

Arbeitsgemeinschaft Selbständiger Unternehmer Bundesverband Junger Unternehmer

Avenue Milcamps 21, 1030 Brussels, Belgium
Tel. (+32) 2-7341102
Fax (+32) 2-7379595
Representative Klaus P. Rohardt

Bundesverband der Freien Berufe

Rue Montoyer 23, 1000 Brussels, Belgium
Tel. (+32) 2-5001052
Fax (+32) 2-5121055
E-mail info-bruessel@freie-berufe.de
URL www.freie-berufe.de
Pres. Dr Ulrich Oesingmann
Man. Dir Arno Metzler

Bundesvereinigung Bauwirtschaft

Rue Jacques de Lalaing 4, Bte 7, 1040
    Brussels, Belgium
Tel. (+32) 2-2301852
Fax (+32) 2-2303451
E-mail a.jung@bv-bauwirtschaft.de
URL www.bv-bauwirtschaft.de
Pres. Heinz-Werner Bonjean
Leader Axel Klaus Jung

Bundesvereinigung der Deutschen Arbeitgeberverbande

Rue du Commerce 31, 1000 Brussels, Belgium
Tel. (+32) 2-2900300
Fax (+32) 2-2900319
E-mail buero-bruessel@bda-online.de
URL www.bda-online.de

Pres. Dr Dieter Hundt
Permanent Delegate Alexandra-Friederike zu
Schoenaich-Carolath

Bundesvereinigung Deutscher Handelsverbande eV (BDH)

Avenue des Nerviens 9/31, 1040 Brussels,
    Belgium
Tel. (+32) 2-2310998
Fax (+32) 2-2308497
E-mail hkrueger.bdhbru@wanadoo.be
Head Horst Kruger

Verband der Anbieter von Telekommunikation und Mediendienste (VATM)

Avenue Livingstone 33, 1000 Brussels,
    Belgium
Tel. (+32) 2-2350980
Fax (+32) 2-2865179
E-mail brussels@vatm.de
URL www.vatm.de
Pres. Gerd Eickers
Chief of Communication and PR Dr Maria
    Knight

GREECE

Greek General Confederation of Labour

Av. Général Eisenhower 104, 1030 Brussels,
    Belgium
Tel. (+32) 2-2167882
Fax (+32) 2-2164613
E-mail gdassis@hol.gr
Pres. Christos Polyzogopoulos
Sec.-Gen. Ioannis Manolis

HUNGARY

Confederation of Hungarian Employers' Organizations for International Co-operation (CEHIC)

Rue du Commerce 31, 1000 Brussels, Belgium
Tel. (+32) 2-5489010
Fax (+32) 2-5489019
E-mail vonosvath@eu-select.com
URL www.cehic.hu/indexe.php
Pres. Janos Vertes
Sec.-Gen. Dr István Komoroczki

ICELAND

Confederation of Icelandic Employers

Avenue de Cortenbergh 168, 1000 Brussels,
  Belgium
Tel. (+32) 2-2800852
Fax (+32) 2-2230805
E-mail kristofer@sa.is

Pres. Ingimundur Sigurpalsson
Permanent Delegate Gustaf Adolf Skulason

ITALY

Unione Italiana del Lavoro (UIL Europa)
Union of Italian Workers

Rue du Gouvernement Provisoire 34, 1000
  Brussels, Belgium
Tel. (+32) 2-2178627
Fax (+32) 2-2199834
E-mail info@uil.it

Sec.-Gen. Luigi Angeletti
Contact Giorgio Liverani

NORWAY

**Brussels Office of the Norwegian
  Confederation of Trade Unions (LO)**

Blvd Du Roi Albert II 5/23, 1210 Brussels,
  Belgium
Tel. (+32) 2-2011810
Fax (+32) 2-2011812
E-mail lo.bru@lono.be

Dir Knut Arne Sanden

SLOVAKIA

**Federation of Employers' Associations of the
  Slovak Republic**

Rue Wiertz 50, 1050 Brussels, Belgium
Tel. (+32) 2-4016899
Fax (+32) 2-4016868

E-mail nanias@nci.be
URL www.azzz.sk
Dir-Gen. František Bruckmayer

SPAIN

**Spanish Confederation of Employers'
  Organizations (CEOE)**

**Confédération espagnole des organisations
  d'employeurs**

Avenue de Tervuren 52, 1040 Brussels,
  Belgium
Tel. (+32) 2-7366080
Fax (+32) 2-7368090
E-mail jirodriguez@ceoe.es
URL www.ceoe.es

Pres. José María Cuevas Salvador
Sec.-Gen. Juan Jiménez Aguilar
Dir José Isaias Rodriguez

SWEDEN

LO-TCO-SACO

Avenue de Tervueren 15, 1040 Brussels,
  Belgium
Tel. (+32) 2-7321800
Fax (+32) 2-7322115
E-mail sven.svensson@bryssel.lo.se
URL www.brysselkontoret.com

Dir Sven Svensson

TURKEY

**Turkish Confederation of Employer
  Associations**

Avenue des Gaulois 13, 1040 Brussels,
  Belgium
Tel. (+32) 2-7364047
Fax (+32) 2-7363993
E-mail kaleagasi@tusiad.org
URL www.tisk.org.tr

Pres. Turgrul Kudatgobilik
Sec.-Gen. Bülent Pirler
Dir Dr Bahadir Kaleagasi

CHAMBERS OF COMMERCE AND INDUSTRY AND TRADE CHAMBERS WITH REPRESENTATIONAL OFFICES IN BRUSSELS

AUSTRIA

Austrian Federal Economic Chamber
Chambre Économique d'Autriche
Wirtschaftskammer Österreich
Avenue de Cortenbergh 30, 1040 Brussels,
    Belgium
Tel. (+32) 2-2865880
Fax (+32) 2-2865899
E-mail eu@eu.austria.be
URL http://wko.at
Pres. Dr Christoph Leitl
Sec.-Gen. Anna Maria Hochhauser
Representative Stefan Pistauer

Handelsdelegation Österreichs
Austrian Trade Commission
Délégation Commerciale d'Autriche
Avenue Louise 479, Bte 52, 1050 Brussels,
    Belgium
Tel. (+32) 2-6451650
Fax (+32) 2-6451669
E-mail bruessel@austriantrade.org
URL www.austriantrade.org
Commercial Counsellor Dr Gustav Gressel

Vereinigung der Österreichischen Industrie
Federation of Austrian Industry
Fédération de l'Industrie Autrichienne
Avenue de Cortenbergh 30, 1040 Brussels,
    Belgium
Tel. (+32) 2-2311847
Fax (+32) 2-2309591
E-mail iv.brussels@iv-net.at
URL www.iv-net.at
Pres. Veit Sorger
Sec.-Gen. Markus Beyrer
Dir Dr Berthold Berger-Henoch

BELGIUM

Agence pour le Commerce Extérieur (ACE)
Agency for Foreign Trade
Blvd du Roi Albert II 30 bte 6, 1000 Brussels,
    Belgium
Tel. (+32) 2-2063511
Fax (+32) 2-2031812
E-mail info@abh-ace.org
URL www.abh-ace.org
Pres. Prince Philippe

Fédération des Entreprises de Belgique (FEB)
Federation of Enterprises of Belgium
Rue Ravenstein 4, 1000 Brussels, Belgium
Tel. (+32) 2-5150811
Fax (+32) 2-5150915
E-mail info@vbo-feb.be
URL www.vbo-feb.be
Pres. Jean-Claude Daoust
Sec.-Gen. Philippe Lambrecht
Dir Diane Struyven

DENMARK

Confederation of Danish Industries (DI)
Avenue de Cortenbergh 168, 1000 Brussels,
    Belgium
Tel. (+32) 2-2850550
Fax (+32) 2-2850555
E-mail bruxafd@di.dk
URL www.di.dk
Pres. Johan Schrøder
Dir-Gen. Hans Skov Christensen

Handvaerksradet
Danish Federation of Small and Medium-Sized Enterprises
Rue Jacques de Lalaing 4, 1040 Brussels,
    Belgium

Tel. (+32) 2-2307599
Fax (+32) 2-2307861
E-mail info@ueapme.com
URL www.di.dkwww.hvr.dk
Pres. Poul R. Ulsøe
Dir Lars Jørgen Nielsen
Contact Christina Lindeholm

FINLAND

Confederation of Finnish Industries EK
**Hauptverband der Finnischen Wirtschaft
EK**
**Confédération des Enterprises Finlandaises
(EK)**
Rue de la Charité 17, 1210 Brussels, Belgium
Tel. (+32) 2-2094311
Fax (+32) 2-2230805
E-mail jukka.ahtela@tt.fi
URL www.ek.fi
Pres. Matti Halmesmäki
Dir Jukka Ahtela

FRANCE

**Assemblée des Chambres Françaises de
Commerce et d'Industrie (ACFCI)**
**Assembly of French Chambers of Commerce
and Industry**
Avenue des Arts 1–2, 1210 Brussels, Belgium
Tel. (+32) 2-2210419
Fax (+32) 2-2176987
E-mail m.chilaud@acfci.cci.fr
URL www.acfci.cci.fr
Pres. Jean-François Bernardin
Dir Henri Malosse

**Association des Chambres de Commerce et
d'Industrie Paris / Ile de France**
Avenue des Arts 36, Boite 4, 1000 Brussels,
Belgium
Tel. (+32) 2-2231840
Fax (+32) 2-2231856
E-mail europe@ccipif.be (central)
Deputy Sandra Penning

**Chambre Française de Commerce et
d'Industrie de Belgique (CFCIB)**
**French Chamber of Trade and Industry of
Belgium**
Artemis Square, Avenue des Arts 8, 1210
Brussels, Belgium

Tel. (+32) 2-5068811
Fax (+32) 2-5068817
E-mail cfcib@cfci.be
URL www.ccife.org/belgique
Pres. Philippe Delaunois
Dir van Cauwenbergh

**Mouvement des Entreprises de France
(MEDEF)**
Rue de Trèves 45, 1040 Brussels, Belgium
Tel. (+32) 2-2310730
Fax (+32) 2-2310838
E-mail medef.brux@skynet.be
URL www.medef.fr
Pres. Laurence Parisot
Permanent Delegate Marie-Christine
Vaccarezza

Provence Alpes Côte d'Azur
Avenue des Celtes 20, 1040 Brussels, Belgium
Tel. (+32) 2-7351370
Fax (+32) 2-7332536
E-mail representation.paca@bruxeurope.be
URL www.cr-paca.fr
Representative Stéphanie Vincent

GERMANY

**Bundesverband der Deutschen Industrie eV
(BDI)**
Federation of German Industries
Rue du Commerce 31, 1000 Brussels, Belgium
Tel. (+32) 2-5489020
Fax (+32) 2-5489029
E-mail Bruessel@bdi-online.de
URL www.bdi-online.de
Pres. Juergen R. Thumann
Dir Bernd Dittmann

Debelux Chamber of Commerce
Debelux Handelskammer
Chambre de Commerce Debelux
Manhattan Office Tower, Bolwerklaan Avenue
du Blvd 21, 1210 Brussels, Belgium
Tel. (+32) 2-2035040
Fax (+32) 2-2032271
E-mail ahk@debelux.org
URL www.debelux.org
Pres. Michel Hahn
Man.Dir Dr Hans-Joachim Maurer

Deutscher Industrie- und Handelskammertag, Vertretung bei der EU

German Chambers of Industry and Commerce Day

Avenue des Arts 19 A–D, 1000 Brussels, Belgium
Tel. (+32) 2-2861611
Fax (+32) 2-2861605
E-mail dihk@bruessel.dihk.de
URL www.dihk.de
Leader Peter Korn

Handelskammer Hamburg

Hamburg Chamber of Commerce

Blvd Clovis 49A, 1000 Brussels, Belgium
Tel. (+32) 2-2861680
Fax (+32 2-2861684
E-mail papaschinopoulou.mary@
　bruessel.dihk.de
URL www.hk24.de
Dir Dr Mary Papaschinopoulou

GREECE

Federation of Greek Industries

Avenue de Cortenbergh 168, 1000 Brussels, Belgium
Tel. (+32) 2-2310053
Fax (+32) 2-2800891
E-mail fgi.bxl@skynet.be
URL www.fgi.org.gr
Chair. Ulysses Kyriacopoulos
Permanent Delegate Irini Yvonni Pari

ICELAND

Federation of Icelandic Industries

Avenue de Cortenbergh 168, 1000 Brussels, Belgium
Tel. (+32) 2-2800852
Fax (+32) 2-2230805
E-mail mottaka@si.is
Permanent Delegate Gustaf Adolf Skulason

IRELAND

Enterprise Ireland

Rue Wiertzstraat 50, 1050 Brussels, Belgium
Tel. (+32) 2-6739866
Fax (+32) 2-6721066

E-mail charlotte.field@enterprise-ireland.com
URL www.enterprise-ireland.com
Man. Charlotte Field

Irish Business Bureau

Avenue de Cortenbergh 89, PO Box 2, 1000 Brussels, Belgium
Tel. (+32) 2-5123333
Fax (+32) 2-5121353
E-mail brussels.ibb@ibec.be
URL www.ibec.ie/ibb
Pres. William Burgess
Asst Dir Arthur Forbes

ITALY

Confederazione Generale Italiana del Commercio

General Confederation of Trade, Tourism, Services and SMEs

Avenue Marnix 30, 1000 Brussels, Belgium
Tel. (+32) 2-2896230
Fax (+32) 2-2896235
E-mail confcomtur@skypro.be
URL www.confcommercio.it
Pres. Sergio Billè
Sec.-Gen. Giacomo Regaldo

Confederazione Nazionale dell'Artigianato e della Piccola e Media Impresa (CNA)

National Confederation of Artisans and Craftsmen of Small and Medium-Sized Enterprises

Rue du Commerce 124, 1000 Brussels, Belgium
Tel. (+32) 2-2307442
Fax (+32) 2-2307219
E-mail bruxelles@cna.ipi
URL www.cnamatera.it
Patrizia Di Mauro

Confindustria – Confederazione Generale dell'Industria Italiana

General Confederation of Italian Industry

Avenue de la Joyeuse Entrée 1, Bte. 11, 1040 Brussels, Belgium
Tel. (+32) 2-2861211
Fax (+32) 2-2302720
E-mail p.pesci@confindustria.be
URL www.confindustria.it
Pres. Luca Cordero di Montezemolo
Permanent Delegate Paolo Nicoletti

Institut Italien pour le Commerce Extérieur (ICE)

Italian Institute for Foreign Trade

Place de la Liberté 12, 1000 Brussels, Belgium
Tel. (+32) 2-2291430
Fax (+32) 2-2231596
E-mail bruxelles@bruxelles.ice.it
URL www.ice.gov.it/estero2/bruxelles
Pres. Umberto Vattani
Dir Barbara Chiappini

Unioncamere

Unione Italiana delle Camera di Commercio Industria, Artigianato e Agricoltura

Rue de l'Industrie 22, 1040 Brussels, Belgium
Tel. (+32) 2-5122240
Fax (+32) 2-5124911
E-mail marco.lopriore@unioncamere.be
URL www.unioncamere.it
Pres. Carlo Sangalli
Delegate Marco Lopriore

JAPAN

Belgium–Japan Association and Chamber of Commerce ASBL-VZW

Association et Chambre de Commerce Belgo-Japonaise

Avenue Louise 287, bte 7, 1050 Brussels, Belgium
Tel. (+32) 2-6441405
Fax (+32) 2-6442360
E-mail info@bja.be
URL www.bja.be
Pres. Luc Willame
Exec. Dir Anja Kellens

JETRO Brussels Center

Rue d'Arlon 69–71, PO Box 2, 1040 Brussels, Belgium
Tel. (+32) 2-2820500
Fax (+32) 2-2802530
E-mail info@jetro.be
URL www.jetro.be
Deputy Dir-Gen. Susumu Tanaka

MALTA

Malta Federation of Industry

Avenue d'Auderghem 289, 1040 Brussels, Belgium

Tel. (+32) 2-5026091
Fax (+32) 2-7360855
E-mail lmizzi@mbb.org.mt
URL www.foi.org.mt
Dir Dr Leonard Mizzi

NETHERLANDS

Dutch Chamber of Commerce for Belgium and Luxembourg

Niederländische Handelskammer für Belgien und Luxemburg

Rue du Congrès 18, 1000 Brussels, Belgium
Tel. (+32) 2-2191174
Fax (+32) 2-2187821
E-mail info@nkvk.be
URL www.nkvk.be
Dir-Gen. Philip Charls

Midden en Klein Bedrijf Nederland (MKB)

Small and Medium-Sized Enterprises

Rue Jacques de Lalaing 4, 4th floor, 1040 Brussels, Belgium
Tel. (+32) 2-2307290
Fax (+32) 2-2301807
E-mail schroder@mkb.nl
URL www.mkb.nl
Pres. Drs L.M.L.H.A. Hermans
Contact Gert Eggermont

Verbond van Nederlandse Ondernemingen (VNO-NCW)

Confederation of Netherlands Industry and Employers

Archimedesstraat 5, Bus 4, 1000 Brussels, Belgium
Tel. (+32) 2-5100880
Fax (+32) 2-5100885
E-mail bou@vno-ncw.nl
URL www.vno-ncw.nl
Pres. Jacques H. Schraven
Permanent Delegate Jan Karelbout

NORWAY

Confederation of Norwegian Enterprise (NHO)

Avenue Cortenbergh 168, Bte 7, 1000 Brussels, Belgium
Tel. (+32) 2-2850560
Fax (+32) 2-2850570

E-mail nho.brussel@nho.no
URL www.nho.no/brussel
Pres. Erling Øverland
Dir Pernille Aga

Norwegian Trade Council
Conseil Norvégien du Commerce Extérieur
Rue Archimède 17, Bte 2, 1000 Brussels,
　Belgium
Tel. (+32) 2-6465070
Fax (+32) 2-6460744
E-mail brussels@ntc.no
URL www.nortrade.com/NTC.aspx
Dir Tore Lasse

PORTUGAL

Associação Industrial Portuguesa (AIP)
Portuguese Association of Industry
Association Industrielle Portugaise
Avenue de Cortenbergh 168, 1000 Brussels,
　Belgium
Tel. (+32) 2-5131994
Fax (+32) 2-5136362
E-mail ipaip@skynet.be
URL www.aip.pt
Pres. Jorge Rocha de Matos
Permanent Delegate Fernando Almeida

Associação Nacional dos Jovens
Empresarios
National Association of Young
Entrepreneurs
Association des Jeunes Entrepreneurs
Portugais
Rue de la Montagne 37, Bte C3, 1000 Brussels,
　Belgium
Tel. (+32) 2-5113447
Fax (+32) 2-5115145
E-mail angebro@unicall.be
URL www.ange.pt
Pres. Armindo Monteiro
Public Relations Dir Goncãlo Leitao

Comércio de Portugal
Portuguese Chamber of Commerce
Chambre de Commerce du Portugal
Rue Joseph II 3, 6e étage, 1000 Brussels,
　Belgium
Tel. (+32) 2-2308323
Fax (+32) 2-2306866

E-mail ccportugal@skynet.be
Pres. Baudouin Dunesm
Dir M.C. Caetano-Thomas

Confederação da Industria Portuguesa
(CIP)
Avenue de Cortenbergh 168, 1000 Brussels,
　Belgium
Tel. (+32) 2-2309270
Fax (+32) 2-2300837
E-mail cipbxl@skynet.be
Permanent Delegate Fernando de Almeida

Investimentos Comércio e Turismo de
Portugal (ICEP)
Rue Blanche 15, 1000 Brussels, Belgium
Tel. (+32) 2-2309625
Fax (+32) 2-2310447
E-mail icep.bruxelas@icep.pt
URL www.icep.pt
Dir Elia Rodrigues

SPAIN

Chambre Officielle de Commerce d'Espagne
en Belgique et au Luxembourg
Cámara Oficial de Comercio de España en
Bélgica y Luxemburgo
Rue Belliard 20, 1040 Brussels, Belgium
Tel. (+32) 2-5171740
Fax (+32) 2-5138805
E-mail info@cocebyl.be
URL www.cocebyl.be
Pres. Juan Rodriguez-Villa
Sec.-Gen. M. Miguel Angel Arrimadas Garcia

Representation of the Spanish Chambers of
Commerce and Industry at the EC
Consejo superior de camaras oficials de
camercio, industria y navegación de
españa
Rue de Luxembourg 19–21, 1000 Brussels,
　Belgium
Tel. (+32) 2-7056750
Fax (+32) 2-7056640
E-mail del.bruselas@cscamaras.es
URL www.camaras.org
Dir-Gen. Ángel Martín Acebes
Dir Fernando Llanos

SWEDEN

Confederation of Swedish Enterprise
Rue du Luxembourg 3, 1000 Brussels, Belgium
Tel. (+32) 2-5015300
Fax (+32) 2-5015320
E-mail bryssel@svensktnaringsliv.se
URL www.swedishenterprise.se
Permanent Delegate Jan Herin

Swedish Trade Council
Rue du Luxembourg 3, 1000 Brussels, Belgium
Tel. (+32) 2-5015354
Fax (+32) 2-5015356
E-mail belgium@swedishtrade.se
URL www.swedishtrade.com/belgium
Pres. Ulf Dinkelspiel
Trade Commission Erik Meurling

SWITZERLAND

Chambre de Commerce Suisse pour la Belgique et le Grand-Duché de Luxembourg
Swiss Chamber of Commerce for Belgium and Grand Duchy of Luxembourg
Square des Nations 24, 1050 Brussels, Belgium
Tel. (+32) 2-6498787
Fax (+32) 2-6498019
URL ccs.blux@swing.be
Administrator Philippe Kenel

Economiesuisse
Verband der Schweizer Unternehmen
Federazione delle imprese svizzere
Fédération des entreprises suisses
Avenue de Cortenbergh 168, 1000 Brussels, Belgium
Tel. (+32) 2-2800844
Fax (+32) 2-2800699
E-mail bruxelles@economiesuisse.ch
URL www.economiesuisse.ch
Pres. Ueli Forster
Delegate Theo Zijdenbos

TURKEY

Turkish Industrialists' and Businessmen's Association (TUSIAD)
Avenue des Gaulois 13, 1040 Brussels, Belgium

Tel. (+32) 2-7364047
Fax (+32) 2-7363993
E-mail kaleagasi@tusiad.org
URL www.tusiad.org
Permanent Delegate Bahadir Kaleagasi

Turkish Research and Business Organizations AISBL (TuR&Bo PPP)
Rue du Luxembourg 14A, 1000 Brussels, Belgium
Tel. (+32) 2-2854020
Fax (+32) 2-2854025
E-mail info@turboppp.org
URL www.turboppp.org
Pres. Ahmet Ecmel Yorganci

Union des Chambres de Commerce, d'Industrie, de Commerce Maritime et des Bourses de Marchandises de Turquie (TOBB)
Union of Chambers of Commerce and Commodity Exchanges of Turkey
C/o Fondation pour le Développement Economique (IKV), Avenue Franklin Roosevelt 148A, 1050 Brussels, Belgium
Tel. (+32) 2-6464040
Fax (+32) 2-6469538
E-mail ikvnet@skynet.be
URL www.tobb.org.tr
Pres. Rifat Hisarcikloglu
Dir Haluk Nuray

Young Businessmen's Association of Turkey (TUGIAD)
Association des Jeunes Hommes d'Affaires de Turquie
Avenue Landhuizenlaan 27, 1850 Grimbergen, Belgium
Tel. (+32) 2-2611808
Fax (+32) 2-2611808
E-mail atthakanhanli@skynet.be
URL www.tugiad.org.tr
Dir Hakan Hanli

UNITED KINGDOM

British Business Bureau (BBB)
Rue Wiertz 50, 1050 Brussels, Belgium
Tel. (+32) 2-2310465
Fax (+32) 2-2309832

E-mail jessica.bauly@cbi.org.uk
URL www.cbi.org.uk
Senior Policy Adviser and Communications
　Jessica Bauly

**British Chamber of Commerce in Belgium
(BCC)**

Blvd Saint-Michel 47, 1040 Brussels,
　Belgium
Tel. (+32) 2-5409030
Fax (+32) 2-5128363

E-mail britcham@britcham.be
URL www.britcham.be
Pres. Russell Patten
Sec.-Gen. Valerie Echard

Confederation of British Industry (CBI)

Rue Wiertz 50, 1050 Brussels, Belgium
Tel. (+32) 2-2310465
Fax (+32) 2-2309832
E-mail andrew.moore@cbi.org.uk
URL www.cbi.org.uk
Dir Andrew Moore

AGRICULTURAL ORGANIZATIONS

AUSTRIA

Präsidentenkonferenz der Landwirtschaftskammern Österreichs

Conference of Presidents of the Austrian Chambers of Agriculture

Conférence des Présidents des Chambres d'Agriculture Autrichiennes

Avenue de Cortenbergh 30, 1040 Brussels, Belgium
Tel. (+32) 2-2854670
Fax (+32) 2-2854671
E-mail pkbrux@pklwk.at
URL www.pklwk.at
Pres. Rudolf Schwarzbock
Sec.-Gen. Augst Astl
Dir Martin Längauer

DENMARK

Danish Bacon & Meat Council

L'Union des Abattoirs Danois, Rue du Luxembourg 47–51, Bte 2, 1050 Brussels, Belgium
Tel. (+32) 2-2302705
Fax (+32) 2-2300098
E-mail ds@agridan.be
URL www.doenskeslagterier.dk
Pres. Anne Birgitte
Dir Knud Buhl

Danish Council of Agriculture

Rue du Luxembourg 47–51, 2ème ètage, Bte 2, 1050 Brussels, Belgium
Tel. (+32) 2-2302705
Fax (+32) 2-2300143
E-mail jbh@agridan.be
URL www.landbrugsraadet.dk
Pres. Peter Gæmelke
Dir Jacob Bagge Hanson

Danish Dairy Board Brussels

Rue de la Science 23–25, Bte 12, 1040 Brussels, Belgium
Tel. (+32) 2-2302705
Fax (+32) 2-2304643
E-mail ddb@agridan.be

Dir Hans Bender
Administrator Paul Andersen

FRANCE

European Association for Information on Local Development

Association Européenne pour l'Information sur le Développement Local (AEIDL)

Chaussée Saint-Pierre 260, 1040 Brussels, Belgium
Tel. (+32) 2-7364960
Fax (+32) 2-7360434
E-mail aeidl@aeidl.be
URL www.aeidl.be
Man. Dir William Van Dingenen

Assemblée Permanente des Chambres d'Agriculture (APCA)

Avenue des Arts 1/2, Bte 9, 1210 Brussels, Belgium
Tel. (+32) 2-2854387
Fax (+32) 2-2854381
E-mail sylvain.lhermitte@apca.chambagri.fr
URL www.apca.chambagri.fr
Representative Sylvain Lhermitte

Association de la Transformation Laitière Française (ATLA)

Avenue des Arts 53, 1000 Brussels, Belgium
Tel. (+32) 2-5020989
Fax (+32) 2-5142337
E-mail jean-pierre.carlier@atla.asso.fr
Pres. Xavier Paul-Renard
Contact Jean-Pierre Carlier

Association Nationale Interprofessionnelle des Fruits et Légumes Transformés (ANIFELT)

Avenue Palmerston 9, 1000 Brussels, Belgium
Tel. (+32) 2-2307110
Fax (+32) 2-2308767
E-mail marie.claude.amphoux@anifelt.com
URL www.anifelt.com
Pres. Jean-Pierre Cuxac
Contact Marie-Claude Amphoux

233

Centre National du Machinisme Agricole, des Eaux et Forêts (DICOVA– CEMAGREF)

Avenue des Arts 8, 1210 Brussels, Belgium
Tel. (+32) 2-5068866
Fax (+32) 2-5068845
E-mail cemagref@clora.net
URL www.cemagref.fr
Sec. Daro Sarr

Confédération Française de la Coopération Agricole (CFCA)

French Confederation for Agricultural Co-operation

Rue de la Science 23–25, Boîte 17, 1040
  Brussels, Belgium
Tel. (+32) 2-2311952
Fax (+32) 2-2306598
E-mail cfca.bxl@pophost.eunet.be
Pres. Balled Joseph
Contact Véronique Guerin

GIE – Bureau Européen de l'Agriculture Française

Rue de la Science 23–25, Bte 17, 1040
  Brussels, Belgium
Tel. (+32) 2-2854380
Fax (+32) 2-2854381
E-mail brigitte.daffargues@skynet.be
Sec. Daffargues

Inter Professionnelle Fruits et Légumes (INTERFEL)

Inter-professional Association of the Fresh Fruit and Vegetable Industry

Avenue Palmerston 9, 1000 Brussels, Belgium
Tel. (+32) 2-2307348
Fax (+32) 2-2308767
E-mail eurodialog@skynet.be
URL www.interfel.com
Dir Jean Ruiz

Union Française des Commerçants en Bestiaux (FFCB / FNICGV)

European Livestock and Meat Trading Union

Rue de la Loi 81A, Bte 9, 1040 Brussels,
  Belgium
Tel. (+32) 2-2304603
Fax (+32) 2-2309400
E-mail uecbv@pophost.eunet.be
URL www.uecbv.eunet.be
Pres. Jean Mazet

Sec.-Gen. Jean-Luc Mériaux
Dir Domenica Barn

GERMANY

Centrale Marketinggesellschaft der Deutschen Agrarwirtschaft mbH (CMA)

Central Marketing Organization of German Agricultural Industries

Rue du Luxembourg 47–51, 1050 Brussels,
  Belgium
Tel. (+32) 2-5053480
Fax (+32) 2-5053481
E-mail info@cma-benelux.be
URL www.cma-exportservice.com
Man. Dir Werner Friedrich

Deutscher Fleischer-Verband

Rue Jacques de Lalaing 4, 1040 Brussels,
  Belgium
Tel. (+32) 2-2306690
Fax (+32) 2-2303451
E-mail info@cibc.be
URL www.cibc.be
Pres. Eugen Nagel
Sec.-Gen. Martin Fuchs
Man. Dir Kirsten Diessner

Milchindustrie-Verband eV

Rue de l'industrie 13, 1000 Brussels, Belgium
Tel. (+32) 2-2850173
Fax (+32) 2-2850174
E-mail anton@milchindustrie.de
URL www.milch-markt.de
Lawyer Alexander Anton

GREECE

Confédération Panhellénique des Unions de Coopératives Agricoles (PASEGES)

Panhellenic Confederation of Unions of Agricultural Co-operatives

Panellenische Verband der Landwirtschaftlichen Genossenschaftlichen Organisationen

Rue des Treves 61, 1040 Brussels, Belgium
Tel. (+32) 2-2306685
Fax (+32) 2-2305915
E-mail paseges@skynet.be
URL www.paseges.gr
Pres. Tzanetos Karamichas
Sec.-Gen. Karagiozopoulos Achilleas
Dir Giannis Kolybas

IRELAND

Irish Co-operative Organisation Society (ICOS)

Rue de la Science 23–25, 1040 Brussels,
  Belgium
Tel. (+32) 2-2310685
Fax (+32) 2-2310698
E-mail mail@icosbrussels.be
URL www.icos.ie
Pres. Donal Cashman
Sec.-Gen. Seamus O'Donohoe
European Affairs Officer Michael Quigley

Irish Dairy Board Benelux SA (IDB)

Radiatorenstraat 1, 1800 Vilvoode, Belgium
Tel. (+32) 2-2516961
Fax (+32) 2-2514318
E-mail james.oregan@idb.be
URL www.idb.be
Man. Dir. Jim O'Regan

Irish Farmers Associations (IFA)

Rue de Trèves 61, 7th Floor, 1040 Brussels,
  Belgium
Tel. (+32) 2-2303137
Fax (+32) 2-2310698
E-mail mail@ifabrussels.be
URL www.ifa.be
Pres. John Dillon
Sec.-Gen. Michael Berkery
Dir Michael Treacy

ITALY

ASSOLATTE

Private Milk Industry & Co-operative

Place de la liberté 12, 1000 Brussels, Belgium
Tel. (+32) 2-2231105
Fax (+32) 2-2194021
E-mail assolatte.bxl@skynet.be
URL www.assolatte.it
Dir Rosanna Pecere

Coldiretti

Agricultural Union

Avenue de Tervuren 27, 1040 Brussels,
  Belgium
Tel. (+32) 2-2309893
Fax (+32) 2-2311478
E-mail bruxelles@coldiretti.it
URL www.coldiretti.it

Pres. Paolo Bedoni
Sec.-Gen. Franco Pasquali
Dir Dr Maurizio Reale

Confederazione Generale dell'Agricoltura Italiano (CONFAGRICOLTURA)

31 Rue Montoyer, Bte 13, 1040 Brussels,
  Belgium
Tel. (+32) 2-2306732
Fax (+32) 2-2309287
E-mail confagricoltura@skynet.be
URL www.confagricoltura.it
Pres. Federico Vecchioni
Sec.-Gen. Vito Bianco
Dir Dr Sandro Mascia

Confederazione Italiana Agricoltori

Rue Philippe le Bon 46, 1000 Brussels,
  Belgium
Tel. (+32) 2-2303012
Fax (+32) 2-2800333
E-mail cia.bxl@skynet.be
URL www.cia.it
Pres. Guiseppe Politi
Dir Dr Claudio Di Rollo

JAPAN

ALIC Europe

Avenue des Arts 10–11, Bte 11, 1210 Brussels,
  Belgium
Tel. (+32) 2-5139093
Fax (+32) 2-5137625
E-mail aliceurope@skynet.be
Pres. Masahiro Seki
Man. Masa Miroseki

NETHERLANDS

LTO Nederland

Wetenschapsstraat 23–25, Bte 21, 1040
  Brussels, Belgium
Tel. (+32) 2-2307500
Fax (+32) 2-2306749
E-mail ibisseling@lto.nl
URL www.lto.nl
Pres. Gerard Doornbos
Sec.-Gen. Dirk Duijzer
Man. Martin van Drial
Contact Lobis

Produktschap Vee en Vlees (PVV)

Cattle and Meat

Rue de la Science 23–25, Bte 21, 1040
  Brussels, Belgium
Tel. (+32) 2-2307500
Fax (+32) 2-2306749
E-mail pvebrus3@skynet.be
Representative Frans van Dongen

**Vereniging van Bloemenveilingen in
Nederland (VBN)**

Dutch Flower Auctions Association

**Association des criées aux fleurs des
Pays-Bas**

Rue de la Science 23–25, Bte 21, 1040
  Brussels, Belgium
Tel. (+32) 2-2315002
Fax (+32) 2-2306749
E-mail pvebrus3@skynet.be
URL www.vbn.nl
EU Representative A. J. M. ton Blom

PORTUGAL

**Associação dos Jovens Agricultores de
Portugal (AJAP)**

Young Farmers Association of Portugal

**Association des Jeunes Agriculteurs du
Portugal**

Rue de la Science 23–25, Bte 28, 1040
  Brussels, Belgium
Tel. (+32) 2-2305708
Fax (+32) 2-2308417
E-mail ajap@skynet.be
URL www.ajap.pt
Contact Paulo Padrol

Confederação dos Agricultores de Portugal

Confédération des Agriculteurs du Portugal

Rue Ste Gertrude 15, 1040 Brussels, Belgium
Tel. (+32) 2-7368528
Fax (+32) 2-7323054
E-mail cap.bxl@skynet.be
URL www.cap.pt
Pres. Joao Pedro Machado
Sec.-Gen. Luis Mira
Delegate Jose Diégo Santiago

**Confederação Nacional da Agricultura
(CNA)**

Confédération de l'Agriculture

Blvd Jamar 53, 1060 Brussels, Belgium
Tel. (+32) 2-5273789
Fax (+32) 2-5273790
Delegate Carla Semeador

SWEDEN

Federation of Swedish Farmers (LRF)

Rue de Trèves 61, 7ème ètage, 1040 Brussels,
  Belgium
Tel. (+32) 2-2800664
Fax (+32) 2-2800608
E-mail rolf.eriksson@lrf.be
URL www.lrf.se
Pres. Caroline Trapp
Dir Rolf Eriksson

UNITED KINGDOM

British Agriculture Bureau

Bureau de l'Agriculture Britannique (BAB)

Rue de Trèves 61, 1040 Brussels, Belgium
Tel. (+32) 2-2850580
Fax (+32) 2-2303928
E-mail BAB@nfuonline.com
Dir Betty Lee

Dairy UK

Rue du Commerce 20/22, 1000 Brussels,
  Belgium
Tel. (+32) 2-5035610
Fax (+32) 2-5035609
E-mail info@dairyUK.org
URL www.dairyuk.org
Dir-Gen. Jim Begg

Meat and Livestock Commission (MLC)

Rue de Trèves 61, 1040 Brussels, Belgium
Tel. (+32) 2-2308668
Fax (+32) 2-2308620
E-mail peter.hardwick@skynet.be
URL www.mlc.org.uk
International Man. Peter Hardwick

REGIONAL AUTHORITIES WITH REPRESENTATION IN BRUSSELS

ASSOCIATIONS WITH LOCAL AND REGIONAL POWERS

Alliance des Intérêts Maritimes Régionaux en Europe

Alliance of Maritime Regional Interests in Europe (AMRIE)

Rue du Commerce 20–22, 1000 Brussels, Belgium
Tel. (+32) 2-7361755
Fax (+32) 2-7352298
E-mail info@amrie.org
URL www.amrie.org
Dir Michael Lloyd

Assemblée des Régions d'Europe (ARE)

Assembly of European Regions (AER)

Versammlung der Regionen Europas (VRE)

Place Sainctelette 2, 1080 Brussels, Belgium
Tel. (+32) 2-4218211
Fax (+32) 2-4218787
E-mail s.cools@a-e-r.org
URL www.a-e-r.org
Pres. Riccardo Illy
Sec.-Gen. Klaus Klipp

Association Européenne des Élus de Montagne (AEM)

European Association of Elected Representatives from Mountain Areas (EAM)

Europäische Vereinigung der Gewählten von Bergregionen (EVB)

Avenue des Arts 1, Bte 9, 1210 Brussels, Belgium
Tel. (+32) 2-2210439
Fax (+32) 2-2176987
E-mail aem@promote-aem.org
URL www.promonte-aem.org
Pres. Luciano Caveri
Sec.-Gen. Sir Carlos Pinto

Communauté de Travail des Régions Alpines

Working Community of the Alpine Countries

Arbeitsgemeinschaft Alpenländer (ARGE ALP)

Avenue de Cortenbergh 52/4, 1000 Brussels, Belgium
Tel. (+32) 2-7432700
Fax (+32) 2-7420980
E-mail info@argealp.org
Pres. Lorenzo Dellai
Sec.-Gen. Dr. Staudigl Fritz

Conférence des Régions Périphériques Maritimes (CRPM)

Conference of Peripheral Maritime Regions of Europe (CPMR)

Square Marie-Louise 77, 1000 Brussels, Belgium
Tel. (+32) 2-2307499
Fax (+32) 2-2802765
E-mail crpm.bruxelles@skynet.be
URL www.cpmr.org
Pres. Claudio Martini
Sec.-Gen. Xavier Gizard
Permanent Delegate Pascal Gruselle

Conseil des Communes et Régions d'Europe (CCRE)

Council of European Municipalities and Regions (CEMR)

Rue d'Arlon 22, 1050 Brussels, Belgium
Tel. (+32) 2-5117477
Fax (+32) 2-5110949
E-mail cemr@ccre.org
URL www.ccre.org
Pres. Dr Michael Häupl
Sec.-Gen. Jeremy Smith
Dir-Gen. Walter Wenzel
Press and Communication Officer Patrizio Fiorilli

Coopération Subrégionale des États de la Mer Baltique (CSREMB)

Baltic Sea States Subregional Co-operation (BSSSC)

Avenue Palmerston 20, 1000 Brussels, Belgium
Tel. (+32) 2-2854643
Fax (+32) 2-2854657
E-mail guenther.schulz@hobru.landsh.de
URL www.bsssc.com
Pres. Brunon Synak
Sec.-Gen. Krystyna Wróblewska
Contact Guenther Schulz

Eurocities

Square de Meeûs 18, 1050 Brussels, Belgium
Tel. (+32) 2-5520888
Fax (+32) 2-5520889
E-mail info@eurocities.be
URL www.eurocities.org
Pres. Richard Leese
Communication Officer Sinead Mullins
Chief Exec. Officer Catherine Parmentier

European Industrial Regions Association (EIRA)

Rue Joseph II 36–38, 1000 Brussels, Belgium
Tel. (+32) 2-2309107
Fax (+32) 2-2302712
E-mail secretariat@eira.org
Pres. Cllr Roger Stone
Policy Officer Maria Domzal

Union des Capitales de l'Union Européenne (UCUE)

Union of Capitals of the European Union

Hôtel de Ville, Grand-Place, 1000 Brussels, Belgium
Tel. (+32) 2-2794952
Fax (+32) 2-2792391
E-mail cabinet.secretaire@brucity.be
URL www.ucue.org
Pres. Gábor Demzky
Contact Francis Deleau

AUSTRIA

Bureau de Liaison de la Haute-Autriche

Liaison Office of Upper Austria to the European Union

Rue Joseph II 36, 1000 Brussels, Belgium

Tel. (+32) 2-2231404
Fax (+32) 2-2192087
E-mail eub.post@ooe.gv.at
URL www.ooe.gv.at
Dir Dr Gérald Lonauer

Bureau de Liaison de Salzbourg

Liaison Office of Salzburg

Rue Frédérick Pelletier 107, 1030 Brussels, Belgium
Tel. (+32) 2-7430760
Fax (+32) 2-7430761
E-mail gritlind.kettl@salzburg.gv.at
Dir Gritlind Kettl

Land Kärnten – Bureau de Liaison

Carinthia Liaison Office

Avenue d'Auderghem 67, 1040 Brussels, Belgium
Tel. (+32) 2-2824910
Fax (+32) 2-2804380
E-mail sekretariat@vbb-kaernten.com
Dir Martina Rattinger

Land Niederösterreich

Lower Austria

Rue Montoyer 14, 1000 Brussels, Belgium
Tel. (+32) 2-5490660
Fax (+32) 2-5026009
E-mail post.noevbb@noel.gv.at
URL www.noel.gv.at
Dir Roland Langthaler Likes

Land Tirol / Tirol Büro

Avenue de Cortenbergh 52, 1000 Brussels, Belgium
Tel. (+32) 2-7432700
Fax (+32) 2-7420980
E-mail info@alpeuregio.org
Head of Office Dr Richard Seeber

Liaison Office of the City of Vienna

Avenue de Tervueren 58, 1040 Brussels, Belgium
Tel. (+32) 2-7438500
Fax (+32) 2-7337058
E-mail post@be.magwien.gv.at
Dir Eva Pretscher

Österreichischer Gemeindebund

Austrian Association of Municipalities

Association des Communes Autrichiennes

Avenue de Cortenbergh 30, 1040 Brussels,
Belgium
Tel. (+32) 2-2820680
Fax (+32) 2-2820688
E-mail oegemeindebund@compuserve.com
URL www.gemeindebund.gv.at
Pres. Helmut Mödlhammer
Sec.-Gen. Dr Robert Hink
Dir Michaela Petz

Österreichischer Stadtebund

Association of Austrian Cities and Towns

Association des villes autrichiennes

Avenue de Cortenbergh 30, 1040 Brussels,
Belgium
Tel. (+32) 2-2820680
Fax (+32) 2-2820682
E-mail stb-bxl@wanadoo.be
URL www.staedtebund.at
Pres. Michael Häupl
Sec.-Gen. Dr Erich Prambock
Dir Simone Wolesa

**Représentation Permanente de l'Autriche –
Représentation des Lander**

**Permanent Representation of Austria –
Representation of the Lander**

Avenue de Cortenbergh 30, 1040 Brussels,
Belgium
Tel. (+32) 2-2305443
Fax (+32) 2-2302544
E-mail klemens.fischer@bruessel.vst.gv.at
Minister Adviser Dr Klemens Fischer

Steiermark Büro

Place des Gueux 8, 1000 Brussels, Belgium
Tel. (+32) 2-7320361
Fax (+32) 2-7321263
E-mail claudia.suppan@stmk.gv.at
URL www.verwaltung.steiermark.at
Dir Erich Korzinek

**Verbindungsbüro des Landes Burgenland
zur Europäischen Union**

**Burgenland Liaison Office at the European
Union**

Rue Montoyer 39, 1000 Brussels, Belgium

Tel. (+32) 2-5143011
Fax (+32) 2-5142391
E-mail andrea.krainer@bgld.gv.at
URL www.burgenland.at
Pres. Walter Prior
Dir Andrea-Maria Krainer

Wiener Wirtschaftsförderungsfonds

Vienna Business Agency

Avenue de Tervueren 58, 1040 Brussels,
Belgium
Tel. (+32) 2-7438516
Fax (+32) 2-7337058
E-mail strohm@wwff.gv.at
URL www.wwff.gv.at
Dir Susanne Strohm

BELGIUM

**Administration Régionale pour les Affaires
Européennes en Belgique pour la
Communauté Germanophone**

Klötzerbahn 32, 4700 Eupen, Belgium
Tel. (+32) 87-596400
Fax (+32) 87-740258
Sec.-Gen. Norbert Heukemes

**Administration Régionale pour les Affaires
Européennes en Belgique pour la
Communauté Germanophone –
Commissariat Général aux Relations
Internationales**

**Regional Administration for European
Affairs in Belgium for the German-
speaking Community – General
Commissariat for International Relations**

Saincteletteplein 2, 1000 Brussels, Belgium
Head of Office Francine Nagels

**Bureau de la Communauté Germanophone à
Brussels**

**Office of the German-speaking Community
in Brussels**

Rue des Minimes 21, 1000 Brussels, Belgium
Tel. (+32) 2-5023080
Fax (+32) 2-5027646
E-mail xavier.kalbusch@dgov.be
Dir Xavier Kalbusch

Bureau de Liaison Bruxelles-Europe

Brussels-Europe Liaison Office

Avenue d'Auderghem 63, 1040 Brussels,
  Belgium
Tel. (+32) 2-2800080
Fax (+32) 2-2800386
E-mail blbe@blbe.irisnet.be
URL www.blbe.irisnet.be
Pres. Nathalie Gilson
Dir Carlo Luyckx

**Délégation Générale de la Communauté
  Française auprès de l'Union Européenne**
**Delegation of the French-speaking
  Community to the European Union**
Rond-Point Schuman 6, 1040 Brussels,
  Belgium
Tel. (+32) 2-2332186
Fax (+32) 2-2803438
E-mail yves.degreef@
  belgoeurop.diplobel.fgov.be
Sec.-Gen. Yves de Greef

**Direction des Relations Extérieures –
  Ministère de la Région de Bruxelles-
  Capitale**
Blvd du Jardin Botanique 20, 1035 Brussels,
  Belgium
Tel. (+32) 2-8003749
Fax (+32) 2-8003820
E-mail cmancel@mbhg.irisnet.be
Associate Sec.-Gen. Nobert de Cooman

**Espace International Wallonie-Bruxelles
  (EIWB)**
Place Sainctelette 2, 1080 Brussels, Belgium
Tel. (+32) 2-4218211
Fax (+32) 2-4218787
E-mail hindey@cgri.cfwb.be
URL www.eiwb.be
Gen. Man. and Gen. Commissioner Philippe
  Suinen
Principal Jean Beelen

**Ministère de la Région Wallonne – Direction
  Générale des Pouvoirs Locaux**
**Directorate-General of the Local Authorities
  of the Ministry for the Walloon Area**
Rue van Opre 91–95, 5100 Jambes, Belgium
Tel. (+32) 81-323711
Fax (+32) 81-309093
E-mail b.fontaine@mrw.wallonie.be
URL mrw.wallonie.be/dgpl
Premier Attaché DLC Bernard Fontaine
Attaché Pierre-Yves Bolen

**Ministère de l'Administration de la
  Communauté Flamande – Section Europe**
Boudewijnlaan 30, 1000 Brussels, Belgium
Tel. (+32) 2-5536177
Fax (+32) 2-5536037
E-mail isabelle.dirkx@coo.vlaanderen.be
Dir-Gen. Diane Verstraeten

**Représentation Permanente de la Région
  Bruxelles-Capitale auprès de l'Union
  Européenne**
Rond Point Schuman 6, 1040 Brussels,
  Belgium
Tel. (+32) 2-2330302
Fax (+32) 2-2804004
E-mail pgoergen@europ.irisnet.be
Representative Pascal Goergen

**Représentation Permanente de la Région
  Flamande auprès des Communautés
  Européennes**
**Permanent Représentation of the Flemish
  area to the European Communities**
Rond Point Schuman 6, 1040 Brussels,
  Belgium
Tel. (+32) 2-2330312
Fax (+32) 2-2330312
E-mail vlaamse@belgoeurop.diplobel.fgov.be
Dir Filip d'Have

Union des Villes et Communes Belges asbl
Union of Belgian Cities and Communes
Rue d'Arlon 53, Bte 4, 1040 Brussels, Belgium
Tel. (+32) 2-2385178
Fax (+32) 2-2311523
E-mail fed@uvcb-vbsg.be
URL www.uvcb-vbsg.be
Pres. M. Jef Gabriels
Sec.-Gen. M. Dominique Laurent
Federal Sec. Thérèse Renier

**Union des Villes et Communes de Wallonie
  asbl**
**Union of the Cities and Communes of
  Wallonia**
Rue d'Arlon 53, Bte 4, 1040 Brussels, Belgium
Tel. (+32) 2-2332003
Fax (+32) 2-2333113
E-mail isabelle.compagnie@uvcw.be
URL www.uvcw.be
Pres. Willy Taminiaux

Sec.-Gen. Louise-Marie Bataille
International Relations Officer Isabelle
  Compagnie

CANADA

Délégation Générale du Québec
General Delegation of Québec
Regierung von Quebec
Avenue des Arts 46, 7th floor, 1000 Brussels,
  Belgium
Tel. (+32) 2-5120036
Fax (+32) 2-5142641
E-mail qc.bruxelles@mri.gouv.qc.ca
URL www.quebec-europe.be
Delegate Gen. Christos Sirros
Adviser on EU Affairs Véronique Guevremont

CZECH REPUBLIC

Association of Agricultural Co-operatives
  and Cities of the Czech Republic (AACC)
Chaussée d'Alsemberg 876, 1180 Brussels,
  Belgium
Tel. (+32) 2-3761081
Fax (+32) 2-3761081
E-mail km.agri@compaqnet.be
Dir Karl Matoušek

Czech European Centre
Rond Point Schuman 6, 1040 Brussels,
  Belgium
Tel. (+32) 2-2828430
Fax (+32) 2-2828431
Dir M. Milan

Delegation of Prague to the EU
Avenue Palmerston 16, 1000 Brussels, Belgium
Tel. (+32) 2-2309491
Fax (+32) 2-2309535
E-mail zdenek.werner@mag.mepnet.cz
Head of Delegation Werner Zdenek

DENMARK

Aarhus EU Office
Av. de Tervuren 35, 1040 Brussels, Belgium
Tel. (+32) 2-2308732
Fax (+32) 2-2308952

E-mail info@bxl.aarhus.dk
URL www.aarhus.dk/bruxelles
Head of Office Lars Holte Nielsen

Association of County Councils in Denmark
Rue de la Science 4, 1000 Brussels, Belgium
Tel. (+32) 2-5501280
Fax (+32) 2-5501275
E-mail arf@arf.be
URL www.arf.dk
Head of Office Asger Andreasen

Copenhagen EU Office
Avenue Palmerston 26, 1000 Brussels, Belgium
Tel. (+32) 2-2854320
Fax (+32) 2-2854329
E-mail adm@copenhagencity.be
URL www.copenhagencity.dk
Head of Section Esther Bulow Davidsen

EURA Ltd
Avenue de Tervuren 35, 1040 Brussels,
  Belgium
Tel. (+32) 2-2307202
Fax (+32) 2-2801759
E-mail eurabxl@eurabxl.com
URL www.eura.dk
Project Man. Ingrida Seduikyte
Business Adviser Hans Kurt Rasmussen
Contact Agnes Uhereczky

EU-Vest
Avenue Palmerston 3, 1000 Brussels, Belgium
Tel. (+32) 2-2803254
Fax (+32) 2-2803329
E-mail jkp@euvest.com
URL www.euvest.com
Man. Johnny Killerup Pedersen

Local Government Denmark (LGDK)
Rue de la Science 4–6, 1000 Brussels, Belgium
Tel. (+32) 2-5501260
Fax (+32) 2-5501272
E-mail tha@kl.dk
URL www.kl.dk
Pres. Ejgil W. Rasmussen
Responsible for relations with the COR Thomas
  Alstrup

North Denmark EU Office

Avenue de Tervuren 35, 1040 Brussels,
Belgium
Tel. (+32) 2-2820373
Fax (+32) 2-2309015
E-mail aalborgeu@aalborg.be
URL www.eu-norddanmark.dk
Pres. Grimur Lund
Project Man. Charlotte Pedersen

Odense Denmark EU Office

Avenue Palmerston 3, 1000 Brussels, Belgium
Tel. (+32) 2-5030904
Fax (+32) 2-5031570
E-mail odense@odense.be
URL www.odense.be
Head of Office Peter T. Saugman

South Denmark European Office

Avenue Palmerston 3, 1000 Brussels, Belgium
Tel. (+32) 2-2804095
Fax (+32) 2-2854099
E-mail jakob.bork@southdenmark.be
Head of Office Jakob Bork
Contact Henrik Esmann

Storstrom Region EU Office

Avenue de Palmerston 3, 1000 Brussels,
Belgium
Tel. (+32) 2-2356653
Fax (+32) 2-2803828
E-mail Kaas@oek.stam.dk
Head of Office Katrine Aadal Andersen

West Zealand EU Office

Avenue de Palmerston 3, 1000 Brussels,
Belgium
Tel. (+32) 2-2356651
Fax (+32) 2-2803828
E-mail info@westzealand.be
URL www.vestamt.dk
Pres. Hans Jørgen Holm
Head of Office Katarina Borgh-Rahm

ESTONIA

Tallinn EU Office

Rue du Luxembourg 3, 1000 Brussels, Belgium
Tel. (+32) 2-5010837
Fax (+32) 2-5010842
E-mail kaido.sirel@tallinnlv.ee
URL http://tallinn.ee
Head of Office Kaido Sirel

FINLAND

Association of Finnish Local and Regional Authorities

Association Finlandaise des Pouvoirs Locaux et Régionaux

Verband der Stadte, Gemeinden und Regionen Finlands

Rue de la Science 4, 1000 Brussels, Belgium
Tel. (+32) 2-5490860
Fax (+32) 2-5027227
E-mail jorma.palola@aflra.fi
URL www.kunnat.net
Pres. Pekka Nousiainen
Permanent Representative Lauri Lamminmäki

City of Turku–Southwest Finland European Office

Avenue des Arts 58, 1000 Brussels, Belgium
Tel. (+32) 2-2871295
Fax (+32) 2-2871209
E-mail european.office@turku.fi
URL www.turku.fi
Head of Office Krista Taipale-Salminen

East Finland EU Office

Scotland House, Rond Point Schuman 6, 1040
Brussels, Belgium
Tel. (+32) 2-2828370
Fax (+32) 2-2828373
E-mail eu.eastfinland@eastfinland.org
URL www.eastfinland.org
Dir Jani Taivalantti
Advisor Lisbeth Mattsson

European North Lapland–Oulu

Rond-Point Schuman 6, PO Box 5, 4th floor,
1040 Brussels, Belgium
Tel. (+32) 2-2346370
Fax (+32) 2-2347911
E-mail seppo.heikkila@lapland-oulu.fi
URL www.lapland-oulu.fi
Dir Seppo Heikkilä
Special Adviser Satu Huuha

Helsinki EU Office

Représentation de Helsinki et de sa Région

Rue Belliard 15–17, 1040 Brussels, Belgium
Tel. GSM: (+32) 473661721
Fax (+32) 2-5035833
E-mail helsinki.euoffice@euhel.be
URL www.helsinki.fi/euoffice
Head of Office Eija Nylund

Rovaniemi–Lapland Office
Rue d'Arlon 38, 1000 Brussels, Belgium
Tel. (+32) 2-2333731
Fax (+32) 2-2302391
E-mail henri.hirvenoja@laplandoffice.be
URL www.rovaniemi.fi
Head of Office Henri Hirvenoja
Rel./CdR Kim Kuivelainen

South Finland EU Office
Bureau Européen du Sud de la Finlande
Avenue Tervuren 35, 1040 Brussels, Belgium
Tel. (+32) 2-2820378
Fax (+32) 2-2820370
E-mail tuula.loikkanen@skynet.be
URL www.southfinland.org
Head of Office Tuula Loikkanen

Tampere Central Region EU Office
Avenue Palmerston 3, 1000 Brussels, Belgium
Tel. (+32) 2-5031489
Fax (+32) 2-5031570
E-mail markku.valtonen@odense.be
URL www.tampere.fi
Sr Delegate Markku Valtonen

West Finland European Office
Rue Joseph II 36–38, 1000 Brussels, Belgium
Tel. (+32) 2-2869081
Fax (+32) 2-2869089
E-mail european.office@westfinland.be
URL www.wfa.fi
Dir Kari Hietala
Information Officer Elina Humala

FRANCE

Antenne Basse-Normandie Europe
Lower-Normandy Agency Europe
Avenue des Gaulois 3, 1040 Brussels, Belgium
Tel. (+32) 2-7324683
Fax (+32) 2-7324767
E-mail info@abne.be
Head of Office Adeline Jacob

Antenne de Bruxelles de la Région de Picardie
Brussels Agency for the Picardy Region
Avenue de la Joyeuse Entrée 1/5, 1040
    Brussels, Belgium
Tel. (+32) 2-2346640
Fax (+32) 2-2346641
E-mail pierre.emmanuel.thomann@skynet.be
Head of Mission Pierre Emmanuel Thomann

Antenne de la Collectivité Territoriale de Corse
Agency of the Local Authority of Corsica
Avenue des Arts 1–2, Bte 9, 1210 Brussels,
    Belgium
Tel. (+32) 2-2210435
Fax (+32) 2-2176612
E-mail ctc.dunyach@pophost.eunet.be
Dir Emmanuelle Thevignot-Dunyach

Association des Maires de France
French Mayors Association
Französische Bürgermeisterverband
Square de Meeûs 21, 1050 Brussels, Belgium
Tel. (+32) 2-5010104
Fax (+32) 2-5111147
E-mail mkeller@amf.asso.fr
URL www.amf.asso.fr
Pres. Jacques Pelissard
Sec.-Gen. André Laignel
Dir François Leonelli
Head of Office Michael Keller

Association des Régions Françaises du Grand-Est
Association of the French Eastern Regions
Rue d'Arlon 55, 1040 Brussels, Belgium
Tel. (+32) 2-2311050
Fax (+32) 2-2303848
E-mail grandest@skynet.be
Dir Christophe Goult

Association Europe–Bretagne–Pays de la Loire
Association Europe–Brittany–Country of the Loire
Avenue de Tervueren 12, 1040 Brussels,
    Belgium
Tel. (+32) 2-7354036
Fax (+32) 2-7352411
E-mail bretloire@bretloire.org
URL www.bretloire.org
Dir Martine Allais

Association Poitou-Charentes Europe (APCE)

Square Marie-Louise 77, 1000 Brussels, Belgium
Tel. (+32) 2-2305551
Fax (+32) 2-2306872
E-mail speyhorgue@apce.org
URL www.apce.org
Head of Mission Estelle Lafond

Association pour la Promotion de l'Alsace
Association for the Promotion of Alsace
Vereinigung für die Förderung von Elsass

Avenue des Arts 1–2, Bte 11, 1210 Brussels, Belgium
Tel. (+32) 2-2210431
Fax (+32) 2-2176612
E-mail b.alsace@easynet.be
URL www.promotion-alsace.org
Pres. Philippe Cailliau
Sec.-Gen. David Schwander
Administrator Odile Dage

Association pour le Développement Européen de l'Ile-de-France (ADEIF)

Rue Guimard 15, 1040 Brussels, Belgium
Tel. (+32) 2-2892510
Fax (+32) 2-5136374
E-mail adeif@adeif.be
URL www.adeif.be
Dir Françoise Chotard

Bureau Aquitaine Europe
Aquitaine Europe Office

Avenue de l'Yser 19, 1040 Brussels, Belgium
Tel. (+32) 2-7380474
Fax (+32) 2-7380475
E-mail info@bureau-aquitaine.be
Permanent Representative Marie-Pierre Mesplede

Bureau de Représentation de Provence– Alpes–Côte d'Azur à Bruxelles
Representative office of Provence–Alps–Côte d'Azur in Brussels

Avenue des Celtes 20, 1040 Brussels, Belgium
Tel. (+32) 2-7351870
Fax (+32) 2-7332536
E-mail representation.paca@bruxeurope.be
Dir Cyrille Perez
Regional Delegate Lila Bettin
Regional Delegate Stéphanie Vincent

Chambres de Commerce Ile-de-France

Avenue des Arts 36, 1040 Brussels, Belgium
Tel. (+32) 2-2231840
Fax (+32) 2-22318 56
E-mail europe@ccipif.be
Dir Sandra Penning

Délégation à l'Aménagement du Territoire et à l'Action Régionale (DATAR Europe)

Place de Louvain 14, 1000 Brussels, Belgium
Tel. (+32) 2-2298471
Fax (+32) 2-2298475
E-mail patricia.pedelabat@diplomatie.gov.fr
Head of Office Gilles Pelurson

Délégation de la Lorraine

Rue des Drapiers 40, 1050 Brussels, Belgium
Tel. (+32) 2-5028840
Fax (+32) 2-5028842
E-mail delegationlorraine@brutele.be
URL www.delegationlorraine.org
Pres. Christine Vandenhaute
Permanent Delegate Patrick Courtin

Délégation de la Polynésie Française

Square Marie-Louise 2, 1000 Brussels, Belgium
Tel. (+32) 2-2301616
Fax (+32) 2-2301400
E-mail delegation@polynesie-paris.com
Head of Office Bruno Peaucellier

Délégation de la Région Limousin

Avenue de Tervuren 12, 1040 Brussels, Belgium
Tel. (+32) 2-7333517
Fax (+32) 2-7342582
E-mail limousin@compaqnet.be
Permanent Delegate Colette Gadioux

Délégation des Côtes d'Armor

Avenue de Gisoul 76, 1200 Brussels, Belgium
Tel. (+32) 2-7715871
Fax (+32) 2-7715871
Dir Bernard Lemarchand

Délégation du Conseil Régional de Haute-Normandie

Rue Montoyer 61, 1000 Brussels, Belgium
Tel. (+32) 2-2350823
Fax (+32) 2-2301320

E-mail haute-normandie@skynet.be
Chargée de mission Barbara Lehembre
Rel./CdR Anuok Hattab

Délégation du Nord–Pas-de-Calais
Rue de l'Industrie 11, 1000 Brussels, Belgium
Tel. (+32) 2-2303036
Fax (+32) 2-2301649
E-mail bureau.nordpasdecalais@skynet.be
Representative Stephane Gerbaud

Délégation Régionale de la Région Rhône-Alpes
Rue de Trèves 49–51, Bte 2, 1040 Brussels, Belgium
Tel. (+32) 2-2820020
Fax (+32) 2-2806071
E-mail deleg.rhone-alpes@skynet.be
URL www.cr-rhone-alpes.fr
Sec.-Gen. Frédérique Barellon

Espace Moselle
Rue des Drapiers 40, 1050 Brussels, Belgium
Tel. (+32) 2-5049700
Fax (+32) 2-5049709
E-mail sales@espace-moselle.be
URL www.espace-moselle.be
Gen. Man. Alain Swinnen

Représentation Midi-Pyrénées
Rue d'Arlon 55, 1040 Brussels, Belgium
Tel. (+32) 2-2800919
Fax (+32) 2-2306783
E-mail office@midipyreneeseurope.be
URL www.midipyreneeseurope.be
Pres. Martin Malvy
Dir Elie Spiroux

GERMANY

Beobachter der Länder
Rue de Trèves 45, 1040 Brussels, Belgium
Tel. (+32) 2-2350270
Fax (+32) 2-2303555
E-mail laenderbeobachter@bruessel.eu-lb.de
Head of Office Herr Martin Bohle

Büro des Landes Berlin
Avenue Michel-Ange 71, 1000 Brussels, Belgium
Tel. (+32) 2-7380070
Fax (+32) 2-7324746

E-mail berlinerbuero@lvbe.verwalt-berlin.de
URL www.berlin.de/EU
Dir Gert Hammer
Deputy Man. (Responsible for CdR) Renate Volpel

Europabüro der Baden-Württembergischen Kommunen
Rue Guimard 7, 1040 Brussels, Belgium
Tel. (+32) 2-5136546
Fax (+32) 2-5138820
E-mail c.glietsch@europabuero-bw.de
URL www.europabuero-bw.de
Head of Office Carsten Glietsch

Europabüro der Bayerischen Kommunen
Rue Guimard 7, 1040 Brussels, Belgium
Tel. (+32) 2-5490700
Fax (+32) 2-5122451
E-mail info@ebbk.de
URL www.ebbk.de
Contact Dr Angelika Poth-Mögele

Europabüro der Deutschen Kommunalen Selbstverwaltung
German Local Government European Office – Eurocommunale
Avenue de la Renaissance 1, 1000 Brussels, Belgium
Tel. (+32) 2-7323596
Fax (+32) 2-7324091
E-mail eurocommunalle@arcadis.be
Dir Dr Ralf von Ameln

Europabüro der Sächsischen Kommunen
Rue Guimard 7, 1040 Brussels, Belgium
Tel. (+32) 2-5136408
Fax (+32) 2-5138820
E-mail info@europabuero-sn.de
Chief of Bureau Carsten Klenke

Europabüro des Deutschen Landkreistages & BAGHKV
Avenue de la Renaissance 1, 1000 Brussels, Belgium
Tel. (+32) 2-7401630
Fax (+32) 2-7401631
E-mail sekretariat.dlt@eurocommunale.org
Head of Office Regine Brunsl

Europabüro des Deutschen Städte und Gemeindebundes

Avenue des Nerviens 9–31 Bte 3, 1040 Brussels, Belgium
Tel. (+32) 2-7401640
Fax (+32) 2-7401641
E-mail dstgb@eurocommunale.org
Dir Dr Klaus Nutzenberger

Europabüro des Deutschen Städtetages

Avenue des Nerviens 9–31, 1040 Brussels, Belgium
Tel. (+32) 2-7401620
Fax (+32) 2-7401621
E-mail walter.leitermann@staedtetag.de
Leader Walter Leitermann

Frankfurt Rhein–Main EU Office

Rue de l'Amazone 2, 1050 Brussels, Belgium
Tel. (+32) 2-5357240
Fax (+32) 2-5349696
E-mail info@belgium.messafrankfurt.com
Representative Jorn Kronenwerth

Hanse Office (Hambourg et Schleswig-Holstein)

Avenue Palmerston 20, 1000 Brussels, Belgium
Tel. (+32) 2-2854640
Fax (+32) 2-2854657
E-mail hanse.office@infomaco.com
Dir Gunter Schulz

Informationsbüro des Landes Mecklenburg-Vorpommern bei der Europäischen Union

Mecklenburg-Vorpommern Information Office at the European Union

Blvd Louis Schmidt 87, 1040 Brussels, Belgium
Tel. (+32) 2-7416000
Fax (+32) 2-7416009
E-mail r.boest@mv.bei-der-eu.de
URL www.mv.bei-der-eu.de
Head of Office Dr Reinhard Boest
Contact Kirsten Schwander

Stuttgart Region European Office in Brussels

Square Vergote 39, 1030 Brussels, Belgium
Tel. (+32) 2-7370408
Fax (+32) 2-7370406
E-mail europa@region-stuttgart.de
URL www.eu.region-stuttgart.de

Pres. Jurgen Fritz
Dir Heike Thumm

Thüringer Büro

Rue Frederic Pelletier 111, 1030 Brussels, Belgium
Tel. (+32) 2-7362060
Fax (+32) 2-7365379
E-mail postbox@TSKBxl.thueringen.de
URL www.thuringer.de/de/tsk/tskbxl
Pres. Dieter Althaus
Dir Dr Paul Brockhausen
Head of Office Christine Holeschovsky

Verbindung des Landes Brandenburg bei der Europäischen Union

Rue Père Eudore Devroye 47, 1040 Brussels, Belgium
Tel. (+32) 2-7377451
Fax (+32) 2-7377469
E-mail poststelle@mdjebrx.brandenburg.de
Dir Dr Marcus Wenig

Verbindungsbüro der Freien Hansestadt Bremen bei der Europäischen Union

Avenue Palmerston 22, 1000 Brussels, Belgium
Tel. (+32) 2-2302765
Fax (+32) 2-2303658
E-mail vertretung@bremen.be
Head of Office Christian Bruns
Responsible for the CdR Constance Ripke

Verbindungsbüro des Landes Sachsen-Anhalt bei der Europäischen Union

Boulevard Saint-Michel 78–80, 1040 Brussels, Belgium
Tel. (+32) 2-7410931
Fax (+32) 2-7410939
E-mail schlemme@vb-bruessel.stk.lsa-net.de
URL www.sachsen-anhalt.de
Dir Juergen Schlemme

Verbindungsbüro des Saarlands bei der Europäischen Gemeinschaften

Avenue de la Renaissance 46, 1000 Brussels, Belgium
Tel. (+32) 2-7430790
Fax (+32) 2-7327370
E-mail office@saarlandbuero.be
Head of Office Herta Adam

Vertretung des Freistaates Bayern bei der Europäischen Union

Blvd Clovis 18, 1000 Brussels, Belgium
Tel. (+32) 2-7430440
Fax (+32) 2-7323225
E-mail Friedrich.vonheusinger@stk.bayern.de
URL www.bayern.de
Dir Edeltraud Boehm-Amtmann
Press Adviser Friedrich von Heusinger

Vertretung des Landes Baden-Würtemberg bei der Europäischen Union

Square Vergote 9, 1200 Brussels, Belgium
Tel. (+32) 2-7417711
Fax (+32) 2-7417799
E-mail poststelle@bruessel.bwl.de
Head of Office Richard Arnold

Vertretung des Landes Hessen bei der Europäischen Union

Avenue de l'Yser 19, 1040 Brussels, Belgium
Tel. (+32) 2-7324220
Fax (+32) 2-7324813
E-mail hessen.eu@lv-bruessel.hessen.de
Dir Dr Hanns-Martin Bachmann

Vertretung des Landes Niedersachsen bei der Europäischen Union

Rue Montoyer 61, 1000 Brussels, Belgium
Tel. (+32) 2-2300017
Fax (+32) 2-2301320
E-mail eu.vertretung@niedersachsen.be
URL www.stk.niedersachsen.de
Dir Michael Bertram
Adviser Dr Wolfgang Pelull

Vertretung des Landes Nordrhein-Westfalen bei der Europäischen Union

Avenue Michel-Ange 10, 1000 Brussels, Belgium
Tel. (+32) 2-7391775
Fax (+32) 2-7391707
E-mail poststelle@lv-eu.nrw.de
Dir Folker Schreiber
Relations with COR Norbert Spinrath

Vertretung des Landes Rheinland-Pfalz bei der Europäischen Union

Avenue de Tervueren 60, 1040 Brussels, Belgium
Tel. (+32) 2-7369729
Fax (+32) 2-7371333
E-mail vertretungbruessel@lv-rlp.de
Dir Hans-Joachim Gunther
Contact Gabrielle Doepgen

GREECE

Agence de Développement de Heraclion

Square de Meeûs 18, 1050 Brussels, Belgium
Tel. (+32) 2-5053443
Fax (+32) 2-5053441
E-mail da.heraklion@brutele.be
Head of Office Eleni Iniotaki

Bureau de la Région de l'Epire

Lancashire House, Rue d'Arlon 28, 1000 Brussels, Belgium
Tel. (+32) 2-2829667
Fax (+32) 2-2829617
E-mail regioeuropa@skynet.be
Dir Athanassios Goumas

Central Union of Municipalities and Communes of Greece

Avenue d'Auderghem 59, 1040 Brussels, Belgium
Tel. (+32) 2-2301376
Fax (+32) 2-2302750
E-mail eetaa@arcadis.be
Dir Katerina Karavola-Bouyer

HUNGARY

Representation of the Regions of Hungary

Square Vergote 5, 1200 Brussels, Belgium
Tel. (+32) 2-73714009
Fax (+32) 2-7356599
E-mail rep.hongrie@skynet.be
Dir Hans Beck
Rel/CdR Magdolona Baranyi

Representation Office of Budapest

Avenue d'Auderghem 63, 1040 Brussels, Belgium
Tel. (+32) 2-2307857
Fax (+32) 2-2309004
E-mail bpoffic@skynet.be
Dir Gizella Kohalmine Matyasi

IRELAND

Irish Regions Office

Rond-Point Schuman 6, 9th floor, 1040
  Brussels, Belgium
Tel. (+32) 2-2828474
Fax (+32) 2-2828475
E-mail robert.collins@iro.ie
URL www.iro.ie
Head of Office Robert Collins

NASC, West Ireland EC Liaison

Rond-Point Schuman 6, 9th floor, 1040
  Brussels, Belgium
Tel. (+32) 2-2828404
Fax (+32) 3-3838406
E-mail bennett@nasc.be
URL www.nasc.ie
Dir John Bennett

ITALY

ANCI-IDEALI Identita Europea per le Autonomie Locali Italiane

Avenue des Arts 39, 1040 Brussels, Belgium
Tel. (+32) 2-2133080
Fax (+32) 2-5135227
E-mail info@ideali.be
URL www.ideali.be
Pres. Leonardo Domenici
Dir Maria Baroni

Conferenza dei Rettori delle Università Italiane (CRUI)

Rond Point Schuman 6, 1040 Brussels,
  Belgium
Tel. (+32) 2-2357342
Fax (+32) 2-2357348
E-mail segreteria@crui.it
URL www.crui.it
Pres. Kurt Kutzler
Delegate Luiss Guido Carli

CRCI Ligurie / Unioncamere Liguri

Rue du Luxembourg 15, 1000 Brussels,
  Belgium
Tel. (+32) 2-2891391
Fax (+32) 2-2891390
E-mail raffaella.bruzzone@casaliguaria.org
Contact Drssa Raffaella Bruzzone

Desk Basilicata

Rue de l'Industrie 22, 1040 Brussels, Belgium
Tel. (+32) 2-5023131
Fax (+32) 2-5025898
E-mail basilicata@easynet.be
URL www.regione.basilicata.it
Head of Office Flavio Burlizzl

Europaregion Tirol-Sudtirol-Trentino

Avenue de Cortenbergh 52, 1000 Brussels,
  Belgium
Tel. (+32) 2-7432700
Fax (+32) 2-7420980
E-mail info@alpeuregio.org
Dir Vittorino Rodaro

Europaregion Tirol-Sudtirol-Trentino (Tirol Buro) (Provincia Autonoma di Bolzano)

Avenue de Cortenbergh 52, 1000 Brussels,
  Belgium
Tel. (+32) 2-7432700
Fax (+32) 2-7420980
E-mail info@alpeuregio.org
Dir Claudio Quaranta

Regione Abruzzo

Rond Point Schuman 6, 1040 Brussels,
  Belgium
Tel. (+32) 2-2868521
Fax (+32) 2-2868528
E-mail i.napolione@regionicentroitalia.org
URL www.regione.abruzzo.it
Pres. Ottaviano Del Turco
Head of Office Isabella Napolione

Regione Autonoma della Sardegna

Avenue des Arts 3–4–5, 1210 Brussels,
  Belgium
Tel. (+32) 2-2194058
Fax (+32) 2-2194105
E-mail sardegna@sardaigne.org
URL www.regionesardegna.it
Pres. Mario Leoni
Head of Office Bianca Bianco

Regione Autonoma Valle d'Aosta
Région autonome Vallée d'Aoste

Rue de Trèves 49/51, 1040 Brussels, Belgium
Tel. (+32) 2-2821850
Fax (+32) 2-2821858

E-mail vda_bruxelles@valleeurope.net
URL www.regione.vda.it
Pres. Carlo Perrin
Head of Office Gian Garancini

Regione Calabria

Rue d'Arlon 55, 1040 Brussels, Belgium
Tel. (+32) 2-2801991
Fax (+32) 2-2802086
E-mail regione.calabria@cercaeuropa.net
URL www.regione.calabria.it
Pres. Agazio Loiero
Dir Giuseppe Amoruso
Contact Giuseppe Mazzotta

Regione Campania

Av. de Cortenbergh 60, 1040 Brussels, Belgium
Tel. (+32) 2-7379180
Fax (+32) 2-7379199
E-mail dario.gargiulo@regionecampania.be
URL www.regione.campania.it
Dir Dario Gargiulo
Contact Claudio D'Aroma

Regione del Veneto

Rue de l'Industrie 22, 1040 Brussels, Belgium
Tel. (+32) 2-5510010
Fax (+32) 2-5510019
E-mail bruxells@regione.veneto.it
URL www.regione.veneto.it
Pres. Giancarlo Giancarlo Galan
Dir Gianlorenzo Martini

Regione Emilia Romagna

Avenue de l'Yser 19, 1040 Brussels, Belgium
Tel. (+32) 2-7323090
Fax (+32) 2-7363190
E-mail emilia-romagna@optinet.be
URL www.regione.emilia-romagna.it
Pres. Vasco Errani
Head of Office Lorenza Badiello

Regione Friuli Venezia Giulia

Rue Wirtz 50/28, 1050 Brussels, Belgium
Tel. (+32) 2-4016130
Fax (+32) 2-4016868
E-mail ines.rubino@regione.fvg.it
URL www.regione.fvg.it
Pres. Riccardo Illy
Co-ordinator Ines Flavia Rubino
Rel./CdR Poclen Luisa

Regione Lazio

Rond Point Schuman 6, 1040 Brussels, Belgium
Tel. (+32) 2-2868534
Fax (+32) 2-2868538
E-mail lazio@regionicentroitalia.org
URL www.regione.lazio.it
Pres. Piero Marrazzo
Dir Franco Oliva
Rel./CdR Fabiano de Leonardis

Regione Liguria

Rue du Luxembourg 15, 1000 Brussles, Belgium
Tel. (+32) 2-2891389
Fax (+32) 2-2891399
E-mail bruxelles@regione.liguria.it
URL www.regione.liguria.it
Pres. Sandro Biasotti
Dir Antonio Parodi

Regione Lombardia

Rue du Luxembourg 3, 1000 Brussels, Belgium
Tel. (+32) 2-5187600
Fax (+32) 2-5187626
E-mail ldelegazione_bruxelles@regione.lombardia.it
URL www.regione.lombardia.it
Dir Prof. Claude Scheiberf
Contact Domenico Beber

Regione Marche
Marches Region

Rond-Point Schuman 14, 1040 Brussels, Belgium
Tel. (+32) 2-2868542
Fax (+32 2) 2868548
E-mail marche@regionicentroitalia.org
URL www.regionicentroitalia.it
Pres. Gerlando Genuardi
Head of Office Vincenzo Cimino
Contact Antonella Passarani

Regione Molise
Molise Region

Rue Point Schuman 6, 1040 Brussels, Belgium
Tel. (+32) 2-2346305
Fax (+32) 2-2347878
E-mail carlo63marinelli@yahoo.it
URL www.regione.molise.it
Pres. Michele Iorio
Responsible Carlo Marinelli

Regione Puglia
Puglia Region
Rue du Luxembourg 3, 1000 Brussels, Belgium
Tel. (+32) 2-5010875
Fax (+32) 2-5010877
E-mail ufficio.bruxelles@regione.puglia.it
Pres. Gabinetto Del
Responsible Carla Capriati

Regione Siciliana
Sicily Region
Place du Champ de Mars 5, 1050 Brussels,
   Belgium
Tel. (+32) 2-5503800
Fax (+32) 2-5503850
E-mail presidenza.bruxelles@
   regionesiciliana.be
URL www.regione.sicilia.it
Pres. Salvatore Cuffaro
Dir Francesco Attaguile
Contact Guido Lo Porto

Regione Toscana
Tuscany Region
Rond Point Schuman 6, 1040 Brussels,
   Belgium
Tel. (+32) 2-2868561
Fax (+32) 2-2868568
E-mail toscana@regionicentroitalia.org
URL www.regione.toscana.it
Pres. Claudio Martini
Responsible Mario Badii

Regione Umbria
Umbria Region
Rond Point Schuman 6, 1040 Brussels,
   Belgium
Tel. (+32) 2-2868571
Fax (+32) 2-2868578
E-mail umbria@regionicentroitalia.org
URL www.regione.umbria.it
Pres. Bruno Bracalente
Responsibile Massimiliano Benelli
Rel./CdR Maria Paola Simone

Union Camere Piemonte
Union of Chambers of Piedmont
Rue de l'Industrie 22, 1040 Brussels, Belgium
Tel. (+32) 2-5500250
Fax (+32) 2-5500259
E-mail sede.bruxelles@
   unioncamerepiemonte.be
URL www.pie.camcom.it
Pres. Renato Viale
Dir Massimo Deandries

Union Camere Veneto
Rue de l'Industrie 22, 1040 Brussels, Belgium
Tel. (+32) 2-5510490
Fax (+32) 2-5510499
E-mail ucv.bxl@ntah.net
URL www.ven.camcom.it
Pres. Paolo Terribile
Responsible Tania Wolski

LITHUANIA
Kaunas Regional Representation
Rue Zinner 1, 1000 Brussels, Belgium
Tel. (+32) 2-2896004
Fax (+32) 2-2896001
E-mail gaile@bce-network.be
Head of Office Gaile Kasmaciauskiene

NETHERLANDS
Amsterdam Eurolink Brussel
Rue des Aduatiques 71–75, 1040 Brussels,
   Belgium
Tel. (+32) 2-7322399
Fax (+32) 2-7320442
E-mail amsterdam@nl-prov.be
URL www.ez.amsterdam.nl
Head of Office Lo Breemer

Association of Netherlands Municipalities (VNG)
Rue de la Science 4, 1000 Brussels, Belgium
Tel. (+32) 2-5501170
Fax (+32) 2-5501272
E-mail Frontoffice@vng.nl
URL www.vng.nl
Pres. Wim Deetman
Chair. Ralph Pans
Head of Office Frank Hilterman

Association of the Provinces of the Netherlands (IPO)
Rue des Aduatiques 71–75, 1040 Brussels,
   Belgium
Tel. (+32) 2-7379958
Fax (+32) 2-7367089

E-mail leeuwen@ipo.nl
URL www.ipo.nl
Deputy Sec. Henk van Leeuwen

Caster Conference and Association of Steel Territories

Avenue de Cortenbergh 118, Bte 13, 1040
Brussels, Belgium
Tel. (+32) 2-7422580
Fax (+32) 2-7422581
E-mail i.vanderstorm@econcepteurope.com
Contact I. van der Storm

East Netherlands Provinces (Overijssel/ Gelderland)

Rue des Aduatiques 71–75, 1040 Brussels,
Belgium
Tel. (+32) 2-7379960
Fax (+32) 2-7379961
E-mail oost.nl@nl-prov.be
Co-ordinator Hein Cannegieter
Dir Rob van Eijkeren

Huis van de Nederlandse Provincies
House of the Dutch Provinces

Aduatukersstraat 71–75, 1040 Brussels,
Belgium
Tel. (+32) 2-7379957
Fax (+32) 2-7379961
E-mail hnp@nl-prov.be
URL www.nl-prov.be
Co-ordinator Hein Cannegieter
Information Officer Karin Schilder

North Netherlands Provinces (Friesland/ Groningen/Dente)

Rue des Aduatiques 71–75, 1040 Brussels,
Belgium
Tel. (+32) 2-7379944
Fax (+32) 2-7379961
E-mail roona@nl-prov.be
Representative Dick Michel
Dir Bert Roona

Province of Flevoland

Rue des Aduatiques 71–75, 1040 Brussels,
Belgium
Tel. (+32) 2-7379953
Fax (+32) 2-7367089
E-mail venema@flevoland.nl
Representative Sidony Venema

Province of Noord-Holland

Rue des Aduatiques 71–75, 1040 Brussels,
Belgium
Tel. (+32) 2-7379952
Fax (+32) 2-7367089
E-mail keulenh@noord-holland.nl
URL www.noord-holland.nl
Representative Marion van Kampen

Province of South-Holland

Rue des Aduatiques 71–75, 1040 Brussels,
Belgium
Tel. (+32) 2-7379951
Fax (+32) 2-7367089
E-mail schim@nl-prov.be
Representative Regina Schim van der Loeff

Province of Utrecht

Rue des Aduatiques 71–75, 1040 Brussels,
Belgium
Tel. (+32) 2-7379953
Fax (+32) 2-7367089
E-mail barg@nl-prov.be
URL www.provincie-utrecht.nl
Adviser Bas van den Barg

Regio Randstad
Randstad Region

Rue des Aduatiques 71–75, 1040 Brussels,
Belgium
Tel. (+32) 2-7379965
Fax (+32) 2-7367089
E-mail pluckel@nl-prov.be
URL www.regio-randstad.nl
Head of Office Hans Pluckel

Southern Netherlands Provinces Zeeland– Noord Brabant–Limburg

Rue des Aduatiques 71–75, 1040 Brussels,
Belgium
Tel. (+32) 2-7379971
Fax (+32) 2-7379961
E-mail degroot@nl-prov.be
Contact Jacqueline De Groot

NORWAY

Kommunenes Sentralforbund
Norwegian Association of Local and Regional Authorities

Rue de la Science 4, 1000 Brussels, Belgium

Tel. (+32) 2-5501291
Fax (+32) 2-5501295
E-mail ks-brussel@ks.no
URL www.ks.no
Representative Ase Erdal

Stavanger-Regionens Europakontor

Rue de la Tourelle 37, 1040 Brussels,
　Belgium
Tel. (+32) 2-2311884
Fax (+32) 2-2800690
E-mail pal@onemarket.be
URL www.one-market.org
Dir Pal Jacob Jacobsen

POLAND

Association of Lower Silesia in the EU

Avenue d'Auberghem 22–28, 1000 Brussels,
　Belgium
Tel. (+32) 2-7402726
Fax (+32) 2-7402720
E-mail alsieu@sn.com.pl
URL www.dolnyslaskwuniieuropejskiej.pl
Pres. Emilian Stańczyszyn
Head of Office Bogna Rodziewicz

**Eastern Poland Euro-Office Lubelskie-
　Podlaskie**

Rue de Trèves 49, bte 7, 1040 Brussels,
　Belgium
Tel. (+32) 2-2850615
Fax (+32) 2-2307035
E-mail obara@taseuro.com
Dir Aneta Obara

Information Office of the Opole Voivodship

Square de Meeûs 18, 1050 Brussels,
　Belgium
Tel. (+32) 2-5501030
Fax (+32) 2-5053441
E-mail opole@brutele.be
Dir Marta Chudzikaewicz

**Pomeranian Permanent Representation to
　the European Union**

Square de Meeûs 18, 1050 Brussels, Belgium
Tel. (+32) 2-5053447
Fax (+32) 2-5053441
E-mail pomerania@brutele.be
Dir Alicja Majewska-Galeziak

**Representation of the Malopolskie
　Voivodship**

Rond Point Schuman 6, 1040 Brussels,
　Belgium
Tel. (+32) 2-2357352
Fax (+32) 2-2357348
E-mail apawl@malopolska.mw.gov.pl
Head of Office Andrzej Pawlica

Representation Office of the Mazovia Region

Avenue Auderghem 63, 1040 Brussels,
　Belgium
Tel. (+32) 2-2309662
Fax (+32) 2-2307083
E-mail anna.burylo@skynet.be
Dir Anna Burylo

PORTUGAL

**Représentation Permanente du Portugal
　auprès de l'Union Européenne**

**Portuguese Permanent Representation to the
　European Union**

Av. de Cortenbergh 12, Kortenberglaan, 1040
　Brussels, Belgium
Tel. (+32) 2-2864211
Fax (+32) 2-2310026
E-mail reper@reper-portugal.be
URL www.reper-portugal.be
Man. Dir Antonia Santos

SLOVAKIA

**Bureau de Liaison de la Région Autonome
　de Bratislava**

Avenue Michel-Ange 75, 1000 Brussels,
　Belgium
Tel. (+32) 2-7420777
Fax (+32) 2-7420791
E-mail bratislava.region@skynet.be
Dir-Rel./CdR Andrea Oel-Brettschneider

SPAIN

Cabildo Insular de Gran Canaria

Rue A. Fauchille 7, 1150 Brussels, Belgium
Tel. (+32) 2-7326585
Fax (+32) 2-7330200
E-mail bruselas@eurovias.com
Pres. Jose Manuel Soria
Contact Rodriguez Ordonez

Centre des Baléares Europe

Centre Balears Europa

Avenue des Arts 3–5–7, 7 pis, 1210 Brussels, Belgium

Tel. (+32) 2-2231410

Fax (+32) 2-2232524

E-mail centre.balears.europa@skynet.be

URL www.cbe.es

Dir Manuel Jaen Palacios

Regional delegate Antoni Costa

Responsible for the COR Margalida Amoros Bauza

Delegación de la Comunidad Valenciana en Bruselas

Rue de la Loi 227, 1040 Brussels, Belgium

Tel. (+32) 2-2302820

Fax (+32) 2-2309019

E-mail ycolorado@delcomval.be

Responsible for the COR Ainara Gomez Lopez

Delegación de la Diputación de Barcelona

Avenue des Arts 3–5, 1050 Brussels, Belgium

Tel. (+32) 2-2233521

Fax (32) 2-2233527

E-mail diba.bxl@skynet.be

Dir Blanca Soler-Tobella

Delegación del Gobierno de Canarias

Avenue Livingstone 21, 1000 Brussels, Belgium

Tel. (+32) 2-5349733

Fax (+32) 2-5349734

E-mail jluebar@gobiernodecanarias.org

URL www.gobiernodecanarias.org

Dir Jose Miguel Luengo Barreto

Rel./CdR Julian Zafra

Delegación del Gobierno de Navarra

Avenue des Arts 3–4–5, 4ème étage, 1210 Brussels, Belgium

Tel. (+32) 2-2237539

Fax (+32) 2-2237542

E-mail europa@navarra.be

Head of Office Maria Lozano Ruiz

Délégation du Pays Basque à Bruxelles (EUSKADI)

Rue des Deux Eglises 27, 1000 Brussels, Belgium

Tel. (+32) 2-2854510

Fax (+32) 2-2854511

E-mail bruselas@ej-gv.es

Delegate Ibon Mendibelzua

Fundación Galicia-Europa

Galicia Europa Foundation

Avenue Milcamps 105, 1030 Brussels, Belgium

Tel. (+32) 2-7355440

Fax (+32) 2-7354678

E-mail bruselas@fundationgalaciaeuropa.org

URL www.fundaciongaliciaeuropa.org

Pres. Manuel Fraga Iribarne

Dir Ana Ramos Barbosa

Rel./CdR Marcos Martin Perez

Gobierno de Aragón

Square de Meeûs 18, 1050 Brussels, Belgium

Tel. (+32) 2-5024344

Fax (+32) 2-5027661

E-mail dga.bxl@brutele.be

URL www.aragob.es

Pres. Marcelino Iglesias Ricou

Dir Mateo Sierra Bardaji

Rel./CdR Pedro Garcia

Instituto de Fomento de la Region de Murcia (INFO)

Avenue des Arts 3–5, 1210 Brussels, Belgium

Tel. (+32) 2-2233348

Fax (+32) 2-2191458

E-mail lucia.huertas@info.carm.es

URL www.ifrm-murcia.es

Dir Lucía Huertas Suanzes

Junta de Andalucia

Avenue des Arts 4 (2e Etage), 1210 Brussels, Belgium

Tel. (+32) 2-2090330

Fax (+32) 2-2090331

E-mail delegacion.bruselas@ junta-andalucia.org

URL www.juntadeandalucia.es

Pres. Manuel Chaves González

Dir Miguel Lucena

Delegate Elvira Saint-Gerons Herrera

Junta de Comunidades de Castilla La Mancha

Rue de la Loi 83–85, Lex Building 1a, 2a Planta, 1040 Brussels, Belgium

Tel. (+32) 2-2311477

Fax (+32) 2-2310313

E-mail castilla-lamancha@jccm.skynet.be
URL www.jccm.es
Dir Javier Jimenez Moratalla
Rel./CdR Abencio Cutanda

Oficina de Asuntos Europeos Principado de Asturias

Avenue des Arts 3–5, 1210 Brussels, Belgium
Tel. (+32) 2-2230214
Fax (+32) 2-2230494
E-mail pasbrus@euronet.be
Dir Javier Fernandez Lopez
Rel./CdR Santiago Martinez Iglesias

Oficina de Extremadura en Bruselas

Sq. Ambiorix 17, 1000 Brussels, Belgium
Tel. (+32) 2-7365950
Fax (+32) 2-7366010
E-mail fomento.bxl@skynet.be
URL www.extremaduraeuropa.org
Dir Teresa Rainha

Oficina de la Comunidad de Madrid en Bruselas

Avenue de la Toison d'Or 55, 3°, 1060
  Brussels, Belgium
Tel. (+32) 2-5347439
Fax (+32) 2-5347431
E-mail comunidad.madrid.oficina@skynet.be
URL www.madrid.org
Dir Alfredo Sánchez Gimeno
Responsible for the COR Pilar Garcia de La
  Cuadra

Oficina de la Junta de Castilla y León en Bruselas

Avenue des Arts,3–4–5, 1210 Brussels,
  Belgium
Tel. (+32) 2-2230255
Fax (+32) 2-2230057
E-mail oficina.cyl@skynet.be
URL www.jcyl.es
Pres. Juan Vicente Herrera Campo
Head of Office Maria José de no Sanchez de
  Leon
Rel./CdR José Juan Rosado Sanchez

Oficina de La Rioja en Brusales

Avenue des Arts 3 (9-ième), 1210 Brussels,
  Belgium
Tel. (+32) 2-2190357
Fax (+32) 2-2193538

E-mail ofirioja1@euronet.be
URL www.larioja.org
Pres. Pedro Sanz
Dir Marta Romo

Oficina del Gobierno de Cantabria en Bruselas

Blvd du Régent 58, 1000 Brussels, Belgium
Tel. (+32) 2-5128101
Fax (+32) 2-5122129
E-mail ue@cantabria.be
URL www.gobcantabria.es
Pres. Miguel Ángel Revilla Roiz
Dir Immaculada Valencia Bayon
Rel./CdR Raquel Rodríguez Fernández

Patronat Catala Pro Europa

Rue de la Loi 227, 1040 Brussels, Belgium
Tel. (+32) 2-2310330
Fax (+32) 2-2302110
E-mail pcpe.bru@infoeuropa.org
URL www.infoeuropa.org
Sec.-Gen. Anna Terrón
Dir Immaculada Buldu-Freixa

SWEDEN

Baltic Sea Seven Islands EU Office

Scotland House, Rond Point Schuman 6, 1040
  Brussels, Belgium
Tel. (+32) 2-2828445
Fax (+32) 2-2828449
E-mail B7@eurodesk.org
URL www.b7.org
Dir Juergen Samuelson
Rel./CdR Jacob Hensen

Central Sweden Brussels Office

Rue du Luxembourg 3, 1000 Brussels, Belgium
Tel. (+32) 2-5010880
Fax (+32) 2-5010749
E-mail info@centralsweden.be
URL www.centralsweden.se
Dir Maria Fogelstrom-Kylberg
Information Officer Eva Bjork

City of Malmo EU Office

Baltic House, Avenue Palmerston 26, 1000
  Brussels, Belgium
Tel. (+32) 2-2854323
Fax (+32) 2-2854329

E-mail ola.nord@malmo.be
URL www.malmo.se
Head of Office Ola Nord

East Sweden EU-Office

Avenue Palmerston 26, 1000 Brussels, Belgium
Tel. (+32) 2-2350011
Fax (+32) 2-2309087
E-mail info@eastsweden.be
URL www.eastsweden.org
Dir Annelie Nylander
Information Officer Maria Möllergren

Federation of Swedish County Councils

Rue de la Science 4, Wetenschapsstraat 4, 1000 Brussels, Belgium
Tel. (+32) 2-5490863
Fax (+32) 2-5027227
E-mail eag@lf.se
URL www.skl.se
Office Man. Elmire af Geijerstam

Mid Scandinavia European Office (Mid Sweden Office)

Rue Guillaume Tell 59B, 1060 Brussels, Belgium
Tel. (+32) 2-5426311
Fax (+32) 2-5431045
E-mail mseo@wanadoo.be
Dir Lisa Jonsson

North Sweden European Office

Avenue Palmerston 26, 1000 Brussels, Belgium
Tel. (+32) 2-2821820
Fax (+32) 2-2821821
E-mail contact@northsweden.org
URL www.northsweden.org
Dir Nils-Olof Forsgren
Head of Office Maria Larsson

South Sweden European Office

Avenue Palmerston 26, 1000 Brussels, Belgium
Tel. (+32) 2-2352660
Fax (+32) 2-2352669
E-mail info@sydsam.be
URL www.sydsam.se
Pres. Roger Kaliff
Dir Sophie Gardestedt
Dir, Communication and Analysis Per Tryding

Stockholm Region

Avenue de Cortenbergh 52, 1000 Brussels, Belgium
Tel. (+32) 2-7400600
Fax (+32) 2-7400616
E-mail asa.fornander@stockholmregion.org
URL www.stockholmregion.org
Man. Dir Thomas Friis Konst

Swedish Association of Local Authorities and Regions

Rue de la Science 4, 1000 Brussels, Belgium
Tel. (+32) 2-5490860
Fax (+32) 2-5027227
E-mail eag@lf.se
URL www.svekom.se
Dir Elmire af Geijerstam

West Sweden EU & Representation Office

Sweden House, Rue du Luxembourg 3, 1000 Brussels, Belgium
Tel. (+32) 2-5010840
Fax (+32) 2-5010842
E-mail kp@westsweden.se
URL www.westsweden.se
Head of Office Kjell Peterson
Rel./CdR Kajsa Sundstrom van Zeveren

SWITZERLAND

Representation of the Swiss Cantons

C/o Oppenheimer Wolff and Donnelly, Avenue Louise 240, Bte 5, 1050 Brussels, Belgium
Tel. (+32) 2-6260500
Fax (+32) 2-6260510
E-mail jrussotto@oppenheimer.com
Esq. Partner Jean Russotto

UNITED KINGDOM

Association of London Government European Service

London House, Rue du Trône 108, 1050 Brussels, Belgium
Tel. (+32) 2-6500819
Fax (+32) 2-6500826
E-mail alg-brussels@gle.co.uk
URL www.alg-europe.gov.uk
Head of Office Amanda Brandellero

Cheshire Brussels Office

North West of England House, Rue du Marteau
21, 1000 Brussels, Belgium
Tel. (+32) 2-2295376
Fax (+32) 2-2295383
E-mail johnstonn@chelsire-brussels.com
Head of Office Nicola Johnston

COSLA / Scottish Local Government

Scotland House, Rond Point Schuman 6, 1040
Brussels, Belgium
Tel. (+32) 2-2828395
Fax (+32) 2-2828429
E-mail cosla@pophost.eunet.be
URL www.cosla.gov.uk
Pres. Cllr Pat Watters
Man. Silke Isbrand

East of England European Partnership

Square de Meeûs 18, Bte 7, 1050 Brussels,
Belgium
Tel. (+32) 2-2891200
Fax (+32) 2-2891209
E-mail brusselsoffice@eastofengland.be
URL www.eastofengland.be
Head of Office Jenny De Rykman
Contact Helen Jackson

East of Scotland European Consortium (ESEC)

Scotland House, Rond Point Schuman 6, 1040
Brussels, Belgium
Tel. (+32) 2-2828428
Fax (+32) 2-2828429
E-mail esec@dundeecity.gov.uk
URL www.esec.org.uk
Head of Office Andrea Schwedler

England's East Midlands European Office (EMEO)

Avenue d'Auderghem 22–28, 1040 Brussels,
Belgium
Tel. (+32) 2-7359938
Fax (+32) 2-7352758
E-mail info@eastmidlandseurope.org
URL www.eastmidlandseurope.org
Dir Iain Derrick

Essex International

Square de Meeûs 18, 1050 Brussels, Belgium
Tel. (+32) 2-5053440
Fax (+32) 2-5053441

E-mail essex@brutele.be
Pres. Steven R Abbott
Head of Office Mark West

Greater Manchester Brussels Office

Rue du Marteau 21, 1000 Brussels, Belgium
Tel. (+32) 2-2295374
Fax (+32) 2-2295383
E-mail catherine.feore@agma-brussels.org
Head of Office Catherine Feore

Hampshire, Isle of Wight Office and West Sussex Office

South East England House, Square de Meeûs
35, 1000 Brussels, Belgium
Tel. (+32) 2-5040720
Fax (+32) 2-5040722
E-mail info@hwws.southeastenglandhouse.net
Dir Daniela Terruso

Highlands and Islands European Office

Scotland House, Rond Point Schuman 6, 1040
Brussels, Belgium
Tel. (+32) 2-2828360
Fax (+32) 2-2828363
E-mail marie.orban@pophost.eunet.be
Head of Office Marie-Yvonne Orban

Kent Partnership Office

South East England House, Square de Meeûs
35, 1000 Brussels, Belgium
Tel. (+32) 2-5040750
Fax (+32) 2-5040755
E-mail brussels.office@kent.gov.uk
Head of European Affairs Marie Dancourt-
Cavanagh
Responsible for European Transactions Stacy
Watts

Lancashire Brussels Office

North West of England House, Rue du Marteau
21, 1000 Brussels, Belgium
Tel. (+32) 2-2295371
Fax (+32) 2-2295383
E-mail alona.bruce@lancashire-brussels.org
Head of Office Alona Bruce
European Policy Officer James Sharples

Local Government International Bureau (LGIB) and Local Government Association – Joint Brussels Office

Rue d'Arlon 22–24, 1050 Brussels, Belgium

Tel. (+32) 2-5023680
Fax (+32) 2-5024035
E-mail brussels.office@lgib.org
Head of Office Richard Kitt
Policy and Co-ordination Officer Dominic
Rowles

**London's European Office, Greater London
Authority**

London House, Leopold Plaza, Rue du Trône
108, 1050 Brussels, Belgium
Tel. (+32) 2-6500800
Fax (+32) 2-6500824
E-mail european.office@london.gov.uk
URL www.london.gov.uk
Head of Office Anna Harradine

Merseyside Brussels Office

North West of England House, Rue du Marteau
21, 1000 Brussels, Belgium
Tel. (+32) 2-2295377
Fax (+32) 2-2295383
E-mail alex.weston@merseyside-europe.org
URL www.merseyside-europe.org
Man. Alex Weston

North of England Office

Avenue de Tervueren 78, 1040 Brussels,
Belgium
Tel. (+32) 2-7353547
Fax (+32) 2-7354074
E-mail euro@neobxl.be
URL www.neobxl.be
Head of Office Stephen Howell

North West Regional Assembly

North West of England House, Rue du Marteau
21, 1000 Brussels, Belgium
Tel. (+32) 2-2295373
Fax (+32) 2-2295383
E-mail abigail.howarth@
northwesthouse-brussels.org
URL www.nwra.gov.uk
Head of Office Abigail Howarth

Office of the Northern Ireland Executive

Rue Wiertz 50, 1050 Brussels, Belgium
Tel. (+32) 2-2901334
Fax (+32) 2-2901332
E-mail info.brusselsoffice@ofmdfmni.gov.uk
Deputy Dir William Dukelow

Scotland Europa

Scotland House, Rond-Point Robert Schuman
6, 1040 Brussels, Belgium
Tel. (+32) 2-2828304
Fax (+32) 2-2828300
E-mail information.desk@scotent.co.uk
URL www.scotlandeuropa.com
Chief Exec. Donald MacInnes
Sec. Anna-Marie de Pillecyn

Scottish Development International
**Agence de développement économique
international de l'Ecosse**

Scotland House, Rond Point Schuman 6, 1040
Brussels, Belgium
Tel. (+32) 2-2828400
Fax (+32) 2-2828414
E-mail maryse.marcherta@cotent.co.uk
URL www.scottishdevelopmentinternational.it
Field Man. Maryse Marcherat

Scottish Executive EU Office

Scotland House, Rond Point Schuman 6, 1040
Brussels, Belgium
Tel. (+32) 2-2828330
Fax (+32) 2-2828345
E-mail seeuo-info@scotland.gsi.gov.uk
URL www.scotland.gov.uk
Head of Office George Calder

Scottish Parliament
Parlement écossais
Schottischen Parlaments

Scotland House, Rond Point Schuman 6, 1040
Brussels, Belgium
Tel. (+32) 2-2828377
E-mail terry.shevlin@scottish.parliament.uk
Contact Terry Shevlin

South and North-East Scotland

Rue Franklin 113, 1000 Brussels, Belgium
Tel. (+32) 2-7355873
Fax (+32) 2-7355766
E-mail dunsmore@compuserve.com
Head of Office Richard Dunsmore

South East Partners

South East England House, Square de Meeûs
35, 1000 Brussels, Belgium
Tel. (+32) 2-5040730
Fax (+32) 2-5040722

E-mail info@southeastpartners.seeh.net
Head of Office Korrina Stewart
Information Asst Nick Allen

South West UK Brussels Office

Avenue Michel-Ange 86, 1000 Brussels,
Belgium
Tel. (+32) 2-7344110
Fax (+32) 2-7344434
E-mail info@southwestuk.be
URL www.westofenglandineurope.org.uk
Head of Office Eleni Marianou

Thames Valley Brussels Office

South East England House, Square de Meeûs
35, 1000 Brussels, Belgium
Tel. (+32) 2-5040736
Fax (+32) 2-5040722
E-mail paola.ottonello@
thamesvalley.southeastenglandhouse.net
URL www.actvar.gov.uk
Head of Office Paola Ottonello

Welsh Local Government Association
Verband der Walisischen Lokalbehörden

Rue Joseph II 20, 1000 Brussels, Belgium
Tel. (+32) 2-5064477
Fax (+32) 2-5028360
E-mail reception@ewrop.com
URL www.wlga.gov.uk

Head of European Office Simon Pascoe
Contact Nia Lewis

West Midlands in Europe

Avenue d'Auderghem 22–28, 1040 Brussels,
Belgium
Tel. (+32) 2-7402710
Fax (+32) 2-7402720
E-mail info@westmidlandsineurope.org
URL www.westmidlandsineurope.org
Dir Glynis Whiting
Rel./CdR Gail Harris

West of Scotland European Consortium

C/o Scotland Europa, Scotland House, Rond
Point Schuman 6, 1040 Brussels, Belgium
Tel. (+32) 2-2828425
Fax (+32) 2-2828429
E-mail cosla@pophost.eunet.be
European Officer Malcolm Leitch

Yorkshire and Humber European Office

Avenue de Cortenbergh 118, PO Box 13, 1000
Brussels, Belgium
Tel. (+32) 2-7353408
Fax (+32) 2-7356214
E-mail european.office@yorkshire.be
URL www.yhassembly.gov.uk
Dir Paul Wardle
Office and Information Man. Filippo Compagni

NATIONAL ASSOCIATIONS WITH REPRESENTATION IN BRUSSELS

AUSTRIA

Österreichische Fremdenverkehrswerbung

Austrian National Tourist Office

Office National Autrichien du Tourisme

Postbus 700, 1050 Brussels, Belgium
Tel. (+32) 2-6460610
Fax (+32) 2-6404693
E-mail info@oewbru.be
URL www.austria-tourism.at

Dir Janauschek

Österreichische Notariatskammer

Austrian Chamber of Notaries

Conseil National du Notariat Autrichien

Rue Newton 1, 1000 Brussels, Belgium
Tel. (+32) 2-7379000
Fax (+32) 2-7379009
E-mail notar@arcadis.be
URL www.notar.at

Permanent Representative Matyk Stefan

Österreichischer Raiffeisenverband

Rue du Commerce 20–22, 1000 Brussels,
  Belgium
Tel. (+32) 2-5490678
Fax (+32) 2-5026407
E-mail raiffbxl@raiffeisenbrussels.be
URL www.raiffeisenverband.at

Pres. Eduardo Baamonde
Representative Dr Helga Steinberger
Sec.-Gen. Dr Ferdinand Maier

DENMARK

Danmarks Rederiforening

Danish Shipowners' Association

Rue du Cornet 83, 1040 Brussels, Belgium
Tel. (+32) 2-2308141
Fax (+32) 2-2308829
E-mail brx@danishshipping.com

Gen. Man. Michael Lund

European Trade Union Confederation (ETUC)

Confédération européenne des syndicats (CES)

Boulevard du Roi Albert II 5, 1210 Brussels,
  Belgium
Tel. (+32) 2-2240411
Fax (+32) 2-2240454
E-mail etuc@etuc.org
URL www.etuc.org

Pres. Candido Mendes
Sec.-Gen. J. Monks
Press Officer Emanuela Bonacina

FRANCE

Agence de l'Environnement et de la Maitrise de l'Énergie (ADEME)

French Environment and Energy Management Agency

Avenue des Arts 53, 1040 Brussels, Belgium
Tel. (+32) 2-5451141
Fax (+32) 2-5139170
E-mail ademe.brux@euronet.be
URL www.ademe.fr

Pres. Michele Pappalardo
Sec.-Gen. Francois Demarcq
Energy Specialist Gérard Saunier

Agence Nationale de Valorisation de la Recherche (ANVAR)

Rue du Luxembourg 3, 1000 Brussels, Belgium
Tel. (+32) 2-5010732
Fax (+32) 2-5010733
E-mail bruxe@anvar.fr
URL www.anvar.fr

Pres. Jean-Pierre Denis
Sec.-Gen. Jean-Marie Sepulchre
Dir Jean-Claude Poree

Association des Ecoles des Mines (ARMINES)

C/o CLORA, Avenue des Arts 8, 1210
  Brussels, Belgium
Tel. (+32) 2-5068864
Fax (+32) 2-5068845

E-mail organisme@clora.net

Association Française des Entreprises Privées (AFEP)

French Association of Private Enterprises

Rue Royale 35, 1000 Brussels, Belgium
Tel. (+32) 2-2199020
Fax (+32) 2-2199506
E-mail afep@skynet.be

Pres. Bertrand Collomb
Project Man. Armand Maheas

Association Nationale des Élus de la Montagne (ANEM)

National Association of the Elected Officials of the Mountain Regions

C/o ACFCI, Avenue des Arts 1–2, bte 9, 1210 Brussels, Belgium
Tel. (+32) 2-2210411
Fax (+32) 2-2176987
E-mail aem@promonte-aem.org
URL www.anem.org

Pres. François Brottes
Sec.-Gen. Martial Saddier

Breiz Europe

Rue Froissart 141, 1040 Brussels, Belgium
Tel. (+32) 2-2304426
Fax (+32) 2-2305183
E-mail breiz.europe@skynet.be

Pres. Jean-Pierre
Dir Christophe Hamon

Bureau Européen de l'Artisanat Français (BEAF)

Rue Jacques de Lalaing 4, 1040 Brussels, Belgium
Tel. (+32) 2-2801443
Fax (+32) 2-2307861
E-mail r.sioldea@ueapme.com

Contact Hubert Delorme

CEMAGREF – La Recherche pour l'Ingénierie de l'Agriculture et de l'Environnement

CEMAGREF – Agricultural and Environmental Engineering Research

C/o CLORA, Avenue des Arts 8, 1210 Brussels, Belgium
Tel. (+32) 2-5068866
Fax (+32) 2-5068845

E-mail info@cemagref.fr
URL www.cemagref.fr

Pres. Augustin Luxin
Sec.-Gen. Alain Vidal

Centre National de la Recherche Scientifique (CNRS)

National Centre for Scientific Research

C/o CLORA, Avenue des Arts 8, 1210 Brussels, Belgium
Tel. (+32) 2-5068840
Fax (+32) 2-5068845
E-mail cnrs@clora.net
URL www.cnrs.fr

Pres. Prof. Bernard Meunier
Dir Monika Dietl

Centre National d'Études Spatiales (CNES)

C/o CLORA, Avenue des Arts 8, 1210 Brussels, Belgium
Tel. (+32) 2-5068802
Fax (+32) 2-5068845
E-mail cnes@clora.net
URL www.cnes.fr

Pres. Yannick d'Escatha
Co-ordinator André Marbach

Club des Organismes de Recherche Associés (CLORA)

Avenue des Arts 8, 1210 Brussels, Belgium
Tel. (+32) 2-5068864
Fax (+32) 2-5068845
E-mail secretariat@clora.net
URL www.clora.net

Sec.-Gen. Marie-Noëlle de Hennin

Commissariat à l'Énergie Atomique (CEA)

French Atomic Energy Commission

C/o CLORA, Avenue des Arts 8, 1210 Brussels, Belgium
Tel. (+32) 2-5068846
Fax (+32) 2-5068845
E-mail cea@clora.net
URL www.cea.fr

Pres. Gary Shapiro
Contact Guillaume Gillet

Conférence des Présidents d'Université (CPU)

Conference of University Presidents (CPU)

C/o CLORA, Avenue des Arts 8, 1210
  Brussels, Belgium
Tel. (+32) 2-5068856
Fax (+32) 2-5068845
E-mail dalle@clora.net
Contact Geneviève Dalle
Contact Patrick Navatte

Délégation des Barreaux de France

Avenue de la Joyeuse Entrée 1, 1040 Brussels,
  Belgium
Tel. (+32) 2-2308331
Fax (+32) 2-2306277
E-mail dbf@dbfbruxelles.com
URL www.dbfbruxelles.com
Dir Laurent Petitjean

**Entreprise Rhône-Alpes International
(ERAI)**

Rue de Trèves 49–51, 1040 Brussels, Belgium
Tel. (+32) 2-2820030
Fax (+32) 2-2806072
E-mail benelux@erai.org
URL www.erai.org
Pres. Perotti Reille
Agency Dir Lionel Dupré

Entreprises Equipement France (EEF)

C/o ACFCI, Avenue Boileau 16, 1040
  Brussels, Belgium
Tel. (+32) 2-2210429
Fax (+32) 2-2176612
E-mail eef@arcadis.be
Contact Alain Jaffre

**Fédération des Industries des Equipements
pour Véhicules (FIEV)**

French Vehicle Equipment Industries

C/o MEDEF, Rue de Trèves 45, 1040 Brussels,
  Belgium
Tel. (+32) 2-2310730
Fax (+32) 2-2310838
E-mail medef.brux@skynet.be
URL www.fiev.fr
Contact Marie Christine Vaccarezza

**Fédération Nationale des Transports
Routiers (FNTR)**

Avenue Louis Gribeaumont 1, Bte 2, 1150
  Brussels, Belgium

Tel. (+32) 2-7726556
Fax (+32) 2-7721126
URL www.fntr.fr
Pres. Petit
Contact Isabelle Maitre

**Institut de Recherche pour le
Développement (IRD)**

Institute of Research for Development

C/o CLORA, Rue Montoyer 47, 1000 Brussels,
  Belgium
Tel. (+32) 2-5068848
Fax (+32) 2-5068845
E-mail brugaillere@clora.net
URL www.ird.fr
Pres. Terry Bergan
Sec.-Gen. Christine d'Argouges
Dir-Gen. Serge Calabre

**Institut Français de Recherche pour
l'Exploitation de la Mer (IFREMER)**

**French Research Institute for Exploitation of
the Sea**

C/o CLORA, Rue Montoyer 47, 1000 Brussels,
  Belgium
Tel. (+32) 2-5068860
Fax (+32) 2-5068845
E-mail ifremer@clora.net
URL www.ifremer.fr
Pres. JeanYves Perrot
Contact Aurélien Carbonnière

**Institut National de la Recherche
Agronomique (INRA)**

C/o CLORA, Rue Montoyer 47, 1000 Brussels,
  Belgium
Tel. (+32) 2-5068854
Fax (+32) 2-5068845
E-mail lamarque@clora.net
URL www.inra.fr
Contact Claudine Lamarque

**Institut National de la Santé et de la
Recherche Médicale (INSERM)**

C/o CLORA, Rue Montoyer 47, 1000 Brussels,
  Belgium
Tel. (+32) 2-5068850
Fax (+32) 2-5068845
E-mail bennigsen@clora.net
URL www.inserm.fr
Contact Elisabeth Benninsen

La Poste

Rue du Luxembourg 3, 1000 Brussels, Belgium
Tel. (+32) 2-5010746
Fax (+32) 2-5010744
E-mail f.mary@laposte.skynet.be
URL www.laposte.fr
Dir F. Mary

Mouvement des Entreprises de France (MEDEF)
Meeting with the French Business Confederation

Rue de Trèves 45, 1040 Brussels, Belgium
Tel. (+32) 2-2310730
Fax (+32) 2-2310838
E-mail medef.brux@skynet.be
Permanent Delegate Marie-Christine Vaccarezza

Office National d'Études et de Recherches Aérospatiales (ONERA)
National Aerospace Research Centre
5 blvd Paul Painlevé, 59045 Lille Cedex, France
Tel. (+33) 3-20-49-69-00
Fax (+33) 3-20-49-69-99
E-mail mainguy@onera.fr
URL www.onera.fr
Dir Anne-Marie Mainguy

Président des Conseillers du Commerce Extérieur de la France
Avenue des Arts 8, 1210 Brussels, Belgium
Tel. (+32) 2-5068811
Fax (+32) 2-5068817
E-mail cfcib@cfci.be
URL www.ccife.org
Pres. Rose Cathy Handy
Dir Andrée Dufau

Réseau Scientifique et Technique (RST) du Ministère de l'Équipement des Transports et du Logement
C/o CLORA, Rue Montoyer 47, 1000 Brussels, Belgium
Tel. (+32) 2-5068874
Fax (+32) 2-5068845
E-mail billotte@clora.net
Sec.-Gen. Michel Binotte

Société de Conseil en marketing et Communication de l'Alimentaire Français (SOPEXA)
Association for Marketing and Communication of the French Food and Drink Industry
Rue du Luxembourg 47–51, 1050 Brussels, Belgium
Tel. (+32) 2-5127969
Fax (+32) 2-5121952
E-mail françois.pommereau@sopexa.com
URL www.sopexa.be
Pres. Dominique Chardon
Dir François Pommereau

Syndicat National de la Restauration Collective (SNRC)
9 Rue de la Trémoille, 75008 Paris, France
Tel. (+33) 1-56-62-16-16
Fax (+33) 1-49-52-05-50
E-mail info@snrc.fr
URL www.snrc.fr
Contact Marie Audrin

Union des Industries Textiles (UIT)
C/o MEDEF, Rue de Trèves 45, 1040 Brussels, France
Tel. (+32) 2-2310730
Fax (+32) 2-2310838
E-mail tnoblot@textile.f
URL www.uit-nord.com
Pres. André Beirnaert
Sec.-Gen. Thierry Noblot

Union Nationale des Industries Carrières et Matériels de Construction (UNICEM)
National Union for the Quarries and Building Materials Industries
3 Rue Alfred Roll, 75849 Paris Cedex 17, France
Tel. (+33) 1-44-01-47-01
Fax (+33) 1-40-54-03-28
E-mail contact@unicem.fr
URL www.unicem.fr
Contact Vaccarella

GERMANY

Aktionsgemeinschaft Wirtschaftlicher Mittelstand eV (AWM)
Active Small and Medium-Sized Enterprises

Place du Luxembourg 11, 1050 Brussels,
   Belgium
Tel. (+32) 2-2309499
Fax (+32) 2-2310601
E-mail info@awm-online
URL www.awm-online.de
Pres. Karl Besse
Sec.-Gen. Silvana Koch Mehrin

**Arbeitsgemeinschaft Berufsständischer
   Versorgungseinrichtungen eV (ABV)**
Rue d'Arlon 50, 1000 Brussels, Belgium
Tel. (+32) 2-2820566
Fax (+32) 2-2820599
E-mail info@abv.de
URL www.abv.de
Contact Michael Prossliner
Contact Madeleine Schavoir

**Arbeitsgemeinschaft Deutscher Tierzüchter
   eV**
Rue du Luxembourg 47–51, 1050 Brussels,
   Belgium
Tel. (+32) 2-2865954
Fax (+32) 2-2854059
E-mail hp.schons@adt.de
Contact Dr Hans-Peter Schons

**Arbeitsgemeinschaft Deutscher
   Verkehrsflughafen (ADV)**
Federal German Airports Association
Gertraudenstr. 20, 10178 Berlin, Germany
Tel. (+49 30) 3101180
Fax (+49 30) 31011890
URL www.adv-net.org
Contact Birgit Schoenrock
Pres. Willi Hermsen

**Ausstellungs- und Messe-Ausschuss der
   Deutschen Wirtschaft eV (AUMA)**
**Association of the German Trade Fair
   Industry**
Rue Grovelines 56, 1000 Brussels, Belgium
Tel. (+32) 2-2801290
Fax (+32) 2-2801290
E-mail a.heidenreich@auma.de
URL www.auma-messen.de
Pres. Thomas H. Hagen
Sec.-Gen. Anna Maria Heidenreich

**Bund für Lebensmittelrecht und
   Lebensmittelkunde eV**
**German Federation of Food Law and Food
   Science**
Avenue des Arts 43, 1040 Brussels, Belgium
Tel. (+32) 2-5081023
Fax (+32) 2-5081021
E-mail bll@bll-online.de
URL www.bll-online.de
Dir Peter Loosen

Bundesagentur für Aussenwirtschaft (BFAI)
Avenue du Boulevard 21, 1210 Brussels,
   Belgium
Tel. (+32) 2-2040173
Fax (+32) 2-2066760
E-mail bruessel@bfai.de
URL www.bfai.de
Dir Kirsten Hungermann

**Bundesarbeitgeberverband Chemie eV
   (BAVC)**
Rue du Commerce 31, 1000 Brussels, Belgium
Tel. (+32) 2-2908980
Fax (+32) 2-2908974
E-mail bruessel@bavc.de
URL www.bavc.de
Dir Markus Handke

**Bundesarbeitsgemeinschaft der Freien
   Wohlfahrtspflege, EU-Vertretung
   (BAGFW)**
Rue de Pascale 6, 1040 Brussels, Belgium
Tel. (+32) 2-2304500
Fax (+32) 2-2305704
E-mail euvertretung@bay-wohlfahrt.de
URL www.caritas.de
Sec.-Gen. Prof. Dr George Cremer

**Bundesarbeitsgemeinschaft der Mittel- und
   Grossbetriebe des Einzelhandels eV
   (BAG)**
Atrium Friedrichstr., 1200 Brussels, Belgium
Tel. (+32) 2-7343289
E-mail femged@pi.be
URL www.bag.de
Pres. Prof. Dr Helmut Merkel

**Bundesarbeitsgemeinschaft der Senioren-
   Organisationen eV**
Rue de la Pacification 65/67, 1000 Brussels,
   Belgium

Tel. (+32) 2-2869021
Fax (+32) 2-2309451
E-mail bagso@easynet.be
URL www.bagso.org
Pres. Roswitha Verhülsdonk
Dir Elke Tippelmann

Bundesarchitektenkammer eV
Federal Chamber of Architects
Avenue de Tervuren 142/144, 1150 Brussels,
　Belgium
Tel. (+32) 2-2197730
Fax (+32) 2-2192494
E-mail bak.brussels@skynet.be
URL www.bak.de
Pres. Prof. Arno Sighart Schmid
Sec.-Gen. Dr Tillman Prinz
Contact Anton Bauch

Bundesingenieurkammer
Federal Chamber of Engineers
Avenue des Arts 12, Bte 15, 1210 Brussels,
　Belgium
Tel. (+32) 2-2197730
Fax (+32) 2-2192494
E-mail ralf.lottes@wanadoo.be
URL www.bingk.de
Dir Ralf Lottes

Bundesnotarkammer
Federal Chamber of Notaries
Conseil Fédéral du Notariat Allemand
Rue Newton 1, 1000 Brussels, Belgium
Tel. (+32) 2-7379000
Fax (+32) 2-7379009
E-mail buero.bruessel@bnotk.de
URL www.bnotk.de
Pres. Dr Hans-Dieter Vaasen
Dr Till Schemmann

Bundesrechtsanwaltskammer
Federal Bar Association
Avenue de Tervuren 142/144, 1150 Brussels,
　Belgium
Tel. (+32) 2-7438646
Fax (+32) 2-7438656
E-mail brak.bxl@brak.be
URL www.brak.de
Pres. Dr Bernhard Dombek
Business Guide Dr Heike Lörcher

Bundessteuerberaterkammer
Federal Tax Advisor Chamber
Avenue de Cortenbergh 52, 1000 Brussels,
　Belgium
Tel. (+32) 2-7430596
Fax (+32) 2-7349117
E-mail bruessel@bstbk.be
Pres. Volker Fasolt
EU referent Karin Sauerteig

Bundesverband der Deutschen Entsorgungswirtschaft eV (BDE)
Federation of the German Waste Management Industry
Fédération Nationale de la Gestion des Déchets
Rue du Commerce 31, 1000 Brussels, Belgium
Tel. (+32) 2-5483890
Fax (+32) 2-5483899
E-mail info@bde-bruessel.be
URL www.bde.org
Pres. Peter Hoffmeyer

Bundesverband der Deutschen Gas- und Wasserwirtschaft (BGW)
Federal Association of the German Gas and Water Industries
Rue Breydel 34, 1040 Brussels, Belgium
Tel. (+32) 2-2350190
Fax (+32) 2-2350199
E-mail aertker@bgw.de
URL www.bgw.de
Pres. Uwe Steckert
Representative Dr Peter Aertker

Bundesverband der Deutschen Volksbanken und Raiffeisenbanken (BVR)
Rue de l'Industrie 26/38, 1040 Brussels,
　Belgium
Tel. (+32) 2-2869848
Fax (+32) 2-2300649
E-mail v.heegemann@bvr.de
Pres. Dr Christopher Pleister
EU Relations Man. Volker Heegemann

Bundesverband der Freien Berufe
Avenue de Cortenbergh 52, 1000 Brussels,
　Belgium
Tel. (+32) 2-7430599
Fax (+32) 2-7345774

E-mail bfbbruessel@compuserve.com
URL www.freie-berufe.de
Pres. Dr Ulrich Oesingmann
Sec.-Gen. Dr Helmut Born
Man. Dir Arno Metzler

**Bundesverband der Mittelstandische
Wirtschaft**

Avenue de la Renaissance 1, 1000 Brussels,
Belgium
Tel. (+32) 2-7396359
Fax (+32) 2-7360571
E-mail info@cea-pme.org
URL www.bvmwonline.de
Pres. Mario Ohoven
Leader Walter Grupp

**Bundesverband des Deutschen
Getränkefachgrosshandels eV**

C/o APRI, Avenue du Boulevard 21, 1210
Brussels, Belgium
Tel. (+32) 2-2040188
Fax (+32) 2- 2034758
E-mail info@apri.web.org
URL www.apri-web.org
Pres. Hans-Joachim Maurer
Dir Matthias Popp

**Bundesverband Güterkraftverkehr Logistik
und Entsorgung (BGL) eV**

Rue d'Arlon 55, 1040 Brussels, Belgium
Tel. (+32) 2-2301082
Fax (+32) 2-2307856
E-mail brussels@bgl-ev.de
URL www.bgl-ev.de
Dir Dirk Saile
Pres. Hermann Grewer

Bundesverband Junger Unternehmer

Avenue Milcamps 21, 1030 Brussels, Belgium
Tel. (+32) 2-7341102
Fax (+32) 2-7345169
E-mail info@bju.de
URL www.bju.de
Man. Dir Michael Kauch

**Bundesverband Öffentlicher Banken
Deutschland, (VÖB)**

Association of German Public Sector Banks

**Association des Banques Publiques
Allemandes**

Avenue de la Joyeuse Entrée 1–5, 1040
Brussels, Belgium
Tel. (+32) 2-2869061
Fax (+32) 2-2310219
E-mail brussels@voeb.de
URL www.voeb.de
Pres. Hans Dietmar Sauer
Dir Lothar Jerzembek

**Bundesvereinigung Deutscher
Apothekenverbande**

Rue Newton 1, 1000 Brussels, Belgium
Tel. (+32) 2-7353057
Fax (+32) 2-7350268
E-mail abda-buero.bruessel@aponet.de
URL www.abda.de
Pres. Heinz-Günter Wolf
Head of European Affairs Dr Susanne Hof

**Bundesvereinigung Deutscher
Handelsverbände eV (BDH)**

Avenue des Nerviens 9–31, 1040 Brussels,
Belgium
Tel. (+32) 2-7354379
Fax (+32) 2-2308497
E-mail bgallus.bdhbru@wanadoo.be
Dir Britta Gallus

Bundeszahnärztekammer

German Dental Association

Chambre Allemande des Dentistes

Avenue de la Renaissance 1, 1000 Brussels,
Belgium
Tel. (+32) 2-7328415
Fax (+32) 2-7355679
E-mail info@bzak.be
URL www.bzaek.de
Pres. Dr Jürgen Weitkamp
Dir Mary van Driel

Büro Brüssel Jugend und Arbeit

Rue de la Pacification 65, 1000 Brussels,
Belgium
Tel. (+32) 2-2304145
Fax (+32) 2- 2309451
E-mail central@bbj.be
URL www.bbj.be
Editor Ulrike Wisser

**Büro der Evangelischen Kirche
Deutschlands in Brüssel**

Rue Joseph II 166, 1000 Brussels, Belgium

Tel. (+32) 2-2301639
Fax (+32) 2-2800108
E-mail ekd.bruessel@ekd.be
URL www.ekd.de
Pres. Manfred Kock
Dir Sabine von Zanthier

Central Marketing-Gesellschaft der Deutschen Agrarwirtschaft (CMA)

Rue du Luxembourg 47–51, 1050 Brussels, Belgium
Tel. (+32) 2-5053480
Fax (+32) 2-5053481
E-mail cma-benelux@skynet.be
URL www.cma.de
Man. Dir Jörn Johann Dwehus

DEKRA eV

Avenue de Cortenbergh 52, 1000 Brussels, Belgium
Tel. (+32) 2-7402490
Fax (+32) 2-6729606
E-mail oliver.deiters.dekra@skynet.be
URL www.dekra.de
Pres. Dietmar Bogk
Man. Dir Oliver Deiters

Deutsche Gesellschaft für Technische Zusammenarbeit (GTZ) GmbH

Avenue d'Auderghem 67, 1040 Brussels, Belgium
Tel. (+32) 2-2309123
Fax (+32) 2-2308750
E-mail gtz.brussels@skynet.be
URL www.gtz.de
Partner Jürgen Koch

Deutsche Postgewerkschaft

Avenue de Tervuren 273/7, 1150 Brussels, Belgium
Tel. (+32) 2-7750221
Fax (+32) 2-7750222
E-mail k.vonbonin@deutschepost.de
URL www.deutschepost.de
Office Man. K. von Bonin

Deutsche Sozialversicherung Europavertretung

Maison Européenne de la Protection Sociale

Rue d'Arlon 50, 1000 Brussels, Belgium
Tel. (+32) 2-2307522
Fax (+32) 2-2307773

E-mail dsv@esip.org
URL www.deutsche-sozialversicherung.de
Dir Dr Franz Terwey

Deutsche Zentrale für Tourismus eV (DZT)
German National Tourist Board

Rue Gulledelle 92, 1200 Brussels, Belgium
Tel. (+32) 2-2459700
Fax (+32) 2-2453980
E-mail gntobru@d-z-t.com
URL www.deutschland-tourismus.de
Pres. Ursula Schörcher
Man. Rijkert Kettelhake

Deutscher Anwaltverein
German Bar Association
Association des avocats allemands

Avenue de la Joyeuse Entrée 1, 1040 Brussels, Belgium
Tel. (+32) 2-2802812
Fax (+32) 2-2802813
E-mail bruessel@anwaltverein.de
URL www.anwaltverein.de
Pres. Rechtsanwalt Hartmut Kilger
Sec.-Gen. Deutscher Anwaltverein

Deutscher Bauernverband eV (DBV)

Rue du Luxembourg 47–51, 1050 Brussels, Belgium
Tel. (+32) 2-2854050
Fax (+32) 2-2854059
E-mail w.kampmann@bauernverband.net
URL www.bauernverband.de
Pres. Gerhard Sonnleitner
Sec.-Gen Helmut Born

Deutscher Beamtenbund (DBB)
Federation of German Civil Servants

Avenue de la Joyeuse Entrée 1–5, 1040 Brussels, Belgium
Tel. (+32) 2-2821870
Fax (+32) 2-2821771
E-mail akademie-europa@cesi.org
URL www.dbb.de
Dir Bernd Rupp

Deutscher Bundeswehrverband (DBwV)
Federal Armed Forces Association
Association des Forces Armées Fédérales Allemandes

Avenue Général de Gaulle 33, 1050 Brussels,
   Belgium
Tel. (+32) 2-6260680
Fax (+32) 2-6260699
E-mail euromil@euromil.org
URL www.dbwv.de
Sec.-Gen. Ulrich A. Hundt

**Deutscher Fleischerverband Vertretung bei
der Europäischen Union**

Rue Jacques de Lalaing 4, 1040 Brussels,
   Belgium
Tel. (+32) 2-2306690
Fax (+32) 2-2303451
E-mail info@cibc.be
URL www.fleischerhandwerk.de
Chief Kirsten Diessner

**Deutscher Gewerkschaftsbund
Verbindungsbüro Brüssel**

Boulevard de l'Empereur 24, 1000 Brussels,
   Belgium
Tel. (+32) 2-5483690
Fax (+32) 2-5483699
E-mail dgb.brux@skynet.be
URL www.dgb.de
Dir of Office Dr Gloria Müller

Deutscher Kohlebergbau

Avenue de Tervuren 168, Bte 5, 1150 Brussels,
   Belgium
Tel. (+32) 2-7724630
Fax (+32) 2-7714104
E-mail prior@eurocoal.org
Contact Crisco Prior

**Deutscher Paritatischer Wohlfahrtsverband
Gesamtverband eV**

Rue Belliard 159, 1040 Brussels, Belgium
Tel. (+32) 2-2381000
Fax (+32) 2-2381009
E-mail info@paritaet.org
Dir Dr Özgür Öner

Deutscher Raiffeisenverband eV

Rue du Luxembourg 47–51, 1050 Brussels,
   Belgium
Tel. (+32) 2-2854050
Fax (+32) 2-2854059
E-mail drv.bxl@raiffeisen.be
URL www.raiffeisen.de
Pres. Manfred Nuessel

Sec.-Gen. Dr Rolf Meyer
Dir Dr Thomas Memmert

Deutscher Sparkassen- und Giroverband

Avenue des Nerviens 9–31, bte 3, 1040
   Brussels, Belgium
Tel. (+32) 2-7401610
Fax (+32) 2-7401617
E-mail info@dsgv.de
URL www.dsgv.de
Pres. Dr Dietrich Hoppenstedt

Deutscher Verkehrssicherheitsrat eV

Avenue des Arts 44, 1040 Brussels, Belgium
Tel. (+32) 2-2134043
Fax (+32) 2-2134049
E-mail mr-consult@t-online.de
Representative Manfred Raisch

Deutsches Aktieninstitut eV

Rue du Commerce 31, 1000 Brussels, Belgium
Tel. (+32) 2-2908990
Fax (+32) 2-2908991
E-mail europa@dai.de
URL www.dai.de
Pres. Max Dietrich Kley
Man. Dir Dr Rüdiger von Rosen

EU-Büro des Deutschen Sports
EU Office of German Sport
Bureau de Liaison auprès de l'UE

Avenue de Cortenbergh 89, 1000 Brussels,
   Belgium
Tel. (+32) 2-7380320
Fax (+32) 2-7380327
E-mail info@eu-sports-office.org
Head of office Tilo Friedmann

**Europavertretung der Deutsche Sozial
Versicherung**
Maison Européenne de la Protection Sociale

Rue d'Arlon 50, 1000 Brussels, Belgium
Tel. (+32) 2-2307522
Fax (+32) 2-2307773
E-mail dsv@esip.org
URL www.deutsche-sozialversicherung.de
Dir Dr Franz Terwey

Friedrich Ebert Stiftung
Friedrich Ebert Foundation

Rue Archimède 5, 1000 Brussels, Belgium

Tel. (+32) 2-2310489
Fax (+32) 2-2307651
E-mail fes@fesbrussels.org
URL www.fes.de
Dir Dr Ernst Stetter

Friedrich Naumann Stiftung
Friedrich Naumann Foundation
Rue Froissart 109, 1040 Brussels, Belgium
Tel. (+32) 2-2820930
Fax (+32) 2-2820931
E-mail ipd@brussels.fnst.org
URL www.fnst.org
Project Officer Hartig Susanne

Gemeinschaft zur Forderung der Privaten Deutschen Pflanzenzuchtung eV
Rue du Luxembourg 47–51, 1050 Brussels, Belgium
Tel. (+32) 2-2820840
Fax (+32) 2-2820841
E-mail gfp-fei@euronet.be
Contact Dr Hilke Riemer

Gesamtverband der Deutschen Textil- und Modeindustrie eV
Umbrella Organization of the German Textile and Fashion Industry
Rue de l'Amazone 2, 1050 Brussels, Belgium
Tel. (+32) 2-5349595
Fax (+32) 2-5349696
E-mail joern.kronenwerth@
belgium.messefrankfurt.com
URL www.gesamttextil.de
Dir J. Kronenwerth

Gesamtverband der Deutschen Versicherungswirtschaft eV
German Insurance Association
Avenue de Cortenbergh 60, 1000 Brussels, Belgium
Tel. (+32) 2-2824730
Fax (+32) 2-2824739
E-mail bruessel@gdv.org
URL www.gdv.org
Pres. Dr Bernd Michaels
Man. Dir Ulf Lemor

Hanns Seidel Stiftung
Hanns Seidel Foundation
Rue de la Loi 155, 1040 Brussels, Belgium

Tel. (+32) 2-2305081
Fax (+32) 2-2307027
E-mail bruessel@hss.de
URL www.hss.de
Dir Markus Russ

Hauptverband der Deutschen Bauindustrie
German Construction Industry
Rue du Commerce 31 (4 tage), 1000 Brussels, Belgium
Tel. (+32) 2-5129597
Fax (+32) 2-5125066
E-mail marleen.heyndrickx@bauindustrie.de
URL www.bauindustrie.de
Pres. Dr Hans-Peter Keitel
Dir Sébastien Richter

Hauptverband der Deutschen Holz und Kunststoffe Verarbeitenden Industrie und Verwandter Industriezweige (HDH)
German Woodworking and Furniture Industry
Rue du Commerce 31, 1000 Brussels, Belgium
Tel. (+32) 2-5030705
Fax (+32) 2-5030707
E-mail j.kurth@hdh-ev.de
URL www.hdh-ev.de
Pres. Helmut Lübke
Contact Jan Kurth

Hauptverband des Deutschen Einzelhandels (HDE)
Federation of the German Retail Trade
Rue Foissart 123–133, 1040 Brussels, Belgium
Tel. (+32) 2-2310998
Fax (+32) 2-2308497
E-mail Horst.Krueger@euronet.be
URL www.einzelhandel.de
Pres. Hermann Franzen
Sec.-Gen. Holger Wenzel
Dir Horst Krueger

Heinrich Böll Stiftung
Heinrich Böll Foundation
Rue d'Arlon 15, 1050 Brussels, Belgium
Tel. (+32) 2-7434100
Fax (+32) 2-7434109
E-mail brussels@boell.de
URL www.boell.be
Dir Claude Weinberg

Institut der Deutschen Wirtschaft eV (IW) Köln

Institut of the German Economy

Institut de l'économie allemande

Avenue des Arts 19 A-D, 1000 Brussels, Belgium
Tel. (+32) 2-2091280
Fax (+32) 2-2091289
E-mail bush@iwkoeln.de
URL www.iwkoeln.de
Pres. Hans-Dietrich Winkhaus
Contact Berthold Bush

Institut der Wirtschaftsprufer in Deutschland eV (IDW)

Rue de Spa 15, 1000 Brussels, Belgium
Tel. (+32) 2-2304290
Fax (+32) 2-2801429
E-mail klaas@idw.de
URL www.idw.de
Head of Office Dr Klaa

Internationale Weiterbildung und Entwicklung GmbH (INWENT)

Capacity Building International

Rue du Commerce 31, 1000 Brussels, Belgium
Tel. (+32) 2-5008961
Fax (+32) 2-5008968
E-mail franck.harbusch@inwent.org
URL www.cdg.de
Contact Franck Harbusch

Kassenärztliche Bundesvereinigung

European Social Insurance Platform

Maison Européenne de la Protection Sociale

Rue d'Arlon 50, 1000 Brussels, Belgium
Tel. (+32) 2-2820560
Fax (+32) 2-2307773
E-mail esip@esip.org
URL www.esip.org
Dir Franz Terwey

Kommission der Bischofskonferenzen der Europäischen Gemeinschaft (COMEC)

Commission of the Bishops' Conferences of the European Community

Commission des Episcopates de la Communauté Européenne

Rue Stévin 42, 1000 Brussels, Belgium
Tel. (+32) 2-2350510
Fax (+32) 2-2303334

E-mail comece@comece.org
URL www.comece.org
Pres. Bishop Josef Homeyer
Sec.-Gen. Mgr Noel Treanor

Konrad-Adenauer-Stiftung eV

Konrad Adenauer Foundation

Avenue de l'Yser 11, 1040 Brussels, Belgium
Tel. (+32) 2-7430743
Fax (+32) 2-7430749
E-mail sekretariat@eukas.be
URL www.kas.de
Pres. Prof. Dr Günter Rinsche
Sec.-Gen. Wilhelm Staudacher
Dir Peter R. Weilemann

Ostasiatischer Verein eV

German–Asia Pacific Business Association

Blvd Clovis 49A, 1000 Brussels, Belgium
Tel. (+32) 2-2861680
Fax (+32) 2-2861684
E-mail papaschinopoulou.mary@ bruessel.dink.de
URL www.oav.de
Dr Mary Papaschinopoulou

Reprasentanz der Berliner Wirtschaft

Representative Office for the Berlin Economy

Avenue Livingstone 33, 1000 Brussels, Belgium
Tel. (+32) 2-2865170
Fax (+32) 2-2865179
E-mail berlin.business@skynet.be
URL www.beoberlin.de
Contact Jorn Exner
Contact Christine Wild

Stahlinstitut VDEh

Steel Institute

Square Marie-Louise 18, Bte 3, 1000 Brussels, Belgium
Tel. (+32) 2-2301855
Fax (+32) 2-2305063
E-mail Alexander.Heck@skynet.be
URL www.stahl-online.de
Chair. Dr Prof. Dieter Ameling
Dir Alexander Heck

VDMA European Office

Diamant Building, Blvd A. Reyers 80, 1030
  Brussels, Belgium
Tel. (+32) 2-7068220
Fax (+32) 2-7068210
E-mail european.office@vdma.org
URL www.vdma.org
Pres. Dr Dieter Brucklacher
Dir Richard Rauch

Verband Beratender Ingenieure (VBI)
German Association of Consulting Engineers

Avenue de la Renaissance 1, 1000 Brussels,
  Belgium
Tel. (+32) 2-7320788
Fax (+32) 2-7320795
E-mail Reinhard.Honert@Liaison-Office.org
URL www.vbi.de
Liaison Officer Reinhard Honert

Verband der Anbieter von Telekommunikations und Mehrwertdiensten eV (VATM)

Avenue Livingstone 33, 1000 Brussels,
  Belgium
Tel. (+32) 2-2350980
Fax (+32) 2-2865179
E-mail brussels@vatm.de
URL www.vatm.de
Pres. Gerd Eickers
Dir Dirk Grewe

Verband der Automobilindustrie eV (VDA)
German Association of the Automotive Industry

Rue du Commerce 31, 1000 Brussels, Belgium
Tel. (+32) 2-5489023
Fax (+32) 2-5489029
E-mail niedenthal@vda.de
URL www.vda.de
Pres. Prof. Dr Bernd Gottschalk
Man.Dir Dr Michael Niedenthal

Verband der Chemischen Industrie eV (VCI)

Rue du Commerce 31, 1000 Brussels, Belgium
Tel. (+32) 2-5480690
Fax (+32) 2-5480699
E-mail quick@bruessel.vci.de
URL www.vci.de
Pres. Dr Jürgen Hambrecht
Dir-Gen. Dr Reinhard Quick

Verband der Deutschen Aromenindustrie eV (DVAI)

Boulevard Charlemagne 96, 1000 Brussels,
  Belgium
Tel. (+32) 2-2343737
Fax (+32) 2-2343739
E-mail vddei-vdrh@aktuell.be
Chair. Horst-Otto Gerberding
Dir Bettina Muermann

Verband der Elektrizitätswerkchaft
German Producers and Distributors of Electricity

Avenue de Tervuren 148, Bte 17, 1150
  Brussels, Belgium
Tel. (+32) 2-7719642
Fax (+32) 2-7630817
E-mail michael.wunnerlich@vdew.net
URL www.vdewNet
Dir Michael Edgar Wunnerlich

Verband der Technischen Uberwachungsvereine eV

Rue Jacques de Lalaing 4, 1040 Brussels,
  Belgium
Tel. (+32) 2-5348277
Fax (+32) 2-5343110
E-mail vdtuev.bruessel@t-online.de
Sec.-Gen. Daniel Pflumm

Verband Deutscher Maschinen und Anlagenbau (VDMA)
German Engineering Federation

Diamant Building, Boulevard A. Reyers 80,
  1030 Brussels, Belgium
Tel. (+32) 2-7068205
Fax (+32) 2-7068210
E-mail european.office@vdma.org
URL www.vdma.org
Pres. Dr Dieter Brucklacher

Verband Deutscher Pfandbriefbanken eV (VDP)
Association of German Pfandbrief Banks

Avenue Michel-Ange 13, 1000 Brussels,
  Belgium
Tel. (+32) 2-7324638
Fax (+32) 2-7324802
E-mail info@hypverband.be
URL www.hypverband.de
Pres. Jurgen Grieger

Department Head Wolfgang Kalberer

Verband Deutscher Verkehrsunternehmen
Rue Sainte-Marie 6, 1080 Brussels, Belgium
Tel. (+32) 2-6636627
Fax (+32) 2-6601072
E-mail constantin.dellis@uitp.com
URL www.uitp.com
Pres. Wolfgang Meyer
Sec.-Gen. Hans Rat

Verband Kommunaler Unternehmen eV (VKU)
Avenue des Nerviens 9–31, Stock 3, 1040
Brussels, Belgium
Tel. (+32) 2-7401650
Fax (+32) 2-7401651
E-mail widmer@vku.de
URL www.vku.de
Dir Beatrix Widmer

Verein Deutscher Ingenieure (VDI)
Association of German Engineers
Association des Ingénieurs Allemands
Rue du Commerce 31, 1000 Brussels, Belgium
Tel. (+32) 2-5008965
Fax (+32) 2-5113367
E-mail bruxelles@vdi.de
URL www.vdi.de
Pres. Dr Eike Lehmann
Office Man. Dr Jorg Niehoff

Vertretung der Deutschen Ärzteschaft
Rue Belliard 197, bte 6, 1040 Brussels,
Belgium
Tel. (+32) 2-2801817
Fax (+32) 2-2308110
E-mail deutschen.arzteschaft@skynet.be
URL www.bundesaerztekammer.de
www.kbv.de
Dir Stefan Graf

Wirtschaftsvereinigung Bergbau
Trade Association of the Mining Industry
Rue du Commerce 31, 1000 Brussels, Belgium
Tel. (+32) 2-2908985
Fax (+32) 2-2908974
E-mail manfred.steinhage@freebel.net
URL www.wv-bergbau.de
Pres. Prof. Dr Friedrich Jakob
Leader Manfred Steinhage

Wirtschaftsvereinigung Stahl
German Steel Federation
Square Marie-Louise 18, Bte 3, 1000 Brussels,
Belgium
Tel. (+32) 2-2301855
Fax (+32) 2-2305063
E-mail Alexander.Heck@skynet.be
URL www.stahl-online.de
Pres. Prof. Dr Dieter Ameling
Dir Alexander Heck

Zentral Verband des Deutschen Handwerks
Central Association of German Handicrafts
Rue Jacques de Lalaing 4, 1040 Brussels,
Belgium
Tel. (+32) 2-2868066
Fax (+32) 2-2302166
E-mail info.brussels@zdh.de
URL www.zdh.de
Pres. Otto Kentzler
Sec.-Gen. Hanns-Eberhard Schleyer

Zentralverband Elektrotechnik- und Elektronikindustrie eV (ZVEI)
Central Association for the Electrical and Electronic Industry
Diamant Building, Blvd A. Reyers 80, 1030
Brussels, Belgium
Tel. (+32) 2-7068258
Fax (+32) 2-7068250
E-mail bruessel@zvei.org
URL www.zvei.de
Pres. Prof. Dr Edward G. Krubasik
Man. Marta Lipczyk

ITALY

Consiglio Nazionale delle Ricerche (CNR)
National Research Council
Rue de la Loi 26, 1040 Brussels, Belgium
Tel. (+32) 2-2194146
Fax (+32) 2-2177415
E-mail cnrbrux@amministrazione.cnr.it
URL www.cnr.it
Pres. Prof. Fabio Pistella
Head Giuseppe Roffi

Federacciai
Rue Belliard 205, 1000 Brussels, Belgium
Tel. (+32) 2-2310285
Fax (+32) 2-2311974

E-mail bruxelles@federacciai.it
URL www.federacciai.it
Pres. Pasini Giuseppe
Dir-Gen. Salvadore Salerno

Federlegno-Arredo
Avenue de la Joyeuse Entrée 1, Bte 11, 1040
  Brussels, Belgium
Tel. (+32) 2-2861211
Fax (+32) 2-2306908
E-mail flabxl@federlegno.it
URL www.federlegno.it
Dir Flippo Perrone Donnorso

Instituto Italiano di Cultura
Italian Cultural Institute
Rue de Livourne 38, 1000 Brussels, Belgium
Tel. (+32) 2-5387704
Fax (+32) 2-5346292
E-mail italculture.bruxelles@euronet.be
Dir Martin Stiglio
Cultural Attaché Sira Moiri

JAPAN

Japan Automobile Manufacturers'
  Association (JAMA)
Avenue Louise 287, 1050 Brussels, Belgium
Tel. (+32) 2-6391430
Fax (+32) 2-6475754
E-mail ga@jama-e.bee
URL www.japanauto.com
Dir-Gen. William C. Duncan

Japan Machinery Centre for Trade
  Investment (JMC)
Rue d'Arlon 69–71, Bte 1, 1040 Brussels,
  Belgium
Tel. (+32) 2-2306992
Fax (+32) 2-2305485
E-mail imai@jmceu.org
URL www.jmcti.org
Exec. Man. Dir Osamu Morimoto

NORWAY

Europanytt
Rue des Confédérés 96, 1000 Brussels,
  Belgium
Tel. (+32) 2-7360572
Fax (+32) 2-7367351

E-mail anders.ulstein@europanytt.no
URL www.europanytt.no
Communication Officer Florence Berteletti-
  Kemp

SWITZERLAND

Swiss Contact Office for Research and
  Higher Education
Rue du Trône 98, 1050 Brussels, Belgium
Tel. (+32) 2-5490980
Fax (+32) 2-5490989
E-mail infodesk@swisscore.org
URL www.swisscore.org
Head of Office Martina Weiss

TAIWAN

National Science Council Taipei
Blvd du Régent 40, 1000 Brussels, Belgium
Tel. (+32) 2-5171730
Fax (+32) 2-2187658
E-mail nsc.taipei@skynet.be
URL www.belgium.nsc.gov.tw
Man. Dir Dr Joseph R.F. Hsu

Taipei Representative Office
Blvd du Regent 40, 1000 Brussels, Belgium
Tel. (+32) 2-5110687
Fax (+32) 2-517-1725
E-mail t.info@skynet.be
URL www.roc-taiwan.be
Dir Lee

TURKEY

Foundation for Professional Training and
  Small Business in Turkey (MEKSA)
Rue du Luxembourg 14A, 1000 Brussels,
  Belgium
Tel. (+32) 2-2854020
Fax (+32) 2-2304025
E-mail eyor@euronet.be
Dir Ahmet Ecmel Yorganci

Organization for the Development of Small
  and Medium-Sized Enterprises
  (KOSGEB)
Rue du Luxembourg 14A, 1000 Brussels,
  Belgium
Tel. (+32) 2-2854020
Fax (+32 2-2854025

E-mail info@turboppp.org
Dir A. Ecmel Yorganci

UNITED KINGDOM

Electricity Association (EA)

Scotland House, Rond-Point 6, 1040 Brussels,
    Belgium
Tel. (+32) 2-2828456
Fax (+32) 2-2828455
E-mail shercock@csi.com
Dir Stuart H.J. Hercock

Freight Transport Association (FTA)

Rue Wiertz 50, 3rd floor, 1050 Brussels,
    Belgium
Tel. (+32) 2-2310321
Fax (+32) 2-2304140
E-mail esc@pophost.eunet.be
URL www.fta.co.uk
Pres. John Russell
Policy Adviser Damian Viccars

Institute of Chartered Accountants in England and Wales

Rue de la Loi 227, 1040 Brussels, Belgium
Tel. (+32) 2-2303272
Fax (+32) 2-2302851
E-mail european.office@icaew.co.uk
URL www.icaew.co.uk
Pres. Paul Druckman
Dir Martin Manuzi

UK Research and Higher Education European Office (UKRHEEO)

Rue de la Loi 83, BP10, 1040 Brussels,
    Belgium

Tel. (+32) 2-2305275
Fax (+32) 2-2304803
E-mail ukro@bbsrc.ac.uk
URL www.ukro.ac.uk
Dir Martin Penny

UNITED STATES OF AMERICA

American Electronics Association Europe (AEA Europe)

Rue des Drapiers 40, 1050 Brussels, Belgium
Tel. (+32) 2-5027015
Fax (+32) 2-5026734
E-mail james_lovegrove@aeanet.org
URL www.aeanet.org
Man. Dir James Lovegrove
Pres. William T. Archey

Motion Picture Association (MPA)

15503 Ventura Blvd., Encino, CA 91436 , USA
Tel. (+1 818) 995-6600
URL www.mpaa.org
Man. Dir Christopher Marcich
Pres. Ken Rutkowski

Society of Plastics Engineers European Office (SPE)

Bistkapellei 44, 2180 Antwerp, Belgium
Tel. (+32) 3-5417755
Fax (+32) 3-5418425
E-mail ypauwels@4spe.org
URL www.4spe.org
Pres. Donna S. Davis
Rep. Yetty Pauwels

DIPLOMATIC CORPS ACCREDITED TO THE EUROPEAN UNION

Afghanistan

Av. de Wolvendael 61, 1180 Brussels, Belgium
Tel. (+32) 2-7613166
Fax (+32) 2-7613167
E-mail ambassade.afghanistan@skynet.be
Head of Mission Umayaun Tandar

Albania

Rue Tenbosch 30, 1000 Brussels, Belgium
Tel. (+32) 2-6443329
Fax (+32) 2-6403177
E-mail albanian.ec1@skynet.be
Head of Mission Arthur Kuko
Counsellor Mimoza Kondo

Algeria

Avenue Molière 209, 1050 Brussels, Belgium
Tel. (+32) 2-3435078
Fax (+32) 2-3435168
E-mail info@algerian-embassy.be
URL www.algerian-embassy.be
Head of Mission Halim Benattalah
Counsellor Ahmed Si Ahmed

Andorra

Rue de la Montagne 10, 1000 Brussels,
  Belgium
Tel. (+32) 2-5021211
Fax (+32) 2-5130741
E-mail ambassade@andorra.be
URL www.andorra.be
Head of Mission Meritxell Mateu i Pi
Counsellor Serge de Behr

Angola

Rue Franz Merjay 182, 1050 Brussels, Belgium
Tel. (+32) 2-3461880
Fax (+32) 2-3440894
E-mail angola.embassy.brussels@skynet.be
Head of Mission Toko Diakenga Serão

Antigua and Barbuda

Rue de Livourne 42, 1000 Brussels, Belgium
Tel. (+32) 2-5342611
Fax (+32) 2-5394009
E-mail ecs.embassies@skynet.be
Head of Mission (vacant)

Argentina

Avenue Louise 225, 7è étage, Bte 2, 1050
  Brussels, Belgium
Tel. (+32) 2-6489371
Fax (+32) 2-6480804
E-mail info@eceur.org
Head of Mission Jorge Remes Lenicov

Armenia

Rue Franz Merjay 157, 1050 Brussels, Belgium
Tel. (+32) 2-3484400
Fax (+32) 2-3484401
E-mail armembel@wanadoo.be
URL www.armenian-embassy.be
Head of Mission Viguen Tchitetchian
Minister Plenipotentiary Edouard Pandian

Australia

Guimard Center, Rue Guimard 6–8, 1040
  Brussels, Belgium
Tel. (+32) 2-2860500
Fax (+32) 2-2306802
E-mail austemb.brussels@dfat.gov.au
Head of Mission Peter Charles Grey
Minister Alison Burrows

Azerbaijan

Av. Molière 464, 1050 Brussels, Belgium
Tel. (+32) 2-3452660
Fax (+32) 2-3459158
E-mail office@azembassy.be
Head of Mission Arif Mamedov

Bahamas
10 Chesterfield Street, London W1X 8AH,
  United Kingdom
Tel. (+44 20) 7408-4488
Fax (+44 20) 7499-9937
E-mail information@bahamashclondon.net
Head of Mission Basil G. O'Brien
Minister-Counsellor Maria T. Zonicle

Bahrain
3 bis place des Etats-Unis, 75016 Paris, France
Tel. (+33) 1-47-23-48-68
Fax (+33) 1-47-20-55-75
E-mail ambassade@ambahrein-france.com
Head of Mission (vacant)
First Sec. Khaled Altamimi

Bangladesh
Rue Jacques Jordaens 29–31, 1000 Brussels,
  Belgium
Tel. (+32) 2-6405500
Fax (+32) 2-6465998
E-mail bdootbrussels@freegate.be
Head of Mission Sayed Maudud Ali
First Sec. Tareq Ahmed

Barbados
Avenue F. D. Roosevelt 100, 1200 Brussels,
  Belgium
Tel. (+32) 2-7321737
Fax (+32) 2-7323266
E-mail brussels@foreign.gov.bb
Head of Mission Errol Humphrey
First Sec. Joy-Ann Skinner

Belarus
Avenue Molière 192, 1050 Brussels, Belgium
Tel. (+32) 2-3400270
Fax (+32) 2-3400287
E-mail embbel@skynet.be
Head of Mission Vladzimir L. Syanko

Belize
Blvd Brand Whitlock 136, 1200 Brussels,
  Belgium
Tel. (+32) 2-7326204
Fax (+32) 2-7326246
E-mail embelize@skynet.be
Head of Mission Yvonne Hyde
First Sec. Keisha Diego

Benin
Avenue de l'Observatoire 5, 1180 Brussels,
  Belgium
Tel. (+32) 2-3749192
Fax (+32) 2-3758326
Head of Mission Euloge Hinvi
Minister-Counsellor Désiré-Auguste Adjahi

Bhutan
Chemin Champ d'Anier 17–19, 1209 Genève,
  Switzerland
Tel. (+41) 22-799-08-90
Fax (+41) 22-799-08-99
Head of Mission Sonam Tobden Rabgye

Bolivia
Avenue Louise 176, Bte 6, 1050 Brussels,
  Belgium
Tel. (+32) 2-6270010
Fax (+32) 2-6474782
E-mail embajada.bolivia@embolbrus.be
Head of Mission Armando Ortuño Yáñez
Minister-Counsellor Arturo Suárez Vargas

Bosnia and Herzegovina
Rue Tenbosch 34, 1000 Brussels, Belgium
Tel. (+32) 2-6442008
Fax (+32) 2-6441698
E-mail mis-eu-nato-bru@skynet.be
Head of Mission Zdenko Martinovic
Minister-Counsellor Nazif Kadric

Botswana
Avenue de Tervuren 169, 1150 Brussels,
  Belgium
Tel. (+32) 2-7352070
Fax (+32) 2-7356318
E-mail botswana@brutele.be
Head of Mission Sasara George
Minister-Counsellor Edith Basadi Tamplin

Brazil
Avenue F. D. Roosevelt 30, 1050 Brussels,
  Belgium
Tel. (+32) 2-6402040
Fax (+32) 2-6488040
E-mail missao@braseuropa.be
Head of Mission José Alfredo Graça Lima
Minister-Counsellor Denis Fonte de Souza
  Pinto
Minister-Counsellor Ligia Maria Scherer

Brunei

Avenue F. D. Roosevelt 238, 1050 Brussels,
  Belgium
Tel. (+32) 2-6750878
Fax (+32) 2-6729358
E-mail kedutaan-brunei.brussels@skynet.be
Head of Mission Dato' Yusof Hamid

Bulgaria

Rue d'Arlon 108, 1140 Brussels, Belgium
Tel. (+32) 2-3748468
Fax (+32) 2-3749188
E-mail info@missionbg.be
Head of Mission Stanislav Daskalov
Minister Plenipotentiary Russi Ivanov
Minister Plenipotentiary Boyan Natan
Minister Plenipotentiary Charlina Vicheva

Burkina Faso

Place d'Arezzo 16, 1180 Brussels, Belgium
Tel. (+32) 2-3459912
Fax (+32) 2-3450612
E-mail ambassade.burkina@skynet.be
Head of Mission Kadré Desiré Ouedraogo

Burundi

Square Marie-Louise 46, 1000 Brussels,
  Belgium
Tel. (+32) 2-2304535
Fax (+32) 2-2307883
Head of Mission Ferdinand Nyabenda
First Counsellor Kaburundi Salvator

Cambodia

Av. de Tervuren 264, 1150 Brussels, Belgium
Tel. (+32) 2-77620372
Fax (+32) 2-7708999
Head of Mission Saphoeun Sun
Minister Plenipotentiary Chant Rith Yao

Cameroon

Avenue Brugmann 131–133, 1190 Brussels,
  Belgium
Tel. (+32) 2-3451870
Fax (+32) 2-3445735
Head of Mission Isabelle Bassong
Minister-Counsellor Iva Tidjani

Canada

Avenue de Tervuren 2, 1040 Brussels, Belgium
Tel. (+32) 2-7410660
Fax (+32) 2-7410629
E-mail canada.eu@arcadis.be

URL www.dfait-maeci.ge.ca/eu-mission
Head of Mission Jeremy K. B. Kinsman
Minister-Counsellor Kevin O'Shea

Cape Verde

Avenue Jeanne 29, 1050 Brussels, Belgium
Tel. (+32) 2-6436270
Fax (+32) 2-6463385
E-mail emb.caboverde@skynet.be
Head of Mission Fernando Jorge Wahnon
  Ferreira

Central African Republic

Boulevard Lambermont 416, 1030 Brussels,
  Belgium
Tel. (+32) 2-2422880
Fax (+32) 2-2151311
E-mail ambassade.centrafricaine@skynet.be
Head of Mission Armand-Guy
  Zounguere-Sokambi
First Counsellor Jean-Pierre Mbazoa

Chad

Blvd Lambermont 52, 1030 Brussels, Belgium
Tel. (+32) 2-2151975
Fax (+32) 2-2163526
E-mail ambassade.tchad@chello.be
Head of Mission Abderahim Yacoub N'Diaye
First Counsellor Idriss Adjideye

Chile

Rue des Aduatiques 106, 1040 Brussels,
  Belgium
Tel. (+32) 2-7433660
Fax (+32) 2-7364994
E-mail misue@misionchile-ue.org
Head of Mission Alberto van Klaveren
Minister-Counsellor José Manuel Silva

China (People's Republic)

Avenue de Tervuren 443–445, 1150 Brussels,
  Belgium
Tel. (+32) 2-7753082
Fax (+32) 2-7753092
E-mail chinaemb-be@mfa.gov.cn
Head of Mission Chengyan Guan
Minister-Counsellor Zhiming Liu

Colombia

Avenue F. D. Roosevelt 96A, 1050 Brussels,
  Belgium
Tel. (+32) 2-6495679
Fax (+32) 2-6465491

Head of Mission Nicolas Echavarría Mesa
Minister Plenipotentiary Victoria Eugenia
 Senior

Comoros

Av. Paul Hymans 128, 1200 Brussels, Belgium
Tel. (+32) 2-7795838
Fax (+32) 2-7795838
E-mail ambacom.bxl@skynet.be
Head of Mission (vacant)

Congo (Democratic Republic)

Av. de Foe 6, 1180 Brussels, Belgium
Tel. (+32) 2-3754796
Fax (+32) 2-3722348
E-mail ambauebruxelles@minaffecirdc.cd
Head of Mission Jean-Pierre
 Mavungu-di-Ngoma

Congo (Republic)

Avenue F. D. Roosevelt 16–18, 1050 Brussels,
 Belgium
Tel. (+32) 2-6483856
Fax (+32) 2-6484213
Head of Mission Jacques Obia
Minister-Counsellor Jean-Paul Engaye

Cook Islands

Rue Berckmans 10, 1060 Brussels, Belgium
Tel. (+32) 2-5431000
Fax (+32) 2-5431001
E-mail cookislands@prmltd.com
Head of Mission Todd McClay

Costa Rica

Avenue Louise 489, 12ème étage, Bte 23, 1050
 Brussels, Belgium
Tel. (+32) 2-6405541
Fax (+32) 2-6483192
E-mail ambcrbel@coditel.net
Head of Mission Maria Salvadora Ortiz Ortiz
Minister-Counsellor Michel Chartier

Côte d'Ivoire

Avenue F. D. Roosevelt 234, 1050 Brussels,
 Belgium
Tel. (+32) 2-6722357
Fax (+32) 2-6720491
E-mail mailbox@ambacibnl.be
URL www.ambassy.bnl.be
Head of Mission Marie Gosset
First Counsellor Konan Narcisse Kouadio

Croatia

Avenue des Arts 50, 1050 Brussels, Belgium
Tel. (+32) 2-5000930
Fax (+32) 2-6465664
E-mail cromiss.eu@mvp.hr
Head of Mission Mirjana Mladineo
Minister Plenipotentiary Jasna Ognjanovac

Cuba

Rue Robert Jones 77, 1180 Brussels, Belgium
Tel. (+32) 2-3430020
Fax (+32) 2-3449691
E-mail consejero@embacuba.be
Head of Mission Rodrigo Malmierca Diaz

Djibouti

Avenue F.D. Roosevelt 204, 1050 Brussels,
 Belgium
Tel. (+32) 2-3476967
Fax (+32) 2-3476963
Head of Mission Mohamed Moussa Chehem

Dominica

Rue de Livourne 42, 1000 Brussels, Belgium
Tel. (+32) 2-5342611
Fax (+32) 2-5394009
E-mail ecs.embassies@skynet.be
Head of Mission Georges Bullen
Minister-Counsellor Arnold Thomas

Dominican Republic

Avenue Bel Air 12, 1180 Brussels, Belgium
Tel. (+32) 2-3464935
Fax (+32) 2-3465152
E-mail embajada@dominicana.be
Head of Mission Federico Alberto Cuello
 Camilo
Minister-Counsellor Rafael Molina Pulgar

Ecuador

Avenue Louise 363, 9è étage, Bte 1, 1050
 Brussels, Belgium
Tel. (+32) 2-6443050
Fax (+32) 2-6442813
E-mail amb.equateur@skynet.be
Head of Mission Méntor Villagomez Merino

Egypt

Avenue de l'Uruguay 19, 1000 Brussels,
 Belgium
Tel. (+32) 2-6635820
Fax (+32) 2-6755888
E-mail embassy.egypt@skynet.be

Head of Mission Soliman Awaad
First Counsellor Magda Baraka

El Salvador
Avenue de Tervuren 171, 7è étage, 1150
  Brussels, Belgium
Tel. (+32) 2-7330485
Fax (+32) 2-7350211
E-mail amb.elsalvador@brutele.be
Head of Mission Hector Gonzalez Urrutia
Minister-Counsellor Anabella
  Machuca-Machuca

Equatorial Guinea
Avenue Jupiter 17, 1190 Brussels, Belgium
Tel. (+32) 2-3462509
Fax (+32) 2-3463309
E-mail guineaecuatorial.brux@skynet.be
Head of Mission Victorino Nka Obiang Naye

Eritrea
Avenue Wolvendael 15–17, 1180 Brussels,
  Belgium
Tel. (+32) 2-3744434
Fax (+32) 2-3720730
E-mail eri_emba_brus@hotmail.com
Head of Mission Aldebrhan Weldegiorgis

Ethiopia
Avenue de Tervuren 231, 1150 Brussels,
  Belgium
Tel. (+32) 2-7713294
Fax (+32) 2-7714914
E-mail etebru@brutele.be
Head of Mission Berhane Gebre-Christos
Deputy Head of Mission Brook Debebe Agden

Fiji
Square Plasky 92–94, 5ème étage, 1030
  Brussels, Belgium
Tel. (+32) 2-7369050
Fax (+32) 2-7361458
E-mail info@fijiembassy.be
URL www.fijiembassy.be
Head of Mission Semeraia Tuinosori Cavuilati

Gabon
Avenue Winston Churchill 112, 1180 Brussels,
  Belgium
Tel. (+32) 2-3406210
Fax (+32) 2-3464669
Head of Mission René Makongo
First Counsellor François Ebibi Mba

Gambia
Avenue F. D. Roosevelt 126, 1050 Brussels,
  Belgium
Tel. (+32) 2-6401049
Fax (+32) 2-6463277
Head of Mission Youssoupha Alyu Kah
Minister-Counsellor Amie Nyan-Alaboson

Georgia
Avenue Orban 58, 1150 Brussels, Belgium
Tel. (+32) 2-7611193
Fax (+32) 2-7611199
E-mail mdvgade@skynet
Head of Mission Konstantin Zaldastanishvili

Ghana
Boulevard Général Wahis 7, 1030 Brussels,
  Belgium
Tel. (+32) 2-7058220
Fax (+32) 2-7056653
E-mail ghanaemb@chello.be
Head of Mission Kobina Wudu
Deputy Head of Mission Clifford N. A. Kotley

Grenada
Rue de Laeken 123, 1er étage, 1000 Brussels,
  Belgium
Tel. (+32) 2-2237303
Fax (+32) 2-2237307
Head of Mission Joan-Marie Countain

Guatemala
Avenue Winston Churchill 185, 1180 Brussels,
  Belgium
Tel. (+32) 2-3459047
Fax (+32) 2-3446499
E-mail obguab@infoboard.be
Head of Mission Edmond Mulet-Lesieur
Minister-Counsellor Jorge Ricardo Putzeys
  Uriguen

Guinea
Blvd Auguste Reyers 108, 1030 Brussels,
  Belgium
Tel. (+32) 2-7710126
Fax (+32) 2-7626036
E-mail ambassadeguinee.bel@skynet.be
Head of Mission Kazaliou Balde

Guinea-Bissau
Avenue F. D. Roosevelt 70, 1050 Brussels,
  Belgium
Tel. (+32) 2-6470890

Fax (+32) 2-6404312
Head of Mission (vacant)
Minister-Counsellor Serafim Ianga

Guyana

Avenue du Brésil 12, 1000 Brussels, Belgium
Tel. (+32) 2-6756216
Fax (+32) 2-6756331
E-mail guyana.embassy@skynet.be
Head of Mission Patrick Ignatius Gomes

Haiti

Chaussée de Charleroi 139, 1060 Brussels,
  Belgium
Tel. (+32) 2-6497381
Fax (+32) 2-6406080
E-mail amb.haiti@brutele.be
Head of Mission (vacant)
Minister-Counsellor Jacques Nixon Myrthil

Honduras

Avenue des Gaulois 3, 5è étage, 1040 Brussels,
  Belgium
Tel. (+32) 2-7340000
Fax (+32) 2-7352626
E-mail ambassade.honduras@chello.be
Head of Mission Teololinda Banegas de Makris
First Counsellor Giampaolo Rizzo Alvarado

Iceland

Rond-Point Schuman 11, 1040 Brussels,
  Belgium
Tel. (+32) 2-2385000
Fax (+32) 2-2306938
E-mail icemb.brussel@utn.stgr.is
Head of Mission Kjartan Jóhansson
Deputy Head of Mission Thórir Ibsen

India

Chaussée de Vleurgat 217, 1050 Brussels,
  Belgium
Tel. (+32) 2-6409140
Fax (+32) 2-6489638
E-mail admin@indembassy.be
Head of Mission Rajendra Madhukar
  Abhyankar

Indonesia

Boulevard de la Woluwe 38, 1200 Brussels,
  Belgium
Tel. (+32) 2-7790915
Fax (+32) 2-7728210
E-mail primebxl@skynet.be
Head of Mission Abdurachman Mattalitti

Iran

Avenue de Tervuren 415, 1150 Brussels,
  Belgium
Tel. (+32) 2-7623745
Fax (+32) 2-7623915
E-mail iran-embassyl@yahoo.com
Head of Mission Ali Ahani
First Counsellor Gholamreza Ebrahim Pour

Iraq

Avenue des Aubépines 23, 1180 Brussels,
  Belgium
Tel. (+32) 2-3745992
Fax (+32) 2-3747615
E-mail ambassade.irak@skynet.be
Head of Mission Jawad al-Doreky
Minister Plenipotentiary Imad al-Ani

Israel

Avenue de l'Observatoire 40, 1180 Brussels,
  Belgium
Tel. (+32) 2-3735500
Fax (+32) 2-3735677
E-mail isr.mis.eu@online.be
Head of Mission Oded Eran
Minister-Counsellor Alon Snir

Jamaica

Av. Hansen-Soulie 77, 1040 Brussels, Belgium
Tel. (+32) 2-2301170
Fax (+32) 2-2346969
E-mail emb.jam.brussels@skynet.be
Head of Mission Evadne Coye
Minister-Counsellor Sharon Saunders

Japan

Square de Meeûs 5–6, 1000 Brussels, Belgium
Tel. (+32) 2-5007711
Fax (+32) 2-5133241
E-mail inf@jmission-eu.be
Head of Mission Kazuo Asakai
Deputy Head of Mission Yoshihisa Kuroda

Jordan

Avenue F. D. Roosevelt 104, 1050 Brussels,
  Belgium
Tel. (+32) 2-6407755
Fax (+32) 2-6402796
E-mail jordan.embassy@skynet.be
Head of Mission Muhyieddeen Shaban Touq

Kazakhstan
Avenue Van Bever 30, 1180 Brussels, Belgium
Tel. (+32) 2-3749562
Fax (+32) 2-3745091
E-mail kazaks@linline.be
Head of Mission Konstantin V. Zhigalov
Counsellor Rustem Kurmanguzhin

Kenya
Avenue Winston Churchill 208, 1180 Brussels,
  Belgium
Tel. (+32) 2-3401040
Fax (+32) 2-3401050
Head of Mission Marx G. N. Kahende
Counsellor Joshua Mugodo

Korea (Democratic People's Republic)
Glinkastr. 5/7, 10117 Berlin, Germany
Tel. (+49 30) 293189
Fax (+49 30) 2293191

Korea (Republic)
Chaussée de La Hulpe 173–175, 1170 Brussels,
  Belgium
Tel. (+32) 2-6755777
Fax (+32) 2-6755221
E-mail eukorea@skynet.be
Head of Mission Haeng-Kyeom Oh
Minister Suk-Bum Park

Kuwait
Avenue F. D. Roosevelt 43, 1050 Brussels,
  Belgium
Tel. (+32) 2-6477950
Fax (+32) 2-6461298
E-mail embassy.kwt@euronet.be
Head of Mission Abdelazeez al-Sharikh

Kyrgyzstan
Rue de l'Abbaye 47, 1050 Brussels, Belgium
Tel. (+32) 2-6401868
Fax (+32) 2-6400131
E-mail kyrgyz.embassy@skynet.be
Head of Mission Chinguiz Aitmatov
Minister-Counsellor Arslan Anarbaev

Laos
Avenue de la Brabançonne 19–21, 1000
  Brussels, Belgium
Tel. (+32) 2-7400950
Fax (+32) 2-7341666
Head of Mission Thongphachanh Sonnasinh

Lebanon
Rue Guillaume Stocq 2, 1050 Brussels,
  Belgium
Tel. (+32) 2-6457765
Fax (+32) 2-6457769
E-mail ambassade.liban@brutele.be
Head of Mission Fawzi Fawaz

Lesotho
Boulevard Général Wahis 44, 1030 Brussels,
  Belgium
Tel. (+32) 2-7053976
Fax (+32) 2-7056779
E-mail lesothobruemb@skynet.be
Head of Mission Moliehi Mathato Adel
  Matlanyane
Counsellor Mabasia Ntsoaki Jeanet Mohabane

Liberia
Avenue du Château 50, 1080 Brussels, Belgium
Tel. (+32) 2-4110112
Fax (+32) 2-4110912
Head of Mission Youngor S. Telewoda

Libya
Avenue Victoria 28, 1000 Brussels, Belgium
Tel. (+32) 2-6493737
Fax (+32) 2-6440155
Head of Mission Ahmed Elhouderi

Liechtenstein
Place du Congrès 1, 1000 Brussels, Belgium
Tel. (+32) 2-2293900
Fax (+32) 2-2193545
E-mail ambassade.liechtenstein@bbru.llv.li
Head of Mission Prince Nicolas de
  Liechtenstein
First Sec. Günther Ettl

Macedonia (Former Yugoslav Republic)
Avenue Louise 209A, 4e étage, 1150 Brussels,
  Belgium
Tel. (+32) 2-7329108
Fax (+32) 2-7329111
Head of Mission Sasko Stefkov
Minister-Counsellor Dimitar Belcev

Madagascar
Avenue de Tervuren 276, 1150 Brussels,
  Belgium
Tel. (+32) 2-7701726
Fax (+32) 2-7723731
E-mail ambassade.madagascar@skynet.be

Head of Mission Jean Beriziky
First Counsellor Pierre Rabarivola

Malawi

Av. Herman Debroux 46, 1160 Brussels,
  Belgium
Tel. (+32) 2-2310980
Fax (+32) 2-2311066
E-mail embassy.malawi@skynet.be
Head of Mission Brian Granthen Bowler
Deputy Head of Mission Antony B. Namisengo

Malaysia

Avenue de Tervuren 414 A, 1150 Brussels,
  Belgium
Tel. (+32) 2-7760340
Fax (+32) 2-7625049
E-mail mwbrusel@euronet.be
Head of Mission Dato' Mohd Ridzam Deva bin
  Abdullah
Minister-Counsellor Zaïnol Abidin bin Omar

Maldives

22 Nottingham Place, London W1U 5NJ,
  United Kingdom
Tel. (+44 20) 7224-2135
Fax (+44 20) 7224-2157
E-mail maldives.high.commission@virgin.net
Head of Mission Hassan Sobir

Mali

Avenue Molière 487, 1050 Brussels, Belgium
Tel. (+32) 2-3457432
Fax (+32) 2-3445700
Head of Mission Ibrahim B. Ba
First Counsellor Labasse Fofana

Mauritania

Avenue de la Colombie 6, 1000 Brussels,
  Belgium
Tel. (+32) 2-6724747 – (+32) 2-6721802
Fax (+32) 2-6722051
E-mail amb.bxl.mauritanie@skynet.be
Head of Mission Sidi Ould Khalifa
Sidi Ould Mohamed Laghdaf

Mauritius

Rue des Bollandistes 68, 1040 Brussels,
  Belgium
Tel. (+32) 2-7339988
Fax (+32) 2-7344021
E-mail ambmaur@skynet.be
Head of Mission Sutiawan Gunessee

Mexico

Avenue F. D. Roosevelt 94, 1050 Brussels,
  Belgium
Tel. (+32) 2-6290711
Fax (+32) 2-6440819
E-mail embamexbel@pophost.eunet.be
Head of Mission Maria de Lourdes Dieck
  Assad
Deputy Head of Mission Francisco Eduardo del
  Rio Lopez

Moldova

Rue Tenbosch 54, 1050 Brussels, Belgium
Tel. (+32) 2-7329659
Fax (+32) 2-7329660
E-mail molda@advalvas.be
Head of Mission Eujen Carpov
Counsellor Natalia Solcan

Monaco

Place Guy d'Arezzo 17, 1180 Brussels,
  Belgium
Tel. (+32) 2-3474987
Fax (+32) 2-3434920
E-mail ambassade.monaco@skynet.be
Head of Mission Jean Pastorelli
First Sec. Pierre-Henri Settimo

Mongolia

Avenue Besme 18, 1190 Brussels, Belgium
Tel. (+32) 2-3446974
Fax (+32) 2-3443215
E-mail sonon@chello.be
URL www.embassy.mongolia.skynet.be
Head of Mission Sodoviin Onon
Counsellor Sed Ochiryn Bayarbaatar

Morocco

Av. Louise 275, 1050 Brussels, Belgium
Tel. (+32) 2-6263410
Fax (+32) 2-6263434
E-mail mission.maroc@skynet.be
Head of Mission Menouar Alem
First Counsellor Nabil Adghoghi

Mozambique

Boulevard Saint-Michel 97, 1040 Brussels,
  Belgium
Tel. (+32) 2-7362564
Fax (+32) 2-7356207
Head of Mission Maria Manuela dos Santos
  Lucas
Minister-Counsellor Mário Saraiva Ngwenya

Myanmar

Rue de Courcelles 60, 75008 Paris, France
Tel. (+33) 1-42-25-56-35
Fax (+33) 1-42-56-49-41
E-mail me-paris@wanadoo.fr
Minister-Counsellor Myint Soe
First Sec. U. Wunna Maung Lwin

Namibia

Avenue de Tervuren 454, 1150 Brussels,
   Belgium
Tel. (+32) 2-7711410
Fax (+32) 2-7719689
E-mail nam.emb@brutele.be
Head of Mission Peter Hitjitevi Katjavivi
Counsellor Sophia Nangombe

Nepal

Av. Brugman 210, 1050 Brussels, Belgium
Tel. (+32) 2-3462658
Fax (+32) 2-3441361
E-mail rne-bru@skynet.be
Head of Mission Naryan Shumshere Thapa

New Zealand

Square de Meeûs 1, 7ème étage, 1000 Brussels,
   Belgium
Tel. (+32) 2-5121040
Fax (+32) 2-5134856
E-mail mark.talbot@mfat.govt.nz
Head of Mission Wade Armstrong
Counsellor Stephen Payton

Nicaragua

Avenue de Wolvendael 55, 1180 Brussels,
   Belgium
Tel. (+32) 2-3756434
Fax (+32) 2-3757188
Head of Mission Lester Mejía Solis

Niger

Avenue F. D. Roosevelt 78, 1050 Brussels,
   Belgium
Tel. (+32) 2-6485058
Fax (+32) 2-6482784
Head of Mission Abdou Abarry
First Counsellor Adani Illo

Nigeria

Avenue de Tervuren 288, 1150 Brussels,
   Belgium
Tel. (+32) 2-7625200
Fax (+32) 2-7623763

E-mail nigeriabrussels@belgacom.net
Head of Mission Clarkson Nwakanma Umelo

Niue

Rue Berckmans 10, 1060 Brussels, Belgium
Tel. (+32) 2-5431000
Fax (+32) 2-5431001
E-mail cookislands@prmltd.com
Head of Mission Todd McClay

Norway

Rue Archimède 17, 1000 Brussels, Belgium
Tel. (+32) 2-2341111
Fax (+32) 2-2341150
E-mail eu.brussels@mfa.no
URL www.eu-norway.org
Head of Mission Bjorn T. Grydeland
Minister Elisabeth Walaas

Oman

Konninginnegracht 27, 2514 AB The Hague,
   Netherlands
Tel. (+31 70) 3615800
Fax (+31 70) 3605464
E-mail embassyoman@wanadoo.nl
Head of Mission Khadija bint Hassan Salman
   al-Lawati

Pakistan

Avenue Delleur 57, 1170 Brussels, Belgium
Tel. (+32) 2-6738007
Fax (+32) 2-6758394
E-mail parepbrussels@skynet.be
Head of Mission Saeed Khalid
Deputy Head of Mission Nasrullah Khan

Panama

Avenue Louise 390–392, Bte 2, 1050 Brussels,
   Belgium
Tel. (+32) 2-6490729
Fax (+32) 2-6489216
E-mail embajada.panama@skynet.be
Head of Mission (vacant)
Minister-Counsellor Elena Barletta de
   Nottebohm

Papua New Guinea

Avenue de Tervuren 430, 1150 Brussels,
   Belgium
Tel. (+32) 2-7790609
Fax (+32) 2-7727088
Head of Mission Isaac Lupari
Counsellor Kapi Maro

Paraguay

Avenue Louise 475, 12è étage, Bte 21, 1050
  Brussels, Belgium
Tel. (+32) 2-6499055
Fax (+32) 2-6474248
E-mail embapar@skynet.be
Head of Mission Emilio Gimenez Franco

Peru

Avenue de Tervuren 179, 1150 Brussels,
  Belgium
Tel. (+32) 2-7333319
Fax (+32) 2-7334819
E-mail comunicaciones@embassy-of-peru.be
Head of Mission Luis Choquihuara Chil
Minister Juan Carlos Gamarra

Philippines

Avenue Molière 297, 1050 Brussels, Belgium
Tel. (+32) 2-3403377
Fax (+32) 2-3456425
Head of Mission (vacant)
Minister Anamarie A. Morales

Qatar

Rue de la Vallée 51, 1050 Brussels, Belgium
Tel. (+32) 2-2231155
Fax (+32) 2-2231166
Head of Mission (vacant)
First Sec. Sheikh Meshal bin Hamad al-Thani

Romania

Rue Montoyer 12, 1000 Brussels, Belgium
Tel. (+32) 2-7000640
Fax (+32) 2-7000641
E-mail bru@roumisue.org
Head of Mission Lazar Comanescu
Minister-Counsellor Viorel Ardeleanu

Russia

Blvd du Régent 31–33, 1050 Brussels, Belgium
Tel. (+32) 2-5021791
Fax (+32) 2-5137649
E-mail misrusce@mail.interpac.be
Head of Mission (vacant)
Deputy Head of Mission Mikhail Petrakov

Rwanda

Avenue des Fleurs 1, 1150 Brussels, Belgium
Tel. (+32) 2-7630721
Fax (+32) 2-7630753
E-mail ambarwanda@skynet.be
URL www.ambarwanda.be

Head of Mission (vacant)
First Counsellor and Chargé d'Affaires a. i.
  Jeanine Kambanda

Saint Christopher and Nevis

Rue de Livourne 42, 1000 Brussels, Belgium
Tel. (+32) 2-5342611
Fax (+32) 2-5394009
E-mail ecf.embassies@skynet.be
Head of Mission Georges Bullen
Minister-Counsellor Arnold Thomas

Saint Lucia

Rue de Livourne 42, 1000 Brussels, Belgium
Tel. (+32) 2-5342611
Fax (+32) 2-5394009
Head of Mission Georges Bullen
Minister-Counsellor Arnold Thomas

Saint Vincent and the Grenadines

Rue de Livourne 42, 1000 Brussels, Belgium
Tel. (+32) 2-5342611
Fax (+32) 2-5394009
E-mail ecs.embassies@skynet.be
Head of Mission Georges Bullen
Minister-Counsellor Arnold Thomas

Samoa

Av. de l'Orée 20, 1000 Brussels, Belgium
Tel. (+32) 2-6608454
Fax (+32) 2-6750336
E-mail samoaembassy@skynet.be
Head of Mission Tauiliili Uili Meredith
Counsellor Annie Meredith

San Marino

Avenue F. D. Roosevelt 62, 1050 Brussels,
  Belgium
Tel. (+32) 2-6442224
Fax (+32) 2-6442057
E-mail amb.rsm.bxl@skynet.be
Head of Mission Savina Zafferani
Counsellor Antonella Benedettini

São Tomé e Príncipe

Avenue de Tervuren 175, 1150 Brussels,
  Belgium
Tel. (+32) 2-7348966
Fax (+32) 2-7348815
E-mail ambassade.sao.tome@skynet.be
Head of Mission (vacant)
First Secretary Antonio de Lima Viegas

Saudi Arabia
Avenue F. D. Roosevelt 45, 1050 Brussels,
　Belgium
Tel. (+32) 2-6492044
Fax (+32) 2-6472492
E-mail ksa.embassy.bxl@skynet.be
Head of Mission Nassir Alassaf
Counsellor Saudi al-Thobaiti

Senegal
Avenue F. D. Roosevelt 196, 1050 Brussels,
　Belgium
Tel. (+32) 2-6730097
Fax (+32) 2-6750460
E-mail senegal.ambassade@coditel.net
Head of Mission Saliou Cisse
Minister-Counsellor Mahmoudou Cheikh Kane

Serbia and Montenegro
Avenue Emile De Mot 19, 1000 Brussels,
　Belgium
Tel. (+32) 2-6498365
Fax (+32) 2-6490878
E-mail mission.rfy@skynet.be
Head of Mission Pavle Jevremovic
Minister-Counsellor Branislava Alendar

Seychelles
Avenue Mozart 51, 75016 Paris, France
Tel. (+33) 1-42-30-57-47
Fax (+33) 1-42-30-57-40
E-mail ambsey@aol.com
Head of Mission Callixte d'Offay

Sierra Leone
Avenue de Tervuren 410, 1150 Brussels,
　Belgium
Tel. (+32) 2-7710053
Fax (+32) 2-7718230
Head of Mission Fode Maclean Dabor
Counsellor James Goodwyll

Singapore
Avenue F. D. Roosevelt 198, 1050 Brussels,
　Belgium
Tel. (+32) 2-6602979
Fax (+32) 2-6608685
E-mail amb.eu@singembbru.be
Head of Mission Walter Woon

Solomon Islands
Avenue Edouard Lacomble 17, 1040 Brussels,
　Belgium
Tel. (+32) 2-7327085
Fax (+32) 2-7326885
E-mail 106255.2155@compuserve.com
Head of Mission Robert Sisilo
Counsellor Joseph Ma'ahanua

South Africa
Rue de la Loi 26, Btes 14–15, 1040 Brussels,
　Belgium
Tel. (+32) 2-2854460
Fax (+32) 2-2854487
E-mail saembassy.belgium@swing.be
Head of Mission Jerry Matthews Matjila
First Sec. Tandjwe Mgxwati

Sri Lanka
Rue Jules Lejeune 27, 1050 Brussels, Belgium
Tel. (+32) 2-3445394
Fax (+32) 2-3446737
E-mail sri.lanka@euronet.be
Head of Mission Chrysantha Jayasinghe

Sudan
Avenue F. D. Roosevelt 124, 1050 Brussels,
　Belgium
Tel. (+32) 2-6479494
Fax (+32) 2-6483499
E-mail sudanbx@yahoo.com
Minister Plenipotentiary Elobeid Mohamed
　Elobeid

Suriname
Avenue Louise 379, Bte 20, 1050 Brussels,
　Belgium
Tel. (+32) 2-6401172
Fax (+32) 2-6463962
E-mail sur.amb.bru@online.be
Head of Mission Gerhard Otmar Hiwat

Swaziland
Avenue Winston Churchill 188, 1180 Brussels,
　Belgium
Tel. (+32) 2-3474771
Fax (+32) 2-3474623
Head of Mission Thembayena Annastasia
　Dlamini

Switzerland

Place de Luxembourg 1, 1050 Brussels,
  Belgium
Tel. (+32) 2-2861311
Fax (+32) 2-2304509
E-mail vertretung@brm.rep.admin.ch
Head of Mission Bernhard Marfurt
Deputy Head of Mission Philippe Guex

Syria

Avenue F. D. Roosevelt 1, 1050 Brussels,
  Belgium
Tel. (+32) 2-5541922
Fax (+32) 2-6464018
E-mail ambsyrie@skynet.be
Head of Mission Mohammad Badi Khattab

Tajikistan

Avenue Louise 363–365, Bte 4, 1060 Brussels,
  Belgium
Tel. (+32) 2-6406933
Fax (+32) 2-6490195
Head of Mission Sharif Rakhimov

Tanzania

Avenue Louise 363, 7è étage, 1050 Brussels,
  Belgium
Tel. (+32) 2-6406500
Fax (+32) 2-6468026
E-mail tanzania@skynet.be
Head of Mission (vacant)
Minister Plenipotentiary P. J. Mbena

Thailand

Square du Val de la Cambre 2, 1050 Brussels,
  Belgium
Tel. (+32) 2-6406810
Fax (+32) 2-6483066
E-mail thaibxl@pophost.eunet.be
Head of Mission Don Pramudvinai
Minister-Counsellor Tomwit Jarnson

Timor-Leste

Av. Cortenbergh 12, 1000 Brussels, Belgium
Tel. (+32) 2-2864289
Fax (+32) 2-2800277
Head of Mission José Antonio Amorim Dias

Togo

Avenue de Tervuren 264, 1150 Brussels,
  Belgium
Tel. (+32) 2-7701791
Fax (+32) 2-7715075
E-mail e-ambassade.togo@skynet.be
Head of Mission Félix Kodjo Sagbo
Minister-Counsellor Anani Kokou Nyawouame

Tonga

36 Molyneux Street, London W1H 6AB,
  United Kingdom
Tel. (+44 20) 7724-5828
Fax (+44 20) 7723-9074
E-mail fetu@btinternet.com
Head of Mission (vacant)
Counsellor Viela Tupou

Trinidad and Tobago

Avenue de la Faisanderie 14, 1150 Brussels,
  Belgium
Tel. (+32) 2-7629400
Fax (+32) 2-7722783
E-mail info@embtrinbago.be
Head of Mission Learie Edgar Rousseau
Minister-Counsellor Susan N. Gordon

Tunisia

Avenue de Tervuren 278, 1150 Brussels,
  Belgium
Tel. (+32) 2-7717395
Fax (+32) 2-7719433
E-mail amb.detunisie@brutele.be
Head of Mission Fethi Merdassi

Turkey

Rue Montoyer 4, 1000 Brussels, Belgium
Tel. (+32) 2-5132836
Fax (+32) 2-5110450
E-mail info@turkdeleg.org
Head of Mission Mustafa Oguz Demiralp
Deputy Permanent Delegate Feza Öztürk

Turkmenistan

Av. Franklin D. Roosevelt 106, 1050 Brussels,
  Belgium
Tel. (+32) 2-6481874
Fax (+32) 2-6481906
E-mail turkmenistan@skynet.be
Head of Mission Niyazlych Nurklychev

Uganda

Avenue de Tervuren 317, 1150 Brussels,
  Belgium
Tel. (+32) 2-7625825
Fax (+32) 2-7630438
Head of Mission Daye Rwabita

285

Ukraine

Avenue Louis Lepoutre 99–101, 1150 Brussels,
Belgium
Tel. (+32) 2-3409860
Fax (+32) 2-3409879
E-mail eu@ukraine-eu.be
Head of Mission Roman Shpek
Minister-Counsellor Kostiantyn Yeliseyev

United Arab Emirates

Avenue F. D. Roosevelt 73, 1050 Brussels,
Belgium
Tel. (+32) 2-6406000
Fax (+32) 2-6462473
E-mail emirates.bxl@infonie.be
Head of Mission Mohammed Salem al-Suweidi

United States of America

Rue Zinner 13, 1000 Brussels, Belgium
Tel. (+32) 2-5082222
Fax (+32) 2-5144339
Head of Mission Rockwell A. Schnabel
Deputy Head of Mission Peter Michael
McKinley

Uruguay

Avenue F. D. Roosevelt 22, 1050 Brussels,
Belgium
Tel. (+32) 2-6401169
Fax (+32) 2-6482909
E-mail uruemb@skynet.be
Head of Mission Elbio Oscar Rosselli Frieri
Minister-Counsellor Julio Tealdi

Uzbekistan

Avenue F. D. Roosevelt 99, 1050 Brussels,
Belgium
Tel. (+32) 2-6728844
Fax (+32) 2-6723946
E-mail ambassador@uzbekistan.be
Head of Mission Vladimir Norov
Counsellor Bakhromjon Alayev

Vatican City State

Avenue Brugmann 289, 1180 Brussels,
Belgium
Tel. (+32) 2-3407700

Fax (+32) 2-3407704
E-mail nuntius.eu@village.eunet.be
Head of Mission André Dupuy

Venezuela

Avenue F. D. Roosevelt 10, 1050 Brussels,
Belgium
Tel. (+32) 2-6390340
Fax (+32) 2-6478820
E-mail embajada@venezuela-eu.org
Head of Mission Luisa Romero Bermudez

Viet Nam

Boulevard Général Jacques 1, 1050 Brussels,
Belgium
Tel. (+32) 2-3792737
Fax (+32) 2-3749376
E-mail vnemb.brussels@skynet.be
Head of Mission Than Thuy Thanh
Minister-Counsellor Dinh Kha Ngo

Yemen

Avenue Franklin D. Roosevelt 114, 1050
Brussels, Belgium
Tel. (+32) 2-6465290
Fax (+32) 2-6462911
E-mail yemen.embassy@skynet.be
Head of Mission Jaffer Mohamed Jaffer
Minister Plenipotentiary Ahmed Abdulkarim
Mohamed Hajar

Zambia

Avenue Molière 469, 1050 Brussels, Belgium
Tel. (+32) 2-3435649
Fax (+32) 2-3474333
Head of Mission Irene Mumba Kamanga
First Sec. J. Mwila

Zimbabwe

Square Joséphine Charlotte 11, 1200 Brussels,
Belgium
Tel. (+32) 2-7625808
Fax (+32) 2-7629605
E-mail zimbrussels@skynet.be
Head of Mission Gift Punungwe
Minister-Counsellor Albert Ranganai
Chimbindi

CONSULTANTS SPECIALIZING IN EU QUESTIONS

At the end of this list is an index of areas of specialization.

2M Public Affairs

Square Vergote 39, 1030 Brussels, Belgium
Tel. (+32) 2-7429456
Fax (+32) 2-7370400
E-mail michel.maroy@2mpublicaffairs.be
URL www.2mpublicaffairs.be
Specialities: Lobbying; Advocacy; Monitoring; Funding opportunities
Contact Michel Maroy

A. T. Kearney

Avenue des Arts 46, 1000 Brussels, Belgium
Tel. (+32) 2-5044811
Fax (+32) 2-5110103
E-mail marie-paule.kirscht@es.atkearney.com
URL www.atkearney.com
Specialities: Aerospace and defence; Automotive industry; Chemicals sector, oil and gas; Consumer and retail sectors; Forest products; Healthcare and pharmaceuticals; Public sector; Telecommunications and electronics; Transport; Utilities; Finance and economics; Manufacturing and supply chain; Strategy and restructuring; Strategic information technology; Strategic sourcing; Change management; Transforming the enterprise; Executive search
Contact Marie-Paule Kirscht

Agra CEAS Consulting Ltd

Imperial College, Wye, Ashford, Kent TN25 5AH, United Kingdom
Tel. (+44 1233) 812181
Fax (+44 1233) 813309
E-mail info@ceasc.com
URL www.ceasc.com
Contact Conrad Caspari

Agra CEAS Consulting Ltd

Rue du Commerce 20–22, 1000 Brussels, Belgium
Tel. (+32) 2-7360088
Fax (+32) 2-7321361
E-mail info@ceasc.com
URL www.ceasc.com
Specialities: Agricultural economics policy; Environmental policy; Marketing; EU accession; Food; Drink
Dr Maria Christodoulou

Anna Macdougald EU Public affairs

Avenue des Arts 50, Bte 20, 1050 Brussels, Belgium
Tel. (+32) 2-5457575
Fax (+32) 2-7339255
E-mail info@macdougald-eu.com
Specialities: Environment; Consumer affairs; Transport; Research and development policy; Enterprise policy; Structural funds; Agriculture; Tourism; Health; Lobbying; Early warning service for clients regarding Commission proposals; Forestry; Food
Contact Anna Macdougald

APCO Associates Inc.

1615 L Street NW, Suite 900, Washington DC 20036, United States of America
Tel. (+1 202) 778-1000
Fax (+1 202) 466-6002
E-mail info@apcoassoc.com
URL www.apcoassoc.com
Contact Margery Kraus

APCO Europe

Rue du Trône 130, 1050 Brussels, Belgium
Tel. (+32) 2-6459811
Fax (+32) 2-6459812
E-mail mail@apco-europe.com
URL www.apco-europe.com
Specialities: Audiovisual; Aviation and transport; Coalition-building; Community relations; Competition policy (mergers and acquisitions); Consumer goods, food and beverages; Corporate events management; Corporate positioning; Crisis communication; Digital Communication; Energy; Enlargement; Environment; Financial services; Government relations;

Healthcare and pharmaceuticals; Information society; Intellectual property; Internal communication; Issues management; Litigation support; Media relations; Mergers and acquisitions; Postal services; Research and intelligence; Sport; Trade

Contact Laurent Chokoualé Datou

Archimède

Rue Joseph II 36, 1000 Brussels, Belgium
Tel. (+32) 2-2173939
Fax (+32) 2-2191842
E-mail richard.steel@euronet.be

Specialities: European Parliament's committees and plenary sessions

Contact Richard Steel

Aromates Independent PR agency

169 Rue d'Aguesseau, 92100 Boulogne Billancourt, France
Tel. (+33) 1-46-99-10-80
Fax (+33) 1-46-04-70-98
E-mail aromates@aromates.fr
URL www.aromates.com

Specialities: Telecommunications and informatics; Internet; Logistics and transport; Business centre

Contact Jacques Marceau

ARPES

Square Ambiorix 32, bte 22, 1000 Brussels, Belgium
Tel. (+32) 2-2305609
Fax (+32) 2-2302898
E-mail etoile@village.unnet.be

Specialities: Agro-industry

Contact Zanarelli

ARPES SRL

Viale G. Mazzini 55, 00195 Rome, Italy
Tel. (+39) 06-3217786
Fax (+39) 06-3217783
E-mail info@arpes.it
E-mail arpesco@tin.it

Contact Christian Benenati

Arthur D. Little

Avenue de Tervuren 270, 1150 Brussels, Belgium
Tel. (+32) 2-7617200
Fax (+32) 2-7620758

E-mail adlittle.brussels@adlittle.com
URL www.adlittle.com

Specialities: Strategy and organization; Change management; Technology management; Informatics; Operations; Industrial, financial and commercial sectors

Contact Frederic Wirtz

Arthur D. Little Inc.

68 Fargo street, Boston, MA 02210, United States of America
Tel. (+1 617) 443-0309
Fax (+1 617) 443-0166
E-mail croufer.edouard@adlittle.com
URL www.adlittle.com

Association for Information Management (ASLIB)

Holywell Centre, 1 Phipp Street, London EC2A 4PS, United Kingdom
Tel. (+44 20) 7613-3031
Fax (+44 20) 7613-5080
E-mail aslib@aslib.com
URL www.aslib.co.uk

Specialities: Information management

B & S Business & Show – Syntagmes

Avenue de la Couronne 340, 1050 Brussels, Belgium
Tel. (+32) 2-6472400
Fax (+32) 2-6405501
E-mail info@bs.be
URL www.bs.be

Specialities: Public relations; Press; Events (organization)

Contact Patrick Lefebvre

Babel P.R.

Rue Royale 326, 1030 Brussels, Belgium
Tel. (+32) 2-2193088
Fax (+32) 2-2190016
E-mail midh.smets@skynet.be

Specialities: Consumer goods; Culture; Leisure

Contact Smets

Baloun, J.C. a Rosehill

N.A. Nekrasova 2, 160 00 Prague 6, Czech Republic
Tel. (+420) 224317374
Fax (+420) 224317298
E-mail boyden_baloun@mbox.vol.cz
URL www.boyden.co

Specialities: Lobbying; Executive search

Contact Chris Clarke

Barabino & Partners Europe S.A.

Rue Thérésienne 7, 1000 Brussels, Belgium

Tel. (+32) 2-5021558

Fax (+32) 2-5024869

E-mail info@barabino.be

URL www.barabinoeurope.com

Specialities: Public affairs; Press; Corporate communication; Crisis management

Contact Federico Steiner

Bennis Porter Novelli

Amsterdamseweg 204, 1182 HL Amstelveen, Netherlands

Tel. (+31 20) 5437600

Fax (+31 20) 5437676

E-mail bennispn.av@bennispn.nl

URL www.bennispn.nl

Specialities: Health; Food; Consumer goods (fast-moving); Industry; Government communication; Information technology; Communications technology

Contact Simon van den Ende

Berkley Associates Sprl

Rue de la Presse 4, 1000 Brussels, Belgium

Tel. (+32) 2-2190532

Fax (+32) 2-2190498

E-mail berkleyassociates@skynet.be

Specialities: SMEs; Education and training; Environment; Research; Enterprise policy; Project management; Training project managers; Fraud prevention training for grant-funded projects

Contact John Stringer

Bioresco Ltd

Bundesstrasse 29, 4054 Basel, Switzerland

Tel. (+41) 61-273-77-00

Fax (+41) 61-273-77-03

E-mail contact@bioresco.ch

URL www.bioresco.ch

Contact Dr Albert Bar

Bioresco Ltd

St Hubertuslaan 4A, 3080 Tervuren, Belgium

Tel. (+32) 2-3050436

Fax (+32) 2-7670274

E-mail bioresco@pandora.be

URL www.bioresco.ch

Specialities: Food; Animal feedstuffs; Food science; Food regulations

Contact Marquard Imfeld

Bureau Européen de Recherches S.A

Rue du Commerce 20–22, 1000 Brussels, Belgium

Tel. (+32) 2-7360088

Fax (+32) 2-7321361

E-mail conrad.caspari@ceas.com

URL www.ceasc.com

Specialities: Common agricultural policy; International trade policy; Farm supply industries; Food processing; Fisheries; Environment; Consumer protection; Regional affairs; Agriculture; Food; Rural environment; EU policy

Contact Conrad Caspari

Bureau Lucy Rozenbaum

Rue Fernand Neuray 8, 1050 Brussels, Belgium

Tel. (+32) 4-75266207

Fax (+32) 2-3440856

E-mail lucy@rozenbaum-associates.net

Specialities: Audiovisual; Communication; Aeronautics

Contact Lucy Rozenbaum

Bureau van Dijk Electronic Publishing

Avenue Louise 250, 1050 Brussels, Belgium

Tel. (+32) 2-6390606

Fax (+32) 2-6488230

E-mail brussels@bvdep.com

URL www.bvdep.it

Specialities: Telecommunications; Statistics; Finance; Electronic publishing; Information and documentation systems; Energy; Strategy; Research and development; Computer applications

Contact Christophe van de Walle

Burson-Marsteller

Avenue de Cortenbergh 118, 1000 Brussels, Belgium

Tel. (+32) 2-7436611

Fax (+32) 2-7336611

E-mail Jeremy_Galbraith@be.bm.com

URL www.bmbrussels.be

Specialities: Public relations; Public affairs; Communication; Government relations

Contact Jeremy Galbraith

Burson-Marsteller AG

Grubenstrasse 40, 8045 Zurich, Switzerland
Tel. (+41) 44-455-84-00
Fax (+41) 44-455-84-01
E-mail info_bm@ch.bm.com
URL www.b-m.ch

Specialities: Marketing communication; Public relations; Advertising

Contact Peter Eberhard

Business Environment Europe S.A.

Rue de l'Industrie 42, bte 16, 1000 Brussels, Belgium
Tel. (+32) 2-2308360
Fax (+32) 2-2308370
E-mail info@bee.be
URL www.bee.be

Specialities: Public affairs (EU); Competition; Environment; Trade; Scenario planning; Strategy; Food and drink; Agriculture; Automobile industry; Energy; Chemicals; Telecommunications; Packaging; Pulp and paper

Contact Bruno Liebhaberg

C. B. Europa

Paseo de la Castellana 46, 28046 Majadahonda (Madrid), Spain
Tel. (+34) 91-4238000
Fax (+34) 91-5760387
E-mail mail@cbeuropa.com
URL www.cbeuropa.com

Specialities: Telecommunications; Energy; Environment; Media; Latin America; Funding

Contact Ignacio Corrochano

Cabinet Stewart

Rue d'Arlon 40, 1000 Brussels, Belgium
Tel. (+32) 2-2307020
Fax (+32) 2-2305043
E-mail cabinetstewart@cabinetstewart.com
URL www.cabinetstewart.com

Specialities: Tailored monitoring; European policy and law; Lobbying strategy; Secretariat services

Contact Catherine Stewart

Centre for European Not-for-Profit Organisations (CENPO)

Rue de la Concorde 57, 1050 Brussels, Belgium
Tel. (+32) 2-7400000
Fax (+32) 2-7400009
E-mail info@cenpo.org
URL www.cenpo.org

Specialities: Third Sector; Not-for-Profit Sector; Aid; Charities; Voluntary work; Arts; Culture; Heritage; Education; Training; Central Europe; Eastern Europe; Social affairs; Health; Development; Research

Contact David Wedgwood

Charlemagne Group

Charlemagne House, 2 Enys Road, Eastbourne BN21 2DE, United Kingdom
Tel. (+44 1323) 434700
Fax (+44 1323) 434702
E-mail enquiries@charlemagne.co.uk
URL www.europe-for-business.co.uk

Specialities: European Union; Information networking and delivery

Contact Peter Barron

Citigate Public Affairs

26 Grosvenor Gardens, London SW1W 0GT, United Kingdom
Tel. (+44 20) 7838-4865
Fax (+44 20) 7838-4801
E-mail warwick.smith@citigatepa.co.uk
URL www.citigatepa.com

Contact Warwick Smith

Citigate Public Affairs

Avenue de Cortenbergh 66, 1000 Brussels, Belgium
Tel. (+32) 2-7368135
Fax (+32) 2-7368847
E-mail johnny.pring@citigopo.com
URL www.citigatepa.com

Specialities: Energy; Transport; Financial services

Contact Thierry Lebeaux

CLAN Public Affairs

Rue Froissart 57, 1040 Brussels, Belgium
Tel. (+32) 2-7365800
Fax (+32) 2-7387120
E-mail clanpa@clan-public-affairs.be
URL www.clan-public-affairs.be

Specialities: Agriculture; Food products;
Health; Automotive industry; Transport;
Financial services; Trade

Contact Serena Catallozzi

Clerens Consulting

Avenue de l'Opale 80, 1030 Brussels, Belgium
Tel. (+32) 2-7432980
Fax (+32) 2-7432990
E-mail patrick@clerens.com

Specialities: Transport; Energy; Environment;
Research and development

Contact Patrick Clerens

Communication Partners

Rue Konkel 105–107, 1150 Brussels, Belgium
Tel. (+32) 2-7724070
Fax (+32) 2-7723065
E-mail comm.partners@skynet.be

Specialities: Crisis management; Internal and
external communication (audits and
strategies); Copywriting; Public affairs;
Press; Evaluation

Contact Jean-Luc Pleunes

Communications Group

Avenue Louise 497, 1050 Brussels, Belgium
Tel. (+32) 2-6409207
Fax (+32) 2-6409224
E-mail terry@eurocom.be
URL www.eurocom.be

Specialities: Technology; Finance; Industry;
EU (relations with)

Contact Terry Davidson

COPCA – Coopération Internationale

Rue Belliard 199, 1040 Brussels, Belgium
Tel. (+32) 2-2309746
Fax (+32) 2-2302612
E-mail copcaue@easynet.be
URL www.copca.com

Specialities: Co-operation for development;
Export promotion

Contact Ana Coelho Rodrigues

Crehan, Kusano & Associates Sprl

Rue d'Arenberg 2, 1000 Brussels, Belgium
Tel. (+32) 2-7421865
Fax (+32) 2-7423763
E-mail Patrick.Crehan@cka.be

Specialities: Hi tech new business
development; RTD innovation; Technology
transfer; Economic and social development;
Industrial co-operation policy; Actions
(design and implementation)

Contact Dr Patrick Crehan

CSM Parliamentary Consultants

72A Rochester Row, London SW1P 1JU,
United Kingdom
Tel. (+44 20) 7233-9090
Fax (+44 20) 7233-9595
E-mail info@csmparl.co.uk
URL www.csmparl.co.uk

Specialities: Internal market; Financial services;
Environment; Consumer affairs; Social
policy; Industrial policy; Energy; Health
policy

Contact Christine Stewart Munro

Deloitte & Touche

Avenue Louise 240, 1050 Brussels, Belgium
Tel. (+32) 2-6006000
Fax (+32) 2-6006001
E-mail pmu@mtsacpeu.org
URL www.deloitte.be

Specialities: Public affairs (Europe); Grants
(EU); Inward investment; Projects (EU);
Evaluation; Economic development

Contact Barry Salzberg

Deloitte & Touche – Tax & Legal

Brussels Airport Business Park, Berkenlaan 7,
1831 Diegem, Belgium
Tel. (+32) 2-6006500
Fax (+32) 2-6006501
E-mail majarrett@deloitte.com
E-mail arainer@deloitte.com
URL www.deloitte.com

Specialities: Competition law (European); State
aids; Taxation law; European Single Market
(entry into); Eastern Europe (business with);
Grants and subsidies; Trade law and customs
procedures (EU); Anti-dumping procedures;
Influencing EU law; Competition issues
(awareness training programmes); Public
procurement law (EU) and its interpretation;
Legislative reviews and monitoring services
(EU)

Contact Madonna Jarrett

Dialogic

Avenue du Colvert 5, 1170 Brussels, Belgium
Tel. (+32) 2-4266466
Fax (+32) 2-4265378
E-mail info@dialogic-agency.com
URL www.dialogic-agency.com

Specialities: Corporate communication; Sports communication; Institutional communication

Contact Philippe Housiaux

Droit et Pharmacie

12 Rue de Lorraine, 92309 Levallois-Perret Cedex, France
Tel. (+33) 1-55-46-91-00
Fax (+33) 1-55-46-91-01
E-mail info@droit-et-pharmacie.fr
URL www.droit-et-pharmacie.fr.

Specialities: Pharmaceutical industry; Legal affairs; Regulatory affairs; Economic affairs; Marketing authorization dossiers

Contact Philippe Conquet

Eamonn Bates Europe Public Affairs SA/NV

Avenue Livingstone 13–15, 1000 Brussels, Belgium
Tel. (+32) 2-2869494
Fax (+32) 2-2869495
E-mail info@eamonnbates.com
URL www.eamonnbates.com

Specialities: Environment; Consumer affairs; Health and safety; Food policy; Public health; Structural funds; Third country representation

Contact Eamonn Bates

Ecotec Research and Consulting

Avenue de Tervuren 13a, 1040 Brussels, Belgium
Tel. (+32) 2-7438949
Fax (+32) 2-7327111
E-mail brussels@ecotec.com
URL www.ecotec.com

Specialities: Economic affairs; Business advice services; Employment; Labour market; Vocational training studies; Regional policy; Feasibility and impact evaluation studies; Town and country planning strategy; Enterprise policy; Tourism; Environmental management and policy; Pollution control technology; Waste management and disposal (research)

Contact John Bell

Ecotec Research and Consulting

12–16 Albert Street, Birmingham B4 7UD, United Kingdom
Tel. (+44 121) 616-3600
Fax (+44 121) 616-3699
E-mail birmingham@ecotec.com
URL www.ecotec.com

Contact Hugh Williams

Edelman Public Relations Worldwide

1500 Broadway, New York, NY 10036, United States of America
Tel. (+1 212) 768-0550
Fax (+1 212) 704-0128
E-mail new.york@edelman.com
URL www.edelman.com

Contact Daniel J. Edelman

Edelman Public Relations Worldwide – Brussels

Rue des Deux Eglises 20, 1000 Brussels, Belgium
Tel. (+32) 2-2276170
Fax (+32) 2-2276189
E-mail brussels@edelman.com
URL www.edelman.be

Contact Teemu Lehtinen

Ellis Publications BV

Wilhelminasingel 105, 6221 BH Maastricht, Netherlands
Tel. (+31 43) 3215313
Fax (+31 43) 3253959
E-mail sales@ellispub.com
URL www.ellispub.com

Specialities: Legal information (EU)

Contact David Fairweather

Enhesa S.A.

Rue du Mail 15, 1050 Brussels, Belgium
Tel. (+32) 2-7759797
Fax (+32) 2-7759799
E-mail enhesa@enhesa.com
URL www.enhesa.com

Specialities: Environmental health and safety law and policy; Occupational health and safety law and policy

Contact Paul Beatley

Entec UK Ltd

Northumbria House, Regent Centre, Gosforth,
  Newcastle upon Tyne NE3 3PX,
  United Kingdom
Tel. (+44 191) 272-6100
Fax (+44 191) 272-6592
E-mail marketing@entecuk.co.uk
URL www.entecuk.com

Specialities: Ground and water management;
  Contaminated land investigation and
  remediation; Water and wastewater
  engineering; Urban and regional planning
  and development; Tourism; Corporate and
  technical risk management; Rural and
  economic development; Fisheries
  development

Contact Simon Armes-Reardon

Environmental Policy Consultants

71 Greencroft Gardens, London NW6 3LJ,
  United Kingdom
Tel. (+44 20) 7328-0050
Fax (+44 20) 7328-0050
E-mail adrian.wilkes@eic-uk.co.uk

Specialities: Environment

Contact Adrian Wilkes

Environmental Resources Management

Visverkopersstraat 13, 1000 Brussels, Belgium
Tel. (+32) 2-5500293
Fax (+32) 2-5500299
E-mail kathleen.goossens@erm.com
URL www.erm.com

Specialities: Waste policy; Environmental
  management; Soil investigation remediation;
  Environmental audits; Sustainable
  development; Environmental strategy;
  Environmental economy and policy

Contact Wim van Breusegem

EPRO SA

Avenue Marnix 19A, 1000 Brussels, Belgium
Tel. (+32) 2-5127980
Fax (+32) 2-5142119
E-mail info@eu-project.org

Specialities: Common Agricultural Policy;
  External relations; Trade policies with third
  countries; Internal industrial and trade
  policies; Customs matters; Public
  procurement; EU funded programmes in
  favour of EU enterprises; EU programmes in

favour of third countries; Economic
  co-operation

Contact Giulio Ripa di Meana

Eric Deakins – International Public Affairs

36 Murray Mews, London NW1 9RJ,
  United Kingdom
Tel. (+44 20) 7267-6196
Fax (+44 20) 7267-3151
E-mail epdeakins@netscapeonline.co.uk

Specialities: International trade; EU–US
  relations; UK government and labour party
  contacts; UK taxation

Contact E. Deakins

Ernst & Young

Avenue Marcel Thiry 204 & 216, 1200
  Brussels, Belgium
Tel. (+32) 2-7749111
Fax (+32) 2-7749090
E-mail info@be.ey.com
URL www.ey.be

Specialities: Services to the EU institutions;
  Evaluations; Public sector; SMEs; ETM
  (interim, management); Taxation; Audit

Contact Gust Herrewijn

ESL & Network

123 avenue des Champs Elysees, 75008 Paris,
  France
Tel. (+33) 1-40-73-14-00
Fax (+33) 1-40-73-14-01
E-mail contact@eslnetwork.com
URL www.eslnetwork.com

Specialities: Finance; Energy; Post, media and
  telecommunications; Telecommunications;
  Industry; EU affairs

Contact C. Calvez

Essor Europe SA

55 Chemin du Moulin Carron, 69130 Ecully,
  France
Tel. (+33) 4-72-86-97-62
Fax (+33) 4-78-33-39-13
E-mail mailbox@essoreurope.fr
URL www.essoreurope.fr

Specialities: Research and development;
  Technology; EU programmes; EUREKA;
  EU projects (establishment of); SMEs;
  Technology transfer; Industrial property;
  Biotechnology; Environment; Transport

Contact Dr Philippe de Montgolfier

Euralia

38 avenue Hoche, 75008 Paris, France
Tel. (+33) 1-45-63-65-00
Fax (+33) 1-45-63-65-05
E-mail info@euralia.com
URL www.euralia.com
Contact Bruno Dupont

Euro-Consejeros S.L.

C/ Cortes de Aragon 35, Entlo Dcha, 50005
  Zaragoza, Spain
Tel. (+34) 976-356812
Fax (+34) 976-561294
E-mail euro-consejeros@red3i.es
URL www.red3i.es/euro
Specialities: EU Law; International commercial
  law
Contact Natalia Morte de Rego

Euro Keys

Avenue de Tervuren 13B, 1040 Brussels,
  Belgium
Tel. (+32) 2-7779979
Fax (+32) 2-7703601
E-mail euro.keys@euro-keys.com
URL www.euro-keys.com
Specialities: Quality control; Energy;
  Transport; Plastics; Chemical sector;
  Environment; Textiles; Pharmaceuticals;
  Food
Contact Monika Derecque-Pois

Euro P.A. Consulting

Rue du Luxembourg 19–21, 1000 Brussels,
  Belgium
Tel. (+32) 2-5124116
Fax (+32) 2-5146932
E-mail info@euro-pa-online.com
URL www.euro-pa-online.com
Specialities: Internal market; Healthcare;
  SMEs; External aid; Research; Environment
Contact Soren Haar

Euro RSCG

2 Allee de Longchamp, 92281 Suresnes Cedex,
  France
Tel. (+33) 1-58-47-90-00
Fax (+33) 1-58-47-99-99
E-mail bernard.sananes@eurorscg.fr
URL www.eurorscg.com
Contact Mercedes Erra

Euro RSCG Brussels

Rue du Doyenné 58, 1180 Brussels, Belgium
Tel. (+32) 2-3483800
Fax (+32) 2-3475911
E-mail christian.d@eurorscg.be
URL www.eurorscg.be
Specialities: European public affairs; Corporate
  communication
Contact Sigrid Ligne

Euro Tec

Rond Point Schuman 9, Bte 15, 1040 Brussels,
  Belgium
Tel. (+32) 2-2820080
Fax (+32) 2-2303168
E-mail info@eurotec.be
Specialities: EU law; Customs and taxation;
  Funding and investment programmes (EU);
  Structural funds; Investment; Venture capital
Contact D'Alessandro

Euro Top Cooperation Partners

Av Louise 486, B14, 1050 Brussels, Belgium
Tel. (+32) 2-6495994
Fax (+32) 2-6403759
E-mail secretariat@eurotop.be
URL www.eurotop.be
Specialities: Technology transfer (energy –
  environment-bioindustry); Project
  management; Feasibility studies; Grants and
  loans; RTD; Web design; Internet
  management tools
Contact Dr Jacques Viseur

Eurocontact

Rue Montoyer 18, 1040 Brussels, Belgium
Tel. (+32) 2-2800062
Fax (+32) 2-2801655
E-mail eurocontact@tin.it
URL www.eurocontact.it
Specialities: SMEs; Tourism; Local authorities;
  Local development; Culture; Information;
  Training
Contact Sergio Diana

Eurofacts OY

Brahenkatu 1 B 4, 20100 Turku, Finland
Tel. (+358 2) 4693030
Fax (+358 2) 4693031
E-mail eurofacts@eurofacts.fi
URL www.eurofacts.fi

Specialities: European affairs;
  Telecommunications; Political risks; Family
  business; Finance; Industrial policy; Trade
  and competition; Information society;
  Taxation; Graphical industry
Contact Anders Blom

Eurofi Ltd

Eurofi House, 37 London Road, Newbury
  RG14 1JL, United Kingdom
Tel. (+44 1635) 31900
Fax (+44 1635) 37370
E-mail eurofi@headoffice.freeserve.co.uk
URL www.eurofi.co.uk
Specialities: Funding (EU); Grants (UK
  government)
Contact B.G.T. Harris

Euromission

6 Blvd St Michel, 84000 Avignon, France
Tel. (+33) 4-90-16-35-03
Fax (+33) 4-90-16-35-01
E-mail Le.Leader@europe-avignon.com
Contact G. Crest

Europa SA

Rue de la Loi 28, 10 étage, bte 1, 1040
  Brussels, Belgium
Tel. (+32) 2-2801195
Fax (+32) 2-2801245
E-mail europa@europa.be
URL www.europa.be
Specialities: Procurement; Goods (supply)
Contact Philip Pickard

**Europabüro für Projektbegleitung GmbH
(EFP)**

Rue le Titien 28, 1000 Brussels, Belgium
Specialities: Social policy; Labour policy;
  Employment Community Initiative (national
  support structure); EQUAL Community
  Initiative (national support structure);
  XENOS (national support structure); Local
  Social Capital programme (national support
  structure)
Contact Dr S. Honnef

**Europabüro für Projektbegleitung GmbH
(EFP)**

Ellerstrasse 48, 53119 Bonn, Germany
Tel. (+49 228) 985-9911

Fax (+49 228) 985-9980
E-mail info@efp-bonn.de
URL www.efp-bonn.de
Contact Dr Sibylle Honnef

Europe Analytica

Ave Livingstone 26, 1000 Brussels, Belgium
Tel. (+32) 2-2311299
Fax (+32) 2-2307658
E-mail info@europe-analytica.com
URL www.europe-analytica.com
Specialities: Political affairs; European Union
  and Member States; Finance; Information
  technology; Food policy; Industrial policy;
  Agriculture
Contact Douglas Herbison

Europe Contact Service (ECOS)

Avenue Adolphe Lacomble 66–68, 1030
  Brussels, Belgium
Tel. (+32) 2-7377700
Fax (+32) 2-7326608
E-mail eis@eis.be
URL www.eis.be
Contact Lucyna Gutman Grauer

Europe Economics

Chancery House, 53–64 Chancery Lane,
  London WC2A 1QU, United Kingdom
Tel. (+44 20) 7831-4717
Fax (+44 20) 7831-4515
E-mail enquiries@europe-economics.com
URL www.europe-economics.com
Specialities: Economic regulation; Competition
  policy; Public policy; Telecommunications;
  Electricity; Gas; Water; Transport;
  Pharmaceuticals; Lotteries and gaming.
Contact Dermot Glynn

Europe for Business

Rue de Lausanne 5, Brussels 1060, Belgium
Tel. (+32) 2-5389275
Fax (+32) 2-5389275
E-mail enquiries@europe-for-business.co.uk
URL www.europe-for-business.co.uk
Specialities: Research and development;
  Funding (EU); Food; Consumer policy;
  Social policy; Environment; Information
  Technology; SMEs; Health; Information
  society; Electronic commerce; Euro
Contact Lindsay Wittenberg

Europe Telematique Information Conseil (ETIC)

Rue Archimède 50, 1040 Brussels, Belgium
Tel. (+32) 2-2306756
Fax (+32) 2-2302306
E-mail etic@skynet.be
URL www.foureuro.com
Specialities: Monitoring of European law; European Parliament
Contact J. Echkenazi

European Advisory Services (EAS)

Rue de l'Association 50, 1000 Brussels, Belgium
Tel. (+32) 2-2181470
Fax (+32) 2-2197342
E-mail info@eas.be
URL www.eas.be
Specialities: Food; Health; Food supplements; Functional foods; Herbal products
Contact Simon Pettman

European Consultants Information Technology

Rue d'Arlon 39–41, 1000 Brussels, Belgium
Tel. (+32) 2-2854010
Fax (+32) 2-2854019
E-mail consult@eurocity.be
URL www.eurocity.be
Specialities: Information technology; Project management; Programme management
Contact Stuart Dowsett

European Consulting Company (ECCO)

Avenue des Gaulois 9, 1040 Brussels, Belgium
Tel. (+32) 2-7365354
Fax (+32) 2-7323427
E-mail info@ecco-eu.com
URL www.ecco.be
Specialities: Agricultural policy; Food law
Contact Alain Galaski

European Development Projects

Avenue des Nerviens 67, 1040 Brussels, Belgium
Tel. (+32) 2-7348791
Fax (+32) 2-7341588
E-mail macarena.ybarra@euronet.be
Specialities: Regional policy; Development aid; Agriculture; Fisheries; Audiovisual; Publishing; Media; Competition policy; Energy; Utilities; Environment; Food; Drink industry; Industrial and intellectual property; SMEs; Telecommunications; Transport
Contact Macarena Ybarra

European Document Research

1100 17th Street NW, Suite 301, Washington DC 20036, United States of America
Tel. (+1 202) 785-8594
Fax (+1 202) 785-8589
E-mail info@europeandocuments.com
URL www.europeandocuments.com
Specialities: EU Documentation; EU Law
Contact George Lesser

European Institute for Public Affairs

Chemin des Moines 1, 1640 Rhode Saint-Genèse, Belgium
Tel. (+32) 2-3581189
Fax (+32) 2-3584566
E-mail c.leclercq@euronet.be
Specialities: Public relations; Press relations; Publications; Seminars; Events; Crisis management; Public affairs
Contact C. Le Clercq

European Multimedia Forum

Rue Hector Denis 55, 1050 Brussels, Belgium
Tel. (+32) 2-2190305
Fax (+32) 2-2191898
E-mail info@e-multimedia.org
URL www.emf.be
Specialities: Information society; Enterprise policy; Internal market
Contact Philippe Wacker

European Policies Research Centre

40 George Street, Glasgow G1 1QE, United Kingdom
Tel. (+44 141) 548-3672
Fax (+44 141) 548-4898
E-mail eprc@strath.ac.uk
URL www.eprc.strath.ac.uk
Specialities: Economic policy; Industrial policy; Regional policy (Western and Eastern Europe); Structural funds; Economic development policy
Contact Jacqui Vance

European Policy Centre

Résidence Palace, Rue de la Loi 155, 1040
  Brussels, Belgium
Tel. (+32) 2-2310340
Fax (+32) 2-2310704
E-mail info@theepc.be
URL www.theepc.be
Specialities: European Union; Political affairs
Contact E. Bisland

European Public Affairs

Rue du Luxembourg 19–21, 1000 Brussels,
  Belgium
Tel. (+32) 2-5068820
Fax (+32) 2-5068825
E-mail info@euralia.com
URL www.euralia.com
Specialities: Banking and finance; Information
  technology; Communications technology;
  Agro-food industry; External relations;
  Development aid; SMEs; Professional
  organizations and associations; European
  Parliament (relations with); Market access/
  WTO
Contact Bruno Dupont

European Public Policy Advisers

Place de Luxembourg 2, 1050 Brussels,
  Belgium
Tel. (+32) 2-7358230
Fax (+32) 2-7354412
E-mail pascal.michaux@eppa.com
URL www.eppa.com
Specialities: Agriculture; Competition;
  Employment; Food; Pharmaceuticals; Media;
  Telecommunications; Trade; Transport;
  Business; Law; Economics; Politics; Public
  administration; Journalism
Contact Pascal Michaux

European Rail Circle

Fontaine Fonteny 8, 1332 Genval, Belgium
Tel. (+32) 2-6336030
Fax (+32) 2-6336029
E-mail clodong@skynet.be
Specialities: Transport; Energy; Trade
Contact André Clodong

European Research Associates (ERA)

Av. des Nerviens 79, 1040 Brussels, Belgium
Tel. (+32) 2-7357260

Fax (+32) 2-7359141
E-mail info@erabrussels.be
URL www.erabrussels.be
Specialities: Economic developments (Europe);
  Political developments (Europe); Industrial
  policy; European Single Market;
  Enlargement; Business regulation (EC);
  Technology transfer; Trade; Trade law;
  Environmental policy and regulation in
  Europe; European industrial co-operation in
  advanced technology sectors; Economic
  Co-operation with EFTA and Eastern
  European countries; Urban and regional
  development; Multinational corporate
  management issues; Telecommunications;
  Information technology; Motor industry;
  Consumer electronics; Pharmaceuticals;
  Biotechnology; Aerospace; Defence;
  Financial services; Environmental
  protection; Energy
Contact Bob Taylor

European Service Network SA

Rue du Collège 27, 1050 Brussels, Belgium
Tel. (+32) 2-6464020
Fax (+32) 2-6404281
E-mail esn@esn.be
URL www.esn.be
Specialities: European affairs; Science and
  technology; Innovation; Information society;
  SMEs; Industry; Environment; Trade;
  Education; Training; Development
  co-operation; Social issues; Human rights;
  Regional policy
Contact Koenraad Tommissen

European Strategy and Lobbying Network

123 avenue des Champs Elysées, 75008 Paris,
  France
Tel. (+33) 1-40-73-14-00
Fax (+33) 1-40-73-14-01
E-mail simonwh@eslnetwork.com
Contact Patrice Allain-Dupré

Europool SA

Rue de l'Industrie 11, 1040 Brussels, Belgium
Tel. (+32) 2-2343057
Fax (+32) 2-2303300
E-mail europool@tiscalinet.be
Specialities: Access to EU markets; Business
  regulation; Phare; Tacis; EDF
Contact Roland Lastenouse

Europublic SA/NV

PO Box 504, Uccle 5, 1180 Brussels, Belgium
Tel. (+32) 2-3437726
Fax (+32) 2-3439330
E-mail mail@europublic.com
URL www.europublic.com
Specialities: Communications strategy; Media relations
Contact Karin Minke

Euroscope: Expertise in the EU and World Economy

Lg Kanaakdijk 62, 6212 AH Maastricht, Netherlands
Tel. (+31 43) 3639189
Fax (+31 43) 3256780
E-mail euroscope@hetnet.nl
Specialities: Internal market strategy; Standards; Telecommunications; Textiles; EU–East Asia relations
Contact J. Pelkmans

Eurostrategies

Avenue des Nerviens 79, 1040 Brussels, Belgium
Tel. (+32) 2-7357260
Fax (+32) 2-7359141
URL es@erabrussels.be
Specialities: Economic consultancy and studies; Telecommunications; Information technology
Contact Robert Taylor

Eurowin Communications

Avenue de la Fontaine 31, 1435 Hevillers, Belgium
Tel. (+32) 1-0658903
Fax (+32) 1-0658448
E-mail marc.callemien@euronet.be
Specialities: European affairs

Excoser S.A.

Rue Maurice Lietart 14, 1150 Brussels, Belgium
Tel. (+32) 2-7722737
Fax (+32) 2-7714439
E-mail excoser.j.agie@skynet.be
URL www.excoser.com
Specialities: Environment; Agri-business; Wood processing and forestry
Contact Joseph Agie de Selsaten

Expertise in Labour Mobility (ELM)

Elandsgracht 17, 1016 TM Amsterdam, Netherlands
Tel. (+31 20) 6836964
Fax (+31 20) 4125295
E-mail info@labourmobility.com
Specialities: Labour mobility
Contact Nannette Ripmeester

FINECO Eurofinancements

Le Florentin, 71 chemin du Moulin Carron, 69570 Dardilly, France
Tel. (+33) 4-78-33-81-79
Fax (+33) 4-78-33-80-63
E-mail contacts@fineco.fr
Specialities: European programmes engineering (RTD); CIS countries (co-operation with); Companies partnership; Technology transfer; Innovation financing
Contact Vasken Pamokdjian

GADESO

C/ Ter 14 (1°), Poligono Son Suster, 07009 Palma de Mallorca, Spain
Tel. (+34) 971-479703
Fax (+34) 971-470042
E-mail fundaciogadeso@gadeso.org
URL www.gadeso.org
Specialities: Tourism; SMEs; Trade; Training
Contact Antoni Tarabini Castellani Cabot

Gerling Belgium S.A.

Avenue de Tervuren 273, 1150 Anvers, Belgium
Tel. (+32) 2-7730811
Fax (+32) 2-7730950
E-mail patrick.thiels@gerling.be
URL www.gerling.com
Specialities: Environmental and safety management; Risk analysis; Risk management; Environmental and safety auditing; Quality management
Contact Patrick Thiels

Gerling Consulting Gruppe GmbH

Institute für Risiko-Consulting Plus Sicherheits-Management GmbH, Frankfurter Strasse 720–726, 51145 Cologne, Germany
Tel. (+49 22) 11442581
Fax (+49 22) 11445604

URL www.gerling.com
Contact Joachim Schmidtke

Global Europe – Consulting Group

Avenue Louise 113, 1050 Brussels, Belgium
Tel. (+32) 2-6401259
Fax (+32) 2-6477328
E-mail global.europe@global-eu.com
URL www.global-eu.com
Specialities: Infrastructure;
  Telecommunications; Environment;
  Transport; RTD; Marketing
Contact D. Villanueva

GPC International

Rue d'Arlon 50, 1000 Brussels, Belgium
Tel. (+32) 2-2300545
Fax (+32) 2-2305706
URL www.gpcinternational.com
Specialities: Food; Pharmaceuticals; Financial
  services; Retailing; Telecommunications;
  Tourism; Trade; Transport; Mergers and
  acquisitions; Taxation; Excise; Health care;
  Company law; Funding (EU); State aids;
  Environment; European Union; North
  America; Eastern Europe
Contact Sam Rowe

Gracious

Rue du Trône 216, 1050 Brussels, Belgium
Tel. (+32) 2-3466059
Fax (+32) 2-3464817
E-mail gracious@village.uunet.be
Specialities: Lifestyle consumer;
  Pharmaceuticals; Goods (fast-moving);
  Computers; Food
Contact I. Peemans

Grantfinder Ltd

Enterprise House, Carlton Road, Worksop
  S81 7QF, United Kingdom
Tel. (+44 19) 0950-1200
Fax (+44 19) 0950-1225
E-mail enquiries@grantfinder.co.uk
URL www.grantfinder.co.uk
Specialities: Grants; Financial opportunities
Contact John Dilworth

Grayling Political Strategy

Rue du Luxembourg 14A, 1000 Brussels,
  Belgium
Tel. (+32) 2-7327040
Fax (+32) 2-7327176
E-mail info@be.garyling.com
URL www.grayling.be
Specialities: Monitoring and analysis; Strategy;
  Lobbying; Media relations; Crisis
  management; Issues and policy monitoring;
  Issues analysis and evaluation; Association
  management
Contact Russell McCleave Pattern

Gullers Group

Hamngatan 11, Box 7004, 10386 Stockholm,
  Sweden
Tel. (+46 8) 679-09-40
Fax (+46 8) 611-07-80
E-mail mats.gullers@gullers.se
URL www.gullers.se
Specialities: Lobbying; Community issues;
  Media relations; Crisis management;
  Strategic planning and analysis;
  Communications strategy
Contact Mats Gullers

Heidi Lambert Communications Sprl

Rue Stévin 212, 1000 Brussels, Belgium
Tel. (+32) 2-7325546
Fax (+32) 2-7353603
E-mail hlc@skynet.be
Specialities: Media; Brussels-based press corps
  of EU correspondents (relations with);
  Conferences
Contact Heidi Lambert

Henley Centre

11–33 St John Street, London EC1M 4PJ,
  United Kingdom
Tel. (+44 20) 7955-1800
Fax (+44 20) 7559-1900
E-mail betterfutures@henleycentre.com
URL www.henleycentre.com
Specialities: Retailing; Food and drink;
  Transport; Telecommunications; Tourism;
  Goods (fast-moving); Media; Financial
  services
Contact Marcus Hickman

Hill and Knowlton Inc

909 Third Avenue, New York, NY 10022, United States of America
Tel. (+1 212) 885-0300
Fax (+1 212) 885-0570
E-mail tom.reno@hillandknowlton.com
URL www.hillandknowlton.com/us
Contact Tom Reno

Hill and Knowlton International Belgium S.A./N.V.

Avenue de Cortenbergh 118, PO Box 8, 1000 Brussels, Belgium
Tel. (+32) 2-7379500
Fax (+32) 2-7379501
E-mail brussels-info@hillandknowlton.com
URL www.hillandknowlton.be
Specialities: Lobbying strategy; Contact building; Crisis management; Media training; Media relations; Legislation (EU)
Contact Elaine Cruikshanks

Hobéon Management Consult BV

Scheveningseweg 46, 2517 KV Den Haag, Netherlands
Tel. (+31 70) 3066800
Fax (+31 70) 3066870
E-mail g.stoltenborg@hobeon.nl
URL www.hobeon.nl
Specialities: Higher education
Contact Hans Stoltenborg

Houston Consulting Europe

Avenue de la Joyeuse Entrée 1–5, 1040 Brussels, Belgium
Tel. (+32) 2-5048040
Fax (+32) 2-5048050
E-mail info@houston-consulting.com
URL www.houston-consulting.com
Specialities: Financial services; Electronic commerce; Consumer protection; Competition; EU–US relations; Economic and social policy in EMU context; Enterprise policy; European Single Market; Telecommunications
Contact Nickolas Reinhardt

Hurlstons Consultancy

2 Ridgmount Street, London WC1E 7AA, United Kingdom
Tel. (+44 20) 7436-9936
Fax (+44 20) 7580-0016
E-mail hurlstons@hurlstons.com
Specialities: Competition; Pharmaceuticals; Employee participation; Agriculture; Social affairs; Trade associations; Packaging; Sunday Trading; Beverages
Contact M. Hurlston

IDOM

Rue de Trèves 49, 1040 Brussels, Belgium
Tel. (+32) 2-2305950
Fax (+32) 2-2307035
E-mail ruiz@taseuro.com
URL www.idom.com
Specialities: Environment; Energy; Telecommunications; Industrial engineering; Civil engineering; Architecture; Project management; Territorial management
Contact Hugo Ruíz Jaime Bernis

IDOM

Lehendakari Aguirre 3, 48014 Bilbao, Spain
Tel. (+34) 94-4797600
Fax (+34) 94-4761804
E-mail info@idom.es
URL www.idom.com
Contact Alberto Tijero

IMC Associates

PO Box 25, Lymington SO41 3WU, United Kingdom
Tel. (+44 1590) 673689
Fax (+44 1590) 670525
E-mail maritime@tcp.co.uk
URL www.homepages.tcp.co.uk/~maritime
Specialities: Industry; Marine industry; Defence industry; International marketing; Business strategy; Business systems
Contact Graham Clarke

Impact

Rue J.S. Bach 33, 1190 Brussels, Belgium
Tel. (+32) 2-7767830
Fax (+32) 2-7767839
E-mail info@impactcommunications.be
URL www.gcibrussels.com
Specialities: Automotive industry; Healthcare; Telecommunications; Consumer affairs; Information technology; Banking; Finance; Biotechnology; Tourism; Leisure
Contact C. Decroix

Infyde – Informacion y Desarrollo S.L

Avda. Zugazarte 8 (3a pl.), 48930 Las Arenas,
  Spain
Tel. (+34) 94-4804095
Fax (+34) 94-4811639
E-mail carlosaleman@infyde.com
Specialities: Regional policy; Technology
  policy; Training policy; Local development;
  Evaluation of policies; European networks
  (design); Innovation; SMEs; RITTS/RIS
Contact Carlos Rivera Alemán

Interel Public Relations & Public Affairs

Avenue de Tervueren 402, 1150 Brussels,
  Belgium
Tel. (+32) 2-7616611
Fax (+32) 2-7776600
E-mail info@interel.be
URL www.interel.be
Specialities: Environment; Social affairs; Food;
  Taxation; Sport; Air transport; Enlargement;
  Telecommunications; Pharmaceuticals;
  Health
Contact Fredrik Lofthagen

International Cooperation Europe Ltd

Blvd du Régent 47–48, 5th floor, 1000
  Brussels, Belgium
Tel. (+32) 2-5030419
Fax (+32) 2-5141342
E-mail icel@pophost.eunet.be
Specialities: Industrial development; Economic
  development; Banking; Environment
Contact Thomas Bourke

**International Development Ireland (IDI)
  Ltd.**

Wilton Park House, Wilton Place, Dublin 2,
  Ireland
Tel. (+353 1) 6625555
Fax (+353 1) 6623133
E-mail idi@dublin.idi.ie
URL www.idi.ie
Contact Ronan Deignan

**International Relations Consulting
  Company (IRELCO)**

Avenue Emile de Mot 19, 1000 Brussels,
  Belgium
Tel. (+32) 2-6401869
Fax (+32) 2-6482161
E-mail general@irelco.com

URL www.irelco.com
Specialities: Information management systems;
  Lobbying; Funding
Contact P. Bähr

**International Technology and Trade
  Associates Inc. (ITTA)**

1330 Connecticut Ave NW, Suite 210,
  Washington, DC 20036-1704, United States
  of America
Tel. (+1 202) 828-2614
Fax (+1 202) 828-2617
E-mail cdyke@itta.com
URL www.itta.com
Contact Charles W. Dyke

**International Technology and Trade
  Associates Inc (ITTA) Europe**

Rue Washington 50, 1050 Brussels, Belgium
Tel. (+32) 2-6408661
Fax (+32) 2-6460915
E-mail baker.mre@skynet.be
URL www.itta.com
Specialities: Trade; Technology; Investment;
  EBRD; Public affairs; International market
  research; International marketing; Defence
  industry; NATO
Contact Ronald E. Baker

Intersalus •

Tarragona 107–115, 9th floor, 08014
  Barcelona, Spain
Tel. (+34) 932-924240
Fax (+34) 932-924238
E-mail internacional@intersalus.com
URL www.intersalus.com
Specialities: Architecture; Engineering;
  Hospitals
Contact Marta Burgell

Ipstrategies

Chaussée de Louvain 490, 1380 Lasne,
  Belgium
Tel. (+32) 2-3510011
Fax (+32) 2-3510114
E-mail info@ipstrategies.be
URL www.ipstrategies.com
Specialities: SMEs; Company development;
  European studies; Technological innovation;
  Strategy and alliance; European aid; Mergers
  and acquisitions; VAT
Contact J.L. MentiorContact A. Pierre

J & A B Associates

3 The Butts, Warwick CV34 4SS,
  United Kingdom
Tel. (+44 1926) 403040
Fax (+44 1926) 403048
E-mail alan.badger@jandab.co.uk
Specialities: European Social Fund; Grants for
  research (EU); Leonardo
Contact Alan Badger

J.M. Didier & Associates S.A.

Avenue Marquis de Villalobar 6, 1050 Brussels,
  Belgium
Tel. (+32) 2-7369910
Fax (+32) 2-7368994
E-mail jmdidier@wanadoo.be
Specialities: Industrial relations; Labour law;
  Worker information, consultation and
  participation; Health and safety; Social
  dialogue
Contact J.M. Didier

Joan Noble Associates Limited

5 Brunswick Gardens, Gregory Place, London
  W8 4AS, United Kingdom
Tel. (+ 44 20) 7727-9345
Fax (+ 44 20) 7792-1992
E-mail joan@joannobleassociates.com
URL www.joannoble.associates.com
Specialities: Food and drinks law;
  Environmental policy; Trade law; Economic
  affairs; Agriculture
Contact Joan Noble

Johnson & Associates Ltd

Little Buckland Farm, Hollywood Lane,
  Lymington SO41 9HD, United Kingdom
Tel. (+44 1590) 688899
Fax (+44 1590) 688950
E-mail johnsonandjones@compuserve.com
URL www.johnsonandjones.co.uk

Keene Public Affairs Consultants Ltd

1st floor, Victory House, 99–101 Regent Street,
  London W1B 4EZ, United Kingdom
Tel. (+44 20) 7287-0652
Fax (+44 20) 7494-0493
E-mail kpac@keenepa.co.uk
URL www.keenepa.co.uk
Specialities: Aviation; Travel; Tourism;
  Pharmaceuticals; Healthcare; Energy;
  Utilities; Chemicals; Trade associations;

Information technology; Transport; Metals;
  Minerals
Contact Anthony Garry Richards

KPMG

Avenue du Bourget 40, 1130 Brussels, Belgium
Tel. (+32) 2-7084900
Fax (+32) 2-7084399
E-mail advisory@kpmg.be
URL www.kpmg.be
Specialities: Business compliance with EU law;
  Business risk; Business opportunities;
  Mergers and acquisitions; External trade;
  Taxation; Grants and loans (EU);
  Competition rules; Audit; Assurance advice;
  Financial advice; Legal advice;
  Management; Banking; Insurance;
  Consumer markets; Communication;
  Entertainment; Industrial markets
Contact Theo Erauw

KPMG European Headquarters

Avenue Louise 54, 1050 Brussels, Belgium
Tel. (+32) 2-5480911
Fax (+32) 2-5480909
E-mail marie-claire.snocks@kpmg.be
URL www.eu.kpmg.net
Specialities: Management; Accounting; Audit;
  Taxation
Contact M.-C. Snocks

KPMG International Headquarters

PO Box 74111, 1070 Amsterdam, Netherlands
Tel. (+31 20) 6566700
Fax (+31 20) 6566777
URL www.kpmg.com
Contact Mike Rake

Kreab AS

Vester Sogade 10, 2, 1601 Kobenhavn V,
  Denmark
Tel. (+45) 88-33-11-00
Fax (+45) 88-33-11-11
E-mail info.sund@kreab.com
URL www.kreab.com
Specialities: Environment; Construction;
  Finance; Lobbying; Health care; Medicine;
  Electronics; Internet; Intranet; Mergers and
  acquisitions; Publications; Corporate
  communication; Financial communication;
  Marketing communication; Competition
Contact Katrine Steen

Kreab Europe

Avenue de Tervueren 2, 1040 Brussels,
  Belgium
Tel. (+32) 2-7376900
Fax (+32) 2-7376940
E-mail info@kreab.com
URL www.kreab.com

Specialities: European affairs; Public affairs;
  Internal relations; Public relations; Investor
  relations; Market communication; Crisis
  management; Events; Exhibitions;
  Campaigns

Contact Georg Danell

Longin & Associés

Avenue des Nerviens 67, 1040 Brussels,
  Belgium
Tel. (+32) 2-2307273
Fax (+32) 2-2308165
E-mail pierre.longin@swing.be

Specialities: Strategic monitoring; Public affairs
  plans; Lobbying; PHARE; TACIS

Contact Pierre Longin

M. P. G. Research Sprl

Avenue H. Hoover 163, 1030 Brussels,
  Belgium
Tel. (+32) 2-2309568
Fax (+32) 2-2309568
E-mail michael.gaum@skynet.be

Specialities: International market; Economic
  research; Automotive industry; Retail trade;
  Wholesale trade; Distribution; Food and
  drink; Textiles; Clothing; Construction;
  Country monitoring; Agriculture

Contact M. Gaum

Maison de l'Europe Avignon-Méditerranée

6 Blvd Saint-Michel, 84000 Avignon, France
Tel. (+33) 4-90-16-35-00
Fax (+33) 4-90-16-35-01
E-mail maison.europe@europe-avignon.com
URL www.europe-avignon.com

Specialities: Europe; Euro

Contact Cyrille Perez

Maxess Sprl

Rue du Coq 87, 1180 Brussels, Belgium
Tel. (+32) 2-3323545
Fax (+32) 2-3323575
E-mail mail@maxessconsult.com

URL www.maxessconsult.com

Specialities: Telecommunications; Technology;
  Marketing

Contact Chris Henny

Metzdorff & Associates

Avenue Louise 109, 1050 Brussels, Belgium
Tel. (+32) 2-5421020
Fax (+32) 2-5421025
E-mail c.metzdorff@aces.be
URL www.metzdorff.com

Specialities: Pharmaceuticals

Contact C. Metzdorff

Mondimpresa Brussels

Rue de l'Industrie 22B, 1040 Brussels,
  Belgium
Tel. (+32) 2-5023131
Fax (+32) 2-5025898
E-mail mondimpresa@easynet.be
URL www.mondimpresa.it

Specialities: European projects; Regional
  desks; Seminars; Conferences; Lobbying

Contact Flavio Burlizzi

Mondimpresa SCPA

Viale Pasteur 10, 00144 Rome, Italy
Tel. (+39) 06-549541
Fax (+39) 06-54954409
E-mail servizi@mondimpresa.it
URL www.mondimpresa.it

Contact Vincenzo Chiriaco

Moores Rowland (MRI)

Sceptre House, 169–173 Regent Street, London
  W1R 7FB, United Kingdom
E-mail info@mri-world.com
URL www.mri-world.com

Contact Paul Hancock

MRI European Co-ordination Office

Avenue Louise 109, 1050 Brussels, Belgium
Tel. (+32) 2-5410750
Fax (+32) 2-5410754
E-mail jerome.adam@mri-europe.be
URL www.mrieurope.com

Specialities: European Union; Central Europe;
  Eastern Europe; CIS

Contact Jerome Adam

National Economic Research Associates (NERA)

Rue de la Loi 23 (7th Floor), 1040 Brussels, Belgium
Tel. (+32) 2-2824340
Fax (+32) 2-2824360
URL www.nera.com

Specialities: Application of micro-economics to regulatory and competition issues, policy evaluation, and business strategy; Competition; Privatization; Market regulation; Law; Economic affairs; Third-party access; International trade; Energy; Transport; Water and sewerage; Telecommunications; Broadcasting; Media; Health; Pharmaceuticals; Environment; Regional policy
Contact Mark Williams

National Economic Research Associates (NERA)

15 Stratford Place, London W1C 1BE, United Kingdom
Tel. (+44 2076) 598500
Fax (+44 2076) 598501
URL www.nera.com
Contact Alison Oldale

Newton 21

Blvd Louis Schmidt 24, 1040 Brussels, Belgium
Tel. (+32) 2-7339760
Fax (+32) 2-7334170
E-mail amahaux@newton21.be
URL www.newton21.com

Specialities: Automotive industry; Finance; Fashion; Food; Environment; Telecommunications; Information technology; Transport; Media; Audiovisual; Television; Events; Sport; Agriculture; Chemicals; Biochemicals; Health
Contact Alain Mahaux

Nicholas Phillips Associates SA

Rue Joseph II 36, Bte 9, 1000 Brussels, Belgium
Tel. (+32) 2-2181370
Fax (+32) 2-2191842
E-mail nicholas.phillips@wanadoo.be
Specialities: European Parliament
Contact Nicholas Hanbury Phillips

Nordic Transport Development (NTU)

Avenue de Tervuren 35, 1040 Brussels, Belgium
Tel. (+45) 9-9300000
Fax (+45) 9-9300001
E-mail ntu-bruxelles@ntu.dk
URL www.ntu.dk
Contact L. Bentzen

Office Kirkpatrick SA

Avenue Wolfers 32, La Hulpe, 1310 Brussels, Belgium
Tel. (+32) 2-6521600
Fax (+32) 2-6521900
E-mail info@office-kirkpatrick.com
Specialities: Industrial property; Patents; Trademarks; Designs
Contact Domenica Hubart

Ogilvy Public Relations Worldwide

Blvd de l'Impératrice 13, 1000 Brussels, Belgium
Tel. (+32) 2-5456600
Fax (+32) 2-5456610
E-mail ogilvypr@ogilvy.be
URL www.ogilvypr.com
Specialities: Health; Medicine; Banking; Pharmaceuticals; Payment systems; Public awareness campaigns; Media training; Crisis communication; Business to business; Public affairs; Public relations co-ordination (Pan-European); Environmental communication; Product launches; Internal communication
Contact Eric Mulders

One Market Sprl

Rue de la Tourelle 37, 1040 Brussels, Belgium
Tel. (+32) 2-2311884
Fax (+32) 2-2800690
E-mail one.market@pop.kpn.be
URL www.one-market.org
Specialities: EU–Scandinavia relations; Training; Marketing; European Union
Contact Pal Jacobsen

PA Consulting Group

Avenue Marcel Thiry 79, Woluwé-Saint-Lambert, 1200 Brussels, Belgium
Tel. (+32) 2-7617900
Fax (+32) 2-7617901
E-mail info@paconsulting.com

URL www.paconsulting.com

Specialities: Economic affairs; Training; Information technology; Customer relations; Business solutions; Technology

Contact Peter Rogers

PA Consulting Group

123 Buckingham Palace Road, London SW1W 9SR, United Kingdom
Tel. (+44 20) 7730-9000
Fax (+44 20) 7333-5050
E-mail info@paconsulting.com
URL www.paconsulting.com
Contact Peter Rogers

Parliamentary & EU News Service

19 Douglas Street, London SW1P 4PA, United Kingdom
Tel. (+44 20) 7233-8283
Fax (+44 20) 7821-9352
E-mail info@parliamentary-monitoring.co.uk
URL www.parliamentary-monitoring.co.uk
Specialities: Publishing and news distribution on EU affairs
Contact Lionel Zetter

Parliamentary Monitoring Services

19 Douglas Street, London SWIP 4PA, United Kingdom
Tel. (+44 20) 7233-8283
Fax (+44 20) 7821-9352
E-mail info@parliamentary-monitoring.co.uk
URL www.parliamentary-monitoring.co.uk
Contact Lionel Zetter

Perchards

1 College Street, St Albans AL3 4PW, United Kingdom
Tel. (+44 1727) 843227
Fax (+44 1727) 843193
E-mail info@perchards.com
URL www.perchards.com
Specialities: Producer responsibility; Waste management; Environment; Consumer affairs
Contact David Perchard

Porter Novelli Brussels

Blvd Louis Mettewielaan 272/5, 1080 Brussels, Belgium
Tel. (+32) 2-4130340

Fax (+32) 2-4130349
E-mail luc.missinne@porternovelli.be
URL www.pnbrussels.com
Specialities: European affairs; Community relations; Media relations
Contact Luc Missinne

Pricewaterhousecoopers

Woluwe Garden, Woluwedal 18, 1932 Brussels, Belgium
Tel. (+32) 2-7104211
Fax (+32) 2-7104299
E-mail davies.mike@be.pwcglobal.com
URL www.pwc.com
Specialities: Public affairs; Accounting; Audit; Taxation
Contact Paul Davies

Profile Corporate Communications

31 Great Peter Street, Westminster, London SW1P 3LR, United Kingdom
Tel. (+44 20) 7654-5600
Fax (+44 20) 7222-2030
E-mail eastoes@profilecc.com
URL www.profilecc.com
Specialities: political contact building; Lobbying; Competition; Media; Trade relations
Contact S. Eastoe

Project Development and Support Ltd

30 Gritstone Road, Matlock DE4 3GD, United Kingdom
Tel. (+44 0162) 957501
Fax (+44 1629) 584972
E-mail pdsl@dial.pipex.com
URL www.esf.uk.com
Specialities: Education; Training; SMEs; Travel; Tourism; Business development; ESF/ERDF/LEADER II; Learning disability; Project monitoring software
Contact J. Roberts

Project Monitor Ltd

30 Gritstone Road, Matlock DE4 3GB, United Kingdom
Tel. (+44 162) 958-3916
Fax (+44 162) 958-4972
E-mail info@projectverify.co.uk
URL www.projectverify.co.uk
Contact Janet Roberts

Public Relations Partners N.V./S.A.

Avenue Roger Vandendriessche 5, 1150
  Brussels, Belgium
Tel. (+32) 2-7620485
Fax (+32) 2-7711959
E-mail eeckman@prp.be
E-mail info@prp.be
URL www.prp.be
Specialities: Communication; Environment;
  Marketing; Media relations; Change
  management
Contact Edgard Eeckman

Rödl & Partner Nürnberg

Äussere-Sulzbacher-Str. 100, 90491
  Nuremberg, Germany
Tel. (+49 911) 919-3
Fax (+49 911) 9193660
E-mail monika.kastl@roedl.de
URL www.roedl.de
Specialities: European Union; Structural funds;
  PHARE; TACIS; Central Europe; Eastern
  Europe; Baltic countries; CIS; Accounting;
  Audit; Public management; Vocational
  training
Contact Monika Kastl

Salustro Reydel

8 Avenue Delcassé, 75008 Paris, France
Tel. (+33) 1-53-77-38-00
Fax (+33) 1-53-77-38-39
E-mail ccroce-spinelli@salustro-reydel.fr
URL www.salustro-reydel.fr
Specialities: Mergers and acquisitions;
  Accounting
Contact Caroline Crocé-Spinelli

Schuman Associates

Rue Archimède 5, 1000 Brussels, Belgium
Tel. (+32) 2-2307439
Fax (+32) 2-2307426
E-mail info@schumanassociates.com
URL www.schumanassociates.com
Specialities: Energy; Transport; Environment;
  Agriculture; External relations; Employment;
  Training; Health; Funding (EU); Technical
  assistance; Consortia creation; Partnerships
Contact Gerard McNamara

Seconde S.L.

Lagsca 36, II Floor F, 28001 Madrid, Spain
Tel. (+34) 91-4358556
Fax (+34) 91-5778360
E-mail eruiz@seconde.org
Specialities: Private sector development;
  Customs; Project management; Institutional
  development
Contact E. Ruiz

Shandwick International

Aldernary House, 15 Queen St, London
  EC4N 1TX, United Kingdom
Tel. (+44 20) 7329-0096
Fax (+44 20) 7329-6009
E-mail hdoesburg@webershandwick.com
Contact H. van Doesburg

Single Market Ventures Sprl

Rue Faider 87, 1050 Brussels, Belgium
Tel. (+32) 2-5372603
Fax (+32) 2-5371078
E-mail info@smv-online.com
URL www.smv-online.com
Specialities: Packaging; Quality control;
  Technical Barriers to Trade (TBT)
Contact Raymond Schonfeld

Skan Europe

Avenue de la Pinède 3, 1380 Lasne, Belgium
Tel. (+32) 2-6532164
Fax (+32) 2-6539389
E-mail skaneurope@compuserve.com
Specialities: EC (relations with);
  Telecommunications; Environment
Contact Strauss

**Société Agence Conseil en Communication
Decitime**

Chaussée de Charleroi 96, 1060 Brussels,
  Belgium
Tel. (+32) 2-5346686
Fax (+32) 2-5346698
E-mail decitime@decitime.be
URL www.decitime.be
Specialities: Institutional communication;
  Financial communication; Crisis
  communication; Internal and external
  communication; Lobbying
Contact Evelyn Gessler

Stern Malkinson & Partners

Rue de Stassart 84, 1050 Brussels, Belgium
Tel. (+32) 2-5520900
Fax (+32) 2-5520911
E-mail info@stern.be
URL www.stern.be

Specialities: EU institutions; EU procedures; EU law; Lobbying; Central Europe; Asia; Public relations; Press

Stratégies & Communication SA

Rue des Hêtres 46, 1630 Linkebeek, Belgium
Tel. (+32) 2-5374400
Fax (+32) 2-5372167
E-mail info@stratcom.be
URL www.stratcom.be

Specialities: Information strategy; Communication; Editorial management; Publications

Contact Luc Dumoulin

Synergon S.A. International Consulting Group

Minoos 10–16, 11743 Athens, Greece
Tel. (+30) 210-9270000
Fax (+30) 210-9270003
E-mail synergon@enet.gr

Contact K. Valleras

Technical Support for European Organisations s.p.r.l. (TESEO)

Avenue de Tervueren 32–34, 7th Floor, 1040 Brussels, Belgium
Tel. (+32) 2-2301090
Fax (+32) 2-2301377
E-mail bianchi@teseo.be
URL www.teseo.be

Specialities: Industrial materials; Environment; Life sciences; Human resources; Worker mobility; Telecommunications; Telematics; Training; Exploitation of technological research; Information industry; SMEs; Conferences; Seminars; Multimedia; Electronic publishing

Contact Gigliola Fioravanti

Touchstone Europe

Rue Wiertz 11, 1050 Brussels, Belgium
Tel. (+32) 2-6440698
Fax (+32) 2-6401084
E-mail andy.erlam@skynet.be
URL www.energychoicesforeurope.com

Specialities: EU institutions (relations with); Funding applications; Public affairs

Contact Andy Erlam

TUV Rheinland Group EU Liaison Office

Square Vergote 39, 1030 Brussels, Belgium
Tel. (+32) 2-7370404
Fax (+32) 2-7370400
E-mail tgrusemann@compuserve.com
URL www.tuev-rheinland.de

Specialities: Environment; Energy; Transport; Certification; Training; Occupational safety and health

Contact Thomas Grusemann

Twijnstra Gudde

POB 907, 3800 Amersfoort, Netherlands
Tel. (+31 33) 4677777
Fax (+31 33) 4677666
E-mail info@tg.nl
URL www.tg.nl

Specialities: Banking; Insurance; Eastern Europe; Environmental control; Health care; Human resources; Information; Logistical management; Project management; Public sector; Privatization management; Strategic management; Quality control

Contact Helmuth Stoop

Value Added Europe

Avenue de Tervueren 233, 1150 Brussels, Belgium
Tel. (+32) 2-7722525
Fax (+32) 2-7725555
E-mail vae@valueaddedeurope.com
URL www.valueaddedeurope.com

Contact Jacques Rassart

Weber Shandwick

Blvd Lambermont 436, 1030 Brussels, Belgium
Tel. (+32) 2-2409760
Fax (+32) 2-2169165
E-mail clevaux@webershandwick.com
URL www.webershandwick.com

Specialities: Strategy analysis; Monitoring EU and national institutions; Lobbying

Contact L. Geothals

Weber Shandwick / Adamson

Park Leopold, Rue Wiertz 50, 1050 Brussels,
  Belgium
Tel. (+32) 2-2409760
Fax (+32) 2-2301496
E-mail jcatlla@webershandwick.com
URL www.webershandwick.com

Specialities: Pharmaceuticals; Environment;
  Media; Audiovisual; Telecommunications;
  Transport; Health care; Energy; Mergers and
  acquisitions; Anti-trust law; Strategic
  communication

Contact Josep Catllà

Westminster

26 Grosvenor Gardens, London SW1W OGT,
  United Kingdom
Tel. (+44 20) 7838-4845
Fax (+44 20) 7233-0335
E-mail rex.osborn@citigatepa.co.uk

Contact Jonathan Curtis

**Yellow Window Management Consultants
NV**

Minderbroedersstraat 14, 2000 Antwerp,
  Belgium
Tel. (+32) 3-2410024
Fax (+32) 3-2035303
E-mail mail@yellowwindow.com
URL www.yellowwindow.com

Specialities: EU regulations; Markets; Industry;
  Companies; Lobbying (technical)

Contact Alian Denis

Zenab Sprl

Avenue Beau Séjour 46, 1180 Brussels,
  Belgium
Tel. (+32) 2-3745911
Fax (+32) 2-3755258
E-mail zenab@skynet.be

Specialities: Audiovisual; Telecommunications;
  Multimedia; Intellectual property

Contact Nicole La Bouverie

INDEX OF CONSULTANTS SPECIALIZING IN EU QUESTIONS

318

Operations
Arthur D. Little, 288

Packaging
Business Environment Europe S.A., 290
Hurlstons Consultancy, 300
Single Market Ventures Sprl, 306

Partnerships
Schuman Associates, 306

Patents
Office Kirkpatrick SA, 304

Payment systems
Ogilvy Public Relations Worldwide, 304

Phare
Europool SA, 297
Longin & Associés, 303
Rödl & Partner Nürnberg, 306

Pharmaceutical industry
Droit et Pharmacie, 292

Pharmaceuticals
Euro Keys, 294
Europe Economics, 295
European Public Policy Advisers, 297
European Research Associates (ERA), 297
GPC International, 299
Gracious, 299
Hurlstons Consultancy, 300
Interel Public Relations & Public Affairs, 301
Keene Public Affairs Consultants Ltd, 302
Metzdorff & Associates, 303
National Economic Research Associates
    (NERA), 304
Ogilvy Public Relations Worldwide, 304
Weber Shandwick / Adamson, 308

Plastics
Euro Keys, 294

Political affairs
Europe Analytica, 295
European Policy Centre, 297

political contact building
Profile Corporate Communications, 305

Political developments (Europe)
European Research Associates (ERA), 297

Political risks
Eurofacts OY, 294

Politics
European Public Policy Advisers, 297

Pollution control technology
Ecotec Research and Consulting, 292

Post, media and telecommunications
ESL & Network, 293

Postal services
APCO Europe, 287

Press
B & S Business & Show – Syntagmes, 288
Barabino & Partners Europe S.A., 289
Communication Partners, 291
Stern Malkinson & Partners, 307

Press relations
European Institute for Public Affairs, 296

Private sector development
Seconde S.L., 306

Privatization
National Economic Research Associates
    (NERA), 304

Privatization management
Twijnstra Gudde, 307

Procurement
Europa SA, 295

Producer responsibility
Perchards, 305

Product launches
Ogilvy Public Relations Worldwide, 304

Professional organizations and associations
European Public Affairs, 297

Programme management
European Consultants Information
    Technology, 296

Project management
Berkley Associates Sprl, 289
Euro Top Cooperation Partners, 294
European Consultants Information
    Technology, 296
IDOM, 300
Seconde S.L., 306
Twijnstra Gudde, 307

Project monitoring software
Project Development and Support Ltd, 305

Projects (EU)
Deloitte & Touche, 291

Public administration
European Public Policy Advisers, 297

LAW FIRMS SPECIALIZING IN THE LAW OF THE EUROPEAN UNION

At the end of this list is an index of areas of specialization.

20 Essex Street

20 Essex Street, London WC2R 3AL, United Kingdom
Tel. (+44 20) 7842-1200
Fax (+44 20) 7842-1270
E-mail clerks@20essexst.com
URL www.20essexst.com

Specialities: Competition law; Free movement of goods; Private international law (Brussels and Rome Conventions); Environmental law; Social law; Institutions

Contact N. Palmer

A & L Goodbody

International Financial Services Centre, North Wall Quay, Dublin 1, Ireland
Tel. (+353 1) 6492000
Fax (+353 1) 6492649
E-mail law@algoodbody.ie
URL www.algoodbody.ie

Specialities: Competition law; Restrictive practices; Anti-trust law; Transport law; Commercial law; Product liability; Non-tariff barriers; Free movement of goods; Free movement of persons; Free movement of services; Free movement of capital; Internal market; EC law in Ireland; Public procurement; Telecommunications; EU law

Contact Vincent Power

Addleshaw Goddard

Avenue de Cortenberg 118, 1000 Brussels, Belgium
Tel. (+32) 2-7322700
Fax (+32) 2-7352352
E-mail tgbrussels@theodoregoddard.co.uk
URL www.addleshawgoddard.com

Specialities: Competition law; State aid; Financial services; Transport law; Anti-dumping; Telecommunications; Informatics; Litigation; WTO

Contact Dan Horovitz

Addleshaw Goddard

150 Aldersgate Street, London EC1A 4EJ, United Kingdom
Tel. (+44 20) 7606-8855
Fax (+44 20) 7606-4390
E-mail tg@theodoregoddard.co.uk
URL www.addleshawgoddard.com
Contact Guy Leigh

Advokat Olav Willadsen

Tunnelvej 7, 2600 Glostrup, Denmark
Tel. (+45) 43-63-26-54

Specialities: Counselling clients; Assisting clients; Court proceedings; EU law; Public procurement

Contact Olav Willadsen

Advokaterne Amaliegade No 42

Amaliegade 42, 1256 Copenhagen K, Denmark
Tel. (+45) 33-11-33-99
Fax (+45) 33-32-46-25
E-mail adv42@amalex.com
URL www.amalex.com

Specialities: Company law; VAT

Contact P.R. Meurs-Gerken

Advokatfirmaet Hjort DA

Avenue Louise 130 A, 1050 Brussels, Belgium
Tel. (+32) 2-2800670
Fax (+32) 2-2307278
E-mail lawoffice.hjort@skynet.be
URL www.hjort.no

Specialities: Competition law; Procurement law; Energy; Free movement of goods; Financial services; Telecommunications; Industrial property rights; Norwegian law; Shipping

Contact Espen Hansteen Fossum

Advokatfirman Lindahl

Box 14240, 10440 Stockholm, Sweden
Tel. (+46 8) 670-58-00
Fax (+46 8) 667-73-80
E-mail reception.stockholm@lindahl.se
URL www.lindahl.se

Specialities: Competition law; Public
  procurement
Contact Staffan Eklöw

Advokatfirman Vinge

Rue du Luxembourg 3, 1000 Brussels, Belgium
Tel. (+32) 2-5010700
Fax (+32) 2-5010707
E-mail olle.rislund@vinge.se
URL www.vinge.se
Specialities: Competition law; Distribution;
  Franchising agreements; Agency
  agreements; Licensing; Joint ventures; EU
  law; Deregulation
Contact Olle Rislund

Advokatfirman Vinge

Smålandsgatan 20, PO Box 1703, 111 87
  Stockholm, Sweden
Tel. (+46 8) 614-30-00
Fax (+46 8) 614-31-90
E-mail michael.wigge@vinge.se
Contact Michael Wigge

AKD Prinsen van Wijmen

POB 4714, 4803 ES Breda, Netherlands
Tel. (+31 76) 5256500
Fax (+31 76) 5142575
E-mail info@akd.nl
URL www.akd.nl
Contact Lars H.E. Møller

AKD Prinsen van Wijmen

Avenue Louise 240, 1050 Brussels, Belgium
Tel. (+32) 2-5345376
Fax (+32) 2-5345535
E-mail info@akd.nl
URL www.akd.be
Contact Pieter Kuypers

Allen & Overy LLP

One New Change, London EC4M 9QQ,
  United Kingdom
Tel. (+44 20) 7330-3000
Fax (+44 20) 7330-9999
E-mail michael.reynolds@allenovery.com
URL www.allenovery.com
Contact Michael. J. Reynolds

Allen & Overy LLP

Avenue de Tervuren 268 A, 1150 Brussels,
  Belgium
Tel. (+32) 2-7802922
Fax (+32) 2-7802244
E-mail michael.reynolds@allenovery.com
URL www.allenovery.com
Contact Michael Reynolds

Andersen Legal

41 Rue Ybry, 92576 Neuilly-sur-Seine Cedex,
  France
Tel. (+33) 1-55-61-10-10
Fax (+33) 1-55-61-15-15
E-mail olivier.chaduteau@fr.ey.com
URL www.ey.com
Specialities: Tax law; Labour law; Commercial
  law; Free movement of goods; Competition
  law; Free movement of services; Distribution
  law; Transfer pricing; Intellectual property
  law; New technologies law; Expatriate
  policy developments; Immigration services
Contact Frédéric Donnedieu de Vabres

Arthur Cox

Earlsfort Centre, Earlsfort Terrace, Dublin 2,
  Ireland
Tel. (+353 1) 6180000
Fax (+353 1) 6180618
E-mail mail@arthurcox.com
URL www.arthurcox.com
Specialities: Competition law; Commercial
  law; Inward investment; Banking services;
  Financial services; Company law;
  Telecommunications; Public procurement;
  Environmental law; Agricultural law;
  Intellectual property rights; Labour law;
  Pharmaceutical law; Food law
Contact James O'Dwyer

Avv. Cesare Trebeschi

Studio Legale Ass. Trebeschi, Via delle
  Battaglie 50, 25122 Brescia, Italy
Tel. (+39) 03-0291599
Fax (+39) 03-03754958
E-mail info@studiotrebeschi.it
Specialities: Administrative law; Civil law;
  Penal law; Agriculture
Contact Tresbeschi Cesare

Avv. Giovanna Andreoni

Via Bellini 12, 20100 Milan, Italy
Tel. (+39) 02-774231
Fax (+39) 02-7742344
E-mail info@nascimbene.com

Specialities: Free movement of persons;
Transport law; Institutional questions; Public
procurement

Contact Bruno Nascimbene

Baker & McKenzie

Avenue Louise 149, 1050 Brussels, Belgium
Tel. (+32) 2-6393611
Fax (+32) 2-6393699
E-mail koen.vanhaerents@bakernet.com
URL www.bakernet.com

Contact Koen Vanhaerents

Baker & McKenzie

One Prudential Plaza, 130 East Randolph
Drive, Chicago, IL 60601, United States of
America
Tel. (+1 312) 861-8000
Fax (+1 312) 861-2899
E-mail Chicago.Information@Bakernet.com
URL www.bakernet.com

Contact Roberta Montafia

Bappert Witz & Selbherr

Rond Point Schuman 9, 1040 Brussels,
Belgium
Tel. (+32) 2-5410330
Fax (+32) 2-5384980
E-mail Brussels@westphalen-law.com
URL www.westphalen-law.com

Contact W. Bachmann

Bappert Witz & Selbherr

Kaiser-Joseph-Strasse 284, 79098 Freiburg,
Germany
Tel. (+49 761) 21808-304
Fax (+49 761) 21808-500
E-mail gerhard.manz@bappert-bws.de
URL www.bappert-bws.com

Contact Gerhard Manz

Barents & Krans

Chaussee de la Hulpe 187, 1170 Brussels,
Belgium
Tel. (+32) 2-6613250
Fax (+32) 2-6753870
E-mail Holant@barentskrans.be

URL www.barentskrans.nl

Contact Laura Parret

Barlow Lyde & Gilbert

Beaufort House, 15 St Botolph Street, London
EC3A 7NJ, United Kingdom
Tel. (+44 20) 7247-2277
Fax (+44 20) 7071-9000
URL www.blg.co.uk

Specialities: Commercial litigation; Arbitration;
EU law in the UK; Insurance; Free
movement of goods; Free movement of
persons; Free movement of services; Free
movement of capital; Reinsurance;
Competition law; Professional indemnity;
Mergers; Acquisitions; Joint ventures;
Company law; Commercial law; Insolvency
law; Marine regulation; Air transport
regulation; Personal injury; Product liability;
Customs; Tax law; Environmental law;
Employment law; Construction law;
Intellectual property law; Information
technology; E-commerce

Contact Richard Dedman

Beachcroft Wansbroughs

100 Fetter Lane, London EC4A 1BN,
United Kingdom
Tel. (+44 20) 7242-1011
Fax (+44 20) 7831-6630
E-mail acrofts@bwlaw.co.uk
URL www.bwlaw.co.uk

Contact Bob Heslett

Beachcroft Wansbroughs

Avenue de Broqueville 116, Bte 10, 1200
Brussels, Belgium
Tel. (+32) 2-7767818
Fax (+32) 2-7704378
E-mail mbroadhurst@bwlaw.co.uk
URL www.bwlaw.co.uk

Specialities: Competition law; Anti-dumping;
Internal market; Agricultural law; Company
law; Consumer law; Education; Employment
law; Environmental law; Pharmaceutical
law; Insurance; Public procurement; EU
structural funds; Telecommunications;
Intellectual property law; Commercial
contracts; Mergers; Acquisitions; Joint
ventures; Commercial law; Water; Lobbying
the EU's institutions

Contact Marisa Broadhurst

Berlioz & Co

Boulevard de Courcelles 68, 75017 Paris,
    France
Tel. (+33) 1-44-01-44-01
Fax (+33) 1-44-15-94-15
E-mail gberlioz@berlioz.com
Contact Georges Berlioz

Berlioz & Co

Avenue Louise 113, 1050 Brussels, Belgium
Tel. (+32) 2-5382234
Fax (+32) 2-5382246
E-mail berlioz@europlaw.com
URL www.berlioz.com

Specialities: Anti-dumping; Audiovisual and
    telecommunications; Banking regulation;
    Competition law; Consumer law; Corporate
    law; EU litigation; Environmental law;
    Financial law; Intellectual property law;
    Labour law; Mergers; Acquisitions; State
    enterprises; Trade regulation; Transport law;
    Telecommunications; Distribution law;
    Energy law; Tax law

Contact Maître Berlioz

Bernhard Gomard

Law Department, Copenhagen Business
    School, Julius Thomsens Plads 10,5, 1925
    Copenhagen-Frederiksberg, Denmark
Tel. (+45) 38-15-26-26
Fax (+45) 38-15-26-10

Berwin Leighton

Adelaide House, London Bridge, London
    EC4R 9HA, United Kingdom
Tel. (+44 20) 7760-1000
Fax (+44 20) 7760-1111
Contact P.F. Stone

Berwin Leighton Paisner

Chaussée de la Hulpe 150, 1170 Brussels,
    Belgium
Tel. (+32) 2-7418630
Fax (+32) 2-7418647
E-mail harold.wouters@blplaw.com
URL www.berwinleighton.com
Contact Harold Wouters

Bircham Dyson Bell

50 Broadway, London SW1H 0BL,
    United Kingdom
Tel. (+44 20) 7227-7000

Fax (+44 20) 7222-3480
E-mail enquirieslondon@bdb-law.co.uk
URL www.bdb-law.co.uk
Contact Jonathan Bracken

Bircham Dyson Bell

Rond-Point Schuman 6, PO Box 5, 1040
    Brussels, Belgium
Tel. (+32) 2-2346306
Fax (+32) 2-2347911
E-mail reception@bdb-law.co.uk
URL www.bdb-law.co.uk
Specialities: Public affairs
Contact David Mundy

Bird & Bird

Rue de la Loi 15, 1040 Brussels, Belgium
Tel. (+32) 2-2826000
Fax (+32) 2-2826011
E-mail simon.topping@twobirds.com
URL www.twobirds.com
Contact Catherine Erkelens

Bird & Bird

90 Fetter Lane, London EC4A 1JP,
    United Kingdom
Tel. (+44 20) 7415-6000
Fax (+44 20) 7415-6111
E-mail morag.macdonald@twobirds.com
Contact Morag Macdonald

Brick Court Chambers

7–8 Essex Street, London WC2R 3LD,
    United Kingdom
Tel. (+44 20) 7379-3550
Fax (+44 20) 7379-3558
E-mail david.vaughan@brickcourt.co.uk
URL www.brickcourt.co.uk
Contact David Vaughan

Brick Court Chambers

Avenue d'Auderghem 36, 1040 Brussels,
    Belgium
Tel. (+32) 2-2303161
Fax (+32) 2-2303347
E-mail fergus.randolph@brickcourt.co.uk
URL www.brickcourt.co.uk
Contact Fergus Randolph

Bristows

3 Lincoln's Inn Fields, London WC2A 3AA,
  United Kingdom
Tel. (+44 20) 7400-8000
Fax (+44 20) 7400-8050
E-mail info@bristows.com
URL www.bristows.com
Contact Helen Hannan

Bufete Dexeus Abogados Asociados

Tuset 8–10, 08006 Barcelona, Spain
Tel. (+34) 932-922266
Fax (+34) 932-373720
E-mail bufetedexeus@icab.es
URL www.bufetedexeus.com
Contact Juan Nunez

Bundesrechtsanwaltskammer

Littenstrasse 9, 10179 Berlin, Germany
Tel. (+49 30) 2849390
Fax (+49 30) 28493911
E-mail zentrale@brak.de
URL www.brak.de
Contact Dr Wolfgang Eichele

Bureau d'Avocats

Rue de Pitteurs 41, 4020 Liège, Belgium
Tel. (+32) 4-3414344
Fax (+32) 4-3437972
E-mail info@misson.be
URL www.misson.be
Specialities: Free movement of goods; Free
  movement of persons; Competition law;
  Sports law
Contact Luc Mission

Cabinet Fontaneau

Blvd Saint Michel 45, 1040 Brussels, Belgium
Tel. (+32) 2-7365944
Fax (+32) 2-7365868
E-mail avocat@fontaneau.com
URL www.fontaneau.com
Specialities: Administrative law; Immigration
  law; Agricultural law; Labour law; Anti-trust
  law; Insurance law; Banking law;
  International contracts; Competition law;
  International private law; Construction law;
  Maritime law; Admiralty law; Consumer
  protection law; Property; Real estate;
  Corporate law; Rent; Leasing; Customs and
  excise; Social security; Employer's liability;
  Transport law; Entertainment; Foreign

investments; Distributorship law; Agency
  law; Franchise law; Environmental law;
  Family law; Health, hospitals and
  malpractice; Intellectual property practice;
  Tax law
Contact Françoise Fontaneau-Vandoren

Cabinet Morera

Corso Venezia 10, 20121 Milan, Italy
Tel. (+39) 02-76022553
Fax (+39) 02-784677
E-mail morera@digibank.it
Contact M. Prandi

Cabinet Pierre Fontaneau

28 Rue de Franqueville, 75116 Paris, France
Tel. (+33) 1-45-03-03-40
Fax (+33) 1-45-03-08-14
E-mail avocats@fontaneau.com
URL www.Fontaneau.com
Contact Pierre Fontaneau

Cabinet Storrer

Avenue Fd Roosevelt 154, 1050 Brussels,
  Belgium
Tel. (+32) 2-6473021
Fax (+32) 2-6460773
E-mail jl.bosteels@storre-law.net
URL www.storrer-law.no
Specialities: Arbitration; Commercial law;
  Foreign law; Civil law; Company law;
  Intellectual property law; Family law;
  Insurance; Labour law
Contact Anne-Marie Storrer

Cappelli e de Caterini Avvocati Associati

Via Nicolo Tartaglia 5, 00197 Rome, Italy
Tel. (+39) 06-8081556
Fax (+39) 06-8080731
E-mail cappelliedecaterini@tiscali.it
Specialities: Environmental law; Agricultural
  law; Anti-trust law; Freedom of
  establishment and services; Public
  procurement
Contact Bandini

Chambers of Mark Watson-Gandy (CWG)

Delacourt House, 3 Delacourt Road,
  Blackheath, London SE3 8XA,
  United Kingdom
Tel. (+ 44 181) 305 -2967
Fax + 44 181) 305 -2968

E-mail eg@cwglaw.com

Specialities: Arbitration; Commercial law; Copyright law; Industrial contracts; Mergers and acquisitions; Accountancy law; Start-ups; Takeovers

Contact Emanuella Giavarra

Chambre de Commerce et d'Industrie Franco-Hellénique

Venizelou Street 43, 546 24 Thessaloniki, Greece

Tel. (+30) 310-235716

Fax (+30) 310-220216

E-mail vosiki@the.forthnet.gr

URL www.ccifhel.org.gr

Specialities: Labour law; Corporate law; Administrative law; Family law; Tax law

Contact M Vosiki

Charriere-Bournazel Champetier de Ribes Spitzer

5 rue de Logelbach, 75017 Paris, France

Tel. (+33) 1-42- 67-57-50

Fax (+33) 1-47-63-32-65

E-mail jpspctzeraccs-scp.avocat.fr

Contact Anne Vitale-Mardyks

Christophoridis & Associates

89–91 Avenue Kifissias, 115 23 Athens, Greece

Tel. (+30) 10-6984734

Fax (+30) 10-6984733

E-mail angchris@otenet.gr

Specialities: Commercial law; Labour law; Banking law; Financial law; Tax law; Industrial property law; Intellectual property law; Public procurement; Transport law; Telecommunications; Insurance law; EU law; International trade

Contact A. Christophoridis

Cleary Gottlieb Steen & Hamilton LLP

Rue de la Loi 57, 1040 Brussels, Belgium

Tel. (+32) 2-2872000

Fax (+32) 2-2311661

E-mail clearygottlieb@cgsh.com

URL www.cgsh.com

Specialities: Anti-dumping; Financial law; Insurance law; Mergers; Acquisitions; Environmental law

Contact Wolfgang Knapp

Cleary Gottlieb Steen & Hamilton LLP

One Liberty Plaza, New York NY 10006-1470, United States of America

Tel. (+1 212) 225-2000

Fax (+1 212) 225-3999

URL www.cgsh.com

Contact Ned Stiles

Cleaver Fulton Rankin

50 Bedford Street, Belfast BT2 7FW, United Kingdom

Tel. (+44 28) 9024-3141

Fax (+44 28) 9024-9096

E-mail n.faris@cfrlaw.co.uk

URL www.cfrlawonline.com

Specialities: Agricultural law; Fisheries law; Civil jurisdictional judgments; Competition law; Consumer protection; Employment law; Environmental law; Intellectual property law; Social policy; State aid

Contact Neil C. Faris

Clifford Chance LLP

Avenue Louise 65, PO Box 2, 1050 Brussels, Belgium

Tel. (+32) 2-5335911

Fax (+32) 2-5335959

E-mail Yves.Herinckx@cliffordchance.com

URL www.cliffordchance.com

Specialities: Anti-trust law; International trade; Single market; Agricultural law; Coal and steel; Environment policy; Company law; Social and employment policy; Product liability; Enforcement of judgments; Tax law; Public procurement; EU funding; Lomé Convention; Transport policy; Telecommunications; Media policy; Computer policy; Intellectual property law; Consumer policy; Appeals from national courts to the Court of Justice of the European Communities; Appeals from national courts to the Court of First Instance of the European Communities

Contact Yves Herinckx

Clifford Chance Pünder

200 Aldersgate Street, London EC1A 4JJ, United Kingdom

Tel. (+44 20) 7600-1000

Fax (+44 20) 7600-5555

E-mail John.Osborne@CliffordChance.com

URL www.CliffordChance.com
Contact John Osborne

CMS Bureau Francis Lefebvre

1–3 Villa Emile Bergerat, 92522 Neuilly
  sur Seine Cedex, France
Tel. (+33) 1-47-38-55-00
Fax (+33) 1-47-38-55-55
E-mail central@bfl-avocats.com
URL www.cms-bfl.com
Contact Francis Delbarre

CMS Bureau Francis Lefebvre

200 Avenue Louise, 1050 Brussels, Belgium
Tel. (+32) 2-6500430
Fax (+32) 2-6262251
E-mail bflbxl@cms-bfl-avocats.be
URL www.cms-bfl.com
Specialities: Competition law; Tax law; Free
  movement of goods; Free movement of
  persons; Litigation; Product liability;
  Commercial law; Environmental law;
  Transport law
Contact Christian Lavabre

CMS Cameron McKenna LLP

Avenue Louise 200, 1050 Brussels, Belgium
Tel. (+32) 2-6262217
Fax (+32) 2-6262309
E-mail robert.maclean@cmck.com
URL www.cmck.com
Specialities: Competition law; Commercial
  law; Internal market; WTO; Litigation
Contact Robert MacLean

CMS Cameron McKenna LLP

Mitre House, 160 Aldersgate Street, London
  EC1A 4DD, United Kingdom
Tel. (+44 20) 7367-3000
Fax (+44 20) 7367-2000
E-mail info@cmck.com
URL www.cmck.com
Contact Duncan Aldred

CMS de Backer

Chaussée de la Hulpe 178, 1170 Brussels,
  Belgium
Tel. (+32) 2-7436900
Fax (+32) 2-7436901
E-mail info@cmsdebacker.be

URL www.debacker.com
Contact Georges Vandersanden

CMS Derks Star Busmann

Avenue Louise 200, 1050 Brussels, Belgium
Tel. (+32) 2-6262300
Fax (+32) 2-6262309
E-mail general@cmsderks.be
URL www.cms.derks.nl
Specialities: Competition law; Anti-dumping;
  Customs law; Commercial law; EEA; Free
  movement of persons; Free movement of
  services; Free movement of goods; Free
  movement of capital; Pharmaceutical law;
  Public procurement
Contact Robert Bosman

CMS Derks Star Busmann

Pythagoraslaan 2, 3584 BB Utrecht,
  Netherlands
Tel. (+31 30) 2121111
Fax (+31 30) 2121333
E-mail utrecht@cms-dsb.com
URL www.cms-dsb.com
Contact Frans Vermeulen

CMS Hasche Sigle

Avenue Louise 200, 1050 Brussels, Belgium
Tel. (+32) 2-6500420
Fax (+32) 2-6500422
E-mail bruessel@cmslegal.de
URL www.cms-hs.com
Specialities: Corporate law; Competition law;
  Subsidies; Procurement law; Banking law;
  Capital market law; Tax law; Distribution
  law; Franchise law; Intellectual property law;
  Maritime law; Transport law; Employment
  law; Energy law; Environmental law;
  Insolvency law; Insurance law; Information
  technology; Telecommunications; Media
  law; Product liability; Real estate law;
  Construction law; Sale of goods; Provision
  of services; Transactions; Mergers and
  acquisitions; Utilities
Contact Dr Michael Bauer

CMS Hasche Sigle

Barckhausstr. 12–16, 60325 Frankfurt am
  Main, Germany
Tel. (+49 69) 71701-0
Fax (+49 69) 71701-110
E-mail Frankfurt@cms-hs.com

URL www.cms-hs.com

Contact Reiner Kurschat

Consejo General de la Abogacia Española

C/ Paseo 2 Recoletos 13, 28004 Madrid, Spain

Tel. (+34) 91-5232593

Fax (+34) 91-5327836

E-mail fela.sanjuan@cgae.es

URL www2.cgae.es

Contact Ruiz Gimenez

Coudert Brothers LLP

Avenue Louise 81, 1050 Brussels, Belgium

Tel. (+32) 2-5428888

Fax (+32) 2-5428989

E-mail pvanderschueren@
belgium.coudert.com

URL www.coudert.com

Contact Stephen O. Spinks

Coudert Brothers LLP

1114 Avenue of the Americas, New York,
NY 10036, United States of America

Tel. (+1 212) 626-4400

Fax (+1 212) 626-4120

E-mail info@.coudert.com

URL www.coudert.com

Contact Clyde E. Rankin

Countrelis & Associés

Rue de la Loi 235, Bte 12, 1040 Brussels,
Belgium

Tel. (+32) 2-2304845

Fax (+32) 2-2308206

E-mail efla_aeda@hotmail.com

Contact André Coutrelis

Countrelis & Associés

55 Avenue Marceau, 75116 Paris, France

Tel. (+33) 1-53-57-47-95

Fax (+33) 1-53-57-47-97

E-mail acoutrelis@coutrelis.com

Contact André Coutrelis

Covington and Burling

Ave des Arts 44, 1040 Brussels, Belgium

Tel. (+32) 2-5495230

Fax (+32) 2-5021598

E-mail dharfst@cov.com

URL www.cov.com

Specialities: Commercial law; Competition
law; Media law; Telecommunications;
Product liability; Food regulations;
Pharmaceuticals regulations; Cosmetics
regulations; Intellectual property law;
Litigation; Arbitration; International trade;
E-commerce; Internet

Contact David L. Harfst

Covington and Burling

1201 Pennsylvania Avenue, NW, Washington,
DC 20004-2401, United States of America

Tel. (+1 202) 662-6000

Fax (+1 202) 662-6291

E-mail jblake@cov.com

URL www.cov.com

Contact Jonathan D. Blake

Crowell and Moring

1001 Pennsylvania Avenue, NW, Washington,
DC 20004, United States of America

Tel. (+1 202) 624-2500

Fax (+1 202) 628-5116

URL www.crowell.com

Contact Terry L. Albertson

Crowell and Moring

Rue Royale 71, 1000 Brussels, Belgium

Tel. (+32) 2-2824082

Fax (+32) 2-2306399

E-mail jashetaylot@crowell.com

URL www.crowell.com

Specialities: Competition law; Mergers and
acquisitions; Banking law; Payment systems;
Tax law; Intellectual property law;
Information technology; Shipping
investment and regulation; Aerospace
industries' investment and regulation;
Environmental law

Contact James Ashe Taylor

Cuatrecasas Abogados Srl

Paseo de Gracia 111, 08008 Barcelona, Spain

Tel. (+34) 932-905500

Fax (+34) 932-905567

E-mail Barcelona@cuatrecasas.com

URL www.cuatrecasas.com

Contact Javier Castrodeza

Cuatrecasas Abogados Srl

Avenue de Cortenbergh 60, 1000 Brussels,
Belgium

Tel. (+32) 2-7433900
Fax (+32) 2-7433901
E-mail Brussels@cuatrecasas.com
URL www.cuatrecasas.com
Contact Cani Fernandez

Dahan, Dahan-Bitton and Dahan

6 Place St Germain des Prés, 75006 Paris,
France
Tel. (+33) 1-45- 49-16-16
Fax (+33) 1-42-22-68-61
E-mail avocats@ddbd.com
URL www.ddbd.com
Contact Maurice Dahan

De Schrijver, van de Gehuchte and Partners

Baarledorpsstraat 93, 9031 Gent, Belgium
Tel. (+32) 9-2244428
Fax (+32) 9-2241870
E-mail office@vocaten.be
URL www.vocaten.be
Specialities: EU law
Contact Dirk van de Gehuchte

De Smedt Philippe Law Offices

391 Avenue Louise, Bte 5, 1050 Brussels,
Belgium
Tel. (+32) 2-6409075
Fax (+32) 2-6409312
E-mail phil.etk@skynet.be
Specialities: Single market; Free movement of
goods; Free movement of services; Free
movement of persons; Free movement of
capital; Financial law; Tax law; EC banking
law; EC investment services law; EC
insurance law; Trade with eastern European
countries; Investment in eastern European
countries; EC commercial law;
Telecommunications; Media law; Transport
law; Public contracts; Environmental law;
Agricultural policy; Intellectual property
law; EC litigation; Transactional law
Contact Philippe de Smedt

Dechert LLP

4000 Bell Atlantic Tower, 1717 Arch Street,
Philadelphia, PA 19103, United States of
America
Tel. (+1 215) 994-4000
Fax (+1 215) 994-2222
E-mail richard.rizzo@dechert.com

URL www.dechert.com
Contact Richard C. Rizzo

Dechert LLP

Avenue Louise 480, 1050 Brussels, Belgium
Tel. (+32) 2-5355411
Fax (+32) 2-5355400
E-mail richard.temko@dechert.com
URL www.dechert.com
Specialities: Competition law;
Telecommunications; Broadcasting;
Environmental law; Food law;
Pharmaceutical law; Tax law; Banking
services; Financial services; Aviation; Public
procurement; Intellectual property law
Contact Richard J. Temko

Dechert LLP

2 Serjeants' Inn, London EC4Y 1LT,
United Kingdom
Tel. (+44 20) 7583-5353
Fax (+44 20) 7353-3683
E-mail steven.fogel@dechert.com
URL www.dechert.com
Specialities: International trade; International
taxation; Customs and excise; Environmental
law; Competition law; Commercial law;
Finance leasing; International arbitration
Contact Steven Fogel

Délégation des Barreaux de France

Avenue de la Joyeuse Entrée 1, 1040 Brussels,
Belgium
Tel. (+32) 2-2308331
Fax (+32) 2-2306277
E-mail dbf@dbfbruxelles.com
URL www.dbfbruxelles.com
Contact Laurent Petitjean

Denton Wilde Sapte

5 Chancery Lane, Clifford's Inn, London
EC4A 2BU, United Kingdom
Tel. (+44 20) 7242-1212
Fax (+44 20) 7404-0087
E-mail info@dentonwildesapte.com
URL www.dentonwildesapte.com

Denton Wilde Sapte

Avenue Louise 140, 1050 Brussels, Belgium
Tel. (+32) 2-2230621
Fax (+32) 2-2230482
E-mail brussels@dentonwildesapte.be

URL www.dentonwildesapte.com
Contact Steven Blakeley

Didier Pierre Avocats

Avenue de Tervueren 163, 1150 Brussels,
  Belgium
Tel. (+32) 2-7350182
Fax (+32) 2-7365253
E-mail didlex@skynet.be
URL http://users.skynet.be/PierreDidier
Contact Pierre Didier

DLA Piper Rudnick Gray Cary UK LLP

Avenue Louise 106, 1050 Brussels, Belgium
Tel. (+32) 2-5001500
Fax (+32) 2-5001600
E-mail steven.deKeyser@dla.com
URL www.dla.com
Contact Yves Brosens

DLA Piper Rudnick Gray Cary UK LLP

3 Noble Street, London EC2V 7EE,
  United Kingdom
Tel. (+44 20) 8700-1111
Fax (+44 20) 7796-6666
E-mail info@dlapiper.com
URL www.dlapiper.com
Contact Steven de Keyser

Echecopar Abogados

Doctor Fleming 3, 28036 Madrid, Spain
Tel. (+34) 91-4589940
Fax (+34) 91-4589949
E-mail madrid@echecopar.es
URL www.echecopar.es
Specialities: Competition law; Customs law
Contact Luis Echecopar Rey

Eduard Marissens

Avenue Molière 183, 1190 Brussels, Belgium
Tel. (+32) 2-3439532
Fax (+32) 2-3436811
E-mail secretariatmarissens@pophost.eunet.be
Specialities: Trade regulation; Anti-trust law;
  Air transport; Telecommunications; Media
  law; Pharmaceutical law; European law
Contact V. Verbist

Ehle and Schiller

Mehlemerstr. 13, 50968 Cologne, Germany
Tel. (+49 221) 937017-0

Fax (+49 221) 9370171-5
E-mail rechtsanwaelte@ehle-schiller.de
URL www.ehle-schiller.de
Specialities: Anti-dumping; Countervailing
  duty; Tax law; Customs duty; Agricultural
  law; Anti-trust law; Food law; State aid
Contact Dr Volker Schiller

Eugene F. Collins

Temple Chambers, 3 Burlington Road, Dublin
  4, Ireland
Tel. (+353 1) 2026400
Fax (+353 1) 6675200
E-mail lawyer@efc.ie
URL www.efc.ie
Specialities: Corporate law; Banking law
Contact Anthony Collins

Fasken Martineau DuMoulin LLP

6th Floor, Hasilwood House, 60 Bishopsgate,
  London EC2N 4AW, United Kingdom
Tel. (+44 20) 7382-6020
Fax (+44 20) 7382-6021
E-mail jlisson@lon.fasken.com
URL www.fasken.com
Specialities: EU law and Canadian
  corporations; EU research and development
  programmes; Competition law;
  Environmental law; Telecommunications;
  Financial issues; Economic issues; Financial
  institutions; Corporate law
Contact James Lisson

Feltgen and Mahaux

Rue du Tabellion 19, 1050 Brussels, Belgium
Tel. (+32) 2-5386080
Fax (+32) 2-5386101
E-mail jeanpierremahaux@compuserve.com
Specialities: Competition law; Equal
  opportunities between women and men;
  Non-contractual liability of institutions
Contact J. P. Mahaux

Fidal

Avenue du Bourget 40, 1130 Brussels, Belgium
Tel. (+32) 2-7084646
Fax (+32) 2-7084645
E-mail frederic.puel@fidal.fr
URL www.fidal.fr
Specialities: Competition law; Distribution law;
  Social law; Tax law; Litigation; Lobbying;

Environmental law; Intellectual property
law; E-commerce; Customs

Contact Frédéric Puel

Field Fisher Waterhouse

41 Vine Street, London EC3N 2AA,
 United Kingdom
Tel. (+44 20) 7861-4000
Fax (+44 20) 7488-0084
E-mail info@ffw.com
URL www.ffwlaw.com

Contact Alex Woodfield

Foley and Lardner LLP

Avenue de Cortenbergh, 118, 1000 Brussels,
 Belgium
Tel. (+32) 2-6392710
Fax (+32) 2-6460311
E-mail sdance@foley.com
URL www.foley.com

Contact Simon E. Dance

Foley and Lardner LLP

777 East Wisconsin Avenue, Milwaukee,
 WI 53202, United States of America
Tel. (+1 414) 271-2400
Fax (+1 414) 297-4900
E-mail nsennett@foley.com
URL www.foley.com

Contact Nancy J. Sennett

Fox Williams

Ten Dominion Street, London EC2M 2EE,
 United Kingdom
Tel. (+44 20) 7628-2000
Fax (+44 20) 7628-2100
E-mail mail@foxwilliams.co.uk
URL www.foxwilliams.co.uk

Contact Jane Mann

Freshfields Bruckhaus Deringer

Bastion Tower, Place du Champ de Mars 5,
 1050 Brussels, Belgium
Tel. (+32) 2-5047000
Fax (+32) 2-5047200
E-mail elizabeth.crossick@freshfields.com
URL www.freshfields.com

Specialities: Competition law; State aid;
 International trade law; Public procurement;
 Environmental law; Liaison with EC
 institutions in relation to proposed
 legislation; Telecommunications and media;

Transport law; Pharmaceutical law; Financial
services; Insurance; Energy; Litigation (EU
law at member state level); Litigation (EU
law at EU level); Litigation (before Court of
Justice); Litigation (before Court of First
Instance); Litigation (before EFTA Court);
EU law implications of transactions taking
place outside the Community; International
corporate matters; International commercial
matters

Contact Elizabeth Crossick

Freshfields Bruckhaus Deringer

65 Fleet Street, London EC4Y 1HS,
 United Kingdom
Tel. (+44 20) 7936-4000
Fax (+44 20) 7936-7001
E-mail anthony.salz@freshfields.com
URL www.freshfields.com

Contact Anthony Salz

Garrigues

Rue Père Eudore Devroye 245, 1150 Brussels,
 Belgium
Tel. (+32) 2-5453700
Fax (+32) 2-5453799
E-mail Stephen.pickard@
 garriguesabogados.com
URL www.garrigues.com

Specialities: Anti-dumping; Financial services;
 Internal market; Intellectual property law;
 Competition law; Technical assistance

Contact Stephen Pickard

Garrigues

José Abascal 45, 28003 Madrid, Spain
Tel. (+34) 91-5145200
Fax (+34) 91-3992408
URL www.garrigues.com

Contact Antonio Garrigues Walker

Geater & Co

Boulevard Brand Whitlock 152, 1200 Brussels,
 Belgium
Tel. (+32) 2-7358272
Fax (+32) 2-7320143
E-mail info@geater-and-co.be
URL www.geater-and-co.be

Specialities: Company law; Competition law;
 Environmental law; Intellectual property
 law; Financial services; Tax law; Fisheries
 law; Commercial law; EU law relating to

various specific sectors of industry; Free movement of goods; Free movement of persons; Free movement of services; Free movement of capital; Energy; Social law; Transport law

Contact Alasdair Geater

Gide Loyrette Nouel

26 Cours Albert 1er, 75008 Paris, France
Tel. (+33) 1-40-75-60-00
Fax (+33) 1-40-75-37-79
E-mail gln.newyork@gide.com
URL www.gide.com

Contact Renaud Baguenault de Puchesse

Gide Loyrette Nouel

Rue de l'Industrie 26–38, 1040 Brussels, Belgium
Tel. (+32) 2-2311140
Fax (+32) 2-2311177
E-mail gln.brussels@gide.com
URL www.gide.fr

Specialities: Competition law; Agricultural law; Corporate law; Transport law; Free movement and freedom of establishment; Environmental law; Customs law; Tax law; Dumping; Social law

Contact Dominique Voillemot

Gleiss Lutz

Rue Guimard 7, 1040 Brussels, Belgium
Tel. (+32) 2-5511020
Fax (+32) 2-5121568
E-mail info@gleisslutz.com
URL www.gleisslutz.com

Specialities: EU law; Competition law; Antitrust law; Mergers and acquisitions; Anti dumping and subsidies; State aid; EC litigation; International trade law

Contact Dr Werner Berg

Gomez-Acebo & Pombo

Castellana 216, 28046 Madrid, Spain
Tel. (+34) 91-5829100
Fax (+34) 91- 5829114
E-mail abogados@gomezacebo-pombo.com
URL www.gomezacebo-pombo.com

Contact Ignacio Gomez-Acebo

Gomez-Acebo & Pombo

Avenue Louise 267, 1050 Brussels, Belgium
Tel. (+32) 2-2311220

Fax (+32) 2-2308035
E-mail abogados.brx@ gomezacebo-pombo.com
URL www.gomezacebo-pombo.com

Contact Emiliano Garayar Gutiérrez

Gorrissen Federspiel Kierkegaard

H.C. Andersens Bd 12, 1553 Copenhagen V, Denmark
Tel. (+45) 33-41-41-41
Fax (+45) 33-41-41-33
E-mail gfk@gfklaw.dk
URL www.gfklaw.uk

Specialities: Competition law; Company law; Banking law; Public procurement; State aid; Employment law; Intellectual property law

Contact Jan-Erik Svensson

Grupp W.G.

Avenue de la Renaissance 1, 1000 Brussels, Belgium
Tel. (+32) 2-7367631
Fax (+32) 2- 7367696

Contact W. Grupp

Hammonds

2 Park Lane, Leeds LS3 1ES, United Kingdom
Tel. (+44 870) 839-0000
Fax (+44 870) 839-7001
URL www.hammonds.com

Contact Ian Greenfield

Hammonds

Avenue Louise 250, PO Box 65, 1050 Brussels, Belgium
Tel. (+32) 2-6277676
Fax (+32) 2-6277686
E-mail konstantinos.adamantopoulos@ hammonds.com
URL www.hammonds.com

Contact Konstantinos Adamantopoulos

Hannes Snellman Attorneys at Law Ltd

PO Box 333, Eteläranta 8, 00131 Helsinki, Finland
Tel. (+358 9) 228841
Fax (+358 9) 177393
E-mail hannes.snellman@hannessnellman.fi
URL www.hannessnellman.fi

Contact Carl-Henrik Wallin

Haver & Mailänder

Lenzhalds 83–85, 70192 Stuttgart, Germany
Tel. (+49 711) 227-440
Fax (+49 711) 2991935
E-mail info@haver-mailaender.de
URL www.haver-mailaender.de
Contact Dr K. Peter Mailander

Haver & Mailänder

Avenue Louise 221, 1050 Brussels, Belgium
Tel. (+32) 2-6394715
Fax (+32) 2-6394728
E-mail bruessel@haver-mailaender.de
URL www.haver-mailaender.de
Specialities: Economic law; Competition law;
Company law; Arbitration
Contact Andreas Bartosch

Heiermann Franke Knipp – Rechtsanwälte

Kettenhofweg 126, 60325 Frankfurt am Main,
Germany
Tel. (+49 69) 9758220
Fax (+49 69) 975822225
E-mail frankfurt@kanzlei-hfk.de
URL www.heiermann-franke-knipp.de
Contact Dr Steffen Hochstadt

Heiermann Franke Knipp – Rechtsanwälte

Rue de la Tourelle 37, 1040 Brussels, Belgium
Tel. (+32) 2-2300924
Fax (+32) 2-2300901
Contact Dr Ing. A. Strub

Hengeler Mueller

Avenue de Cortenbergh 118, bte 2, 1000
Brussels, Belgium
Tel. (+32) 2-7885500
Fax (+32) 2-7885599
E-mail hmwwbrx@hengeler.com
URL www.hengeler.com
Contact Dr Bernhard M. Maassen

Hengeler Mueller Weitzel Wirtz

Bockenheimer Landstr. 51, 60325 Frankfurt am
Main, Germany
Tel. (+49 69) 170 950
Fax (+49 69) 725 773
Contact Dr O. de Lousanoff

Herbert Smith LLP

Exchange House, Primrose Street, London
EC2A 2HS, United Kingdom
Tel. (+44 20) 7374-8000
Fax (+44 20) 7374-0888
E-mail contact@herbertsmith.com
URL www.herbertsmith.com
Contact Richard Fleck

Herbert Smith

Rue Guimard 15, 1040 Brussels, Belgium
Tel. (+32) 2-5117450
Fax (+32) 2-5117772
E-mail nicola.hanly@herbertsmith.com
URL www.herbertsmith.com
Specialities: Competition law; Public
procurement; Trade/WTO issues; Media/
sport; Regulations; Commercial law;
Environmental law; State aid; Mergers
Contact Nicola Hanly

Heuking Kühn Lüer Wojtek

Cecilienallee 5, 40474 Düsseldorf, Germany
Tel. (+49 211) 6005500
Fax (+49 211) 60055050
E-mail duesseldorf@heuking.de
URL www.heuking.de
Contact Dirk W. Kolvenbach

Heuking Kühn Lüer Wojtek

Avenue Louise 140, 1050 Brussels, Belgium
Tel. (+32) 2-6462000
Fax (+32) 2-6462040
E-mail brussels@heuking.de
URL www.heuking.de
Specialities: EU law; Anti-trust law;
International trade law; International customs
law; EU trade law; EU customs law;
Environmental regulations; Health
regulations; Safety regulations;
Telecommunications; Media law; Intellectual
property rights; Transport law; Information
technology law; Computer law; Employment
law; Mergers and acquisitions; Tax law;
Arbitration
Contact Gabrielle H. Williamson

Hjort Law Office DA

Akersgaten 2, PO Box 471 Sentrum, 0105
Oslo, Norway
Tel. (+47) 22-47-18-00
Fax (+47) 22-47-18-18

E-mail advokatfirma@hjort.no
URL www.hjort.no
Contact Jan Petter Romsaas

Hoche Demolin Brulard Barthélémy

Avenue des Arts 46, 1000 Brussels, Belgium
Tel. (+32) 2-2131450
Fax (+32) 2-2131460
E-mail info@be.hochelaw.com
URL www.hochelaw.com
Contact Peirre Demolin

Hoffmann & Partners

Avenue Louise 385/1, 1050 Brussels, Belgium
Tel. (+32) 2-6480970
Fax (+32) 2-6402779
E-mail ehoffmann@hoffmann-partners.com
URL www.hoffmann-partners.com
Specialities: Competition law; Lobbying
Contact Dr Elisabeth Hoffmann

Hogan & Hartson LLP

Thirteenth Street 555 NW, Washington,
   DC 20004-1109, United States of America
Tel. (+1 202) 637-5600
Fax (+1 202) 637-5910
E-mail jwgorrell @hhlaw.com
URL www.hhlaw.com
Contact J. Warren Gorrell

Hogan & Hartson LLP

Rue de l'Industrie 26, 1040 Brussels, Belgium
Tel. (+32) 2-5050911
Fax (+32) 2-5050996
E-mail chatton@hhlaw.com
URL www.hhlaw.com
Specialities: Food law; Cosmetics; Agricultural
   law; Commercial law; Telecommunications
   and satellites; Pharmaceutical products;
   Competition regulation; Trade regulation;
   Environmental law; Safety law; Aviation;
   Industrial standards; Technical standards;
   Public procurement; State aid; Labour law;
   Free movement of persons; Free movement
   of goods; Free movement of services;
   Litigation (before Court of Justice);
   Litigation (before Court of First Instance);
   Mergers and acquisitions; International trade;
   International investment; Data protection
Contact Catriona Hatton

Holman Fenwick & Willan

Marlow House, Lloyd's Avenue, London
   EC3N 3AL, United Kingdom
Tel. (+44 20) 7488-2300
Fax (+44 20) 7481-0316
E-mail holmans@hfw.co.uk
URL www.hfw.com
Contact Philip A Wareham

Hydrolex

Rue Hydraulique 6, 1210 Brussels, Belgium
Tel. (+32) 2-2173990
Fax (+32) 2-2180672
E-mail avocats@grollet-partners.be
URL www.grollet-partners.be
Contact Christine Rygaert

International Bar Association (IBA)

271 Regent Street, London W1B 2AQ,
   United Kingdom
Tel. (+44 20) 7629-1206
Fax (+44 20) 7409-0456
E-mail member@int-bar.org
URL www.ibanet.org
Contact Mark Ellis

International Law Chambers

ILC House, Avenue Emile Max 91–93, 1030
   Brussels, Belgium
Tel. (+32) 2-7325663
Fax (+32) 2-7325570
E-mail ilcuk@aol.com
Contact M. Joseph

International Law Chambers

ILC House, 77 Chepstow Road, Bayswater,
   London W2 5QR, United Kingdom
Tel. (+44 20) 7221-5685
Fax (+44 20) 7221-0193
E-mail ilcuk@aol.com
Contact T. Kennedy

International Legal Counsel Sprl

Avenue Ernest Cambier 23, 1030 Brussels,
   Belgium
Tel. (+32) 2-2163655
Fax (+32) 2-2164278
Specialities: Intellectual property law; Energy
   law; Environmental law; Tax law
Contact T. B. Trumpy

J. P. Karsenty et Associés

Avenue de Broqueville 116, Bte 10, 1200
  Brussels, Belgium
Tel. (+32) 2-7767818
Fax (+32) 2-7704378
E-mail jnazerali@bwlaw.co.uk
URL www.bwlaw.co.uk

Specialities: Competition law; Anti-dumping;
  Internal market; Agricultural law; Company
  law; Consumer law; Education; Employment
  law; Environmental law; Pharmaceutical
  law; Insurance; Public procurement; Funding
  under EU Structural Funds;
  Telecommunications; Intellectual property
  law; Commercial contracts; Mergers and
  acquisitions; Joint ventures; Commercial
  law; Water

Contact Julie Nazerali

J. P. Karsenty et Associés

70 Bd de Courcelles, 75017 Paris, France
Tel. (+33) 1-47-63-74-75
Fax (+33) 1-46-22-33-27
E-mail mkarsenty@jpkarsenty.com
Contact Martine Karsenty-Ricard

Jalles Advogados

Rue J A Demot 23, 1040 Brussels, Belgium
Tel. (+32) 2-2301318
Fax (+32) 2-2307907
E-mail 106043.1322@compuserve.com

Specialities: Competition law; Trade barriers;
  Dumping; Information technology; Freedom
  of establishment; Food law; Pharmaceutical
  law; International trade; EC public function;
  Free movement of services; Relations with
  ACP countries; Social law; Environmental
  law; Transport law; Customs; Banking law;
  Insurance; Telecommunications; Industrial
  property law; Intellectual property law;
  Contract law; Company law; Agricultural
  law; State aid

Contact Isabel Jalles

Jalles Advogados

Av. Alvares Cabral 34 – 6°, 1250-018 Lisbon,
  Portugal
Tel. (+351) 213884095
Fax (+351) 213881955
E-mail 106115,20@compuserve.com

Contact Isabel Jalles

Japan Science and Technology Agency

65 Avenue Louise, Box 11, 1050 Brussels,
  Belgium
Tel. (+32) 2-5357840
Fax (+32) 2-5357700
E-mail RNakamura@nih.gov
URL www.jst.go.jp

Contact Dr Richard Nakamura

Jean van Riel

Rue de l'Aurore 2/24, 1000 Brussels, Belgium
Tel. (+32) 2-6260735
Fax (+32) 2-6461136
E-mail vanriel@skynet.be

Contact J. van Riel

Jonas Bruun

Bredgade 38, 1260 Copenhagen K, Denmark
Tel. (+45) 33-47-88-00
Fax (+45) 33-47-88-88
E-mail jsk@jblaw.dk
URL www.jonasbruun.com

Specialities: EU law; Competition law; Free
  movement of goods; Free movement of
  services; Free movement of capital;
  Establishment; Procurement of public supply
  contracts; Procurement of public works
  contracts; Telecommunications; Trade mark
  law

Contact Jeppe Skadhauge

Jones Day

North Point, 901 Lakeside Avenue, Cleveland,
  OH 44114-1190, United States of America
Tel. (+1 216) 586-3939
Fax (+1 216) 579-0212
E-mail office@jonesday.com
URL www.jonesday.com

Contact Robert H. Rawson

Jones Day

Blvd Brand Whitlock 165, 1200 Brussels,
  Belgium
Tel. (+32) 2-6451411
Fax (+32) 2-6451445
E-mail office@jonesday.com
URL www.jonesday.com

Contact Luc G. Houben

Juridisk Institut Copenhagen Business School

Howitzvej 13, 3. sal, 2000 Frederiksberg, Denmark
Tel. (+45) 38-15-26-26
Fax (+45) 38-15-26-10
E-mail st.jur@cbs.dk
URL www.cbs.dk/law
Contact Steen Treumer

Juriscope

2 Teleport, Avenue René Cassin, 86960 Futuroscope Cedex, France
Tel. (+33) 5-49-49-41-41
Fax (+33) 5-49-49-00-66
E-mail contact@juriscope.org
URL www.juriscope.org
Contact Laure Bernuau

Katrin Markus Rechtsanwältin

Avenue de la Renaissance 1/8, 1000 Brussels, Belgium
Tel. (+32) 2-7359939
Fax (+32) 2-7351076
E-mail info@brussel.diplo.de
Specialities: Family Law
Contact Katrin Markus

Keller and Heckman LLP

Rue Blanche 25, 1060 Brussels, Belgium
Tel. (+32) 2-5410570
Fax (+32) 2-5410580
E-mail info_brussels@khlaw.com
URL www.khlaw.com
Contact Jean-Philippe Montfort

Keller and Heckman LLP

1001 G Street NW, Washington, DC 20001, United States of America
Tel. (+1 202) 434-4100
Fax (+1 202) 434-4646
E-mail info_washington@khlaw.com
URL www.khlaw.com
Contact John S. Eldred

Kelley Drye & Warren LLP

101 Park Avenue, New York, NY 10178, United States of America
Tel. (+1 212) 808-78 00
Fax (+1 212) 808-7897
E-mail jcallagy@kelleydrye.com
URL www.kelleydrye.com
Contact John Callagy

Kelley Drye & Warren LLP

Avenue Louise 106, 1050 Brussels, Belgium
Tel. (+32) 2-6461110
Fax (+32) 2-6400589
E-mail avanlanduyt@kelleydrye.com
URL www.kelleydrye.com
Specialities: Financial law; Commercial law; EU law
Contact André van Landuyt

Kemmler Rapp Böhlke

Rond Point Schuman 9, Box 9, 1040 Brussels, Belgium
Tel. (+32) 2-2309075
Fax (+32) 2-2301416
E-mail krb&c@eurojura.be
URL www.eurojura.be
Specialities: Competition law; Free movement of goods; Free movement of services; Free movement of persons; Indirect taxation; State aid; Telecommunications; Air transport; Energy; External trade
Contact Barbara Rapp-Jung

Kiethe Rechtsanwälte

Vollmannstrasse 59, 81925 Munich, Germany
Tel. (+49 89) 920010
Fax (+49 89) 92001111

Kiethe Rechtsanwälte

Avenue Louise 179, 1050 Brussels, Belgium
Tel. (+32) 2-6467072
Fax (+32) 2-6463347
Specialities: EU law; Commercial law; Banking law; Financial law; Mergers and acquisitions; Public law; Competition law; Anti-trust law
Contact Dr Kiethe

Kokkinos & Associates, European Legal Consultancy

Hippocratous Str 4, 106 79 Athens, Greece
Tel. (+30) 210-3613379
Fax (+30) 210-3612084
E-mail eurolegal@attglobal.net
URL www.euro-legal.net
Contact Constantine Kokkinos

Kromann Reumert

Rue du Luxembourg 3, 1000 Brussels, Belgium
Tel. (+32) 2-5010700
Fax (+32) 2-5010701
E-mail bru@kromannreumert.com
URL www.kromannreumert.com

Specialities: Competition law;
  Telecommunications; Free movement of
  goods; Public procurement

Contact Henrik Stenbjerre

Kromann Reumert

Sundkrogsgade 5, 2100 Copenhagen, Denmark
Tel. (+45) 70-12-12-11
Fax (+45) 70-12-13-11
E-mail cph@kromannreumert.com
URL www.kromannreumert.com

Contact Jens Munk Plum

**Lafarge – Flecheux – Campana – Le
Blevennec**

24 Rue de Prony, 75809 Paris Cedex 17, France
Tel. (+33) 1-44-29-32-32
Fax (+33) 1-44-29-31-00
E-mail lfc@24rueprony.fr

Contact Michel Bazex

Lafili, van Crombrugghe & Partners

Drève des Renards 6, Bte 1, 1180 Brussels,
  Belgium
Tel. (+32) 2-3730910
Fax (+32) 2-3754525
E-mail office.bru@lafili-law.be
URL www.lafili-law.be

Specialities: Notification procedure (Art 81);
  Distributorship agreements; Franchise
  agreements; Agency; Know-how licensing
  (Reg 556/89); Patent licensing (Reg 2349/
  84); Mergers and acquisitions (Reg 4064/
  89); Product liability (Dir 25071985);
  Aviation, ground handling (Dir 98/67); CRS;
  Dominant position (Art 82)

Contact Louis Lafili

Lallemand et Legros

Avenue Emile de Mot 19, 1000 Brussels,
  Belgium
Tel. (+32) 2-6487530
Fax (+32) 2-6487841

Contact David Pardes

Lambert & Associés

Avenue Defré 19, 1180 Brussels, Belgium
Tel. (+32) 2-3755973
Fax (+32) 2-3755980
E-mail desk@lambert.be
URL www.lavocat.com

Specialities: Public law; Construction law;
  Pharmaceutical law; International law;
  European law; Press; Audiovisual
  communication; Social law

Contact Nadine Kalamian

Lamy Associés

40 Rue de Bonnel, 69484 Lyon Cedex 03,
  France
Tel. (+33) 4-78-62-14-00
Fax (+33) 4-78-62-14-99
E-mail info@lamy-ribeyre.com
URL www.lamy-ribeyre.com

Contact Christoph Martin Radtke

Law Offices Dr F. Schwank

Stock Exchange Building, Wipplingerstrasse
  34, 1010 Vienna, Austria
Tel. (+43 1) 5335704
Fax (+43 1) 5335706
E-mail offices@schwank.com
URL www.schwank.com

Contact Dr Friedrich Schwank

Law Offices Dr F. Schwank

Avenue Coghen 198/2, 1180 Brussels, Belgium
Tel. (+32) 2-479489710
Fax (+32) 2-3457934
E-mail offices@schwank.com
URL www.schwank.com

Contact Gaetan Zeyen

LeBoeuf, Lamb, Greene & Macrae LLP

Arts/Lux Building, Rue du Luxemburg 14A,
  1000 Brussels, Belgium
Tel. (+32) 2-2270900
Fax (+32) 2-2270909
E-mail vnuyts@llgm.sprint.com
URL www.llgm.com

Specialities: Competition law; Commercial
  law; Customs; Environmental law;
  Telecommunications; Insurance; Financial
  services; Public procurement; EEA and
  Eastern Europe; Energy law; Free movement
  of goods; Free movement of persons; Free

movement of services; Free movement of capital; Audiovisual communication

Contact Etienne R. Claes

LeBoeuf, Lamb, Greene & Macrae LLP

125 West 55th Street, New York, NY 10019-5389, United States of America

Tel. (+1 212) 424-8000

Fax (+1 212) 424-8500

URL www.llgm.com

Contact Steven H. Davis

Lett & Co

Radhuspladsen 4, 1550 København V, Denmark

Tel. (+45) 33-77-00-00

Fax (+45) 33-77-00-01

E-mail lettco@lettco.dk

URL www.lettco.dk

Specialities: Company law; Competition law; Mergers; Insurance; Banking law; Litigation (before Court of Justice); Litigation (before Court of First Instance); Food law; Public procurement; Labour law

Contact Georg Lett

Liedekerke.Wolters.Waelbroeck. Kirkpatrick

Blvd de l'Empereur 3, 1000 Brussels, Belgium

Tel. (+32) 2-5511515

Fax (+32) 2-5511414

E-mail info@liedekerke-law.be

URL www.liedekerke-law.be

Contact John Kirkpatrick

Linklaters de Bandt

Rue Brederode 13, 1000 Brussels, Belgium

Tel. (+32) 2-5019411

Fax (+32) 2-5019494

E-mail europe.infor@linklaters.com

URL www.linklaters.com

Linnells

Seacourt Tower West Way, Oxford OX2 0FB, United Kingdom

Tel. (+44 186) 524-8607

Fax (+44 186) 572-8445

E-mail info@bllaw.co.uk

URL www.linnells.co.uk

Contact Joss Saunders

Lovells

Avenue Louise 523, 1050 Brussels, Belgium

Tel. (+32) 2-6470660

Fax (+32) 2-6471124

E-mail thomas.mcquail@lovells.com

URL www.lovells.com

Contact Thomas McQuail

Lovells

Atlantic House, Holborn Viaduct, London EC1A 2FG, United Kingdom

Tel. (+44 20) 7296-2000

Fax (+44 20) 7296-2001

E-mail firstname.surname@lovells.com

URL www.lovells.com

Contact Andrew Foyle

Loyens Advocaten

Woluwe Atrium, Neerveldstraat 101–103, 1200 Brussels, Belgium

Tel. (+32) 2-7434343

Fax (+32) 2-7434310

E-mail information@loyens.com

URL www.loyens.com

Specialities: Competition law; Merger control; State aid; Energy law; Telecommunications; Transport law; Environmental law; Public procurement; Free movement

Contact Christian Chéruy

Luis Brito Correia Advogados

Av. Alvares Cabral 84-2°, 1200 Lisboa, Portugal

Tel. (+351) 213703600

Fax (+351) 213882554

E-mail lbricor@mail.telepac.pt

URL www.eureseau.com

Contact Dr Luis Brito Correia

Macfarlanes

10 Norwich Street, London EC4A 1BD, United Kingdom

Tel. (+44 20) 7831-9222

Fax (+44 20) 7831-9607

URL www.macfarlanes.com

Contact Penny Rutterford

Macfarlanes

Avenue Louise 165, 1050 Brussels, Belgium

Tel. (+32) 2-6477350

Fax (+32) 2-6406499

E-mail jane.whittaker@macfarlanes.com

URL www.macfarlanes.com

Specialities: Competition law; Commercial law; Free movement of goods; Free movement of financial services; Transport law; Entertainment; Telecommunications; Environmental law

Contact Jane Whittaker

MacRoberts

152 Bath Street, Glasgow G2 4TB, United Kingdom
Tel. (+44 141) 332-9988
Fax (+44 141) 332 -8886
E-mail maildesk@macroberts.com
URL www.macroberts.com

Specialities: Corporate law; Commercial law; Competition law

Contact David Flint

Magnusson Wahlin Qvist Stanbrook

Advokataktieselskab Pilestræde 58, 1112 Copenhagen, Denmark
Tel. (+45) 33-12- 45-22
Fax (+45) 33-93-60-23
E-mail copenhagen@dk.maqs.com
URL www.maqs.com

Contact Jens H. Elmerkjær

Mannheimer Swartling

Avenue de Tervueren 13, 1040 Brussels, Belgium
Tel. (+32) 2-7322222
Fax (+32) 2-7369652
E-mail jc@msa.se
URL www.msa.se

Contact Johan Coyet

Mannheimer Swartling

Norrmalmstorg 4, Box 1711, 111 87 Stockholm, Sweden
Tel. (+46 8) 50-57-65-00
Fax (+46 8) 50-57-65-01
E-mail lexner@msa.se
URL www.mannheimerswartling.se.

Contact Sven Lexner

Martinez Lage & Asociados

Claudio Coello 37, 28001 Madrid, Spain
Tel. (+34) 91-4264470
Fax (+34) 91-5773774
E-mail info@martinezlarge.com
URL www.martinezlage.com

Specialities: EC institutions; Litigation; Competition law; State aid; Intellectual property law; EC freedoms; Public contracts; Concentration of companies; Dumping; Transport law; EU aids and subsidies

Contact Santiago Martinez Lage

McCann FitzGerald Solicitors

International Financial Services Centre, 2 Harbourmaster Place, Dublin 1, Ireland
Tel. (+353 1) 8290000
Fax (+353 1) 8290010
E-mail wemaster@mccann.fitzgerald.ie
URL www.mccann-fitzgerald.ie

Contact Gerald FitzGerald

McCann FitzGerald Solicitors

Avenue de Cortenbergh 89, 1000 Brussels, Belgium
Tel. (+32) 2-7400370
Fax (+32) 2-7400371
E-mail damian.collins@mccann-fitzgerald.ie
URL www.mccann-fitzgerald.ie

Specialities: Anti-trust law; State aid; Public undertakings; Mergers and acquisitions; Intellectual property law; Exclusive distribution; Joint ventures; Commercial law; Internal market; Agricultural law; Fisheries law; Banking law; Financial services; Telecommunications; Environmental law; Air transport; Public procurement; Regional issues; Structural funds

Contact Damian Collins

Michael G. Papaconstantinou

Queen Sophia Avenue 4, 10674 Athens, Greece
Tel. (+30) 210-7295750
Fax (+30) 210-7295756
E-mail hpaplaw@ath.forthnet.gr

Contact Helen Papaconstantinou

Miller, Bolle and Partners

Avenue Louise 283, Box 19, 1050 Brussels, Belgium
Tel. (+32) 2-6404400
Fax (+32) 2-6489995
E-mail office@millerlaw.be
URL www.millerlaw.be

Specialities: Commercial law; Company law; Corporate law; Financial law; Tax law; Mergers and acquisitions

Contact Shiloh Miller

Moltke-Leth Advokater

Amaliegade 12, 1256 Copenhagen K, Denmark
Tel. (+45) 33-11-65-11
Fax (+45) 33-11-49-11
E-mail law@moltke-leth.dk
URL www.moltke-leth.dk
Specialities: Competition law; Purchase of
  businesses; Sale of businesses
Contact Grethe Jorgensen

Moons

Blvd Brand Whitlock 158 B.6, 1200 Brussels,
  Belgium
Tel. (+32) 2-7367177
Fax (+32) 2-7366591
E-mail moons.@advocaten.de
URL www.advocaten.de/moons.htm
Specialities: Contract law; Commercial law;
  Company law; Corporate law; Labour law;
  EU law; Arbitration
Contact Dr Eric J.H. Moons

Morgan Lewis & Bockius LLP

1701 Market Street, Philadelphia, PA 19103,
  United States of America
Tel. (+1 215) 963-5000
Fax (+1 215) 963- 5001
URL www.morganlewis.com
Contact J. Gordon Cooney

Morgan, Lewis & Bockius LLP

Rue Guimard 7, 1040 Brussels, Belgium
Tel. (+32) 2-5077500
Fax (+32) 2-5077555
E-mail isinan@morganlewis.com
URL www.morganlewis.com
Specialities: Anti-trust law; Competition law;
  Commercial law; Customs; IPR; Consumer
  protection; Public procurement;
  Environmental law
Contact S. Alan Hamburger

Morrison & Foerster LLP

Avenue Molière 262, 1180 Brussels, Belgium
Tel. (+32) 2-3470400
Fax (+32) 2-3471824
E-mail tvinje@mofo.com
URL www.mofo.com
Contact Thoms C. Vinge

Nabarro Nathanson

Avenue Louise 209A, 1050 Brussels, Belgium
Tel. (+32) 2-6260740
Fax (+32) 2-6260752
E-mail r.bickler@nabarro.com
URL www.nabarro.com
Specialities: Competition law; Commercial
  law; Information technology;
  Telecommunications; Anti-dumping; Public
  procurement; Customs and origin legislation;
  Energy; Single market; Financial services
Contact Rachel Bickler

Nabarro Nathanson

Lacon House, 2 Theobald's Court, Theobald's
  Road, London WC1X 8RW, United Kingdom
Tel. (+44 20) 7524-6000
Fax (+44 20) 7524-6524
E-mail info@nabarro.com
URL www.nabarro.com
Contact C. Mehta

Nauta Dutilh

Weena 750, POB 1110, 3014 DA Rotterdam,
  Netherlands
Tel. (+31 10) 2240000
Fax (+31 10) 4148444
E-mail info@nautadutilh.com.
URL www.nautadutilh.com
Contact J.J. Feenstra

Nauta Dutilh

Terhulpsesteenweg 177, 1170 Brussels,
  Belgium
Tel. (+32) 2-5668000
Fax (+32) 2-5668001
E-mail ndbru@nautadutilh.com
URL www.nautadutilh.com
Specialities: EU law
Contact Marc van der Woude

Nebelong & Partnere

Ostergade 16, Postboks 1051, 1007
  Copenhagen K, Denmark
Tel. (+45) 33-11-75-22
Fax (+45) 33-32-47-75
E-mail nebelong@nebelong.dk
URL www.nebelong.dk
Contact Henrik C. Winkel

Norton Rose

Kempson House, 35–37 Camomile Street,
London EC3A 7AN, United Kingdom
Tel. (+44 20) 7283-6000
Fax (+44 20) 7283-6500
E-mail marketing@nortonrose.com
URL www.nortonrose.com
Contact Peter Martyr

Norton Rose

Avenue Louise 489, 1050 Brussels, Belgium
Tel. (+32) 2-2376111
Fax (+32) 2-2376136
URL www.nortonrose.com
Specialities: EU law
Contact Riccardo Celli

Oppenheimer Wolff & Donnelly LLP

Avenue Louise 240, Bte 5, 1050 Brussels,
Belgium
Tel. (+32) 2-6260500
Fax (+32) 2-6260510
E-mail jrussotto@owdlaw.com
URL www.owdlaw.com
Specialities: Competition law; Commercial
law; Free movement of goods; Free
movement of services; Free movement of
capital; Customs; Environmental law;
Consumer protection; Company law; Tax
law; Internal market; Harmonization of
technical standards; Banking sector;
Information technology sector; Chemicals
sector; Motor vehicles sector;
Pharmaceutical law; Telecommunications;
Food sector; Biotechnology sector; Financial
services sector; Consumer products sector;
Medical devices sector; Sports sector
Contact Eric Osterweil

Oppenheimer Wolff & Donnelly LLP

Plaza VII, 45 South Seventh Street, Suite 3300,
Minneapolis, MN 55402-1609, United States
of America
Tel. (+1 612) 607-7000
Fax (+1 612) 607-7100
E-mail info@oppenheimer.com
URL www.owdlaw.com
Contact P. Middleton

Pillsbury Winthrop Shaw Pittman LLP

One Battery Park Plaza, New York, NY 10004-
1490, United States of America

Tel. (+1 212) 858-1000
Fax (+1 212) 858-1500
E-mail info@pillsburylaw.com
URL www.pillsburywinthrop.com
Contact Mark Riedy

PLMJ

Edificio Eurolex, Av. da Liberdade 224, 1250-
148 Lisbon, Portugal
Tel. (+351) 213197300
Fax (+351) 213197400
E-mail jcv@plmj.pt
URL www.plmj.com
Contact Jose Luis da Cruz Vilaça

Pritchard Englefield

14 New Street, London EC2M 4HE,
United Kingdom
Tel. (+44 20) 7972-9720
Fax (+44 20) 7972-9722
E-mail po@pe-legal.com
URL www.pritchardenglefield.co.uk
Contact David Glass

RadcliffesleBrasseur

5 Great College Street, Westminster, London
SW1P 3SJ, United Kingdom
Tel. (+44 20) 7222-7040
Fax (+44 20) 7222- 6208
E-mail info@rlb-law.com
URL www.rlb-law.com
Specialities: Intellectual property; Consumer
agency; Competition law; Environmental
law; Public procurement; Employment law;
Equal opportunities; Company law;
Establishment of businesses; Monitoring of
forthcoming EU legislation; Lobbying
Contact Roland Gillott

Richards Butler

Avenue Louise 149, Bte 40, 1050 Brussels,
Belgium
Tel. (+32) 2-5357474
Fax (+32) 2-5357475
E-mail law@richardsbutler.com
URL www.richardsbutler.com
Contact Katherine Holmes

Richards Butler

Beaufort House, 15 St Botolph Street, London
EC3A 7EE, United Kingdom
Tel. (+44 20) 7247-6555

Fax (+44 20) 7247-5091
E-mail kmh@richardsbutler.com
URL www.richardsbutler.com
Contact Kathering Holmes

Roca Junyent

Aribau 198, 08036 Barcelona, Spain
Tel. (+34) 932-419200
Fax (+34) 934-145030
E-mail bcn@rocajunyent.com
URL www.rocajunyent.com
Specialities: Anti-trust law; Agency
  agreements; Distribution agreements;
  Intellectual property law; Directives;
  Regulations; Free movement of goods; EU
  proceedings; Mergers and acquisitions
Contact Roser Ràfols

**Rui Peixoto Duarte & Associados –
Advogados**

Rua Antonio Patricio 203/205, 4150-100 Porto,
  Portugal
Tel. (+351) 226067908
Fax (+351) 226001816
E-mail info@rpda-law.com
URL www.rpda-law.com
Contact Rui Peixoto Duarte

S. J. Berwin

Square de Meeûs 19, Bte 3, 1050 Brussels,
  Belgium
Tel. (+32) 2-5115340
Fax (+32) 2-5115917
E-mail brussels@sjberwin.com
URL www.sjberwin.com
Specialities: Competition law; Anti-trust law;
  Anti-dumping regulations; Customs
  regulations; Free movement of goods;
  Intellectual property law; Common
  agricultural policy; State aid; Grants;
  Financial services; Banking sector; Securities
  sector; Finance sector; Telecommunications;
  Information technology law; Tax law;
  Environmental law; Civil liability for waste;
  Mergers and acquisitions; Commercial
  policy; Regulations; EC-based litigation
  before domestic courts; EC-based litigation
  before the European Court of Justice;
  Fisheries sector
Contact Ramon Gallardo

S. J. Berwin

222 Gray's Inn Road, London WC1X 8XF,
  United Kingdom
Tel. (+44 20) 75332222
Fax (+44 20) 75332000
E-mail info@sjberwin.com
URL www.sjberwin.com
Contact Elaine Gibson-Bolton

SCP Granrut

89/91 rue du Faubourg Saint-Honoré, 75008
  Paris, France
Tel. (+33) 1-53-43-15-15
Fax (+33) 1-53-43-15-00
E-mail s.micheli@granrut.com
Contact Stéphane Micheli

Simmons & Simmons

Avenue Louise 149 b.16, 1050 Brussels,
  Belgium
Tel. (+32) 2-5420960
Fax (+32) 2-5420961
E-mail anthony.orr@simmons-simmons.com
URL www.simmons-simmons.com
Specialities: EU law; Competition law; Public
  procurement; Transport law; State aid; Free
  movement of goods; Agricultural law; Anti-
  dumping; European Commission; Litigation
  (before Court of Justice); EU law
Contact Anthony Orr

Simmons & Simmons

City Point, One Ropemaker Street, London
  EC2Y 9SS, United Kingdom
Tel. (+44 20) 7628-2020
Fax (+44 20) 7528-2070
E-mail mark.dawkins@simmons-simmons.com
URL www.simmons-simmons.com
Contact Mark Dawkins

Skadden, Arps, Slate, Meagher & Flom LLP

Avenue Louise 523, Box 30, 1050 Brussels,
  Belgium
Tel. (+32) 2-6390300
Fax (+32) 2-6390339
E-mail bhawk@skadden.com
URL www.skadden.com
Contact Henry L. Huser

Skadden, Arps, Slate, Meagher & Flom LLP

Four Times Square New York, New York,
  NY 10036, United States of America

Tel. (+1 212) 735-3000
Fax (+1 212) 735-2000
E-mail bhawk@skadden.com
URL www.skadden.com
Contact Wallace L. Schwartz

Slaughter and May

One Bunhill Row, London EC1Y 8YY,
United Kingdom
Tel. (+44 20) 7600-1200
Fax (+44 20) 7090-5000
E-mail tim.clark@slaughterandmay.com
URL www.slaughterandmay.com
Contact Tim Clark

Slaughter and May

Avenue de Cortenbergh 118, 1000 Brussels,
Belgium
Tel. (+32) 2-7379400
Fax (+32) 2-7379401
E-mail John.boyce@slaughterandmay.com
URL www.slaughterandmay.com
Specialities: Competition law; State aids;
Public procurement; Commercial law; Air
transport
Contact John Boyce

Souriadakis, Frangakis and Associates

Rue Kriezotou 6, 106 71 Athens, Greece
Tel. (+30) 210-3626888
Fax (+30) 210-3631631
E-mail sofralaw@otenet.gr
URL www.sofralaw.gr
Specialities: Competition law; State aids;
Institutional affairs; External relations; Free
movement of capital; Company law; Energy;
Litigation (before Court of Justice); Public
contracts; Free movement of goods; Free
movement of workers and social policy;
Freedom of establishment; Freedom to
provide services; Industrial policy and the
internal market; Transport law
Contact Dr Nikos Frangakis

Spandre et Associés

Rond Point Schuman 9, Bte 3, 1040 Brussels,
Belgium
Tel. (+32) 2-2309180
Fax (+32) 2-2302124
E-mail mario.spandre@infoboard.be
Contact Spandre

Squire Sanders & Dempsey LLP

Avenue Louise 165, Box 13-14, 1050 Brussels,
Belgium
Tel. (+32) 2-6271111
Fax (+32) 2-6271100
E-mail bhartnett@ssd.com
URL www.ssd.com
Specialities: Competition law;
Telecommunications regulation; Information
technology; Environmental law;
Pharmaceutical law; Energy law; Mergers
Contact Brain N. Hartnett

Stanbrook & Hooper S.C.

Rue Père Eudore Devroye 245, 1150 Brussels,
Belgium
Tel. (+32) 2-2305059
Fax (+32) 2-2305713
E-mail stanbrook.hooper@stanbrook.com
URL www.stanbrook.com
Specialities: International trade; Competition
law; 1992 programme for the completion of
the single market; Customs; Transport law;
Intellectual property law; Free movement of
goods; Free movement of persons; Free
movement of services; Environmental law;
Public procurement; Financial services; Food
law; Energy; Telecommunications; Public
utilities
Contact Clive Stanbrook

Stewart and Stewart

Blvd Dewandre 13, 6000 Charleroi, Belgium
Tel. (+32) 71-325131
Fax (+32) 71-323526
E-mail spinoit.wese@brutele.be
URL www.stewartlaw.com
Specialities: Anti-dumping; Anti-subsidies;
Customs; Competition law; International
trade
Contact Bernard Spinoit

Stewart and Stewart

2100 M Street NW, Suite 200, Washington, DC
20037, United States of America
Tel. (+1 202) 785-4185
Fax (+1 202) 466-1286
E-mail general@stewartlaw.com
URL www.stewartlaw.com
Contact Terence P. Stewart

Stibbe Simont Monahan Duhot

Rue Henri Wafelaertsstraat 47–51, 1060
    Brussels, Belgium
Tel. (+32) 2-5335211
Fax (+32) 2-5335212
E-mail info@stibbe.be
URL www.stibbe.com

Specialities: Competition law; State aids;
    Media law; Telecommunications;
    Pharmaceutical law; Cosmetics;
    Environmental law; Agricultural law;
    Energy; Tax law; Anti-dumping; Trade
    protection laws; Pension law; Banking law;
    Transport law; Free movement of goods;
    Free movement of capital; Free movement of
    persons; Intellectual property; Industrial
    property; Foodstuffs sector

Contact Olivier Clevenbergh

Stibbe

Strawinskylaan 2001, POB 75640, 1070 AP
    Amsterdam, Netherlands
Tel. (+31 20) 5460606
Fax (+31 20) 5460123
E-mail info@stibbe.nl
URL www.stibbe.com

Contact Joost van Lanschot

Studio Legale Bonelli Erede Pappalardo

Rue Montoyer 8, 1000 Brussels, Belgium
Tel. (+32) 2-5520070
Fax (+32) 2-5520071
E-mail bep.bxl@beplex.com

Contact Merola Massimo

Studio Legale Corapi

Via Flaminia 318, 00196 Rome, Italy
Tel. (+39) 06-3218563
Fax (+39) 06-3200992
E-mail info@studiolegalecorapi.it
URL www.studiolegalecorapi.it

Specialities: Arbitration; Corporate law;
    Financial markets; Banking sector; Insurance
    sector; Construction contracts

Contact Diego Corapi

Studio Legale Sabelli

Via Parigi 11, 00185 Rome, Italy
Tel. (+39) 06-4888701
Fax (+39) 06-48887057
E-mail info@sofralaw.gr
URL www.sabellilawfirm.it

Contact Luca Sabelli

Studio Legale Sergio Diana

Rue Montoyer 18b, 1040 Brussels, Belgium
Tel. (+32) 2-2800062
Fax (+32) 2-2801655
E-mail eurocontact@eurocontact.it
URL www.eurocontact.it

Contact S. Di Guisto

Studio Legale Sergio Diana

Piazza Repubblica 4, 09125 Cagliari, Italy
Tel. (+39) 07-044813
Fax (+39) 07-0456263
E-mail eurocontact@eurocontact.it
URL www.eurocontact.it

Contact S. Diana

Studio Legale Tonucci

Via Principessa Clotilde 7, 00196 Rome, Italy
Tel. (+39) 06-362271
Fax (+39) 06-3235161
E-mail SGrisolia@tonucci.it
URL www.tonucci.it

Specialities: Telecommunications; Energy law;
    Environmental law; Company law;
    Commercial property law; Industrial
    property law; Free movement of persons;
    Free movement of goods; Free movement of
    services; EU public procurement;
    Competition law; Anti-trust law; Multimedia
    law; Computer law; Data protection law

Contact Stefano Grisolia

Studio Steccanella Maurizio

Via Aurelio Saffi 23, 20123 Milan, Italy
Tel. (+39) 02-4692838
Fax (+39) 02-4692838
E-mail stecca.maur@id.it

Contact M. Steccanella

Taylor Wessing

Trône House, Rue du Trône 4, 1000 Brussels,
    Belgium
Tel. (+32) 2-2896060
Fax (+32) 2-2896070
E-mail brussels@taylorwessing.com
URL www.taylorwessing.com

Specialities: Competition law; Commercial
    law; Free movement of goods; Public
    procurement; EC energy; Environmental
    law; Telecommunications; Intellectual

property law; Biotechnology; Employment law

Contact Peter Willis

Taylor Wessing

Carmelite, 50 Victoria Embankment,
Blackfriars, London EC4Y 0DX,
United Kingdom
Tel. (+44 20) 7300-7000
Fax (+44 20) 7300-7100
E-mail london@taylorwessing.com
URL www.taylorwessing.com
Contact Gordon Jackson

Terry R. Broderick, Esq.

Avenue Pierre Curie 51, 1050 Brussels,
Belgium
Tel. (+32) 2-6460019
Fax (+32) 2-6460152
E-mail terry.broderick@pop.kpn.be
URL www.terry-broderick.com

Specialities: Company law; Competition law
and procedure; Distribution; Franchising;
Internal market developments; Intellectual
property; Licensing; Joint ventures; Mergers
and acquisitions; Commercial law and
procedure

Contact Terry Broderick

**Thommessen Krefting Greve Lund AS –
Advokatfirma**

Rue du Luxembourg 3, 1000 Brussels, Belgium
Tel. (+32) 2-5010700
Fax (+32) 2-5010701
E-mail brussels@thommessen.no
URL www.tkgl.no

Specialities: Competition law; Merger control;
Distribution systems; Cartel cases; Public
procurement; Internal market; Information
technology; Media law; Maritime sector

Contact Eivind J. Vesterkjær

**Thommessen, Krefting & Greve Lund AS –
Advokatfirma**

Haakon VII Gate 10, PO Box 1484 Vika, 0116
Oslo, Norway
Tel. (+47) 23-11-11-11
Fax (+47) 23-11-10-10
E-mail siri.teigum@tkgl.no
URL www.tkgl.no
Contact Siri Teigum

**Trans European Law Firms Alliance
(TELFA)**

Avenue Louise 208, 1050 Brussels, Belgium
Tel. (+32) 2-6462759
Fax (+32) 2-6422793
E-mail info@telfa.be
URL www.telfa.org
Contact Giancarlo Agace

Travers Smith Braithwaite

10 Snow Hill, London EC1A 2AL,
United Kingdom
Tel. (+44 20) 7295-3000
Fax (+44 20) 7295-3500
URL www.traverssmith.com
Contact Chris Carroll

Uettwiller Grelon Gout Canat & Associés

Avenue Albert-Elisabeth 46, Box 1, 1200
Brussels, Belgium
Tel. (+32) 2-7366614
Fax (+32) 2-7366818
E-mail pvandoorn@uggc-law.be
URL www.uggc-law.be

Specialities: European business law; Tax law;
VAT

Contact P. van Doorn

Van Bael & Bellis

Avenue Louise 165, 1050 Brussels, Belgium
Tel. (+32) 2-6477350
Fax (+32) 2-6406499
E-mail brussels@vanbaelbellis.com
URL www.vanbaelbellis.com

Specialities: Anti-trust law; Anti-dumping;
Customs; Commercial law; EU law;
Competition law; Deregulation; Free
movement of goods

Contact Bellis

Van Cutsem Wittamer Marnef et Associés

Avenue Louise 137/1, 1050 Brussels, Belgium
Tel. (+32) 2-5430200
Fax (+32) 2-5381378
E-mail legal@vancutsem.be
URL www.vancutsem.be
Contact Bertrand Wittamer

Wedlake Bell

52 Bedford Row, London WC1R 4LR,
United Kingdom

Tel. (+44 20) 7395-3000
Fax (+44 20) 7395-3100
E-mail legal@wedlakebell.com
URL www.wedlakebell.com
Contact Adrian Heath-Saunders

Weil, Gotshal & Manges LLP

767 Fifth Avenue, New York, NY 10153,
  United States of America
Tel. (+1 212) 310-8000
Fax (+1 212) 310-8007
E-mail john.neary@weil.com
URL www.weil.com

Contact John Neary

Weil, Gotshal & Manges LLP

Avenue Louise 81, Box 9-10, 1050 Brussels,
  Belgium
Tel. (+32) 2-5437460
Fax (+32) 2-5437489
E-mail Shay.ben-shaool@weil.com
URL www.weil.com

Specialities: Competition law; State aid;
  Telecommunications; EU law

Contact Shay Ben-Shaool

Weser & Partners

Avenue Armand Huysmans 22, 1050 Brussels,
  Belgium
Tel. (+32) 2-6401249
Fax (+32) 2-6401249

Specialities: Competition law; Contractual
  obligations; Arbitration before national
  courts; Arbitration before international
  courts; Litigation before national courts;
  Litigation before international courts; EU
  grants; EU loans; Banking law; Financial
  law; Intellectual property law; Audiovisual
  communication; Telecommunications; Free
  movement of persons; Free movement of
  services; Free movement of capital;
  Dumping; Abuse of dominant position;
  Subsidiaries; Investment in EU countries;
  Investment in eastern European countries;
  Free movement of judgments; Comparative
  social law; Mergers; Holdings; Joint
  ventures; Appeals to the Court of Justice of
  the EC; Litigation (before Court of First
  Instance); Product liability; Foreign
  companies; Tax law; International
  conventions between EU countries;
  International conventions between EU

countries and other countries; Consumer
  protection; Environmental law; Lobbying;
  Goods and finance

Contact M. Wester

White & Case LLP

Rue de la Loi 62, 1040 Brussels, Belgium
Tel. (+32) 2-2191620
Fax (+32) 2-2191626
E-mail PLindfelt@whitecase.com
URL www.whitecase.com

Contact Jacob Borum

White & Case LLP

1155 Avenue of the Americas, New York,
  NY 10036-2787, United States of America
Tel. (+1 212) 819-8200
Fax (+1 212) 354-8113

Contact Duane D. Wall

Wilmer Cutler & Pickering

Bastion Tower, Place du Champ de Mars 5,
  1050 Brussels, Belgium
Tel. (+32) 2-2854900
Fax (+32) 2-2854949
E-mail Marco.bronckers@wilmer.com
URL www.wilmer.com

Specialities: Telecommunications regulations;
  Media regulations; Intellectual property law;
  Competition law; EU trade law; Aviation
  regulations; European transactional work

Contact Marco Bronckers

Wilmer Cutler & Pickering

2445 M Street, NW, Washington, DC 20037,
  United States of America
Tel. (+1 202) 663-6000
Fax (+1 202) 663-6363
E-mail william.perlstein@wilmerhale.com
URL www.wilmer.com

Contact William J. Perlstein

Zepos & Yannopoulos

Katehaki & Kiffissias Avenue 75, 115 25
  Athens, Greece
Tel. (+30) 210-6967000
Fax (+30) 210-699464
E-mail info@zeya.com
URL www.zeya.com

Contact Dimitris J. Zepos

INDEX OF LAW FIRMS SPECIALIZING IN THE LAW OF THE EU

INDEX OF ACRONYMS IN PART II

Index of Acronyms in Part II

INDEX OF FULL NAMES IN PART II

Index of Full Names in Part II

405

410

INDEX OF KEYWORDS IN PART II

(Keywords in this index are derived from the sections *Trade and Professional Associations*, *Interest Groups and Non-Governmental Organizations*, *European Church Associations*, *Miscellaneous*, and *Employer Organizations and Trade Union Organizations*. Separate indexes of specialities, which occur earlier in the book, fulfil a similar function for the sections *Consultants Specializing in EU Questions* and *Law Firms Specializing in the Law of the European Union*.)

421